An English Language

SUFFIXIONARY

A Rhyming Dictionary

The easiest-to-use rhyming dictionary on the market

Formatted like a regular dictionary so you look up full words and not endings

25,500 words and commonly used proper nouns and phrases

Booksurge Publishing LLC
North Charleston, SC

Printed by
BOOKSURGE Publishing LLC
5341 Dorchester Rd., Suite 16
North Charleston, SC 29418
www.booksurge.com

Copyright © 2004 by Tim Blanchard
ISBN 1-59457-705-6
Place Orders at www.suffixionary.com

Printed in the U.S.A.

The trademark Suffixionary® is registered in the U.S. Patent and Trademark Office.

Dedication

To my mother, Lillian Blanchard, who has had a life-long interest and involvement in clear and substantive writing and teaching

To my wife, Barbara, who is a skilled craftsman with words and a master at writing and speaking with creativity and impact

To my daughter, Jean, from whom words flows with clarity and insight in her writing, speaking and counseling practice and

To my son, David, whose entrepreneurial mind and marketing savvy created a new word, Suffixionary, to be the title of this work

PREFACE

This suffixionary is a dictionary of 25,500 words that are linked to others words with the same sound endings, known as suffixes. The user simply looks up a word like in a dictionary and the link is listed so the group of words with which it rhymes can be easily found. All other rhyming dictionaries require the user to determine and then look up the ending of a word for which they want to find words that rhyme. Looking up endings can be an awkward and complicated process compared to simply looking up whole words.

Finding words that rhyme can be helpful when formulating an outline, writing poetry or musical lyrics, developing a catchy advertisement, determining a book or article title, creatively expressing humor, or simply formulating a memorable phrase or statement.

For example, an article about how wealth destroyed a marriage might be entitled "A Casualty of Prosperity" rather than "How Money Destroyed My Marriage". An outline on success might include- "Success Requires Determination, Organization and Action" rather then "Success Requires Hard Work, Orderliness and Performance".

Making a statement interesting and striking is a desirable goal for every creative communicator. This Suffixionary can readily assist those who want to succeed in engaging the attention and minds of others by using words that rhyme.

This volume doesn't include technical words from various fields like medicine and science that are not commonly understood and used. For example, the word *septicemia*, which describes a condition where there are poisonous bacteria in the blood, is not included. Technical abbreviations like ADP [automatic data processing] and AEC [Atomic Energy Commission] are also not included.

GUIDELINES FOR USAGE

This Suffixionary is structured like a dictionary. When you want to find a list of words with the same suffix sound as a word you are using, or would like to use, simply look up the word as you would in a dictionary. Following each word, there is either a list of words that rhyme with it or a word in brackets that refers you to the list of words that rhyme with it.

For example, if you look up the word **alcove,** you'll see:

> **alcove,** clove, cookstove, cove, dove, drove,
> grove, rove, stove, strove, trove, wove

If you look up the word **left**, you'll see:

> **left,** [aleft]

> Look up **aleft**, and you'll see all the words that rhyme with **left**:

> **aleft,** bereft, cleft, deft, heft, left, theft

If you are working with a word you cannot find in this Suffixionary, try to think of another word that ends with the same sound. For example, if you couldn't find the word **ache**, you might think of a word like **take**. That word would lead you to the list of words that rhyme with **ache.** Note: Some words have no commonly used words with which they rhyme. Those words are not included in this volume.

A few suffixes are very common. Hundreds of words have those endings. This volume often divides those large lists into several smaller ones. This enables the user to narrow the list of words that more closely rhyme with the word(s) he is using. For example, the first word in the Suffixionary is **a capella**. The basic ending is **a,** but in this book all the words listed as rhyming with **a capella** not only contain the **a** ending/sound but also the **la** ending/sound.

At the end of the **a capella** list, there are a number of other words placed in brackets- (see also **addenda, alfalfa** [various endings], **angelica, anathema, alumna, abracadabra, aorta, alleluia**). These all have the *a* ending/sound as well, but each word has a different letter before the *a*. Thus, they are grouped and listed separately because there are a number of words that contain those same double endings/sounds.

For example, if you look up **addenda**, you will find a list of words with the *da* ending, **angelica** and you will find a list of words with the *ka* sound ending, **anathema** with the *ma* ending, **alumna** with the *na* ending, **abracadabra** with the *ra* ending, **aorta** with the *ta* ending, and **alleluia** with the *ya* sound ending, etc. The remaining words with the *a* sound ending, like *fa, sa, pa* and more are grouped together under **alfalfa** since there are not enough words with each of those endings to show them separately. That is why after **alfalfa** there is a bracket entitled [remaining endings]. So, if you are looking for words that have an *a* ending, but they do not fit with one of the other separately listed endings, you'll find them under the word with the [remaining endings] next to it.

If you cannot find a word or words under the specific double ending that both rhyme with and have the meaning you want, you might look under the other words with only the common *a* ending. For example, you might want to communicate in a paper that adding an **addenda** is a bad idea. If there is no word with a *da* ending that means "a bad idea", you might want to use **anathema**, i.e., "an addenda is anathema". The *da* and *ma* endings don't sound exactly alike, but they still sound okay together because of the common *a* ending.

The English language also has some unique characteristics that require special attention and a decision when working with suffixes and rhymes. Some words are spelled the same but are pronounced differently depending on the usage. One pronunciation indicates that the word is a verb and another that the word is a noun or adjective. For example, the word **affiliate** can be both a verb, *a-fill-e-ate,* and a noun, *a-fill-e-ut*. Another is **abuse**, which can be either a noun, *a-buse,* or a verb, *a-buze*. Those words with two pronunciations and usages will be shown separately, with **[verb]** following one and **[noun]** following the other. The user will have to decide which pronunciation is appropriate.

Some words also have the same suffix sound, but can have two meanings and usages. The difference between the two is where the pronunciation emphasis is placed. For example, **contest** can be both a noun and a verb. The noun places the emphasis on the first syllable, *con*, [*con*-test] while the verb places the emphasis on the second syllable, *test,* [con-*test*]. Since the spelling and sound of the suffix are the same, both usages refer back to the same list, under **abreast**. As the user looks through the list of words that rhyme, he will have to discern which words in that list are verbs and which are nouns.

a capella, ancilla, areola,
ayatollah, bola, braciola,
cabala, cabriolet, camarilla,
candela, canola, chinchilla,
cola, copula, flotilla, formula,
gala, gladiola, gondola,
gorilla, granola, guerrilla,
hula, hyperbola, mandala,
mozzarella, mullah, nebula,
panatela, parabola, payola,
peninsula, salmonella,
scintilla, selah, spaetzle,
spatula, tarantula, tequila,
umbrella, valvula, vanilla,
villa, viola, wallah (see also
addenda, alfalfa [remaining
endings], **angelica,
anathema, alumna,
abracadabra, aorta,
alleluia**)
aah, aba, abaca, ah, aha,
aliyah, aloha, aw, awe, bah,
blah, blaw, bourgeois, bra,
brava, brouhaha, bucksaw,
bylaw, caw, claw, coleslaw,
craw, denouement, draw,
éclat, entrechat, flaw,
foofaraw, forepaw, gaga,
gnaw, grandma, grandpa,
guffaw, hacksaw, handsaw,
hoopla, hurrah, jaw, jigsaw,
law, lockjaw, ma, mackinaw,
maw, moola, oompah,
outlaw, overdraw, paw,
pshaw, rah, raw, redraw,
rickshaw, ripsaw, saw,
seesaw, shaw, slaw,
southpaw, spa, squaw, straw,
thaw, whipsaw, withdraw,

whoopla
aardvark, arc, ark, ballpark,
bark, benchmark, birthmark,
bookmark, dark, disembark,
earmark, embark, hallmark,
hark, hierarch, landmark,
lark, mark, matriarch,
meadowlark, monarch, narc,
park, patriarch, pockmark,
postmark, remark, shark,
sitzmark, spark, stark,
tetrarch, trademark,
watermark
ab, blob, bob, cob, corncob,
daub, doorknob, fob, glob,
gob, heartthrob, hob, hobnob,
job, kabob, knob, lob,
macabre, mob, nob, rob,
skibob, slob, snob, sob,
squab, swab, throb
aba, [aah]
abaca, [aah]
aback, air pack, alack,
almanac, aphrodisiac,
applejack, back, backpack,
backtrack, bareback,
biofeedback, bivouac, black,
blackjack, bootjack, brush
back, bushwhack, buyback,
callback, cardiac, carry back,
claque, coast rack, cognac,
comeback, cornerback,
cossack, counterattack,
crack, crackerjack, demoniac,
drawback, fallback, fast-track,
feedback, flack, flak, flapjack,
flashback, fullback, giveback,
greenback, gripsack,
gunnysack, hack, halfback,

hardback, hardtack,
hatchback, haversack,
haystack, hemophiliac,
hijack, hopsack, horseback,
hypochondriac, jack,
kickback, kleptomaniac,
knack, knapsack, kayak, lack,
leaseback, maniac, medevac,
megalomaniac, multitrack,
off-track, pack, paperback,
Pasternak, payback,
piggyback, plaque, playback,
Pontiac, pullback, quack,
quarterback, racetrack, rack,
ransack, razorback, rollback,
runback, sac, sack,
sacroiliac, scatback, serac,
setback, shack, shellac,
sidetrack, skipjack, slack,
slapjack, slotback, smack,
smoke jack, smokestack,
snack, snow pack, stack,
steeplejack, tach, tack,
tailback, throwback,
thumbtack, thwack, tieback,
touchback, track, Union Jack,
unpack, wetback, whack,
wingback, wisecrack, wrack,
yashmak, zodiac, zwieback
abacus, amicus, auto focus,
caducous, carcass, caucus,
circus, cuss, discus, discuss,
focus, fracas, locus, mucous,
mucus, raucous, rediscuss,
refocus, ruckus (see also
antibias [remaining endings],
**abbess, abstemious,
amorphous, analogous,
adscititious, advantageous,**

**acropolis, allonymous,
agribusiness, auspice,
actress, alkalosis, afflatus,
ambiguous)**
abaft, aft, aircraft, antiaircraft,
back draft, camshaft,
crankshaft, downdraft, draft,
driveshaft, engraft, graft,
handicraft, kraft, overdraft,
raft, redraft, shaft, spacecraft,
stagecraft, understaffed,
watercraft, witchcraft,
woodcraft
abalone, aborigine,
accompany, acne, acrimony,
agony, agrimony, alimony,
antiphony, any, assignee,
attorney, balcony, baloney,
barony, beanie, benny, bikini,
blarney, bologna, bonny,
bony, botany, brainy, brawny,
briny, brownie, bunny,
calumny, canny, ceremony,
chimney, chutney, cine,
colony, company, coney,
corny, cosmogony, cottony,
cranny, crony, designee,
destiny, detainee,
disharmony, donee, downy,
epiphany, euphony, fanny,
felony, fettuccine, funny,
genie, gluttony, gooney,
grainy, granny, gurney,
harmony, hegemony, honey,
hootenanny, horny, ignominy,
irony, jitney, journey, kidney,
knee, larceny, linguine, litany,
loony, macaroni, mahogany,
many, martini, matrimony,

meanie, minestrone,
miscellany, misogyny,
money, monogyny,
monotony, moony, mutiny,
nanny, ninny, nominee,
padrone, palimony,
parsimony, patrimony, penny,
pepperoni, phony, pony,
progeny, puny, rainy,
scrawny, scrutiny, shinny,
shiny, simony, sixpenny,
skinny, sonny, spaghettini,
spoony, spumoni, stony,
sunny, symphony, tawny,
teeny, telephony, testimony,
tetrazzini, theogony,
theophany, thorny, tiffany,
timpani, tinny, tiny, tony,
tortellini, tourney, trainee,
tyranny, uncanny, wahine,
weenie, wienie, zany,
zucchini (see also **buoy**
[remaining endings], **abbey,
acidy, anastrophe, aggie,
blotchy, banshee, apathy,
newsworthy, analogy,
achy, ably, academy,
apocope, accusatory,
ancestry, absorbency,
abatis (pronounced *te*),
anchovy, colloquy,
advisee)**
abandonment, abasement,
abatement, abetment,
abutment, accompaniment,
accomplishment,
accouterment, achievement,
acknowledgment, adamant,
adjournment, adjustment,

advancement, advertisement,
advisement, agreement,
ailment, aliment, alignment,
allotment, allurement,
amazement, amendment,
ament, amusement,
announcement, annulment,
antiestablishment,
antidevelopment,
antiestablishment,
antigovernment, apartment,
appeasement, appointment,
apportionment, arbitrament,
argument, armament,
arraignment, arrangement,
assessment, assignment,
assortment, astonishment,
atonement, attachment,
attainment, basement,
battlement, bereavement,
betterment, bewilderment,
chastisement, clamant,
clement, commandment,
commencement, comment,
commitment, compartment,
complement, compliment,
condiment, confinement,
consignment, containment,
contentment, deferment,
defilement, department,
deployment, deportment,
detachment, detriment,
development, disagreement,
disappointment,
disarmament, disbursement,
discernment,
discouragement,
disinvestment, displacement,
divestment, document,

dormant, easement, element,
embankment,
embarrassment,
embellishment, embodiment,
emolument, emplacement,
employment, encampment,
encouragement, endearment,
endorsement, endowment,
engagement, enhancement,
enjambment, enjoyment,
enlargement, enlightenment,
enlistment, enrichment,
enrollment, entanglement,
entertainment, entitlement,
entrapment, environment,
equipment, establishment,
estrangement, excitement,
excrement, experiment,
figment, filament, firmament,
foment, fragment, fulfillment,
garment, garnishment,
government, habiliment,
harassment, impeachment,
impediment, implement,
improvement, inclement,
increment, indictment,
inducement, informant,
infotainment, infringement,
installment, instrument,
interment, inurement,
investment, involvement,
judgment, lament, ligament,
liniment, management,
measurement, merriment,
micromanagement,
misstatement, mistreatment,
moment, monument,
movement, nonachievement,
noncommitment,

noninvolvement,
nonpayment, nourishment,
ointment, ornament,
outplacement, overpayment,
parchment, parliament,
pavement, payment,
pediment, pigment,
placement, predicament,
preretirement, procurement,
punishment, puzzlement,
raiment, readjustment,
realignment, reappointment,
rearrangement,
reassessment, reassignment,
recruitment, redevelopment,
reenactment, refinement,
refreshment, regiment,
reimbursement,
reinforcement, reinstatement,
reinvestment, repayment,
replacement, replenishment,
requirement, resentment,
retirement, rudiment,
sacrament, sediment, self-
abasement, self-
advancement, self-
aggrandizement, self-
assessment, self-betterment,
self-development, self-
employment, self-fulfillment,
self-government, self-
improvement, self-
management,
semiretirement, sentiment,
settlement, shipment,
statement, supplement,
temperament, tenement,
testament, tournament,
treatment, underemployment,

5

undergarment,
unemployment, varmint,
vehement, vestment,
wonderment (see also
accordant, abeyant
[remaining endings],
**abundant, ambivalent,
abandonment, abstinent,
aberrant, absent, adjacent,
abirritant)**
abase, ace, aerospace,
airspace, anyplace, apace,
backspace, base, basket
case, birthplace, bookcase,
bootlace, bouillabaisse,
brace, briefcase, case,
chase, commonplace,
crankcase, database,
debase, deface, disgrace,
displace, efface, embrace,
emplace, encase, enchase,
enlace, erase, face, firebase,
fireplace, footrace, freebase,
grace, headspace, hiding
place, horse race, interface,
interlace, lace, lactase,
lightface, mace, marketplace,
millrace, misplace, nutcase,
outpace, pace, paleface,
pillowcase, place, race, rat
race, replace, retrace,
shoelace, showcase,
showplace, slipcase,
someplace, space, staircase,
steeplechase, suitcase,
tenace, test case, trace,
typeface, vase, wheelbase,
workplace
abased, aftertaste, barefaced,

baste, boldfaced, chaste,
distaste, foretaste, haste,
lambaste, moonfaced,
pantywaist, paste, placed,
posthaste, shamefaced,
straitlaced, taste, toothpaste,
unchaste, unplaced, waist,
waste
abasement, [abandonment]
abash, ash, backlash,
backslash, balderdash, bash,
brash, cache, calash, cash,
clash, crash, dash, eyelash,
flash, gash, gnash, hash, hot
flash, lash, mash, mishmash,
mustache, noncash,
panache, rash, rehash, sash,
slash, smash, splash, stash,
thrash, trash, whiplash
abate, acerbate, approbate,
bait, conglobate, debate,
exacerbate, incubate,
masturbate, probate, rebate,
reprobate (see also **ate**
[remaining endings],
**accommodate, create,
abnegate, abdicate, ablate,
acclimate, abominate,
anticipate, accelerate,
acetate, activate,
accentuate)**
abatement, [abandonment]
abatis, ability, abnormality,
absentee, absurdity, acclivity,
accountability, acerbity,
acidity, activity, actuality,
acuity, adaptability, adoptee,
adversity, affinity,
affordability, agility, alacrity,

almighty, ambiguity, amenity,
amity, amnesty, amputee,
angioplasty, animosity,
annuity, anonymity, ante,
antiauthority, antiobescenity,
antipoverty, antiquity, anxiety,
aplenty, appointee, arty,
asperity, atrocity, audacity,
austerity, authenticity,
authority, availability, avidity,
batty, beauty, bestiality,
bhakti, bitty, bloodthirsty,
bootie, booty, bounty, brevity,
brutality, busty, caducity,
calamity, canonicity,
capability, capacity,
cappelletti, captivity,
carnality, casualty, catty,
causality, cavity, celebrity,
centrality, certainty,
champerty, charity, chastity,
chatty, chayote, chesty,
churchianity, city, civility,
clarity, collegiality, comity,
committee, commodity,
commonality, community,
complexity, complicity,
concinnity, conductivity,
confetti, conformity,
congruity, constitutionality,
continuity, cordiality,
cotrustee, county, crafty,
creativity, credibility,
creditability, credulity,
crotchety, cruelty, crusty,
culpability, cupidity, curiosity,
cutie, dainty, deductibility,
deformity, deity, density,
depravity, deputy, devotee,

dexterity, difficulty, dignity,
dirty, disability, discontinuity,
dishonesty, disrespectability,
disunity, disutility, ditty,
diversity, divinity, dotty,
doughty, drafty, duplicity,
dusty, duty, dynasty,
ecumenicity, eighty, elasticity,
electricity, empty, enmity,
enormity, entity, ethnicity,
equality, equanimity, equity,
eternity, extremity, facility,
faculty, fallibility, falsity,
familiarity, fatality, fatty,
faulty, feasibility, fecundity,
feisty, felicity, femininity,
ferocity, fertility, festivity,
fidelity, fidgety, fifty, finality,
flighty, fluidity, formality, forty,
fragility, frailty, fraternity,
frigidity, frivolity, frosty, fruity,
futility, futurity, gaiety,
garrulity, generosity, gentility,
goatee, grantee, gratuity,
gravity, gritty, guarantee,
guaranty, guilty, hasty,
haughty, hearty, hefty,
heredity, honesty, hospitality,
hostility, humanity, humidity,
humility, hyperactivity,
identity, illuminati, immaturity,
immensity, immorality,
immortality, immunity,
impiety, impossibility,
impropriety, impunity,
impurity, inability, incapacity,
incompatibility, indemnity,
indignity, individuality,
inductee, inequality, inequity,

infertility, infidelity, infinity,
infirmity, ingenuity,
inhumanity, iniquity, insanity,
insecurity, instability,
integrity, intensity, intercity,
invincibility, invulnerability,
irregularity, irresponsibility,
jetty, karate, kitty, knotty,
laity, lefty, legality, legatee,
levity, liability, liberality,
liberty, liquidity, locality, lofty,
longevity, loyalty, lusty,
machete, magnanimity,
majesty, majority, manicotti,
maternity, maturity, meaty,
mediocrity, mendacity,
mentality, mighty, minority,
misty, modality, modernity,
modesty, moiety,
monstrosity, morality,
morbidity, mortality, mufti,
multicity, multiplicity,
multiversity, municipality,
musty, mutability, mutuality,
nasty, nationality, nativity,
naughty, necessity, neutrality,
nicety, nifty, nightie, ninety,
nobility, nonconformity,
nonentity, nonfatty,
nonnecessity, notoriety,
novelty, nudity, nutty, obesity,
objectivity, obscenity,
obscurity, opacity,
opportunity, originality,
overhasty, parity, partiality,
party, passivity, paternity,
patty, paucity, peculiarity,
penalty, perpetuity,
perplexity, persnickety,

personality, personalty, petty,
peyote, piety, pity, plenty,
pliability, plurality, polarity,
polity, popularity, porosity,
possibility, posterity,
potentiality, potty, pouty,
poverty, pretty, principality,
priority, privity, probability,
probity, proclivity,
productivity, profanity,
profundity, promiscuity,
propensity, property,
propinquity, propriety,
prosperity, proximity, puberty,
publicity, punctuality, purity,
putty, quality, quantity,
rapidity, rarity, rationality,
ratty, readability, reality,
reciprocity, regularity,
relativity, reliability, repartee,
responsibility, rickety, rigidity,
royalty, rusty, safety,
sagacity, salty, sanctity,
sanity, satiety, scanty,
scarcity, security, self-
identity, senility, seniority,
sensibility, sensitivity,
sensuality, sentimentality,
serendipity, serenity, settee,
seventy, severity, sexuality,
shanty, shifty, similarity,
simplicity, sincerity,
singularity, sixty, smutty,
snooty, snotty, sobriety,
sociability, society, sodality,
softy, solemnity, solidarity,
solidity, sorority, sortie,
sovereignty, spaghetti,
sparsity, specialty, specificity,

spirituality, spontaneity, sporty, spotty, squatty, stability, sterility, stupidity, subjectivity, subspecialty, subtlety, suitability, superfluity, superiority, surety, susceptibility, sweaty, tasty, tatty, tea, technicality, tee, temerity, temporality, tenacity, tensity, tenuity, testy, thirsty, thirty, thrifty, throaty, timidity, toasty, totality, touristy, tranquility, travesty, treaty, trustee, trusty, turgidity, tutti, twenty, ubiquity, unanimity, unity, uncertainty, undesirability, uniformity, university, unreality, uppity, utility, vacuity, validity, vanity, vapidity, variability, variety, varsity, velleity, velocity, velvety, veracity, verity, versatility, viability, vicinity, vigilante, vinosity, virginity, virility, virtuosity, viscosity, visibility, vitality, volatility, voracity, vulgarity, wapiti, warrantee, warranty, weighty, witty, zesty (see also **buoy** [remaining endings], **abbey, acidy, anastrophe, aggie, blotchy, banshee, apathy, newsworthy, analogy, achy, ably, academy, abalone, apocope, accessory, ancestry, accountancy, anchovy, colloquy, advisee**)

abattoir, afar, ajar, are, autocar, avatar, bar, bazaar, bizarre, boudoir, boxcar, boyar, car, catarrh, caviar, char, cigar, commissar, costar, couloir, crossbar, crowbar, czar, daystar, debar, devoir, disbar, drawbar, exemplar, falling star, far, flatcar, guar, guitar, handlebar, insofar, jaguar, jar, lodestar, lonestar, memoir, minicar, morning star, motor car, north star, our, par, quasar, radar, railcar, registrar, repertoire, reservoir, sandbar, scar, seminar, shofar, shooting star, sidebar, sidecar, sonar, spar, star, streetcar, subpar, superstar, tar, tow bar, trolley car, tsar
abaxial, actuarial, adverbial, adversarial, aerial, alluvial, arterial, axial, bacterial, bestial, bicentennial, biennial, bilabial, binomial, burial, celestial, centennial, ceremonial, coaxial, collegial, colloquial, colonial, congenial, connubial, corporeal, cranial, custodial, dictatorial, editorial, ethereal, equatorial, filial, genial, gubernatorial, immaterial, imperial, industrial, jovial, lineal, marmoreal, material, matrimonial, memorial, menial, mercurial, millennial,

ministerial, monomial,
multinomial, noncustodial,
parochial, perennial, pictorial,
polynomial, postmillennial,
premillennial, primordial,
proverbial, quadrennial,
radial, remedial, serial,
sidereal, terrestrial, territorial,
testimonial, tonsorial, triaxial,
trivial, tutorial, venereal,
venial, wool (see also **agile**
[remaining endings], **accrual,
able, antipodal, anneal,
apocryphal, angle, abbatial,
aisle, acoustical, abnormal,
aboriginal, abdominal,
broil, airfoil, ample,
admiral, apostle,
accidental, adjectival,
accrual, aswhirl, appraisal)**
abbatial, antisocial, artificial,
asocial, beneficial, biosocial,
biracial, bushel,
circumstantial, commercial,
confidential, controversial,
credential, crucial,
differential, especial,
essential, existential,
experiential, facial, financial,
glacial, impartial,
inconsequential, inferential,
influential, infomercial, initial,
interracial, judicial, marshal,
martial, multiracial,
noncommercial,
nonconfidential,
noncontroversial,
nonessential, nonfinancial,
nonracial, nonresidential,

nuptial, official, palatial,
partial, postnuptial, potential,
preferential, prejudicial,
prenuptial, presidential,
providential, provincial,
prudential, racial, residential,
reverential, sacrificial,
sequential, social, spatial,
special, substantial,
superficial, tangential,
torrential, uncial,
uncommercial, unessential,
unofficial, unsocial (see
abaxial)
abbess, airbus, blunderbuss,
bus, buss, minibus, omnibus,
rebus, succubus, syllabus,
trolleybus (see **abacus)**
abbey, adobe, baby, bee,
bobby, booby, brumby,
bumblebee, busby, chubby,
crabby, crybaby, derby,
dobby, flabby, freebie, gabby,
grabby, grandbaby, grubby,
hobby, honeybee, hubby,
lobby, nubby, ruby, rugby,
scrubby, shabby, stubby,
tabby, tubby, wallaby, zombie
(see also **abalone)**
abbot, abut, ambit, but, butt,
celibate, cohabit, cubit, debit,
exhibit, gambit, gibbet, habit,
halibut, hobbit, inhabit, inhibit,
orbit, prohibit, rabbit, rebut,
scuttlebutt, sherbet, turbot
(see also **accredit** [remaining
endings], **affiliate, agate,
advocate, aglet, animate,**

acuminate, accurate,
acquit, apposite)
abbreviation, abdication,
abduction, aberration,
abjection, abjuration,
ablation, ablution,
abnegation, abolition,
abomination, abortion,
abreaction, absolution,
absorption, abstention,
abstraction, academician,
acceleration, accentuation,
acceptation, accession,
acclamation, acclimation,
accommodation,
accreditation, accretion,
acculturation, accumulation,
accusation, action, activation,
actualization, acquisition,
adaptation, addiction,
addition, adjudication,
administration, admiration,
admission, admonition,
adoption, adoration,
adulteration, adumbration,
advection, affectation,
affection, affiliation,
affirmation, affliction,
agglomeration, agglutination,
aggravation, aggregation,
aggression, agitation,
alienation, alimentation,
allegation, alliteration,
allegorization, allocation,
allocution, alteration,
altercation, alternation,
amalgamation, ambition,
amelioration, ammunition,
amortization, amplification,

angulation, animation,
annexation, annihilation,
annotation, annunciation,
antichristian, anticipation,
antidepression,
antidiscrimination,
antievolution, antifashion,
anti-inflation, anti-integration,
antipollution, antiprostitution,
apparition, appellation,
apperception application,
apportion, apposition,
appreciation, apprehension,
approbation, appropriation,
approximation, arbitration,
argumentation, arithmetician,
articulation, articulation,
ascension, ascription, ashen,
asphyxiation, aspiration,
assassination, assertion,
assignation, assimilation,
association, assumption,
attention, attenuation,
attestation, attraction,
attribution, attrition, auction,
audition, augmentation,
auscultation, authentication,
authorization, automation,
autosuggestion, avocation,
avulsion, beatification,
beautification, benediction,
bifurcation, calcification,
calculation, calibration,
cancellation, capitalization,
capitation, capitulation,
caption, carburetion,
carnation, castigation,
castration, categorization,
catherization, causation,

caution, celebration,
certification, cessation,
characterization, circulation,
circumlocution,
circumscription,
circumvolution, citation,
civilization, clarification,
classification, clinician,
coagulation, coalition,
codification, coeducation,
coercion, cogitation,
cognition, cohabitation,
collaboration, collection,
colonization, coloration,
combination, commendation,
commemoration,
commercialization,
commission, commotion,
communication,
commutation, compaction,
compassion, compensation,
competition, compilation,
completion, complexion,
complication, composition,
comprehension,
compression, compulsion,
compunction, computation,
computerization, conception,
concession, concoction,
concussion, condemnation,
condensation,
condescension, condition,
conduction, confection,
confederation, confession,
configuration, confirmation,
confiscation, conflagration,
conformation, confrontation,
confutation, congestion,
conglomeration,

congratulation, congregation,
conjugation, conjunction,
connection, conniption,
connotation, conscription,
consecration, conservation,
consideration, consolation,
consolidation, conspiration,
constellation, consternation,
constipation, constitution,
constriction, construction,
consubstantiation,
consultation, consummation,
consumption, contamination,
contemplation, contention,
continuation, contortion,
contraception, contraction,
contradiction, contraption,
contribution, contrition,
convection, convention,
conversation, conviction,
convocation, convolution,
convulsion, cooperation,
coordination, copulation,
coronation, corporation,
correction, correlation,
corroboration, corruption,
coruscation,
counterdemonstration,
counter suggestion,
counterrevolution, creation,
cremation, cross-
examination, cross-
fertilization, crucifixion,
culmination, cultivation,
cushion, cybernation,
dalmatian, damnation,
deactivation, debarkation,
decapitation, deceleration,
decentralization, deception,

decertification,
dechlorination, declaration,
declassification, declension,
decommission,
decompression,
deconstruction, decoration,
decriminalization, decryption,
dedication, deduction, de-
escalation, defalcation,
defamation, defection,
defibrillation, definition,
deflation, deflection,
defoliation, deforestation,
degeneration, degradation,
dehydration, dejection,
delegation, deletion,
deliberation, delineation,
delusion, demarcation,
demolition, demonization,
demonstration, denegation,
denigration, denomination,
denotation, denunciation,
depersonalization, depiction,
depletion, deportation,
deposition, depravation,
depreciation, depression,
deprivation, deputation,
deputization, deregulation,
dereliction, derivation,
description, desecration,
desegregation, desertion,
designation, desolation,
desperation, destination,
destitution, destruction,
detection, deterioration,
determination, detonation,
detoxification, detraction,
devaluation, devastation,
deviation, devolution,

devotion, diagnostician,
dictation, diction, dietitian,
differentiation, diffraction,
digitalization, digression,
dilatation, dilation, dilution,
dimension, diminutive,
direction, discoloration,
discretion, discrimination,
discussion, disinflation,
disintegration, disjunction,
disinformation, dislocation,
dispassion, dispensation,
disposition, disproportion,
disputation, disqualification,
dissatisfaction, dissection,
dissension, dissertation,
dissimilation, dissimulation,
dissipation, dissolution,
distillation, distinction,
distortion, distraction,
distribution, divagation,
divarication, diversification,
diversion, divination,
documentation,
domestication, domination,
donation, dramatization,
duplication, duration,
dysfunction, ebullition,
edification, edition, education,
effusion, egression,
ejaculation, ejection, elation,
election, electrician,
electrocution, elevation,
elimination, elocution,
elongation, elucidation,
eluviation, emancipation,
emasculation, embrocation,
emendation, emigration,
emission, emotion,

emulation, emulsion,
enumeration, epilation,
equalization, erection,
erudition, eruption,
estimation, evacuation,
evaluation, evangelization,
evaporation, eviction,
evolution, exaggeration,
exaltation, examination,
exasperation, excavation,
exception, exclamation,
excommunication, excretion,
execution, exemption,
exertion, exhilaration,
exhortation, expansion,
expectation, expedition,
experimentation, expatiation,
expiration, explanation,
exploitation, exploration,
exposition, expression,
expropriation, expulsion,
extension, extermination,
extinction, extortion,
extraction, extradition,
extrapolation, extrication,
extroversion, exultation,
fabrication, faction,
fascination, fashion,
federation, fermentation,
fertilization, fibrillation, fiction,
figuration, filiation, filtration,
fixation, flagellation, flexion,
flotation, fluctuation, fluxion,
foliation, foreordination,
forestation, formation,
formulation, fornication,
fortification, foundation,
fraction, fragmentation,
fraternization, friction, fruition,

frustration, fumigation,
function, furcation, gelation,
generalization, generation,
germination, gestation,
gesticulation, globalization,
glorification, gradation,
graduation, granulation,
gratification, gravitation,
gumption, gustation, gyration,
habituation, hallucination,
hesitation, hospitalization,
humiliation, hypertension,
hyperventilation,
hypotension, identification,
idolization, ignition, illation,
illumination, illustration,
imagination, imitation,
immigration, impartation,
impassion, imperfection,
implantation, implementation,
implication, importation,
imposition, imprecision,
impression, improvisation,
impulsion, imputation,
inaction, inattention,
inauguration, incantation,
incarnation, inception,
inclination, inclusion,
incubation, indentation,
indication, indignation,
indiscretion, indoctrination,
induction, industrialization,
inebriation, infection,
infiltration, inflammation,
inflation, inflection,
information, infraction,
infusion, inhalation, inhibition,
initiation, injection, injunction,
innovation, inoculation,

inquisition, inscription,
insertion, insinuation,
insolation, integration,
intension, intention,
interaction, interception,
intercession, intercorrelation,
intergeneration, interjection,
intermission, interpolation,
interposition, interpretation,
interrogation, intersection,
intercession, interruption,
intonation, intoxication,
introduction, introspection,
intrusion, intuition, invasion,
invention, inversion,
invitation, invocation,
irrigation, irritation, isolation,
itemization, jactitation,
jubilation, junction,
jurisdiction, justification,
juxtaposition, laceration,
lactation, lamentation,
lamination, lavation, legation,
legislation, levitation, libation,
liberalization, liberation,
limitation, liposuction,
liquidation, literation,
litigation, location,
locomotion, logician, lotion,
lubrication, machination,
magician, magnification,
maladaption, malediction,
malformation, malfunction,
malnutrition, manifestation,
manipulation, mansion,
manumission, martian,
masturbation, mathematician,
maturation, maximization,
mediation, medication,

meditation, memorization,
menstruation, mention,
migration, ministration,
misallocation, misapplication,
miscalculation,
mischaracterization,
misclassification,
miscommunication,
miscomprehension,
miscomputation,
misconception,
misconnection,
misconstruction, misdirection,
misevaluation, misfunction,
misidentification,
misinformation,
misperception,
mispronunciation,
misquotation, mistranslation,
mitigation, mobilization,
moderation, modernization,
modification, modulation,
molestation, monition,
mortification, motion,
motivation, multifunction,
multiplication, munition,
mutation, narration, natation,
nation, nationalization,
navigation, negation,
negotiation, nidification,
nomination, nonaction,
nonadmission,
nonaggression,
noncomprehension,
noncontradiction,
noncooperation,
nondiscrimination,
nonmusician,
nonproliferation,

normalization, notation, notification, notion, novation, nutrition, obfuscation, objection, objurgation, oblation, obligation, obliteration, observation, obsession, obstruction, obturation, occupation, omission, operation, opposition, oppression, option, oration, orchestration, ordination, organization, orientation, oscillation, osculation, ostentation, ovation, over exaggeration, overexertion, overexpansion, overgeneralization, overproduction, overprotection, overreaction, overregulation, overpopulation, ovulation, oxidation, pagination, palpitation, participation, partition, parturition, penetration, pension, perception, percussion, perdition, perfection, perforation, permission, peroration, persecution, perseveration, personification, perspiration, petition, pigmentation, pincushion, plantation, polarization, pollination, pollution, population, portion, position, possession, post conception, post depression, post graduation, postposition, potation, potion,

preadmission, precaution, preelection, precession, precipitation, precognition, preconception, precondition, predestination, predetermination, predication, prediction, predilection, premeditation, premonition, preoccupation, preparation, preposition, prequalification, preregistration, prescription, presentation, preservation, presumption, pretension, prevention, privation, proabortion, probation, procession, proclamation, procreation, production, profession, prognostication, progression, prohibition, projection, proliferation, prolongation, promotion, promulgation, pronunciation, propagation, propitiation, proportion, proposition, propulsion, prosecution, prostitution, prostration, protection, protestation, protraction, provocation, publication, pulsation, punctuation, purification, putrefaction, qualification, quotation, ramification, rationalization, reacquisition, reaction, reactivation, readmission, reaffirmation, realization, reapportion, reauthorization, recalculation, recapitalization, recension,

reception, recession,
reciprocation, recitation,
reclamation, reclassification,
recognition, recollection,
recommendation,
recommission,
recomputation, reconciliation,
recondition, reconnection,
reconsecration,
reconstruction, reconviction,
recreation, recrimination,
rectification, recuperation,
redaction, rededication,
redemption, redirection,
redistribution, reduction,
reduplication, reeducation,
reelection, reevaluation,
reexamination, refashion,
refection, reflection,
reforestation, reformation,
refraction, refrigeration,
refutation, regeneration,
regimentation, registration,
regression, regulation,
regurgitation, rehabilitation,
refection, reincarnation,
reinterpretation, reinvention,
reinvestigation, rejection,
rejuvenation, relation,
realization, reelection,
relegation, relocation,
remission, remonstration,
remuneration, renegotiation,
rendition, renovation,
renunciation, reorganization,
reparation, repartition,
repercussion, repetition,
replantation, repletion,
replication, reposition,

repossession, representation,
repression, reprobation,
reproduction, republication,
repudiation, repulsion,
reputation, requisition,
resection, reservation,
resignation, resolution,
respiration, restitution,
restoration, restriction,
resumption, resurrection,
resuscitation, retaliation,
retardation, retention,
retraction, retranslation,
retribution, retrogression,
reunification, revelation,
reverberation, revitalization,
revocation, revolution,
revulsion, rotation, ruination,
salvation, salutation,
sanctification, sanction,
sanitation, satiation,
satisfaction, saturation,
scansion, scintillation,
secession, secretion, section,
sedation, sedition, seduction,
segmentation, segregation,
selection, self-actualization,
self-condemnation, self-
deception, self-evaluation,
self-promotion, self-
protection, self-regulation,
self-absorption, self-
contradiction, self-
determination, self-
examination, self-glorification,
self-gratification, self-
incrimination, self-
justification, self-preservation,
self-realization, self-

revelation, self-satisfaction,
sensation, separation,
serration, session,
sexploitation, shun,
simplification, simulation,
situation, slumpflation,
solicitation, solution,
sophistication, sortition,
spallation, specialization,
specification, speculation,
spiritualization, spoliation,
stabilization, stagflation,
standardization, starvation,
station, statistician,
sterilization, stimulation,
stipulation, strangulation,
stratification, striation,
subjugation, sublimation,
submission, subordination,
subreption, subrogation,
subscription, subsection,
substantiation, substation,
substitution, succession,
suction, suffocation,
suggestion, summation,
superstition, supposition,
suppression, suspension,
suspicion, syncopation,
syndication, tactician,
tarnation, taxation,
technician,
telecommunication,
teleportation, temptation,
tension, termination,
tessellation, titillation,
toleration, torsion, traction,
tradition, transaction,
transcription, transfiguration,
transformation,

transgression, transition,
translation, transmission,
transmutation, transportation,
transposition,
transubstantiation,
trepidation, tribulation,
trituration, tuition, ulceration,
unction, undulation,
unification, unionization,
urbanization, urination,
usurpation, utilization,
vacation, vaccination,
vacillation, validation,
valuation, variation,
variegation, vaticination,
vegetation, veneration,
ventilation, verbalization,
verbigeration, verification,
versification, vexation,
vibration, vilification,
vindication, vinification,
violation, visitation,
visualization, vituperation,
vivisection, vocation, volition,
westernization, workstation
abdicate, adjudicate,
advocate, allocate, altercate,
authenticate, bifurcate, cate,
cheapskate, collocate,
communicate, complicate,
confiscate, coruscate,
dedicate, defalcate, defecate,
demarcate, deprecate,
dislocate, divaricate,
domesticate, duplicate,
educate, equivocate,
eradicate, excommunicate,
explicate, exsiccate,
extricate, fabricate, falcate,

fornicate, hypothecate,
imbricate, implicate,
imprecate, inculcate, indicate,
intoxicate, locate, lubricate,
masticate, medicate,
misallocate, obfuscate,
overmedicate, overeducate,
placate, plicate, pontificate,
predicate, prefabricate,
prevaricate, prognosticate,
reallocate, rededicate,
reciprocate, reduplicate,
reeducate, relocate, replicate,
saccate, skate, sophisticate,
suffocate, sulcate, supplicate,
syndicate, triplicate, truncate,
vacate, vindicate(see also
abate)
abdication, [abbreviation]
abdomen, acumen, afikomen,
airman, albumen, alderman,
alderwoman, anchorman,
anchorwoman,
anchorwoman, atman,
axman, backgammon,
backwoodsman, bagman,
bagwoman, ballsman,
batsman, bellman, bitumen,
boatman, bondman,
bondsman, bondwoman,
bookman, bowman,
brakeman, cacodemon,
cameraman, camerawoman,
chairman, chairwoman,
churchman, cinnamon,
clansman, clergyman,
clergywoman, cochairman,
common, congressman,
councilman, craftsman,

cross-examine, dairyman,
defenseman, demon,
determine, draftsman,
examine, famine, fireman,
fisherman, fisherwoman,
flagman, fly man, foreman,
forewoman, freshman,
frontiersman, gammon,
garbage man, gentleman,
gravamen, groomsman,
guardsman, gunman,
hangman, helmsman,
henchman, herdsman,
highwayman, human, hymen,
illumine, inhuman,
journeyman, kinsman,
lawman, layman, laywoman,
lemon, letterman, lineman,
linesman, mammon,
marksman, midshipman,
militiaman, milkman,
multivitamin, newsman,
nobleman, nonhuman,
numen, oarsman, oilman,
omen, ombudsman,
packman, penman, pitchman,
plowman, policeman,
postman, predetermine,
pressman, reexamine,
regimen, riflemen, salesman,
salmon, seaman, semen,
sermon, shaman, shipman,
showman, signalman,
spearman, specimen,
spokesman, spokeswoman,
sportsman, sportswoman,
stamen, statesman,
stickman, stillman, stockman,
stuntman, stuntwoman,

19

subhuman, summon,
superhuman, switchman,
swordsman, tales man,
talisman, tallyman, trash
man, ultra human,
uncommon, underclassman,
vermin, vitamin, watchman,
waterman, wingman, woman,
woodman, workingman,
yardman, yeoman (see also
antiphon [remaining
endings], **abecedarian,
bandwagon, abrasion,
awaken, pressrun, arson,
antitoxin, abbreviation,
antiunion, artisan**)
abdominal, affectional, anal,
antiphonal, atonal, banal,
bidirectional, cacuminal,
carnal, channel, charnel,
colonel, communal,
confessional, confrontational,
congregational,
constitutional, coronal,
criminal, deaconal,
denominational, devotional,
diagonal, directional,
dispensational, diurnal,
doctrinal, eternal, external,
final, flannel, fractional,
fraternal, funnel, gravitational,
infernal, instructional,
interdenominational,
intergenerational, internal,
intestinal, invitational, journal,
kennel, kernel, maternal,
nocturnal, nominal,
multichannel,
nonconfrontational,

nonconventional
nondenominational,
nonfunctional,
nonoperational, nonpersonal,
nonrational, nontraditional,
occupational, organizational,
original, panel, paternal,
penal, phenomenal,
propositional, quarterfinal,
rational, regnal, renal,
sectional, semifinal, seminal,
sensational, shrapnel, signal,
seminal, situational, spinal,
subliminal, supernal, tonal,
transformational, tribunal,
tunnel, unintentional,
unprofessional, untraditional,
urinal, vaginal, venal, vernal,
vinyl, virginal, vocational (see
also **abaxial, aboriginal**
[similar sound])
abduct, adduct, aqueduct,
conduct, construct, deduct,
duct, eruct, induct, instruct,
misconduct, obstruct,
product, reconstruct, self-
destruct, usufruct, viaduct
abduction, [abbreviation]
abductor, accelerator,
activator, actor, actuator,
adapter, adjuster,
administrator, aerometer,
aflutter, after, agitator,
alcoholmeter, algometer,
alligator, altar, alter,
alternator, altimeter, amateur,
amphitheater, animator,
annihilator, annunciator,
applicator, arbiter, arbitrator,

aspirator, auditor, aviator,
backwater, banter,
barometer, barter, batter,
beater, benefactor, better,
bitter, blatter, blotter,
breakwater, bullfighter,
butter, calculator, candle
lighter, canter, cantor, captor,
carburetor, carpenter, cater,
catheter, center, centimeter,
chanter, chapiter, chapter,
character, charter, chatter,
cheater, chiropractor, clatter,
clutter, coadjutor,
coconspirator, codirector,
coeditor, coexecutor,
collaborator, collator,
collector, comforter,
commentator, communicator,
commuter, compactor,
competitor, computer,
conciliator, conductor,
conservator, conspirator,
contractor, converter,
copromoter, coproprietor,
copywriter, corrupter, cotter,
coulter, counter, crater,
creator, creditor, critter,
cultivator, curator, cutter,
daughter, debtor, decameter,
decanter, decorator,
defibrillator, dehydrator,
delegator, demonstrator,
denominator, depositor,
detector, deter, detonator,
diameter, dictator, dimeter,
director, distributor, doctor,
donator, doubter, drifter,
dumbwaiter, duplicator,

editor, educator, eggbeater,
ejector, elevator, embitter,
emulator, encounter, enter,
epicenter, equator, escalator,
estimator, executor, exhibitor,
exhorter, expediter, exporter,
expositor, exterminator,
facilitator, factor, falter, fetter,
fighter, filter, firefighter,
firewater, flatter, flitter,
floater, floodwater, flutter,
flyswatter, forequarter,
fornicator, foxhunter,
frankfurter, freighter,
freshwater, fritter, fumigator,
gaiter, garter, gator,
generator, gladiator, glitter,
goiter, granddaughter,
grantor, greater,
groundwater, gunfighter,
gutter, hairsplitter, halter,
headhunter, headwaiter,
heater, helicopter, hereafter,
hindquarter, hunter,
hypocenter, idolater, idolator,
illustrator, imitator,
implementer, incinerator,
incubator, indicator, infiltrator,
inhibitor, innovator, inspector,
instructor, inter, interpreter,
interrogator, investigator,
interpolator, intimidator,
inventor, janitor, jetsetter,
jitter, keynoter, kilometer,
kilter, lamplighter, later, latter,
laughter, letter, lighter,
liquidator, liter, litigator, litter,
loiter, malefactor,
manipulator, marketer,

martyr, matter, mediator,
metacenter, meter,
midwinter, minicomputer,
miter, moderator, monitor,
mortar, motivator, motor,
mutter, navigator, nectar,
neuter, newsletter,
nomenclator, nonfactor,
nonvoter, nonwriter,
nonstarter, numerator,
objector, operator, orator,
orbiter, otter, ouster, outer,
pacesetter, painter, palter,
parameter, patter, percolator,
perimeter, persecutor, peter,
pewter, pinsetter, placater,
planter, platter, plotter,
pointer, polluter, porter,
potter, predator,
predestinator, presbyter,
presenter, primogenitor,
printer, proctor, procurator,
progenitor, prognosticator,
projector, promoter,
promulgator, propagator,
propitiator, proprietor,
prosecutor, prospector,
protector, protractor, pulsator,
punter, putter, quarter,
quitter, raconteur, radiator,
rafter, reactor, reconnoiter,
recruiter, rector, redactor,
redecorator, reenter,
reflector, refractor,
refrigerator, regenerator,
regulator, renovator, renter,
reporter, respirator,
resuscitator, revelator,
ripsnorter, rotor, router,

saboteur, saltpeter, saltwater,
saunter, scatter, scepter,
scooter, scriptwriter, sculptor,
seawater, sector, self-starter,
semiconductor, senator,
sequitur, setter, shatter,
shelter, shooter, shoplifter,
shutter, simulator, sinter,
sitter, skater, skeeter, skelter,
skitter, slaughter, smatter,
smelter, snifter, solicitor,
songwriter, sorter, spatter,
spectator, specter,
speculator, speechwriter,
speedometer, splatter,
splinter, splitter, splutter,
sportswriter, spotter,
springwater, sprinter, sputter,
starter, steamfitter,
stepdaughter, stonecutter,
stutter, subchapter,
subcontractor, subsector,
suiter, suitor, supercomputer,
supplanter, supporter,
sweater, swelter, tacometer,
tartar, tatter, teeter,
telemarketer, teleprinter,
teletypewriter, tempter,
terminator, testator, theater,
thermometer, tidewater, titter,
tormentor, totter, tractor,
traitor, translator, transmitter,
trapshooter, trendsetter,
trotter, troubleshooter,
trumpeter, tutor, tweeter,
twitter, typesetter, typewriter,
underwater, underwriter,
utter, valuator, vaulter,
vector, ventilator, vibrator,

victor, visitor, voltmeter,
volumeter, voter, waiter,
wastewater, water, welter,
wildcatter, winter, woodcutter,
writer (see also **arbitrager**
remaining endings], **amber,
adder, buffer, agar,
acupuncture, acupressure,
altogether, admeasure,
amplifier, armiger, angler,
armor, afterburner,
barkeeper, aggressor,
administer, achiever,
airpower, ballplayer,
adviser)**
abeam, academe, agleam,
airstream, beam, blaspheme,
bloodstream, cream,
daydream, deem, double-
team, downstream, dream,
esteem, extreme, gleam,
grapheme, ice cream,
inseam, lexeme, mainstream,
midstream, moonbeam,
ream, redeem, regime,
scheme, scream, seam,
seem, self-esteem, steam,
stream, subtheme, supreme,
taxeme, team, teem, theme,
upstream
abecedarian, accordion,
aeolian, agrarian, alien,
alluvion, amphibian,
antediluvian, antinomian,
antitotalitarian, antiquarian,
apiarian, arcadian,
authoritarian, barbarian,
carrion, centenarian,
champion, circadian, clarion,

cochampion, collegian,
comedian, contrarian,
countian, criterion, custodian,
disciplinarian,
documentarian, draconian,
egalitarian, enchiridion,
equestrian, grammarian,
guardian, halcyon, lesbian,
librarian, median, meridian,
millenarian, nickelodeon,
nonauthoritarian,
nonsectarian, oblivion,
octogenarian, paean,
parliamentarian, pedestrian,
plebeian, predestinarian,
premillenarian, proletarian,
ruffian, salutatorian, scorpion,
sectarian, seminarian,
sexagenarian, subterranean,
thespian, totalitarian,
trinitarian, unitarian,
utilitarian, valedictorian,
valetudinarian, vegetarian,
veterinarian (see also
abdomen)
abed, acid head, aforesaid,
ahead, airhead, amulet,
arrowhead, audiocassette,
baldhead, barrelhead,
bassinet, bayonet,
beachhead, bed, bedspread,
bedstead, behead, bighead,
biped, blackhead, bled,
blessed, blockhead,
bloodshed, bobsled,
bonehead, bread, brunette,
bullhead, clarinet, coed,
cokehead, coronet,
crossbred, dead, deadhead,

deathbed, dogsled,
dopehead, dread, drumhead,
dumbhead, dunkerhead, ed,
egghead, embed, farmstead,
fathead, featherbed, fed,
figurehead, flatbed, fled,
forget, fountainhead, gazette,
gingerbread, godhead, head,
highbred, homestead,
hothead, inbred, infrared,
instead, lead, led, letterhead,
limited, loggerhead,
masthead, meathead, met,
misled, moped, net,
newlywed, overfed,
overhead, ped, pinhead,
pled, pothead, premed,
purebred, quadruped, read,
red, retread, riverbed, said,
shed, shewbread,
shortbread, shred, skinhead,
sled, sorehead, spearhead,
sped, spread, stead,
subhead, sweetbread,
swellhead, thickhead,
thoroughbred, thread,
thunderhead, toolshed,
towhead, trailhead, tread,
truebred, unread, unsaid,
unwed, warhead, watershed,
wed, well-bred, well-read,
whitehead, widespread,
woodenhead, woodshed
aberrant, abhorrent,
accelerant, adherent, affront,
antiperspirant, apparent,
arrant, aspirant, battlefront,
beachfront, belligerent,
breakfront, brunt,

cobelligerent, concurrent,
confront, cormorant,
crosscurrent, currant, current,
deodorant, deterrent,
different, emigrant, errant,
expectorant, exuberant,
flagrant, forefront, fragrant,
front, fulgurant, gerent,
godparent, grandparent,
grunt, houseparent, hydrant,
ignorant, immigrant,
incoherent, indifferent,
inerrant, inherent, irreverent,
itinerant, lakefront, migrant,
nonrecurrent, oceanfront,
operant, quadrant,
recalcitrant, recurrent,
referent, refrigerant,
registrant, restaurant,
reverent, riverfront, runt,
shorefront, spirant,
stepparent, storefront,
tolerant, torrent, transparent,
tyrant, undercurrent, vagrant,
vibrant, warrant, waterfront
(see also **abandonment**)
aberration, [abbreviation]
abet, alphabet, asset,
bachelorette, backset,
baguette, barrette, becket,
beget, beset, bet, blanquette,
brevet, briolette, briquette,
brochette, cadet, calumet,
cassette, cigarette, coquette,
corvette, coset,
counterthreat, debt, duet,
diskette, epithet, fret, get,
godet, handset, headset,
heavyset, inlet, inset, jet, let,

majorette, maquette, minuet,
motet, octet, offset, onset,
outlet, pet, pirouette, quartet,
quintet, regret, reset, roulette,
septet, set, sextet, silhouette,
soubrette, soviet, statuette,
stylet, sublet, subset,
suffragette, sunset, sweat,
taboret, tacet, threat, toilette,
towellette, turbojet, typeset,
upset, usherette, vedette, vet,
videocassette, vignette, wet,
whet, yet (see also **bassinet**)
abetment, [abandonment]
abeyance, abhorrence,
absence, abstinence,
abundance, acceptance,
accidence, acquaintance,
adherence, admittance,
adolescence, affluence,
allegiance, alliance,
allowance, ambience,
ambivalence, ambulance,
annoyance, antiviolence,
appearance, appliance,
appurtenance, arrogance,
ascendance, assistance,
assonance, assurance,
attendance, audience,
balance, belligerence,
beneficence, benevolence,
brilliance, buoyance,
clairvoyance, clearance,
coexistence, cognizance,
coherence, coincidence,
coinsurance, comeuppance,
competence, compliance,
concomitance, concurrence,
condolence, conference,

confidence, confluence,
congruence, conscience,
continence, continuance,
convenience, convergence,
conveyance,
correspondence,
countenance,
counterbalance,
counterintelligence,
credence, dalliance,
decadence, deference,
defiance, deliverance,
dependence, deterrence,
deviance, diffidence,
diligence, disappearance,
discontinuance,
disobedience, dissidence,
dissonance, distance,
disturbance, divergence,
dominance, dunce,
ebullience, effulgence,
elegance, eloquence,
emergence, eminence,
encumbrance, endurance,
entrance, equivalence,
esperance, events,
excellence, exorbitance,
existence, expedience,
experience, extravagance,
exuberance, flamboyance,
flatulence, forbearance,
fragrance, frequence,
furtherance, grandiloquence,
grievance, hesitance,
hindrance, ignorance,
imbalance, immanence,
imminence, impatience,
impermanence, impertinence,
importance, impotence,

impudence, incidence,
incoherence, incompetence,
inconvenience,
independence, indifference,
indigence, indulgence,
inelegance, inexperience,
inference, influence,
inheritance, innocence,
insignificance, insistence,
insolence, instance,
insurance, insurgence,
intelligence, intemperance,
interference, intermittence,
intolerance, intransigence,
irradiance, irrelevance,
irreverence, issuance,
magnificence,
magniloquence,
maintenance, maleficence,
malevolence, negligence,
nescience, noncompliance,
nonconference,
nonconfidence,
nonexistence,
nonperformance,
nonresistance, nonsense,
nonviolence, obedience,
observance, occurrence,
offense, omnipotence,
omniscience, once, opulence,
ordinance, ordnance,
outdistance, overabundance,
overconfidence,
overindulgence, parlance,
patience, penance,
penitence, performance,
permanence, perseverance,
persistence, pertinence,
pestilence, petulance,

precedence, preclearance,
preeminence, preexistence,
preponderance, prescience,
prevalence, prominence,
providence, province,
purtenance, purveyance,
radiance, reassurance,
recalcitrance, recognizance,
reconnaissance, redolence,
refulgence, reinsurance,
relevance, reliance,
reluctance, remembrance,
repugnance, resemblance,
residence, resilience,
resistance, resonance,
resplendence, resurgence,
reticence, reverence,
riddance, sapience, science,
self-existence, self-
confidence, self-indulgence,
self-insurance, semblance,
sentience, sequence,
severance, significance,
silence, sixpence,
subsistence, substance,
superabundance,
surveillance, sustenance,
teleconference, temperance,
tolerance, transcendence,
transference, truculence,
turbulence, utterance,
valance, valence, variance,
vengeance, vigilance,
violence, virulence(see also
accordance)
abeyant, abortifacient,
absorbent, adjuvant, affiant,
affluent, ambient, ancient,
anti-incumbent, aperient,

applicant, arrogant, brilliant,
bunt, buoyant, chatoyant,
circumambient, clairvoyant,
client, clinquant, coefficient,
cognizant, communicant,
compliant, congruent,
constituent, convenient,
convent, defiant, deficient,
defoliant, delinquent, deviant,
discrepant, disobedient,
ebullient, efficient, elegant,
elephant, eloquent, eluant,
emollient, euphoriant,
expedient, extravagant,
fervent, flamboyant, flippant,
fluent, fumigant, giant,
gradient, grandiloquent, hunt,
impatient, incipient,
inconvenient, inefficient,
inelegant, ineloquent, infant,
infrequent, ingredient,
inpatient, insignificant,
insolvent, insufficient,
intoxicant, irrelevant,
lambent, lenient, litigant,
lubricant, luxuriant,
magniloquent, maidservant,
manhunt, mendicant,
merchant, multiclient,
nescient, nonaffluent,
nondelinquent,
nonincumbent,
nonparticipant, nonrelevant,
nutrient, obedient, observant,
occupant, omniscient, orient,
outpatient, overextravagent,
participant, parturient,
patient, peccant, penchant,
piquant, pliant, poignant,

prescient, proficient, prurient,
punt, pursuant, quotient,
radiant, rampant, recipient,
recreant, recumbent,
relevant, reliant, represent,
resilient, salient, sapient, self-
reliant, self-sufficient,
sentient, serpent, servant,
shunt, significant, solvent,
somnifacient, subsequent,
subservient, sufficient,
superefficient, supplicant,
sycophant, transient,
trenchant, triumphant, truant,
ultraefficient, vacant, valiant,
variant (see also
abandonment)
abhor, adore, afore, albacore,
anaphor, antiwar, anymore,
ashore, backdoor, bedsore,
before, boar, bookstore, bore,
carnivore, chore,
commodore, confiteor,
conquistador, core, corps,
décor, deplore, devisor,
dinosaur, door, downpour,
drugstore, encore, evermore,
explore, floor, folklore, for,
fore, forevermore, four,
fourscore, frore, furor,
furthermore, galore, gore,
guarantor, hardcore,
heretofore, hoar, ignore,
implore, indoor, lakeshore,
legislator, lessor, lore,
matador, manticore, mentor,
metaphor, more, mortgagor,
nevermore, nonpoor, nor,
oar, offshore, onshore, or,

ore, outdoor, outscore,
pinafore, pompadour, pore,
postwar, pour, rapport,
restore, roar, score,
seashore, sensor, shore,
signor, snore, soar, softcore,
sophomore, sore, spore,
stevedore, store, subfloor,
superstore, swore, sycamore,
therefore, theretofore,
threescore, tore, transferor,
troubadour, underscore,
uproar, war, wherefore,
whore, yore
abhorrence, [abeyance]
abhorrent, [aberrant]
abide, aborticide, allied,
alongside, amide, applied,
aside, astride, backside,
backslide, beachside,
bedside, beside, bestride,
betide, bide, biocide,
blindside, bonafide, bride,
broadside, bromide, certified,
chide, citywide, classified,
cockeyed, coincide, collide,
confide, countryside,
countrywide, courtside,
cowhide, crosseyed,
curbside, cyanide, decide,
deride, dignified, dissatisfied,
diversified, divide, double-
wide, downside, downslide,
elide, eventide, farside,
feticide, fireside, flip side,
fluoride, formaldehyde,
fortified, fratricide, fried,
fungicide, genocide,
germicide, glide, glorified,

graveside, guide, hayride,
herbicide, hide, hillside,
homicide, horsehide,
infanticide, insecticide, inside,
ironside, joyride, justified,
lakeside, landslide, matricide,
miticide, mountainside,
nationwide, nightside,
nondiversified, noonside,
offside, onside, outride,
outside, overqualified,
override, overstride,
parricide, patricide, peroxide,
pesticide, poolside,
preoccupied, preside, pride,
provide, purified, qualified,
rarefied, rawhide, refried,
reside, ride, ringside, riptide,
riverside, roadside, seaside,
self-satisfied, side, signified,
slide, snide, spermicide,
stateside, statewide,
storewide, stride, subdivide,
subside, suicide, tide,
topside, tried, ultrawide,
uncertified, unclarified,
undignified, unidentified,
unjustified, unmodified,
unsatisfied, unspecified,
unoccupied, unqualified,
untried, verbicide, wayside,
weakside, wide, worldwide,
yuletide
ability, [abatis]
abject, affect, aftereffect,
architect, aspect, bisect,
circumspect, codirect, collect,
confect, connect, convect,
correct, deflect, defect,

deject, detect, dialect, direct,
disaffect, disconnect,
disinfect, disrespect, dissect,
effect, eject, elect, erect,
expect, genuflect, incorrect,
indirect, infect, inflect, inject,
inspect, intellect, interject,
intersect, introject, necked,
neglect, nonelect,
overprotect, pandect, project,
prospect, protect, recollect,
reconnect, redirect, reelect,
reflect, reinspect, reject,
resect, respect, resurrect,
retrospect, ripple effect, sect,
select, self-respect, subject,
suspect, vivisect
abjection, [abbreviation]
abjuration, [abbreviation]
abjure, adjure, allure, amour,
aperture, armature, assure,
boor, brochure, calenture,
caricature, cocksure, coiffure,
coinsure, confiture, contour,
couture, coverture, cure,
curvature, demure, detour,
divestiture, embouchure,
endure, ensure, epicure,
forfeiture, immature,
imprimatur, impure, insecure,
insure, inure, investiture,
ligature, literature, lure,
manicure, manure, mature,
miniature, obscure, overture,
paramour, pedicure, perdure,
poor, premature, procure,
pure, reassure, reinsure, self-
insure, signature, spoor,

sure, temperature, tour,
velour, velure
ablate, accumulate, adulate,
ambulate, annihilate,
apostolate, articulate,
assimilate, blate, breastplate,
calculate, cantillate,
capitulate, chelate, circulate,
circumvallate, coagulate,
collate, confabulate, conflate,
congratulate, contemplate,
copulate, correlate, cucullate,
cumulate, deescalate,
defibrillate, deflate, delate,
depopulate, deregulate,
desolate, dilate,
discombobulate, dissimulate,
distillate, drawplate,
ejaculate, elate, emasculate,
emulate, encapsulate,
escalate, etiolate,
expostulate, extrapolate,
fellate, fibrillate, flagellate,
flocculate, formulate,
gesticulate, granulate,
gratulate, hyperventilate,
immolate, inflate, inoculate,
insulate, interpellate,
interpolate, interrelate,
invigilate, isolate, jubilate,
late, legislate, manipulate,
matriculate, miscalculate,
mistranslate, modulate,
mutilate, nameplate, oblate,
obnubilate, oscillate,
osculate, overinflate,
overpopulate, overregulate,
overstimulate, ovulate,
peculate, perambulate,

percolate, plait, plate,
populate, postulate, prolate,
pullulate, recalculate,
recapitulate, recirculate,
reformulate, regulate,
reinflate, relate, repopulate,
retranslate, scintillate,
simulate, slate,
somnambulate, speculate,
stimulate, stipulate,
strangulate, stridulate,
tabulate, tessellate, titillate,
toeplate, translate,
triangulate, ululate, undulate,
vacillate, vallate, ventilate,
violate(see also **abate**)
ablation, [abbreviation]
ablative, abortive,
accumulative, accusative,
acquisitive, active, adaptive,
additive, adjective
administrative, adoptive,
adventive, adversative,
affective, affirmative,
alternative, amative,
annotative, appelative,
appointive, appreciative,
argumentative, ascriptive,
assertive, associative,
attentive, attractive,
attributive, authoritative,
automotive, calmative,
captive, cognitive, collective,
combative, commemorative,
communicative, comparative,
competitive, connective,
connotative, consecutive,
conservative, constitutive,
contemplative, contraceptive,

corrective, correlative,
constructive, cooperative,
costive, counterproductive,
creative, cumulative, curative,
dative, deceptive, declarative,
decretive, deductive,
defective, definitive,
degenerative, derivative,
demonstrative, descriptive,
destructive, detective,
determinative, digestive,
diminutive, directive,
disjunctive, disruptive,
distinctive, distributive,
durative, effective, elective,
executive, exhaustive,
expletive, festive, figurative,
fixative, formative, fugitive,
furtive, genitive, hortative,
hyperactive, illative,
imperative, inactive,
inattentive, incentive,
inchoative, indicative,
inductive, ineffective,
infinitive, informative,
initiative, innovative,
inoperative, inquisitive,
inscriptive, insensitive,
instinctive, instructive,
interactive, interrogative,
intransitive, introspective,
intuitive, invective, inventive,
irrespective, iterative,
laxative, legislative, locative,
locomotive, lucrative,
maladaptive, manipulative,
meditative, motive, narrative,
native, negative, nominative,
nonaddictive, nonassertive,

noncombative,
noncommunicative,
noncompetitive,
nonconsecutive,
nonconstructive,
noncooperative, noncreative,
noncumulative,
nondeductive,
nondescriptive,
nondestructive, nondirective,
nondisruptive, noneffective,
nonelective, nonnegative,
nonobjective, nonproductive,
nonquantitative, nonreactive,
nonrestrictive, normative,
objective, octave, operative,
optative, overprotective,
oversensitive, overactive,
participative, pejorative,
perceptive, perspective,
plaintive, positive,
postoperative, predictive,
preemptive, prerogative,
prescriptive, preservative,
preventative, preventive,
primitive, privative, proactive,
productive, prohibitive,
prospective, provocative,
punitive, putative, qualitative,
quantitative, radioactive,
reactive, receptive, recitative,
redemptive, reflective,
relative, repetitive,
representative, reproductive,
respective, restive, restrictive,
retributive, retroactive,
retrospective, sedative,
selective, self-protective,
sensitive, speculative,

sportive, stative, subjective,
subjunctive, substantive,
suggestive, superlative,
supersensitive, supportive,
susceptive, talkative,
tentative, transitive,
ultraconservative,
unattractive,
uncommunicative,
uncompetitive,
uncooperative, uncreative,
undemonstrative,
underactive, unproductive,
unreceptive, vegetative,
vindictive, vituperative,
vocative, volitive, votive(see
also **forgive** [remaining
endings], **abrasive**)
ablaut, afoot, barefoot,
clubfoot, flatfoot, foot, hotfoot,
input, kaput, output,
pussyfoot, put, soot,
tenderfoot, throughput,
underfoot, webfoot
ablaze, agaze, always, amaze,
anyways, appraise, baize,
blaze, bordelaise, braise,
braze, chaise, craze, daze,
emblaze, faze, gaze, glaze,
graze, haze, hollandaise,
lase, laze, maize, malaise,
mayonnaise, maze, mores,
nowadays, paraphrase,
phase, phrase, praise, raise,
rase, raze, reappraise,
rephrase, sideways,
stargaze, upraise, weekdays
able, abominable, abubble,
acceptable, accessible,

accountable, achievable,
actionable, adaptable,
adjustable, admirable,
admissible, adoptable,
adorable, advisable, affable,
affordable, agreeable,
alienable, allowable, amble,
amenable, amiable,
amicable, answerable,
applicable, appreciable,
apprehensible, approachable,
approvable, arable, arguable,
assemble, assignable,
assumable, atremble,
attainable, audible, available,
avoidable, babble, bailable,
bankable, barbel, bauble,
bearable, believable, bible,
biodegradable, blamable,
bobble, brabble, bramble,
breakable, bubble, bumble,
burble, cable, callable,
cannibal, capable, certifiable,
changeable, charitable,
chasuble, chewable, cobble,
collapsible, collectible,
combustible, comestible,
comfortable, commendable,
communicable, comparable,
compatible, comprehensible,
conceivable, conformable,
conscionable, considerable,
constable, contemptible,
convertible, correctable,
corrigible, corruptible,
credible, creditable,
crossable, crucible, crumble,
culpable, curable, cymbal,
dabble, debatable, decibel,

deductible, defensible,
definable, degradable,
delectable, demonstrable,
deniable, dependable,
deplorable, depreciable,
desirable, despicable,
destructible, detachable,
detestable, dibble, digestible,
dirigible, disable,
disagreeable, disassemble,
discernible, disciplinable,
discussable, dishonorable,
dispensable, disposable,
disputable, disreputable,
disrespectable, dissemble,
dissoluble, divisible, double,
drabble, dribble, durable,
eatable, edible, educable,
electable, eligible, enable,
enforceable, ennoble,
ensemble, enumerable,
enviable, equitable, evitable,
excitable, exhaustible,
expandable, expendable,
explainable, explicable, fable,
fallible, fashionable,
favorable, feasible, feeble,
flammable, flappable, flexible,
foible, forcible, foreseeable,
forgettable, formidable,
frangible, friable, fribble,
fumble, gabble, gable,
gamble, garble, global,
gobble, grabble, grumble,
gullible, habile, herbal,
hobble, honorable, horrible,
hospitable, humble,
identifiable, ignoble, illegible,
imaginable, immersible,

immobile, immovable,
immutable, impalpable,
impassible, impeachable,
impeccable, impenetrable,
imperceptible, imperishable,
impermissible, implacable,
implausible, imponderable,
impossible, impracticable,
impressionable, improbable,
inaccessible, inadmissible,
inadvisable, inalienable,
inalterable, inapplicable,
inapproachable, inaudible,
incalculable, incapable,
incombustible, incomparable,
incompatible,
incomprehensible,
inconceivable, incorrigible,
incorruptible, incredible,
incurable, indefatigable,
indefectible, indefensible,
indefinable, indelible,
indescribable, indestructible,
indigestible, indispensable,
indisputable,
indistinguishable, indivisible,
indomitable, indubitable,
inedible, ineffable,
ineffaceable, ineligible,
inequitable, inescapable,
inestimable, inevitable,
inexcusable, inexhaustible,
inexorable, inexplicable,
inexpressible,
inextinguishable, inextricable,
infallible, inflammable,
inflatable, inflexible,
inhospitable, inimitable,
innumerable, inoperable,

insatiable, inscrutable,
insensible, inseparable,
insoluble, insolvable,
insatiable, insuperable,
insurable, insurmountable,
intangible, intelligible,
interchangeable,
interminable, intolerable,
intractable, invaluable,
invariable, inviable, invincible,
inviolable, invisible, irascible,
irreconcilable, irreducible,
irrefutable, irreparable,
irreplaceable, irreplaceable,
irrepressible, irreproachable,
irresistible, irresolvable,
irresponsible, irreversible,
irrevocable, irritable, jumble,
justifiable, kibble, label,
lamentable, laudable,
laughable, legible, liable,
libel, likable, livable, lovable,
makable, malleable,
manageable, marble,
marketable, marriageable,
memorable, mendable,
mensurable, miserable,
mislabel, mobile, moldable,
movable, multivariable,
mumble, mutable, negligible,
negotiable, nibble, nimble,
noble, nonbreakable,
noncombustible,
nonconvertible,
nondeductible,
nondepletable,
nonflammable,
nonmeasurable,
nonnegotiable,

nonperishable,
nonquantifiable,
nonrefundable,
nonrenewable,
nonreturnable, nonreusable,
nontaxable, nontransferable,
nonverbal, notable,
noticeable, nubble,
observable, operable,
ostensible, palatable,
palpable, parable, passable,
payable, peaceable, pebble,
penetrable, perceivable,
perceptible, perdurable,
perishable, permeable,
permissible, personable,
pitiable, plausible,
pleasurable, pliable, portable,
possible, potable, practicable,
preamble, predictable,
preferable, presentable,
preventable, printable,
probably, profitable,
promotable, psychobabble,
publishable, punishable,
questionable, quibble,
quotable, rabble, ramble,
reassemble, reasonable,
rebel, receivable,
reconcilable, redouble,
referable, refillable,
reformable, refutable, relabel,
reliable, remarkable,
remissible, removable,
renegotiable, renewable,
repairable, reparable,
repeatable, reprehensible,
reproducible,
reprogrammable, reputable,

resemble, resolvable,
respectable. responsible,
restrainable, retractable,
retrievable, returnable,
reusable, reversible,
revocable, rotatable, rubble,
ruble, rumble, sable, satiable,
scrabble, scramble, scribble,
scrutable, scumble,
searchable, seasonable,
sensible, shamble, sizable,
sociable, soluble, solvable,
spreadable, squabble, stable,
stubble, stumble,
submersible, suitable,
susceptible, sustainable,
syllable, symbol, table,
tangible, taxable, teachable,
tenable, terrible, testable,
thimble, tillable, timetable,
tolerable, touchable,
traceable, tractable,
treasonable, treatable, treble,
tremble, tribal, trouble,
trustable, tumble, turntable,
unable, unacceptable,
unaccountable, unalterable,
unanswerable,
unapproachable,
unassailable, unattainable,
unavailable, unavoidable,
unbearable, unbeatable,
unbelievable, unbendable,
unbreakable, unchangeable,
uncomfortable,
unconscionable,
uncontrollable, undebatable,
undeliverable, undeniable,
undependable, undigestible,

undrinkable, uneducable,
unelectable, unemployable,
unenforceable,
unexplainable,
unfashionable, unfathomable,
unfavorable, unforgettable,
unforeseeable, unforgivable,
uninsurable, unintelligible,
unjustifiable, unknowable,
unlovable, unmanageable,
unmentionable, unobtainable,
unpalatable, unpardonable,
unpredictable, unprintable,
unprofitable, unpublishable,
unquenchable,
unquestionable,
unreasonable,
unrecognizable,
unreconcilable,
unredeemable, unreliable,
unremarkable, unresolvable,
unsalable, unsalvageable,
unscramble, unsearchable,
unseasonable, unsellable,
unshakable, unsinkable,
unsociable, unspeakable,
unstable, unstoppable,
unsuitable, unsupportable,
unsurpassable,
unsustainable, untamable,
unteachable, untenable,
unthinkable, untouchable,
unutterable, unverifiable,
unwearable, unwinnable,
unworkable, valuable,
variable, vegetable, verbal,
verifiable, veritable, viable,
vincible, visible, vocable,
voidable, voluble, vulnerable,

wamble, warble, washable,
wearable, wobble, workable,
worktable (see also **abaxial**)
abloom, anteroom, assume,
baby boom, backroom,
ballroom, barroom, bathroom,
bedroom, bloom, boardroom,
boom, bridegroom,
broadloom, broom, brume,
cloakroom, consume,
costume, courtroom,
darkroom, doom, elbowroom,
entomb, exhume, flume,
fume, gloom, greenroom,
groom, guardroom,
headroom, heirloom,
homeroom, legroom, legume,
loom, lunchroom, mudroom,
mushroom, newsroom,
perfume, playroom, plume,
poolroom, pressroom,
presume, resume, room,
salesroom, schoolroom,
showroom, sickroom, spume,
stillroom, stockroom,
storeroom, subsume,
sunroom, tearoom, tomb,
toolroom, vacuum,
wardroom, wareroom,
washroom, whom, womb,
workroom, zoom
abluted, accepted, accredited,
affected, adjusted, affiliated,
animated, articulated,
assorted, augmented,
automated, belated, belted,
benighted, big-hearted,
blasted, bloated, busted,
calculated, capsulated,

celebrated, chested,
closefisted, coldhearted,
committed, complected,
complicated, conceited,
conjugated, connected,
constipated, contented,
convoluted, coordinated,
corrugated, cultivated, dated,
decaffeinated, dedicated,
deep-rooted, deep-seated,
dejected, delighted,
demented, departed,
devoted, dilapidated, dilated,
directed, disaffected,
disappointed, disconnected,
disinterested, disjointed,
dispirited, disseminated,
dissipated, distracted,
distributed, double-breasted,
double-jointed, downhearted,
educated, elated, elevated,
enlisted, farsighted, fetid,
fitted, fixated, flat-footed,
foliated, freehearted, frosted,
gifted, greathearted,
halfhearted, hardhearted,
heated, heavyhearted,
hyphenated, impacted,
imputed, incorporated,
inebriated, inflated,
interrelated, intoxicated,
irritated, knotted, lamented,
laminated, liberated,
maladapted, maladjusted,
monounsaturated,
multifaceted, multitalented,
nearsighted, nonaccredited,
nonactivated, nonaffiliated,
nonassociated,

noncommitted, nonelected,
nonrated, nonregulated,
nonrestricted, noted,
openhearted, oriented,
outdated, overeducated,
overexcited, overinflated,
overopinionated, overrated,
parted, patented, perforated,
pointed, polyunsaturated,
potted, premeditated,
purported, repeated,
restricted, sainted, saturated,
scented, segregated,
selected, self-directed, self-
inflicted, self-motivated, self-
oriented, self-appointed,
shortsighted, simulated,
skirted, softhearted,
sophisticated, spirited, stilted,
stouthearted, stud,
supersophisticated,
syncopated, talented,
tenderhearted, tested,
tightfisted, truehearted,
twisted, unabated,
unaccepted, unadulterated,
unaffected, unaffiliated,
unallocated, unanticipated,
unappreciated,
unappropriated, unassisted,
unassociated, unaudited,
unbudgeted, uncalculated,
uncarpeted, uncharted,
uncirculated, uncommitted,
uncompleted, uncomplicated,
unconsecrated, uncontested,
unconverted, uncoordinated,
uncorrected, uncorroborated,
undated, undaunted,

undecorated, undedicated,
undefeated, undelegated,
underappreciated,
underbudgeted,
undereducated,
underinflated,
underpopulated,
underrepresented,
understated, undesignated,
undirected, undisputed,
undocumented, undoubted,
unedited, uneducated,
unexpected, unexploited,
unformulated,
unincorporated, unindicted,
uninfected, uninhabited,
uninhibited, uninspected,
uninstructed, uninsulated,
uninterested, united,
uninterrupted, unintimidated,
uninvited, unirrigated,
unliberated, unlimited,
unlisted, unmedicated,
unmerited, unmitigated,
unmotivated, unobstructed,
unprecedented, unprotected,
unrated, unreported,
unrepresented, unrequited,
unsaturated, unscented,
unscripted, unsegregated,
unsolicited, unsophisticated,
unspotted, unstated,
unsubstantiated, untainted,
untalented, untranslated,
untreated, unvisited,
unwanted, unwarranted,
variegated, vaulted, vaunted,
warmhearted, wasted,
weighted, well-adjusted,

wholehearted, worsted (see
acid [remaining endings],
absentminded)
ablution, [abbreviation]
ably, absolutely, abundantly,
abusively, abysmally,
academically, acceptability,
accessibility, accidentally,
accordingly, accurately,
actually, adequately,
advisedly, aesthetically,
aimlessly, aioli, alee, alley,
amole, amphiboly, amply,
anomaly, antimonopoly,
appellee, assembly, badly,
bally, barely, barley, belly,
billy, biweekly, biyearly,
bodily, boldly, bristly,
broccoli, brotherly, bubbly,
bully, burley, burly,
campanile, cannoli, challis,
chili, chilly, civilly, collie, colly,
comely, conclusively, coolie,
costly, coulee, counselee,
cowardly, crackly, creaturely,
cuddly, cully, curly, daily,
dally, dastardly, deli,
diametrically, diddly, dilly,
dillydally, directly, doily, dolly,
dully, duopoly, early, earthly,
easily, elderly, especially,
facsimile, family, filly, finale,
flea, flee, fleshly, folly, frijole,
fully, galilee, galley, gally,
gangly, generally, ghastly,
gingerly, girlie, glee, goalie,
golly, gravelly, grisly, grizzly,
guacamole, gully, haole,
heartily, hillbilly, hilly, holly,

holy, homely, homily, hourly,
hurly, hyperbole, jelly, jolly,
jubilee, lee, leisurely, likely,
lily, lively, lonely, lovely,
lowly, majorly, mallee,
mannerly, masterly, measly,
medley, melancholy,
monopoly, monthly, motley,
nonfamily, oily, oligopoly,
only, orderly, paisley,
panoply, parley, parsley,
partially, pearly, plea,
potbelly, prickly, primarily,
princely, probably, pulley,
rally, ravioli, reveille, ruly,
sally, scaly, scholarly,
scraggly, semimonthly,
shapely, sickly, sightly, silly,
simile, simply, sisterly,
slovenly, sluggardly, smelly,
sowbelly, spindly, sprightly,
stately, steely, stepfamily,
stilly, straggly, sully, surely,
tally, tamale, telefacsimile,
temporarily, timely, tingly,
trolley, truly, ugly, ukulele,
unruly, unscholarly,
unfriendly, ungodly,
unhappily, unholy, unlikely,
unlovely, unmanly,
unmannerly, unseemly,
unsightly, untimely,
unworldly, valley, verily,
vermicelli, virtually, valley,
wally, whirly, wiggly, wily,
womanly, worldly, yearly (see
also **abalone**)
abnegate, abrogate,
aggregate, arrogate,

castigate, congregate,
conjugate, corrugate,
delegate, derogate,
desegregate, divagate,
elongate, expurgate,
floodgate, fumigate, fustigate,
gait, gate, headgate,
instigate, interrogate,
investigate, irrigate, legate,
litigate, mitigate, navigate,
negate, obligate, promulgate,
propagate, reinvestigate,
relegate, runagate,
segregate, subjugate,
subrogate, surrogate,
tailgate, tollgate, variegate,
vulgate(see also **abate**)
abnegation, [abbreviation]
abnormal, abysmal, animal,
baptismal, brumal, camel,
caramel, decimal, dismal,
duodecimal, enamel, formal,
geothermal, infinitesimal,
informal, maximal, minimal,
mull, nonformal, nonoptimal,
normal, optimal, paranormal,
pommel, primal, pummel,
semiformal, subnormal,
suboptimal, thermal, trammel
(see also **abaxial**)
abnormality, [abatis]
aboard, aboveboard, adored,
afford, backboard,
backsword, baseboard,
billboard, blackboard, board,
breadboard, buckboard,
cardboard, chalkboard,
checkerboard, chipboard,
clipboard, dartboard,

dashboard, duckboard,
fiberboard, fingerboard,
floorboard, footboard, ford,
freeboard, gourd, headboard,
horde, inboard, keyboard,
mortarboard, motherboard,
onboard, outboard,
overboard, paddleboard,
paperboard, pressboard,
punchboard, reboard,
sailboard, scoreboard,
shuffleboard, skateboard,
smorgasbord, snowboard,
soundboard, splashboard,
springboard, storyboard,
surfboard, switchboard,
sword, tackboard, tagboard,
unexplored, wallboard,
washboard [see also **accord**]
abode, anode, antinode,
antipode, area code,
armload, backload, bode,
bowed, busload, carload,
caseload, cathode, code,
commode, corrode,
crossroad, decode,
download, encode, episode,
epode, erode, explode,
forebode, freeload, genetic
code, goad, hallowed,
implode, inroad, load, lode,
miscode, mode, Morse code,
node, ode, overload,
palinode, payload, planeload,
railroad, reload, road, rode,
strode, toad, trainload,
truckload, unload, upload,
workload
abolish, accomplish,

admonish, anguish, apish,
astonish, baitfish, banish,
bearish, blandish, blemish,
bookish, boorish, boyish,
brackish, brandish, bullish,
burnish, catfish, cherish,
childish, churlish, clannish,
co-publish, cultish, darkish,
demolish, dervish, devilish,
diminish, dish, distinguish,
doggish, dovish, embellish,
establish, extinguish, famish,
fetish, feverish, fiendish,
finish, fish, flourish, folkish,
foolish, freakish, furbish,
furnish, garish, garnish,
gibberish, girlish, goldfish,
grayish, greenish, hawkish,
hellish, hoggish, horseradish,
impish, impoverish, jellyfish,
languish, lavish, licorice,
loutish, mannish, modish,
mulish, nebbish, nightmarish,
orangish, outlandish, parish,
peevish, perish, pish, polish,
prudish, publish, punish,
qualmish, ravish, reestablish,
reddish, refinish, refurbish,
relinquish, relish, replenish,
republish, roguish, rubbish,
schottische, selfish,
sheepish, sickish, skirmish,
skittish, slavish, slobbish,
sluggish, snobbish, sottish,
squeamish, squish, standish,
standoffish, stylish, swish,
tarnish, ticklish, unselfish,
vanish, varnish, viperish,
voguish, waggish, whish,

wish
abolition, [abbreviation]
abolitionism, absenteeism,
absolutism, activism,
agnosticism, alcoholism,
altruism, anachronism,
anarchism, aneurysm,
animism, antagonism,
anthropomorphism,
anthropopathism, antielitism,
antifeminism, antiracism,
aphorism, asceticism,
astigmatism, atavism,
atheism, athleticism,
atomism, atticism, autism,
autoeroticism, baptism,
barbarism, behavorism,
besom, bolshevism, bosom,
bruxism, cannibalism,
capitalism cataclysm,
catechism, chasm,
chauvinism, chiasm, chrism,
colonialism, colloquialism,
communism,
congregationalism,
conservatism,
countercriticism, creationism,
criticism, cronyism, cynicism,
denominationalism,
despotism, determinism,
diabolism, dogmatism,
druidism, dualism,
ecumenism, egalitarianism,
egotism, elitism, empiricism,
enthusiasm,
environmentalism, eroticism,
euphemism, evangelism,
exhibitionism, existentialism,
exorcism, expansionism,

expressionism, extremism,
fascism, fatalism, favoritism,
feminism, fetishism,
feudalism, formalism,
fraternalism, funambulism,
fundamentalism, futurism,
globalism, gnosticism,
gradualism, heathenism,
hedonism, henotheism,
heroism, humanism,
hypnotism, idealism,
imperialism, individualism,
isolationism, journalism,
legalism, lesbianism,
liberalism magnetism,
mannerism, masochism,
materialism, mechanism,
mercantilism, metabolism,
methodism, microorganism,
microcosm, militarism,
millennialism, misoneism,
modernism, monetarism,
monism, monotheism,
moralism, multiculturalism,
mysticism, narcissism,
nationalism, naturalism,
nepotism, nihilism,
obstructionism, occultism,
opportunism, optimism,
organism, orgasm, pacifism,
paganism, pantheism,
parallelism, paroxysm,
passivism, paternalism,
patriotism, perfectionism,
pessimism, phantasm,
pharisaism, photojournalism,
pietism, plagiarism,
pleonasm, pluralism,
polytheism, populism,

positivism, pragmatism,
premillennialism, prism,
professionalism,
protectionism, provincialism,
pugilism, puritanism,
quietism, racism, rationalism,
realism, rebaptism,
recidivism, reductionism,
regionalism, relativism,
revivalism, rheumatism,
ritualism, sacerdotalism,
sacramentalism, sadism,
sadomasochism, sarcasm,
satanism, schism, sciolism,
secularism, self-criticism,
sensationalism, sensualism,
sentimentalism, separatism,
sexism, shamanism,
skepticism, socialism,
solecism, solipsism,
somnambulism, sophism,
spasm, spiritism, spiritualism,
statism, stoicism,
subjectivism, surrealism,
syllogism, symbolism,
syncretism, syndicalism,
synergism, televangelism,
terrorism, theism, tokenism,
totalitarianism, tourism,
traditionalism, tribalism,
tritheism, truism,
ultranationalism,
universalism, utilitarianism,
utopianism, vandalism,
ventriloquism, volunteerism,
voodooism, welfarism,
witticism
abolitionist, abortionist,
accompanist, agonist,

antagonist, anticommunist,
antievolutionist, antifeminist,
arsonist, balloonist, botanist,
cartoonist, chauvinist,
colonist, columnist,
communist, conservationist,
contortionist, cosmogonist,
creationist, ecumenist,
evolutionist, exhibitionist,
expansionist, expressionist,
hedonist, humanist, hygienist,
illusionist, impressionist,
insurrectionist, integrationist,
internist, isolationist,
liberationist, machinist,
modernist, monist,
noncommunist, nutritionist,
opportunist, organist,
percussionist, perfectionist,
pianist, proabortionist,
prohibitionist, projectionist,
protagonist, protectionist,
reductionist, receptionist,
religionist, revisionist,
revolutionist, secessionist,
segregationist, separationist,
shamanist,
ultrasegregationist (see also
activist [remaining endings],
**allergist, aerialist,
alchemist, allegorist,
assist, absolutist**)
abominable, [able]
abominate, adnate,
agglutinate, agnate, alienate,
alternate, assassinate,
bicarbonate, bombinate,
cachinnate, carbonate,
cognate, connate,

consternate, contaminate,
coordinate, coronate,
crenate, criminate, culminate,
dechlorinate, decontaminate,
deracinate, designate,
detonate, discriminate,
disseminate, dominate,
donate, eliminate, emanate,
exterminate, fascinate,
festinate, fluorinate,
fractionate, fulminate,
geminate, germinate,
hallucinate, hibernate,
hyphenate, illuminate,
impersonate, impregnate,
incarnate, incriminate,
indoctrinate, innate,
inseminate, intonate,
laminate, machinate,
magnate, marinate, neonate,
nominate, originate, ornate,
oxygenate, paginate,
peregrinate, perennate,
personate, phonate, pollinate,
predestinate, predominate,
procrastinate, proportionate,
ratiocinate, reincarnate,
rejuvenate, renominate,
repristinate, resonate,
ruminate, stagnate,
subordinate, terminate,
urinate, vaccinate,
vaticinate(see also **abate**)
abomination, [abbreviation]
aboriginal, additional, annul,
antieducational, arsenal,
attitudinal, cardinal,
coeducational, coeternal,
conditional, congressional,

conventional, conversational,
delusional, dimensional,
emotional, exceptional,
fictional, foundational,
functional, germinal,
heptagonal, hymnal,
impersonal, institutional,
intentional, international,
interpersonal, irrational,
jurisdictional, marginal,
medicinal, motivational,
multidimensional,
multidirectional,
multigenerational,
multinational, national,
nonemotional,
nonprofessional, notional,
null, occasional, octagonal,
optional, ordinal,
overemotional,
paraprofessional, personal,
processional, positional,
professional, proportional,
recessional, regional,
relational, retinal, seasonal,
semiprofessional, sentinel,
subpanel, terminal,
traditional, transnational,
transitional, ultraprofessional,
unconditional,
unconstitutional,
unconventional, unemotional,
unidimensional,
unidirectional, vaticinal,
volitional (see also **abaxial,**
   abdominal [similar sound])
aborigine, [abalone]
abort, assort, athwart, bort,
cavort, cohort, consort,

contort, distort, escort,
exhort, extort, heliport, ort,
presort, quart, resort, retort,
short, snort, sort, swart,
thwart, tort, wart, worrywart
aborticide, [abide]
abortifacient, [abeyant]
abortion, [abbreviation]
abortionist, [abolitionist]
abortive, [ablative]
abound, aboveground,
aground, around, astound,
background, battleground,
belowground, bloodhound,
bound, campground,
chowhound, clothbound,
cofound, compound,
confound, dumbfound,
earthbound, eastbound,
elkhound, expound,
fairground, fogbound,
foreground, found,
greyhound, ground,
hardbound, hell bound,
hidebound, home bound,
hound, housebound,
impound, inbound, merry-go-
round, middle ground,
mound, outbound,
playground, pound, profound,
propound, rebound, redound,
renowned, resound,
rockhound, round, runaround,
snowbound, sound,
southbound, spellbound,
surround, turnaround,
ultrasound, unbound,
underground, unsound,

westbound, wound,
wraparound
about, bailout, blackout,
blowout, boy scout, bout,
breakout, brownout, burnout,
buyout, carryout, checkout,
closeout, clout, cookout, cop-
out, cutout, devout, doubt,
downspout, dropout, drought,
dugout, fallout, flat-out,
foldout, gadabout, gout,
groundout, grout, handout,
hangout, hideout, holdout,
knockout, layout, lockout,
lookout, lout, misroute, out,
payout, pig out, pitchout,
pout, printout, pullout, putout,
rainspout, readout, reroute,
rollout, roundabout, rout,
route, runabout, sauerkraut,
scout, self-doubt, sellout,
setout, shakeout, shout,
shutout, snout, spout, sprout,
stakeout, standout, stout,
strikeout, takeout,
thereabout, throughout, tout,
trout, tryout, turnabout,
turnout, umlaut, walkout,
washout, waterspout,
whereabout, whiteout,
wipeout, without, workout
above, dove, glove, ladylove,
love, of, self-love, shove,
thereof, turtledove, whereof
aboveboard, [aboard]
aboveground, [abound]
abracadabra, agora, algebra,
aura, aurora, bora, bravura,
caesura, caldera, cathedra,

camera, candelabra,
cataphora, chakra, chimera,
cholera, cobra, contra,
diaspora, era, etcetera, extra,
fedora, flora, genre, infra,
libra, mantra, marimba,
marinara, mascara, menorah,
okra, opera, orchestra,
palaestra, pandora, plethora,
primipara, senora, sierra,
signora, tempura, terra,
tundra, ultra, umbra,
vertebra, zebra (see also **a capella**)
abrade, accolade, afraid, aid,
aide, aquacade, arcade,
barmaid, barricade, blade,
blockade, braid, bridesmaid,
brigade, brocade, cade,
cannonade, cascade,
cavalcade, centigrade,
chambermaid, charade,
chiffonade, colonnade,
corrade, crusade, dairymaid,
decade, defilade, degrade,
dissuade, downgrade,
escalade, escapade, evade,
everglade, fade, glade,
grade, grenade, handmade,
homemade, housemaid,
inlaid, invade, jade, lade, laid,
lemonade, limeade, made,
maid, marinade, marmalade,
masquerade, medicaid,
mermaid, motorcade,
nursemaid, orangeade, paid,
palisade, parade, persuade,
pervade, plantigrade,
postpaid, promenade, raid,

renegade, retrograde, self-
made, serenade, shade,
spade, spayed, staid,
stockade, subgrade, suede,
sunshade, switchblade,
tirade, trade, unafraid,
unpaid, wade
Abraham, [aerogram]
abrasion, abscission,
adhesion, affusion, allusion,
animadversion, aspersion,
aversion, circumcision,
civilization, coercion,
cohesion, collision, collusion,
conclusion, confusion,
contusion, conversion,
corrosion, decision, delusion,
derision, diffusion, disillusion,
dispersion, division, effusion,
elision, elusion, emersion,
emulsion, envision, equation,
erosion, evasion, emulsion,
excision, exclusion,
excursion, explosion,
extroversion, fusion, illusion,
immersion, implosion,
incision, inclusion, indecision,
infusion, introversion,
invasion, lesion, nondecision,
obtrusion, occasion,
occlusion, persuasion,
perversion, precision,
prevision, profusion,
protrusion, provision,
recursion, reinvasion,
rescission, reversion,
revision, scission, seclusion,
self-delusion, suasion,
subdivision, submersion,

subversion, supervision,
television, transfusion,
version, vision (see also
abdomen)
abrasive, abusive, adhesive,
aggressive, allusive,
apprehensive,
antisubversive, coercive,
comprehensive, compulsive,
conclusive, conducive,
convulsive, corrosive,
counteroffensive, corrosive,
cursive, decisive, defensive,
depressive, derisive, divisive,
effusive, elusive, embracive,
evasive, excessive,
exclusive, excursive,
expansive, expensive,
explosive, expressive,
extensive, illusive, impassive,
impressive, impulsive,
incisive, inclusive,
inconclusive, indecisive,
inexpensive, inexpressive,
ingressive, inoffensive,
intensive, intrusive, invasive,
jussive, massive, missive,
nonabrasive, nonadhesive,
nonaggressive, nonintrusive,
nonpermissive,
nonprogressive,
nonpurposive,
nonresponsive, obsessive,
obtrusive, offensive,
oppressive, ostensive,
passive, pensive, percussive,
permissive, persuasive,
pervasive, possessive,
progressive, purposive,

recessive, recursive,
reflexive, regressive,
repressive, repulsive,
responsive, submissive,
successive, ultraexclusive,
unexpressive, unobtrusive,
unpersuasive, unresponsive
(see also **ablative**)
abreaction, [abbreviation]
abreast, alkahest, anapest,
armrest, arrest, attest,
backrest, behest, bequest,
best, blest, breast, chest,
compressed, congest,
conquest, contest, crest,
depressed, detest, digest,
disinvest, distressed, divest,
dressed, footrest, gabfest,
guest, hard-pressed,
headrest, hillcrest,
houseguest, imprest, incest,
infest, ingest, inquest, invest,
jest, lest, manifest, Midwest,
molest, nest, obsessed,
palimpsest, pest, possessed,
pretest, professed, protest,
quest, rearrest, repressed,
retest, reinvest, request, rest,
self-addressed, slugfest,
songfest, southwest, suggest,
test, unconfessed,
undressed, unexpressed,
unimpressed, unprocessed,
unrest, vest, west, wrest, zest
abridge, acreage, anchorage,
average, beverage, borage,
bridge, brokerage, carriage,
cartridge, courage, coverage,
discourage, disparage,

45

drawbridge, encourage,
flybridge, footbridge, forage,
fridge, hemorrhage,
intermarriage, leverage,
marriage, miscarriage,
moorage, partridge, porridge,
remarriage, ridge, storage,
suffrage, undercarriage,
umbrage (see also
acknowledge [remaining
endings], **appanage**)
abroach, approach, broach,
brooch, caroche, coach,
cockroach, encroach,
outcoach, poach, reproach,
roach, stagecoach
abroad, applaud, aubade,
awed, ballade, baud, bawd,
bigarade, broad, clawed,
clod, cod, couvade, death
squad, decapod, defraud,
ephod, esplanade, facade,
fraud, fusillade, god,
goldenrod, hod, jihad, laud,
maraud, mod, nod, odd, plod,
pod, prod, quad, ramrod, rod,
roughshod, shod, slipshod,
sod, squad, tightwad, tripod,
trod, wad
abrogate, [abnegate]
abrupt, bankrupt, corrupt,
developed, disrupt, erupt,
interrupt, irrupt, undeveloped
abscess, acquiesce, access,
address, aggress, assess,
bless, caress, chess,
coalesce, compress, confess,
convalesce, cress,
decompress, depress,

digress, dispossess, distress,
dress, duress, egress,
evanesce, express, fess,
finesse, guess, headdress,
impress, inverness, largesse,
less, mess, obsess, oppress,
outdress, outguess,
overdress, press, profess,
reassess, recrudesce,
redress, regress, repossess,
repress, reprocess, stress,
success, sundress, suppress,
transgress, tress, undress,
unless, watercress,
winepress, yes
abscind, backwind, crosswind,
disciplined, downwind,
exscind, rescind, skinned,
tailwind, undisciplined,
unexamined, whirlwind, wind,
woodwind
abscise, anglicize, assize,
capsize, circumcise, criticize,
depoliticize, emphasize,
excise, exercise, exorcise,
fantasize, hypothesize,
incise, italicize, metastasize,
midsize, ostracize,
overemphasize,
overexercise, oversize,
plasticize, politicize,
publicize, reemphasize,
romanticize, size, synthesize,
underemphasize (see also
advise [remaining endings],
**actualize, agnize,
accessorize, absolutize**)
abscission, [abrasion]
abscond, beyond, blond,

bond, correspond, fishpond,
fond, gourmand, junk bond,
millpond, pond, respond,
vagabond, wand
absence, [abhorrence]
absent, acquiescent, anti-
convulsant, beneficent,
innocent, magnificent,
maleficent, munificent,
nonadjacent, relaxant,
reticent (see also
abandonment)
absentee, [abatis]
absenteeism, [abolitionism]
absentminded, backhanded,
bearded, bedded, bladed,
braided, broadminded,
candid, clearheaded,
confounded, decided,
degraded, divided, dud,
eggheaded, embedded,
extended. fairminded,
feebleminded, guarded,
hooded, intended, landed,
loaded, minded, misguided,
multisided, pigheaded,
prerecorded, retarded,
rounded, secluded, self-
deluded, shorthanded,
simpleminded, single-
handed, single-minded,
sordid, splendid, stranded,
thickheaded, unaided,
unbounded, undecided,
undefended, underhanded,
undivided, unfounded,
unfunded, unguarded,
unheralded, unintended,
unleaded, unrecorded,

unrewarded, unseeded,
untended, well-founded, well-
grounded, well-rounded,
wooded, wounded,
wrongheaded (see also
abluted)
absolute, acute, astute,
attribute, bathing suit, beaut,
birthday suit, boot, bruit, brut,
brute, butte, cahoot, chute,
comminute, commute,
compute, confute, constitute,
contribute, convolute, coot,
crapshoot, cute, deaf-mute,
depute, destitute, dilute,
dispute, disrepute, dissolute,
dress suit, electrocute, elute,
execute, firstfruit, flute, fruit,
grapefruit, gym suit, hirsute,
hoot, impute, institute,
irresolute, jumpsuit, jute,
lawsuit, loot, lute, minute,
moot, mute, offshoot,
outshoot, overshoot, pantsuit,
parachute, passion fruit,
permute, persecute, playsuit,
pollute, prosecute, prostitute,
pursuit, reboot, recompute,
reconstitute, recruit, refute,
repute, resolute, root, route,
salute, scoot, shoot, snoot,
snowsuit, space suit, square
root, statute, substitute, suit,
sunsuit, sweat suit, swimsuit,
taproot, telecommute, toot,
transmute, tribute,
troubleshoot, uproot, wet suit
absolutely, [ably]
absolution, [abbreviation]

absolutism, [abolitionism]
absolutist, anecdotist,
anesthetist, artist, baptist,
cultist, dogmatist, egotist,
leftist, obscurantist, occultist,
parachutist, pietist,
pragmatist, scientist,
separatist, spiritist, ultraleftist,
ultrarightist (see also
abolitionist)
absolutize, acclimatize,
advertise, alphabetize,
amortize, anesthetize,
apostatize, baptize, chastise,
demagnetize, demonetize,
deputize, desensitize,
digitize, dramatize, expertize,
hypnotize, hypostatize,
magnetize, monetize,
overdramatize, prioritize,
privatize, proselytize,
rebaptize, sanitize, sensitize,
stigmatize, syncretize,
systematize, traumatize (see
also **abscise**)
absolve, devolve, dissolve,
evolve, involve, resolve,
revolve, solve
absorb, adsorb, orb
absorbancy, accountancy,
accuracy, addressee,
adequacy, advocacy, agency,
antsy, apoplexy, apostasy,
argosy, aristocracy, artsy,
ascendancy, astromancy,
autocracy, autopsy,
bankruptcy, biopsy, bitsy,
bossy, bouncy, brassy,
bureaucracy, candidacy,

cataplexy, celibacy, chassis,
chintzy, chiromancy, classy,
clemency, codependency,
competency, complacency,
confederacy, consistency,
conspiracy, constancy,
constituency, contingency,
controversy, courtesy,
currency, curtesy, curtsy,
cutesy, decency, deficiency,
delicacy, delinquency,
democracy, dependency,
dicey, diplomacy,
discrepancy, dicey, divorcee,
dormancy, dressy, dropsy,
ecstasy, efficacy, efficiency,
embassy, emcee,
emergency, epilepsy, epoxy,
equivalency, errancy,
excellency, expectancy,
expediency, fallacy, falsie,
fancy, fantasy, flossy,
fluency, folksy, foresee, foxy,
frequency, fricassee, fussy,
galaxy, gassy, glossy,
grassy, greasy, gutsy, gypsy,
heresy, hissy, horsy, hussy,
hydromancy, hypocrisy, icy,
idiocy, idiosyncrasy,
immediacy, inaccuracy,
inadequacy, inconsistency,
indecency, inefficiency,
infancy, insufficiency,
interdependency, intimacy,
jealousy, juicy, lassie, legacy,
legitimacy, leniency, leprosy,
lessee, literacy, lunacy,
malignancy, maxi, mercy,
messy, missy, mossy,

mousy, narcolepsy,
necromancy, neo-orthodoxy,
nonemergency,
nonresidency, normalcy,
occupancy, ochlocracy,
odyssey, orthodoxy, oversee,
papacy, patsy, pharisee,
pharmacy, piracy, pixie,
pleurisy, plutocracy, policy,
posse, potency, presidency,
pricey, primacy, prissy,
privacy, proficiency,
profligacy, prophecy, proxy,
pungency, pussy, racy,
redundancy, regency,
relevancy, renitency,
residency, ritzy, sassy,
saucy, sea, secrecy, see,
self-sufficiency, sexy,
sightsee, sissy, spicy,
sufficiency, supremacy, taxi,
tenacity, tendency,
theocracy, theodicy, tipsy,
tootsie, transparency,
truancy, ultimacy, undersea,
urgency, vacancy, vagrancy,
vibrancy (see also **abalone**)
absorbency, [absorbancy]
absorbent, [abeyant]
absorption, [abbreviation]
abstain, acid rain, afterpain,
airplane, amain, appertain,
arcane, arraign, ascertain,
attain, bane, biplane,
birdbrain, blain, bloodstain,
brain, campaign, cane,
cellophane, chain,
champagne, champaign,
chicane, chilblain, chow

mein, cinquain, cocaine,
complain, constrain, contain,
crane, deign, deplane,
destain, detain, detrain,
disdain, distrain, domain,
drain, drivetrain, enchain,
engrain, entertain, entrain,
explain, eyestrain, fain,
featherbrain, feign, floodplain,
foreordain, gain, germane,
grain, humane, hurricane,
hydroplane, inane, ingrain,
inhumane, insane, lain,
lamebrain, lane, lightplane,
main, maintain, mane,
membrane, methane,
migraine, monoplane,
multigrain, mundane, obtain,
ordain, outgain, pain, pane,
pertain, plain, plane, profane,
quatrain, rain, rattlebrain,
regain, refrain, reign, rein,
remain, restrain, retain,
retrain, romaine, sane,
scatterbrain, seaplane,
seatrain, seine, slain, sprain,
stain, strain, sugarcane,
sustain, swain, tearstain,
terrain, train, twain, urbane,
vain, vane, vein, volplane,
wane, warplane, windowpane
abstemious, acrimonious,
alias, amphibious, aqueous,
atrabilious, beauteous,
bilious, bounteous, capias,
ceremonious,
contemporaneous, copious,
courteous, curios,
deleterious, delirious,

devious, discourteous,
disharmonious, dubious,
envious, erroneous,
euphonious,
extemporaneous,
extraneous, fastidious,
felonious, furious, gaseous,
glorious, gregarious,
harmonious, heterogeneous,
hideous, hilarious,
ignominious, illustrious,
insidious, instantaneous,
imperious, impervious,
industrious, inglorious,
injurious, laborious,
lascivious, luxurious,
melodious, meritorious,
miscellaneous, multifarious,
mysterious, nefarious,
nonhomogeneous, notorious,
nucleus, oblivious,
obsequious, obvious, odious,
pancreas, parsimonious,
pervious, plenteous,
precarious, previous,
punctilious, radius,
sanctimonious, serious,
simultaneous, spontaneous,
spurious, studious, tedious,
vagarious, vainglorious,
various, vicarious, victorious
(see also **abacus**)
abstention, [abbreviation]
abstinence, [abhorrence]
abstinent, appurtenant,
component, consonant,
continent, covenant,
culminant, deponent,
determinant, dissonant,

dominant, eminent, exponent,
immanent, imminent,
impermanent, impertinent,
incontinent, lieutenant,
malignant, opponent,
pennant, permanent,
pertinent, predominant,
preeminent, pregnant,
prominent, proponent,
recombinant, regnant,
repugnant, resonant,
stagnant, tenant (see also
abandonment)
abstract, act, attacked, attract,
backed, cataract, compact,
contract, counteract, detract,
distract, enact, exact, extract,
fact, impact, inact, matter-of-
fact, pact, react, redact, re-
enact, refract, retract,
subtract, tact, tract, transact
abstraction, [abbreviation]
abstruse, abuse, adduce,
burnoose, caboose,
calaboose, conduce, deduce,
deuce, douce, educe,
excuse, footloose, goose,
hypotenuse, induce,
introduce, juice, loose,
moose, multiuse, noose,
nous, obtuse, overproduce,
produce, profuse, puce,
recluse, reduce, reproduce,
ruse, seduce, sluice, spruce,
traduce, transduce, truce,
unloose, use, vamoose,
verjuice
absurd, afterward, awkward,
backward, bastard, begird,

billiard, biohazard, bird,
blackbird, blizzard, bluebird,
bollard, bustard, buzzard,
buzzword, byword,
clapboard, crossword,
cupboard, curd, custard,
dastard, dotard, downward,
drunkard, dullard, eastward,
foreword, forward, froward,
gird, gizzard, haggard,
haphazard, hazard, heard,
heaven-ward, herd,
homeward, inward, jailbird,
laggard, leeward, leopard,
lizard, lovebird, mallard,
mockingbird, mustard, nerd,
niggard, nonstandard,
onward, orchard, outward,
overheard, oxford, password,
placard, record, registered,
reword, seaward, shepherd,
skyward, sluggard, snowbird,
southward, standard,
starboard, steward,
straightforward, structured,
substandard, surd, tabard,
third, toward, turd, upward,
vineyard, vizard, watchword,
wayward, westward,
windward, wizard, word
absurdity, [abatis]
abubble, [able]
abulia, academia, acedia,
acequia, acrophobia,
agoraphobia, ailurophobia,
alexia, alopecia, ambrosia,
amentia, analgesia, anemia,
anhedonia, anomia, anorexia,
antonomasia, aphasia,

aphonia, apnea, apraxia,
arcadia, area, aria,
arrhythmia, asphyxia,
asthenia, ataxia, bacteria,
bohemia, bulimia, cachexia,
cafeteria, chlamydia,
claustrophobia, cornea,
cornucopia, diarrhea,
dementia, diphtheria,
dipsomania, dyslexia,
dyspepsia, effluvia,
egomania, encyclopedia,
euphoria, euthanasia,
exurbia, fascia, galactorrhea,
galleria, gonorrhea,
hemophilia, hernia,
homophobia, hydrophobia,
hypothermia, hysteria, idea,
inertia, insignia, insomnia,
intelligentsia, kleptomania,
lamia, leukemia, luminaria,
malaria, mania, media,
megalomania, memorabilia,
miliaria, minutia, monomania,
multimedia, nausea,
panacea, paronomasia,
pedophilia, phantasmagoria,
phobia, pizzeria, poinsettia,
pyromania, quesadilla,
schizophrenia, sententia,
sinfonia, souvlakia, stadia,
stria, suburbia, technophobia,
toxemia, trachea, trivia,
utopia, xenophobia, zirconia
abundance, [abhorrence]
abundant, accident,
antioxidant, appendant,
ascendant, attendant,
candent, codefendant,

codependent, coincident,
confident, correspondent,
decadent, defendant,
descendant, despondent,
diffident, dissident, evident,
fondant, impendent,
impudent, incident,
independent, interdependent,
nondependent, nonresident,
overconfident,
overdependent, oxidant,
pendant, precedent,
president, redundant,
resident, resplendent,
respondent, self-confident,
self-evident, splendent,
superabundant,
superconfident, transcendent
(see also **abandonment**)
abundantly, [ably]
abuse [noun], [abstruse]
abuse [verb], [amuse]
abusive, [abrasive]
abusively, [ably]
abut, [abbot]
abutment, [abandonment]
abuzz, bananas, britches,
  buzz, does, fuzz, missus,
  molasses, pajamas, riches,
  was
abysmal, [abnormal]
abysmally, [ably]
abyss, amanuensis, amiss,
  bliss, classis, deixis, dismiss,
  entasis, hiss, kiss, miss, piss,
  reminisce, remiss, sis, this
academe, [abeam]
academia, [abulia]
academic, adynamic, anemic,

atomic, autonomic, bulimic,
ceramic, comic, cosmic,
dynamic, economic, emic,
endemic, epidemic, gimmick,
gnomic, hypodermic,
miasmic, mimic, nonatomic,
noneconomic, orgasmic,
pandemic, panoramic,
polemic, rhythmic, seismic,
subatomic, systemic (see
also **acidic** [remaining
endings], **acerbic,
anthropomorphic, acyclic,
allergenic, aleatoric,
airsick, acoustic**)
academically, [ably]
academician, [abbreviation]
academy, acme, agame,
  agronomy, alchemy,
  anatomy, anomie, antinomy,
  appendectomy, archenemy,
  army, astronomy, atomy,
  autonomy, balmy, bigamy,
  blasphemy, bonhomie,
  chamois, chummy, clammy,
  commie, crummy, dichotomy,
  digamy, doomy, dormie,
  dreamy, dummy, economy,
  enemy, epitome, eponymy,
  filmy, foamy, gimme, gloomy,
  grimy, gummy, homey,
  infamy, jimmy, mammy,
  mastectomy, me, metonymy,
  misogamy, mommy,
  monogamy, mummy, origami,
  pastrami, polygamy, preemie,
  pygmy, roomy, rummy,
  salami, sashimi, sesame,
  shammy, shimmy, slimy,

smarmy, sodomy, squirmy,
steamy, stormy, stymie,
swami, taxidermy, taxonomy,
theonomy, tonsillectomy,
trichotomy, tsunami, tummy,
vasectomy, whammy, wormy,
yummy (see also **abalone**)
accede, airspeed, antecede,
bead, birdseed, bleed,
bodied, bourride, breed,
candied, cede, centipede,
colead, concede, cottonseed,
creed, crossbreed, deed,
exceed, feed, flaxseed,
frenzied, Godspeed, greed,
hackneyed, half-breed,
hayseed, heed, hurried,
impede, inbreed, indeed,
intercede, keyed, knead,
lead, linseed, married, mead,
misdeed, mislead, misread,
moneyed, multistoried, need,
nosebleed, plead, precede,
proceed, proofread, ragweed,
read, recede, reed, reread,
reseed, salaried, screed,
seaweed, secede, seed, self-
feed, speed, stampede,
steed, storied, succeed,
supersede, swede,
tumbleweed, tweed,
understudied, unmarried,
unsalaried, unsullied, weed
accelerate, acculturate,
administrate, adulterate,
adumbrate, aerate,
agglomerate, airfreight,
alliterate, ameliorate,
arbitrate, aspirate,

asseverate, berate, birthrate,
calibrate, carbohydrate,
castrate, celebrate,
cerebrate, collaborate,
commemorate, commiserate,
concentrate, confederate,
conglomerate, consecrate,
cooperate, corroborate, crate,
curate, cut-rate, deaerate,
decelerate, decorate,
deflagrate, degenerate,
dehydrate, deliberate,
demonstrate, denigrate,
desecrate, desiderate,
deteriorate, disintegrate,
edulcorate, elaborate,
elucubrate, emigrate,
enumerate, equilibrate,
evaporate, exaggerate,
exasperate, execrate,
exenterate, exhilarate,
exonerate, expectorate,
exuberate, federate, filtrate,
freight, frustrate, generate,
grate, great, gyrate, hydrate,
illustrate, immigrate,
impetrate, inaugurate,
incarcerate, incinerate,
incorporate, indurate,
infiltrate, ingrate,
interpenetrate, invigorate,
irate, iterate, itinerate,
lacerate, liberate, macerate,
magistrate, maturate,
meliorate, mercurate,
migrate, moderate, narrate,
nitrate, obliterate, operate,
orate, orchestrate,
overexaggerate, overrate,

53

penetrate, perforate,
perorate, perpetrate, prate,
preponderate, proliferate,
prorate, prostrate, quadrate,
rate, recalibrate,
reconsecrate, recuperate,
redecorate, refrigerate,
regenerate, rehydrate,
reintegrate, reiterate,
remonstrate, remunerate,
reoperate, reorchestrate,
reverberate, saturate,
separate, serrate, straight,
strait, tolerate, trait,
transliterate, transmigrate,
triturate, underrate, ulcerate,
venerate, vertebrate, vibrate,
vituperate, vociferate (see
also **abate**)
acceleration, [abbreviation]
accelerator, [abductor]
accent, ascent, assent, bent,
cent, circumvent, concent,
convent, dent, descent,
discontent, disorient, dissent,
event, extent, frequent, gent,
indent, intent, invent,
malcontent, misrepresent,
nonevent, outspent, pent,
percent, portent, prevent,
reorient, reinvent, relent, rent,
repellent, repent, represent,
resent, scent, sent, spent,
superintendent, tent, vent
accentuate, antiquate,
actuate, counterweight,
deadweight, devaluate,
effectuate, equate, evacuate,
evaluate, eventuate,

extenuate, featherweight,
fluctuate, flyweight, graduate,
habituate, heavyweight,
infatuate, insinuate,
lightweight, menstruate,
middleweight, misevaluate,
overweight, paperweight,
perpetuate, punctuate,
reevaluate, situate,
superheavyweight,
underweight, valuate, wait,
weight, welterweight (see
also **abate**)
accentuation, [abbreviation]
accept, adept, backswept,
concept, crept, except, inept,
intercept, kept, leapt,
overslept, percept, precept,
slept, swept, wept, windswept
acceptability, [ably]
acceptable, [able]
acceptance, [abhorrence]
acceptation, [abbreviation]
accepted, [abluted]
access, acquiesce, abscess,
address, aggress, assess,
bless, caress, chess,
coalesce, compress, confess,
convalesce, cress,
decompress, depress,
digress, dispossess, distress,
dress, duress, egress,
evanesce, excess, express,
fatherless, fathomless, fess,
finesse, governess, guess,
headdress, impress,
inverness, largesse, less,
meaningless, measureless,
merciless, mess, motherless,

obsess, oppress, outdress,
outguess, overdress,
possess, press, profess,
progress, prophetess,
reassess, recrudesce,
redress, regress, repossess,
repress, reprocess,
stewardess, stress, success,
sundress, suppress,
transgress, tress, undress,
unless, watercress,
winepress, yes
accessibility, [ably]
accessible, [able]
accession, [abbreviation]
accessorize, acculturize,
allegorize, apprise, apprize,
arborize, arise, authorize,
barbarize, bowdlerize,
burglarize, categorize,
catherize, cauterize,
characterize, comprise,
contemporize, demilitarize,
denuclearize, deodorize,
depressurize, emprise,
enterprise, extemporize,
familiarize, glamorize,
memorize, mesmerize,
militarize, miniaturize,
mischaracterize, moisturize,
motorize, notarize,
pasteurize, plagiarize,
polarize, popularize,
pressurize, prize, pulverize,
reauthorize, reprise, rise,
satirize, secularize,
summarize, sunrise, surprise,
temporize, tenderize,
terrorize, theorize, vaporize,

vulgarize, weatherize (see
also **abscise**)
accessory, accusatory,
actuary, adultery, adversary,
advisory, agree, airy,
aleatory, amatory, ambry,
ambulatory, ancillary, angry,
anniversary, anticipatory,
antievolutionary, antimilitary,
antislavery, apiary, a
posteriori, apothecary,
apriori, arbitrary, archery,
armory, artery, artillery,
auditory, augury, auxiliary,
bakery, bawdry, baneberry,
belfry, battery, beneficiary,
berry, bicentenary, binary,
bindery, blackberry, bleary,
boundary, bowery,
boysenberry, brasserie,
bravery, breviary, brewery,
bribery, burglary, burry, bury,
butchery, buttery, calorie,
cannery, calvary,
camaraderie, canary,
capillary, carefree, carry,
category, cavalry, celery,
cemetery, century, chary,
cheery, chemistry, cherry,
chicanery, chicory, chivalry,
citizenry, clary, comfrey,
commendatory, commentary,
commissary, compensatory,
complementary,
complimentary, compulsory,
confectionary, confectionery,
conservatory, consistory,
contemporary, contrary,
contradictory, cookery,

corollary, coronary,
creamery, crematory,
culinary, curry, cursory,
customary, daiquiri, dairy,
debauchery, debris,
declamatory, decree,
dedicatory, degree, delivery,
depository, deprecatory,
derogatory, devilry, diablerie,
diary, dictionary, dietary,
dignitary, dilatory, directory,
disagree, disciplinary,
discovery, discretionary,
discriminatory, disinflationary,
dispensary, dissatisfactory,
documentary, doggery,
dormitory, dory, dowry,
drapery, dreary, drollery,
drudgery, dungaree, duty-
free, dysentery, eatery, eerie,
eleemosynary, elementary,
embracery, embroidery,
emery, emissary, empery,
enginery, entry, epistolary,
esprit, estuary, every,
evolutionary, explanatory,
exploratory, expository,
extraordinary, extrasensory,
factory, fairy, ferry, fiduciary,
fiery, filigree, finery, fishery,
flattery, fleury, floury, flowery,
flurry, foolery, forestry,
forgery, formicary, foundry,
fragmentary, free, furry, fury,
gallery, germfree, gimmickry,
glory, glossary, gory, granary,
greenery, grocery, gunnery,
haberdashery, hairy,
hatchery, hereditary, hickory,

history, hoary, honorary,
hortatory, hosiery, hungry,
hurry, husbandry, illusory,
imagery, imaginary,
incendiary, infirmary
inflammatory, inflationary,
injury, inquiry, interlibrary,
intermarry, intermediary,
interplanetary, introductory,
inventory, involuntary,
itinerary, ivory, jamboree,
jewelry, jittery, judiciary, jury,
knavery, laboratory, lapidary,
laudatory, laundry, lavatory,
leathery, lechery, lectionary,
legionary, legendary, library,
literary, livery, lottery,
luminary, luxury, machinery,
mandatory, marry, masonry,
mastery, memory,
menagerie, mercenary,
mercury, merry monastery,
military mimicry, minatory,
miscarry, misery, missionary,
mockery, momentary,
monetary, monitory,
mortuary, multistory, mystery,
napery, necessary,
nonarbitrary,
noncomplimentary,
noncontemporary, nondairy,
nondiscretionary,
nondiscriminatory,
nonheriditary,
noninflammatory,
nonmonetary,
nonparticipatory, notary,
nugatory, nursery, obituary,
obligatory, observatory,

offertory, olfactory, oratory,
ordinary, ornery, orphrey,
ovary, palmistry, paltry,
pantry, papery, paramilitary,
parliamentary, parry,
participatory, pastry,
pecuniary, pedigree,
penitentiary, penury,
peppery, peremptory,
perfunctory, perphery,
perjury, perry, phylactery,
planetary, plenary,
postsecondary, potpourri,
pottery, powdery, prairie,
precatory, predatory,
preliminary, preprimary,
presbytery, primary,
probationary, promissory,
propitiatory, proprietary,
provisory, purgatory,
quackery, quandary, quarry,
query, rapparee, raspberry,
remarry, reactionary,
recovery, rectory, referee,
refinery, reformatory,
refractory, regulatory,
repertory, repository, retiree,
revelry, reverie, revolutionary,
rivalry, robbery, rosary,
rosemary, rotary, rotisserie,
rubbery, safari, salary,
salutary, sanctuary, sanitary,
savagery, savory, scary,
scenery, scullery, scurry,
secondary, secretary,
sedentary, self-glory, self-
mastery, seminary, sensory,
serry, sherry, shikari,
shivaree, shrubbery,

skullduggery, slavery,
slippery, snobbery, solitary,
sorcery, sorry, spree, starry,
stationary, stationery,
statuary, statutory, story,
strawberry, subcategory,
subsidiary, substitutionary,
sugary, summary, sundry,
supplementary, suppository,
surgery, surrey, tannery,
tarry, teary, temporary,
ternary, territory, tertiary,
theory, thievery, three,
tomfoolery, topiary, trajectory,
transferee, transitory,
treachery, treasury, tributary,
trickery, twittery,
ultrarevolutionary,
uncomplimentary,
undersecretary, unitary,
unnecessary, unsanitary,
unsatisfactory, unsavory,
unwary, upholstery, urinary,
usury, vagary, vainglory,
valedictory, vary, venery,
venire, very, vestiary, victory,
visionary, vocabulary,
voluntary, voluptuary, votary,
waggery, wary, watery,
weary, winery, wiry, wizardry,
worry, yakitori (see **abalone**)
accidence, [abhorrence]
accident, [abundant]
accidental, acquittal,
anecdotal, battle, beetle,
belittle, bottle, brattle, brittle,
brutal, cantle, capital, capitol,
cattle, centripetal, chattel,
chortle, coincidental,

57

committal, congenital, continental, contrapuntal, covenantal, dactyl, decretal, dental, departmental, detrimental, developmental, digital, disgruntle, dismantle, dotal, dottle, ductile, elemental, embattle, embrittle, entitle, epicontinental, experimental, fatal, fertile, fetal, fettle, footle, frontal, futile, genital, gentle, gruntle, horizontal, hospital, hostel, hostile, hurtle, immortal, incidental, infertile, instrumental, intercontinental, interdepartmental, intertestamental, judgmental, kettle, kirtle, lentil, lintel, listel, little, mantel, mantle, marital, mental, metal, mettle, mistitle, monumental, mortal, motile, mottle, natal, neonatal, nettle, noncommittal, nonfatal, nonhostile, nonjudgmental, orbital, oriental, ornamental, palatal, parental, parietal, pedestal, perinatal, petal, pistil, pistol, pivotal, portal, postal, postnatal, pottle, prattle, premarital, prenatal, prattle, prenatal, projectile, rattle, rebuttal, recital, rectal, regimental, remittal, rental, requital, sacerdotal, sacramental, scuttle, sentimental, settle, shuttle,

societal, spittle, startle, subtitle, subtle, subtotal, supplemental, tactile, tattle, teakettle, teetotal, temperamental, throttle, title, tittle, tottle, total, transcendental, transcontinental, turtle, unsettle, versatile, victual, vital, volatile, wattle, whittle (see also **abaxial**)
accidentally, [ably]
acclaim, aflame, aim, aspartame, became, blame, brand name, came, claim, counterclaim, dame, declaim, defame, disclaim, endgame, exclaim, fame, flame, frame, game, inflame, lame, maim, mainframe, misaim, misname, name, nickname, overcame, postgame, pregame, proclaim, quitclaim, rename, reclaim, same, shame, surname, tame, video game, war game
acclamation, [abbreviation]
acclimate, amalgamate, animate, approximate, automate, bedmate, checkmate, chromate, classmate, consummate, cremate, crewmate, cyclamate, decimate, desquamate, diplomate, estimate, helpmate, housemate, inmate, intimate, legitimate, mate, overestimate, palmate,

playmate, primate,
roommate, schoolmate,
shipmate, stalemate,
sublimate, teammate,
underestimate (see also
abate)
acclimation, [abbreviation]
acclimatize, [absolutize]
acclivity, [abatis]
accolade, [abrade]
accommodate, airdate,
antedate, backdate,
candidate, consolidate, date,
depredate, dilapidate,
double-date, elucidate,
fluoridate, intimidate,
inundate, invalidate, liquidate,
mandate, mithridate,
noncandidate, postdate,
redate, sedate, update,
validate (see also **abate**)
accommodation,
[abbreviation]
accompaniment,
[abandonment]
accompanist, [abolitionist]
accompany, [abalone]
accomplish, [abolish]
accomplishment,
[abandonment]
accord, award, chord,
concord, cord, discord, fjord,
Ford, harpsichord, landlord,
lord, misrecord, record,
reward, slumlord, sword,
ward, warlord, whipcord (see
also **aboard**)
accordance, acquiescence,
advertence, avoidance,

cadence, candescence,
complaisance, concordance,
concupiscence,
convalescence,
effervescence, efflorescence,
effluence, emittance,
essence, evanescence,
florescence, fluorescence,
guidance, imprudence,
iridescence, jurisprudence,
license, malfeasance,
nuisance, obeisance,
obsolescence,
omnipresence, pittance,
preadolescence, presence,
prudence, pubescence,
puissance, recrudescence,
reminiscence, remittance
(see also **abeyance**)
accordant, accountant,
advertent, antecedent,
ardent, blatant, cadent,
combatant, consultant,
decedent, discordant,
effluent, imprudent,
inadvertent, intermittent,
latent, mordant, natant,
noncombatant, omnipresent,
patent, peasant, pedant,
pheasant, pleasant, pollutant,
potent, precedent, present,
prudent, remittent, repentant,
resultant, retardant, rodent,
statant, strident, student,
unimportant, unrepentant,
unpleasant, verdant (see also
abeyant)
accordingly, [ably]
accordion, [abecedarian]

59

accost, cost, defrost, double-crossed, embossed, exhaust, frost, holocaust, lost, Pentecost, permafrost
accoucheur, acupressure, dishwasher, excelsior, fissure, flasher, flexure, glacier, gusher, haberdasher, indenture, kosher, licensure, pressure, publisher, pusher, refinisher, refresher, rupture, scripture, slasher, thrasher, thresher, unsure, usher, venture, washer, well-wisher (see also abductor)
account, amount, count, discount, dismount, fount, mount, paramount, recount, rediscount, remount, surmount, tantamount, viscount
accountability, [abatis]
accountable, [able]
accountancy, [absorbancy]
accountant, [accordant]
accouterment, [abandonment]
accredit, adequate, affidavit, albeit, arcuate, audit, aureate, bandit, banquet, budget, buffet, carpet, comfit, conduit, covet, crotchet, cruet, crumpet, cut, decrepit, despot, diet, digit, discomfit, discredit, disquiet, divot, double-digit, edit, elegit, eluate, episcopate, fidget, forfeit, fussbudget, gadget, graduate, hatchet, hut, inadequate, inchoate, incipit,

infatuate, intercollegiate, intuit, invertebrate, jut, latchet, midget, nongraduate, nonprofit, pandit, parapet, pivot, plaudit, poet, postgraduate, precipitate, private, profit, prophet, pundit, puppet, putt, quiet, ratchet, respite, riot, rivet, roseate, scut, semiprivate, shut, snippet, soffit, somewhat, strumpet, suet, surfeit, trivet, trumpet, undergraduate, velvet, what, whiffet, widget (see also abbot)
accreditation, [abbreviation]
accredited, [abluted]
accrete, aesthete, afterbeat, athlete, backbeat, backseat, balance sheet, beat, backstreet, bedsheet, beet, biathlete, bittersweet, bleat, broadsheet, browbeat, buckwheat, cheat, cleat, compete, complete, conceit, concrete, deadbeat, deadheat, deadmeat, deceit, defeat, delete, deplete, discreet, discrete, downbeat, drumbeat, eat, effete, elite, entreat, excrete, exegete, feat, feet, fleet, greet, heartbeat, heat, helpmeet, hoofbeat, incomplete, indiscreet, judgment seat, maltreat, meat, meet, mesquite, mete, mincemeat, mistreat, neat, nonathlete,

obsolete, offbeat,
outcompete, overeat,
overheat, overtreat,
paraclete, parakeet, peat,
pentathlete, petite, pleat,
preheat, reheat, receipt,
repeat, replete, retreat, seat,
secrete, sheet, skeet, sleet,
street, spreadsheet, suite,
sweet, treat, triathlete, tweet,
unseat, upbeat, wheat
accretion, [abbreviation]
accrual, actual, annual,
antihomosexual, asexual,
audiovisual, avowal,
biannual, bilingual, bisexual,
casual, conceptual,
consensual, contextual,
continual, contractual, duel,
effectual, eventual, factual,
gradual, habitual,
heterosexual, homosexual,
individual, ineffectual,
manual, menstrual,
monolingual, multilingual,
mutual, noncontractual,
nonhomosexual,
nonintellectual, nonsexual,
pansexual, perceptual,
perpetual, psychosexual,
punctual, residual, ritual, self-
renewal, semiannual,
sensual, sexual, spiritual,
televisual, textual,
transsexual, ultracasual,
unequal, unspiritual, unusual,
usual, virtual, visual (see also
abaxial)
accrue, adieu, ado, ague,

anew, argue, askew, avenue,
babu, ballyhoo, bamboo,
bayou, barbecue, bestrew,
bijou, blew, blue, boo,
booboo, breakthrough, brew,
buckaroo, bugaboo, burgoo,
cachou, callaloo, canoe,
caribou, cashew, chew, clew,
clue, cockapoo, continue,
construe, coo, corkscrew,
coup, crew, cuckoo, cue,
curfew, curlicue, debut,
detinue, devalue, dew,
discontinue, do, doodoo,
doux, drew, due, ecru, Elihu,
endue, ensue, eschew, ewe,
few, flew, flu, flue, fondue,
foreknew, glue, golf shoe,
goo, grew, gumshoe, guru,
haiku, hairdo, hereinto,
hereto, hew, Hindu,
homebrew, honeydew,
horseshoe, hue, hullabaloo,
igloo, imbue, impromptu,
interview, into, issue, Jesu,
Jew, kangaroo, kazoo, knew,
lieu, lulu, Malibu, manitou,
marabou, Matthew, menu,
mildew, milieu, miscue,
misconstrue, mountain dew,
muumuu, nephew, new, onto,
ooh, outdo, overdo, overdue,
overshoe, overthrew,
overvalue, overview, peek-a-
boo, pew, phew, pooh,
preview, purlieu, pursue,
purview, queue, ragout, redo,
reissue, rendezvous, renew,
rescue, residue, revalue,

revenue, review, revue, rue,
screw, shampoo, shoe,
shrew, sinew, skew, slew,
slough, snafu, snowshoe,
soft-shoe, sous, spew,
statue, stew, strew, subdue,
sue, superglue, surtout,
taboo, tattoo, teleview,
thereto, thew, threw, through,
thumbscrew, tissue, to, tofu,
too, true, tutu, two,
undervalue, undo, unglue,
unscrew, unto, untrue, value,
vendue, venue, view, virtue,
voodoo, wahoo, waterloo,
well-to-do, whew, who,
withdrew, woo, worldview,
yahoo, you, zoo
acculturalize, [accessorize]
acculturate, [accelerate]
acculturation, [abbreviation]
accumulate, [ablate]
accumulation, [abbreviation]
accumulative, [ablative]
accuracy, [absorbancy]
accurate, agglomerate,
  alliterate, barbiturate, carat,
  caret, carrot, cofavorite,
  commensurate, confederate,
  conglomerate, considerate,
  corporate, culprit, curate,
  degenerate, deliberate,
  demerit, desperate,
  directorate, disinherit,
  disparate, doctorate,
  elaborate, electorate,
  emirate, favorite, federate,
  ferret, floret, garret, illiterate,
  immoderate, inaccurate,

inconsiderate, indurate,
inherit, intemperate, interpret,
inveterate, karat, lacerate,
levirate, literate, merit,
misinterpret, moderate,
noncorporate, nonliterate,
obdurate, parrot, pastorate,
pirate, portrait, protectorate,
regenerate, reinterpret, rut,
secret, self-portrait,
semiliterate, separate, spirit,
strut, temperate, triumvirate,
turret, unregenerate,
vertebrate, vinaigrette (see
also **abbot**)
accurately, [ably]
accursed, [athirst]
accusation, [abbreviation]
accusative, [ablative]
accusatory, [accessory]
accuse, [abuse]
accustom, antemortem,
  arboretum, atom, autumn,
  bantam, bottom, custom,
  datum, dictum, ecosystem,
  item, momentum, phantom,
  postmortem, postpartum,
  quantum, rectum, sanctum,
  scrotum, sputum, stratum,
  substratum, symptom,
  system, tomentum, totem,
  ultimatum, verbatim, victim
ace, [abase]
acedia, [abulia]
acequia, [abulia]
acerbate, [abate]
acerbic, aerobic, agoraphobic,
  alembic, amebic, anaerobic,
  claustrophobic, cubic,

hydrophobic, pubic, syllabic
(see also **academic**)
acerbity, [abatis]
acetate, agitate, amputate,
annotate, apartheid,
apostate, aspartate,
auscultate, capitate, cogitate,
commentate, commutate,
corotate, crepitate, debilitate,
decapitate, devastate,
dictate, downstate, estate,
excogitate, facilitate,
felicitate, gravitate, habilitate,
hebetate, hesitate, imitate,
incapacitate, ingurgitate,
instate, interstate, intestate,
intrastate, irritate, lactate,
levitate, meditate, militate,
misstate, multistate, mutate,
necessitate, orientate,
overstate, palpitate,
potentate, precipitate,
premeditate, prostate,
punctate, regurgitate,
rehabilitate, reinstate,
reluctate, restate, resuscitate,
rotate, state, substate,
testate, tractate, tristate,
understate, upstate (see also
abate)
acetylene, alkaline, ampicillin,
billon, bowline, chamberlain,
chaplain, colon, crestfallen,
crinoline, decathlon, eidolon,
felon, gallon, goblin, gremlin,
insulin, javelin, kremlin,
lanolin, marlin, masculine,
maudlin, melon, muskmelon,
muslin, pentathlon, pollen,

poplin, porcelain, self-
discipline, semicolon, solon,
stolen, sullen, swollen, talon,
tarpaulin, tefillin, triathlon,
unmasculine, villain,
watermelon, zeppelin (see
also **abdomen**)
ache, [awake]
achievable, [able]
achieve, aggrieve, apperceive,
believe, bereave, breve,
cleave, conceive, deceive,
disbelieve, eve, greave,
grieve, heave, interweave,
leave, make believe,
misconceive, misperceive,
naive, overachieve, peeve,
perceive, preconceive, reave,
receive, relieve, reprieve,
retrieve, self-deceive,
sheave, shirtsleeve, sleave,
sleeve, weave
achievement, [abandonment]
achiever, allover, aquiver,
aver, beaver, believer,
cabdriver, cadaver,
cantilever, caregiver,
carryover, changeover,
cleaver, clever, clover, cover,
crossover, deceiver, deliver,
discover, disfavor, dissever,
diver, downriver, driver,
dustcover, duumvir,
earthmover, endeavor, ever,
favor, fervor, fever, flavor,
forever, giver, graver,
hangover, hardcover,
holdover, hover, however,
laver, lawgiver, layover,

leftover, lever, lifesaver, liver,
louver, lover, makeover,
maneuver, moreover, mover,
never, nonbeliever, observer,
outmaneuver, over,
overachiever, palaver,
passover, popover, pullover,
pushover, quaver,
quicksilver, quiver, redeliver,
receiver, recover, rediscover,
reliever, reprover, retriever,
revolver, river, rover, saver,
screwdriver, server, sever,
shaver, shiver, silver,
slipcover, sliver, spillover,
stiver, stopover, stover,
strikeover, takeover,
timesaver, triumvir, trover,
turnover, unbeliever,
uncover, underachiever,
undercover, waiver, waver,
whatever, whatsoever,
whenever, wherever,
whichever (see also
abalone)
achy, anarchy, autarchy,
autarky, balky, bookie,
bouzouki, bulky, cay, chunky,
clunky, cocky, colicky,
cookie, corky, cranky, creaky,
crikey, croquis, dickey, dinky,
donkey, doohickey, dorky,
ducky, dusky, dyarchy,
finicky, flaky, fluky, flunky,
frisky, funky, hankie, hanky,
hickey, hierarchy, hockey,
hokey, hokey pokey, honky,
hooky, husky, icky, jerky,
jockey, junkie, karaoke, key,

khaki, kinky, kooky, lackey,
lanky, latchkey, leaky, lucky,
malarkey, marquee,
matriarchy, milky, monarchy,
monkey, mucky, murky,
nitpicky, nooky, oligarchy,
panicky, perky, pesky, picky,
pinkie, plucky, poky, porky,
quickie, rekey, risky, rocky,
rookie, shaky, silky, slinky,
smoky, sneaky, sparky,
spooky, spunky, squeaky,
staticky, sticky, stinky, stocky,
streaky, sukiyaki, sulky,
synecdoche, tacky, talky,
teriyaki, tetrarchy, tiki,
triarchy, tricky, turkey,
turnkey, unlucky, wacky,
whacky, whiskey, yucky (see
also **abatis**)
acid rain, [abstain]
acid, acrid, aged, algid,
antacid, aphid, arid, avid,
ballad, bicuspid, blood,
bowlegged, bud, crooked,
crud, cud, cupid, cursed,
dogged, fervid, flaccid, flood,
florid, fluid, forehead, forked,
frigid, gelid, gravid, hatred,
horrid, hotblood, humid,
hundred, hybrid, insipid,
intrepid, invalid, jagged,
kindred, languid, learned,
lifeblood, lipid, liquid, livid,
lucid, lurid, method, morbid,
mud, myriad, naked,
nonliquid, nonvalid, orchid,
pallid, pavid, period, placid,
putrid, rabid, ragged, rancid,

rapid, rigid, rosebud, rugged,
sacred, salad, sapid, scud,
self-hatred, semiarid, solid,
spud, squalid, stolid, stupid,
synod, tepid, thud, timid,
torpid, torrid, trepid, tumid,
turbid, turgid, unlearned,
valid, vapid, vivid, wicked,
wretched (see also **abluted**)
acidhead, [abed]
acidic, algebraic, allergic,
anagogic, anthropic,
aperiodic, archaic, aspic,
bailiwick, candlewick, carsick,
chick, civic, dropkick,
empathic, encyclopedic,
epic, episodic, ethic, fleishig,
handpick, heroic, hick, kick,
lethargic, lithic, logic, magic,
medic, melodic, microscopic,
monolithic, mosaic, nit-pick,
nomadic, nonallergic,
nostalgic, nutpick, orthopedic,
orthoscopic, paramedic,
paraplegic, periodic,
pharisaic, philanthropic, pic,
pick, placekick, priapic,
prosaic, psychic,
quadriplegic, quick, sidekick,
slick, sociopathic, spasmodic,
sporadic, stoic, strategic,
telescopic, thick, toothpick,
topic, tragic, wick (see also
academic)
acidity, [abatis]
acidy, already, antibody,
anybody, attendee, baddie,
baglady, baldie, bandy,
bardy, bawdy, birdie, bloody,

body, brandy, buddy,
burgundy, busybody, caddie,
candy, chickadee, cloudy,
comedy, corody, cuddy,
custody, daddy, dandy,
disembody, dowdy, dramedy,
eddy, embody, everybody,
foolhardy, garibaldi, gaudy,
giddy, goody, grandee,
greedy, handy, hardy, heady,
homebody, howdy, jeopardy,
laddie, lady, landlady,
malady, melody, middy, midi,
milady, moldy, moody,
muddy, needy, nobody,
noddy, pandowdy, parody,
perfidy, prosody, psalmody,
ready, remedy, rhapsody,
rowdy, ruddy, sandy, seedy,
self-study, shady, shoddy,
somebody, speedy, spondee,
steady, study, sturdy,
subsidy, sundae, tardy, tidy,
tragedy, trendy, underbody,
underhandy, understudy,
unsteady, unwieldy, vendee,
waddy, wadi, weedy, wieldy,
windy, woody, wordy (see
also **abalone**)
acknowledge, adage,
advantage, afterimage,
appendage, assemblage,
bandage, baggage, blockage,
bondage, breakage,
brockage, burgage, cabbage,
cartage, cartilage, cleavage,
college, corkage, cottage,
cribbage, damage,
disadvantage, dockage,

dosage, dotage, drayage,
driftage, embassage,
ensilage, envisage, foliage,
footage, foreknowledge,
freightage, frontage, garbage,
heritage, homage, hostage,
image, knowledge, language,
leafage, leakage, lineage,
linkage, luggage, message,
mileage, millage, mintage,
mispackage, misusage,
mortgage, outage, package,
parentage, passage,
percentage, pilgrimage,
pillage, portage, postage,
postcollege, pottage,
poundage, precollege,
prepackage, presage,
privilege, ravage, repackage,
roughage, rummage,
sacrilege, salvage, sausage,
savage, scrimmage,
seepage, self-image,
sewage, shortage, shrinkage,
silage, sinkage, slanguage,
slippage, sortilege, spillage,
spoilage, stoppage, stowage,
stumpage, sullage, tillage,
tutelage, ullage, usage,
vantage, verbiage, vestige,
village, vintage, visage,
voltage, voyage, wattage,
wreckage, yardage (see also
abridge)
acknowledgment,
[abandonment]
acme, [academy]
acne, [abalone]
acorn, adorn, airborne, althorn,

antiporn, born, bourn,
bullhorn, corn, earthborn,
firstborn, flugelhorn, foghorn,
forewarn, forlorn, forsworn,
freeborn, greenhorn, horn,
inborn, longhorn, lovelorn,
morn, mourn, newborn,
peppercorn, popcorn, porn,
reborn, scorn, shoehorn,
shopworn, shorn, stillborn,
sworn, thorn, timeworn,
tinhorn, torn, unborn, unicorn,
warn, weatherworn
acoustic, acrobatic, acrostic,
aeromagnetic, aeronautic,
aesthetic, agnostic, altruistic,
anabatic, anaclitic, analeptic,
anachronistic, analytic,
anesthetic, animistic,
antagonistic, antic, antibiotic,
anticlimactic, antihumanistic,
antiseptic, antithetic, aoristic,
apathetic, aphoristic,
apocalyptic, apodictic,
apologetic, apoplectic,
aposematic, aquatic, arctic,
arthritic, aristocratic,
arithmetic, aromatic, artistic,
ascetic, aseptic, asthmatic,
astigmatic, asymptomatic,
ataractic, atheistic, athletic,
attic, authentic, autistic,
autocratic, automatic,
axiomatic, ballistic, bathetic,
biotic, broomstick, bombastic,
bureaucratic, candlestick,
cannibalistic, capitalistic,
catalectic, cataleptic,
catalytic, cathartic, caustic,

chaotic, characteristic,
charismatic, chauvinistic,
chiropractic, chopstick,
chromatic, cinematic,
climatic, communistic,
copacetic, cosmetic, critic,
cryptic, cystic, dalmatic,
deictic, democratic, deontic,
despotic, diabetic, diagnostic,
dialectic, didactic,
diagrammatic, dietetic,
diplomatic, dipstick, diuretic,
docetic, dogmatic, domestic,
dramatic, drastic, drumstick,
eclectic, ecstatic, eidetic,
elastic, emblematic, emetic,
empathetic, emphatic,
enclitic, energetic, enigmatic,
enthusiastic, epileptic, eristic,
erotic, erratic, evangelistic,
exotic, fanatic, fantastic,
fatalistic, fiddlestick, flagstick,
frantic, frenetic, futuristic,
galactic, genetic, gigantic,
gnostic, gymnastic, hectic,
hedonistic, hemistich, heretic,
heuristic, holistic, homiletic,
humanistic, hypnotic,
iconoclastic, idealistic,
idiomatic, idiotic,
impressionistic, inauthentic,
inelastic, intergalactic,
interscholastic, joystick,
lactic, legalistic, linguistic,
lipstick, logistic, lunatic,
magnetic, majestic, mantic,
masochistic, matchstick,
materialistic, mechanistic,
melodramatic, militaristic,

modernistic, monastic,
monotheistic, moralistic,
morganatic, mystic,
narcoleptic, narcotic,
nationalistic, naturalistic,
neurotic, nightstick, nihilistic,
noetic, nonaesthetic,
nonartistic, nonathletic,
noncharismatic,
nondemocratic, nontheistic,
ontic, operatic, opportunistic,
optic, optimistic, orgiastic,
overemphatic, overenergetic,
overenthusiastic,
overoptimistic, panchromatic,
pantheistic, paternalistic,
paralytic, perfectionistic,
periphrastic, pathetic,
patriotic, patristic, pedantic,
peptic, peripatetic,
periphrastic, pessimistic,
phatic, phlegmatic, phonetic,
pietistic, plastic, pluralistic,
plutocratic, pneumatic,
poetic, polygenetic,
polytheistic, positivistic,
pragmatic, problematic,
prophetic, prophylactic,
prosthetic, psychosomatic,
psychotic, quadratic, quixotic,
realistic, relativistic, ritualistic,
robotic, romantic, rustic,
sadistic, sadomasochistic,
sarcastic, schematic,
schismatic, scholastic,
semantic, semiautomatic,
separatistic, septic, shtick,
simplistic, skeptic, slapstick,
socialistic, somatic, spastic,

spiritistic, spiritualistic, static,
statistic, stick, stigmatic,
stylistic, styptic, surrealistic,
symbiotic, sympathetic,
symptomatic, syncretic,
synergistic, synoptic,
synthetic, systematic, tactic,
theistic, thematic, theocratic,
therapeutic, tic, tick, tonetic,
traumatic, tritheistic,
ultranationalistic,
ultrapatriotic, unapologetic,
uncharacteristic,
undemocratic, undiplomatic,
unenthusiastic, unpatriotic,
unrealistic, unromantic,
unstick, unsympathetic,
unsystematic, uptick, vatic,
wholestick, yardstick(see also
academic)
acoustical, aeronautical,
agrochemical, allegorical,
alphabetical, analogical,
anatomical, ankle, analytical,
apical, apolitical,
archaeological, analytical,
article, antithetical,
astrological, astronomical,
asymmetrical, atypical,
autobiographical, barnacle,
besprinkle, biblical, bicycle,
bifocal, biochemical,
bioethical, biographical,
biological, biomedical,
botanical, buckle, buckle,
cackle, canonical, canticle,
carbuncle, categorical,
chemical, chicle, chronicle,
chronological, chuckle,

clinical, circle, classical,
clerical, cockle, comical,
cosmical, conical, crackle,
crinkle, critical, cubical,
cubicle, cull, cuticle, cycle,
cyclical, cylindrical, cynical,
darkle, debacle, deckle,
demonical, diabolical,
diacritical, dialectical,
dialogical, domical,
dominical, dramatical,
ecclesiastical, economical,
ecumenical, egotistical,
electrical, elliptical, empirical,
encircle, encyclical, epical,
epicycle, epochal, equivocal,
eschatological, ethical,
evangelical, exegetical,
fanatical, farcical, fickle,
fiscal, focal, follicle, furuncle,
genealogical, geographical,
geological, geometrical,
geophysical, geopolitical,
grammatical, graphical,
hackle, heckle, heretical,
hierarchical, historical,
honeysuckle, hypercritical,
hypothetical, icicle, identical,
illogical, impractical, inimical,
ironical, jackal, juridical,
knuckle, lackadaisical,
Levitical, lexical, liturgical,
local, logical, lyrical, magical,
manacle, maniacal,
mathematical, mechanical,
medical, metaphysical,
metaphorical, methodical,
methodological, metrical,
miracle, monarchal,

monarchical, monocle,
motorcycle, musical,
mythical, mythological,
nautical, nickel, nonclinical,
noncritical, noncyclical,
nonlogical, nonphilosophical,
nonphysical, nonpolitical,
nonreciprocal, nonsensical,
nontechnical, nontheological,
numerical, numskull,
obstacle, ontological, optical,
oracle, oratorical, overcritical,
parabolical, paradoxical,
parenthetical, particle,
pathological, pedagogical,
periodical, pharisaical,
pharmaceutical,
philosophical, physical,
pickle, pinnacle, polemical,
political, pontifical, practical,
prickle, problematical,
prophetical, psychological,
pumpernickel, puritanical,
quizzical, radical,
ramshackle, rankle, rascal,
receptacle, reciprocal,
recycle, rhetorical, sabbatical,
satirical, self-critical,
semicircle, shackle, shekel,
sickle, skeptical, skull,
snorkel, sociological,
sociopolitical, spackle,
sparkle, speckle, spectacle,
spherical, spiracle, sprinkle,
statistical, stereotypical,
stickle, suckle, supercritical,
surgical, swashbuckle,
symbolical, symmetrical,
tabernacle, tackle, tactical,

tautological, technical,
technological, teleological,
tentacle, testicle, theatrical,
theological, theoretical,
theosophical, tickle, tinkle,
topical, topological, trickle,
tricycle, tropical, truckle,
twinkle, typical,
typographical, typological,
tyrannical, ultracritical,
ultraradical, umbilical,
unbiblical, uncle, uncritical,
unequivocal, unethical,
unicycle, unpolitical,
unshackle, untypical, vehicle,
veridical, versickle, vertical,
vocal, vortical, whimsical,
wrinkle, zoological
acoustics, acrobatics,
aerobatics, aeronautics,
aerostatics, aesthetics,
apologetics, athletics,
ballistics, cybernetics,
dietetics, dogmatics,
genetics, geopolitics,
gymnastics, hermeneutics,
homiletics, linguistics,
logistics, mathematics,
numismatics, optics,
orthodontics, phonetics,
politics, prosthetics, robotics,
semantics, slimnastics,
statistics, tactics
acquaint, ain't, attaint,
complaint, constraint, faint,
feint, paint, plaint, quaint,
repaint, restraint, saint, self-
restraint, taint, unrestraint
acquaintance, [abhorrence]

acquiesce, [abscess]
acquiescence, [accordance]
acquiescent, anti-convulsant,
  absent, beneficent, innocent,
  magnificent, maleficent,
  munificent, nonadjacent,
  relaxant, reticent (see also
  abandonment)
acquire, admire, afire, aspire,
  attire, backfire, barbwire,
  bonfire, brushfire, campfire,
  conspire, desire, dire,
  drumfire, empire, enquire,
  entire, esquire, expire, fire,
  haywire, hellfire, inquire,
  inspire, ire, lyre, mire, misfire,
  perspire, quagmire,
  reacquire, rehire, rewire,
  require, respire, retire,
  retrofire, sapphire, satire,
  sire, spire, spitfire, squire,
  surefire, suspire, tire,
  transpire, umpire, vampire,
  wildfire, wire
acquisition, [abbreviation]
acquisitive, [ablative]
acquit, admit, armpit, basket,
  befit, benefit, bit, bitt,
  bowsprit, cabinet, cenobite,
  chit, cockpit, commit,
  counterfeit, credit, definite,
  dimwit, emit, fit, flit, frostbit,
  gigabit, grit, half-wit, hit,
  hypocrite, intermit, it, kit, knit,
  lit, manumit, misfit, mishit,
  mitt, nit, nitwit, obit, omit,
  outhit, outfit, outwit,
  overcommit, permit, pit,
  pulpit, quit, readmit, refit,

resubmit, recommit, remit,
  retrofit, shit, sit, skit, slit, spit,
  split, submit, tidbit, tit,
  transmit, turnspit, twit, unfit,
  whit, wit, writ, zit
acquittal, [accidental]
acre, anchor, attacker,
  automaker, backer, baker,
  banker, beaker, bicker, biker,
  blinker, bloodsucker,
  boilermaker, bookmaker,
  breaker, broker, bunker,
  bushwacker, busker,
  cabinetmaker, canker,
  caretaker, caseworker,
  checker, choker, clinker,
  clunker, coanchor, comaker,
  concur, conquer, corker,
  coworker, cracker, croaker,
  cur, dicker, docker,
  donnicker, double-decker,
  dressmaker, drinker,
  drugmaker, exchequer, faker,
  filmmaker, firecracker,
  flanker, flicker, footlocker,
  freethinker, glassmaker,
  groundbreaker, hacker,
  hanker, haymaker,
  heartbreaker, homemaker,
  hooker, hunker, icebreaker,
  incur, jawbreaker, joker,
  junker, kicker, knocker,
  lacquer, lawbreaker,
  lawmaker, linebacker,
  liqueur, liquor, locker,
  loudspeaker, lucre, maker,
  marker, massacre,
  matchmaker, mocker,
  moniker, moviemaker,

nightwalker, noisemaker,
nondrinker, nonsmoker,
nonworker, nutcracker, occur,
onlooker, owner, pacemaker,
peacemaker, piker,
placekicker, playmaker,
poker, porker, pricker,
pucker, quaker, rancor, recur,
reoccur, rocker, sacker,
saltshaker, seeker,
seersucker, sepulcher,
shaker, shocker, sinker,
slacker, sleepwalker, slicker,
smacker, sneaker, snicker,
snooker, soccer, spanker,
speaker, spelunker,
squeaker, stacker, sticker,
stinker, stockbroker, stoker,
streaker, streetwalker,
strikebreaker, striker, succor,
sucker, sunseeker,
supertanker, tanker,
tearjerker, ticker, tiebreaker,
tinker, toolmaker,
troublemaker, trucker,
undertaker, vicar, walker,
watchmaker, whicker,
whisker, wicker, windbreaker,
wiseacre, woodpecker,
woodworker, worker, younker
[see also **arbitrager**
[remaining endings], **barber,
acupuncture, adder, confer,
eager, pressure, author,
closure, dryer, ledger,
angler, clamor, owner,
copper, dancer, abductor,
mister, favor, power, layer,
razor]**

acreage, [abridge]
acrid, [acid]
acrimonious, [abstemious]
acrimony, [abalone]
acrobat, aerostat, Arafat,
Ararat, aristocrat, at,
autocrat, bat, begat, blat,
bobcat, brat, bureaucrat,
butterfat, cat, chat, chitchat,
combat, concordat, copycat,
cravat, defat, democrat,
dingbat, diplomat, doormat,
drat, fat, fat cat, flat, format,
frat, gnat, habitat, hard hat,
hat, jurat, kittycat,
laundromat, magnificat, mat,
matte, muscat, muskrat,
noncombat, nonfat, pat,
photostat, plat, plutocrat,
polecat, pussycat, rat,
reformat, rheostat, sat, scat,
slat, spat, splat, sprat,
standpat, stat, strawhat, tat,
technocrat, that, theocrat,
thermostat, tomcat, top hat,
vat, wildcat, ziggurat
acrobatic, [acoustic]
acrobatics, [acoustics]
acronym, antonym, brim,
cherubim, dim, eponym, glim,
grim, gym, Hasidim, him,
homonym, hymn, limb,
prelim, prim, pseudonym, rim,
seraphim, skim, slim, swim,
synonym, teraphim, trim, vim,
whim
acrophobia, [abulia]
acropolis, ageless, aimless,
annulus, affectless,

anomalous, atlas, bibulous,
bolus, bottomless, boundless,
brainless, breathless,
calculus, callous, callus,
careless, chalice,
changeless, childless,
classless, cloudless, clueless
colorless, cordless,
countless, crapulous,
credulous, cumulus, cutlass,
dauntless, debtless, digitalis,
doubtless, effortless,
emotionless, expressionless,
fantabulous, faultless,
fearless, flawless, flocculus,
frivolous, fruitless, gallus,
garrulous, goalless, godless,
gormless, graceless,
groundless, guiltless, gutless,
hapless, harmless, heartless,
heedless, helpless,
homeless, hopeless,
incredulous, irregardless,
jealous, jobless, joyless,
libelous, lifeless, limitless,
listless, malice, marvelous,
matchless, meaningless,
measureless, megapolis,
merciless, meticulous,
metropolis, mindless,
miraculous, motherless,
motionless, nebulous,
necklace, necropolis,
needless, overzealous,
painless, palace, penniless,
perilous, phallus, pitiless,
plus, populace, populous,
powerless, priceless,
purposeless, rebellious,

reckless, regardless,
relentless, restless,
ridiculous, ruthless,
sacrilegious, scandalous,
scoreless, scrupulous,
scurrilous, seamless,
selfless, senseless,
shameless, shiftless, sinless,
sleepless, sleeveless, solace,
solicitous, soulless,
spineless, spiritless, spotless,
stainless, starless, stimulus,
strapless, stridulous, stylus,
surplus, syphilis, tactless,
tasteless, thornless,
thoughtless, timeless,
tireless, toneless, topless,
trackless, trellis, tremulous,
unscrupulous, useless,
valueless, virtueless,
weightless, winless, wireless,
witless, wordless, worthless,
zealous (see also **abacus**)
across, albatross, applesauce,
backcross, bathos, boss,
chaos, crisscross, cross,
demitasse, doss, double-
cross, dross, emboss, epos,
eros, ethos, floss, gloss,
gravitas, lacrosse, loss,
moss, omphalos, pathos,
sauce, semigloss, telos,
topos, toss
acrostic, [acoustic]
acrylic, acyclic, alcoholic,
anabolic, angelic, apostolic,
click, clique, diabolic, flick,
frolic, garlic, hydraulic,
hyperbolic, idyllic, italic, lick,

melancholic, metabolic,
metallic, nonalcoholic,
parabolic, phallic, philatelic,
psychedelic, public, relic,
rollick, slick, symbolic, telic,
vitriolic, workaholic (see also
academic)
act, [abstract]
action, [abbreviation]
actionable, [able]
activate, aggravate, captivate,
cultivate, deactivate, derivate,
elevate, enervate, estivate,
excavate, innervate,
innovate, motivate,
reactivate, renovate, salivate
(see also **abate**)
activation, [abbreviation]
activator, [abductor]
active, [ablative]
activism, [abolitionism]
activist, anarchist, archivist,
atheist, coexist, copyist,
deist, escapist, essayist,
exist, fist, linguist, lobbyist,
marimbist, masochist,
melodist, methodist,
monotheist, nontheist, nudist,
orchardist, pacifist, pantheist,
passivist, philanthropist,
polytheist, positivist, preexist,
propagandist, recidivist,
relativist, reservist, sadist,
sadomasochist, sexist,
soloist, sophist, theist,
tritheist, twist, typist,
vibraharpist, ventriloquist
(see also **abolitionist**)
activity, [abatis]

actor, [abductor]
actress, adulteress,
adulterous, adventurous,
ambidextrous, amorous,
anarthrous, anhydrous,
apterous, arras, authoress,
avarice, barbarous,
boisterous, buttress,
cadaverous, cancerous,
cantankerous, carnivorous,
chivalrous, chorus, cirrus,
citrus, clamorous, clitoris,
congress, cypress,
dangerous, dentifrice,
desirous, dexterous,
directress, disastrous,
dolorous, embarrass,
empress, fibrous, fortress,
generous, glamorous,
headmistress, heiress,
hubris, humorous, ingress,
iris, idolatrous, leprous,
ludicrous, lustrous,
malodorous, mattress,
misaddress, mistress,
monstrous, murderous,
noncancerous,
nonglamorous, nulliparous,
numerous, obstreperous,
odoriferous, odorous,
omnivorous, onerous,
overgenerous, papyrus,
ponderous, porous,
precancerous, preposterous,
progress, prosperous,
rancorous, rhinoceros,
rigorous, seamstress,
slanderous, slaughterous,
slumberous, sonorous,

sorceress, splendiferous,
sudoriferous, temptress,
tenebrous, terrace,
thesaurus, thunderous,
timorous, torturous,
treacherous, truss, tumurous,
ultraglamorous, uterus,
vaporous, venturous,
vigorous, viperous, virus,
viviparous, vociferous,
waitress, walrus, wondrous
(see also **abacus**)
actual, [accrual]
actuality, [abatis]
actualization, [abbreviation]
actualize, allies, analyze,
animalize, annualize,
brutalize, cannibalize,
capitalize, capsulize,
catalyze, centralize, civilize,
commercialize,
compartmentalize,
conceptualize,
constitutionalize,
contextualize, cross-fertilize,
crystallize, decentralize,
decriminalize, demoralize,
denationalize,
departmentalize,
depersonalize, despiritualize,
destabilize, devitalize,
editorialize, emotionalize,
equalize, evangelize,
externalize, federalize,
fertilize, fictionalize, finalize,
formalize, generalize,
hospitalize, idealize, idolize,
immobilize, impersonalize,
individualize, industrialize,

initialize, institutionalize,
internalize, internationalize,
journalize, legalize, liberalize,
localize, marginalize,
materialize, memorialize,
metabolize, mobilize,
monopolize, moralize,
nationalize, naturalize,
neutralize, normalize,
overgeneralize, overutilize,
paralyze, penalize,
personalize, psychoanalyze,
rationalize, reanalyze,
reconceptualize, realize,
recapitalize, regionalize,
remobilize, revitalize,
scandalize, sensationalize,
sensualize, serialize,
socialize, specialize,
spiritualize, stabilize, sterilize,
stylize, tantalize, territorialize,
tranquilize, trivialize,
universalize, utilize,
vandalize, verbalize,
visualize, vitalize, vocalize
(see also **abscise**)
actually, [ably]
actuarial, [abaxial]
actuary, [accessory]
actuate, [accentuate]
actuator, [abductor]
acuity, [abatis]
acumen, [abdomen]
acuminate, affectionate,
baronet, bayonet, beechnut,
bonnet, butternut, chestnut,
coconut, compassionate,
concatenate, coordinate,
determinate, diaconate,

dispassionate,
disproportionate, donut,
doughnut, effeminate,
emarginate, fortunate, garnet,
geminate, granite, hornet,
illuminate, importunate,
incarnate, indefinite,
indeterminate, indiscriminate,
infinite, inordinate,
insubordinate, laminate,
locknut, magnet, minute, nut,
obstinate, ordinate,
passionate, peanut, planet,
pomegranate, predominate,
proportionate, senate, sennit,
signet, sonnet, spinet,
subordinate, sunbonnet,
tenet, unfortunate, unit,
walnut,
whodunit (see **abbot**)
acupressure, [accoucheur]
acupuncture, admixture,
adventure, agriculture,
apiculture, aquaculture,
archer, architecture,
bleacher, blucher, butcher,
capture, catcher, censure,
churr, cincture, clincher,
cloture, conjecture,
coresearcher, counterculture,
creature, culture, debenture,
denture, departure,
dispatcher, dogcatcher,
enrapture, expenditure,
feature, fixture, fletcher,
floriculture, flycatcher,
fracture, furniture, future,
garniture, gesture,
horticulture, imposture,

infrastructure, juncture,
keypuncher, launcher,
lecture, legislature,
manufacture, misadventure,
mixture, moisture, multure,
nature, nomenclature,
nurture, pasture,
peradventure, picture,
pitcher, poacher, posture,
preacher, puncture, rancher,
rapture, recapture,
remanufacture, restructure,
scorcher, sculpture, stature,
stretcher, stricture, structure,
subculture, substructure,
superstructure, suture,
teacher, texture, thatcher,
tincture, torture, trencher,
vesture, viticulture, voucher,
vulture, watcher (see also
abductor)
acute, astute, attribute, beaut,
boot, bruit, brut, brute, butte,
cahoot, chute, comminute,
commute, compute, confute,
constitute, contribute,
convolute, coot, crapshoot,
cute, depute, destitute, dilute,
dispute, disrepute, dissolute,
distribute, electrocute, elute,
execute, flute, fruit,
grapefruit, hirsute, hoot,
impute, institute, irresolute,
jumpsuit, jute, lawsuit, loot,
lute, minute, moot, mute,
offshoot, outshoot, overshoot,
pantsuit, parachute, permute,
persecute, playsuit, pollute,
prosecute, prostitute, pursuit,

reboot, recompute,
reconstitute, recruit, refute,
repute, resolute, root, route,
salute, scoot, shoot, snoot,
snowsuit, statute, substitute,
suit, sunsuit, swimsuit,
taproot, telecommute, toot,
transmute, tribute,
troubleshoot, uproot
acyclic, [acrylic]
ad hoc, [aftershock]
ad lib, [bib]
ad, armpad, bad, brad, cad,
chad, chiliad, clad, comrade,
crawdad, dad, doodad, dyad,
ennead, fad, footpad,
forbade, gad, glad, grad,
granddad, had, helipad,
heptad, ironclad, keypad, lad,
launchpad, Leningrad, mad,
monad, nomad, notepad,
olympiad, pad, pentad, plaid,
rad, sad, scad, tad, triad,
Trinidad, unclad, ungrad
adage, acknowledge
adamant, [abandonment]
adapt, apt, handicapped,
nonhandicapped, rapt,
snowcapped, untapped
adaptability, [abatis]
adaptable, [able]
adaptation, [abbreviation]
adapter, [abductor]
adaptive, [ablative]
addend, amend, append,
apprehend, ascend, attend,
backbend, befriend, bend,
blend, bookend, boyfriend,
commend, comprehend,

condescend, contend,
defend, depend, descend,
dividend, downtrend, emend,
end, expend, extend, fend,
friend, godsend, impend,
intend, lend, mend, minuend,
misapprehend, missend,
misspend, offend, outspend,
overextend, overspend,
portend, pretend,
recommend, rend, repetend,
reprehend, resend, send,
spend, stipend, subtend,
subtrahend, superintend,
suspend, tend, transcend,
trend, uptrend, vend,
weekend
addenda, aficionada, agenda,
alameda, anaconda, armada,
barracuda, coda, enchilada,
gravida, hacienda, pagoda,
panada, panda, posada,
propaganda, rotunda,
schadenfreude, soda,
tostada, veranda (see also **a
capella**)
addendum, album, alum,
amalgam, aluminum,
antebellum, anthem, asylum,
become, bedlam, benumb,
boredom, brummagem,
bubblegum, buckram, bum,
bunkum, carom, cerebellum,
chrysanthemum, chum,
column, come, condom,
continuum, conundrum,
corrigendum, crumb,
curriculum, decorum, denim,
drum, dumb, dumdum,

eardrum, emblem,
exemplum, forum, freedom,
from, fulcrum, gingham,
glum, gum, harem, hokum,
honorarium, hoodlum, hum,
humdrum, income, interim,
kingdom, macadam, madam,
maelstrom, martyrdom,
maximum, medium,
memorandum, minimum,
modem, modicum, mum,
numb, optimum, opusculum,
origanum, outcome,
overcome, pendulum,
peplum, pilgrim, plum, plumb,
poem, pogrom, practicum,
premium, problem, quorum,
random, referendum,
rostrum, rum, scrum, scum,
seldom, serfdom, serum,
slalom, slum, solemn,
spectrum, stardom, sternum,
stickum, stratagem, strum,
stumblebum, suboptimum,
succumb, sugarplum, swum,
tandem, tarmacadam,
theorem, therefrom, thumb,
unwelcome, variorum,
vellum, venom, volume,
wampum, welcome, wisdom
adder, alder, alexander,
ambassador, ardor, asunder,
attainder, backorder,
backslider, bandleader,
bartender, binder, blender,
blinder, blunder, boarder,
bondholder, border, boulder,
breeder, broider, builder,
bystander, calendar,

camcorder, candleholder,
candor, cardholder, cedar,
cheddar, cheerleader,
chowder, cider, cinder,
cofounder, coholder,
colander, coleader, collider,
commander, condor,
consider, contender,
coriander, corridor, cylinder,
dander, decoder, defender,
disorder, divider, dodder,
doubleheader, elder,
embroider, engender,
faultfinder, feeder, fender,
fielder, finder, flounder,
fodder, folder, founder,
freeloader, gallbladder,
gander, gender,
gerrymander, girder, glider,
goaltender, grader, gridder,
grinder, grounder,
gunpowder, header, heder,
hinder, holder, infielder,
insider, intruder, joinder,
ladder, landholder, larder,
launder, lavender, leader,
loader, lowlander, malodor,
maunder, meander, murder,
nonattender, nonreader,
odor, offender, order,
outrider, outsider, pander,
penholder, persuader,
philander, plodder, plunder,
policyholder, ponder, powder,
presider, pretender,
proofreader, provider, raider,
rebounder, reconsider,
recorder, rejoinder,
remainder, render, reorder,

rider, ringleader, roughrider,
rudder, salamander, sander,
seder, seeder, self-surrender,
shareholder, sheepherder,
shipbuilder, shoulder,
shudder, slander,
slaveholder, slender, slider,
smolder, solder, spellbinder,
spender, spider, splendor,
spreader, squander,
stakeholder, stepladder,
stockbreeder, stockholder,
strider, sunder, surfboarder,
surrender, suspender, tender,
thereunder, thunder, tinder,
titleholder, toolholder, trader,
transponder, udder, under,
vendor, viewfinder, wader,
wander, weeder, welder,
wider, wonder, yonder (see
also **abductor**)
addict, afflict, benedict,
conflict, constrict, contradict,
convict, depict, derelict,
district, edict, evict, imperfect,
inflict, interdict, object,
perfect, predict, reconvict,
redistrict, relict, restrict, strict,
subdistrict, subject, ticked,
unperfect, verdict
addiction, [abbreviation]
addition, [abbreviation]
additional, [aboriginal]
additive, [ablative]
address, [acquiesce]
addressee, [absorbancy]
adduce, [abstruse]
adduct, [abduct]

adenoid, alkaloid, android,
aneroid, anthropoid, asteroid,
avoid, celluloid, deltoid,
devoid, fibroid, flavonoid,
Freud, hemorrhoid,
meteoroid, overjoyed,
paranoid, schizoid, self-
employed, steroid, tabloid,
thyroid, typhoid,
underemployed, unemployed,
void
adept, [accept]
adequacy, [absorbancy]
adequate, [accredit]
adequately, [ably]
adhere, ampere, appear,
arrear, atmosphere,
auctioneer, austere,
balladeer, beer, belvedere,
bemire, besmear, bier, blear,
bombardier, boutonniere,
brassiere, brigadier,
buccaneer, budgeteer,
career, cashier, cashmere,
cassimere, cavalier,
chandelier, chanticleer,
charioteer, cheer, clear,
cohere, commandeer,
compeer, dear, deer,
disappear, domineer, ear,
ecosphere, electioneer, emir,
endear, engineer, exosphere,
fear, financier, fleer, frontier,
gear, headgear, hear,
hemisphere, here, insincere,
interfere, jeer, lavaliere,
marketeer, mere, midyear,
mountaineer, muleteer,
multiyear, musketeer,

mutineer, nadir, near, peer,
persevere, pier, pioneer,
premier, profiteer, pulpiteer,
puppeteer, queer, racketeer,
reappear, rear, reindeer,
revere, sear, seer, severe,
shear, sheer, sincere, smear,
sneer, souvenir, spear,
sphere, steer, stratosphere,
tear, tier, veer, veneer,
volunteer, year, yesteryear
adherence, [abhorrence]
adherent, [aberrant]
adhesion, [abrasion]
adhesive, [abrasive]
adieu, [accrue]
adios, adipose, bellicose,
caespitose, cellulose, close,
comatose, dextrose,
diagnose, dose, engross,
fructose, glucose, grandiose,
granulose, gross, lactose,
megadose, morose, mythos,
nodose, operose, otiose,
overdose, sucrose,
tomentose, varicose, verbose
adipose, [adios]
adjacent, adolescent,
antidepressant, candescent,
canescent, complacent,
complaisant, convalescent,
conversant, crescent, decent,
depressant, docent,
effervescent, efflorescent,
evanescent, fluorescent,
incandescent, incessant,
indecent, iridescent, lucent,
luminescent, nascent,
opalescent, pubescent,

puissant, quiescent, recent,
relucent, reminiscent,
renascent, suppressant,
translucent (see also
abandonment)
adjectival, anvil, approval,
arrival, bevel, carnival, cavil,
civil, corrival, daredevil, devil,
disapproval, dishevel, drivel,
estival, evil, festival, frivol,
gavel, gravel, grovel, hovel,
interval, level, marvel,
medieval, naval, navel, novel,
oval, primeval, ravel,
removal, retrieval, revel,
revival, rival, shovel, shrivel,
snivel, sublevel, survival,
swivel, travel, uncivil, unravel,
vaudeville, weevil (see also
abaxial)
adjective, [ablative]
adjoin, coin, conjoin, enjoin,
groin, join, loin, purloin,
rejoin, sirloin, tenderloin
adjourn, andiron, astern,
attorn, auburn, burn, cavern,
churn, cistern, concern,
discern, downturn, earn,
eastern, epergne, fern,
govern, gridiron, heartburn,
intern, iron, lantern, learn,
lectern, misgovern, modern,
nocturne, northern,
overgovern, overturn, pattern,
postern, postmodern, relearn,
return, slattern, sojourn,
southern, spurn, stern,
stubborn, sunburn, taciturn,
tavern, turn, ultramodern,

unlearn, upturn, urn,
windburn, yearn
adjournment, [abandonment]
adjudge, begrudge, budge,
drudge, fudge, grudge, judge,
misjudge, nudge, prejudge,
sludge, smudge, trudge
adjudicate, [abdicate]
adjudication, [abbreviation]
adjunct, conjunct, defunct,
disjunct
adjure, [abjure]
adjust, adust, allegorist,
amethyst, analyst, antielitist,
antitrust, aorist, august,
ballast, biased, breakfast,
bust, catalyst, crust, cyclist,
dentist, dichotomist, disgust,
dishonest, disinterest,
distrust, dust, earnest, eldest,
encrust, enthusiast, entrust,
environmentalist, farthest,
finest, forest, furthest, gust,
gymnast, harvest, honest,
immodest, interest, just,
latest, locust, lust, mistrust,
modest, must, nonsexist,
overearnest, piecrust,
readjust, robust, rust,
sawdust, self-interest,
stardust, tempest, thinnest,
thrust, trust, unbiased,
unitrust, unjust, wanderlust,
youngest
adjustable, [able]
adjusted, [abluted]
adjuster, [abductor]
adjustment, [abandonment]
adjutant, annuitant, assistant,

coexistent, concomitant,
consistent, constant,
contestant, decongestant,
detent, disinfectant, distant,
equidistant, existent,
exorbitant, expectant, extant,
exultant, hesitant, impenitent,
important, impotent,
incompetent, inconsistent,
inconstant, inhabitant,
insistent, instant, irritant,
militant, nonmilitant,
nonresistant, omnicompetent,
omnipotent, penitent,
persistent, precipitant,
protestant, reluctant, renitent,
resistant, self-existent,
sextant, stunt, ultradistant,
ultramilitant (see also
abandonment)
adjuvant, [abeyant]
adman, Afghan, African, also-
ran, an, anchorman, Ann,
bagman, ban, bedpan,
began, best man, boardman,
boogeyman, bran,
businessman, caftan,
cameraman, cancan,
caravan, catamaran,
caveman, clan, cornerman,
Dan, deadpan, divan,
doorman, dustpan,
Englishman, fan, flan,
frogman, funnyman, gagman,
handyman, headman, Iran,
Klan, Koran, Ku Klux Klan,
madman, mailman, man,
medicine man, middleman,
minivan, minuteman, oat

bran, oilcan, outman, outran,
overran, pan, pivotman, plan,
preplan, ran, rattan,
repairman, sandman,
sauceman, scan, sedan,
serviceman, snowman,
soundman, spaceman, span,
strongman, suntan,
superman, swingman, tan,
than, trepan, van,
weatherman, wingspan
admass, alas, amass, ass,
bass, bluegrass, brass,
bypass, class, crabgrass,
crass, crevasse, demitasse,
en masse, fiberglass, first-
class, frass, gas, glass,
grass, hourglass, harass,
impasse, jackass, landmass,
lass, looking glass, lower-
class, mass, middle-class,
morass, outclass, overpass,
pass, sass, sassafras,
second-class, spyglass,
subclass, sunglass, surpass,
teargas, trespass,
underclass, underpass,
upper-class, vas, wineglass,
wiseass, working-class
admeasure, azure, brazier,
closure, composure,
countermeasure, crosier,
disclosure, displeasure,
embrasure, enclosure,
exposure, foreclosure,
leisure, measure,
nondisclosure, pleasure,
seizure, treasure (see also
abductor)

administer, alabaster,
ancestor, aster, astir,
bandmaster, baluster,
banister, barrister, bestir,
bister, blister, blockbuster,
bluster, bolster, booster,
broadcaster, buster,
cadastre, canister, caster,
castor, chorister, cloister,
cluster, clyster, coaster,
coinvestor, concertmaster,
defroster, dexter, disaster,
dockmaster, dopester,
dragster, drillmaster, duster,
enregister, fester, filibuster,
fluster, forecaster, forester,
foster, gagster, gamester,
gangbuster, gangster,
hamster, harbormaster,
headmaster, hipster, holster,
huckster, imposter, investor,
jester, keister, klister,
lackluster, lamster, lobster,
luster, master, minister,
minster, mister, mobster,
molester, monster, muster,
nester, ouster, oyster, pastor,
paymaster, pester, plaster,
pollster, polyester, poster,
postmaster, prankster,
preregister, punster,
quartermaster, quizmaster,
register, resistor, ringmaster,
roadster, roaster, rooster,
roster, scoutmaster,
seamster, semester,
sequester, shyster, sinister,
sister, sodbuster, songster,
speedster, spinster,

sportscaster, spymaster,
stationmaster, stepsister, stir,
taskmaster, taster, teamster,
telecaster, thruster, toaster,
toastmaster, transistor,
trickster, twister, upholster,
weathercaster, yardmaster,
youngster (see also
abductor)
administrate, [accelerate]
administration, [abbreviation]
administrative, [ablative]
administrator, [abductor]
administratrix, admix,
aerodynamics, aesthetics,
affix, appendix, avionics,
bioethics, bionics, biophysics,
bollix, calisthenics, calix,
cervix, cicatrix, civics,
commix, crucifix,
demographics, didactics,
dominatrix, dynamics,
econometrics, economics,
electronics, ergonomics,
eugenics, executrix, fix,
genetics, helix, histrionics,
hydraulics, hysterics,
intermix, matrix, mechanics,
mediatrix, metaphysics, mix,
mnemonics, nix, obstetrics,
onyx, orthopedics, pediatrics,
phonics, physics, prefix,
premix, pyrotechnics, radix,
six, suffix, theatrics, transfix
admirable, [able]
admiral, amoral, ancestral,
apparel, architectural,
atemporal, balmoral, barrel,
beryl, bicameral, bicultural,
bilateral, cadastral, carrel,
cathedral, central, cerebral,
collateral, conjectural, coral,
corporal, countercultural,
cultural, doctoral, doggerel,
electoral, ephemeral,
equilateral, federal, floral,
funeral, general, guttural,
immoral, imperil, inaugural,
intercultural, intramural,
lateral, laurel, liberal, literal,
mackerel, mandrel, mayoral,
mineral, minstrel, monaural,
mongrel, monocultural,
moral, multicultural,
multilateral, mural, natural,
neoliberal, neutral, numeral,
oral, orchestral, pastoral,
pectoral, peril, peripheral,
petrol, plural, postdoctoral,
procedural, puerile,
quadrilateral, referral, rural,
sacral, scoundrel, scriptural,
several, spiral, sterile,
structural, supernatural,
temporal, timbrel,
transcultural, trilateral, trull,
ultraliberal, unicameral,
unilateral, unnatural,
unscriptural, viral, virile,
visceral (see also **abaxial**)
admiration, [abbreviation]
admire, [acquire]
admissible, [able]
admission, [abbreviation]
admit, [acquit]
admittance, [abhorrence]
admix, [administratrix]
admixture, [acupuncture]

admonish, [abolish]
admonition, [abbreviation]
adnate, [abominate]
ado, [accrue]
adobe, [abbey]
adolescence, [abhorrence]
adolescent, [adjacent]
adopt, opt
adoptable, [able]
adoptee, [abatis]
adoption, [abbreviation]
adoptive, [ablative]
adorable, [able]
adoration, [abbreviation]
adore, [abhor]
adored, [aboard]
adorn, [acorn]
adrift, airlift, chairlift, deadlift,
    downshift, drift, facelift,
    forklift, gearshift, gift, grift, lift,
    makeshift, miffed, rift, shift,
    shoplift, sift, snowdrift,
    spendthrift, spindrift, swift,
    thrift, uplift
adroit, droit, exploit, introit
adscititious, ambitious,
    anxious, atrocious,
    audacious, auspicious,
    avaricious, bodacious,
    bumptious, capricious,
    captious, cautious,
    conscientious, conscious,
    contentious, curvaceous,
    delicious, efficacious,
    expeditious, facetious,
    factious, fallacious, ferocious,
    fictitious, flagitious, flirtatious,
    gracious, inauspicious,
    inefficacious, infectious,

judicious, licentious,
    loquacious, luscious,
    malicious, mendacious,
    meretricious, nauseous,
    noninfectious, noxious,
    nutritious, obnoxious,
    ostentatious, overambitious,
    overanxious, overcautious,
    pernicious, perspicacious,
    precious, precocious,
    pretentious, propitious,
    pugnacious, rambunctious,
    rapacious, repetitious,
    sagacious, salacious,
    scrumptious, sebaceous,
    self-conscious,
    semiconscious, sententious,
    spacious, specious,
    subconscious, superstitious,
    surreptitious, suspicious,
    tenacious, tendentious, ultra-
    cautious, unambitious,
    unconscious, ungracious,
    unpretentious, veracious,
    vicious, vivacious, voracious
    (see also **abacus**)
adscript, conscript, crypt,
    encrypt, manuscript,
    nondescript, postscript,
    rescript, script, subscript,
    transcript
adsorb, [absorb]
adulate, [ablate]
adult, antepenult, catapult,
    consult, cult, difficult, exult,
    insult, occult, penult, result,
    tumult
adulterate, [accelerate]
adulteration, [abbreviation]

adulterer, armor bearer,
adventurer, bearer,
conqueror, deliverer,
devourer, emperor, error,
explorer, feuhrer, horror,
juror, laborer, manufacturer,
mirror, murderer, pallbearer,
philanderer, reinsurer, scorer,
sorcerer, squanderer,
talebearer, terror,
torchbearer, treasurer,
usurer, wanderer,
wayfarer(see also **abductor**)
adulteress, [actress]
adulterous, [actress]
adultery, [accessory]
adulthood, babyhood,
bachelorhood, boyhood,
brotherhood, childhood,
cottonwood, could,
deadwood, driftwood,
falsehood, firewood,
godhood, good, hardwood,
hood, knighthood, likelihood,
livelihood, manhood,
misunderstood, motherhood,
neighborhood, parenthood,
plywood, priesthood,
pulpwood, redwood,
sainthood, servanthood,
should, statehood, stood,
understood, widowerhood,
widowhood, withstood,
womanhood, wood,
wormwood, would
adumbrate, [accelerate]
adumbration, [abbreviation]
adust, [adjust]

advance, askance, break
dance, chance,
circumstance, dance,
enhance, expanse, finance,
France, freelance, glance,
happenstance, lance, manse,
nance, perchance, prance,
refinance, romance, stance,
sweatpants, trance,
underfinance, underpants
advancement, [abandonment]
advantage, [acknowledge]
advantageous, aegis,
burgess, contagious,
courageous, egregious,
gorgeous, interreligious,
irreligious, litigious,
noncontagious, nonreligious,
outrageous, prestigious,
prodigious, religious,
sacrilegious (see also
abacus)
advection, [abbreviation]
adventive, [ablative]
adventure, [acupuncture]
adventurer, [adulterer]
adventuresome, awesome,
balsam, blithesome, blossom,
bothersome, burdensome,
buxom, cumbersome,
darksome, dolesome,
fearsome, flotsam, foursome,
fulsome, gruesome, gypsum,
handsome, irksome, jetsam,
loathsome, lonesome,
maxim, meddlesome,
noisome, quarrelsome,
ransom, some, sum,
threesome, tiresome,

toilsome, toothsome,
troublesome, twosome,
unwholesome, venturesome,
wearisome, wholesome,
winsome, worrisome
adventurous, [actress]
adverb, blurb, curb, disturb,
exurb, herb, perturb, proverb,
suburb, superb, verb
adverbial, [abaxial]
adversarial, [abaxial]
adversary, [accessory]
adversative, [ablative]
adverse, amerce, asperse,
averse, burse, coerce,
commerce, converse, curse,
disburse, disperse, diverse,
hearse, immerse,
intersperse, inverse, nurse,
obverse, perverse, purse,
rehearse, reimburse, reverse,
submerse, terse, traverse,
universe, verse, worse
adversity, [abatis]
advert, alert, ambivert, assert,
avert, blurt, braggart, comfort,
concert, controvert, convert,
covert, culvert, curt, desert,
dessert, discomfort, divert,
effort, evert, exert, expert,
extrovert, filbert, flirt, girt,
hurt, inert, insert, introvert,
invert, miniskirt, nightshirt,
outskirt, overexert, overt,
pert, pervert, redshirt, revert,
shirt, skirt, spurt, squirt,
stalwart, subvert, sweatshirt,
undershirt, underskirt, unhurt,
wort, yogurt

advertence, [accordance]
advertent, [accordant]
advertise, [absolutize]
advertisement,
[abandonment]
advice, concise, de-ice,
device, dice, edelweiss,
entice, ice, imprecise, lice,
merchandise, mice, nice,
paradise, precise, price, rice,
sacrifice, self-sacrifice, slice,
spice, splice, suffice, thrice,
twice, ultraprecise, vice, vise
advisable, [able]
advise, anatomize, anodize,
apologize, atomize,
bastardize, catechize,
clockwise, compromise,
contrariwise,
counterclockwise, crabwise,
crosswise, customize,
demise, demythologize,
despise, devise, disguise,
economize, edgewise,
empathize, energize,
epitomize, eulogize, flatwise,
franchise, gormandize, guise,
improvise, itemize,
jeopardize, legitimize,
lengthwise, likewise,
maximize, merchandise,
methodize, minimize,
misadvise, optimize,
otherwise, oxidize,
philosophize, propagandize,
psychologize, reenergize,
relativize, remise, revise,
sodomize, standardize,
stepwise, strategize,

streetwise, subjectivize, subsidize, supervise, surmise, syllogize, sympathize, televise, theologize, unwise, victimize, wise (see also **abscise**)

advisedly, [ably]

advisee, ballsy, booboisie, bourgeoisie, breezy, busy, cheesy, chimpanzee, clumsy, cosy, cozy, crazy, daisy, devisee, dizzy, doozy, dozy, drowsy, easy, flimsy, floozy, franchisee, frenzy, frizzy, fubsy, fuzzy, guernsey, hazy, jazzy, jersey, kamikaze, lazy, lousy, mosey, muzzy, newsy, noisy, nosy, overbusy, palsy, pansy, paparazzi, poesy, posy, prosy, queasy, rosy, scuzzy, sleazy, snazzy, speakeasy, tizzy, uneasy, wheezy, whimsy (see also **abalone**)

advisement, [abandonment]

adviser, allegorizer, appetizer, atomizer, blazer, boozer, brownnoser, browser, bruiser, bulldozer, buzzer, cleanser, closer, composer, compromiser, cruiser, deodorizer, divisor, equalizer, fertilizer, franchiser, freezer, geezer, geyser, greaser, hellraiser, journalizer, laser, lazar, loser, mazer, miser, nonuser, organizer, plagiarizer, proselytizer, rationalizer, razor, riser,

scissor, stabilizer, stargazer, stripteaser, supervisor, sympathizer, synthesizer, teaser, trailblazer, tranquilizer, trouser, tweezer, vaporizer, visor, womanizer (see also **abductor**)

advisory, [accessory]

advocacy, [absorbancy]

advocate, [noun] affricate, aftermarket, ascot, becket, biscuit, blanket, bracket, brisket, bucket, casket, certificate, circuit, coquet, cricket, crocket, croquette, crosscut, dedicate, delicate, docket, ducat, duplicate, etiquette, frisket, gasket, gutbucket, haircut, imbricate, indelicate, intricate, jacket, junket, locket, market, musket, packet, picket, pickpocket, precut, predicate, pricket, racket, recut, reduplicate, replicate, rocket, shortcut, skyrocket, socket, sophisticate, sprocket, straightjacket, supermarket, syndicate, thicket, ticket, tourniquet, trinket, triplicate, undercut, uncut, uppercut, wastebasket, wicket (see also **abbot**)

advocate, [verb] [abdicate]

adynamic, [academic]

aegis, [advantageous]

aeolian, [abecedarian]

aerate, [accelerate]

aerial, [abaxial]

aerialist, agriculturalist,
   anticapitalist,
   anticonversationalist,
   backlist, blacklist, capitalist,
   checklist, congregationalist,
   conversationalist, editorialist,
   enlist, evangelist,
   existentialist, fatalist,
   federalist, finalist,
   fundamentalist, globalist,
   hairstylist, idealist,
   individualist, industrialist,
   instrumentalist,
   internationalist, journalist,
   legalist, list, loyalist,
   materialist, medalist,
   mercantilist, monopolist,
   moralist, nationalist,
   naturalist, nihilist, novelist,
   panelist, philatelist,
   photojournalist, populist,
   postmillennialist,
   premillennialist, pugilist,
   rationalist, realist, reenlist,
   revivalist, ritualist, royalist,
   sacramentalist,
   sensationalist, shortlist,
   socialist, specialist,
   spiritualist, stylist, surrealist,
   televangelist, traditionalist,
   vitalist, vocalist (see also
   abolitionist)
aerobatics, [acoustics]
aerobic, [acerbic]
aerodynamics, [administratrix]
aerodyne, Abraham, affine,
   alpine, Amsterdam, asinine,
   assign, battering ram, benign,
   Birmingham, bovine, brine,

calamine, calcimine, canine,
   caprine, chine, cline,
   combine, concubine,
   condign, confine, consign,
   cosine, countersign, define,
   design, dine, divine,
   enshrine, entwine, fine,
   grapevine, intertwine, iodine,
   ma'am, malign, milligram,
   mine, monkeyshine,
   moonshine, nine, opine,
   outshine, palatine, pine,
   porcupine, reassign, redefine,
   redesign, refine, repine,
   resign, shine, shrine, sign,
   spine, stein, strychnine,
   sunshine, swine, thine,
   turpentine, twine, undermine,
   valentine, Viet Nam, vine,
   whine, wine (see also **airline**)
aerogram, am, anagram,
   angiogram, bam, cablegram,
   clam, cram, cryptogram,
   dam, damn, diagram,
   diaphragm, doorjamb,
   epigram, exam, flam,
   flimflam, gam, gram, ham,
   hologram, jam, kilogram, lam,
   lamb, logjam, madame,
   monogram, overprogram,
   pictogram, program, ram,
   reprogram, scam, scram,
   sham, sine, slam, sonogram,
   supine, swam, telegram,
   tram, wham, yam
aeromagnetic, [acoustic]
aerometer, [abductor]
aeronaut, aforethought,
   afterthought, aliquot, allot,

antipot, apricot, aquanaut,
ascot, astronaut, aught,
begot, besot, big shot,
bloodshot, blot, bought,
brought, boycott, buckshot,
Camelot, cannot, caught,
caveat, cheap shot, chip
shot, clot, cocotte, coffee pot,
cosmonaut, cot, counterplot,
crackpot, culotte, distraught,
dogtrot, dot, drylot, dry-rot,
earshot, feedlot, flowerpot,
forethought, forget-me-not,
forgot, fought, fraught, got,
gunshot, hot, hotshot,
jackpot, jot, juggernaut,
kilowatt, knot, long shot, lot,
marplot, mascot, nightspot,
not, nought, onslaught,
ought, overshot, plot,
polkadot, polyshot, pot,
potshot, red-hot, robot, rot,
sandlot, savate, self-taught,
sexpot, shot, skat, slapshot,
slingshot, slipknot, slot,
snapshot, snot, sought, spot,
squat, stinkpot, stockpot,
subplot, sunspot, swat,
taught, taut, teapot, thought,
tommyrot, topknot, tot, trot,
untaught, upshot, watt,
whatnot, white-hot, woodlot,
wrought, yacht
aeronautic, [acoustic]
aeronautical, [acoustical]
aeronautics, [acoustics]
aerosol, alcohol, all, appall,
awl, baby doll, backhaul, ball,
banquet hall, baseball,

basketball, bawl, beanball,
befall, birdcall, blackball,
bradawl, brawl, butterball,
cabal, call, cannonball,
carryall, catcall, catchall,
cholesterol, cornball, coverall,
crawl, curveball, doll,
downfall, drawl, drywall,
enthrall, ethanol, eyeball, fall,
fastball, fireball, football,
forestall, forkball, free fall,
gall, gasohol, goofball, hall,
handball, hardball, haul,
highball, install, judgment
hall, knuckleball, loll, lowball,
mall, maul, meatball,
menthol, moll, mothball,
nightfall, oddball, off-the-wall,
overall, overhaul, paddleball,
pall, pitfall, protocol,
racquetball, rainfall, recall,
reinstall, scall, scrawl,
screwball, shawl, shortfall,
sidewall, sleazeball,
slimeball, small, snowball,
softball, spall, speedball,
spitball, sprawl, squall, stall,
stickball, stonewall, tall,
tetherball, thrall, trackball,
trumpet call, urban sprawl,
volleyball, wall, waterfall,
wherewithal, whitewall,
windfall, withal
aerospace, [abase]
aerostat, [acrobat]
aerostatics, [acoustics]
aesthete, [accrete]
aesthetic, [acoustic]
aesthetically, [ably]

aesthetics, [acoustics]
afar, [abattoir]
affable, [able]
affair, aftercare, aglare, air,
   airfare, antiwelfare, armchair,
   artware, aware, bare,
   beachwear, bear, beware,
   billionaire, blare, chinaware,
   compare, coheir, compare,
   concessionaire, cookware,
   courseware, dare, debonair,
   declare, despair, dinnerware,
   dishware, disrepair,
   doctrinaire, earthenware,
   eclair, ensnare, fair, fanfare,
   fare, flair, flare, flatware,
   footwear, forbear, forebear,
   forswear, foursquare, glair,
   glare, glassware, hair,
   hardware, heir, impair,
   knitwear, legionnaire,
   longhair, mare, medicare,
   midair, millionaire,
   multibillionaire,
   multimillionaire, neckwear,
   nightmare, pair, pare, pear,
   playwear, prayer, prepare,
   questionnaire, rare, repair,
   share, silverware, sleepwear,
   slipware, snare, software,
   solitaire, spare, sportswear,
   square, stair, stare,
   stemware, stoneware, swear,
   swimwear, tableware, tare,
   there, thoroughfare,
   threadbare, tinware,
   unaware, underwear, unfair,
   ware, warfare, wear, welfare,

   workfare [see also
   anywhere]
affect, [abject]
affectation, [abbreviation]
affected, [abluted]
affection, [abbreviation]
affectional, [abdominal]
affectionate, [acuminate]
affective, [ablative]
affectless, [acropolis]
affiant, [abeyant]
affiliate, [noun]
   baccalaureate, chariot,
   cheviot, collegiate,
   compatriot, deviate,
   expatriate, fiat, foliate, idiot,
   immediate, inappropriate,
   intermediate, lariat, laureate,
   mediate, opiate, patriot,
   proletariat, secretariat (see
   also **abbot**)
affiliate, [verb] [create]
affiliated, [abluted]
affiliation, [abbreviation]
affine, [aerodyne]
affined, behind, bind, blind,
   color-blind, combined,
   confined, disinclined, double-
   blind, find, grind, hind,
   humankind, inclined, kind,
   mankind, mastermind, mind,
   nonaligned, rebind, refind,
   remind, rewind, rind,
   spellbind, streamlined,
   undefined, undermined,
   undersigned, unkind,
   ultrarefined, unrefined,
   unsigned, unwind, well-
   defined, wind, womankind

affinity, [abatis]
affirm, angiosperm,
    angleworm, berm, bookworm,
    confirm, disaffirm, earthworm,
    ectotherm, firm, germ,
    heartworm, hookworm, infirm,
    midterm, pachyderm, perm,
    pinworm, reaffirm, reconfirm,
    ringworm, silkworm, sperm,
    squirm, tapeworm, term,
    therm, worm
affirmation, [abbreviation]
affirmative, [ablative]
affix, [administratrix]
afflatus, apparatus,
    appendicitis, apprentice,
    armistice, arthritis, asbestos,
    brattice, bronchitis, bursitis,
    cactus, calamitous, cantus,
    circuitous, coitus, cohostess,
    colitis, conceptus, countess,
    covetous, cultus, emeritus,
    eucalyptus, felicitous, fetus,
    flatus, fortuitous, fremitus,
    gingivitis, gratis, gratuitous,
    hepatitis, hiatus, hostess,
    ictus, impetus, injustice,
    justice, laryngitis, lattice,
    lettuce, malpractice, mastitis,
    meningitis, momentous,
    neuritis, notice, poetess,
    portentous, poultice, practice,
    precipitous, priestess,
    prospectus, riotous, situs,
    solicitous, solstice, status,
    stratus, tendonitis, tinnitus,
    tonsillitis, tortoise, treatise,
    ubiquitous (see also **abacus**)
afflict, [addict]

affliction, [abbreviation]
affluence, [abhorrence]
affluent, [abeyant]
afflux, crux, deluxe, efflux, flux,
    influx, reflux, shucks
afford, [aboard]
affordability, [abatis]
affordable, [able]
affray, array, astray, betray,
    bray, cabaret, cadre, defray,
    disarray, dray, émigré,
    entree, foray, fray, gray,
    hombre, hooray, lingerie,
    padre, portray, pray, prey,
    puree, ray, sempre, spray,
    stingray, stray, tray, trey (see
    also **agape [noun]**
    (remaining endings), **clay,
    away**)
affricate, [advocate]
affright, airtight, alexandrite,
    alight, alright, appetite, aright,
    backbite, backlight, bipartite,
    birthright, bite, blight,
    bobwhite, bombsight, bright,
    bullfight, byte, campsite,
    candlelight, catfight, cellulite,
    cite, contrite, copyright,
    daylight, delight, despite,
    disunite, dogfight, downright,
    droplight, dynamite, erudite,
    excite, expedite, extradite,
    eyesight, fight, finite, firefight,
    fistfight, flashlight, fleabite,
    flight, floodlight, foresight,
    forthright, fortnight, fright,
    frostbite, gaslight,
    gesundheit, ghostwrite,
    gigabyte, graphite, gunfight,

headlight, height, highlight, hindsight, homesite, ignite, impolite, incite, indict, indite, insight, invite, kite, knight, light, limelight, lite, megabyte, meteorite, midnight, might, millwright, miswrite, mite, moonlight, multipartite, neophyte, night, nitrite, nonwhite, outfight, outright, overbite, overnight, oversight, overwrite, parasite, partite, penlight, playwright, plebiscite, plight, polite, prefight, preflight, prizefight, proselyte, quite, recite, recondite, reignite, requite, reunite, rewrite, right, rite, satellite, searchlight, sidelight, sight, site, skintight, skylight, skywrite, sleight, slight, smite, snakebite, socialite, spaceflight, spite, spotlight, sprite, stalactite, stalagmite, starlight, stoplight, streetlight, stylite, sunlight, supertight, taillight, termite, tight, tonight, topflight, torchlight, toxophilite, transvestite, tripartite, trite, twilight, ultraright, underwrite, unite, upright, uptight, wainwright, watertight, weeknight, white, write

affront, [aberrant]
affusion, [abrasion]
Afghan, [adman]
aficionada, [addenda]
aficionado, albedo, avocado,

bandeau, bravado, commando, condo, credo, crescendo, dado, desperado, dido, do, dodo, doe, dough, foreshadow, incommunicado, innuendo, judo, kudo, libido, lido, meadow, mikado, ordo, overshadow, parlando, pseudo, scherzando, shadow, sourdough, strappado, tardo, tornado, torpedo, tournedos, tuxedo, weirdo, widow, window (see also **afterglow** [remaining endings], **arpeggio, foe, ago, alfresco, afterglow, albino, allegro, also, aggiornamento, bozo**)

afikomen, [abdomen]
afire, [acquire]
aflame, [acclaim]
afloat, anecdote, antidote, asymptote, banknote, bloat, boat, capote, coat, connote, coyote, creosote, cutthroat, demote, denote, devote, dote, dreamboat, emote, endnote, ferryboat, fireboat, float, flyboat, foldboat, footnote, gloat, goat, gunboat, houseboat, housecoat, keynote, lifeboat, misquote, moat, mote, motorboat, note, oat, overcoat, overpromote, paddleboat, petticoat, powerboat, promote, quote, raincoat, remote, revote, riverboat, rote, rowboat,

sailboat, scapegoat,
showboat, smote, sore throat,
speedboat, steamboat,
sugarcoat, tailcoat, throat,
topcoat, tote, towboat,
tugboat, turncoat, undercoat,
vote, wainscot, wrote, zygote
aflutter, [abductor]
afoot, [ablaut]
afore, [abhor]
aforesaid, [abed]
aforethought, [aeronaut]
afraid, [abrade]
afresh, bobeche, caleche,
crèche, enmesh, flesh, fresh,
mesh, refresh, synchromesh,
thresh
African, [adman]
aft, [abaft]
after, [abductor]
afterbeat, [accrete]
afterbirth, childbirth, berth,
birth, dearth, earth, girth,
mirth, self-worth, stillbirth,
unearth, worth
afterburner, airliner, banner,
barnburner, beginner, boner,
breadwinner, burner,
campaigner, cleaner,
columnar, commissioner,
commoner, conditioner,
consigner, container,
convener, co-owner,
coparcener, corner, coroner,
crooner, demeanor, designer,
detainer, diner, dinner,
discipliner, dishonor, diviner,
donor, downer, entertainer,
entrepreneur, executioner,
extortioner, eyeliner,
foreigner, forerunner, garner,
governor, gunner, gunrunner,
hardliner, headliner, honor,
inner, jetliner, joiner,
kindergartner, landowner,
learner, liner, listener, loaner,
loner, lunar, manner, manor,
mariner, minor,
misdemeanor, mourner, non-
owner, non-signer, nor,
opener, parishioner, partner,
pensioner, practitioner,
prisoner, prizewinner,
recliner, restrainer, retainer,
runner, scanner, schooner,
shiner, sinner, sojourner,
sooner, spanner, spinner,
strainer, streamliner,
sustainer, sweetener, tanner,
tenor, thinner, toner, tuner,
vintner, wagoner, whitener,
wiener, winner(see also
abductor)
aftercare, [affair]
afterclap, backslap, backwrap,
bootstrap, burlap, cap,
catnap, chap, clap, claptrap,
crap, entrap, firetrap, flap,
frap, gap, gingersnap,
handicap, heeltap, hubcap,
jockstrap, kidnap, knap,
kneecap, lap, map, mishap,
mousetrap, nap, nightcap,
overlap, pap, rap, rattletrap,
rattrap, recap, rewrap, sap,
satrap, scrap, shiplap,
skullcap, skycap, slap, snap,
snowcap, stopgap, strap, tap,

thunderclap, trap, unsnap,
unstrap, unwrap, whitecap,
wiretap, wrap, yap, zap
afterdeck, backcheck, beck,
bedeck, bottleneck,
breakneck, check,
countercheck, cross-check,
deck, discotheque, double-
check, dreck, fleck,
forecheck, foredeck,
hatcheck, heck, henpeck,
home ec, leatherneck, neck,
neck-and-neck, paycheck,
quarterdeck, rain check,
recheck, redneck, roughneck,
rubber check, rubberneck,
shipwreck, spec, speck,
sundeck, tech, trek,
turtleneck, wreck
aftereffect, [abject]
afterglow, aglow, airflow,
armadillo, bedfellow, bellow,
below, bibelot, billow, blow,
bolo, bordello, buffalo,
bungalow, callow, cello,
cembalo, cigarillo,
counterblow, fallow, fellow,
follow, furlough, gigolo, glow,
hallow, halo, hello, hollo,
hollow, lo, low, marshmallow,
mellow, outflow, overflow,
peccadillo, piccolo, pillow,
polo, pueblo, shallow, silo,
slow, solo, swallow, tableau,
tallow, violoncello, wallow,
willow, yellow(see also
aficionado)
afterimage, [acknowledge]
afterlife, alewife, drawknife,

fife, housewife, jackknife,
knife, life, lowlife, midlife,
midwife, nightlife,
pocketknife, pro-life, rife,
right-to-life, strife, wife,
wildlife
aftermarket, [advocate]
aftermath, bath, birdbath,
bloodbath, footbath, lath,
math, naturopath, path,
psychopath, sociopath,
strath, sunbath, warpath,
wrath
aftermost, almost, bedpost,
boast, coast, cohost,
compost, doorpost,
engrossed, farthermost,
foremost, furthermost,
gatepost, ghost, glasnost,
goalpost, guidepost,
hindmost, host, impost,
inmost, innermost, lamppost,
most, outpost, post, provost,
roast, seacoast, signpost,
toast, undermost, uppermost,
utmost, uttermost
afternoon, aswoon, attune,
autoimmune, baboon,
balloon, bassoon, boon,
buffoon, cartoon, cocoon,
commune, coon, croon,
dragoon, dune, forenoon,
goon, half-moon, harpoon,
honeymoon, immune,
importune, impugn,
inopportune, lagoon,
lampoon, loon, macaroon,
maroon, monsoon, moon,
noon, opportune, pantaloon,

picayune, platoon, pontoon,
prune, raccoon, repugn,
saloon, soon, spittoon,
spoon, strewn, swoon,
tablespoon, teaspoon,
tribune, triune, tune, tycoon,
typhoon
afterpain, [abstain]
afterpiece, altarpiece, apiece,
caprice, cease, centerpiece,
coulisse, crease, decease,
decrease, degrease,
earpiece, fleece, frontispiece,
geese, grease, hairpiece,
headpiece, heelpiece,
increase, lease, masterpiece,
mouthpiece, niece,
nosepiece, obese, peace,
piece, police, release,
showpiece, sublease,
tailpiece, timepiece, toepiece,
workpiece
after-rake, [awake]
aftershave, behave, brave,
cave, concave, conclave,
crave, deprave, enclave,
engrave, enslave, forgave,
gave, grave, knave, lave,
microwave, misbehave, nave,
pave, rave, save, shave,
short-wave, slave, stave, tidal
wave, unpave, waive, wave
aftershock, ad hoc, antilock,
armlock, backtalk, balk,
bangkok, bedrock, bibcock,
bloc, block, boardwalk, bock,
cakewalk, calk, catwalk,
caulk, chalk, chock, clock,
cock, coldcock, cornstock,
crock, crosswalk, deadlock,
defrock, doc, dock, doubletalk, dreadlock, dry-dock,
duckwalk, earlock, flintlock,
floc, flock, frock, gamecock,
gawk, gridlock, hammerlock,
hawk, headlock, hemlock,
hock, hollyhock, interlock,
jaywalk, jock, knock,
laughingstock, lilac, livestock,
lock, matchlock, mock,
nighthawk, overstock,
padlock, peacock, pock,
poppycock, restock,
roadblock, rock, schlock,
shamrock, sherlock, shock,
shoptalk, sidewalk, skywalk,
smock, sock, stock, squawk,
stalk, stumblingblock,
sunblock, talk, tarok, ticktock,
tomahawk, unlock, walk,
warlock, weathercock,
wedlock, wristlock
aftertaste, [abased]
afterthought, [aeronaut]
afterward, [absurd]
afterworld, dreamworld,
netherworld, underworld,
world
ag, bag, battle flag, beanbag,
brag, carpetbag, crag,
dirtbag, dishrag, drag, fag,
flag, fleabag, gag, hag,
handbag, jag, jet lag, lag,
litterbag, lollygag, mailbag,
nag, rag, ragbag, ragtag,
saddlebag, sag, sandbag,
scumbag, shag, sleazebag,
snag, sprag, stag, swag, tag,

wag, washrag, zag, zigzag
again, amen, ben,
comedienne, den, glen, hen,
julienne, pen, pigpen,
playpen, ten, then, weaken,
when, wren, yen
against, commenced,
condensed, dispensed,
evidenced, experienced,
fenced, incensed,
inexperienced, influenced,
reverenced, sensed
agame, [academy]
agape, [noun or adjective]
antigay, appliqué, assay,
attaché, atelier, ave, aye,
bay, beignet, bidet, birthday,
blasé, bobstay, bouquet,
buffet, bustier, cachet, cafe,
cantatrice, chardonnay, chez,
cliché, communiqué,
consommé, convey, crochet,
croquet, daresay, day, decay,
dismay, disobey, dolce,
doomsday, dossier, duce,
duende, eh, embay,
entremets, essay, everyday,
expose, fay, fey, fiancé,
flambé, forte, frappe,
gainsay, gay, gourmet, hay,
hearsay, hey, heyday,
holiday, macramé, mainstay,
matinee, may, midday,
naiveté, nay, negligee, neigh,
nongay, noonday, nosegay,
obey, overpay, overstay,
parfait, parquet, passé, pay,
payday, protégé, purvey,
rappee, reconvey, repay,

resume, risqué, roturier, roué,
sauté, say, soiree, sorbet,
stay, survey, they, today,
touché, toupee, underpay,
vivache, volante, weekday,
workaday, workday, yea,
yesterday (see also **airplay,
affray, airway**)
agape, [verb] ape, audiotape,
cape, chape, cityscape,
crape, crepe, drape, escape,
gape, grape, jape, landscape,
nape, rape, reshape, scape,
serape, seascape, shape,
shipshape, snowscape,
streetscape, tape, videotape,
waterscape
agar, anger, auger, augur,
bagger, beggar, beleaguer,
booger, bugger, burger,
carpetbagger, cheeseburger,
chigger, clanger, clangor,
comanager, cougar, dagger,
defogger, dinger, ditchdigger,
dragger, eager, finger,
footdragger, forefinger,
hamburger, humdinger,
hunger, jigger, jogger,
ladyfinger, lager, languor,
linger, longer, malinger,
meager, monger, mugger,
nigger, ogre, outrigger,
overeager, pettifogger, rigger,
rigor, slugger, stagger, sugar,
swagger, tiger, trigger, vigor,
vinegar, vulgar, warmonger,
younger (see also **abductor**)
agate, [aggregate]
agaze, [ablaze]

age, assuage, atomic age,
backstage, birdcage, cage,
disengage, downstage,
encage, engage, enrage,
gage, gauge, middle age,
misguage, offstage, old age,
onstage, outrage, overage,
page, rage, rampage, sage,
soundstage, stage, teenage,
underage, upstage, wage
aged, [acid]
ageless, [acropolis]
agelong, along, belong, bong,
daylong, dingdong,
diphthong, evensong, furlong,
gong, headlong, headstrong,
lifelong, long, nightlong,
oblong, prolong, prong,
singsong, song, strong,
tagalong, thong, throng,
weeklong, wrong
agency, [absorbancy]
agenda, [addenda]
agent, argent, astringent,
cogent, contingent,
convergent, detergent,
diligent, divergent, emergent,
exigent, fulgent, indigent,
indulgent, insurgent,
intelligent, intransigent,
negligent, noncontingent,
overindulgent, pageant,
plangent, pungent, refulgent,
regent, resurgent, self-
indulgent, sergeant, stringent,
superintelligent, tangent,
unintelligent, urgent (see also
abandonment)

aggie, baggy, bogey, boogie,
buggy, corgi, craggy, doggy,
draggy, druggie, foggy, fogy,
groggy, hoagie, leggy,
muggy, piggy, scraggy,
shaggy, smoggy, soggy,
springy, stringy, yogi (see
also **abalone**)
aggiornamento, agitato,
allegretto, alto, antipasto,
bestow, burrito, canto,
chateau, concerto, contralto,
ditto, falsetto, gelato, ghetto,
grotto, gusto, incognito,
legato, lotto, magneto,
manifesto, memento,
mistletoe, molto, mosquito,
motto, obbligato, perfecto,
photo, pimento, pinto,
plateau, portmanteau, potato,
presto, pronto, rialto,
spiccato, spinto, staccato,
stiletto, stow, stretto,
telephoto, tenuto, tiptoe, toe,
tomato, tow, undertow, veto,
vibrato, wirephoto (see also
aficionado)
agglomerate, [noun]
[accurate]
agglomerate, [verb]
[accelerate]
agglomeration, [abbreviation]
agglutinate, [abominate]
agglutination, [abbreviation]
aggravate, [activate]
aggravation, [abbreviation]
aggregate, [noun] [agate]
aggregate, [verb] [abnegate]
aggregation, [abbreviation]

aggress, [acquiesce]
aggression, [abbreviation]
aggressive, [abrasive]
aggressor, announcer,
  answer, assessor, bouncer,
  boxer, bracer, bursar, cancer,
  censer, censor, chaser,
  chasseur, compressor,
  condenser, confessor,
  connoisseur, co-producer,
  cosponsor, cursor, dancer,
  dispenser, douceur, dresser,
  duplexer, elixir, enforcer,
  enhancer, farceur, flexor,
  gasser, grocer, hairdresser,
  howitzer, intercessor, juicer,
  lancer, lesser, masseur,
  microprocessor, mixer, non-
  answer, officer, oppressor,
  parser, predecessor,
  processor, producer,
  professor, purchaser, racer,
  re-possessor, saucer, seltzer,
  silencer, sir, spencer,
  sponsor, spritzer, stressor,
  successor, tracer, transducer,
  transgressor, trespasser,
  ulcer, vinedresser (see also
  abductor)
aggrieve, [achieve]
aghast, backcast, bast,
  bedfast, blast, bombast,
  broadcast, cablecast, cast,
  caste, cineast, clast,
  colorfast, contrast, downcast,
  encomiast, enthusiast, fast,
  flabbergast, forecast, gassed,
  gast, half-mast, holdfast,
  iconoclast, last, lightfast,

mast, miscast, newscast,
  outcast, outlast, overcast,
  past, pederast, precast,
  rebroadcast, recast, repast,
  sandblast, simulcast,
  sportscast, steadfast,
  superfast, telecast, typecast,
  vast, ultrafast, unsurpassed,
  videocast, weathercast
agile, angel, archangel,
  betrothal, bowel, brothel,
  coequal, cordial, crewel,
  cudgel, dowel, duel, dull,
  embowel, equal, evangel,
  fragile, gruel, hull, jewel,
  lethal, lingual, lull, nonlethal,
  renewal, satchel, sequel,
  spaniel, towel, tranquil,
  trowel, vagile, vigil, vowel,
  withdrawal (see also **abaxial**)
agility, [abatis]
agitate, [acetate]
agitation, [abbreviation]
agitato, [aggiornamento]
agitator, [abductor]
agitprop, airdrop, atop,
  backdrop, backstop,
  barbershop, barhop, bebop,
  bellhop, blacktop, bop,
  carhop, cartop, chap, chop,
  clop, coffee shop, coin-op,
  cooktop, cop, countertop,
  crop, desktop, doorstop,
  drop, eardrop, eavesdrop,
  flattop, flop, fop, glop,
  gumdrop, hardtop, hilltop,
  hop, laptop, lollipop, lop,
  mop, mountaintop, nonstop,
  plop, pop, prop, raindrop,

rooftop, shop, shortstop, slop,
sop, stop, strop, swap,
sweatshop, tabletop,
teardrop, teenybop, tiptop,
top, treetop, turboprop, whop,
wineshop
aglare, [affair]
agleam, [abeam]
aglet, amulet, anklet, annulate,
annulet, apiculate, appellate,
armlet, articulate, autopilot,
ballot, billet, booklet, boomlet,
bracelet, brooklet, bullet,
camlet, chaplet, charlotte,
chocolate, circlet, coagulate,
collet, consulate, copilot,
correlate, couplet, coverlet,
cullet, cutlet, desolate,
disconsolate, driblet, droplet,
eaglet, eyelet, fillet, flagellate,
frontlet, gauntlet, geniculate,
gimlet, glut, goblet, gullet,
hamlet, harlot, housetop,
immaculate, inarticulate,
inviolate, karate chop, leaflet,
mallet, millet, omelet,
outcrop, palate, palette,
pallet, pamphlet, pawn shop,
pellet, piglet, pilot, postulate,
prelate, pullet, quintuplet, rest
stop, ringlet, scarlet,
sextuplet, share crop, skillet,
sleevelet, slut, starlet, soda
pop, tablet, template, tiptop,
toilet, traffic stop triplet,
ultraviolet, undulate, varlet,
violet, wallet, wiglet, wristlet,
zealot (see also abbot)
aglow, [afterglow]

agnate, [abominate]
agnize, agonize, aluminize,
antagonize, balkanize,
canonize, colonize,
dehumanize, demonize,
disorganize, galvanize,
gorgonize, harmonize,
homogenize, immunize,
latinize, lionize, mechanize,
modernize, organize,
overorganize, solemnize,
suburbanize, synchronize,
tyrannize, unionize, urbanize,
westernize, womanize (see
also abscise)
agnostic, [acoustic]
agnosticism, [abolitionism]
ago, amigo, archipelago,
bingo, bongo, cargo, ego,
embargo, escargot, flamingo,
forego, forgo, go, gringo,
imago, impetigo, indigo,
largo, lingo, logo, mango,
marengo, outgo, superego,
tango, undergo, vertigo,
virago (see also aficionado)
agog, analog, apologue,
backlog, bandog, bog,
bulldog, bullfrog, catalog,
clog, cog, decalogue, defog,
demagogue, dialogue, dog,
duologue, eclogue, eggnog,
epilogue, flog, fog, frog,
gulag, hedgehog, hog,
hotdog, ideologue, jog,
leapfrog, log, miscatalog,
monologue, nog, pedagogue,
Prague, prologue, slog,
smog, stalag, synagogue,

theologue, tog, travelogue,
underdog, watchdog,
waterlog
agonist, [abolitionist]
agonize, [agnize]
agony, [abalone]
agora, [abracadabra]
agoraphobia, [abulia]
agoraphobic, [acerbic]
agrarian, [abecedarian]
agree, [accessory]
agreeable, [able]
agreement, [abandonment]
agribusiness, alumnus,
androgynous, anise,
antogenous, anus, baroness,
blindness, boldness, bonus,
brightness, business,
cacophonous, caliginous,
cavernous, consciousness,
cornice, coterminous,
covetousness, craftiness,
craziness, crispness,
culpableness, deaconess,
deadness, divisiveness,
emptiness, erogenous,
eyewitness, finis, fitness,
foolishness, forgiveness,
fuliginous, fullness, furnace,
genus, gluttonous, goodness,
governess, graciousness,
happiness, hardness,
harness, heaviness, heinous,
highness, holiness,
indebtedness, indigenous,
intravenous, kindness,
laziness, lewdness, likeness,
lioness, loneliness, loudness,
loveliness, luminous,

madness, meekness,
mellowness, menace,
merriness, messiness, minus,
monotonous, mountainous,
multitudinous, mutinous,
nervousness, nonpoisonous,
nothingness, ominous, onus,
penis, permissiveness,
plentifulness, poisonous,
pretentiousness,
propitiousness, ravenous,
reasonableness,
rebelliousness, redness,
righteousness, roughness,
ruinous, selfishness,
seriousness, serpiginous,
shininess, shyness, sickness,
sinus, sloppiness, soreness,
spaciousness, splendidness,
spunkiness, stateliness,
steadfastness, steadiness,
steeliness, sternness,
stickiness, stiffness, stillness,
stodginess, strenuousness,
stubbornness, suddenness,
sultriness, sweetness,
tactfulness, tediousness,
tenderness, tennis,
tenuousness, terminus,
terribleness, terseness,
tetanus, thankfulness,
thanklessness, thickness,
thoroughness, thriftiness,
tightness, timeliness,
tirelessness, togetherness,
touchiness, trustfulness,
turgidness, ungodliness,
unrighteousness,
uprightness, usefulness,

variableness, verminous,
villainous, vindictiveness,
vinous, vividness,
voluminous, weakness,
wellness, whiteness,
wickedness, wilderness,
witness, worldliness,
worthiness (see also **abacus**)
agriculturalist, [aerialist]
agriculture, [acupuncture]
agrimony, [abalone]
agrochemical, [acoustical]
agronomy, [academy]
aground, [abound]
ague, [accrue]
ah, [aah]
aha, [aah]
ahead, [abed]
ahold, behold, billfold,
blindfold, bold, cajoled,
centerfold, cold, controlled,
eightfold, enfold, fingerhold,
fivefold, fold, foothold,
foretold, fourfold, freehold,
gold, handhold, hold,
household, leasehold,
manifold, manyfold, marigold,
mold, ninefold, old, onefold,
overenrolled, oversold, refold,
retold, scold, self-controlled,
sevenfold, sheepfold, sixfold,
sold, stranglehold,
stronghold, threefold,
threshhold, toehold, told,
twofold, uncontrolled, unfold,
unsold, untold, uphold,
withhold
ahoy, alloy, annoy, batboy,
beachboy, boy, busboy,

callboy, cloy, convoy,
corduroy, cowboy, coy,
decoy, deploy, destroy,
employ, enjoy, envoy, flyboy,
goy, homeboy, hoy, joy,
killjoy, lowboy, newsboy,
paperboy, playboy, plowboy,
ploy, poi, redeploy, soy,
tomboy, toy, unemploy,
viceroy
aid, [abrade]
aid-de-camp, amp, camp,
champ, clamp, cramp, damp,
decamp, encamp, gramp,
lamp, minicamp, preamp,
ramp, revamp, samp, scamp,
stamp, sunlamp, tamp,
tramp, vamp
aide, [abrade]
ail, airmail, ale, assail, avail,
baal, bail, bale, betrayal,
bewail, Bloomingdale, brail,
braille, broad scale,
Chippendale, curtail, dale,
derail, detail, doornail,
empale, entail, exhale, fail,
fairy tale, flail, frail, gale,
ginger ale, grail, greenmail,
hail, hale, hobnail, Holy Grail,
impale, inhale, jail, kale, mail,
male, martingale, nail, pail,
pale, percale, portrayal,
prevail, quail, rail, regale,
rescale, sail, sale, scale,
shale, sliding scale, snail,
stale, surveil, swale, tail, tale,
trail, travail, unveil, upscale,
vail, vale, veil, wail, wale,
whale (see also **blackmail**)

ailment, [abandonment]
ailurophobia, [abulia]
aim, [acclaim]
aimless, [acropolis]
aimlessly, [ably]
ain't, [acquaint]
aioli, [ably]
air, [affair]
airborne, [acorn]
airbrush, blush, brush,
  bulrush, crush, flush, gush,
  hairbrush, hush, lush, mush,
  onrush, paintbrush, plush,
  rush, shush, slush,
  toothbrush, underbrush
airbus, [abbess]
aircraft, [abaft]
airdate, [accommodate]
airdrop, [agitprop]
airdry, alkali, ally, apply, awry,
  aye, banzai, barfly, belie,
  bonsai, buckeye, butterfly,
  canaille, comply, counterspy,
  cry, deadeye, decry, deny,
  descry, die, dry, dye, eye, fie,
  firefly, fly, fry, gadfly, guy, hi,
  high, hogtie, horsefly, imply,
  lie, lye, magi, misapply,
  multiply, my, necktie, nigh,
  occupy, outcry, oversupply,
  pie, pigsty, ply, potpie,
  prophesy, pry, quasi, reapply,
  reoccupy, rely, reply, rye,
  shanghai, shoofly, shy, sigh,
  sky, sly, spry, spy, sty,
  superspy, supply, thigh, thy,
  tie, try, ultradry, untie, vie,
  walleye, why, wry (see also
  alibi, amplify)

airfare, [affair]
airfield, backfield, battlefield,
  chesterfield, field, grainfield,
  infield, midfield, minefield,
  outfield, playfield, windshield
airflow, [afterglow]
airfoil, gargoyle, subsoil, tinfoil,
  topsoil, turmoil (see also
  broil)
airfreight, [accelerate]
airhead, [abed]
airhose, appose, arose,
  bellows, brownnose,
  bulldoze, chose, close,
  clothes, cloze, compose,
  counterpose, decompose,
  depose, disclose, dispose,
  doze, enclose, expose,
  foreclose, froze, gallows,
  hose, impose, interpose,
  juxtapose, metamorphose,
  nachos, nose, oppose,
  overexpose, pose,
  predispose, presuppose,
  primrose, propose, prose,
  recompose, repose, rose,
  superimpose, suppose,
  those, transpose,
  underexpose
airlift, [adrift]
airline, align, alkaline, aquiline,
  balkline, baseline, beeline,
  bloodline, borderline,
  bottomline, breadline,
  bustline, byline, clothesline,
  coastline, dateline, deadline,
  decline, dragline, driveline,
  feline, fraulein, frontline,
  guideline, hairline, headline,

hemline, hipline, incline, lifeline, line, mainline, misalign, outline, pipeline, plotline, realign, recline, redline, roofline, shoreline, sideline, skyline, streamline, timberline, touchline, truckline, underline, waistline, waterline (see also **aerodyne**)

airliner, [afterburner]

airmail, [ail]

airman, [abdomen]

airpack, [aback]

airpipe, antitype, archetype, aristotype, bagpipe, blowpipe, calotype, drainpipe, gripe, hype, mistype, overripe, pinstripe, pipe, prototype, retype, ripe, sideswipe, snipe, standpipe, stenotype, stereotype, stripe, swipe, tailpipe, teletype, tripe, type, unripe, windpipe, wipe

airplane, [abstain]

airplay, allay, allee, ballet, belay, boule, byplay, chalet, clay, counterplay, delay, display, downplay, flay, foreplay, gunplay, horseplay, inlay, interlay, interplay, lay, lei, melee, mislay, misplay, outplay, outlay, overlay, overplay, parlay, play, relay, replay, screenplay, slay, sleigh, soufflé, splay, teleplay, underlay, underplay, valet, waylay, wordplay (see also **agape**)

airport, aport, backcourt, carport, comport, court, crosscourt, davenport, deport, downcourt, export, forecourt, fort, half-court, import, multisport, missort, nonsupport, passport, port, purport, report, seaport, spoilsport, sport, support, transport

airpower, bower, brainpower, candlepower, cauliflower, cower, deflower, devour, dour, dower, empower, fewer, firepower, flower, follower, horsepower, hour, interviewer, lower, mayflower, nonchurchgoer, nonviewer, overpower, persuer, power, repower, reviewer, scour, sewer, shower, skewer, snowblower, sour, sunflower, superpower, thundershower, tower, viewer, wallflower, waterpower, were, widower, wildflower, wrongdoer (see also **abductor**)

airship, apostleship, assistantship, authorship, battleship, brinkmanship, censorship, chairmanship, championship, citizenship, companionship, co-ownership, courtship, dealership, dictatorship, directorship, discipleship, eldership, entrepreneurship, fellowship, flagship, followership, friendship,

gamesmanship,
guardianship, gunship,
headship, internship,
interrelationship, kingship,
kinship, leadership, lordship,
marksmanship, membership,
ownership, partisanship,
partnership, penmanship,
principalship, proprietorship,
receivership, relationship,
salesmanship, scholarship,
ship, spaceship,
sportsmanship, sonship,
sponsorship, starship,
statesmanship, steamship,
stewardship, survivorship,
swordsmanship, township,
trusteeship, warship,
workmanship, worship (see
also **airstrip**)

airshow, akimbo, although,
apropos, arroyo, backhoe,
banjo, beau, bimbo, bow,
bravo, capo, carbo, cheapo,
combo, criollo, crossbow,
demo, depot, dojo, duo,
duomo, dynamo, elbow,
embryo, expo, flambeau, floe,
flow, foe, oxbow, fortissimo,
gaucho, gazebo, gazpacho,
gestapo, gizmo, gumbo,
hobo, hoe, honcho, hypo, joe,
jumbo, kayo, limbo, limo,
litho, machismo, macho,
majordomo, mayo, memo,
mojo, mow, nacho, nouveau,
oboe, oh, owe, oxbow,
placebo, poncho, primo,
rainbow, rancho, repo, salvo,

show, sideshow, sunbow,
talleyho, tempo, though,
turbo, typo, whoa, woe (see
also **aficionado**)

airsick, analgesic, anorexic,
banausic, basic, carsick,
classic, extrinsic, forensic,
geodesic, heartsick, intrinsic,
lovesick, music, nontoxic,
seasick, sic, sick, toxic (see
also **academic**)

airspace, [abase]

airspeed, [accede]

airstream, [abeam]

airstrip, backflip, blip, blue
chip, bullwhip, catnip, chip,
clip, dip, drip, equip, filmstrip,
fingertip, flip, grip, grippe,
gyp, handgrip, hairlip, hip,
horsewhip, lip, microchip, nip,
outstrip, parsnip, pip, quip,
rip, scrip, sip, skip, slip, snip,
strip, tip, trip, unzip, whip, yip,
zip (see also **airship**)

airtight, [affright]

airtime, anytime, bedtime,
begrime, chime, climb, crime,
daytime, dime, dinnertime,
doubletime, downtime,
enzyme, flextime, full-time,
grime, halftime, harvesttime,
lifetime, lime, longtime,
lunchtime, maritime,
mealtime, meantime, mime,
nighttime, noontime,
overtime, pantomime,
paradigm, part-time,
peacetime, playtime, prime,
ragtime, rhyme, slime,

sometime, springtime,
sublime, summertime,
suppertime, teatime, thyme,
time, uptime, wartime,
wintertime
airway, aisleway, alway,
anyway, archway, areaway,
away, beltway, breakaway,
breezeway, byway,
castaway, causeway,
crawlway, cutaway, doorway,
driveway, entryway,
expressway, fadeaway,
fairway, fallaway, faraway,
floodway, flyaway, flyway,
foldaway, folkway, foul play,
freeway, gangway, gateway,
getaway, giveaway,
greenway, guideway,
halfway, hallway, headway,
hideaway, highway, layaway,
leeway, midway, outweigh,
parkway, passageway,
pathway, raceway, railway,
roadway, runaway, runway,
segue, sideway, skyway,
someway, speedway,
spillway, stairway, sternway,
stowaway, straightway,
subway, superhighway,
taxiway, tearaway, thataway,
thoughtway, throwaway,
tollway, tramway, underway,
walkway, walkaway,
waterway, way, weigh, whey
(see also **agape**)
airy, [accessory]
aisle, argyle, awhile, beguile,
bile, compile, defile, denial,

dial, ensile, file, guile, isle,
lifestyle, mile, misfile, misdial,
mistrial, pile, pretrial, redial,
resile, retrial, revile, self-
denial, smile, stile, style,
sundial, tile, trial, unpile, vial,
vile, viol, while, wile,
worthwhile (see also **abaxial**)
aisleway, [airway]
ajar, [abattoir]
akimbo, [airshow]
akin, backspin, begin, bin, blin,
buckskin, chagrin, chin,
clothespin, deerskin, din,
discipline, duckpin, dustbin,
fin, foreskin, gin, grin, hairpin,
hatpin, headpin, in, inn, kin,
kingpin, linchpin, mandolin,
maximin, mortal sin,
munchkin, pigskin, pin,
pushpin, redskin, saimin,
sheepskin, shin, sin, skin,
spin, stickpin, superthin,
tailspin, tenpin, therein, thin,
tin, topspin, twin, underpin,
unpin, violin, wherein, win,
wineskin, within
alabaster, [administer]
alack, [aback]
alacrity, [abatis]
alameda, [addenda]
alarm, arm, barm, charm,
disarm, farm, firearm, fire
alarm, forearm, gendarme,
harm, rearm, schoolmarm,
sidearm, underarm
alarmist, alchemist, anatomist,
animist, atomist, bigamist,
biochemist, chemist,

conformist, economist, mist,
monogamist, nonconformist,
optimist, polemist, pogromist,
polygamist, psalmist,
taxidermist (see also
abolitionist)
alas, [admass]
albacore, [abhor]
albatross, [across]
albedo, [aficionado]
albino, amino, bambino,
campesino, cappuccino,
casino, chino, domino,
foreknow, inferno, kimono,
know, makimono,
maraschino, merino, minnow,
no, piano, snow, soprano,
vino, volcano, winnow, wino
(see also **aficionado**)
album, [addendum]
albumen, [abdomen]
alchemist, [alarmist]
alchemy, [academy]
alcohol, [aerosol]
alcoholic, [acyclic]
alcoholism, [abolitionism]
alcoholmeter, [abductor]
alcove, clove, cookstove,
cove, dove, drove, grove,
rove, stove, strove, trove,
wove
alder, [adder]
alderman, [abdomen]
alderwoman, [abdomen]
ale, [ail]
aleatoric, alphanumeric,
anthropocentric, atmospheric,
auric, baldrick, barbaric,
bigeneric, brick, choleric,

cleric, concentric, crick,
derrick, eccentric, egocentric,
electric, empiric, esoteric,
ethnocentric, exocentric,
fabric, gastric, generic,
geocentric, geometric,
geriatric, goldbrick, historic,
hydroelectric, limerick, lyric,
maverick, meteoric, metric,
numeric, pinprick, prehistoric,
prick, rhetoric, rubric,
sophomoric, symmetric,
theocentric, trick (see also
academic)
aleatory, [accessory]
alee, [ably]
aleft, bereft, cleft, deft, heft,
left, theft
alehouse, backhouse, blouse,
birdhouse, blockhouse,
boathouse, bughouse,
chouse, clearinghouse,
coffeehouse, clubhouse,
courthouse, customhouse,
doghouse, dollhouse, douse,
farmhouse, firehouse,
flophouse, full house,
greenhouse, grouse,
guardhouse, hothouse,
house, icehouse, jailhouse,
lighthouse, madhouse,
mouse, nuthouse, outhouse,
packinghouse, penthouse,
playhouse, poorhouse,
porterhouse, powerhouse,
safe house, schoolhouse,
slaughterhouse,
smokehouse, souse, spouse,
statehouse, storehouse,

teahouse, tollhouse,
warehouse, White House,
whorehouse
alembic, [acerbic]
aleph, chef, clef, deaf
alert, [advert]
alewife, [afterlife]
alexander, [adder]
alexandrine, almandine,
amine, amphetamine,
antihistamine, aquamarine,
Augustine, bean, beguine,
between, bombazine,
caffeine, canteen, carbine,
careen, casein, chlorine,
choline, clean, codeine,
contravene, convene,
cuisine, dean, demean,
dentine, dopamine, dry-clean,
dudeen, duvetyn, eighteen,
epicene, evergreen, fifteen,
figurine, fluorine, foreseen,
fourteen, gabardine,
gadarene, gangrene,
gasoline, gene, glean, go-
between, green, grenadine,
guillotine, Halloween,
histamine, holstein,
houseclean, hygiene,
internecine, intervene, jean,
jellybean, kerosene, keen,
kidney bean, latrine, lean,
libertine, lien, lima bean,
limousine, machine,
magazine, marine, mean,
mesne, mezzanine, mien,
moline, morphine,
mousseline, navy bean,
Nazarene, nectarine,

newsmagazine, nicotine,
nineteen, nonobscene,
obscene, offscreen,
oleomargarine, overseen,
Pauline, peen, piscine,
praline, preen, preteen,
pristine, protein, quarantine,
queen, ravine, reconvene,
routine, saline, saltine,
sardine, scene, screen, seen,
serene, serpentine,
seventeen, sewing machine,
sheen, sixteen, soybean,
spleen, split screen,
submarine, subroutine,
sunscreen, subteen,
tambourine, tangerine, teen,
thirteen, tontine, trampoline,
tureen, ultraclean, umpteen,
unclean, unforeseen, unseen,
vaccine, velveteen, wean,
windscreen, wintergreen,
wolverine
alexandrite, [affright]
alexia, [abulia]
alfalfa, alpha, amoeba, anlage,
apocrypha, aqua, bertha,
boa, bodega, bonanza, bulla,
bursa, cadenza, chautauqua,
chimichanga, chutzpah,
credenza, diva, djellabah,
extravaganza, geisha, guava,
huh, inertia, influenza, java,
kava, larva, lava, lingua,
maharaja, matzo, mesa,
messiah, mestiza, militia,
minutia, mitzvah, neuralgia,
ninja, nostalgia, nova,
omega, ottava, papa,

papaya, piazza, pizza, plaza,
rumba, rutabaga, saga,
saliva, salsa, scuba, shiva,
stanza, the, toga, tuba, via,
visa, vulva, yeshiva, yoga
(see also **a capella**)
alfresco, banko, broncho,
bucko, bunco, calico, coco,
cocoa, disco, echo, fiasco,
fresco, loco, magnifico,
morocco, pekoe, pinko,
portico, psycho, reecho,
stucco, taco, tobacco, wacko,
whacko (see also
aficionado)
algebra, [abracadabra]
algebraic, [acidic]
algid, [acid]
algometer, [abductor]
algorithm, biorhythm, fathom,
rhythm, them
alias, [abstemious]
alibi, buy, by, bye, driveby,
flyby, hereby, lullaby, nearby,
passerby, rabbi, standby,
thereby, whereby (see also
aye, defy)
alien, [abecedarian]
alienable, [able]
alienate, [abominate]
alienation, [abbreviation]
alight, [affright]
align, [airline]
alignment, [abandonment]
alike, bike, businesslike,
childlike, counterstrike, dike,
dislike, dyke, godlike, hike,
hitchhike, kike, ladylike,
lifelike, like, mike, minibike,

motorbike, pike, psych,
shunpike, spike, strike,
thunderstrike, turnpike,
unbusinesslike, unlike,
unsportsmanlike, warlike,
workmanlike
aliment, [abandonment]
alimentation, [abbreviation]
alimony, [abalone]
aliquot, [aeronaut]
alive, archive, arrive, beehive,
chive, connive, contrive,
deprive, derive, dive, drive,
endive, five, hive, jive, live,
nosedive, outdrive, overdrive,
revive, rive, skive, strive,
survive, thrive
aliyah, [aah]
alkahest, [abreast]
alkali, [airdry]
alkaline, [adjective]
[acetylene]
alkaline, [noun] [airline]
alkaloid, [adenoid]
alkalosis, amaurosis, amitosis,
amniocentesis, anabasis,
anacrusis, analysis,
antithesis, aphesis, apodosis,
aposiopesis, apotheosis,
arsis, ascesis, axis, basis,
biogenesis, catachresis,
catalexis, catalysis, catharsis,
census, cirrhosis, colossus,
consensus, crisis, diagnosis,
dialysis, diaphoresis,
diocese, eisegesis, ellipsis,
emesis, emphasis,
epexegesis, excursus,
exegesis, genesis, gnosis,

halitosis, hypnosis, hypothesis, ketosis, metamorphosis, misemphasis, mononucleosis, narcissus, narcosis, nemesis, neurosis, nexus, oasis, osmosis, overemphasis, paralysis, parenthesis, photosynthesis, polygenesis, praxis, princess, proboscis, process, prognosis, prolepsis, prophylaxis, prosthesis, protasis, psychoanalysis, psychosis, sclerosis, scoliosis, self-analysis, self-hypnosis, stasis, suss, symbiosis, synopsis, synthesis, telekinesis, telesis, thesis, thrombosis, tuberculosis, underemphasis, versus (see also **abacus**)

all, [aerosol]

allay, [airplay]

allee, [airplay]

allegation, [abbreviation]

allege, cutting edge, dredge, edge, fledge, hedge, ledge, pledge, sledge, straightedge, wedge

allegiance, [abhorrence]

allegorical, [acoustical]

allegorist, [adjust]

allegorist, amorist, behaviorist, centrist, florist, futurist, grist, guitarist, jurist, manicurist, monetarist, motorist, optometrist, purist, satirist, secularist, terrorist, theorist, tourist, tryst, wrist (see also **abolitionist**)

allegorization, [abbreviation]

allegorize, [accessorize]

allegorizer, [adviser]

allegretto, [aggiornamento]

allegro, arrow, barrow, bistro, bolero, borough, brocero, bro, bureau, burgh, burro, burrow, caballero, crow, embarcadero, escrow, farrow, furrow, giro, grow, gyro, harrow, hero, hydro, maestro, marrow, metro, misthrow, morrow, narrow, outgrow, overthrow, pharaoh, politburo, pro, ranchero, repro, roe, row, scarecrow, semipro, sombrero, sorrow, sparrow, superhero, tarot, thorough, throw, tomorrow, wheelbarrow, zero (see also **aficionado**)

alleluia, azalea, begonia, cabana, dahlia, encaenia, gardenia, genitalia, hallelujah, lasagna, magnolia, mantilla, paraphernalia, petunia, pneumonia, regalia, tortilla (see also **a capella**)

allergen, androgen, antigen, bludgeon, burgeon, carcinogen, contagion, curmudgeon, dudgeon, dungeon, engine, estrogen, hallucinogen, halogen, hydrogen, imagine, legion, margin, nitrogen, origin, oxygen, pidgin, pigeon,

region, religion, smidgen,
sturgeon, surgeon,
theologian, virgin (see also
abdomen)
allergenic, anthropogenic,
arsenic, asthenic, aphonic,
atonic, beatnik, bionic,
calisthenic, cariogenic,
catatonic, chronic, clinic,
cynic, demonic, draconic,
dysgenic, electronic, ethnic,
eugenic, galvanic,
hallucinogenic, harmonic,
histrionic, hygienic, inorganic,
interoceanic, irenic, ironic,
laconic, manic, mechanic,
messianic, mnemonic,
monophonic, moronic,
multiethnic, nonacademic,
nonantagonistic,
noncarcinogenic, nick,
oceanic, organic, panic,
peacenik, phonic,
photogenic, picnic, platonic,
polytechnic, quadraphonic,
refusenik, sardonic, satanic,
scenic, schizophrenic, sonic,
sputnik, stereophonic,
supersonic, symphonic,
telegenic, telephonic, titanic,
tonic, tunic, volcanic (see
also **academic**)
allergic, [acidic]
allergist, anthropologist,
apologist, cosmetologist,
cosmologist, criminologist,
demonologist, futurologist,
gemologist, genealogist, gist,
morphologist, musicologist,

neurologist, pathologist,
philologist, radiologist,
seismologist, sociologist,
strategist, syllogist,
thanatologist, thaumaturgist
(see also **abolitionist**)
allergy, analogy,
anesthesiology, angelology,
anthology, anthropology,
apiology, apogee, apology,
archaeology, astrology,
bibliology, biology, bungee,
cagey, campanology,
cardiology, chronology,
clergy, climatology,
cosmetology, cosmology,
counterstrategy, criminology,
demonology, dermatology,
dingy, dodgy, doxology,
dramaturgy, ecclesiology,
ecology, edgy, effigy, elegy,
energy, epistemology,
eschatology, etiology,
etymology, eulogy, gee,
gemology, genealogy,
geology, geophagy,
gerontology, grungy,
gynecology, hematology,
ideology, lethargy, liturgy,
mangy, metallurgy,
methodology, mingy,
misology, missiology,
morphology, mortgagee,
musicology, mythology,
necrology, neurology,
numerology, oncology,
ontology, orgy,
parapsychology, pathology,
pedagogy, penology,

pharmacology, phenomenology, philology, phraseology, physiology, pneumatology, prodigy, psychology, pudgy, radiology, refugee, scroungy, seismology, sociology, soteriology, speleology, spongy, squeegee, stagy, stingy, stodgy, strategy, synergy, tautology, technology, teleology, terminology, thanatology, thaumaturgy, theology, theurgy, topology, toxicology, typology, veggie, wedgie, wedgy, zoology (see also **abalone**)

alley, [ably]

alley-oop, coop, coupe, croup, droop, dupe, goop, group, hoop, loop, nincompoop, poop, recoup, regroup, scoop, sloop, snoop, soup, stoop, stoup, stupe, subgroup, swoop, troop, troupe, whoop

alliance, [abhorrence]

allied, [abide]

allies, [actualize]

alligator, [abductor]

alliterate, [noun] [accurate]

alliterate, [verb] [accelerate]

alliteration, [abbreviation]

allocate, [abdicate]

allocation, [abbreviation]

allocution, [abbreviation]

allograph, autograph, behalf, better-half, calf, carafe,

cenotaph, chaff, choreograph, decaf, distaff, epigraph, epitaph, flagstaff, gaff, giraffe, graph, half, half-and-half, holograph, laugh, lithograph, mimeograph, monograph, paragraph, phonograph, photograph, pictograph, polygraph, riff-raff, sclaff, seismograph, serigraph, staff, subparagraph, telegraph

allonymous, amice, anadromous, animus, anonymous, autonomous, blasphemous, borborygmus, calamus, chiasmus, cosmos, dichotomous, enormous, famous, grimace, hippopotamus, ignoramus, imprimis, infamous, isthmus, litmus, magnanimous, mittimus, monogamous, polygamous, pomace, posthumous, prechristmas, premise, promise, pumice, pusillanimous, synonymous, thermos, unanimous, venomous (see also **abacus**)

allot, [aeronaut]

allotment, [abandonment]

allover, [achiever]

allow, anyhow, avow, bough, bow, bowwow, brow, cacao, chow, ciao, cow, disallow, disavow, endow, eyebrow, gangplow, haymow, highbrow, hoosegow, how, kowtow, landau, lowbrow,

luau, meow, mow, nohow,
now, ow, plow, pow, pow-
wow, scow, snowplow,
somehow, sough, sow, thou,
vow, wow
allowable, [able]
allowance, [abhorrence]
allowed, [aloud]
alloy, [ahoy]
allude, brood, collude,
conclude, continued, crude,
delude, denude, dude, elude,
exclude, extrude, exude,
feud, fast food, food, hued,
include, interlude, intrude,
lewd, mood, nude, obtrude,
occlude, postlude, preclude,
prelude, protrude, prude,
pseud, rude, seafood,
seclude, shrewd, unissued,
unglued (see also **altitude)**
allure, [abjure]
allurement, [abandonment]
allusion, [abrasion]
allusive, [abrasive]
alluvial, [abaxial]
alluvion, [abecedarian]
ally, [airdry]
almanac, [aback]
almandine, [alexandrine]
almighty, [abatis]
almond, brigand,
cummerbund, diamond,
errand, fecund, fund, garland,
gerund, headland, highland,
holland, husband, island,
jocund, legend, midland,
moribund, obtund, refund,
reverend, rotund, second,

secund, shunned, stunned,
thousand, underfund,
vilipend, woodland
almost, [aftermost]
aloft, croft, hayloft, loft, soft
aloha, [aah]
alone, backbone, ballon,
baritone, bemoan, birthstone,
blown, bombardon, bone,
brimstone, brownstone,
calzone, Capone, capstone,
car phone, cell phone,
chanson, chaperon,
cheekbone, clone,
cobblestone, collarbone,
cologne, condone, cone,
cornerstone, cornpone,
cortisone, crone, cyclone,
debone, depone, dethrone,
diaphone, dictaphone,
disown, drone, earphone,
end zone, enthrone, epigone,
flown, footstone, foreknown,
frisson, full-blown, full-grown,
funny bone, gallstone,
gemstone, gravestone,
grindstone, groan, grown,
hailstone, handblown,
headphone, hearthstone,
herringbone, homegrown,
hone, hormone, impone,
ingrown, jawbone, known,
loan, lone, megaphone,
mellophone, methadone,
microphone, mignon, moan,
orgone, overblown,
overgrown, overthrown, own,
ozone, phone, pinecone,
postpone, prednisone, prone,

rezone, sandstone,
saxophone, scone, sewn,
shone, shown, silicone,
speakerphone, tailbone,
telephone, testosterone,
throne, thrown, tombstone,
trombone, undertone,
unknown, whetstone,
windblown, wishbone,
xylophone, zone (see also
atone)
along, [agelong]
alongside, [abide]
aloof, bulletproof, childproof,
crushproof, fireproof,
foolproof, goof, leakproof,
lightproof, mothproof, poof,
proof, rainproof, reroof,
reproof, roof, shockproof,
spoof, sunroof, tamperproof,
waterproof, weatherproof,
windproof
alopecia, [abulia]
aloud, allowed, becloud,
bowed, cloud, crowd,
enshroud, loud, overcrowd,
overloud, proud, shroud,
stroud, thundercloud,
unbowed
alp, scalp
alpha, [alfalfa]
alphabet, [abet]
alphabetical, [acoustical]
alphabetize, [absolutize]
alphanumeric, [aleatoric]
alpine, [aerodyne]
already, [acidy]
alright, [affright]
also, arioso, basso, calypso,

espresso, expresso, fatso,
grandioso, lasso, miso, peso,
piso, scherzo, sew, so, torso,
vigoroso, virtuoso (see also
aficionado)
also-ran, [adman]
altar, [abductor]
altarpiece, [afterpiece]
altazimuth, behemoth,
bismuth, doth, mammoth,
sabbath, shibboleth, zenith
alter, [abductor]
alteration, [abbreviation]
altercate, [abdicate]
altercation, [abbreviation]
alternate, [abominate]
alternation, [abbreviation]
alternative, [ablative]
alternator, [abductor]
althorn, [acorn]
although, [airshow]
altimeter, [abductor]
altitude, amplitude, aptitude,
attitude, beatitude, certitude,
crassitude, finitude, fortitude,
gratitude, habitude,
hebetude, inaptitude,
ineptitude, infinitude,
ingratitude, inquietude,
lassitude, latitude, longitude,
magnitude, mansuetude,
multitude, platitude,
plenitude, pulchritude,
quietude, rectitude, servitude,
similitude, solicitude, solitude,
turpitude, vastitude,
vicissitude (see also **allude**)
alto, [aggiornamento]
altogether, another, anther,

author, bellwether, blather,
bother, brother, coauthor,
dither, either, ether, farther,
father, feather, forefather,
further, gather, godfather,
godmother, grandfather,
grandmother, hither, lather,
leather, mother, neither,
nether, other, panther,
pother, rather, slather, slither,
smother, stepbrother,
stepfather, stepmother,
swither, tether, thither, tither,
together, weather, whether,
whither, wither, zither (see
also **abductor**)
altruism, [abolitionism]
altruistic, [acoustic]
alum, [addendum]
aluminize, [agnize]
aluminum, [addendum]
alumna, angina, antenna,
arena, ballerina, banana,
bandanna, bwana, cantilena,
cantina, carina, catena,
cavatina, china, corona,
duenna, farina, fauna,
fontina, hosanna, hyena,
mana, manana, manna,
marijuana, marina, mina,
nirvana, novena, parmigiana,
persona, phenomena,
piranha, retina, sauna,
stamina, subpoena, tuna,
vagina (see also **a capella**)
alumnus, [agribusiness]
alway, [airway]
always, [ablaze]
am, [aerogram]

amain, [abstain]
amalgam, [addendum]
amalgamate, [acclimate]
amalgamation, [abbreviation]
amanuensis, [abyss]
amass, [admass]
amateur, [abductor]
amative, [ablative]
amatory, [accessory]
amaurosis, [alkalosis]
amaze, [ablaze]
amazement, [abandonment]
amazon, anacoluthon, ancon,
anon, asyndeton, autobahn,
awn, baton, begone, biathlon,
blouson, bonbon, boron,
bouillon, bourguignon,
boustrophedon, brawn,
bygone, cabochon, caisson,
carillon, carryon,
chateaubriand, chiffon,
chignon, con, conn, coupon,
crayon, crepon, cretonne,
crouton, cyclotron,
dawndoggone, don, drawn,
echelon, elan, electron,
epsilon, fawn, foregone,
gone, head-on, hexagon,
hogan, icon, john, lawn,
leprechaun, lexicon, liaison,
marathon, marzipan,
mastodon, moron, neon,
neutron, noumenon, nylon,
octagon, on, oxymoron,
pantheon, paragon, pawn,
pecan, pentagon,
phenomenon, polygon,
prawn, prolegomenon,
proton, python, radon, rayon,

salon, spawn, swan,
talkathon, tampon, telethon,
thereon, thereupon, upon,
walkathon, walk-on, wan,
withdrawn, woebegone,
yawn, yon
ambassador, [adder]
amber, antechamber, arbor,
barber, belabor, blabber,
blubber, bobber, burr, caliber,
camber, chamber, clamber,
clobber, clubber, cucumber,
cumber, dismember, ember,
encumber, fiber, gibber,
goober, harbor, jabber,
jobber, labor, landlubber,
libber, limber, lubber, lumber,
member, neighbor,
nonmember, number,
outnumber, prenumber,
renumber, remember, robber,
rubber, saber, slobber,
slumber, sober, somber,
subscriber, tabor, timber,
timbre, transcriber (see also
abductor)
ambidextrous, [actress]
ambience, [abhorrence]
ambient, [abeyant]
ambiguity, [abatis]
ambiguous, arduous,
assiduous, conspicuous,
contemptuous, contiguous,
continuous, discontinuous,
disingenuous, fastuous,
fatuous, flexuous, impetuous,
incongruous, inconspicuous,
ingenuous, innocuous,
mellifluous, nocuous,

nonambiguous,
noncontiguous, perspicuous,
presumptuous, promiscuous,
prowess, sensuous,
strenuous, sumptuous,
tempestuous, tenuous,
tortuous, tumultuous,
unambiguous, vacuous,
virtuous, voluptuous
ambit, [abbot]
ambition, [abbreviation]
ambitious, [adscititious]
ambivalence, [abhorrence]
ambivalent, ambulant,
appellant, assailant,
benevolent, blunt, callant,
coolant, corpulent,
equivalent, esculent,
excellent, exhalant, flagellant,
flatulent, flocculent,
fraudulent, indolent, inhalant,
insolent, jubilant, malevolent,
nonviolent, opulent, petulant,
postulant, prevalent, redolent,
sealant, silent, somnolent,
stimulant, succulent, talent,
truculent, turbulent,
ultraviolent, vigilant, violent,
virulent, volant (see also
abandonment)
ambivert, [advert]
amble, [able]
ambrosia, [abulia]
ambry, [accessory]
ambulance, [abhorrence]
ambulant, [ambivalent]
ambulate, [ablate]
ambulatory, [accessory]

ambush, bush, push,
 rosebush, tush
amebic, [acerbic]
ameliorate, [accelerate]
amelioration, [abbreviation]
amen, [again]
amenable, [able]
amend, [addend]
amendment, [abandonment]
amenity, [abatis]
ament, [abandonment]
amentia, [abulia]
amerce, [adverse]
amethyst, [adjust]
amiable, [able]
amicable, [able]
amice, [allonymous]
amicus, [abacus]
amid, bid, did, druid, eyelid,
 forbid, grid, hid, id, kid, lid,
 mid, outbid, outdid, overbid,
 overdid, pyramid, rebid, rid,
 skid, slid, squid, underbid
amide, [abide]
amidst, midst
amigo, [ago]
amine, [alexandrine]
amino, [albino]
amiss, [abyss]
amitosis, [alkalosis]
amity, [abatis]
ammunition, [abbreviation]
amnesty, [abatis]
amniocentesis, [alkalosis]
amoeba, [alfalfa]
amok, amuck, awestruck,
 bannock, barrack, buck,
 bullock, buttock, chuck, cluck,
 dead duck, duck,

dumbstruck, dybbuk, elegiac,
 epoch, eunuch, fast buck,
 fuck, guck, hammock,
 hassock, havoc, lameduck,
 luck, megabuck, moonstruck,
 muck, nip and tuck, puck,
 pluck, potluck, puck, roebuck,
 shuck, stage-struck,
 starstruck, struck, stuck,
 stomach, struck, stuck, suck,
 thunderstruck, truck, tuck,
 unstuck, woodchuck, yuck,
 yuk
amole, [ably]
among, dung, flung, high
 strung, hung, lung, mother
 tongue, rung, strung, slung,
 sprung, stung, sung, swung,
 tongue, unsung,
 weltanschauung, wrung,
 young
amoral, [admiral]
amorist, [allegorist]
amorous, [actress]
amorphous, aphis, artifice,
 benefice, boniface, doofus,
 edifice, fuss, interoffice,
 office, orifice, preface,
 resurface, surface (see also
 abacus)
amortization, [abbreviation]
amortize, [absolutize]
amount, [account]
amour, [abjure]
amp, [aid-de-camp]
ampere, [adhere]
ampersand, analysand, and,
 armband, backhand, band,
 bandstand, beforehand,

bellyband, bland, brand, cabstand, canned, command, contraband, countermand, cowhand, demand, disband, Disneyland, dockhand, dreamland, dryland, expand, farmhand, farmland, firebrand, firsthand, flatland, forehand, freehand, gangland, gland, grand, fairyland, fatherland, grandstand, grassland, hand, handstand, hatband, headband, headstand, heartland, hinterland, hired hand, Holy Land, homeland, inkstand, inland, kickstand, land, longhand, mainland, manned, marshland, meadowland, misunderstand, motherland, multiplicand, name brand, narrowband, newstand, nightstand, offhand, operand, quicksand, remand, reprimand, Rio Grande, sand, secondhand, shorthand, southland, stagehand, stand, strand, summand, sweatband, thirdhand, timberland, undermanned, understand, unmanned, unplanned, vacationland, waistband, wasteband, wasteland, watchband, withstand, wonderland, wristband
amphetamine, [alexandrine]
amphibian, [abecedarian]
amphibious, [abstemious]

amphiboly, [ably]
amphitheater, [abductor]
ampicillin, [acetylene]
ample, apple, carpel, chapel, couple, cripple, crumple, dapple, dimple, disciple, duple, empurple, episcopal, estoppel, example, gospel, grapple, laypeople, manciple, maple, multiple, municipal, nipple, papal, participle, people, pimple, pineapple, principal, principle, pupil, purple, quadruple, quintuple, ripple, rumple, salespeople, sample, scalpel, scruple, sextuple, simple, staple, steeple, stipple, supple, temple, topple, townspeople, trample, triple, uncouple (see also **abaxial**)
amplification, [abbreviation]
amplifier, briar, brier, choir, crier, drier, dryer, flier, friar, frier, gunfire, gyre, hire, humidifier, liar, magnifier, modifier, multiplier, prior, qualifier, sanctifier (see also **abductor**)
amplify, beautify, certify, clarify, classify, codify, crucify, decertify, declassify, defy, dehumidify, deify, detoxify, dignify, disqualify, diversify, dulcify, edify, emulsify, exemplify, falsify, fortify, fructify, glorify, gratify, horrify, humidify, identify, indemnify, intensify, justify,

liquefy, lithify, magnify,
misclassify, misidentify,
modify, mortify, mummify,
mystify, notify, nullify,
objectify, ossify, oversimplify,
pacify, personify, petrify,
purify, putrefy, qualify,
quantify, rarefy, ratify,
reclassify, recodify, refortify,
recertify, rectify, reify, revivify,
sanctify, satisfy, scarify,
signify, simplify, solemnify,
solidify, specify, stratify,
stultify, stupefy, terrify, testify,
typify, unify, verify, vilify,
vinify, vitrify, vivify (see also
airdry [remaining endings],
alibi)
amplitude, [altitude]
amply, [ably]
amputate, [acetate]
amputee, [abatis]
Amsterdam, [aerogram]
amuck, [amok]
amulet, [aglet]
amuse, abuse, bemuse, blues,
booze, bruise, chanteuse,
chartreuse, choose, confuse,
cruise, cruse, defuse, diffuse,
disuse, effuse, enthuse,
excuse, fuse, infuse, lose,
masseuse, misuse, muse,
news, ooze, overuse, peruse,
recuse, refuse, ruse,
schmooze, snooze, suffuse,
whose
amusement, [abandonment]
an, [adman]
anabasis, [alkalosis]

anabatic, [acoustic]
anabolic, [acyclic]
anachronism, [abolitionism]
anachronistic, [acoustic]
anaclitic, [acoustic]
anacoluthon, [amazon]
anaconda, [addenda]
anacrusis, [alkalosis]
anadromous, [allonymous]
anaerobic, [acerbic]
anaglyph, cliff, handkerchief,
if, midriff, miff, riff, sniff, spiff,
stiff, tiff, whiff
anagogic, [acidic]
anagram, [aerogram]
anal, [abdominal]
analeptic, [acoustic]
analgesia, [abulia]
analgesic, [airsick]
analog, [agog]
analogical, [acoustical]
analogous, asparagus, bogus,
esophagus, fungus,
humongous, magus (see also
abacus)
analogy, [allergy]
analysand, [ampersand]
analysis, [alkalosis]
analyst, [adjust]
analytic, [acoustic]
analytical, [acoustical]
analyze, [actualize]
anapest, [abreast]
anaphor, [abhor]
anarchism, [abolitionism]
anarchist, [activist]
anarchy, [achy]
anarthrous, [actress]
anastrophe, [antipornography]

117

anathema, anima, aroma,
asthma, bema, carcinoma,
charisma, chiasma, cinema,
coma, comma, cyclorama,
dharma, dilemma, diploma,
docudrama, dogma,
drachma, drama, duma,
eczema, edema,
emphysema, enema, enigma,
glaucoma, hematoma,
karma, kerygma, magma,
mamma, melanoma,
melodrama, miasma, pajama,
panorama, penultima,
plasma, pneuma,
psychodrama, sarcoma,
schema, sigma, soma,
stigma, stoma, summa,
trauma (see also **a capella**)
anatomical, [acoustical]
anatomist, [alchemist]
anatomize, [advise]
anatomy, [academy]
ancestor, see administer]
ancestral, [admiral]
ancestry, artistry, axletree,
baptistry, bigotry,
biochemistry, cabinetry,
cantatrice, carpentry,
casuistry, chantry, circuitry,
country, dentistry, gallantry,
gantry, gentry, geometry,
idolatry, industry, infantry,
ministry, optometry,
peasantry, pleasantry, poetry,
poultry, psaltery, psychiatry,
puppetry, reentry, registry,
rocketry, satisfactory, sentry,
sophistry, sultry, symmetry,

tapestry, telemetry, toiletry,
tree, trigonometry, vestry
(see also **abalone**)
anchor, [acre]
anchorage, [abridge]
anchorman, [abdomen]
anchorman, [adman]
anchorperson, [abdomen)
anchorwoman, [abdomen]
anchovy, bevy, civvy, covey,
divvy, envy, gravy, groovy,
heavy, ivy, jayvee, levee,
levy, movie, navy, nervy,
privy, savvy, scurvy, skivvy,
ultraheavy, wavy (see also
abalone)
ancient, [abeyant]
ancilla, [a capella]
ancillary, [accessory]
ancon, [amazon]
and, [ampersand]
andiron, [adjourn]
androgen, [allergen]
androgynous, [agribusiness]
android, [adenoid]
anecdotal, [accidental]
anecdote, [afloat]
anecdotist, [absolutist]
anemia, [abulia]
anemic, [academic]
aneroid, [adenoid]
anesthesiology, [allergy]
anesthetic, [acoustic]
anesthetist, [absolutist]
anesthetize, [absolutize]
aneurysm, [abolitionism]
anew, [accrue]
angel food cake, [awake]
angel, [agile]

angelica, babushka, barranca,
basilica, bazooka, botanica,
circa, coca, dumka, erotica,
eureka, harmonica, mecca,
mocha, paprika, parka,
perestroika, pica, plica, polka,
replica, swastika, tapioca,
troika, vodka, yarmulke (see
also **a capella**)
angelology, [allergy]
anger, [agar]
angina, [alumna]
angiogram, [aerogram]
angioplasty, [abatis]
angiosperm, [affirm]
angle, bagel, bangle, beagle,
bedraggle, boggle, bogle,
boondoggle, bugle,
centrifugal, comingle,
commingle, conjugal, cringle,
dangle, dingle, disentangle,
draggle, eagle, embrangle,
entangle, finagle, frugal,
gaggle, gargle, giggle,
goggle, gull, gurgle, haggle,
illegal, intermingle, jangle,
jiggle, jingle, juggle, jungle,
kugel, legal, madrigal,
mangle, mingle, mogul,
niggle, ogle, paralegal,
prodigal, quadrangle,
rectangle, regal, shingle,
single, smuggle, snuggle,
spangle, squiggle, straggle,
strangle, struggle, tangle,
tingle, toggle, triangle,
untangle, waggle, wangle,
wiggle, wrangle, wriggle (see
also **abaxial**)

angler, angular, annular,
antler, bachelor, binocular,
bipolar, blur, boiler,
bookseller, bottler, bowler,
broiler, bubbler, buckler,
burglar, butler, cackler,
caterpillar, cellar, cellular,
chancellor, chandler,
channeler, circular, chiller,
cobbler, collar, color,
compiler, comptroller,
controller, cooler, co-ruler,
counselor, coupler, crawler,
cuddler, curler, cutler,
dawdler, dealer, discolor,
dissimilar, distiller, dollar,
dolor, extracurricular, feeler,
filar, filler, fireballer, gentler,
granular, handler, hauler,
healer, heeler, holler,
hosteler, hustler, inhaler,
installer, irregular, jailer,
jeweler, jocular, juggler, killer,
knuckler, mailer, middler,
miler, miller, modular, molar,
molecular, monocular,
muffler, multicolor, muscular,
ocular, painkiller, pallor,
panhandler, parlor, particular,
perpendicular, pillar, polar,
poplar, popular, preschooler,
propeller, prowler, rambler,
reseller, reconciler,
rectangular, regular, revealer,
roller, rototiller, ruler, sailer,
sailor, saltcellar, sampler,
scalar, schiller, scholar,
sealer, secular, similar,
singular, sizzler, slur,

smuggler, sniffler, solar, sparkler, spectacular, spoiler, sprinkler, squaller, squalor, squealer, stapler, steamroller, stellar, storyteller, straggler, stroller, tabular, tailor, tattler, teetotaler, teller, thriller, tickler, tiller, titular, toddler, trailer, traveler, trawler, triangular, tumbler, unspectacular, unpopular, valor, vascular, vehicular, vernacular, vocabular, volar, wassailer, watercolor, watercooler, whaler, whistler, wholesaler, wiggler, wrangler, wrestler (see also **abductor**)

angleworm, [affirm]
anglicize, [abscise]
angry, [accessory]
anguish, [abolish]
angular, [angler]
angulation, [abbreviation]
anhedonia, [abulia]
anhydrous, [actress]
anile, crocodile, domicile, erstwhile, exile, freestyle, gentile, hairstyle, infantile, juvenile, labile, meanwhile, nubile, pedophile, percentile, profile, quartile, refile, retile, reconcile, reptile, sandpile, senile, stabile, stockpile, subfile, turnstile, woodpile, xenophile
anima, [anathema]
animadversion, [abrasion]
animal, [abnormal]
animalize, [actualize]

animate, [adjective]
approximate, climate, comet, consummate, estimate, exanimate, guestimate, helmet, hermit, illegitimate, inanimate, intimate, legitimate, limit, misestimate, mutt, penultimate, plummet, proximate, smut, summit, ultimate, vomit (see also **abbot**)
animate, [verb] [acclimate]
animated, [abluted]
animation, [abbreviation]
animator, [abductor]
animism, [abolitionism]
animist, [alchemist]
animistic, [acoustic]
animosity, [abatis]
animus, [allonymous]
anise, [agribusiness]
ankh, clonk, conk, honk, wonk, zonk
ankle, [acoustical]
anklet, [aglet]
anlage, [alfalfa]
Ann, [adman]
annals, cockles, durables, genitals, measles, oodles, shambles, shingles
anneal, appeal, bastille, ceil, conceal, congeal, creel, deal, difficile, eel, feel, freewheel, genteel, heal, heel, ideal, incorporeal, keel, kneel, meal, nonmaterial, ordeal, peal, peel, presbyterial, real, reel, repeal, reveal, seal, senatorial, spiel, squeal,

steal, steel, surreal, teal,
trinomial, unreal, veal, weal,
wheel, zeal (see also
abaxial)
annex, apex, bellowdecks,
circumflex, codex, complex,
convex, cortex, desex,
duplex, ex, flex, fourplex,
hex, index, latex, lex,
multiplex, narthex, perplex,
reflex, sex, simplex, spandex,
specs, telex, triplex, unisex,
vertex, vex, vortex
annexation, [abbreviation]
annihilate, [ablate]
annihilation, [abbreviation]
annihilator, [abductor]
anniversary, [accessory]
annotate, [acetate]
annotation, [abbreviation]
annotative, [ablative]
announce, bounce, denounce,
enounce, flounce,
mispronounce, ounce,
pounce, pronounce,
renounce, trounce
announcement,
[abandonment]
announcer, [aggressor]
annoy, [ahoy]
annoyance, [abhorrence]
annual, [accrual]
annualize, [actualize]
annuitant, [abirritant]
annuity, [abatis]
annul, [aboriginal]
annular, [angler]
annulate, [aglet]
annulet, [aglet]

annulment, [abandonment]
annulus, [acropolis]
annunciation, [abbreviation]
annunciator, [abductor]
anode, [abode]
anodize, [advise]
anoint, appoint, ballpoint,
checkpoint, conjoint,
counterpoint, disappoint,
gunpoint, joint, knifepoint,
midpoint, needlepoint,
outpoint, pinpoint, point,
reappoint, standpoint,
viewpoint
anomalous, [acropolis]
anomaly, [ably]
anomia, [abulia]
anomie, [academy]
anon, [amazon]
anonymity, [abatis]
anonymous, [allonymous]
anorexia, [abulia]
anorexic, [airsick]
another, [altogether]
answer, [aggressor]
answerable, [able]
ant, aslant, aunt, cant, can't,
chant, decant, descant,
eggplant, enceinte, enchant,
gallant, gallivant, grant,
implant, incant, pant, plant,
rant, recant, replant, scant,
slant, supplant, transplant
antacid, [acid]
antagonism, [abolitionism]
antagonist, [abolitionist]
antagonistic, [acoustic]
antagonize, [agnize]
ante, [abatis]

121

antebellum, [addendum]
antecede, [accede]
antecedent, [accordant]
antechamber, [amber]
antedate, [accommodate]
antediluvian, [abecedarian]
antelope, aslope, biotope, cantaloupe, cope, coup, dope, downslope, elope, envelope, fluoroscope, grope, gyroscope, hope, horoscope, interlope, kaleidoscope, lope, microscope, mope, nope, periscope, pope, rope, scope, slope, soap, stethoscope, taupe, telescope, tightrope, tope, towrope, trope
antemortem, [accustom]
antenna, [alumna]
antepenult, [adult]
anterior, barrier, bilinear, carrier, clothier, copier, courier, courtier, couturier, couturiere, easier, ball carrier, exterior, farrier, furrier, interior, interlinear, linear, meteor, nuclear, overseer, posterior, pronuclear, superior, tarrier, thermonuclear, ulterior, warrior (see also **abductor)**
anteroom, [abloom]
anthem, [addendum]
anther, [altogether]
anthology, [allergy]
anthrax, anticlimax, ax, battle ax, climax, earwax, excise tax, fax, flax, income tax, lax, max, minimax, overtax, pax,

pretax, relax, saks, sales tax, sealing wax, surtax, syntax, tax, thorax, wax
anthropic, [acidic]
anthropocentric, [aleatoric]
anthropogenic, [allergenic]
anthropoid, [adenoid]
anthropologist, [allergist]
anthropology, [allergy]
anthropomorphic, antipornographic, beatific, catastrophic, dimorphic, ectomorphic, endomorphic, frigorific, geographic, graphic, hieroglyphic, holographic, honorific, horrific, magnific, malefic, pacific, phonographic, photographic, pornographic, prescientific, prolific, salvific, scientific, soporific, specific, stenographic, strophic, sudorific, telegraphic, tenebrific, terrific, traffic (see also **academic**)
anthropomorphism, [abolitionism]
anthropopathism, [abolitionism]
anthurium, aquarium, atrium, auditorium, axiom, barium, become, biennium, cafetorium, calcium, cilium, coliseum, colosseum, colloquium, compendium, condominium, consortium, cranium, crematorium, criterium, delirium, effluvium, emporium, encomium,

equilibrium, geranium,
gymnasium, helium, idiom,
linoleum, lithium, magnesium,
mausoleum, millennium,
moratorium, museum,
natatorium, odeum, opium,
opprobrium, petroleum,
planetarium, plutonium,
podium, potassium,
presidium, quadrennium,
quadrivium, requiem,
sanitarium, sanitorium,
sodium, solarium, solatium,
stadium, sudatorium,
symposium, tedium, uranium
antiaircraft, [abaft]
antibias, bias, bodice,
canthus, canvas, congruous,
cowardice, crevice,
disservice, duchess, exodus,
fulvous, genius, goddess,
grievous, hazardous,
horrendous, impious,
ingenious, jaundice, Jesus,
joyous, mischievous,
nervous, nidus,
nonhazardous, novice, pelvis,
pious, purchase, repurchase,
righteous, seditious, self-
righteous, service,
stewardess, stupendous,
subreptitious, superfluous,
thus, tremendous, us (see
also **abacus**)
antibiotic, [acoustic]
antibody, [acidy]
antic, [acoustic]
anticapitalist, [aerialist]

antichrist, Christ, enticed,
heist, poltergeist, zeitgeist
antichristian, [abbreviation]
antichurch, besmirch, birch,
church, interchurch, lurch,
perch, research, search,
smirch
anticipate, constipate,
dissipate, emancipate,
exculpate, extirpate, palpate,
participate, pate, spate,
syncopate (see also **abate**)
anticipation, [abbreviation]
anticipatory, [accessory]
anticlimactic, [acoustic]
anticlimax, [anthrax]
anticommunist, [abolitionist]
anticonversationalist,
[aerialist]
anti-convulsant, [acquiescent]
antidepressant, [adjacent]
antidepression, [abbreviation]
antidevelopment,
[abandonment]
antidiscrimination,
[abbreviation]
antidote, [afloat]
antieducational, [aboriginal]
antielitism, [abolitionism]
antielitist, [adjust]
antiestablishment,
[abandonment]
antievolution, [abbreviation]
antievolutionary, [accessory]
antievolutionist, [abolitionist]
antifashion, [abbreviation]
antifeminism, [abolitionism]
antifeminist, [abolitionist]
antifreeze, appease,

asperges, baggies, betise,
big cheese, boonies, breeze,
cacoethes, camise,
Cantonese, caries, cheese,
chemise, Chinese,
computerese, crises,
diabetes, disease, displease,
ease, expertise, feces, feeze,
freeze, frieze, herpes,
indices, Japanese, jeez,
ladies, legalese, litotes,
miniseries, overseas, please,
rabies, reprise, seize, series,
sleaze, sneeze, soubise,
species, squeeze, striptease,
sundries, tease, tennies
antigay, [agape]
antigen, [allergen]
antigovernment,
   [abandonment]
antihistamine, [alexandrine]
antihomosexual, [accrual]
antihumanistic, [acoustic]
antiincumbent, [abeyant]
anti-inflation, [abbreviation]
anti-integration, [abbreviation]
antilock, [aftershock]
antimilitary, [accessory]
antimonopoly, [ably]
antinode, [abode]
antinomian, [abecedarian]
antinomy, [academy]
antiobescenity, [abatis]
antioxidant, [abundant]
antipasto, [aggiornamento]
antipathy, apathy,
   blameworthy, breathy,
   couthie, creditworthy, earthy,
   empathy, filthy, frothy,

healthy, lengthy, mouthy,
   pithy, sympathy, telepathy,
   toothy, unhealthy, wealthy
   (see also **abalone**)
antiperspirant, [aberrant]
antiphon, beckon, chicken,
   deafen, driven, embolden,
   everyone, fun, given,
   interurban, interwoven,
   misshapen, nonchristian,
   olden, outdone, postchristian,
   ripen, roughen, someone,
   suburban, toughen, tun,
   unchristian, undone, uneven,
   unshaven (see also
   abdomen)
antiphonal, [abdominal]
antiphony, [abalone]
antipodal, astraddle,
   backpaddle, backpedal,
   beadle, befuddle, biocidal,
   boodle, botryoidal, bridal,
   bridle, brindle, buddle,
   bundle, caboodle, candle,
   caudal, citadel, coddle,
   conchoidal, cradle, cuddle,
   curdle, dandle, dawdle,
   decadal, diddle, dirndl,
   doodle, dreidel, dwindle,
   engirdle, enkindle, feudal,
   fiddle, fondle, fuddle,
   germicidal, girdle, griddle,
   handle, heddle, homicidal,
   huddle, hurdle, idle, idol,
   kindle, ladle, manhandle,
   medal, meddle, middle,
   mishandle, modal, model,
   mollycoddle, muddle, needle,
   nodal, noodle, paddle,

panhandle, parricidal, pedal,
peddle, piddle, poodle,
puddle, rekindle, remodel,
riddle, rundle, saddle, sandal,
scandal, seidel, sidesaddle,
sidle, skedaddle, softpedal,
spindle, spraddle, straddle,
strudel, suicidal, supermodel,
swaddle, swindle, tidal,
toddle, trundle, twaddle,
twiddle, unsaddle, vandal,
waddle, wheedle, yodel (see
also **abaxial**)
antipode, [abode]
antipollution, [abbreviation]
antiporn, [acorn]
antipornographic,
[anthropomorphic]
antipornography,
[anastrophe]
antipot, [aeronaut]
antipoverty, [abatis]
antiprostitution, [abbreviation]
antiquarian, [abecedarian]
antiquate, [accentuate]
antique, apeak, beak, beek,
bespeak, bezique, bleak,
boutique, cacique, cheek,
chic, cleek, clinique, creak,
creek, critique, debeak,
doublespeak, eke, freak,
geek, Greek, hide-and-seek,
Holy Week, leak, leek, meek,
midweek, misspeak,
mystique, newspeak, oblique,
peak, peek, physique,
pipsqueak, pique, reek, seek,
shriek, sleek, sneak, speak,
squeak, streak, technique,

tweak, unique, weak, week,
workweek, wreak
antiquity, [abatis]
antiracism, [abolitionism]
antiseptic, [acoustic]
antislavery, [accessory]
antisocial, [abbatial]
antistrophe, [anastrophe]
antisubversive, [abrasive]
antithesis, [alkalosis]
antithetic, [acoustic]
antithetical, [acoustical]
antitotalitarian, [abecedarian]
antitoxin, anchorperson,
comparison, grandson, son,
sponson, stepson, sun,
tocsin, toxin, unison, venison,
vixen (see also **abdomen**)
antitrust, [adjust]
antitype, [airpipe]
antiunion, aphelion, banyan,
bastion, battalion, billion,
bullion, bunion, canyon,
chameleon, civilian,
communion, companion,
disunion, dominion, doyenne,
hellion, jillion, medallion,
million, minion, minyan,
multimillion, nonunion,
opinion, pavilion, rebellion,
reunion, scallion, scullion,
stallion, union (see also
abdomen)
antiviolence, [abhorrence]
antiwar, [abhor]
antiwelfare, [affair]
antler, angler]
antogenous, [agribusiness]
antonomasia, [abulia]

antonym, [acronym]
antsy, [absorbancy]
anus, [agribusiness]
anvil, [adjectival]
anxiety, [abatis]
anxious, [adscititious]
any, [abalone]
anybody, [acidy]
anyhow, [allow]
anymore, [abhor]
anyplace, [abase]
anything, bowstrong, bring,
bullring, cling, ding, ding-a-
ling, evening, everything,
fling, handspring, heartstring,
king, mainspring, offspring,
ping, plaything, ring, sing,
sling, spring, sting, swing,
thing, ting, underling,
wedding, wing, wring
anytime, [airtime]
anyway, [airway]
anyways, [ablaze]
anywhere, care, chair,
derriere, elsewhere, ere,
everywhere, nowhere,
plowshare, scare,
somewhere, timeshare,
wheelchair, where [see also
affair]
aorist, [adjust]
aoristic, [acoustic]
aorta, arista, ballista, beta,
betta, biretta, bota, cabaletta,
cabretta, canasta, cantata,
casita, cheetah, data, delta,
emerita, errata, fajita, fiesta,
forta, frittata, granita, iota,
junta, manta, margarita,
operetta, pancetta, pasta,
pelota, perfecta, pinata, pita,
placenta, quota, regatta,
ricotta, senorita, sonata,
taffeta, to, toccata, vendetta,
vista, vita, yenta (see also a
capella)
apace, [abase]
apart, art, cart, chart,
counterpart, dart, depart, fart,
flowchart, forepart, handcart,
heart, impart, kart, lionheart,
mart, outsmart, oxcart, part,
pushcart, rampart, restart,
shopping cart, smart, start,
start-of-the-art, supersmart,
sweetheart, tart, ultrasmart,
upstart
apartheid, [acetate]
apartment, [abandonment]
apathetic, [acoustic]
apathy, [antipathy]
ape, [agape]
apeak, [antique]
aperient, [abeyant]
aperiodic, [acidic]
aperitif, beef, belief, brief,
chief, cloverleaf, debrief,
disbelief, flyleaf, grief,
kerchief, leaf, motif, reef,
relief, sheaf, thief, unbelief
aperture, [abjure]
apex, [annex]
aphasia, [abulia]
aphelion, [antiunion]
aphesis, [alkalosis]
aphid, [acid]
aphis, [amorphous]
aphonia, [abulia]

aphonic, [allergenic]
aphorism, [abolitionism]
aphoristic, [acoustic]
aphrodisiac, [aback]
apiarian, [abecedarian]
apiary, [accessory]
apical, [acoustical]
apiculate, [agle]
apiculture, [acupuncture]
apiece, [afterpiece]
apiology, [allergy]
apish, [abolish]
aplenty, [abatis]
aplomb, atom bomb, bomb,
bombe, car bomb, firebomb,
glom, Guam, hydrogen
bomb, imam, intercom, letter
bomb, mail bomb, mom,
napalm, palm, phenom,
pompom, prom, psalm,
qualm, sitcom, smoke bomb,
supermom, wigwam [see also
palm]
apnea, [abulia]
apocalypse, eclipse, ellipse,
snips
apocalyptic, [acoustic]
apocope, aromatherapy,
bibliotherapy, bumpy, buppie,
calliope, canapé, canopy,
chemotherapy, chippy,
choppy, copy, crappy,
creepy, crispy, dopey, drippy,
droopy, dumpy, entropy,
epopee, escapee, flappy,
floppy, frumpy, gossipy,
groupie, grumpy, guppy,
happy, hippie, jalopy, jumpy,
lumpy, mopey, multicopy,

nippy, orthoepy, pea, pee,
peppy, pericope,
philanthropy, photocopy,
poppy, preppy,
psychotherapy, puppy, raspy,
recopy, recipe, rupee,
scampi, scrappy, skimpy,
sleepy, sloppy, snappy,
snippy, snoopy, soapy,
soppy, soupy, stumpy,
syncope, teepee, therapy,
unhappy, whippy, whoopee,
wispy, yippee, yippie, yuppie,
zippy (see also abalone)
apocrypha, [alfalfa]
apocryphal, artful, aweful,
awful, baffle, baleful, baneful,
bashful, basketful, beautiful,
blissful, boastful, bountiful,
bucketful, careful, cheerful,
chockful, coffle, colorful,
deceitful, delightful, direful,
disdainful, distasteful,
distressful, distrustful, doleful,
doomful, doubtful, dreadful,
dutiful, earful, eventful,
faithful, fanciful, fateful,
fearful, fistful, forceful,
forgetful, fretful, frightful,
fruitful, graceful, grateful,
harmful, hateful, helpful,
hopeful, hurtful, insightful,
joyful, lawful, lustful,
masterful, meaningful,
merciful, mindful, mournful,
mouthful, offal, painful,
peaceful, pitiful, playful,
plentiful, powerful, prayerful,
prideful, purposeful, raffle,

regretful, remorseful,
resentful, reshuffle,
resourceful, respectful, restful
revengeful, riffle, rifle, rightful,
rueful, ruffle, sackful,
scornful, scuffle, shameful,
shovelful, shuffle, sinful,
skillful, slothful, snaffle,
sniffle, sorrowful, spiteful,
stifle, stressful, successful,
suspenseful, tactful, tasteful,
tearful, thankful, thoughtful,
trifle, triumphal, truffle,
trustful, truthful, ultracareful,
ultrapowerful, uneventful,
unfaithful, unfruitful,
ungraceful, ungrateful,
unhealthful, unhelpful,
unlawful, unmerciful,
unskillful, unsuccessful,
untruthful, useful, vengeful,
waffle, wakeful, wasteful,
watchful, whiffle, willful,
wishful, wistful, woeful,
wonderful, worshipful,
wrathful, wrongful, youthful,
zestful (see also **abaxial**)
apodictic, [acoustic]
apodosis, [alkalosis]
apogee, [allergy]
apolitical, [acoustical]
apologetic [acoustic]
apologetics, [acoustics]
apologist, [allergist]
apologize, [advise]
apologue, [agog]
apology, [allergy]
apoplectic, [acoustic]
apoplexy, [absorbancy]

aport, [airport]
aposematic, [acoustic]
aposiopesis, [alkalosis]
apostasy, [absorbancy]
apostate, [acetate]
apostatize, [absolutize]
aposteriori, [accessory]
apostle, axle, basal, bristle,
bustle, cancel, capsule,
castle, chancel, codicil,
colossal, corpuscle, council,
counsel, diesel, dismissal,
docile, dorsal, encapsule,
epistle, facile, fossil, gristle,
hassle, hustle, imbecile,
jostle, missal, missile, morsel,
muscle, nestle, outhustle,
outmuscle, parcel, passel,
pencil, pestle, pretzel,
proconsul, rehearsal,
reversal, rustle, schnitzel,
stencil, tassel, tensile, thistle,
tinsel, tonsil, trestle, tussle,
universal, utensil, vassal,
vessel, wassail, whistle,
wrestle (see also **abaxial**)
apostleship, [airship]
apostolate, [ablate]
apostolic, [acyclic]
apostrophe, [anastrophe]
apothecary, [accessory]
apothegm, Bethlehem,
condemn, contemn, diadem,
gem, hem, mayhem, phlegm,
phloem, proem, protem, stem
apotheosis, [alkalosis]
appall, [aerosol]
appalled, auld, bald,
blackballed, so-called

appanage, baronage, carnage,
coinage, co-manage,
drainage, dunnage, lineage,
manage, micromanage,
mismanage, orphanage,
overmanage, parsonage,
patronage, personage,
signage, tonnage, vicinage
(see also **abridge**)
apparatus, [afflatus]
apparel, [admiral]
apparent, [aberrant]
apparition, [abbreviation]
appeal, [anneal]
appear, [adhere]
appearance, [abhorrence]
appease, [antifreeze]
appeasement, [abandonment]
appelative, [ablative]
appellant, [ambivalent]
appellate, [aglet]
appellation, [abbreviation]
appellee, [ably]
append, [addend]
appendage, [acknowledge]
appendant, [abundant]
appendectomy, [academy]
appendicitis, [afflatus]
appendix, [administratrix]
apperceive, [achieve]
apperception [abbreviation]
appertain, [abstain]
appetite, [affright]
appetizer, [adviser]
applaud, [abroad]
applause, cause, clause,
gauze, menopause, pause
apple, [ample]
applejack, [aback]

applesauce, [across]
appliance, [abhorrence]
applicable, [able]
applicant, [abeyant]
application, [abbreviation]
applicator, [abductor]
applied, [abide]
appliqué, [agape]
apply, [airdry]
appoint, [anoint]
appointee, [abatis]
appointive, [ablative]
appointment, [abandonment]
apportion, [abbreviation]
apportionment,
[abandonment]
appose, [airhose]
apposite, chemisette, closet,
composite, deposit, exit,
exquisite, opposite,
perquisite, posit, prerequisite,
redeposit, reposit, requisite,
revisit, visit (see also **abbot**)
apposition, [abbreviation]
appraisal, arousal, bamboozle,
basil, bedazzle, bezel,
causal, chisel, damsel,
dazzle, disposal, drizzle,
easel, embezzle, espousal,
fizzle, foozle, frazzle, frizzle,
gazelle, grizzle, guzzle,
muzzle, nasal, nozzle,
nuzzle, perusal, proposal,
puzzle, reappraisal, refusal,
reprisal, sizzle, spousal,
swizzle, tousle, weasel (see
also **abaxial**)
appraise, [ablaze]
appreciable, [able]

appreciation, [abbreviation]
appreciative, [ablative]
apprehend, [addend]
apprehensible, [able]
apprehension, [abbreviation]
apprehensive, [abrasive]
apprentice, [afflatus]
apprise, [accessorize]
apprize, [accessorize]
approach, [abroach]
approachable, [able]
approbate, [abate]
approbation, [abbreviation]
appropriation, [abbreviation]
approvable, [able]
approval, [adjectival]
approve, behoove, commove,
   disapprove, disprove, groove,
   improve, move, preapprove,
   prove, reapprove, remove,
   reprove
approximate, [acclimate]
approximate, [animate]
approximation, [abbreviation]
appurtenance, [abhorrence]
appurtenant, [abstinent]
apraxia, [abulia]
apricot, [aeronaut]
apriori, [accessory]
apropos, [airshow]
apse, chaps, collapse, craps,
   elapse, lapse, perhaps,
   prolapse, relapse, synapse,
   taps
apt, [adapt]
apterous, [actress]
aptitude, [altitude]
aqua, [alfalfa]
aquacade, [abrade]

aquaculture, [acupuncture]
aquamarine, [alexandrine]
aquanaut, [aeronaut]
aquanaut, aeronaut,
   aforethought, afterthought,
   aliquot, allot, antipot, apricot,
   astronaut, aught, begot,
   besot, bloodshot, bought,
   brought, boycott, buckshot,
   caught, caveat, clot, cocotte,
   cosmonaut, cot, counterplot,
   crackpot, culotte, distraught,
   dogtrot, dot, drylot, dry-rot,
   earshot, feedlot, flowerpot,
   forethought, fraught, gunshot,
   hot, hotshot, jackpot, jot,
   juggernaut, knot, lot, marplot,
   mascot, nightspot, not,
   nought, onslaught, ought,
   overshot, plot, polyshot,
   robot, rot, sandlot, savate,
   self-taught, sexpot, shot,
   skat, slingshot, slipknot, slot,
   snapshot, snot, spot, squat,
   stinkpot, stockpot, subplot,
   sunspot, swat, taut, teapot,
   thought, tommyrot, topknot,
   tot, trot, untaught, upshot,
   watt, whatnot, woodlot,
   wrought, yacht
aquarium, [anthurium]
aquatic, [acoustic]
aqueduct, [abduct]
aqueous, [abstemious]
aquiline, [airline]
aquiver, [achiever]
arabesque, burlesque,
   copydesk, desk, grotesque,
   picturesque, statuesque

arable, [able]
Arafat, [acrobat]
arbiter, [abductor]
arbitrage, barrage, cabotage,
  camouflage, collage,
  corsage, counterespionage,
  decoupage, dressage,
  empennage, entourage,
  espionage, frottage, fuselage,
  garage, gavage, massage,
  menage, mirage, montage,
  moulage, sabotage, triage
arbitrager, biographer, doer,
  drawer, err, folksinger,
  hanger, her, mudslinger,
  paperhanger, ringer, secure,
  singer, stinger, straphanger,
  stringer, swinger, wringer,
  zinger (see also **abductor**)
arbitrament, [abandonment]
arbitrate, [accelerate]
arbitration, [abbreviation]
arbitrator, [abductor]
arbor, [amber]
arboretum, [accustom]
arborize, [accessorize]
arc, [aardvark]
arcade, [abrade]
arcadia, [abulia]
arcadian, [abecedarian]
arcane, [abstain]
arch, cornstarch, march,
  outmarch, parch, starch,
  overarch
archaeological, [acoustical]
archaeology, [allergy]
archaic, [acidic]
archangel, [agile]

archbishop, backup, bangup,
  bishop, blowup, breakup,
  buildup, catchup, checkup,
  cleanup, collop, cup, cutup,
  develop, dollop, envelop,
  fillip, follow-up, gallop,
  gossip, hangup, hiccup,
  holdup, hookup, hup, hyssop,
  ketchup, layup, letup, lineup,
  linkup, lockup, makeup,
  markup, matchup,
  overdevelop, parsnip,
  pasteup, pickup, pileup,
  pinup, polyp, pup, redevelop,
  roundup, scallop, screwup,
  setup, slipup, smashup,
  speedup, stickup, stirrup,
  sup, syrup, tiptop, tulip,
  turnip, up, wallop, windup,
  work, worship
archduke, cuke, duke, fluke,
  gook, juke, kook, nuke, puke,
  rebuke, souk, spook
archenemy, [academy]
archer, [acupuncture]
archery, [accessory]
archetype, [airpipe]
archfiend, fiend
archipelago, [ago]
architect, [abject]
architectural, [admiral]
architecture, [acupuncture]
archive, [alive]
archivist, [activist]
archway, [airway]
arctic, [acoustic]
arcuate, [adequate]
ardent, [accordant]
ardor, [adder]

arduous, [ambiguous]
are, [abattoir]
area code, [abode]
area, [abulia]
areaway, [airway]
arena, [alumna]
areola, [a capella]
areole, atoll, aureole,
  banderole, bankroll, beadroll,
  beanpole, black hole,
  blowhole, bole, boll, bowl,
  buttonhole, cabriole, cajole,
  camisole, capriole, casserole,
  charcoal, coal, cole, condole,
  console, control, creole,
  croquignole, cubbyhole, dole,
  droll, drumroll, enroll, ensoul,
  extol, farandole, fishbowl,
  fishing pole, flagpole, foal,
  foxhole, girandole, goal, half-
  sole, hellhole, hole, innersole,
  insole, Interpol, jelly roll,
  keyhole, knoll, knothole,
  loophole, manhole, midsole,
  mole, multirole, oriole, parole,
  patrol, payroll, peephole,
  pigeonhole, pighole, pinhole,
  pole, poll, porthole, posthole,
  pothole, punch bowl, reenroll,
  remote control, rigmarole,
  rock and roll, role, roll, scroll,
  self-control, sheol, shoal,
  sinkhole, skoal, slipsole, sole,
  soul, stole, stroll, Super Bowl,
  tadpole, telephone, thole, toll,
  troll, washbowl, whole
argent, [agent]
argosy, [absorbancy]
argot, [agate]

arguable, [able]
argue, [accrue]
argument, [abandonment]
argumentation, [abbreviation]
argumentative, [ablative]
argyle, [aisle]
aria, [abulia]
arid, [acid]
aright, [affright]
arioso, [also]
arise, [accessorize]
arista, [aorta]
aristocracy, [absorbancy]
aristocrat, [acrobat]
aristocratic, [acoustic]
aristotype, [airpipe]
arithmetic, [acoustic]
arithmetician, [abbreviation]
ark, [aardvark]
arm, [alarm]
armada, [addenda]
armadillo, [afterglow]
armageddon, bedridden,
  bidden, broaden, burden,
  cordon, deaden,
  downtrodden, forbidden,
  garden, handmaiden, harden,
  hidden, hoyden, laden,
  leaden, madden, maiden,
  overburden, pardon, ridden,
  sodden, trodden, unburden,
  warden, widen (see also
  abdomen)
armament, [abandonment]
armature, [abjure]
armband, [ampersand]
armchair, [affair]
armiger, astrologer, badger,
  bordure, challenger, charger,

codger, conjure, danger,
derringer, dodger, dowager,
edger, encourager,
endanger, forger, ginger,
grandeur, granger, harbinger,
injure, integer, ledger, major,
manager, manger, merger,
messenger, micromanager,
ordure, pager, passenger,
perjure, plunger, procedure,
ranger, reinjure, scavenger,
soldier, stranger,
supercharger, verdure,
villager, wager (see also
abductor)
armistice, [afflatus]
armlet, [aglet]
armload, [abode]
armlock, [aftershock]
armor, astronomer,
beachcomber, blasphemer,
bloomer, boomer, bomber,
bummer, charmer, clamor,
comer, consumer, costumer,
creamer, customer,
daydreamer, demur, dimmer,
disclaimer, dreamer,
drummer, dulcimer, emmer,
enamor, farmer, former,
framer, gamer, glamour,
glimmer, gossamer,
grammar, hammer, humor,
informer, jackhammer,
latecomer, midsummer,
misnomer, murmur, myrrh,
newcomer, nonconsumer,
nonperformer, omer,
performer, plumber, primer,
programmer, redeemer,

reformer, rumor, schemer,
screamer, shimmer, simmer,
skimmer, slammer,
sledgehammer, stammer,
steamer, streamer, summer,
timer, transformer, tremor,
trimmer, tumor, warmer,
windjammer, yammer (see
also **abductor**)
armorbearer, [adulterer]
armory, [accessory]
armpad, [ad]
armpatch, attach, Bach,
bandersnatch, batch, catch,
cratch, detach, dispatch,
hatch, latch, match,
mismatch, patch, potlatch,
reattach, rematch, scratch,
snatch, thatch
armpit, [acquit]
armrest, [abreast]
army, [academy]
aroma, [anathema]
aromatherapy, [apocope]
aromatic, [acoustic]
arose, [airhose]
around, [abound]
arousal, [appraisal]
arouse, browse, carouse,
dowse, drowse, espouse,
rouse
arpeggio, audio, barrio, brio,
cameo, cheerio, fellatio, folio,
imbroglio, impresario,
mustachio, nuncio, oratorio,
patio, polio, portfolio,
presidio, punctilio, radio,
ratio, rodeo, scenario, stereo,
studio, trio, video (see also

aficionado)
arraign, [abstain]
arraignment, [abandonment]
arrange, change, derange,
downrange, estrange,
exchange, grange,
interchange, multirange,
prearrange, range, rearrange,
shortchange, shortrange,
strange
arrangement, [abandonment]
arrant, [aberrant]
arras, [actress]
array, [affray]
arrear, [adhere]
arrest, [abreast]
arrhythmia, [abulia]
arrival, [adjectival]
arrive, [alive]
arrogance, [abhorrence]
arrogant, [abeyant]
arrogate, [abnegate]
arrow, [allegro]
arrowhead, [abed]
arroyo, [airshow]
arsenal, [aboriginal]
arsenic, [allergenic]
arsis, [alkalosis]
arson, assassin, basin, bison,
boatswain, businessperson,
cameraperson, chairperson,
chasten, chosen, christen,
delicatessen, fasten, fission,
glisten, hasten, layperson,
lessen, lesson, listen, loosen,
mason, moisten, parson,
person, salesperson,
spokesperson, stonemason,
superperson, unfasten,
unloosen, washbasin,
weatherperson, worsen see
also **antitoxin**]
arsonist, [abolitionist]
art, apart, cart, chart,
counterpart, dart, depart, fart,
flowchart, forepart, handcart,
heart, impart, kart, mart,
outsmart, oxcart, part,
pushcart, rampart, restart,
smart, start, supersmart,
sweetheart, tart, ultrasmart,
upstart
arterial, [abaxial]
artery, [accessory]
artful, [apocryphal]
arthritic, [acoustic]
arthritis, [afflatus]
artichoke, awoke, backstroke,
baroque, bespoke,
breaststroke, broke, choke,
cloak, coke, convoke,
counterstroke, cowpoke,
croak, downstroke, evoke,
folk, heatstroke, hoke,
invoke, joke, kinfolk, kinsfolk,
masterstroke, oak, okeydoke,
poke, presoak, provoke,
revoke, sidestroke, slowpoke,
smoke, soak, space walk,
spoke, stoke, stroke,
sunstroke, thunderstroke,
toque, upstroke, woke,
womenfolk, yoke, yolk
article, [acoustical]
articulate, [noun or adjective]
[aglet]
articulate, [verb] [ablate]
articulated, [abluted]

articulation, [abbreviation]
artifice, [amorphous]
artificial, [abbatial]
artillery, [accessory]
artisan, bartizan, benison, bipartisan, citizen, courtesan, cousin, cozen, crimson, denizen, noncitizen, nonpartisan, partisan (see also abdomen)
artist, [absolutist]
artistic, [acoustic]
artistry, [ancestry]
artsy, [absorbancy]
artware, [affair]
artwork, beadwork, berserk, bodywork, bulwark, burke, busywork, cabinetwork, casework, chirk, cirque, clerk, clockwork, dirk, drawnwork, ductwork, falsework, fieldwork, firework, footwork, framework, frostwork, grillwork, groundwork, guesswork, handiwork, handwork, homework, housework, irk, jerk, legwork, lifework, lurk, metalwork, millwork, murk, needlework, network, outwork, overwork, paperwork, patchwork, perk, piecework, quirk, rework, roadwork, salesclerk, schoolwork, shirk, slopwork, smirk, stickwork, stonework, teamwork, timework, tinwork, wonderwork, woodwork, work
arty, [abatis]
as, has, jazz, pizzazz, razz, spaz, topaz, whereas
asbestos, [afflatus]
ascend, [addend]
ascendance, [abhorrence]
ascendancy, [absorbancy]
ascendant, [abundant]
ascension, [abbreviation]
ascent, [accent]
ascertain, [abstain]
ascesis, [alkalosis]
ascetic, [acoustic]
asceticism, [abolitionism]
ascot, [advocate]
ascribe, bribe, circumscribe, conscribe, describe, diatribe, gibe, imbibe, inscribe, jibe, mistranscribe, overprescribe, oversubscribe, prescribe, proscribe, scribe, subscribe, transcribe, tribe, vibe
ascription, [abbreviation]
ascriptive, [ablative]
aseptic, [acoustic]
asexual, [accrual]
ash, [abash]
ashen, [abbreviation]
ashore, [abhor]
aside, [abide]
asinine, [aerodyne]
ask, bask, cask, casque, flask, mask, task, unmask
askance, [advance]
askew, [accrue]
aslant, [ant]
asleep, beep, bleep, bopeep, cheap, cheep, creep, deep, heap, jeep, keep, leap, oversleep, peep, reap, seep, sheep, sleep, steep, sweep,

veep, weep
aslope, [antelope]
asocial, [abbatial]
asparagus, [analogous]
aspartame, [acclaim]
aspartate, [acetate]
aspect, [abject]
asperges, [antifreeze]
asperity, [abatis]
asperse, [adverse]
aspersion, [abrasion]
asphalt, assault, basalt, cobalt,
    default, exalt, fault, halt,
    gestalt, malt, salt,
    somersault, vault
asphyxia, [abulia]
asphyxiation, [abbreviation]
aspic, [acidic]
aspirant, [aberrant]
aspirate, [accelerate]
aspiration, [abbreviation]
aspirator, [abductor]
aspire, [acquire]
ass, [admass]
assail, [ail]
assailant, [ambivalent]
assassin, [anchorperson]
assassinate, [abominate]
assassination, [abbreviation]
assault, [asphalt]
assay, [agape]
assemblage, [acknowledge]
assemble, [able]
assembly, [ably]
assent, [accent]
assert, [advert]
assertion, [abbreviation]
assertive, [ablative]
assess, [acquiesce]

assessment, [abandonment]
assessor, [aggressor]
asset, [abet]
asseverate, [accelerate]
assiduous, [ambiguous]
assign, [aerodyne]
assignable, [able]
assignation, [abbreviation]
assignee, [abalone]
assignment, [abandonment]
assimilate, [ablate]
assimilation, [abbreviation]
assist, bassist, bioethicist,
    consist, cyst, desist, encyst,
    ethicist, exorcist, fascist,
    geneticist, insist, lyricist,
    persist, pharmacist, physicist,
    polemicist, publicist, racist,
    resist, romanticist, solipsist,
    subsist, supremacist (see
    also **abolitionist**)
assistance, [abhorrence]
assistant, [abirritant]
assistantship, [airship]
assize, [abscise]
association, [abbreviation]
associative, [ablative]
assonance, [abhorrence]
assort, [abort]
assorted, [abluted]
assortment, [abandonment]
assuage, [age]
assumable, [able]
assume, [abloom]
assumption, [abbreviation]
assurance, [abhorrence]
assure, [abjure]
aster, [administer]
asterisk, bisque, brisk, disc,

disk, floppy disk, frisk,
obelisk, risk, tamarisk,
videodisk, whisk
astern, [adjourn]
asteroid, [adenoid]
asthenia, [abulia]
asthenic, [allergenic]
asthma, [anathema]
asthmatic, [acoustic]
astigmatic, [acoustic]
astigmatism, [abolitionism]
astir, [administer]
astonish, [abolish]
astonishment, [abandonment]
astound, [abound]
astraddle, [antipodal]
astral, [barrel]
astray, [affray]
astride, [abide]
astringent, [agent]
astrodome, catacomb,
chrome, chromosome, comb,
coxcomb, dome, foam,
gnome, home, honeycomb,
metronome, monochrome,
motorhome, ohm, roam,
shalom, Superdome,
syndrome, tome, velodrome
astrologer, [armiger]
astrological, [acoustical]
astrology, [allergy]
astromancy, [absorbancy]
astronaut, [aeronaut]
astronomer, [armor]
astronomical, [acoustical]
astronomy, [academy]
astute, [acute]
asunder, [adder]
aswarm, barnstorm,

brainstorm, chloroform,
conform, cribriform,
cuneiform, deform, dorm,
ensiform, firestorm, form,
hailstorm, inform, lukewarm,
misinform, norm, outperform,
perform, pisiform, platform,
rainstorm, reform, sandstorm,
snowstorm, storm, swarm,
thunderstorm, transform,
uniform, warm, windstorm
aswirl, awhirl, burl, cowgirl,
curl, earl, furl, girl, hurl, pearl,
playgirl, salesgirl, showgirl,
squirrel, swirl, twirl, unfurl,
whirl (see also **abaxial**)
aswoon, [afternoon]
asylum, [addendum]
asymmetrical, [acoustical]
asymptomatic, [acoustic]
asymptote, [afloat]
asyndeton, [amazon]
at, [acrobat]
ataractic, [acoustic]
atavism, [abolitionism]
ataxia, [abulia]
ate, compensate, fate, fixate,
hate, inspissate, phosphate,
pulsate, self-hate, sensate
(see also **abate**)
atelier, [agape]
atemporal, [admiral]
atheism, [abolitionism]
atheist, [activist]
atheistic, [acoustic]
athirst, accursed, bratwurst,
burst, cloudburst, downburst,
durst, first, groundburst,
headfirst, knockwurst,

liverwurst, outburst, sunburst, thirst, wienerwurst, worst
athlete, [accrete]
athletic, [acoustic]
athleticism, [abolitionism]
athletics, [acoustics]
athwart, [abort]
atilt, bloodguilt, built, guilt, hilt, jilt, kilt, lilt, quilt, rebuilt, silt, spilt, stilt, tilt, wilt
atlas, [acropolis]
atman, [abdomen]
atmosphere, [adhere]
atmospheric, [aleatoric]
atoll, [areole]
atom bomb, [aplomb]
atom, [accustom]
atomic age, [age]
atomic, [academic]
atomism, [abolitionism]
atomist, [alchemist]
atomize, [advise]
atomizer, [adviser]
atomy, [academy]
atonal, [abdominal]
atone, baritone, halftone, headstone, intone, limestone, milestone, millstone, monotone, stone, tone, touchstone, touch-tone, two-tone (see also **alone**)
atonement, [abandonment]
atonic, [allergenic]
atop, [agitprop]
atrabilious, [abstemious]
atremble, [able]
atrium, [anthurium]
atrocious, [adscititious]
atrocity, [abatis]

atrophy, [anastrophe]
attach, [armpatch]
attaché, [agape]
attachment, [abandonment]
attack, [aback]
attacked, [abstract]
attacker, [acre]
attain, [abstain]
attainable, [able]
attainder, [adder]
attainment, [abandonment]
attaint, [acquaint]
attempt, contempt, dreamt, exempt, preempt, self-contempt, tax-exempt, tempt, unkempt
attend, [addend]
attendance, [abhorrence]
attendant, [abundant]
attendee, [acidy]
attention, [abbreviation]
attentive, [ablative]
attenuation, [abbreviation]
attest, [abreast]
attestation, [abbreviation]
attic, [acoustic]
atticism, [abolitionism]
attire, [acquire]
attitude, [altitude]
attitudinal, [aboriginal]
attorn, [adjourn]
attorney, [abalone]
attract, [abstract]
attraction, [abbreviation]
attractive, [ablative]
attribute, [acute]
attribution, [abbreviation]
attributive, [ablative]
attrition, [abbreviation]

attune, [afternoon]
atypical, [acoustical]
aubade, [abroad]
auburn, [adjourn]
auction, [abbreviation]
auctioneer, [adhere]
audacious, [adscititious]
audacity, [abatis]
audible, [able]
audience, [abhorrence]
audio, [arpeggio]
audiocassette, [abet]
audiotape, [agape]
audiovisual, [accrual]
audit, [adequate]
audition, [abbreviation]
auditor, [abductor]
auditorium, [anthurium]
auditory, [accessory]
auger, [agar]
aught, [aeronaut]
augmentation, [abbreviation]
augmented, [abluted]
augur, [agar]
augury, [accessory]
august, [adjust]
Augustine, [alexandrine]
auld, [appalled]
aunt, [ant]
aura, [abracadabra]
aureate, [adequate]
aureole, [areole]
auric, [aleatoric]
aurora, s[abracadabra]
auscultate, [acetate]
auscultation, [abbreviation]
auspice, campus, carpus,
    compass, corpus,
    encompass, hospice,

multicampus, multipurpose,
    octopus, opus, pompous,
    porpoise, purpose, pus,
    rumpus, trespass (see also
    abacus)
auspicious, [adscititious]
austere, [adhere]
austerity, [abatis]
autarchy, [achy]
authentic, [acoustic]
authenticate, [abdicate]
authentication, [abbreviation]
authenticity, [abatis]
author, [altogether]
authoress, [actress]
authoritarian, [abecedarian]
authoritative, [ablative]
authority, [abatis]
authorization, [abbreviation]
authorize, [accessorize]
authorship, [airship]
autism, [abolitionism]
autistic, [acoustic]
autobahn, [amazon]
autobiographical, [acoustical]
autobiography, [anastrophe]
autocar, [abattoir]
autocracy, [absorbancy]
autocrat, [acrobat]
autocratic, [acoustic]
autoeroticism, [abolitionism]
autofocus, [abacus]
autograph, [allograph]
autoimmune, [afternoon]
automaker, [acre]
automate, [acclimate]
automated, [abluted]
automatic, [acoustic]
automation, [abbreviation]

automobile, bonspiel,
cartwheel, commonweal,
flywheel, mercantile,
newsreel, oatmeal,
piecemeal, pinwheel, reseal,
snowmobile, waterwheel
automotive, [ablative]
autonomic, [academic]
autonomous, [allonymous]
autonomy, [academy]
autopilot, [aglet]
autopsy, [absorbancy]
autosuggestion,
[abbreviation]
autumn, [accustom]
auxiliary, [accessory]
avail, [ail]
availability, [abatis]
available, [able]
avalanche, blanch, branch,
interbranch, ranch
avante-guard, [backyard]
avarice, [actress]
avaricious, [adscititious]
avatar, [abattoir]
avaunt, bouffant,
commandant, confidant,
croissant, daunt, debutante,
détente, dilettante, flaunt,
font, gaunt, haunt, jaunt,
nonchalant, savant, taunt,
vaunt, want
ave, [agape]
avenge, revenge, scavenge
avenue, [accrue]
aver, [achiever]
average, [abridge]
averse, [adverse]
aversion, [abrasion]

avert, [advert]
aviator, [abductor]
avid, [acid]
avidity, [abatis]
avionics, [administratrix]
avocado, [aficionado]
avocation, [abbreviation]
avoid, [adenoid]
avoidable, [able]
avoidance, [accordance]
avouch, couch, crouch,
debouch, grouch, ouch,
pouch, slouch, vouch
avow, [allow]
avowal, [accrual]
avulsion, [abbreviation]
aw, see [aah]
awake, ache, after-rake, angel
food cake, backache, bake,
beefsteak, bellyache, betake,
brake, break, cake,
cheesecake, coffee break,
cornflake, crake, cupcake,
daybreak, devil's food cake,
drake, doubletake, earache,
earthquake, fake, firebreak,
flake, forsake, fruitcake,
garter snake, griddle cake,
grubstake, hand brake,
handshake, headache,
heartache, hoecake, hotcake,
intake, jailbreak, keepsake,
lake, mackintosh, make, milk
shake, mandrake, mistake,
muckrake, namesake,
newsbreak, opaque,
outbreak, overtake, pancake,
partake, piece of cake,
quake, rake, rattlesnake,

remake, retake, reawake,
sake, shake, shortcake,
slake, snake, snowflake,
stake, steak, stomachache,
strake, sweepstake, take,
toothache, undertake,
uptake, wake, water break,
wedding cake, wide-awake,
windbreak, youthquake
awaken, bacon, barbican,
beacon, betoken, bodkin,
bracken, broken, bumpkin,
buskin, can, cannikin, darken,
deacon, drunken, falcon,
godforsaken, hearken,
housebroken, liken, manikin,
mannequin, napkin,
outspoken, pelican, publican,
pumpkin, quicken, reawaken,
reckon, republican, sicken,
silken, slacken, softspoken,
spoken, stricken, sunken,
thicken, token, well-spoken,
unbroken, unshaken,
unspoken (see also
abdomen)
award, chord, concord, cord,
discord, fjord, harpsichord,
landlord, lord, misrecord,
record, reward, slumlord,
sword, ward, warlord,
whipcord
aware, [affair]
awash, backwash, bosh,
brainwash, cosh, downwash,
frosh, galosh, gosh, goulash,
hogwash, josh, kibosh,
midrash, mouthwash, posh,
quash, rewash, slosh,

squash, swash, wash,
whitewash
away, [airway]
awe, [aah]
awed, [abroad]
aweful, [apocryphal]
awesome, [adventuresome]
awestruck, [amok]
awful, [apocryphal]
awhile, [aisle]
awhirl, [aswirl]
awkward, [absurd]
awl, [aerosol]
awn, [amazon]
awoke, [artichoke]
awry, [airdry]
ax, [anthrax]
axial, [abaxial]
axiom, [anthurium]
axiomatic, [acoustic]
axis, [alkalosis]
axle, [apostle]
axletree, [ancestry]
axman, [abdomen]
ayatollah, [a capella]
aye, [agape]
aye, [airdry]
azalea, [alleluia]
azure, [admeasure]
baal, [ail]
babble, [able]
baboon, [afternoon]
babu, [accrue]
babushka, [angelica]
baby boom, [abloom]
baby doll, [aerosol]
baby, [abbey]
babyhood, [adulthood]
baccalaureate, [affiliate]

bach, [armpatch]
bachelor, [angler]
bachelorette, [abet]
bachelorhood, [adulthood]
back, [aback]
backache, [awake]
backbeat, [accrete]
backbend, [addend]
backbite, [affright]
backboard, [aboard]
backbone, [alone]
backcast, [aghast]
backcheck, [afterdeck]
backcourt, [airport]
backcross, [across]
backdate, [accommodate]
backdoor, [abhor]
backdraft, [abaft]
backdrop, [agitprop]
backed, [abstract]
backer, [acre]
backfield, [airfield]
backfill, bill, brill, chill,
chlorophyll, daffodil, dill,
distill, downhill, drill, dullsville,
dunghill, fill, foothill, freewill,
frill, fulfill, grill, goodwill, grill,
grille, gristmill, handbill, hill,
ill, instill, kill, kiln, laetrile,
landfill, mil, mill, molehill, nil,
overbill, overkill, pill, quill,
refill, roadkill, rototill, sawmill,
self-will, shill, shrill, sigil, sill,
skill, spadille, spill, standstill,
still, swill, thrill, till, treadmill,
trill, twill, until, uphill, waybill,
will, windchill, windmill,
windowsill
backfire, [acquire]

backflip, [airstrip]
backgammon, [abdomen]
background, [abound]
backhand, [ampersand]
backhanded, [absentminded]
backhaul, [aerosol]
backhoe, [airshow]
backhouse, [alehouse]
backlash, [abash]
backlight, [affright]
backlist, [aerialist]
backload, [abode]
backlog, [agog]
backorder, [adder]
backpack, [aback]
backpaddle, [antipodal]
backpedal, [antipodal]
backrest, [abreast]
backroom, [abloom]
backrub, bathtub, bub, carob,
cherub, club, cub, drub, dub,
flub, grub, hub, hubbub,
nightclub, nub, pub, rub,
scrub, shrub, snub, stub, sub,
tub, washtub
backseat, [accrete]
backset, [abet]
backside, [abide]
backslap, [afterclap]
backslash, [abash]
backslide, [abide]
backslider, [adder]
backspace, [abase]
backspin, [akin]
backstab, blab, cab, confab,
crab, dab, drab, flab, gab,
grab, jab, lab, landgrab, nab,
prefab, rehab, scab, slab,
stab, tab, taxicab

backstage, [age]
backstairs, downstairs,
upstairs
backstitch, bewitch, bitch,
cross-stitch, ditch, eldritch,
enrich, flitch, glitch,
hemstitch, hitch, itch, niche,
ostrich, pitch, rich, sandwich,
snitch, spinach, stitch, switch,
twitch, ultrahitch, unhitch,
which, witch
backstop, [agitprop]
backstreet, [accrete]
backstretch, etch, fetch,
homestretch, retch, sketch,
stretch, wretch
backstroke, [artichoke]
backswept, [accept]
backsword, [aboard]
backtalk, [aftershock]
backtrack, [aback]
backup, bishop, blowup,
breakup, buildup, buttercup,
catchup, checkup, cleanup,
close-up, collop, cup, cutup,
develop, dollop, envelop,
fillip, follow-up, gallop,
Gallup, getup, gossip, grown-
up, hangup, hard up, hiccup,
holdup, hookup, hup, hyssop,
ketchup, layup, letup, lineup,
linkup, lockup, makeup,
markup, matchup,
overdevelop, parsnip,
pasteup, pickup, pileup,
pinup, polyp, pup, redevelop,
roundup, scallop, screwup,
setup, slipup, smashup,
speedup, stickup, stirrup,

sup, syrup, tea cup, toss-up,
tulip, turnip, up, wallop,
warm-up, windup, worship
backward, [absurd]
backwash, [awash]
backwater, [abductor]
backwind, [abscind]
backwoodsman, [abdomen]
backwrap, [afterclap]
backyard, avant-garde,
bankcard, bard, barnyard,
barred, blowhard, boatyard,
bodyguard, bombard,
boulevard, brassard,
brickyard, canard, card,
chard, churchyard, courtyard,
diehard, discard, disregard,
dockyard, farmyard,
graveyard, guard, hard,
junkyard, lard, leotard,
lifeguard, lumberyard,
mudguard, nard, noseguard,
postcard, regard, retard,
safeguard, scorecard, shard,
shipyard, spikenard,
stockyard, undercard,
unguard, vanguard, yard
bacon, [awaken]
bacteria, [abulia]
bacterial, [abaxial]
bad, [ad]
baddie, [acidy]
badger, [armiger]
badly, [ably]
badminton, [anchorperson]
badmouth, bigmouth,
foulmouth, loudmouth,
motormouth, mouth, south
baffle, [apocryphal]

bag, [ag]
bagatelle, barbell, bell, belle,
bethel, bombshell, bridewell,
brocatel, carousel, cartel,
cell, chandelle, citadel,
clientele, cockleshell, compel,
cowbell, dell, dispel, doorbell,
dumbbell, dwell, eggshell,
Emmanuel, excel, expel,
farewell, fell, foretell, freckle,
gel, groundswell, handbell,
hard-shell, hell, hotel,
Immanuel, impel, indwell,
infidel, inkwell, knell, jell,
lapel, mademoiselle,
misspell, motel, Nobel, noel,
nonpareil, nutshell, outsell,
oversell, parallel, pastel,
personnel, presell, propel,
quell, rappel, resell, repel,
seashell, sell, shell, smell,
soft sell, spell, stairwell,
swell, tell, undersell, well
bagel, [angle]
baggage, [acknowledge]
bagger, [agar]
baggies, [antifreeze]
baggy, [aggie]
baglady, [acidy]
bagman, [noun] [abdomen]
bagman, [noun] [adman]
bagpipe, [airpipe]
baguette, [abet]
bagwoman, [abdomen]
bah, [aah]
bail, [ail]
bailable, [able]
bailiwick, [acidic]
bailout, [about]

bait, [abate]
baitfish, [abolish]
baize, [ablaze]
bake, [awake]
baker, [acre]
bakery, [accessory]
baksheesh, corniche,
microfiche, hashish, leash,
quiche, unleash
balance sheet, [accrete]
balance, [abhorrence]
balcony, [abalone]
bald, [appalled]
balderdash, [abash]
baldhead, [abed]
baldie, [acidy]
baldrick, [aleatoric]
bale, [ail]
baleful, [apocryphal]
balk, [aftershock]
balkanize, [agnize]
balkline, [airline]
balky, [achy]
ball carrier, [anterior]
ball, [aerosol]
ballad, [acid]
ballade, [abroad]
balladeer, [adhere]
ballast, [adjust]
ballerina, [alumna]
ballet, [airplay]
ballista, [aorta]
ballistic, [acoustic]
ballistics, [acoustics]
ballon, [alone]
balloon, [afternoon]
balloonist, [abolitionist]
ballot, [aglet]
ballpark, [aardvark]

ballplayer, behavior,
  bricklayer, configure,
  conveyor, destroyer,
  disfigure, doomsayer,
  doomsdayer, failure, familiar,
  figure, foyer, interlayer,
  junior, lawyer, layer,
  misbehavior, monseigneur,
  monsingnor, monsieur,
  multiplayer, naysayer,
  peculiar, player, purveyor,
  refigure, reconfigure, savior,
  seigneur, senior, soothsayer,
  prayer, surveyor, taxpayer,
  tenure, transfigure,
  unfamiliar, voyeur, your (see
  also **abductor**)
ballpoint, [anoint]
ballroom, [abloom]
ballsman, [abdomen]
ballsy, [advisee]
bally, [ably]
ballyhoo, [accrue]
balm, becalm, calm, embalm,
  Islam, semi-calm (see also
  aplomb)
balmoral, [admiral]
balmy, [academy]
baloney, [abalone]
balsam, [adventuresome]
baluster, [administer]
bam, [aerogram]
bambino, [albino]
bamboo, [accrue]
bamboozle, [appraisal]
ban, [adman]
banal, [abdominal]
banana, [alumna]
bananas, [abuzz]

banausic, [airsick]
band, [ampersand]
bandage, [acknowledge]
bandanna, [alumna]
bandbox, boondocks, box,
  chatterbox, chickenpox,
  cowpox, detox, equinox,
  firebox, fox, gearbox, hard
  knocks, hatbox, heterodox,
  icebox, idiot box, jukebox,
  lockbox, mailbox, matchbox,
  neo-orthodox, orthodox, ox,
  paradox, pillbox, pox,
  sandbox, skybox, smallpox,
  soapbox, strongbox,
  sweatbox, tinderbox, toolbox,
  ultra-orthodox, unorthodox,
  xerox
bandeau, [aficionado]
banderole, [areole]
bandersnatch, [armpatch]
bandit, [adequate]
bandleader, [adder]
bandmaster, [administer]
bandog, [agog]
bandstand, [ampersand]
bandwagon, bargain, begun,
  brogan, bun, cardigan,
  dragon, gorgon, gun,
  handgun, hooligan, jargon,
  mulligan, noggin, one, none,
  num, organ, outgun,
  overdone, pagan, pun,
  shotgun, slogan, speargun,
  spun, stun, toboggan, ton,
  wagon, wanigan, won (see
  also **abdomen**)
bandwidth, width
bandy, [acidy]

bane, [abstain]
baneberry, [accessory]
baneful, [apocryphal]
bang, big bang, boomerang,
 clang, dang, defang, fang,
 gang, hang, harangue,
 meringue, mustang,
 orangutan, overhang, pang,
 rang, sang, sank, savings
 bank, shebang, slang, spang,
 sprang, tang, twang,
 whizbang, yang
bangkok, [aftershock]
bangle, [angle]
bangup, [backup]
banish, [abolish]
banister, [administer]
banjo, [airshow]
bank, blank, crank, dank,
 databank, drank, flank, franc,
 frank, gangplank, interbank,
 lank, mountebank, outflank,
 outrank, plank, prank, rank,
 riverbank, shank, shrank,
 snowbank, spank, stank,
 swank, tank, thank, yank
bankable, [able]
bankbook, billhook, book,
 brook, buttonhook, casebook,
 cashbook, checkbook,
 codebook, cook, crook,
 donnybrook, fishhook,
 forsook, guidebook,
 handbook, hook, hymnbook,
 look, matchbook, mistook,
 nook, notebook, outlook,
 overcook, overbook,
 overlook, partook, passbook,
 playbook, pocketbook, rook,

 scrapbook, shook, skyhook,
 songbook, sourcebook,
 storybook, textbook, took,
 unhook, workbook, yearbook
bankcard, [backyard]
banker, [acre]
banknote, [afloat]
banko, [alfresco]
bankroll, [areole]
bankrupt, [abrupt]
bankruptcy, [absorbancy]
banner, [afterburner]
bannock, [amok]
banquet hall, [aerosol]
banquet, [adequate]
banshee, bushy, chichi, cushy,
 dishy, fishy, flashy, fleshy,
 garnishee, gushy, maharashi,
 marshy, mushy, pushy, she,
 slushy, specie, splashy,
 squishy, sushi, trashy (see
 also **abalone**)
bantam, [accustom]
banter, [abductor]
banyan, [antiunion]
banzai, [airdry]
baptism, [abolitionism]
baptismal, [abnormal]
baptist, [absolutist]
baptistry, [ancestry]
baptize, [absolutize]
bar, [abattoir]
barb, carb, garb, rhubarb
barbarian, [abecedarian]
barbaric, [aleatoric]
barbarism, [abolitionism]
barbarize, [accessorize]
barbarous, [actress]
barbecue, [accrue]

barbel, [able]
barbell, [bagatelle]
barber, [amber]
barbershop, [agitprop]
barbican, [awaken]
barbiturate, [accurate]
barbwire, [acquire]
bard, [backyard]
bardy, [acidy]
bare, [affair]
bareback, [aback]
barefaced, [abased]
barefoot, [ablaut]
barely, [ably]
barf, scarf
barfly, [airdry]
bargain, [bandwagon]
barge, charge, countercharge,
  discharge, enlarge, large,
  mischarge, overcharge,
  recharge, sparge,
  supercharge, surcharge,
  undercharge
barhop, [agitprop]
baritone, [atone]
barium, [anthurium]
bark, [aardvark]
barkeeper, beekeeper,
  beeper, blooper, bookkeeper,
  bumper, caliper, camper,
  caper, capper, chipper,
  chopper, clipper, clodhopper,
  co-developer, cooper, coper,
  copper, creeper, crimper,
  crisper, cropper, damper,
  dapper, developer, diaper,
  dipper, distemper,
  doorkeeper, double-dipper,
  dropper, flapper, flipper,
  flypaper, gamekeeper,
  gatekeeper, goalkeeper,
  gossiper, grasshopper,
  groundskeeper, helper,
  hopper, housekeeper, hyper,
  improper, innkeeper, jasper,
  jumper, juniper, keeper,
  kidnapper, leaper, leper,
  lockkeeper, minesweeper,
  newspaper, notepaper,
  pamper, paper, paratrooper,
  pauper, per, popper, proper,
  prosper, purr, rapper, reaper,
  romper, sandpaper,
  sandpiper, scamper, scooper,
  scorekeeper, scrapper,
  scupper, shopkeeper,
  shopper, showstopper,
  simper, skipper, skyscraper,
  sleeper, slipper, spur, stock-
  keeper, stopper, stop-keeper,
  strapper, stripper, stupor,
  super, supper, sweeper,
  tamper, taper, teenybopper,
  temper, timekeeper, tipper,
  topper, torpor, tripper,
  trooper, trouper, upper,
  vapor, vesper, viper (see also
  abductor)
barley, [ably]
barm, [alarm]
barmaid, [abrade]
barn, darn, tarn, yarn
barnacle, [acoustical]
barnburner, [afterburner]
barnstorm, [aswarm]
barnyard, [backyard]
barometer, [abductor]
baronage, [appanage]

baroness, [agribusiness]
baronet, [acuminate]
barony, [abalone]
baroque, [artichoke]
barrack, [amok]
barracuda, [addenda]
barrage, [arbitrage]
barranca, [angelica]
barred, [backyard]
barrel, [admiral]
barrelhead, [abed]
barrette, [abet]
barricade, [abrade]
barrier, [anterior]
barrio, [audio]
barrister, [administer]
barroom, [abloom]
barrow, [allegro]
bartender, [adder]
barter, [abductor]
bartizan, [artisan]
basal, [apostle]
basalt, [asphalt]
bascule, befool, boulle,
  carpool, cesspool, cool, cruel,
  cupule, dirty pool, drool, dual,
  ductule, faldstool, fool,
  footstool, fuel, gene pool,
  ghoul, granule, minuscule,
  misrule, module, molecule,
  mule, nodule, opuscule,
  overcool, overrule, pool,
  preschool, pule, refuel,
  reschedule, retool, ridicule,
  rule, schedule, school, self-
  rule, spool, stool, supercool,
  toadstool, tomfool, tool,
  ultracool, uncool, undercool,
  vestibule, whirlpool, yule

base, [abase]
baseball, [aerosol]
baseboard, [aboard]
baseline, [airline]
basement, [abandonment]
bash, [abash]
bashful, [apocryphal]
basic, [airsick]
basil, [appraisal]
basilica, [angelica]
basin, [anchorperson]
basis, [alkalosis]
bask, [ask]
basket case, [abase]
basket, [acquit]
basketball, [aerosol]
basketful, [apocryphal]
bass, [admass]
bassinet, bobbinet, brunet,
  canzonet, castanet, clarinet,
  cornet, coronet, dinette,
  dragnet, fishnet, kitchenette,
  luncheonette, marionette,
  martinet, net, sermonette
  (see also abet)
bassist, [assist]
basso, [also]
bassoon, [afternoon]
bast, [aghast]
bastard, [absurd]
bastardize, [advise]
baste, [abased]
bastille, [anneal]
bastion, [antiunion]
bat, [acrobat]
batboy, [ahoy]
batch, [armpatch]
bath, [aftermath]
bathe, lathe, scathe, sunbathe

bathetic, [acoustic]
bathing suit, [absolute]
bathos, [across]
bathrobe, disrobe, earlobe,
  enrobe, garderobe, globe,
  homophobe, Job, lobe,
  microbe, probe, robe, strobe,
  wardrobe, xenophobe
bathroom, [abloom]
bathtub, [backrub]
baton, [amazon]
batsman, [abdomen]
battalion, [antiunion]
batten, beaten, begotten,
  brighten, browbeaten,
  bulletin, button, canton,
  carton, certain, cosmopolitan,
  cotton, cretin, curtain,
  dishearten, enlighten, fatten,
  frighten, gluten, glutton,
  gratin, hearten, heighten,
  kindergarten, kitten, lighten,
  manhattan, metropolitan,
  mitten, molten, mountain,
  mutton, puritan, rotten, satin,
  shorten, skeleton, smarten,
  straighten, straten, sultan,
  sweeten, tarlatan, tartan,
  threaten, tighten, titan,
  unbeaten, uncertain,
  unwritten, verboten, wanton,
  written (see also **abdomen**)
batter, [abductor]
battering, [aerogram]
battery, [accessory]
battle ax, [anthrax]
battle flag, [ag]
battle, [accidental]
battlefield, [airfield]

battlefront, [aberrant]
battleground, [abound]
battlement, [abandonment]
battleship, [airship]
batty, [abatis]
bauble, [able]
baud, [abroad]
bawd, [abroad]
bawdry, [accessory]
bawdy, [acidy]
bawl, [aerosol]
bay, [agape]
bayonet, [abet]
bayou, [accrue]
bazaar, [abattoir]
bazooka, [angelica]
beach, beech, beseech,
  bleach, breach, breech, each,
  impeach, leach, leech,
  outreach, peach, preach,
  reach, screech, speech,
  teach, overreach
beachboy, [ahoy]
beachcomber, [armor]
beachfront, [aberrant]
beachhead, [abed]
beachside, [abide]
beachwear, [affair]
beacon, [awaken]
bead, [accede]
beadle, [antipodal]
beadroll, [areole]
beadwork, [artwork]
beagle, [angle]
beak, antique
beaker, [acre]
beam, [abeam]
bean, [alexandrine]
beanbag, [ag]

beanball, [aerosol]
beanie, [abalone]
beanpole, [areole]
bear, [affair]
bearable, [able]
bearded, [absentminded]
bearer, [adulterer]
bearish, [abolish]
beast, ceased, deceased,
  east, feast, fleeced, least,
  Middle East, Mideast,
  modiste, northeast, priest,
  southeast, yeast
beat, [accrete]
beaten, [anchorperson]
beater, [abductor]
beatific, [anthropomorphic]
beatification, [abbreviation]
beatitude, [altitude]
beatnik, [allergenic]
beau, [airshow]
beaut, [acute]
beauteous, [abstemious]
beautification, [abbreviation]
beautiful, [apocryphal]
beautiful, [apocryphal]
beautify, [amplify]
beauty, [abatis]
beaver, [achiever]
bebop, [agitprop]
becalm, [balm]
became, [acclaim]
beck, [afterdeck]
becket, [abet]
becket, [advocate]
beckon, [antiphon]
becloud, [aloud]
become, [addendum]
bed, [abed]

bedazzle, [appraisal]
bedbug, billbug, bug, chug,
  chugalug, debug, doodlebug,
  drug, dug, earplug, firebug,
  fireplug, fug, hug, humbug,
  jitterbug, jug, ladybug,
  litterbug, lovebug, lug, mug,
  plug, pug, rug, shrug, slug,
  smug, snug, thug, tug, ugh
bedded, [absentminded]
bedeck, [afterdeck]
bedevil, [anvil]
bedfast, [aghast]
bedfellow, [afterglow]
bedlam, [addendum]
bedmate, [acclimate]
bedpan, [adman]
bedpost, [aftermost]
bedraggle, [angle]
bedraggled, bespectacled,
  disabled, double-barreled,
  emerald, fabled, gnarled,
  herald, marbled, multileveled,
  newfangled, noncredentialed,
  preassembled, principled,
  ribald, scaffold, softboiled,
  sozzled, springald, tangled,
  troubled, unassembled,
  uncredentialed, unlabeled,
  unprincipled, unrivaled,
  unruffled, untroubled, veiled
bedridden, [anchorperson]
bedrock, [aftershock]
bedroom, [abloom]
bedsheet, [accrete]
bedside, [abide]
bedsore, [abhor]
bedspread, [abed]
bedstead, [abed]

bedtime, [airtime]
bee, [abbey]
beech, [beach]
beechnut, [acuminate]
beef, [aperitif]
beefsteak, [awake]
beehive, [alive]
beek, [antique]
beekeeper, [barkeeper]
beeline, [airline]
beep, [asleep]
beeper, [barkeeper]
beer, [adhere]
beet, [accrete]
beetle, [accidental]
befall, [aerosol]
befit, [acquit]
befool, [bascule]
before, [abhor]
beforehand, [ampersand]
befriend, [addend]
befuddle, [antipodal]
beg, bootleg, bowleg, dogleg,
    dreg, egg, goose egg, keg,
    leg, nutmeg, peg
began, [adman]
begat, [acrobat]
beget, [abet]
beggar, [agar]
begin, [akin]
beginner, [afterburner]
begird, [absurd]
begone, [amazon]
begonia, [alleluia]
begot, [aeronaut]
begotten, [anchorperson]
begrime, [airtime]
begrudge, [adjudge]
beguiled, child, foster-child,

love child, mild, self-styled,
    wild
beguine, [alexandrine]
begun, [bandwagon]
behalf, [allograph]
behave, [aftershave]
behavior, [ballplayer]
behaviorist, [allegorist]
behavorism, [abolitionism]
behead, [abed]
behemoth, [altazimuth]
behest, [abreast]
behind, [affined]
behold, [ahold]
behoove, [approve]
beignet, [agape]
belabor, [amber]
belated, [abluted]
belay, [airplay]
belch, squelch
beleaguer, [agar]
belvedere, [adhere]
belfry, [accessory]
belie, [airdry]
belief, [aperitif]
believable, [able]
believe, [achieve]
believer, [achiever]
belittle, [accidental]
bell, [bagatelle]
belle, [bagatelle]
bellhop, [agitprop]
bellicose, [adios]
belligerence, [abhorrence]
belligerent, [aberrant]
bellman, [abdomen]
bellow, [afterglow]
bellowdecks, [annex]
bellows, [airhose]

bellwether, [altogether]
belly, [ably]
bellyache, [awake]
bellyband, [ampersand]
bellyful, [apocryphal]
below, [afterglow]
belowground, [abound]
belt, dealt, dwelt, felt, heartfelt,
  melt, pelt, smelt, snowmelt,
  svelte, welt
belted, [abluted]
beltway, [airway]
bema, [anathema]
bemire, [adhere]
bemoan, [alone]
bemuse, [abuse]
ben, [again]
bench, blench, drench,
  entrench, french, quench,
  retrench, stench, trench,
  wench, workbench, wrench
benchmark, [aardvark]
bend, [addend]
beneath, bequeath, heath,
  sheath, underneath, wreath
benedict, [addict]
benediction, [abbreviation]
benefactor, [abductor]
benefice, [amorphous]
beneficence, [abhorrence]
beneficent, [acquiescent]
beneficial, [abbatial]
beneficiary, [accessory]
benefit, [acquit]
benevolence, [abhorrence]
benevolent, [ambivalent]
benighted, [abluted]
benign, [aerodyne]
benison, [artisan]

benny, [abalone]
bent, [accent]
benumb, [addendum]
bequeath, [beneath]
bequest, [abreast]
berate, [accelerate]
bereave, [achieve]
bereavement, [abandonment]
bereft, [aleft]
berm, [affirm]
berry, [accessory]
berserk, [artwork]
berth, [afterbirth]
bertha, [alfalfa]
beryl, [admiral]
beseech, [beach]
beset, [abet]
beside, [abide]
besiege, siege
besmear, [adhere]
besmirch, [antichurch]
besom, [abolitionism]
besot, [aeronaut]
bespeak, [antique]
bespectacled, [bedraggled]
bespoke, [artichoke]
besprinkle, [acoustical]
best man, [adman]
best, [abreast]
bestial, [abaxial]
bestiality, [abatis]
bestir, [administer]
bestow, [aggiornamento]
bestrew, [accrue]
bestride, [abide]
bet, [abet]
beta, [aorta]
betake, [awake]
bethel, [bagatelle]

bethink, blink, bobolink, brink, chink, clink, dink, double-think, downlink, drink, fink, groupthink, hoodwink, ink, interlink, jink, link, mink, oink, outdrink, overdrink, pink, plink, preshrink, rethink, rink, shrink, sink, slink, stink, think, uplink, wink, zinc
Bethlehem, [apothegm]
betide, [abide]
betise, [antifreeze]
betoken, [awaken]
betray, [affray]
betrayal, [ail]
betroth, both, growth, nongrowth, oath, outgrowth
betrothal, [agile]
betta, [aorta]
better, [abductor]
better-half, [allograph]
betterment, [abandonment]
between, [alexandrine]
bevel, [adjectival]
beverage, [abridge]
bevy, [anchovy]
bewail, [ail]
beware, [affair]
bewilderment, [abandonment]
bewitch, [backstitch]
beyond, [abscond]
bezel, [appraisal]
bezique, [antique]
bhakti, [abatis]
biannual, [accrual]
bias, [antibias]
biased, [adjust]
biathlete, [accrete]
biathlon, [amazon]

bib, ad lib, crib, drib, fib, glib, lib, nib, rib, sahib, sib, squib
bibcock, [aftershock]
bibelot, [afterglow]
bible, [able]
biblical, [acoustical]
bibliography, [anastrophe]
bibliology, [allergy]
bibliotherapy, [apocope]
bibulous, [acropolis]
bicameral, [admiral]
bicarbonate, [abominate]
bicentenary, [accessory]
bicentennial, [abaxial]
biceps, forceps, quadriceps, triceps
bicker, [acre]
bicultural, [admiral]
bicuspid, [acid]
bicycle, [acoustical]
bid, [amid]
bidden, [anchorperson]
bide, [abide]
bidet, [agape]
bidirectional, [abdominal]
biennial, [abaxial]
biennium, [anthurium]
bier, [adhere]
bifocal, [acoustical]
bifurcate, [abdicate]
big bang, [bang]
big cheese, [antifreeze]
big shot, [aeronaut]
big, bigwig, brig, dig, earwig, fig, frig, guinea pig, gig, grig, jig, pig, prig, renege, rig, shindig, sprig, swig, thimblerig, thingamajig, twig, whirligig, wig, zig

bigamist, [alchemist]
bigamy, [academy]
bigarade, [abroad]
bigeneric, [aleatoric]
bighead, [abed]
big-hearted, [abluted]
bigmouth, [badmouth]
bigot, [agate]
bigotry, [ancestry]
bigwig, [big]
bijou, [accrue]
bike, [alike]
biker, [acre]
bikini, [abalone]
bilabial, [abaxial]
bilateral, [admiral]
bile, [aisle]
bilinear, [anterior]
bilingual, [accrual]
bilious, [abstemious]
bilk, buttermilk, ilk, milk, silk
bill, [backfill]
billboard, [aboard]
billbug, [bedbug]
billet, [aglet]
billfold, [ahold]
billhook, [bankbook]
billiard, [absurd]
billiards, innards
billion, [antiunion]
billionaire, [affair]
billon, [acetylene]
billow, [afterglow]
billy, [ably]
bimbo, [airshow]
bin, [akin]
binary, [accessory]
bind, [affined]
binder, [adder]

bindery, [accessory]
binge, constringe, cringe,
    fringe, hinge, impinge,
    infringe, orange, singe,
    springe, syringe, tinge,
    twinge
bingo, [ago]
binocular, [angler]
binomial, [abaxial]
biochemical, [acoustical]
biochemist, [alchemist]
biochemistry, [ancestry]
biocidal, [antipodal]
biocide, [abide]
biodegradable, [able]
bioethical, [acoustical]
bioethicist, [assist]
bioethics, [administratrix]
biofeedback, [aback]
biogenesis, [alkalosis]
biographer, [arbitrager]
biography, [anastrophe]
biohazard, [absurd]
biological, [acoustical]
biology, [allergy]
biomedical, [acoustical]
bionic, [allergenic]
bionics, [administratrix]
biophysics, [administratrix]
biopsy, [absorbancy]
biorhythm, [algorithm]
biosocial, [abbatial]
biotic, [acoustic]
biotope, [antelope]
bipartisan, [artisan]
bipartite, [affright]
biped, [abed]
biplane, [abstain]
bipolar, [angler]

biracial, [abbatial]
birch, [antichurch]
birdbath, [aftermath]
birdbrain, [abstain]
birdcage, [age]
birdcall, [aerosol]
birdhouse, [alehouse]
birdie, [acidy]
birdseed, [accede]
biretta, [aorta]
Birmingham, [aerogram]
birth, [afterbirth]
birthday suit, [backup]
birthday, [agape]
birthmark, [aardvark]
birthplace, [abase]
birthrate, [accelerate]
birthright, [affright]
birthstone, [alone]
biscuit, [advocate]
bisect, [abject]
bisexual, [accrual]
bishop, [backup]
bismuth, [altazimuth]
bison, [anchorperson]
bisque, [asterisk]
bister, [administer]
bistro, [allegro]
bit, [acquit]
bitch, [backstitch]
bite, [affright]
bitsy, [absorbancy]
bitt, [acquit]
bitter, [abductor]
bittersweet, [accrete]
bitty, [abatis]
bitumen, [abdomen]
bivouac, [aback]
biweekly, [ably]

biyearly, [ably]
bizarre, [abattoir]
blab, [backstab]
blabber, [amber]
black hole, [areole]
black, [aback]
blackball, [aerosol]
blackballed, [appalled]
blackberry, [accessory]
blackbird, [absurd]
blackboard, [aboard]
blackhead, [abed]
blackjack, [aback]
blacklist, [aerialist]
blackmail, bobtail, cattail,
    coattail, cocktail, contrail,
    cottontail, dovetail,
    downscale, ducktail, e-mail,
    fantail, female, fingernail,
    fishtail, folktale, foxtail,
    guardrail, handrail, hangnail,
    monorail, pigtail, ponytail,
    resale, retail, shirttail,
    subscale, tattletale, telltale,
    thumbnail, whitetail,
    wholesale [see also ail]
blackout, [about]
blacksmith, coppersmith, fifth,
    kith, locksmith, monolith,
    myth, pith, silversmith, smith,
    swith, whitesmith, wordsmith
blacktop, [agitprop]
bladder, [adder]
blade, [abrade]
bladed, [absentminded]
blah, [aah]
blain, [abstain]
blamable, [able]
blame, [acclaim]

blameworthy, [apathy]
blanch, [avalanche]
bland, [ampersand]
blandish, [abolish]
blank, [bank]
blanket, [advocate]
blanquette, [abet]
blare, [affair]
blarney, [abalone]
blasé, [agape]
blaspheme, [abeam]
blasphemer, [armor]
blasphemous, [allonymous]
blasphemy, [academy]
blast, [aghast]
blasted, [abluted]
blat, [acrobat]
blatant, [accordant]
blate, [ablate]
blather, [altogether]
blatter, [abductor]
blaw, [aah]
blaze, [ablaze]
blazer, [adviser]
blazon, blazon, brazen,
  chosen, dozen, emblazon,
  frozen, fusion, horizon,
  imprison, poison, prison,
  raisin, reason, resin, risen,
  season, treason, unfrozen
  (see also **abdomen**)
bleach, [beach]
bleacher, [acupuncture]
bleak, [antique]
blear, [adhere]
bleary, [accessory]
bleat, [accrete]
bleb, cobweb, ebb, spiderweb,
  web

bled, [abed]
bleed, [accede]
bleeder, [adder]
bleep, [asleep]
blemish, [abolish]
blench, [bench]
blend, [addend]
blender, [adder]
bless, [acquiesce]
blessed, [abed]
blest, [abreast]
blew, [accrue]
blight, [affright]
blimp, chimp, crimp, gimp,
  imp, limp, pimp, shrimp,
  skimp, wimp
blin, [akin]
blind, [affined]
blinder, [adder]
blindfold, [ahold]
blindness, [agribusiness]
blindside, [abide]
blink, [bethink]
blinker, [acre]
blip, [airstrip]
bliss, [abyss]
blissful, [apocryphal]
blister, [administer]
blithe, lithe, scythe, tithe,
  writhe
blithesome, [adventuresome]
blitz, ditz, glitz, grits, spritz
blitzkrieg, colleague, fatigue,
  intrigue, league, little league,
  major league, minor league
blizzard, [absurd]
bloat, [afloat]
bloated, [abluted]
blob, [ab]

bloc, [aftershock]
block, [aftershock]
blockade, [abrade]
blockage, [acknowledge]
blockbuster, [administer]
blocked, concoct, crocked,
   half-cocked, landlocked,
   stalked
blockhead, [abed]
blockhouse, [alehouse]
blond, [abscond]
blood, [acid]
bloodbath, [aftermath]
bloodguilt, [atilt]
bloodhound, [abound]
bloodline, [airline]
bloodshed, [abed]
bloodshot, [aeronaut]
bloodstain, [abstain]
bloodstream, [abeam]
bloodsucker, [acre]
bloodthirsty, [abatis]
bloody, [acidy]
bloom, [abloom]
bloomer, [armor]
Bloomingdale, [ail]
blooper, [barkeeper]
blossom, [adventuresome]
blotch, botch, butterscotch,
   crotch, deathwatch, debauch,
   hopscotch, notch, scotch,
   splotch, stopwatch, swatch,
   watch, wristwatch
blotchy, boccie, catchy,
   churchy, crunchy, duchy,
   grouchy, hibachi, kimchi,
   litchi, mariachi, patchy,
   paunchy, peachy, preachy,
   punchy, raunchy, scratchy,

sketchy, slouchy, tetchy,
   touchy, twitchy (see also
   abalone)
blotter, [abductor]
blouse, [alehouse]
blouson, [amazon]
blow, [afterglow]
blowhard, [backyard]
blowhole, [areole]
blown, [alone]
blowout, [about]
blowpipe, [airpipe]
blowtorch, scorch, torch
blowup, [backup]
blubber, [amber]
blucher, [acupuncture]
bludgeon, [allergen]
blue chip, [airstrip]
blue, [accrue]
bluebird, [absurd]
bluegrass, [admass]
blueprint, calamint, dint,
   fingerprint, flint, footprint,
   glint, handprint, hint,
   hoofprint, imprint, lint, mint,
   misprint, newsprint, overprint,
   peppermint, print, remint,
   reprint, skinflint, spearmint,
   splint, sprint, squint, stint,
   thumbprint, tint, voiceprint,
   wunderkind
blues, [abuse]
bluff, buff, chuff, cuff, dandruff,
   duff, earmuff, enough, fluff,
   foodstuff, gruff, guff,
   handcuff, huff, muff,
   overstuff, puff, rebuff, rough,
   ruff, scruff, scuff, snuff, stuff,
   teraph, tough

blunder, [adder]
blunderbuss, [abbess]
blunt, [ambivalent]
blur, [angler]
blurb, [adverb]
blurt, [advert]
blush, [airbrush]
bluster, [administer]
boa, [alfalfa]
boar, [abhor]
board, [aboard]
boarder, [adder]
boardman, [adman]
boardroom, [abloom]
boardwalk, [aftershock]
boast, [aftermost]
boastful, [apocryphal]
boat, [afloat]
boathouse, [alehouse]
boatman, [abdomen]
boatswain, [anchorperson]
boatyard, [backyard]
bob, [ab]
bobber, [amber]
bobbinet, [bassinet]
bobble, [able]
bobby, [abbey]
bobcat, [acrobat]
bobeche, [afresh]
bobolink, [bethink]
bobsled, [abed]
bobstay, [agape]
bobtail, [blackmail]
bobwhite, [affright]
boccie, [blotchy]
bock, [aftershock]
bodacious, [adscititious]
bode, [abode]
bodega, [alfalfa]

bodice, [antibias]
bodily, [ably]
bodkin, [awaken]
body, [acidy]
bodyguard, [backyard]
bodysurf, enserf, serf, surf,
  turf, windsurf
bodywork, [artwork]
boff, checkoff, cough, cutoff,
  doff, face-off, kickoff,
  knockoff, layoff, leadoff, liftoff,
  off, payoff, pilaf, rip-off,
  runoff, scoff, send-off, setoff,
  shutoff, sing-off, standoff,
  takeoff, trough, turnoff, well-
  off
bog, [agog]
bogey, [aggie]
boggle, [angle]
bogle, [angle]
bogus, [analogous]
bohemia, [abulia]
bohunk, bunk, chipmunk,
  chunk, clunk, debunk, drunk,
  dunk, flunk, funk, gunk, hunk,
  junk, monk, plunk, punk,
  shrunk, slunk, skunk, spunk,
  stunk, sunk, thunk, trunk
boidoir, [abattoir]
boil, [broil]
boiler, [angler]
boilermaker, [acre]
boisterous, [actress]
bola, [a capella]
bold, [ahold]
boldfaced, [abased]
boldly, [ably]
boldness, [agribusiness]
bole, [areole]

bolero, [allegro]
boll, [areole]
bollard, [absurd]
bollix, [administratrix]
bolo, [afterglow]
bologna, [abalone]
bolshevism, [abolitionism]
bolster, [administer]
bolt, colt, dolt, jolt, molt, revolt,
  thunderbolt, volt
bolus, [acropolis]
bomb, [aplomb]
bombard, [backyard]
bombardier, [adhere]
bombardon, [alone]
bombast, [aghast]
bombastic, [acoustic]
bombazine, [alexandrine]
bombe, [aplomb]
bomber, [armor]
bombinate, [abominate]
bombshell, [bagatelle]
bombsight, [affright]
bonafide, [abide]
bonanza, [alfalfa]
bonbon, [amazon]
bond, [abscond]
bondage, [acknowledge]
bondholder, [adder]
bondman, [abdomen]
bondsman, [abdomen]
bondwoman, [abdomen]
bone, [alone]
bonehead, [abed]
boner, [afterburner]
bonfire, [acquire]
bong, [agelong]
bongo, [ago]
bonhomie, [academy]

boniface, [amorphous]
bonkers, checkers, druthers,
  headquarters, horsefeathers,
  knickers, pliars, scissors,
  theirs, tweezers, vespers
bonnet, [acuminate]
bonny, [abalone]
bonsai, [airdry]
bonspiel, [automobile]
bonus, [agribusiness]
bony, [abalone]
boo, [accrue]
boob, cube, drawtube,
  flashcube, lube, tube
booboisie, [advisee]
booboo, [accrue]
booby, [abbey]
boodle, [antipodal]
booger, [agar]
boogeyman, [adman]
boogie, [aggie]
book, [bankbook]
bookcase, [abase]
bookend, [addend]
bookie, [achy]
bookish, [abolish]
bookkeeper, [barkeeper]
booklet, [aglet]
bookmaker, [acre]
bookman, [abdomen]
bookmark, [aardvark]
bookseller, [angler]
bookshelf, elf, herself, himself,
  itself, myself, oneself, self,
  shelf, yourself
bookstore, [abhor]
bookworm, [affirm]
boom, [abloom]
boomer, [armor]

boomlet, [aglet]
boomtown, breakdown,
  brown, clown, comedown,
  countdown, crackdown,
  crown, down, downtown,
  drawdown, drown, frown,
  gown, hoedown, hometown,
  knockdown, letdown,
  lockdown, lowdown,
  markdown, meltdown,
  midtown, nightgown, noun,
  pronoun, putdown, renown,
  rubdown, shakedown,
  shantytown, showdown,
  shutdown, slowdown,
  splashdown, sundown,
  takedown, teardown,
  touchdown, town, turndown,
  uptown
boon, [afternoon]
boondocks, [bandbox]
boondoggle, [angle]
boonies, [antifreeze]
boor, [abjure]
boorish, [abolish]
boost, loosed, roost
booster, [administer]
boot, [acute]
booth, bucktooth, couth,
  forsooth, half-truth, ruth,
  sawtooth, sleuth, tollbooth,
  tooth, truth, uncouth,
  vermouth, youth
bootie, [abatis]
bootjack, [aback]
bootlace, [abase]
bootleg, [beg]
bootstrap, [afterclap]
booty, [abatis]

booze, [abuse]
boozer, [adviser]
bop, [agitprop]
bopeep, [asleep]
bora, [abracadabra]
borage, [abridge]
borborygmus, [allonymous]
bordelaise, [ablaze]
bordello, [afterglow]
border, [adder]
borderline, [airline]
bordure, [armiger]
bore, [abhor]
boredom, [addendum]
born, [acorn]
boron, [amazon]
borough, [allegro]
bort, [abort]
bosh, [awash]
bosk, kiosk, mosque
bosom, [abolitionism]
boss, [across]
bossy, [absorbancy]
bota, [aorta]
botanica, [angelica]
botanical, [acoustical]
botanist, [abolitionist]
botany, [abalone]
botch, [blotch]
both, [betroth]
bother, [altogether]
bothersome, [adventuresome]
botryoidal, [antipodal]
bottle, [accidental]
bottleneck, [afterdeck]
bottler, [angler]
bottom, [accustom]
bottomless, [acropolis]
bottomline, [airline]

bouffant, [avaunt]
bough, [allow]
bought, [aeronaut]
bouillabaisse, [abase]
bouillon, [amazon]
boulder, [adder]
boule, [airplay]
boulevard, [backyard]
boulle, [bascule]
bounce, [announce]
bouncy, [absorbancy]
bound, [abound]
boundary, [accessory]
boundless, [acropolis]
bounteous, [abstemious]
bountiful, [apocryphal]
bounty, [abatis]
bouquet, [agape]
bourgeois, [aah]
bourgeoisie, [advisee]
bourguignon, [amazon]
bourn, [acorn]
bourride, [accede]
boustrophedon, [amazon]
bout, [about]
boutique, [antique]
boutonniere, [adhere]
bouzouki, [achy]
bovine, [aerodyne]
bow, [noun] [airshow]
bow, [verb] [allow]
bowdlerize, [accessorize]
bowed, [adjective] [abode]
bowed, [verb] [aloud]
bowel, [agile]
bower, [airpower]
bowery, [accessory]
bowl, [areole]
bowleg, [beg]

bowlegged, [acid]
bowler, [angler]
bowline, [acetylene]
bowman, [abdomen]
bowsprit, [acquit]
bowstring, [anything]
bowwow, [allow]
box, [bandbox]
boxcar, [abattoir]
boxer, [aggressor]
boy scout, [about]
boy, [ahoy]
boyar, [abattoir]
boycott, [aeronaut]
boyfriend, [addend]
boyhood, see adulthood]
boyish, [abolish]
boysenberry, [accessory]
bozo, garbanzo, gonzo,
    mestizo, orzo, proviso (see
    also **aficionado**))
bra, [aah]
brabble, [able]
brace, [abase]
bracelet, [aglet]
bracer, [aggressor]
braciola, [a capella]
bracken, [awaken]
bracket, [advocate]
brackish, [abolish]
brad, [ad]
bradawl, [aerosol]
brag, [ag]
braggart, [advert]
braid, [abrade]
braided, [absentminded]
brail, [ail]
braille, [ail]
brain, [abstain]

brainchild, godchild,
grandchild, stepchild,
undefiled
brainless, [acropolis]
brainpower, [power]
brainstorm, [aswarm]
brainwash, [awash]
brainy, [abalone]
braise, [ablaze]
brake, [awake]
brakeman, [abdomen]
bramble, [able]
bran, [adman]
branch, [avalanche]
brand name, [acclaim]
brand, [ampersand]
brandish, [abolish]
brandy, [acidy]
brash, [abash]
brass, [admass]
brassard, [backyard]
brasserie, [accessory]
brassiere, [adhere]
brassy, [absorbancy]
brat, [acrobat]
brattice, [afflatus]
brattle, [accidental]
bratwurst, [athirst]
brava, [aah]
bravado, [aficionado]
brave, [aftershave]
bravery, [accessory]
bravo, [airshow]
bravura, [abracadabra]
brawl, [aerosol]
brawn, [amazon]
brawny, [abalone]
bray, [affray]
braze, [ablaze]

brazen, [anchorperson]
brazier, [admeasure]
breach, [beach]
bread, [abed]
breadboard, [aboard]
breadline, [airline]
breadwinner, [afterburner]
break, [awake]
breakable, [able]
breakage, [acknowledge]
breakaway, [airway]
breakdance, [advance]
breakdown, [boomtown]
breaker, [acre]
breakfast, [adjust]
breakfront, [aberrant]
breakneck, [afterdeck]
breakout, [about]
breakthrough, [accrue]
breakup, [backup]
breakwater, [abductor]
breast, [abreast]
breastplate, [ablate]
breaststroke, [artichoke]
breath, death, depth
breathe, ensheathe, seethe,
sheathe, teethe, wreathe
breathless, [acropolis]
breathy, [apathy]
breech, [beach]
breed, [accede]
breeder, [adder]
breeze, [antifreeze]
breezeway, [airway]
breezy, [advisee]
breve, [achieve]
brevet, [abet]
breviary, [accessory]
brevity, [abatis]

brew, [accrue]
brewery, [accessory]
briar, [amplifier]
bribe, [ascribe]
bribery, [accessory]
brick, [aleatoric]
bricklayer, [ballplayer]
brickyard, [backyard]
bridal, [antipodal]
bride, [abide]
bridegroom, [abloom]
bridesmaid, [abrade]
bridewell, [bagatelle]
bridge, [abridge]
bridle, [antipodal]
brief, [aperitif]
briefcase, [abase]
brier, [amplifier]
brig, [big]
brigade, [abrade]
brigadier, [adhere]
brigand, [almond]
bright, [affright]
brighten, [anchorperson]
brightness, [agribusiness]
brill, [backfill]
brilliance, [abhorrence]
brilliant, [abeyant]
brim, [acronym]
brimstone, [alone]
brindle, [antipodal]
brine, [aerodyne]
bring, [anything]
brink, [bethink]
brinkmanship, [airship]
briny, [abalone]
brio, [audio]
brioche, cloche, gauche
briolette, [abet]

briquette, [abet]
brisance, ensconce, nuance,
    ordonnance, outrance,
    renaissance, response,
    sconce, séance
brisk, [asterisk]
bristle, [apostle]
bristly, [ably]
britches, [abuzz]
brittle, [accidental]
bro, [allegro]
broach, [abroach]
broad, [abroad]
broadcast, [aghast]
broadcaster, [administer]
broadcloth, broth,
    cheesecloth, cloth, froth,
    moth, sackcloth, sloth, swath,
    tablecloth, troth, washcloth,
    wroth
broaden, [anchorperson]
broadloom, [abloom]
broadminded, [absentminded]
broadscale, [ail]
broadsheet, [accrete]
broadside, [abide]
brocade, [abrade]
brocatel, [bagatelle]
broccoli, [ably]
brocero, [allegro]
brochette, [abet]
brochure, [abjure]
brockage, [acknowledge]
brogan, [bandwagon]
brogue, rogue, vogue
broider, [adder]
broil, boil, charbroil, coil,
    despoil, disembroil, disloyal,
    embroil, foil, hoyle, loyal,

moil, oil, recoil, roil, royal,
soil, spoil, toil, turmoil, uncoil
(see also **abaxial, airfoil**)
broiler, [angler]
broke, [artichoke]
broken, [awaken]
broker, [acre]
brokerage, [abridge]
bromide, [abide]
bronchitis, [afflatus]
broncho, [alfresco]
brooch, [abroach]
brood, [allude]
brook, [bankbook]
brooklet, [aglet]
broom, [abloom]
broomstick, [acoustic]
broth, [broadcloth]
brothel, [agile]
brother, [altogether]
brotherhood, [adulthood]
brotherly, [ably]
brought, [aeronaut]
brouhaha, [aah]
brow, [allow]
browbeat, [accrete]
browbeaten, [anchorperson]
brown, [boomtown]
brownie, [abalone]
brownnose, [airhose]
brownnoser, [adviser]
brownout, [about]
brownstone, [alone]
browse, [arouse]
browser, [adviser]
bruise, [abuse]
bruiser, [adviser]
bruit, [acute]
brumal, [abnormal]

brumby, [abbey]
brume, [abloom]
brummagem, [addendum]
brunch, bunch, counterpunch,
crunch, hunch, keypunch,
lunch, munch, outpunch,
punch, scrunch
brunet, [bassinet]
brunette, [abet]
brunt, [aberrant]
brush, [airbrush]
brushback, [aback]
brushfire, [acquire]
brut, [acute]
brutal, [accidental]
brutality, [abatis]
brutalize, [actualize]
brute, [acute]
bruxism, [abolitionism]
bub, [backrub]
bubble, [able]
bubblegum, [addendum]
bubbler, [angler]
bubbly, [ably]
buccal, [acoustical]
buccaneer, [adhere]
buck, [amok]
buckaroo, [accrue]
buckboard, [aboard]
bucket, [advocate]
bucketful, [apocryphal]
buckeye, [airdry]
buckle, [acoustical]
buckler, [angler]
bucko, [alfresco]
buckram, [addendum]
bucksaw, [aah]
buckshot, [aeronaut]
buckskin, [akin]

bucktooth, [booth]
buckwheat, [accrete]
bud, [acid]
buddle, [antipodal]
buddy, [acidy]
budge, [adjudge]
budget, [adequate]
budgeter, [adhere]
buff, [bluff]
buffalo, [afterglow]
buffer, calligrapher, camphor,
    candlesnuffer, chamfer,
    chauffeur, cinematographer,
    cipher, coffer, coiffeur,
    confer, conifer, counteroffer,
    cryptographer, decipher,
    defer, differ, duffer, encipher,
    fir, fur, gaffer, gofer, goffer,
    gopher, heifer, infer, laugher,
    lifer, loafer, offer,
    philosopher, photographer,
    pilfer, pornographer, prefer,
    proffer, reefer, refer, scoffer,
    snuffer, staffer, stenographer,
    stuffer, suffer, sulfur,
    seismographer, surfer,
    thurifer, topographer,
    transfer, typographer, wafer,
    woofer, zephyr (see also
    abductor)
buffet, [adequate]
buffet, [agape]
buffoon, [afternoon]
bug, [bedbug]
bugaboo, [accrue]
bugger, [agar]
buggy, [aggie]
bughouse, [alehouse]
bugle, [angle]

build, chilled, gild, guild,
    multiskilled, overbuild,
    rebuild, self-willed, skilled,
    unfulfilled, unskilled, willed
builder, [adder]
buildup, [backup]
built, [atilt]
bulb, flashbulb, lightbulb
bulge, divulge, indulge,
    overindulge
bulimia, [abulia]
bulimic, [academic]
bulk, hulk, skulk, sulk
bulky, [achy]
bull, [apocryphal]
bulla, [alfalfa]
bulldog, [agog]
bulldoze, [airhose]
bulldozer, [adviser]
bullet, [aglet]
bulletin, [anchorperson]
bulletproof, [aloof]
bullfight, [affright]
bullfighter, [abductor]
bullfinch, chinch, cinch, clinch,
    finch, flinch, grinch, inch,
    lynch, pinch, squinch, winch
bullfrog, [agog]
bullhead, [abed]
bullhorn, [acorn]
bullion, [antiunion]
bullish, [abolish]
bullock, [amok]
bullring, [anything]
bullwhip, [airstrip]
bully, [ably]
bulrush, [airbrush]
bulwark, [artwork]
bum, [addendum]

bumble, [able]
bumblebee, [abbey]
bummer, [armor]
bump, callithump, chump,
  clump, crump, dump, flump,
  frump, grump, hump, jump,
  lump, mugwump, plump,
  pump, rump, slump, stump,
  sump, thump, trump, tump,
  ump, whump
bumper, [barkeeper]
bumpkin, [awaken]
bumptious, [adscititious]
bumpy, [apocope]
bun, [bandwagon]
bunch, [brunch]
bunco, [alfresco]
bundle, [antipodal]
bungalow, [afterglow]
bungee, [allergy]
bunion, [antiunion]
bunk, [bohunk]
bunker, [acre]
bunkum, [addendum]
bunny, [abalone]
bunt, [abeyant]
buoy, dinghy, doughy,
  employee, facetiae, flooey,
  gooey, he, payee, prexy,
  thee, ye (see also abalone)
buoyance, [abhorrence]
buoyant, [abeyant]
buppie, [apocope]
burble, [able]
burden, [anchorperson]
burdensome,
  [adventuresome]
bureau, [allegro]
bureaucracy, [absorbancy]

bureaucrat, [acrobat]
bureaucratic, [acoustic]
burg, homburg, iceberg]
burgage, [acknowledge]
burgeon, [allergen]
burger, [agar]
burgh, [allegro]
burglar, [angler]
burglarize, [accessorize]
burglary, [accessory]
burgoo, [accrue]
burgundy, [acidy]
burial, [abaxial]
burke, [artwork]
burl, [aswirl]
burlap, [afterclap]
burlesque, [arabesque]
burley, [ably]
burly, [ably]
burn, [adjourn]
burner, [afterburner]
burnish, [abolish]
burnoose, [abstruse]
burnout, [about]
burnsides, ides
  burp, chirp, slurp, stirp,
  twerp, usurp
burr, [amber]
burrito, [aggiornamento]
burro, [allegro]
burrow, [allegro]
burry, [accessory]
bursa, [alfalfa]
bursar, [aggressor]
burse, [adverse]
bursitis, [afflatus]
burst, [athirst]
bury, [accessory]
bus, [abbess]

busboy, [ahoy]
busby, [abbey]
bush, [ambush]
bushel, [abbatial]
bushwacker, [acre]
bushwhack, [aback]
bushy, [banshee]
business, [agribusiness]
businesslike, [alike]
businessman, [adman]
businessperson,
    [anchorperson]
busker, [acre]
buskin, [awaken]
busload, [abode]
buss, [abbess]
bust, [adjust]
bustard, [absurd]
busted, [abluted]
buster, [administer]
bustier, [agape]
bustle, [apostle]
bustline, [airline]
busty, [abatis]
busy, [advisee]
busybody, [acidy]
busywork, [artwork]
but, [abbot]
butch, putsch
butcher, [acupuncture]
butchery, [accessory]
butler, [angler]
butt, [abbot]
butte, [acute]
butter, [abductor]
butterball, [aerosol]
buttercup, [backup]
butterfat, [acrobat]
butterfly, [airdry]

buttermilk, [bilk]
butternut, [acuminate]
butterscotch, [blotch]
buttery, [accessory]
buttock, [amok]
button, [anchorperson]
buttonhole, [areole]
buttonhook, [bankbook]
buttress, [actress]
buxom, [adventuresome]
buy, [alibi]
buyback, [aback]
buyout, [about]
buzz, [as]
buzzard, [absurd]
buzzer, [adviser]
buzzword, [absurd]
bwana, [alumna]
by, [alibi]
bye, [alibi]
bygone, [amazon]
bylaw, [aah]
byline, [airline]
bypass, [admass]
byplay, [airplay]
bystander, [adder]
byte, [affright]
byway, [airway]
byword, [absurd]
cab, [backstab]
cabal, [aerosol]
cabala, [a capella]
cabaletta, [aorta]
caballero, [allegro]
cabana, [alleluia]
cabaret, [affray]
cabbage, [acknowledge]
cabdriver, [achiever]
cabinet, [acquit]

cabinetmaker, [acre]
cabinetry, [ancestry]
cabinetwork, [artwork]
cable, [able]
cablecast, [aghast]
cablegram, [aerogram]
cabochon, [amazon]
caboodle, [antipodal]
caboose, [abstruse]
cabotage, [arbitrage]
cabretta, [aorta]
cabriole, [areole]
cabriolet, [a capella]
cabstand, [ampersand]
cacao, [allow]
cache, [abash]
cachet, [agape]
cachexia, [abulia]
cachinnate, [abominate]
cachou, [accrue]
cacique, [antique]
cackle, [acoustical]
cackler, [angler]
cacodemon, [abdomen]
cacography, [anastrophe]
cacophonous, [agribusiness]
cacpoethes, [antifreeze]
cactus, [afflatus]
cacuminal, [abdominal]
cad, [ad]
cadastral, [admiral]
cadastre, [administer]
cadaver, [achiever]
cadaverous, [actress]
caddie, [acidy]
cade, [abrade]
cadence, [accordance]
cadent, [accordant]
cadenza, [alfalfa]

cadet, [abet]
cadre, [affray]
caducity, [abatis]
caducous, [abacus]
caespitose, [adios]
caesura, [abracadabra]
café, [agape]
cafeteria, [abulia]
cafetorium, [anthurium]
caffeine, [alexandrine]
caftan, [adman]
cage, [age]
cagey, [allergy]
cahoot, [acute]
cahoots, firstfruits, grassroots
caisson, [amazon]
cajole, [areole]
cajoled, [ahold]
cake, [awake]
cakewalk, [aftershock]
calaboose, [abstruse]
calamine, [aerodyne]
calamint, [blueprint]
calamitous, [afflatus]
calamity, [abatis]
calamus, [allonymous]
calash, [abash]
calcification, [abbreviation]
calcimine, [aerodyne]
calcium, [anthurium]
calculate, [ablate]
calculated, [abluted]
calculation, [abbreviation]
calculator, [abductor]
calculus, [acropolis]
caldera, [abracadabra]
caleche, [afresh]
calendar, [adder]
calenture, [abjure]

calf, [allograph]
caliber, [amber]
calibrate, [accelerate]
calibration, [abbreviation]
calico, [alfresco]
caliginous, [agribusiness]
caliper, [barkeeper]
calisthenic, [allergenic]
calisthenics, [administratrix]
calix, [administratrix]
calk, [aftershock]
call, [aerosol]
callable, [able]
callaloo, [accrue]
callant, [ambivalent]
callback, [aback]
callboy, [ahoy]
calligrapher, [buffer]
calligraphy, [anastrophe]
calliope, [apocope]
callithump, [bump]
callous, [acropolis]
callow, [afterglow]
callus, [acropolis]
calm, [balm]
calmative, [ablative]
calorie, [accessory]
calotype, [airpipe]
calumet, [abet]
calumny, [abalone]
calvary, [accessory]
calve, halve, have, salve
calypso, [also]
calzone, [alone]
camaraderie, [accessory]
camarilla, [a capella]
camber, [amber]
camcorder, [adder]
came, [acclaim]

camel, [abnormal]
Camelot, [aeronaut]
cameo, [audio]
camera, [abracadabra]
cameraman, [noun]
    [abdomen]
cameraman, [noun] [adman]
cameraperson,
    [anchorperson]
camerawoman, [abdomen]
camise, [antifreeze]
camisole, [areole]
camlet, [aglet]
camouflage, [arbitrage]
camp, [aid-de-camp]
campaign, [abstain]
campaigner, [afterburner]
campanile, [ably]
campanology, [allergy]
camper, [barkeeper]
campesino, [albino]
campestral, [barrel]
campfire, [acquire]
campground, [abound]
camphor, [buffer]
campsite, [affright]
campus, [auspice]
camshaft, [abaft]
can, [awaken]
can't, [ant]
canaille, [airdry]
canal, chorale, corral, decal,
    gal, locale, morale, musicale,
    pal, rationale
canapé, [apocope]
canard, [backyard]
canary, [accessory]
canasta, [aorta]
cancan, [adman]

cancel, [apostle]
cancellation, [abbreviation]
cancer, [aggressor]
cancerous, [actress]
candela, [a capella]
candelabra, [abracadabra]
candent, [abundant]
candescence, [accordance]
candescent, [adjacent]
candid, [absentminded]
candidacy, [absorbancy]
candidate, [accommodate]
candle, [antipodal]
candleholder, [adder]
candlelight, [affright]
candlelighter, [abductor]
candlepower, [airpower]
candlesnuffer, [buffer]
candlestick, [acoustic]
candlewick, [acidic]
candor, [adder]
candy, [acidy]
cane, [abstain]
canescent, [adjacent]
canine, [aerodyne]
canister, [administer]
canker, [acre]
canned, [ampersand]
cannery, [accessory]
cannibal, [able]
cannibalism, [abolitionism]
cannibalistic, [acoustic]
cannibalize, [alize]
cannikin, [awaken]
cannoli, [ably]
cannonade, [abrade]
cannonball, [aerosol]
cannot, [aeronaut]
canny, [abalone]

canoe, [accrue]
canola, [a capella]
canonical, [acoustical]
canonicity, [abatis]
canonize, [agnize]
canopy, [apocope]
cant, [ant]
cantaloupe, [antelope]
cantankerous, [actress]
cantata, [aorta]
cantatrice, [plural] [ancestry]
cantatrice, [singular] [agape]
canteen, [alexandrine]
canter, [abductor]
canthus, [antibias]
canticle, [acoustical]
cantilena, [alumna]
cantilever, [achiever]
cantillate, [ablate]
cantina, [alumna]
cantle, [accidental]
canto, [aggiornamento]
canton, [anchorperson]
Cantonese, [antifreeze]
cantor, [abductor]
cantus, [afflatus]
canvas, [antibias]
canyon, [antiunion]
canzonet, [bassinet]
cap, [afterclap]
capability, [abatis]
capable, [able]
capacity, [abatis]
cape, [agape]
caper, [barkeeper]
capias, [abstemious]
capillary, [accessory]
capital, [accidental]
capitalism, [abolitionism]

capitalist, [aerialist]
capitalistic, [acoustic]
capitalization, [abbreviation]
capitalize, [actualize]
capitate, [acetate]
capitation, [abbreviation]
capitol, [accidental]
capitulate, [ablate]
capitulation, [abbreviation]
capo, [airshow]
capone, [alone]
capote, [afloat]
cappelletti, [abatis]
capper, [barkeeper]
cappuccino, [albino]
caprice, [afterpiece]
capricious, [adscititious]
caprine, [aerodyne]
capriole, [areole]
capsize, [abscise]
capstone, [alone]
capsulated, [abluted]
capsule, [apostle]
capsulize, [actualize]
caption, [abbreviation]
captious, [adscititious]
captivate, [activate]
captive, [ablative]
captivity, [abatis]
captor, [abductor]
capture, [acupuncture]
car bomb, [aplomb]
car phone, [alone]
car, [abattoir]
carafe, [allograph]
caramel, [abnormal]
carat, [accurate]
caravan, [adman]
carb, [barb]

carbine, [alexandrine]
carbo, [airshow]
carbohydrate, [accelerate]
carbonate, [abominate]
carbuncle, [acoustical]
carburetion, [abbreviation]
carburetor, [abductor]
carcass, [abacus]
carcinogen, [allergen]
carcinoma, [anathema]
card, [backyard]
cardboard, [aboard]
cardholder, [adder]
cardiac, [aback]
cardigan, [bandwagon]
cardinal, [aboriginal]
cardiology, [allergy]
care, [anywhere]
careen, [alexandrine]
career, [adhere]
carefree, [accessory]
careful, [apocryphal]
caregiver, [achiever]
careless, [acropolis]
caress, [acquiesce]
caret, [accurate]
caretaker, [acre]
cargo, [ago]
carhop, [agitprop]
caribou, [accrue]
caricature, [abjure]
caries, [antifreeze]
carillon, [amazon]
carina, [alumna]
cariogenic, [allergenic]
carload, [abode]
carnage, [appanage]
carnal, [abdominal]
carnality, [abatis]

carnation, [abbreviation]
carnival, [adjectival]
carnivore, [abhor]
carnivorous, [actress]
carob, [backrub]
caroche, [abroach]
carol, [barrel]
carom, [addendum]
carouse, [arouse]
carp, [harp]
carpel, [ample]
carpenter, [abductor]
carpentry, [ancestry]
carpet, [adequate]
carpetbag, [ag]
carpetbagger, [agar]
carpool, [bascule]
carport, [airport]
carpus, [auspice]
carrel, [admiral]
carriage, [abridge]
carrier, [anterior]
carrion, [abecedarian]
carrot, [accurate]
carry, [accessory]
carryall, [aerosol]
carryback, [aback]
carryon, [amazon]
carryout, [about]
carryover, [achiever]
carsick, [acidic]
cart, [apart]
cartage, [acknowledge]
carte-blanch, [haunch]
cartel, [bagatelle]
cartilage, [acknowledge]
cartography, [anastrophe]
carton, [anchorperson]
cartoon, [afternoon]

cartoonist, [abolitionist]
cartop, [agitprop]
cartouche, douche, swoosh,
   whoosh
cartridge, [abridge]
cartwheel, [automobile]
carve, starve
cascade, [abrade]
case, [abase]
casebook, [bankbook]
casein, [alexandrine]
caseload, [abode]
casework, [artwork]
caseworker, [acre]
cash, [abash]
cashbook, [bankbook]
cashew, [accrue]
cashier, [adhere]
cashmere, [adhere]
casino, [albino]
casita, [aorta]
cask, [ask]
casket, [advocate]
casque, [ask]
casserole, [areole]
cassette, [abet]
cassimere, [adhere]
cast, [aghast]
castanet, [bassinet]
castaway, [airway]
caste, [aghast]
caster, [administer]
castigate, [abnegate]
castigation, [abbreviation]
castle, [apostle]
castor, [administer]
castrate, [accelerate]
castration, [abbreviation]
casual, [accrual]

casualty, [abatis]
casuistry, [ancestry]
cat, [acrobat]
catachresis, [alkalosis]
cataclysm, [abolitionism]
catacomb, [astrodome]
catalectic, [acoustic]
cataleptic, [acoustic]
catalexis, [alkalosis]
catalog, [agog]
catalysis, [alkalosis]
catalyst, [adjust]
catalytic, [acoustic]
catalyze, [actualize]
catamaran, [adman]
cataphora, [abracadabra]
cataplexy, [absorbancy]
catapult, [adult]
cataract, [abstract]
catastrophe, [anastrophe]
catastrophic,
    [anthropomorphic]
catatonic, [allergenic]
catcall, [aerosol]
catch, [armpatch]
catchall, [aerosol]
catcher, [acupuncture]
catchup, [backup]
catchy, [blotchy]
cate, [abdicate]
catechism, [abolitionism]
catechize, [advise]
categorical, [acoustical]
categorization, [abbreviation]
categorize, [accessorize]
category, [accessory]
catena, [alumna]
cater, [abductor]
caterpillar, [angler]

catfight, [affright]
catfish, [abolish]
catgut, [agate]
catharsis, [alkalosis]
cathartic, [acoustic]
cathedra, [abracadabra]
cathedral, [admiral]
catherization, [abbreviation]
catherize, [accessorize]
catheter, [abductor]
cathode, [abode]
catnap, [afterclap]
catnip, [airstrip]
cattail, [blackmail]
cattle, [accidental]
catty, [abatis]
catwalk, [aftershock]
caucus, [abacus]
caudal, [antipodal]
caught, [aeronaut]
cauliflower, [airpower]
caulk, [aftershock]
causal, [appraisal]
causality, [abatis]
causation, [abbreviation]
cause, [applause]
causeway, [airway]
caustic, [acoustic]
cauterize, [accessorize]
caution, [abbreviation]
cautious, [adscititious]
cavalcade, [abrade]
cavalier, [adhere]
cavalry, [accessory]
cavatina, [alumna]
cave, [aftershave]
caveat, [aeronaut]
caveman, [adman]
cavern, [adjourn]

cavernous, [agribusiness]
caviar, [abattoir]
cavil, [adjectival]
cavity, [abatis]
cavort, [abort]
caw, [aah]
cay, [achy]
cease, [afterpiece]
ceased, [beast]
cedar, [adder]
cede, [accede]
ceil, [anneal]
celebrate, [accelerate]
celebrated, [abluted]
celebration, [abbreviation]
celebrity, [abatis]
celery, [accessory]
celestial, [abaxial]
celibacy, [absorbancy]
celibate, [abbot]
cell phone, [alone]
cell, [bagatelle]
cellar, [angler]
cello, [afterglow]
cellophane, [abstain]
cellular, [angler]
cellulite, [affright]
celluloid, [adenoid]
cellulose, [adios]
cembalo, [afterglow]
cemetery, [accessory]
cenobite, [acquit]
cenotaph, [allograph]
cense, commence, condense,
   consequence, defense,
   dense, dispense, expense,
   fens, flense, frankincense,
   gents, hence, immense,
   incense, intense, mense,

pretense, recompense,
   sense, suspense, tense,
   thence, whence
censer, [aggressor]
censor, [aggressor]
censorship, [airship]
censure, [acupuncture]
census, [alkalosis]
cent, [accent]
centenarian, [abecedarian]
centennial, [abaxial]
center, [abductor]
centerfold, [ahold]
centerpiece, [afterpiece]
centigrade, [abrade]
centimeter, [abductor]
centipede, [accede]
central, [admiral]
centrality, [abatis]
centralize, [actualize]
centrifugal, [angle]
centrifuge, deluge, huge,
   kludge, refuge, scrouge,
   stooge, subterfuge
centripetal, [accidental]
centrist, [allegorist]
century, [accessory]
ceramic, [academic]
cerebellum, [addendum]
cerebral, [admiral]
cerebrate, [accelerate]
ceremonial, [abaxial]
ceremonious, [abstemious]
ceremony, [abalone]
certain, [anchorperson]
certainty, [abatis]
certifiable, [able]
certificate, [advocate]
certification, [abbreviation]

certified, [abide]
certify, [amplify]
certify, [beautify]
certitude, [altitude]
cervix, [administratrix]
cessation, [abbreviation]
cesspool, [bascule]
chad, [ad]
chafe, fail-safe, safe, strafe,
  unsafe, vouchsafe, waif
chaff, [allograph]
chagrin, [akin]
chain, [abstain]
chair, [anywhere]
chairlift, [adrift]
chairman, [abdomen]
chairmanship, [airship]
chairperson, [anchorperson]
chairwoman, [abdomen]
chaise, [ablaze]
chakra, [abracadabra]
chalet, [airplay]
chalice, [acropolis]
chalk, [aftershock]
chalkboard, [aboard]
challenge, expunge, lozenge,
  lunge, plunge, sponge
challenger, [armiger]
challis, [ably]
chamber, [amber]
chamberlain, [acetylene]
chambermaid, [abrade]
chameleon, [antiunion]
chamfer, [buffer]
chamois, [academy]
champ, [aid-de-camp]
champagne, [abstain]
champaign, [abstain]
champerty, [abatis]

champion, [abecedarian]
championship, [airship]
chance, [advance]
chancel, [apostle]
chancellor, [angler]
chandelier, [adhere]
chandelle, [bagatelle]
chandler, [angler]
change, [arrange]
changeable, [able]
changeless, [acropolis]
changeover, [achiever]
channel, [abdominal]
channeler, [angler]
chanson, [alone]
chant, [ant]
chanter, [abductor]
chanteuse, [amuse]
chanticleer, [adhere]
chantry, [ancestry]
chaos, [across]
chaotic, [acoustic]
chap, [noun] [afterclap]
chap, [noun] [agitprop]
chape, [agape]
chapel, [ample]
chaperon, [alone]
chapiter, [abductor]
chaplain, [acetylene]
chaplet, [aglet]
chaps, [apse]
chapter, [abductor]
char, [abattoir]
character, [abductor]
characteristic, [acoustic]
characterization,
  [abbreviation]
characterize, [accessorize]
charade, [abrade]

charbroil, [broil]
charcoal, [areole]
chard, [backyard]
chardonnay, [agape]
charge, [barge]
charger, [armiger]
chariot, [affiliate]
charioteer, [adhere]
charisma, [anathema]
charismatic, [acoustic]
charitable, [able]
charity, [abatis]
charlotte, [aglet]
charm, [alarm]
charmer, [armor]
charnel, [abdominal]
chart, [apart]
charter, [abductor]
chartreuse, [amuse]
chary, [accessory]
chase, [abase]
chaser, [aggressor]
chasm, [abolitionism]
chasseur, [aggressor]
chassis, [absorbancy]
chaste, [abased]
chasten, [anchorperson]
chastise, [absolutize]
chastisement, [abandonment]
chastity, [abatis]
chasuble, [able]
chat, [acrobat]
chateau, [aggiornamento]
chateaubriand, [amazon]
chatoyant, [abeyant]
chattel, [accidental]
chatter, [abductor]
chatterbox, [bandbox]
chatty, [abatis]

chauffeur, [buffer]
chautauqua, [alfalfa]
chauvinism, [abolitionism]
chauvinist, [abolitionist]
chauvinistic, [acoustic]
chayote, [abatis]
cheap shot, [aeronaut]
cheap, [asleep]
cheapo, [airshow]
cheapskate, [abdicate]
cheat, [accrete]
cheater, [abductor]
check, [afterdeck]
checkbook, [bankbook]
checker, [acre]
checkerboard, [aboard]
checkers, [bonkers]
checklist, [aerialist]
checkmate, [acclimate]
checkoff, [boff]
checkout, [about]
checkpoint, [anoint]
checkup, [backup]
cheddar, [adder]
cheek, [antique]
cheekbone, [alone]
cheep, [asleep]
cheer, [adhere]
cheerful, [apocryphal]
cheerio, [audio]
cheerleader, [adder]
cheery, [accessory]
cheese, [antifreeze]
cheeseburger, [agar]
cheesecake, [awake]
cheesecloth, [broadcloth]
cheesy, [advisee]
cheetah, [aorta]
chef, [aleph]

chelate, [ablate]
chemical, [acoustical]
chemise, [antifreeze]
chemisette, [apposite]
chemist, [alchemist]
chemistry, [accessory]
chemotherapy, [apocope]
cherish, [abolish]
cherry, [accessory]
cherub, [backrub]
cherubim, [acronym]
chess, [acquiesce]
chest, [abreast]
chested, [abluted]
chesterfield, [airfield]
chestnut, [acuminate]
chesty, [abatis]
cheviot, [affiliate]
chew, [accrue]
chewable, [able]
chez, [agape]
chiasm, [abolitionism]
chiasma, [anathema]
chiasmus, [allonymous]
chic, [antique]
chicane, [abstain]
chicanery, [accessory]
chichi, [banshee]
chick, [acidic]
chickadee, [acidy]
chicken, [antiphon]
chickenpox, [bandbox]
chicle, [acoustical]
chicory, [accessory]
chide, [abide]
chief, [aperitif]
chiffon, [amazon]
chiffonade, [abrade]
chigger, [agar]

chignon, [amazon]
chilblain, [abstain]
child, [beguiled]
childbirth, [afterbirth]
childish, [abolish]
childless, [acropolis]
childlike, [alike]
childproof, [aloof]
chili, [ably]
chiliad, [ad]
chill, [backfill]
chilled, [build]
chiller, [angler]
chilly, [ably]
chime, [airtime]
chimera, [abracadabra]
chimichanga, [alfalfa]
chimney, [abalone]
chimp, [blimp]
chimpanzee, [advisee]
chin, [akin]
china, [alumna]
chinaware, [affair]
chinch, [bullfinch]
chinchilla, [a capella]
chine, [aerodyne]
Chinese, [antifreeze]
chink, [bethink]
chino, [albino]
chintzy, [absorbancy]
chip shot, [aeronaut]
chip, [airstrip]
chipboard, [aboard]
chipmunk, [bohunk]
Chippendale, [ail]
chipper, [barkeeper]
chippy, [apocope]
chirk, [artwork]
chirography, [anastrophe]]

chiromancy, [absorbancy]
chiropractic, [acoustic]
chiropractor, [abductor]
chirp, [burp]
chisel, [appraisal]
chit, [acquit]
chitchat, [acrobat]
chivalrous, [actress]
chivalry, [accessory]
chive, [alive]
chlamydia, [abulia]
chlorine, [alexandrine]
chloroform, [aswarm]
chlorophyll, [backfill]
chock, [aftershock]
chockful, [apocryphal]
chocolate, [aglet]
choice, invoice, pro-choice,
   rejoice, voice
choir, [amplifier]
choke, [artichoke]
choker, [acre]
cholera, [abracadabra]
choleric, [aleatoric]
cholesterol, [aerosol]
choline, [alexandrine]
chomp, comp, pomp, romp,
   swamp, tromp, whomp
choose, [abuse]
chopper, [barkeeper]
choppy, [apocope]
chops, cyclops, eyedrops, tops
chopstick, [acoustic]
choral, [barrel]
chorale, [canal]
chord, [award]
chore, [abhor]
choreograph, [allograph]
choreography, [anastrophe]

chorister, [administer
chortle, [accidental]
chorus, [actress]
chose, [airhose]
chosen, [anchorperson]
chouse, [alehouse]
chow mein, [abstain]
chow, [allow]
chowder, [adder]
chowhound, [abound]
chrism, [abolitionism]
Christ, [antichrist]
christen, [anchorperson]
chromate, [acclimate]
chromatic, [acoustic]
chrome, [astrodome]
chromosome, [astrodome]
chronic, [allergenic]
chronicle, [acoustical]
chronological, [acoustical]
chronology, [allergy]
chrysanthemum, [addendum]
chubby, [abbey]
chuck, [amok]
chuckle, [acoustical]
chuff, [bluff]
chuffy, [anastrophe]
chug, [bedbug]
chugalug, [bedbug]
chum, [addendum]
chummy, [academy]
chump, [bump]
chunk, [bohunk]
chunky, [achy]
church, [antichurch]
churchianity, [abatis]
churchman, [abdomen]
churchy, [blotchy]
churchyard, [backyard]

churlish, [abolish]
churn, [adjourn]
churr, [acupuncture]
chute, [acute]
chutney, [abalone]
chutzpah, [alfalfa]
ciao, [allow]
cicatrix, [administratrix]
cider, [adder]
cigar, [abattoir]
cigarette, [abet]
cigarillo, [afterglow]
cilium, [anthurium]
cinch, [bullfinch]
cinder, [adder]
cine, [abalone]
cineast, [aghast]
cinema, [anathema]
cinematic, [acoustic]
cinematographer, [buffer]
cinematography, [anastrophe]
cinnamon, [abdomen]
cinquain, [abstain]
cipher, [buffer]
circa, [angelica]
circadian, [abecedarian]
circle, [acoustical]
circlet, [aglet]
circuit, [advocate]
circuitous, [afflatus]
circuitry, [ancestry]
circular, [angler]
circulate, [ablate]
circulation, [abbreviation]
circumambient, [abeyant]
circumcise, [abscise]
circumcision, [abrasion]
circumference, cross-
reference, difference,

preference, reference
circumflex, [annex]
circumlocution, [abbreviation]
circumscribe, [ascribe]
circumscription,
[abbreviation]
circumspect, [abject]
circumstance, [advance]
circumstantial, [abbatial]
circumvallate, [ablate]
circumvent, [accent]
circumvolution,
[abbreviation]
circus, [abacus]
cirque, [artwork]
cirrhosis, [alkalosis]
cirrus, [actress]
cistern, [adjourn]
citadel, [noun] [antipodal]
citadel, [noun] [bagatelle]
citation, [abbreviation]
cite, [affright]
citizen, [artisan]
citizenry, [accessory]
citizenship, [airship]
citrus, [actress]
city, [abatis]
cityscape, [agape]
citywide, [abide]
civic, [acidic]
civics, [administratrix]
civil, [adjectival]
civilian, [antiunion]
civility, [abatis]
civilization, [abbreviation]
civilize, [actualize]
civilly, [ably]
civvy, [anchovy]
clad, [ad]

claim, [acclaim]
clairvoyance, [abhorrence]
clairvoyant, [abeyant]
clam, [aerogram]
clamant, [abandonment]
clamber, [amber]
clammy, [academy]
clamor, [armor]
clamorous, [actress]
clamp, [aid-de-camp]
clan, [adman]
clanger, [agar]
clangor, [agar]
clannish, [abolish]
clansman, [abdomen]
clap, [afterclap]
clapboard, [absurd]
claptrap, [afterclap]
claque, [aback]
clarification, [abbreviation]
clarify, [amplify]
clarinet, [abet]
clarion, [abecedarian]
clarity, [abatis]
clary, [accessory]
clash, [abash]
clasp, enclasp, gasp, grasp,
  rasp
class, [admass]
classic, [airsick]
classical, [acoustical]
classification, [abbreviation]
classified, [abide]
classify, [amplify]
classis, [abyss]
classless, [acropolis]
classmate, [acclimate]
classy, [absorbancy]
clast, [aghast]

clatter, [abductor]
clause, [applause]
claustrophobia, [abulia]
claustrophobic, [acerbic]
claw, [aah]
clawed, [abroad]
clay, [airplay]
clean, [alexandrine]
cleaner, [afterburner]
cleanse, lens
cleanser, [adviser]
cleanup, [backup]
clear, [adhere]
clearance, [abhorrence]
clearheaded, [absentminded]
clearinghouse, [alehouse]
cleat, [accrete]
cleavage, [acknowledge]
cleave, [achieve]
cleaver, [achiever]
cleek, [antique]
clef, [aleph]
cleft, [aleft]
clemency, [absorbancy]
clement, [abandonment]
clergy, [allergy]
clergyman, [abdomen]
clergywoman, [abdomen]
cleric, [aleatoric]
clerical, acoustical]
clerk, [artwork]
clever, [achiever]
clew, [accrue]
cliché, [agape]
click, [acyclic]
client, [abeyant]
clientele, [bagatelle]
cliff, [anaglyph]
climate, [animate]

climatic, [acoustic]
climatology, [allergy]
climax, [anthrax]
climb, [airtime]
clinch, [bullfinch]
clincher, [acupuncture]
cline, [aerodyne]
cling, [anything]
clinic, [allergenic]
clinical, [acoustical]
clinician, [abbreviation]
clinique, [antique]
clink, [bethink]
clinker, [acre]
clinquant, [abeyant]
clip, [airstrip]
clipboard, [aboard]
clipper, [barkeeper]
clique, [acyclic]
clitoris, [actress]
cloak, [artichoke]
cloakroom, [abloom]
clobber, [amber]
cloche, [brioche]
clock, [aftershock]
clockwise, [advise]
clockwork, [artwork]
clod, [applaud]
clodhopper, [barkeeper]
clog, [agog]
cloister, [administer]
clone, [alone]
clonk, [ankh]
close [verb], [airhose]
close, [noun] [adios]
closefisted, [abluted]
closeout, [about]
closer, [adviser]
closet, [apposite]

close-up, [backup]
closure, [admeasure]
clot, [aeronaut]
cloth, [broadcloth]
clothbound, [abound]
clothe, loathe
clothes, [airhose]
clothesline, [airline]
clothespin, [akin]
clothier, [anterior]
cloture, [acupuncture]
cloud, [aloud]
cloudburst, [athirst]
cloudless, [acropolis]
cloudy, [acidy]
clout, [about]
clove, [alcove]
clover, [achiever]
cloverleaf, [aperitif]
clown, [boomtown]
cloy, [ahoy]
cloze, [airhose]
club, [backrub]
clubber, [amber]
clubfoot, [ablaut]
clubhouse, [alehouse]
cluck, [amok]
clue, [accrue]
clueless [acropolis]
clump, [bump]
clumsy, [advisee]
clunk, [bohunk]
clunker, [acre]
clunky, [achy]
cluster, [administer]
clutch, crutch, dutch,
    forasmuch, hutch, inasmuch,
    much, retouch, such, touch
clutter, [abductor]

clyster, [administer]
coach, [abroach]
coadjutor, [abductor]
coagulate, [noun] [aglet]
coagulate, [verb] [ablate]
coagulation, [abbreviation]
coal, [areole]
coalesce, [acquiesce]
coalition, [abbreviation]
coanchor, [acre]
coarse, concourse, course,
  deforce, discourse, divorce,
  enforce, force, hoarse,
  intercourse, midcourse,
  minicourse, racecourse,
  recourse, reenforce,
  reinforce, resource, source,
  telecourse, watercourse,
  workforce [see also endorse]
coast, [aftermost]
coaster, [administer]
coastline, [airline]
coastrack, [aback]
coat, [afloat]
coattail, [blackmail]
coauthor, [altogether]
coax, hoax
coaxial, [abaxial]
cob, [ab]
cobalt, [asphalt]
cobble, [able]
cobbler, [angler]
cobblestone, [alone]
cobelligerent, [aberrant]
cobra, [abracadabra]
cobweb, [bleb]
coca, [angelica]
cocaine, [abstain]
cochairman, [abdomen]

cochampion, [abecedarian]
cock, [aftershock]
cockapoo, [accrue]
cockeyed, [abide]
cockle, [acoustical]
cockles, [annals]
cockleshell, [bagatelle]
cockpit, [acquit]
cockroach, [abroach]
cocksure, [abjure]
cocktail, [blackmail]
cocky, [achy]
coco, [alfresco]
cocoa, [alfresco]
coconspirator, [abductor]
coconut, [acuminate]
cocoon, [afternoon]
cocotte, [aeronaut]
cod, [abroad]
coda, [addenda]
coddle, [antipodal]
code, [abode]
codebook, [bankbook]
codefendant, [abundant]
codeine, [alexandrine]
codependency, [absorbancy]
codependent, [abundant]
co-developer, [barkeeper]
codex, [annex]
codger, [armiger]
codicil, [apostle]
codification, [abbreviation]
codify, [amplify]
codirect, [abject]
codirector, [abductor]
coed, [abed]
coeditor, [abductor]
coeducation, [abbreviation]
coeducational, [aboriginal]

coefficient, [abeyant]
coequal, [agile]
coerce, [adverse]
coercion, [noun] [abrasion]
coercion,[noun]
  [abbreviation]
coercive, [abrasive]
coeternal, [aboriginal]
coexecutor, [abductor]
coexist, [activist]
coexistence, [abhorrence]
coexistent, [abirritant]
cofavorite, [accurate]
coffee break, [awake]
coffee pot, [aeronaut]
coffee shop, [agitprop]
coffee, [anastrophe]
coffeehouse, [alehouse]
coffer, [buffer]
coffle, [apocryphal]
cofound, [abound]
cofounder, [adder]
cog, [agog]
cogent, [agent]
cogitate, [acetate]
cogitation, [abbreviation]
cognac, [aback]
cognate, [abominate]
cognition, [abbreviation]
cognitive, [ablative]
cognizance, [abhorrence]
cognizant, [abeyant]
cohabit, [abbot]
cohabitation, [abbreviation]
coheir, [affair]
cohere, [adhere]
coherence, [abhorrence]
cohesion, [abrasion]
coholder, [adder]

cohort, [abort]
cohost, [aftermost]
cohostess, [afflatus]
coiffeur, [buffer]
coiffure, [abjure]
coil, [broil]
coin, [adjoin]
coinage, [appanage]
coincide, [abide]
coincidence, [abhorrence]
coincident, [abundant]
coincidental, [accidental]
coin-op, [agitprop]
coinsurance, [abhorrence]
coinsure, [abjure]
coinvestor, [administer]
coitus, [afflatus]
coke, [artichoke]
cokehead, [abed]
cola, [a capella]
colander, [adder]
cold, [ahold]
coldcock, [aftershock]
coldhearted, [abluted]
cole, [areole]
colead, [accede]
coleader, [adder]
coleslaw, [aah]
colicky, [achy]
coliseum, [anthurium]
colitis, [afflatus]
collaborate, [accelerate]
collaboration, [abbreviation]
collaborator, [abductor]
collage, [arbitrage]
collapse, [apse]
collapsible, [able]
collar, [angler]
collarbone, [alone]

collate, [ablate]
collateral, [admiral]
collator, [abductor]
colleague, [blitzkrieg]
collect, [abject]
collectible, [able]
collection, [abbreviation]
collective, [ablative]
collector, [abductor]
college, [acknowledge]
collegial, [abaxial]
collegiality, [abatis]
collegian, [abecedarian]
collegiate, [affiliate]
collet, [aglet]
collide, [abide]
collider, [adder]
collie, [ably]
collision, [abrasion]
collocate, [abdicate]
collop, [backup]
colloquial, [abaxial]
colloquialism, [abolitionism]
colloquium, [anthurium]
colloquy, [dewy]
collude, [allude]
collusion, [abrasion]
colly, [ably]
cologne, [alone]
colon, [acetylene]
colonel, [abdominal]
colonial, [abaxial]
colonialism, [abolitionism]
colonist, [abolitionist]
colonization, [abbreviation]
colonize, [agnize]
colonnade, [abrade]
colony, [abalone]
color, [angler]

coloration, [abbreviation]
color-blind, [affined]
colorfast, [aghast]
colorful, [apocryphal]
colorless, [acropolis]
colossal, [apostle]
colosseum, [anthurium]
colossus, [alkalosis]
colt, [bolt]
column, [addendum]
columnar, [afterburner]
columnist, [abolitionist]
coma, [anathema]
comaker, [acre]
co-manage, [appanage]
comanager, [agar]
comatose, [adios]
comb, [astrodome]
combat, [acrobat]
combatant, [accordant]
combative, [ablative]
combination, [abbreviation]
combine, [aerodyne]
combined, [affined]
combo, [airshow]
combustible, [able]
come, [addendum]
comeback, [aback]
comedian, [abecedarian]
comedienne, [again]
comedown, [boomtown]
comedy, [acidy]
comely, [ably]
comer, [armor]
comestible, [able]
comet, [animate]
comeuppance, [abhorrence]
comfit, [adequate]
comfort, [advert]

comfortable, [able]
comforter, [abductor]
comfrey, [accessory]
comfy, [anastrophe]
comic, [academic]
comical, [acoustical]
comingle, [angle]
comity, [abatis]
comma, [anathema]
command, [ampersand]
commandant, [avaunt]
commandeer, [adhere]
commander, [adder]
commandment,
   [abandonment]
commando, [aficionado]
commemorate, [accelerate]
commemoration,
   [abbreviation]
commemorative, [ablative]
commence, [cense]
commenced, [against]
commencement,
   [abandonment]
commend, [addend]
commendable, [able]
commendation, [abbreviation]
commendatory, [accessory]
commensurate, [accurate]
comment, [abandonment]
commentary, [accessory]
commentate, [acetate]
commentator, [abductor]
commerce, [adverse]
commercial, [abbatial]
commercialization,
   [abbreviation]
commercialize, [actualize]
commie, [academy]

commingle, [angle]
comminute, [acute]
commiserate, [accelerate]
commissar, [abattoir]
commissary, [accessory]
commission, [abbreviation]
commissioner, [afterburner]
commit, [acquit]
commitment, [abandonment]
committal, [accidental]
committed, [abluted]
committee, [abatis]
commix, [administratrix]
commode, [abode]
commodity, [abatis]
commodore, [abhor]
common, [abdomen]
commonality, [abatis]
commoner, [afterburner]
commonplace, [abase]
commonweal, [automobile]
commonwealth, health,
   stealth, wealth
commotion, [abbreviation]
commove, [approve]
communal, [abdominal]
commune, [afternoon]
communicable, [able]
communicant, [abeyant]
communicate, [abdicate]
communication, [abbreviation]
communicative, [ablative]
communicator, [abductor]
communion, [antiunion]
communiqué, [agape]
communism, [abolitionism]
communist, [abolitionist]
communistic, [acoustic]
community, [abatis]

commutate, [acetate]
commutation, [abbreviation]
commute, [acute]
commuter, [abductor]
comp, [chomp]
compact, [abstract]
compaction, [abbreviation]
compactor, [abductor]
companion, [antiunion]
companionship, [airship]
company, [abalone]
comparable, [able]
comparative, [ablative]
compare, [affair]
comparison, [antitoxin]
compartment, [abandonment]
compartmentalize, [actualize]
compass, [auspice]
compassion, [abbreviation]
compassionate, [acuminate]
compatible, [able]
compatriot, [affiliate]
compeer, [adhere]
compel, [bagatelle]
compendium, [anthurium]
compensate, [ate]
compensation, [abbreviation]
compensatory, [accessory]
compete, [accrete]
competence, [abhorrence]
competency, [absorbancy]
competition, [abbreviation]
competitive, [ablative]
competitor, [abductor]
compilation, [abbreviation]
compile, [aisle]
compiler, [angler]
complacency, [absorbancy]
complacent, [adjacent]

complain, [abstain]
complaint, [acquaint]
complaisance, [accordance]
complaisant, [adjacent]
complected, [abluted]
complement, [abandonment]
complementary, [accessory]
complete, [accrete]
completion, [abbreviation]
complex, [annex]
complexion, [abbreviation]
complexity, [abatis]
compliance, [abhorrence]
compliant, [abeyant]
complicate, [abdicate]
complicated, [abluted]
complication, [abbreviation]
complicity, [abatis]
compliment, [abandonment]
complimentary, [accessory]
comply, [airdry]
component, [abstinent]
comport, [airport]
compose, [airhose]
composer, [adviser]
composite, [apposite]
composition, [abbreviation]
compost, [aftermost]
composure, [admeasure]
compound, [abound]
comprehend, [addend]
comprehensible, [able]
comprehension,
    [abbreviation]
comprehensive, [abrasive]
compress, [acquiesce]
compressed, [abreast]
compression, [abbreviation]
compressor, [aggressor]

comprise, [accessorize]
compromise, [advise]
compromiser, [adviser]
comptroller, [angler]
compulsion, [abbreviation]
compulsive, [abrasive]
compulsory, [accessory]
compunction, [abbreviation]
computation, [abbreviation]
compute, [acute]
computer, [abductor]
computerese, [antifreeze]
computerization,
    [abbreviation]
comrade, [ad]
con, [amazon]
concatenate, [acuminate]
concave, [aftershave]
conceal, [anneal]
concede, [accede]
conceit, [accrete]
conceited, [abluted]
conceivable, [able]]
conceive, [achieve]
concent, [accent]
concentrate, [accelerate]
concentric, [aleatoric]
concept, [accept]
conception, [abbreviation]
conceptual, [accrual]
conceptualize, [actualize]
conceptus, [afflatus]
concern, [adjourn]
concert, [advert]
concertmaster, [administer]
concerto, [aggiornamento]
concession, [abbreviation]
concessionaire, [affair]
conchoidal, [antipodal]

conciliator, [abductor]
concinnity, [abatis]
concise, [advice]
conclave, [aftershave]
conclude, [allude]
conclusion, [abrasion]
conclusive, [abrasive]
conclusively, [ably]
concoct, [blocked]
concoction, [abbreviation]
concomitance, [abhorrence]
concomitant, [abirritant]
concord, [award]
concordance, [accordance]
concordat, [acrobat]
concourse, [coarse]
concrete, [accrete]
concubine, [aerodyne]
concupiscence, [accordance]
concur, [acre]
concurrence, [abhorrence]
concurrent, [aberrant]
concussion, [abbreviation]
condemn, [apothegm]
condemnation, [abbreviation]
condensation, [abbreviation]
condense, [cense]
condensed, [against]
condenser, [aggressor]
condescend, [addend]
condescension, [abbreviation]
condign, [aerodyne]
condiment, [[abandonment]
condition, [abbreviation]
conditional, [aboriginal]
conditioner, [afterburner]
condo, [aficionado]
condole, [areole]
condolence, [abhorrence]

condom, [addendum]
condominium, [anthurium]
condone, [alone]
condor, [adder]
conduce, [abstruse]
conducive, [abrasive]
conduct, [abduct]
conduction, [abbreviation]
conductivity, [abatis]
conductor, [abductor]
conduit, [adequate]
cone, [alone]
coney, [abalone]
confab, [backstab]
confabulate, [ablate]
confect, [abject]
confection, [abbreviation]
confectionary, [accessory]
confectionery, [accessory]
confederacy, [absorbancy]
confederate, [adjective]
    [accurate]
confederate, [verb]
    [accelerate]
confederation, [abbreviation]
confer, [buffer]
conference, [abhorrence]
confess, [acquiesce]
confession, [abbreviation]
confessional, [abdominal]
confessor, [aggressor]
confetti, [abatis]
confidant, [avaunt]
confide, [abide]
confidence, [abhorrence]
confident, [abundant]
confidential, [abbatial]
configuration, [abbreviation]
configure, [ballplayer]

confine, [aerodyne]
confined, [affined]
confinement, [abandonment]
confirm, [affirm]
confirmation, [abbreviation]
confiscate, [abdicate]
confiscation, [abbreviation]
confit, [anastrophe]
confiteor, [abhor]
confiture, [abjure]
conflagration, [abbreviation]
conflate, [ablate]
conflict, [addict]
confluence, [abhorrence]
conform, [aswarm]
conformable, [able]
conformation, [abbreviation]
conformist, [alchemist]
conformity, [abatis]
confound, [abound]
confounded, [absentminded]
confront, [aberrant]
confrontation, [abbreviation]
confrontational, [abdominal]
confuse, [abuse]
confusion, [abrasion]
confutation, [abbreviation]
confute, [acute]
congeal, [anneal]
congenial, [abaxial]
congenital, [accidental]
congest, [abreast]
congestion, [abbreviation]
conglobate, [abate]
conglomerate, [noun]
    [accurate]
conglomerate, [verb]
    [accelerate]

conglomeration, [abbreviation]
congratulate, [ablate]
congratulation, [abbreviation]
congregate, [abnegate]
congregation, [abbreviation]
congregational, [abdominal]
congregationalism, [abolitionism]
congregationalist, [aerialist]
congress, [actress]
congressional, [aboriginal]
congressman, [abdomen]
congruence, [abhorrence]
congruent, [abeyant]
congruity, [abatis]
congruous, [antibias]
conical, [acoustical]
conifer, [buffer]
conjectural, [admiral]
conjecture, [acupuncture]
conjoin, [adjoin]
conjoint, [anoint]
conjugal, [angle]
conjugate, [adjective] [agate]
conjugate, [verb] [abnegate]
conjugated, [abluted]
conjugation, [abbreviation]
conjunct, [adjunct]
conjunction, [abbreviation]
conjure, [armiger]
conk, [ankh]
conn, [amazon]
connate, [abominate]
connect, [abject]
connected, [abluted]
connection, [abbreviation]
connective, [ablative]
conniption, [abbreviation]

connive, [alive]
connoisseur, [aggressor]
connotation, [abbreviation]
connotative, [ablative]
connote, [afloat]
connubial, [abaxial]
conquer, [acre]
conqueror, [adulterer]
conquest, [abreast]
conquistador, [abhor]
conscience, [abhorrence]
conscientious, [adscititious]
conscionable, [able]
conscious, [adscititious]
consciousness, [agribusiness]
conscribe, [ascribe]
conscript, [adscript]
conscription, [abbreviation]
consecrate, [accelerate]
consecration, [abbreviation]
consecutive, [ablative]
consensual, [accrual]
consensus, [alkalosis]
consequence, [cense]
conservation, [abbreviation]
conservationist, [abolitionist]
conservatism, [abolitionism]
conservative, [ablative]
conservator, [abductor]
conservatory, [accessory]
conserve, curve, deserve, nerve, observe, preserve, reserve, self-serve, serve, swerve, unnerve, unreserve, verve
consider, [adder]
considerable, [able]
considerate, [accurate]

consideration, [abbreviation]
consign, [aerodyne]
consigner, [afterburner]
consignment, [abandonment]
consist, [assist]
consistency, [absorbancy]
consistent, [abirritant]
consistory, [accessory]
consolation, [abbreviation]
console, [areole]
consolidate, [accommodate]
consolidation, [abbreviation]
consommé, [agape]
consonant, [abstinent]
consort, [abort]
consortium, [anthurium]
conspicuous, [ambiguous]
conspiracy, [absorbancy]
conspiration, [abbreviation]
conspirator, [abductor]
conspire, [acquire]
constable, [able]
constancy, [absorbancy]
constant, [abirritant]
constellation, [abbreviation]
consternate, [abominate]
consternation, [abbreviation]
constipate, [anticipate]
constipated, [abluted]
constipation, [abbreviation]
constituency, [absorbancy]
constituent, [abeyant]
constitute, [acute]
constitution, [abbreviation]
constitutional, [abdominal]
constitutionality, [abatis]
constitutionalize, [actualize]
constitutive, [ablative]
constrain, [abstain]

constraint, [acquaint]
constrict, [addict]
constriction, [abbreviation]
constringe, [binge]
construct, [abduct]
construction, [abbreviation]
constructive, [ablative]
construe, [accrue]
consubstantiation,
  [abbreviation]
consulate, [aglet]
consult, [adult]
consultant, [accordant]
consultation, [abbreviation]
consume, [abloom]
consumer, [armor]
consummate, [adjective]
  [animate]
consummate, [verb]
  [acclimate]
consummation, [abbreviation]
consumption, [abbreviation]
contagion, [allergen]
contagious, [advantageous]
contain, [abstain]
container, [afterburner]
containment, [abandonment]
contaminate, [abominate]
contamination, [abbreviation]
contemn, [apothegm]
contemplate, [ablate]
contemplation, [abbreviation]
contemplative, [ablative]
contemporaneous,
  [abstemious]
contemporary, [accessory]
contemporize, [accessorize]
contempt, [attempt]
contemptible, [able]

contemptuous, [ambiguous]
contend, [addend]
contender, [adder]
contented, [abluted]
contention, [abbreviation]
contentious, [adscititious]
contentment, [abandonment]
contest, [verb] [abreast]
contest, [noun] [abreast]
contestant, [abirritant]
context, next, oversexed,
   perplexed, pretext, sexed,
   subtext, teletext, text, vexed,
   videotext
contextual, [accrual]
contextualize, [actualize]
contiguous, [ambiguous]
continence, [abhorrence]
continent, [abstinent]
continental, [accidental]
contingency, [absorbancy]
contingent, [agent]
continual, [accrual]
continuance, [abhorrence]
continuation, [abbreviation]
continue, [accrue]
continued, [allude]
continuity, [abatis]
continuous, [ambiguous]
continuum, [addendum]
contort, [abort]
contortion, [abbreviation]
contortionist, [abolitionist]
contour, [abjure]
contra, [abracadabra]
contraband, [ampersand]
contraception, [abbreviation]
contraceptive, [ablative]
contract, [abstract]

contraction, [abbreviation]
contractor, [abductor]
contractual, [accrual]
contradict, [addict]
contradiction, [abbreviation]
contradictory, [accessory]
contrail, [blackmail]
contralto, [aggiornamento]
contraption, [abbreviation]
contrapuntal, [accidental]
contrarian, [abecedarian]
contrariwise, [advise]
contrary, [accessory]
contrast, [aghast]
contravene, [alexandrine]
contribute, [acute]
contribution, [abbreviation]
contrite, [affright]
contrition, [abbreviation]
contrive, [alive]
control, [areole]
controlled, [ahold]
controller, [angler]
controversial, [abbatial]
controversy, [absorbancy]
controvert, [advert]
contusion, [abrasion]
conundrum, [addendum]
convalesce, [acquiesce]
convalescence, [accordance]
convalescent, [adjacent]
convect, [abject]
convection, [abbreviation]
convene, [alexandrine]
convener, [afterburner]
convenience, [abhorrence]
convenient, [abeyant]
convent, [accent]
convention, [abbreviation]

conventional, [aboriginal]
converge, demiurge, dirge,
  diverge, emerge, immerge,
  merge, purge, resurge,
  scourge, splurge, submerge,
  surge, upsurge, urge, verge
convergence, [abhorrence]
convergent, [agent]
conversant, [adjacent]
conversation, [abbreviation]
conversational, [aboriginal]
conversationalist, [aerialist]
converse, [adverse]
conversion, [abrasion]
convert, [advert]
converter, [abductor]
convertible, [able]
convex, [annex]
convey, [agape]
conveyance, [abhorrence]
conveyor, [ballplayer]
convict, [addict]
conviction, [abbreviation]
convince, evince, mince,
  prince, rinse, shin splints,
  since, wince
convocation, [abbreviation]
convoke, [artichoke]
convolute, [acute]
convoluted, [abluted]
convolution, [abbreviation]
convoy, [ahoy]
convulse, impulse, pulse,
  repulse
convulsion, [abbreviation]
convulsive, [abrasive]
coo, [accrue]
cook, [bankbook]
cookery, [accessory]

cookie, [achy]
cookout, [about]
cookstove, [alcove]
cookware, [affair]
cool, [bascule]
coolant, [ambivalent]
cooler, [angler]
coolie, [ably]
coon, [afternoon]
coop, coupe, croup, droop,
  dupe, goop, group, hoop,
  loop, nincompoop, poop,
  recoup, regroup, scoop,
  sloop, snoop, soup, stoop,
  stoup, stupe, subgroup,
  swoop, troop, troupe, whoop
cooper, [barkeeper]
cooperate, [accelerate]
cooperation, [abbreviation]
cooperative, [ablative]
coordinate, [noun]
  [acuminate]
coordinate, [verb] [abominate]
coordinated, [abluted]
coordination,
  [abbreviation]
coot, [acute]
co-owner, [afterburner]
co-ownership, [airship]
cop, [agitprop]
copacetic, [acoustic]
coparcener, [afterburner]
cope, [antelope]
coper, [barkeeper]
copier, [anterior]
copilot, [aglet]
copious, [abstemious]
cop-out, [about]
copper, [barkeeper]

coppersmith, [blacksmith]
co-producer, [aggressor]
copromoter, [abductor]
coproprietor, [abductor]
co-publish, [abolish]
copula, [a capella]
copulate, [ablate]
copulation, [abbreviation]
copy, [apocope]
copycat, [acrobat]
copydesk, [arabesque]
copyist, [activist]
copyright, [acquit]
copywriter, [abductor]
coquet, [advocate]
coquette, [abet]
coral, [admiral]
cord, [award]
cordial, [agile]
cordiality, [abatis]
cordless, [acropolis]
cordon, [anchorperson]
corduroy, [ahoy]
core, [abhor]
coresearcher, [acupuncture]
corf, dwarf, ectomorph,
  endomorph, wharf
corgi, [aggie]
coriander, [adder]
cork, dork, fork, pitchfork,
  stork, torque, uncork
corkage, [acknowledge]
corker, [acre]
corkscrew, [accrue]
corky, [achy]
cormorant, [aberrant]
corn, [acorn]
cornball, [aerosol]
corncob, [ab]

cornea, [abulia]
corner, [afterburner]
cornerback, [aback]
cornerman, [adman]
cornerstone, [alone]
cornet, [bassinet]
cornflake, [awake]
cornice, [agribusiness]
corniche, [baksheesh]
cornpone, [alone]
cornstalk, [aftershock]
cornstarch, [arch]
cornucopia, [abulia]
corny, [abalone]
corody, [acidy]
corollary, [accessory]
corona, [alumna]
coronal, [abdominal]
coronary, [accessory]
coronate, [abominate]
coronation, [abbreviation]
coroner, [afterburner]
coronet, [bassinet]
corotate, [acetate]
corporal, [admiral]
corporate, [accurate]
corporation, [abbreviation]
corporeal, [abaxial]
corps, [abhor]
corpulent, [ambivalent]
corpus, [auspice]
corpuscle, [apostle]
corrade, [abrade]
corral, [canal]
correct, [abject]
correctable, [able]
correction, [abbreviation]
corrective, [ablative]
correlate, [verb] [ablate]

correlate, [noun] [aglet]
correlation, [abbreviation]
correlative, [ablative]
correspond, [abscond]
correspondence, [abhorrence]
correspondent, [abundant]
corridor, [adder]
corrigendum, [addendum]
corrigible, [able]
corrival, [adjectival]
corroborate, [accelerate]
corroboration, [abbreviation]
corrode, [abode]
corrosion, [abrasion]
corrosive, [abrasive]
corrugate, [abnegate]
corrugated, [abluted]
corrupt, [abrupt]
corrupter, [abductor]
corruptible, [able]
corruption, [abbreviation]
corsage, [arbitrage]
corset, cresset, deficit, dulcet,
    elicit, explicit, facet, faucet,
    illicit, implicit, licit, russet,
    solicit, tacit, transit, whatsit
    (see also **abbot**)
cortege, manege
cortex, [annex]
cortisone, [alone]
co-ruler, [angler]
coruscate, [abdicate]
coruscation, [abbreviation]
corvette, [abet]
coset, [abet]
cosh, [awash]
cosine, [aerodyne]
cosmetic, [acoustic]
cosmetologist, [allergist]

cosmetology, [allergy]
cosmic, [academic]
cosmical, [acoustical]
cosmogonist, [abolitionist]
cosmogony, [abalone]
cosmography, [anastrophe]
cosmologist, [allergist]
cosmology, [allergy]
cosmonaut, [aeronaut]
cosmopolitan, [anchorperson]
cosmos, [allonymous]
cosponsor, [aggressor]
cossac, [aback]
cost, [accost]
costar, [abattoir]
costive, [ablative]
costly, [ably]
costume, [abloom]
costumer, [armor]
cot, [aeronaut]
coterminous, [agribusiness]
cotrustee, [abatis]
cottage, [acknowledge]
cotter, [abductor]
cotton, [anchorperson]
cottonseed, [accede]
cottontail, [blackmail]
cottonwood, [adulthood]
cottony, [abalone]
couch, [avouch]
cougar, [agar]
cough, [boff]
could, [adulthood]
coulee, [ably]
coulisse, [afterpiece]
couloir, [abattoir]
coulter, [abductor]
council, [apostle]
councilman, [abdomen]

counsel, [apostle]
counselee, [ably]
counselor, [angler]
count, [account]
countdown, [boomtown]
countenance, [abhorrence]
counter, [abductor]
counteract, [abstract]
counterattack, [aback]
counterbalance, [abhorrence]
counterblow, [afterglow]
countercharge, [barge]
countercheck, [afterdeck]
counterclaim, [acclaim]
counterclockwise, [advise]
countercriticism,
    [abolitionism]
countercultural, [admiral]
counterculture, [acupuncture]
counterdemonstration,
    [abbreviation]
counterespionage, [arbitrage]
counterfeit, [acquit]
counterintelligence,
    [abhorrence]
countermand, [ampersand]
countermeasure, [admeasure]
counteroffensive, [abrasive]
counteroffer, [buffer]
counterpart, [apart]
counterplay, [airplay]
counterplot, [aeronaut]
counterpoint, [anoint]
counterpoise, equipoise,
    hoise, noise, poise, turquoise
counterpose, [airhose]
counterproductive, [ablative]
counterpunch, [brunch]

counterrevolution,
    [abbreviation]
countersign, [aerodyne]
counterspy, [airdry]
counterstrategy, [allergy]
counterstrike, [alike]
counterstroke, [artichoke]
countersuggestion,
    [abbreviation]
counterthreat, [abet]
countertop, [agitprop]
counterweight, [accentuate]
countess, [afflatus]
countian, [abecedarian]
countless, [acropolis]
country, [ancestry]
countryside, [abide]
countrywide, [abide]
county, [abatis]
coup, [noun] [accrue]
coup, [verb] [antelope]
coupe, [coop]
couple, [ample]
coupler, [angler]
couplet, [aglet]
coupon, [amazon]
courage, [abridge]
courageous, [advantageous]
courier, [anterior]
course, [coarse]
courseware, [affair]
court, [airport]
courteous, [abstemious]
courtesan, [artisan]
courtesy, [absorbancy]
courthouse, [alehouse]
courtier, [anterior]
courtroom, [abloom]
courtship, [airship]

courtside, [abide]
courtyard, [backyard]
cousin, [artisan]
couth, [booth]
couthie, [apathy]
couture, [abjure]
couturier, [anterior]
couturiere, [anterior]
couvade, [abroad]
cove, [alcove]
covenant, [abstinent]
covenantal, [accidental]
cover, [achiever]
coverage, [abridge]
coverall, [aerosol]
coverlet, [aglet]
covert, [advert]
coverture, [abjure]
covet, [adequate]
covetous, [afflatus]
covetousness, [agribusiness]
covey, [anchovy]
cow, [allow]
cowardice, [antibias]
cowardly, [ably]
cowbell, [bagatelle]
cowboy, [ahoy]
cower, [airpower]
cowgirl, [aswirl]
cowhand, [ampersand]
cowhide, [abide]
coworker, [acre]
cowpoke, [artichoke]
cowpox, [bandbox]
coxcomb, [astrodome]
coy, [ahoy]
coyote, [afloat]
cozen, [artisan]
cozy, [advisee]

crab, [backstab]
crabby, [abbey]
crabgrass, [admass]
crabwise, [advise]
crack, [aback]
crackdown, [boomtown]
cracker, [acre]
crackerjack, [aback]
crackle, [acoustical]
crackly, [ably]
crackpot, [aeronaut]
cradle, [antipodal]
craftiness, [agribusiness]
craftsman, [abdomen]
crafty, [abatis]
crag, [ag]
craggy, [aggie]
crake, [awake]
cram, [aerogram]
cramp, [aid-de-camp]
crane, [abstain]
cranial, [abaxial]
cranium, [anthurium]
crank, [bank]
crankcase, [abase]
crankshaft, [abaft]
cranky, [achy]
cranny, [abalone]
crap, [afterclap]
crape, [agape]
crappy, [apocope]
craps, [apse]
crapshoot, [acute]
crapulous, [acropolis]
crash, [abash]
crass, [admass]
crassitude, [altitude]
cratch, [armpatch]
crate, [accelerate]

crater, [abductor]
cravat, [acrobat]
crave, [aftershave]
craw, [aah]
crawdad, [ad]
crawl, [aerosol]
crawler, [angler]
crawlway, [airway]
crayon, [amazon]
craze, [ablaze]
craziness, [agribusiness]
crazy, [advisee]
creak, [antique]
creaky, [achy]
cream, [abeam]
creamer, [armor]
creamery, [accessory]
crease, [afterpiece]
create, [disaffiliate]
creation, [abbreviation]
creationism, [abolitionism]
creationist, [abolitionist]
creative, [ablative]
creativity, [abatis]
creator, [abductor]
creature, [acupuncture]
creaturely, [ably]
crèche, [afresh]
credence, [abhorrence]
credential, [abbatial]
credenza, [alfalfa]
credibility, [abatis]
credible, [able]
credit, [acquit]
creditability, [abatis]
creditable, [able]
creditor, [abductor]
creditworthy, [apathy]
credo, [aficionado]

credulity, [abatis]
credulous, [acropolis]
creed, [accede]
creek, [antique]
creel, [anneal]
creep, [asleep]
creeper, [barkeeper]
creepy, [apocope]
cremate, [acclimate]
cremation, [abbreviation]
crematorium, [anthurium]
crematory, [accessory]
crenate, [abominate]
creole, [areole]
creosote, [afloat]
crepe, [agape]
crepitate, [acetate]
crepon, [amazon]
crept, [accept]
crescendo, [aficionado]
crescent, [adjacent]
cress, [acquiesce]
cresset, [corset]
crest, [abreast]
crestfallen, [acetylene]
cretin, [anchorperson]
cretonne, [amazon]
crevasse, [admass]
crevice, [antibias]
crew, [accrue]
crewel, [agile]
crewmate, [acclimate]
crib, [bib]
cribbage, [acknowledge]
cribriform, [aswarm]
crick, [aleatoric]
cricket, [advocate]
crier, [amplifier]
crikey, [achy]

crime, [airtime]
criminal, [abdominal]
criminate, [abominate]
criminologist, [allergist]
criminology, [allergy]
crimp, [blimp]
crimper, [barkeeper]
crimson, [artisan]
cringe, [binge]
crinkle, [acoustical]
crinoline, [acetylene]
criollo, [airshow]
cripple, [ample]
crises, [antifreeze]
crisis, [alkalosis]
crisp, lisp, wisp
crisper, [barkeeper]
crispness, [agribusiness]
crispy, [apocope]
crisscross, [across]
criterion, [abecedarian]
criterium, [anthurium]
critic, [acoustic]
critical, [acoustical]
criticism, [abolitionism]
criticize, [abscise]
critique, [antique]
critter, [abductor]
croak, [artichoke]
croaker, [acre]
crochet, [agape]
crock, [aftershock]
crocked, [blocked]
crocket, [advocate]
crocodile, [anile]
croft, [aloft]
croissant, [avaunt]
crone, [alone]
crony, [abalone]

cronyism, [abolitionism]
crook, [bankbook]
crooked, [acid]
croon, [afternoon]
crooner, [afterburner]
crop, [agitprop]
cropper, [barkeeper]
croquet, [agape]
croquette, [advocate]
croquignole, [areole]
croquis, [achy]
crosier, [admeasure]
cross, [across]
crossable, [able]
crossbar, [abattoir]
crossbow, [airshow]
crossbred, [abed]
crossbreed, [accede]
cross-check, [afterdeck]
crosscourt, [airport]
crosscurrent, [aberrant]
crosscut, [advocate]
cross-examination,
　[abbreviation]
cross-examine, [abdomen]
cross-eyed, [abide]
cross-fertilization,
　[abbreviation]
cross-fertilize, [actualize]
crossover, [achiever]
cross-reference,
　[circumference]
crossroad, [abode]
cross-stitch, [backstitch]
crosswalk, [aftershock]
crosswind, [abscind]
crosswise, [advise]
crossword, [absurd]
crotch, [blotch]

crotchet, [adequate]
crotchety, [abatis]
crouch, [avouch]
croup, [coop]
crouton, [amazon]
crow, [allegro]
crowbar, [abattoir]
crowd, [aloud]
crown, [boomtown]
crowstep, doorstep, footstep,
  hep, instep, lockstep,
  misstep, overstep, pep, prep,
  rep, quickstep, step
crucial, [abbatial]
crucible, [able]
crucifix, [administratrix]
crucifixion, [abbreviation]
crucify, [amplify]
crud, [acid]
crude, [allude]
cruel, [bascule]
cruelty, [abatis]
cruet, [adequate]
cruise, [abuse]
cruiser, [adviser]
crumb, [addendum]
crumble, [able]
crummy, [academy]
crump, [bump]
crumpet, [adequate]
crumple, [ample]
crunch, [brunch]
crusade, [abrade]
cruse, [amuse]
crush, [airbrush]
crushproof, [aloof]
crust, [adjust]
crusty, [abatis]
crutch, [clutch]

crux, [afflux]
cry, [airdry]
crybaby, [abbey]
crypt, [adscript]
cryptic, [acoustic]
cryptogram, [aerogram]
cryptographer, [buffer]
cryptography, [anastrophe]
crystallize, [actualize]
cub, [backrub]
cubbyhole, [areole]
cube, [boob]
cubic, [acerbic]
cubical, [acoustical]
cubicle, [acoustical]
cubit, [abbot]
cuckoo, [accrue]
cucullate, [ablate]
cucumber, [amber]
cud, [acid]
cuddle, [antipodal]
cuddler, [angler]
cuddly, [ably]
cuddy, [acidy]
cudgel, [agile]
cue, [accrue]
cuff, [bluff]
cuisine, [alexandrine]
cuke, [archduke]
culinary, [accessory]
cull, [acoustical]
cullet, [aglet]
cully, [ably]
culminant, [abstinent]
culminate, [abominate]
culmination, [abbreviation]
culotte, [aeronaut]
culpability, [abatis]
culpable, [able]

culpableness, [agribusiness]
culprit, [accurate]
cult, [antepenult]
cultish, [abolish]
cultist, [absolutist]
cultivate, [activate]
cultivated, [abluted]
cultivation, [abbreviation]
cultivator, [abductor]
cultural, [admiral]
culture, [acupuncture]
cultus, [afflatus]
culvert, [advert]
cumber, [amber]
cumbersome,
  [adventuresome]
cummerbund, [almond]
cumulate, [ablate]
cumulative, [ablative]
cumulus, [acropolis]
cuneiform, [aswarm]
cup, [backup]
cupboard, [absurd]
cupcake, [awake]
cupful, [apocryphal]
cupid, [acid]
cupidity, [abatis]
cupule, [bascule]
cur, [acre]
curable, [able]
curate, [accelerate]
curate, [accurate]
curative, [ablative]
curator, [abductor]
curb, [adverb]
curbside, [abide]
curd, [absurd]
curdle, [antipodal]
cure, [abjure]

curfew, [accrue]
curios, [abstemious]
curiosity, [abatis]
curl, [aswirl]
curler, [angler]
curlicue, [accrue]
curly, [ably]
curmudgeon, [allergen]
currant, [aberrant]
currency, [absorbancy]
current, [aberrant]
curriculum, [addendum]
curry, [accessory]
curse, [adverse]
cursed, [acid]
cursive, [abrasive]
cursor, [aggressor]
cursory, [accessory]
curt, [advert]
curtail, [ail]
curtain, [anchorperson]
curtesy, [absorbancy]
curtsy, [absorbancy]
curvaceous, [adscititious]
curvature, [abjure]
curve, [conserve]
curveball, [aerosol]
cushion, [abbreviation]
cushy, [banshee]
cuss, [abacus]
custard, [absurd]
custodial, [abaxial]
custodian, [abecedarian]
custody, [acidy]
custom, [accustom]
customary, [accessory]
customer, [armor]
customhouse, [alehouse]
customize, [advise]

cut, [adequate]
cutaway, [airway]
cute, [acute]
cutesy, [absorbancy]
cuticle, [acoustical]
cutie, [abatis]
cutlass, [acropolis]
cutler, [angler]
cutlet, [aglet]
cutoff, [boff]
cutout, [about]
cutrate, [accelerate]
cutter, [abductor]
cutthroat, [afloat]
cutting edge, [allege]
cutup, [backup]
cyanide, [abide]
cybernation, [abbreviation]
cybernetics, [acoustics]
cyborg, morgue
cyclamate, [acclimate]
cycle, [acoustical]
cyclical, [acoustical]
cyclist, [adjust]
cyclone, [alone]
cyclops, [chops]
cyclorama, [anathema]
cyclotron, [amazon]
cylinder, [adder]
cylindrical, [acoustical]
cymbal, [able]
cynic, [allergenic]
cynical, [acoustical]
cynicism, [abolitionism]
cypress, [actress]
cyst, [assist]
cystic, [acoustic]
czar, [abattoir]
dab, [backstab]

dabble, [able]
dactyl, [accidental]
dad, [ad]
daddy, [acidy]
dado, [aficionado]
daffodil, [backfill]
daffy, [anastrophe]
dagger, [agar]
dahlia, [alleluia]
daily, [ably]
dainty, [abatis]
daiquiri, [accessory]
dairy, [accessory]
dairymaid, [abrade]
dairyman, [abdomen]
daisy, [advisee]
dale, [ail]
dalliance, [abhorrence]
dally, [ably]
dalmatian, [abbreviation]
dalmatic, [acoustic]
dam, [aerogram]
damage, [acknowledge]
dame, [acclaim]
damn, [aerogram]
damnation, [abbreviation]
damp, [aid-de-camp]
damper, [barkeeper]
damsel, [appraisal]
Dan, [adman]
dance, [advance]
dancer, [aggressor]
dander, [adder]
dandle, [antipodal]
dandruff, [bluff]
dandy, [acidy]
danger, [armiger]
dangerous, [actress]
dangle, [angle]

dank, [bank]
dapper, [barkeeper]
dapple, [ample]
dare, [affair]
daredevil, [adjectival]
daresay, [agape]
dark, [aardvark]
darken, [awaken]
darkish, [abolish]
darkle, [acoustical]
darkroom, [abloom]
darksome, [adventuresome]
darn, [barn]
dart, [apart]
dartboard, [aboard]
dash, [abash]
dashboard, [aboard]
dastard, [absurd]
dastardly, [ably]
data bank, [bank]
data, [aorta]
database, [abase]
date, [accommodate]
dated, [abluted]
dateline, [airline]
dative, [ablative]
datum, [accustom]
daub, [ab]
daughter, [abductor]
daunt, [avaunt]
dauntless, [acropolis]
davenport, [airport]
dawdle, [antipodal]
dawdler, [angler]
dawn, [amazon]
day, [agape]
daybreak, [awake]
daydream, [abeam]
daydreamer, [armor]

daylight, [affright]
daylong, [agelong]
daystar, [abattoir]
daytime, [airtime]
daze, [ablaze]
dazzle, [appraisal]
deacon, [awaken]
deaconal, [abdominal]
deaconess, [agribusiness]
deactivate, [activate]
deactivation, [abbreviation]
dead duck, [amok]
dead, [abed]
deadbeat, [accrete]
deaden, [anchorperson]
deadeye, [airdry]
deadhead, [abed]
deadheat, [accrete]
deadlift, [adrift]
deadline, [airline]
deadlock, [aftershock]
deadmeat, [accrete]
deadness, [agribusiness]
deadpan, [adman]
deadweight, [accentuate]
deadwood, [adulthood]
deaerate, [accelerate]
deaf, [aleph]
deafen, [antiphon]
deaf-mute, [backup]
deal, [anneal]
dealer, [angler]
dealership, [airship]
dealt, [belt]
dean, [alexandrine]
dearth [afterbirth]
death squad, [abroad]
death, [breath]
deathbed, [abed]

deathwatch, [blotch]
debacle, [acoustical]
debar, [abattoir]
debarkation, [abbreviation]
debase, [abase]
debatable, [able]
debate, [abate]
debauch, [blotch]
debauchery, [accessory]
debeak, [antique]
debenture, [acupuncture]
debilitate, [acetate]
debit, [abbot]
debonair, [affair]
debone, [alone]
debouch, [avouch]
debrief, [aperitif]
debris, [accessory]
debt, [abet]
debtless, [acropolis]
debtor, [abductor]
debug, [bedbug]
debunk, [bohunk]
debut, [accrue]
debutante, [avaunt]
decadal, [antipodal]
decade, [abrade]
decadence, [abhorrence]
decadent, [abundant]
decaf, [allograph]
decaffeinated, [abluted]
decal, [canal]
decalogue, [agog]
decameter, [abductor]
decamp, [aid-de-camp]
decant, [ant]
decanter, [abductor]
decapitate, [acetate]
decapitation, [abbreviation]

decapod, [abroad]
decathlon, [acetylene]
decay, [agape]
decease, [afterpiece]
deceased, [beast]
decedent, [accordant]
deceit, [accrete]
deceitful, [apocryphal]
deceive, [achieve]
deceiver, [achiever]
decelerate, [accelerate]
deceleration, [abbreviation]
decency, [absorbancy]
decent, [adjacent]
decentralization,
   [abbreviation]
decentralize, [actualize]
deception, [abbreviation]
deceptive, [ablative]
decertification, [abbreviation]
decertify, [amplify]
dechlorinate, [abominate]
dechlorination, [abbreviation]
decibel, [able]
decide, [abide]
decided, [absentminded]
decimal, [abnormal]
decimate, [acclimate]
decipher, [buffer]
decision, [abscission]
decisive, [abrasive]
deck, [afterdeck]
deckle, [acoustical]
declaim, [acclaim]
declamatory, [accessory]
declaration, [abbreviation]
declarative, [ablative]
declare, [affair]

declassification,
  [abbreviation]
declassify, [amplify]
declension, [abbreviation]
decline, [airline]
decode, [abode]
decoder, [adder]
decommission, [abbreviation]
decompose, [airhose]
decompress, [acquiesce]
decompression, [abbreviation]
decongestant, [abirritant]
deconstruction, [abbreviation]
decontaminate, [abominate]
decor, [abhor]
decorate, [accelerate]
decoration, [abbreviation]
decorator, [abductor]
decorum, [addendum]
decoupage, [arbitrage]
decoy, [ahoy]
decrease, [afterpiece]
decree, [accessory]
decrepit, [adequate]
decretal, [accidental]
decretive, [ablative]
decriminalization,
  [abbreviation]
decriminalize, [actualize]
decry, [airdry]
decryption, [abbreviation]
dedicate, [adjective]
  [advocate]
dedicate, [verb] [abdicate]
dedicated, [abluted]
dedication, [abbreviation]
dedicatory, [accessory]
deduce, [abstruse]
deduct, [abduct]

deductibility, [abatis]
deductible, [able]
deduction, [abbreviation]
deductive, [ablative]
deed, [accede]
deem, [abeam]
deep, [asleep]
deep-rooted, [abluted]
deep-seated, [abluted]
deer, [adhere]
deerskin, [akin]
deescalate, [ablate]
de-escalation, [abbreviation]
deface, [abase]
defalcate, [abdicate]
defalcation, [abbreviation]
defamation, [abbreviation]
defame, [acclaim]
defat, [acrobat]
default, [asphalt]
defecate, [abdicate]
defect, [abject]
defection, [abbreviation]
defective, [ablative]
defend, [addend]
defendant, [abundant]
defender, [adder]
defense, [cense]
defenseman, [abdomen]
defensible, [able]
defensive, [abrasive]
defer, [buffer]
deference, [abhorrence]
deferential, [facial]
deferment, [abandonment]
defiance, [abhorrence]
defiant, [abeyant]
defibrillate, [ablate]
defibrillation, [abbreviation]

defibrillator, [abductor]
deficiency, [absorbancy]
deficient, [abeyant]
deficit, [corset]
defilade, [abrade]
defile, [aisle]
defilement, [abandonment]
definable, [able]
define, [aerodyne]
definite, [acquit]
definition, [abbreviation]
definitive, [ablative]
deflagrate, [accelerate]
deflate, [ablate]
deflation, [abbreviation]
deflect, [abject]
deflection, [abbreviation]
deflower, [airpower]
defog, [agog]
defogger, [agar]
defoliant, [abeyant]
defoliation, [abbreviation]
deforce, [coarse]
deforestation, [abbreviation]
deform, [aswarm]
deformity, [abatis]
defraud, [abroad]
defray, [affray]
defrock, [aftershock]
defrost, [accost]
defroster, [administer]
deft, [aleft]
defunct, [adjunct]
defuse, [amuse]
defy, [amplify]
degenerate, [adjective]
  [accurate]
degenerate, [verb]
  [accelerate]

degeneration, [abbreviation]
degenerative, [ablative]
degradable, [able]
degradation, [abbreviation]
degrade, [abrade]
degraded, [absentminded]
degrease, [afterpiece]
degree, [accessory]
dehumanize, [agnize]
dehumidify, [amplify]
dehydrate, [accelerate]
dehydration, [abbreviation]
dehydrator, [abductor]
de-ice, [advice]
deictic, [acoustic]
deify, [amplify]
deign, [abstain]
deist, [activist]
deity, [abatis]
deixis, [abyss]
deject, [abject]
dejected, [abluted]
dejection, [abbreviation]
delate, [ablate]
delay, [airplay]
delectable, [able]
delegate, [noun] [agate]
delegate, [verb] [abnegate]
delegation, [abbreviation]
delegator, [abductor]
delete, [accrete]
deleterious, [abstemious]
deletion, [abbreviation]
deli, [ably]
deliberate, [adjective]
  [accurate]
deliberate, [verb] [accelerate]
deliberation, [abbreviation]
delicacy, [absorbancy]

delicate, [advocate]
delicatessen, [anchorperson]
delicious, [adscititious]
delight, [affright]
delighted, [abluted]
delightful, [apocryphal]
delineation, [abbreviation]
delinquency, [absorbancy]
delinquent, [abeyant]
delirious, [abstemious]
delirium, [anthurium]
deliver, [achiever]
deliverance, [abhorrence]
deliverer, [adulterer]
delivery, [accessory]
dell, [bagatelle]
delta, [aorta]
deltoid, [adenoid]
delude, [allude]
deluge, [centrifuge]
delusion, [abbreviation]
delusion, [abrasion]
delusional, [aboriginal]
deluxe, [afflux]
delve, helve, shelve, twelve
demagnetize, [absolutize]
demagogue, [agog]
demand, [ampersand]
demarcate, [abdicate]
demarcation, [abbreviation]
demean, [alexandrine]
demeanor, [afterburner]
demented, [abluted]
dementia, [abulia]
demerit, [accurate]
demilitarize, [accessorize]
demise, [advise]
demitasse, [noun] [across]
demitasse, [noun] [admass]

demiurge, [converge]
demo, [airshow]
democracy, [absorbancy]
democrat, [acrobat]
democratic, [acoustic]
demographics, [administratrix]
demography, [anastrophe]
demolish, [abolish]
demolition, [abbreviation]
demon, [abdomen]
demonetize, [absolutize]
demoniac, [aback]
demonic, [allergenic]
demonical, [acoustical]
demonization, [abbreviation]
demonize, [agnize]
demonologist, [allergist]
demonology, [allergy]
demonstrable, [able]
demonstrate, [accelerate]
demonstration, [abbreviation]
demonstrative, [ablative]
demonstrator, [abductor]
demoralize, [actualize]
demote, [afloat]
demur, [armor]
demure, [abjure]
demythologize, [advise]
den, [again]
denationalize, [actualize]
denegation, [abbreviation]
deniable, [able]
denial, [aisle]
denigrate, [accelerate]
denigration, [abbreviation]
denim, [addendum]
denizen, [artisan]
denomination, [abbreviation]
denominational, [abdominal]

denominationalism,
[abolitionism]
denominator, [abductor]
denotation, [abbreviation]
denote, [afloat]
denouement, [aah]
denounce, [announce]
dense, [cense]
density, [abatis]
dent, [accent]
dental, [accidental]
dentifrice, [actress]
dentine, [alexandrine]
dentist, [adjust]
dentistry, [ancestry]
denture, [acupuncture]
denuclearize, [accessorize]
denude, [allude]
denunciation, [abbreviation]
deny, [airdry]
deodorant, [aberrant]
deodorize, [accessorize]
deodorizer, [adviser]
deontic, [acoustic]
depart, [apart]
departed, [abluted]
department, [abandonment]
departmental, [accidental]
departmentalize, [actualize]
departure, [acupuncture]
depend, [addend]
dependable, [able]
dependence, [abhorrence]
dependency, [absorbancy]
depersonalization,
[abbreviation]
depersonalize, [actualize]
depict, [addict]
depiction, [abbreviation]

deplane, [abstain]
deplete, [accrete]
depletion, [abbreviation]
deplorable, [able]
deplore, [abhor]
deploy, [ahoy]
deployment, [abandonment]
depoliticize, [abscise]
depone, [alone]
deponent, [abstinent]
depopulate, [ablate]
deport, [airport]
deportation, [abbreviation]
deportment, [abandonment]
depose, [airhose]
deposit, [apposite]
deposition, [abbreviation]
depositor, [abductor]
depository, [accessory]
depot, [airshow]
depravation, [abbreviation]
deprave, [aftershave]
depravity, [abatis]
deprecate, [abdicate]
deprecatory, [accessory]
depreciable, [able]
depreciation, [abbreviation]
depredate, [accommodate]
depress, [acquiesce]
depressant, [adjacent]
depressed, [abreast]
depression, [abbreviation]
depressive, [abrasive]
depressurize, [accessorize]
deprivation, [abbreviation]
deprive, [alive]
depth, [breath]
deputation, [abbreviation]
depute, [acute]

deputization, [abbreviation]
deputize, [absolutize]
deputy, [abatis]
deracinate, [abominate]
derail, [ail]
derange, [arrange]
derby, [abbey]
deregulate, [ablate]
deregulation, [abbreviation]
derelict, [addict]
dereliction, [abbreviation]
deride, [abide]
derision, [abrasion]
derisive, [abrasive]
derivate, [activate]
derivation, [abbreviation]
derivative, [ablative]
derive, [alive]
dermatology, [allergy]
derogate, [abnegate]
derogatory, [accessory]
derrick, [aleatoric]
derriere, [anywhere]
derringer, [armiger]
dervish, [abolish]
descant, [ant]
descend, [addend]
descendant, [abundant]
descent, [accent]
describe, [ascribe]
description, [abbreviation]
descriptive, [ablative]
descry, [airdry]
desecrate, [accelerate]
desecration, [abbreviation]
desegregate, [abnegate]
desegregation, [abbreviation]
desensitize, [absolutize]
desert, [advert]

desertion, [abbreviation]
deserve, [conserve]
desex, [annex]
desiderate, [accelerate]
design, [aerodyne]
designate, [abominate]
designation, [abbreviation]
designee, [abalone]
designer, [afterburner]
desirable, [able]
desire, [acquire]
desirous, [actress]
desist, [assist]
desk, [arabesque]
desktop, [agitprop]
desolate, [ablate]
desolate, [aglet]
desolation, [abbreviation]
despair, [affair]
desperado, [aficionado]
desperate, [accurate]
desperation, [abbreviation]
despicable, [able]
despiritualize, [actualize]
despise, [advise]
despite, [affright]
despoil, [broil]
despondent, [abundant]
despot, [adequate]
despotic, [acoustic]
despotism, [abolitionism]
desquamate, [acclimate]
dessert, [advert]
destabilize, [actualize]
destain, [abstain]
destination, [abbreviation]
destiny, [abalone]
destitute, [acute]
destitution, [abbreviation]

destroy, [ahoy]
destroyer, [ballplayer]
destructible, [able]
destruction, [abbreviation]
destructive, [ablative]
detach, [armpatch]
detachable, [able]
detachment, [abandonment]
detail, [ail]
detain, [abstain]
detainee, [abalone]
detainer, [afterburner]
detect, [abject]
detection, [abbreviation]
detective, [ablative]
detector, [abductor]
detent, [abirritant]
détente, [avaunt]
deter, [abductor]
detergent, [agent]
deteriorate, [accelerate]
deterioration, [abbreviation]
determinant, [abstinent]
determinate, [acuminate]
determination, [abbreviation]
determinative, [ablative]
determine, [abdomen]
determinism, [abolitionism]
deterrence, [abhorrence]
deterrent, [aberrant]
detest, [abreast]
detestable, [able]
dethrone, [alone]
detinue, [accrue]
detonate, [abominate]
detonation, [abbreviation]
detonator, [abductor]
detour, [abjure]
detox, [bandbox]

detoxification, [abbreviation]
detoxify, [amplify]
detract, [abstract]
detraction, [abbreviation]
detrain, [abstain]
detriment, [abandonment]
detrimental, [accidental]
deuce, [abstruse]
devaluate, accentuate]
devaluation, [abbreviation]
devalue, [accrue]
devastate, [acetate]
devastation, [abbreviation]
develop, [backup]
developed, [abrupt]
developer, [barkeeper]
development, [abandonment]
developmental, [accidental]
deviance, [abhorrence]
deviant, [abeyant]
deviate, [affiliate]
deviation, [abbreviation]
device, [advice]
devil, [adjectival]
devil's food cake, [awake]
devilish, [abolish]
devilry, [accessory]
devious, [abstemious]
devise, [advise]
devisee, [advisee]
devisor, [abhor]
devitalize, [actualize]
devoid, [adenoid]
devoir, [abattoir]
devolution, [abbreviation]
devolve, [absolve]
devote, [afloat]
devoted, [abluted]
devotee, [abatis]

devotion, [abbreviation]
devotional, [abdominal]
devour, [airpower]
devourer, [adulterer]
devout, [about]
dew, [accrue]
dewy, [colloquy]
dexter, [administer]
dexterity, [abatis]
dexterous, [actress]
dextrose, [adios]
dharma, [anathema]
diabetes, [antifreeze]
diabetic, [acoustic]
diablerie, [accessory]
diabolic, [acyclic]
diabolical, [acoustical]
diabolism, [abolitionism]
diaconate, [acuminate]
diacritical, [acoustical]
diadem, [apothegm]
diagnose, [adios]
diagnosis, [alkalosis]
diagnostic, [acoustic]
diagnostician, [abbreviation]
diagonal, [abdominal]
diagram, [aerogram]
diagrammatic, [acoustic]
dial, [aisle]
dialect, [abject]
dialectic, [acoustic]
dialectical, [acoustical]
dialogical, [acoustical]
dialogue, [agog]
dialysis, [alkalosis]
diameter, [abductor]
diametrically, [ably]
diamond, [almond]
diaper, [barkeeper]

diaphone, [alone]
diaphoresis, [alkalosis]
diaphragm, [aerogram]
diarrhea, [abulia]
diary, [accessory]
diaspora, [abracadabra]
diatribe, [ascribe]
dibble, [able]
dibs, nibs, spareribs
dice, [advice]
dicey, [absorbancy]
dichotomist, [adjust]
dichotomous, [allonymous]
dichotomy, [academy]
dicker, [acre]
dickey, [achy]
Dictaphone, [alone]
dictate, [acetate]
dictation, [abbreviation]
dictator, [abductor]
dictatorial, [abaxial]
dictatorship, [airship]
diction, [abbreviation]
dictionary, [accessory]
dictum, [accustom]
did, [amid]
didactic, [acoustic]
didactics, [administratrix]
diddle, [antipodal]
diddly, [ably]
dido, [aficionado]
die, [airdry]
diehard, [backyard]
diesel, [apostle]
diet, [adequate]
dietary, [accessory]
dietetic, [acoustic]
dietetics, [acoustics]
dietitian, [abbreviation]

differ, [buffer]
difference, [circumference]
different, [aberrant]
differential, [abbatial]
differentiation, [abbreviation]
difficile, [anneal]
difficult, [adult]
difficulty, [abatis]
diffidence, [abhorrence]
diffident, [abundant]
diffraction, [abbreviation]
diffuse, [abuse]
diffusion, [abrasion]
dig, [big]
digamy, [academy]
digest, [abreast]
digestible, [able]
digestive, [ablative]
digit, [adequate]
digital, [accidental]
digitalis, [acropolis]
digitalization, [abbreviation]
digitize, [absolutize]
dignified, [abide]
dignify, [amplify]
dignitary, [accessory]
dignity, [abatis]
digress, [acquiesce]
digression, [abbreviation]
dike, [alike]
dilapidate, [accommodate]
dilapidated, [abluted]
dilatation, [abbreviation]
dilate, [ablate]
dilated, [abluted]
dilation, [abbreviation]
dilatory, [accessory]
dilemma, [anathema]
dilettante, [avaunt]

diligence, [abhorrence]
diligent, [agent]
dill, [backfill]
dilly, [ably]
dillydally, [ably]
dilute, [acute]
dilution, [abbreviation]
dim, [acronym]
dime, [airtime]
dimension, [abbreviation]
dimensional, [aboriginal]
dimeter, [abductor]
diminish, [abolish]
diminutive, [ablative]
dimmer, [armor]
dimorphic, [anthropomorphic]
dimple, [ample]
dimwit, [acquit]
din, [akin]
dine, [aerodyne]
diner, [afterburner]
dinette, [bassinet]
ding, [anything]
ding-a-ling, [anything]
dingbat, [acrobat]
dingdong, [agelong]
dinger, [agar]
dinghy, [buoy]
dingle, [angle]
dingy, [allergy]
dink, [bethink]
dinky, [achy]
dinner, [afterburner]
dinnertime, [airtime]
dinnerware, [affair]
dinosaur, [abhor]
dint, [blueprint]
diocese, [alkalosis]
dip, [airstrip]

diphtheria, [abulia]
diphthong, [agelong]
diploma, [anathema]
diplomacy, [absorbancy]
diplomat, [acrobat]
diplomate, [acclimate]
diplomatic, [acoustic]
dipper, [barkeeper]
dipsomania, [abulia]
dipstick, [acoustic]
dire, [acquire]
direct, [abject]
directed, [abluted]
direction, [abbreviation]
directional, [abdominal]
directive, [ablative]
directly, [ably]
director, [abductor]
directorate, [accurate]
directorship, [airship]
directory, [accessory]
directress, [actress]
direful, [apocryphal]
dirge, [converge]
dirigible, [able]
dirk, [artwork]
dirndl, [antipodal]
dirtbag, [ag]
dirty pool, [bascule]
dirty, [abatis]
disability, [abatis]
disable, [able]
disabled, [bedraggled]
disadvantage, [acknowledge]
disaffect, [abject]
disaffected, [abluted]
disaffiliate, [create]
disaffirm, [affirm]
disagree, [accessory]

disagreeable, [able]
disagreement, [abandonment]
disallow, [allow]
disappear, [adhere]
disappearance, [abhorrence]
disappoint, [anoint]
disappointed, [abluted]
disappointment,
  [abandonment]
disapproval, [adjectival]
disapprove, [approve]
disarm, [alarm]
disarmament, [abandonment]
disarray, [affray]
disassemble, [able]
disaster, [administer]
disastrous, [actress]
disavow, [allow]
disband, [ampersand]
disbar, [abattoir]
disbelief, [aperitif]
disbelieve, [achieve]
disburse, [adverse]
disbursement, [abandonment]
disc, [asterisk]
discard, [backyard]
discern, [adjourn]
discernible, [able]
discernment, [abandonment]
discharge, [barge]
disciple, [ample]
discipleship, [airship]
disciplinable, [able]
disciplinarian, [abecedarian]
disciplinary, [accessory]
discipline, [akin]
disciplined, [abscind]
discipliner, [afterburner]
disclaim, [acclaim]

disclaimer, [armor]
disclose, [airhose]
disclosure, [admeasure]
disco, [alfresco]
discolor, [angler]
discoloration, [abbreviation]
discombobulate, [ablate]
discomfit, [adequate]
discomfort, [advert]
disconnect, [abject]
disconnected, [abluted]
disconsolate, [aglet]
discontent, [accent]
discontinuance, [abhorrence]
discontinue, [accrue]
discontinuity, [abatis]
discontinuous, [ambiguous]
discord, [award]
discordant, [accordant]
discotheque, [afterdeck]
discount, [account]
discourage, [abridge]
discouragement,
  [abandonment]
discourse, [coarse]
discourteous, [abstemious]
discover, [achiever]
discovery, [accessory]
discredit, [adequate]
discreet, [accrete]
discrepancy, [absorbancy]
discrepant, [abeyant]
discrete, [accrete]
discretion, [abbreviation]
discretionary, [accessory]
discriminate, [abominate]
discrimination,
  [abbreviation]
discriminatory, [accessory]

discus, [abacus]
discuss, [abacus]
discussable, [able]
discussion, [abbreviation]
disdain, [abstain]
disdainful, [apocryphal]
disease, [antifreeze]
disembark, [aardvark]
disembody, [acidy]
disembroil, [broil]
disengage, [age]
disentangle, [angle]
disfavor, [achiever]
disfigure, [ballplayer]
disgrace, [abase]
disgruntle, [accidental]
disguise, [advise]
disgust, [adjust]
dish, [abolish]
disharmonious, [abstemious]
disharmony, [abalone]
dishearten, [anchorperson]
dishevel, [adjectival]
dishonest, [adjust]
dishonesty, [abatis]
dishonor, [afterburner]
dishonorable, [able]
dishrag, [ag]
dishware, [affair]
dishwasher, [acupressure]
dishy, [banshee]
disillusion, [abrasion]
disinclined, [affined]
disinfect, [abject]
disinfectant, [abirritant]
disinflation, [abbreviation]
disinflationary, [accessory]
disinformation, [abbreviation]
disingenuous, [ambiguous]

disinherit, [accurate]
disintegrate, [accelerate]
disintegration, [abbreviation]
disinterest, [adjust]
disinterested, [abluted]
disinvest, [abreast]
disinvestment, [abandonment]
disjointed, [abluted]
disjunct, [adjunct]
disjunction, [abbreviation]
disjunctive, [ablative]
disk, [asterisk]
diskette, [abet]
dislike, [alike]
dislocate, [abdicate]
dislocation, [abbreviation]
dislodge, dodge, garage,
  hodgepodge, lodge, stodge
disloyal, [broil]
dismal, [abnormal]
dismantle, [accidental]
dismay, [agape]
dismember, [amber]
dismiss, [abyss]
dismissal, [apostle]
dismount, [account]
Disneyland, [ampersand]
disobedience, [abhorrence]
disobedient, [abeyant]
disobey, [agape]
disorder, [adder]
disorganize, [agnize]
disorient, [accent]
disown, [alone]
disparage, [abridge]
disparate, [accurate]
dispassion, [abbreviation]
dispassionate, [acuminate]
dispatch, [armpatch]

dispatcher, [acupuncture]
dispel, [bagatelle]
dispensable, [able]
dispensary, [accessory]
dispensation, [abbreviation]
dispensational, [abdominal]
dispense, [cense]
dispensed, [against]
dispenser, [aggressor]
disperse, [adverse]
dispersion, [abrasion]
dispirited, [abluted]
displace, [abase]
displacement, [abandonment]
display, [airplay]
displease, [antifreeze]
displeasure, [admeasure]
disposable, [able]
disposal, [appraisal]
dispose, [airhose]
disposition, [abbreviation]
dispossess, [acquiesce]
disproportion, [abbreviation]
disproportionate, [acuminate]
disprove, [approve]
disputable, [able]
disputation, [abbreviation]
dispute, [acute]
disqualification, [abbreviation]
disqualify, [amplify]
disquiet, [adequate]
disregard, [backyard]
disrepair, [affair]
disreputable, [able]
disrepute, [acute]
disrespect, [abject]
disrespectability, [abatis]
disrespectable, [able]
disrobe, [bathrobe]

disrupt, [abrupt]
disruptive, [ablative]
dissatisfaction, [abbreviation]
dissatisfactory, [accessory]
dissatisfied, [abide]
dissect, [abject]
dissection, [abbreviation]
dissemble, [able]
disseminate, [abominate]
disseminated, [abluted]
dissension, [abbreviation]
dissent, [accent]
dissertation, [abbreviation]
disservice, [antibias]
dissever, [achiever]
dissidence, [abhorrence]
dissident, [abundant]
dissimilar, [angler]
dissimilation, [abbreviation]
dissimulate, [ablate]
dissimulation, [abbreviation]
dissipate, [anticipate]
dissipated, [abluted]
dissipation, [abbreviation]
dissoluble, [able]
dissolute, [acute]
dissolution, [abbreviation]
dissolve, [absolve]
dissonance, [abhorrence]
dissonant, [abstinent]
dissuade, [abrade]
distaff, [allograph]
distance, [abhorrence]
distant, [abirritant]
distaste, [abased]
distasteful, [apocryphal]
distemper, [barkeeper]
distill, [backfill]
distillate, [ablate]

distillation, [abbreviation]
distiller, [angler]
distinct, extinct, indistinct,
   instinct, linked, precinct,
   succinct, unlinked
distinction, [abbreviation]
distinctive, [ablative]
distinguish, [abolish]
distort, [abort]
distortion, [abbreviation]
distract, [abstract]
distracted, [abluted]
distraction, [abbreviation]
distrain, [abstain]
distraught, [aeronaut]
distress, [acquiesce]
distressed, [abreast]
distressful, [apocryphal]
distribute, [acute]
distributed, [abluted]
distribution, [abbreviation]
distributive, [ablative]
distributor, [abductor]
district, [addict]
distrust, [adjust]
distrustful, [apocryphal]
disturb, [adverb]
disturbance, [abhorrence]
disunion, [antiunion]
disunite, [affright]
disunity, [abatis]
disuse, [amuse]
disutility, [abatis]
ditch, [backstitch]
ditchdigger, [agar]
dither, [altogether]
ditto, [aggiornamento]
ditty, [abatis]
ditz, [blitz]

diuretic, [acoustic]
diurnal, [abdominal]
diva, [alfalfa]
divagate, [abnegate]
divagation, [abbreviation]
divan, [adman]
divaricate, [abdicate]
divarication, [abbreviation]
dive, [alive]
diver, [achiever]
diverge, [converge]
divergence, [abhorrence]
divergent, [agent]
diverse, [adverse]
diversification, [abbreviation]
diversified, [abide]
diversify, [amplify]
diversion, [abbreviation]
diversity, [abatis]
divert, advert]
divest, [abreast]
divestiture, [abjure]
divestment, [abandonment]
divide, [abide]
divided, [absentminded]
dividend, [addend]
divider, [adder]
divination, [abbreviation]
divine, [aerodyne]
diviner, [afterburner]
divinity, [abatis]
divisible, [able]
division, [abrasion]
divisive, [abrasive]
divisiveness, [agribusiness]
divisor, [adviser]
divorce, [coarse]
divorcee, [absorbancy]
divot, [adequate]

divulge, [bulge]
divvy, [anchovy]
dizzy, [advisee]
djellabah, [alfalfa]
do, [noun] [aficionado]
do, [verb] [accrue]
dobbin, [anchorperson]
dobby, [abbey]
doc, [aftershock]
docent, [adjacent]
docetic, [acoustic]
docile, [apostle]
dock, [aftershock]
dockage, [acknowledge]
docker, [acre]
docket, [advocate]
dockhand, [ampersand]
dockmaster, [administer]
dockyard, [backyard]
doctor, [abductor]
doctoral, [admiral]
doctorate, [accurate]
doctrinaire, [affair]
doctrinal, [abdominal]
docudrama, [anathema]
document, [abandonment]
documentarian, [abecedarian]
documentary, [accessory]
documentation, [abbreviation]
dodder, [adder]
dodge, [dislodge]
dodger, [armiger]
dodgy, [allergy]
dodo, [aficionado]
doe, [aficionado]
doer, [arbitrager]
does, [abuzz]
doff, [boff]
dog, [agog]

dogcatcher, [acupuncture]
dogfight, [affright]
dogged, [acid]
doggerel, [admiral]
doggery, [accessory]
doggish, [abolish]
doggone, [amazon]
doggy, [aggie]
doghouse, [alehouse]
dogleg, [beg]
dogma, [anathema]
dogmatic, [acoustic]
dogmatics, [acoustics]
dogmatism, [abolitionism]
dogmatist, [absolutist]
dogsled, [abed]
dogtrot, [aeronaut]
doily, [ably]
dojo, [airshow]
dolce, [agape]
dole, [areole]
doleful, [apocryphal]
dolesome, [adventuresome]
doll, [aerosol]
dollar, [angler]
dollhouse, [alehouse]
dollop, [backup]
dolly, [ably]
dolor, [angler]
dolorous, [actress]
dolt, [bolt]
domain, [abstain]
dome, [astrodome]
domestic, [acoustic]
domesticate, [abdicate]
domestication, [abbreviation]
domical, [acoustical]
domicile, [anile]
dominance, [abhorrence]

dominant, [abstinent]
dominate, [abominate]
domination, [abbreviation]
dominatrix, [administratrix]
domineer, [adhere]
dominical, [acoustical]
dominion, [antiunion]
domino, [albino]
don, [amazon]
donate, [abominate]
donation, [abbreviation]
donator, [abductor]
donee, [abalone]
donkey, [achy]
donnicker, [acre]
donnybrook, [bankbook]
donor, [afterburner]
donut, [acuminate]
doodad, [ad]
doodle, [antipodal]
doodlebug, [bedbug]
doodoo, [accrue]
doofus, [amorphous]
doohickey, [achy]
doom, [abloom]
doomful, [apocryphal]
doomsayer, [ballplayer]
doomsday, [agape]
doomsdayer, [ballplayer]
doomy, [academy]
door, [abhor]
doorbell, [bagatelle]
doorjamb, [aerogram]
doorkeeper, [barkeeper]
doorknob, [ab]
doorman, [adman]
doormat, [acrobat]
doornail, [ail]
doorpost, [aftermost]

doorstep, [crowstep]
doorstop, [agitprop]
doorway, [airway]
doozy, [advisee]
dopamine, [alexandrine]
dope, [antelope]
dopehead, [abed]
dopester, [administer]
dopey, [apocope]
dork, [cork]
dorky, [achy]
dorm, [aswarm]
dormancy, [absorbancy]
dormant, [abandonment]
dormie, [academy]
dormitory, [accessory]
dorp, gorp, warp
dorsal, [apostle]
dory, [accessory]
dosage, [acknowledge]
dose, [adios]
doss, [across]
dossier, [agape]
dot, [aeronaut]
dotage, [acknowledge]
dotal, [accidental]
dotard, [absurd]
dote, [afloat]
doth, [altazimuth]
dottle, [accidental]
dotty, [abatis]
double take, [awake]
double, [able]
double-barreled, [bedraggled]
double-blind, [affined]
double-breasted, [abluted]
double-check, [afterdeck]
double-cross, [across]
double-crossed, [accost]

double-date, [accommodate]
double-decker, [acre]
double-digit, [adequate]
double-dipper, [barkeeper]
doubleheader, [adder]
double-jointed, [abluted]
doublespeak, [antique]
doubletalk, [aftershock]
double-team, [abeam]
double-think, [bethink]
doubletime, [airtime]
double-wide, [abide]
doubt, [about]
doubter, [abductor]
doubtful, [apocryphal]
doubtless, [acropolis]
douce, [abstruse]
douceur, [aggressor]
douche, [cartouche]
dough, [aficionado]
doughnut, [acuminate]
doughty, [abatis]
doughy, [buoy]
dour, [airpower]
douse, [alehouse]
doux, [accrue]
dove, [noun] [above]
dove, [verb] [alcove]
dovetail, [blackmail]
dovish, [abolish]
dowager, [armiger]
dowdy, [acidy]
dowel, [agile]
dower, [airpower]
down, [boomtown]
downbeat, [accrete]
downburst, [athirst]
downcast, [aghast]
downcourt, [airport]

downdraft, [abaft]
downer, [afterburner]
downfall, [aerosol]
downgrade, [abrade]
downhearted, [abluted]
downhill, [backfill]
downlink, [bethink]
download, [abode]
downplay, [airplay]
downpour, [abhor]
downrange, [arrange]
downright, [affright]
downriver, [achiever]
downscale, [blackmail]
downshift, [adrift]
downside, [abide]
downslide, [abide]
downslope, [antelope]
downspout, [about]
downstage, [age]
downstairs, [backstairs]
downstate, [acetate]
downstream, [abeam]
downstroke, [artichoke]
downtime, [airtime]
downtown, [boomtown]
downtrend, [addend]
downtrodden, [anchorperson]
downturn, [adjourn]
downward, [absurd]
downwash, [awash]
downwind, [abscind]
downy, [abalone]
dowry, [accessory]
dowse, [arouse]
doxology, [allergy]
doyenne, [antiunion]
doze, [airhose]
dozen, [anchorperson]

dozy, [advisee]
drab, [backstab]
drabble, [able]
drachma, [anathema]
draconian, [abecedarian]
draconic, [allergenic]
draft, [abaft]
draftsman, [abdomen]
drafty, [abatis]
drag, [ag]
dragger, [agar]
draggle, [angle]
draggy, [aggie]
dragline, [airline]
dragnet, [bassinet]
dragon, [bandwagon]
dragoon, [afternoon]
dragster, [administer]
drain, [abstain]
drainage, [appanage]
drainpipe, [airpipe]
drake, [awake]
drama, [anathema]
dramatic, [acoustic]
dramatical, [acoustical]
dramatization, [abbreviation]
dramatize, [absolutize]
dramaturgy, [allergy]
dramedy, [acidy]
drank, [bank]
drape, [agape]
drapery, [accessory]
drastic, [acoustic]
drat, [acrobat]
draw, [aah]
drawback, [aback]
drawbar, [abattoir]
drawbridge, [abridge]
drawdown, [boomtown]

drawee, [colloquy]
drawer, [arbitrager]
drawknife, [afterlife]
drawl, [aerosol]
drawn, [amazon]
drawnwork, [artwork]
drawplate, [ablate]
drawtube, [boob]
dray, [affray]
drayage, [acknowledge]
dread, [abed]
dreadful, [apocryphal]
dreadlock, [aftershock]
dream, [abeam]
dreamboat, [afloat]
dreamer, [armor]
dreamland, [ampersand]
dreamt, [attempt]
dreamworld, [afterworld]
dreamy, [academy]
dreary, [accessory]
dreck, [afterdeck]
dredge, [allege]
dreg, [beg]
dreidel, [antipodal]
drench, [bench]
dress suit, [backup]
dress, [acquiesce]
dressage, [arbitrage]
dressed, [abreast]
dresser, [aggressor]
dressmaker, [acre]
dressy, [absorbancy]
drew, [accrue]
drib, [bib]
dribble, [able]
driblet, [aglet]
drier, [amplifier]
drift, [adrift]

driftage, [acknowledge]
drifter, [abductor]
driftwood, [adulthood]
drill, [backfill]
drillmaster, [administer]
drink, [bethink]
drinker, [acre]
drip, [airstrip]
drippy, [apocope]
drive, [alive]
driveby, [alibi]
drivel, [adjectival]
driveline, [airline]
driven, [antiphon]
driver, [achiever]
driveshaft, [abaft]
drivetrain, [abstain]
driveway, [airway]
drizzle, [appraisal]
droit, [adroit]
droll, [areole]
drollery, [accessory]
drone, [alone]
drool, [bascule]
droop, [coop]
droopy, [apocope]
drop, [agitprop]
dropkick, [acidic]
droplet, [aglet]
droplight, [affright]
dropout, [about]
dropper, [barkeeper]
dropsy, [absorbancy]
dross, [across]
drought, [about]
drove, [alcove]
drown, [boomtown]
drowse, [arouse]
drowsy, [advisee]

drub, [backrub]
drudge, [adjudge]
drudgery, [accessory]
drug, [bedbug]
drugget, [agate]
druggie, [aggie]
drugmaker, [acre]
drugstore, [abhor]
druid, [amid]
druidism, [abolitionism]
drum, [addendum]
drumbeat, [accrete]
drumfire, [acquire]
drumhead, [abed]
drummer, [armor]
drumroll, [areole]
drumstick, [acoustic]
drunk, [bohunk]
drunkard, [absurd]
drunken, [awaken]
druthers, [bonkers]
dry, [airdry]
dry-clean, [alexandrine]
dry-dock, [aftershock]
dryer, [amplifier]
dryland, [ampersand]
drylot, [aeronaut]
dry-rot, [aeronaut]
drywall, [aerosol]
dual, [bascule]
dualism, [abolitionism]
dub, [backrub]
dubious, [abstemious]
ducat, [advocate]
duce, [agape]
duchess, [antibias]
duchy, [blotchy]
duck, [amok]
duckboard, [aboard]

duckpin, [akin]
ducktail, [blackmail]
duckwalk, [aftershock]
ducky, [achy]
duct, [abduct]
ductile, [accidental]
ductule, [bascule]
ductwork, [artwork]
dud, [absentminded]
dude, [allude]
dudeen, [alexandrine]
dudgeon, [allergen]
due, [accrue]
duel, [accrual]
duende, [agape]
duenna, [alumna]
duet, [abet]
duff, [bluff]
duffer, [buffer]
dug, [bedbug]
dugout, [about]
duke, [archduke]
dulcet, [corset]
dulcify, [amplify]
dulcimer, [armor]
dull, [agile]
dullard, [absurd]
dullsville, [backfill]
dully, [ably]
duma, [anathema]
dumb, [addendum]
dumbbell, [bagatelle]
dumbfound, [abound]
dumbhead, [abed]
dumbstruck, [amok]
dumbwaiter, [abductor]
dumdum, [addendum]
dumka, [angelica]
dummy, [academy]

dump, [bump]
dumpy, [apocope]
dunce, [abhorrence]
dune, [afternoon]
dung, [among]
dungaree, [accessory]
dungeon, [allergen]
dunghill, [backfill]
dunk, [bohunk]
dunkerhead, [abed]
dunnage, [appanage]
duo, [airshow]
duodecimal, [abnormal]
duologue, [agog]
duomo, [airshow]
duopoly, [ably]
dupe, [coop]
duple, [ample]
duplex, [annex]
duplexer, [aggressor]
duplicate, **[adjective]**
  [advocate]
duplicate, **[verb]** [abdicate]
duplication, [abbreviation]
duplicator, [abductor]
duplicity, [abatis]
durable, [able]
durables, [annals]
duration, [abbreviation]
durative, [ablative]
duress, [acquiesce]
durst, [athirst]
dusk, husk, musk, tusk
dusky, [achy]
dust, [adjust]
dustbin, [akin]
dustcover, [achiever]
duster, [administer]
dustpan, [adman]

dusty, [abatis]
dutch, [clutch]
dutiful, [apocryphal]
duty, [abatis]
duty-free, [accessory]
duumvir, [achiever]
duvetyn, [alexandrine]
dwell, [bagatelle]
dwelt, [belt]
dwindle, [antipodal]
dyad, [ad]
dyarchy, [achy]
dybbuk, [amok]
dye, [airdry]
dynamic, [academic]
dynamics, [administratrix]
dynamite, [affright]
dynamo, [airshow]
dynasty, [abatis]
dysentery, [accessory]
dysfunction, [abbreviation]
dysgenic, [allergenic]
dyslexia, [abulia]
dyspepsia, [abulia]
dystrophy, [anastrophe]
each, [beach]
eager, [agar]
eagle, [angle]
eaglet, [aglet]
ear, [adhere]
earache, [awake]
eardrop, [agitprop]
eardrum, [addendum]
earful, [apocryphal]
earl, [aswirl]
earlobe, [bathrobe]
earlock, [aftershock]
early, [ably]
earmark, [aardvark]

earmuff, [bluff]
earn, [adjourn]
earnest, [adjust]
earphone, [alone]
earpiece, [afterpiece]
earplug, [bedbug]
earshot, [aeronaut]
earth, [afterbirth]
earthborn, [acorn]
earthbound, [abound]
earthenware, [affair]
earthly, [ably]
earthmover, [achiever]
earthquake, [awake]
earthworm, [affirm]
earthy, [apathy]
earwax, [anthrax]
earwig, [big]
ease, [antifreeze]
easel, [appraisal]
easement, [abandonment]
easier, [anterior]
easily, [ably]
east, [beast]
eastbound, [abound]
eastern, [adjourn]
eastward, [absurd]
easy, [advisee]
eat, [accrete]
eatable, [able]
eatery, [accessory]
eavesdrop, [agitprop]
ebb, [bleb]
ebullience, [abhorrence]
ebullient, [abeyant]
ebullition, [abbreviation]
eccentric, [aleatoric]
ecclesiastical, [acoustical]
ecclesiology, [allergy]

echelon, [amazon]
echo, [alfresco]
éclair, [affair]
éclat, [aah]
eclectic, [acoustic]
eclipse, [apocalypse]
eclogue, [agog]
ecocatastrophe, [anastrophe]
ecology, [allergy]
econometrics, [administratrix]
economic, [academic]
economical, [acoustical]
economics, [administratrix]
economist, [alchemist]
economize, [advise]
economy, [academy]
ecosphere, [adhere]
ecosystem, [accustom]
ecru, [accrue]
ecstasy, [absorbancy]
ecstatic, [acoustic]
ectomorph, [corf]
ectomorphic,
    [anthropomorphic]
ectotherm, [affirm]
ecumenical, [acoustical]
ecumenicity, [abatis]
ecumenism, [abolitionism]
ecumenist, [abolitionist]
eczema, [anathema]
ed, [abed]
eddy, [acidy]
edelweiss, [advice]
edema, [anathema]
edge, [allege]
edger, [armiger]
edgewise, [advise]
edgy, [allergy]
edible, [able]

edict, [addict]
edification, [abbreviation]
edifice, [amorphous]
edify, [amplify]
edit, [adequate]
edition, [abbreviation]
editor, [abductor]
editorial, [abaxial]
editorialist, [aerialist]
editorialize, [actualize]
educable, [able]
educate, [abdicate]
educated, [abluted]
education, [abbreviation]
educator, [abductor]
educe, [abstruse]
edulcorate, [accelerate]
eel, [anneal]
eerie, [accessory]
efface, [abase]
effect, [abject]
effective, [ablative]
effectual, [accrual]
effectuate, [accentuate]
effeminate, [acuminate]
effervescence, [accordance]
effervescent, [adjacent]
effete, [accrete]
efficacious, [adscititious]
efficacy, [absorbancy]
efficiency, [absorbancy]
efficient, [abeyant]
effigy, [allergy]
efflorescence, [accordance]
efflorescent, [adjacent]
effluence, [accordance]
effluent, [accordant]
effluvia, [abulia]
effluvium, [anthurium]

efflux, [afflux]
effort, [advert]
effortless, [acropolis]
effulgence, [abhorrence]
effuse, [amuse]
effusion, [abbreviation]
effusive, [abrasive]
egalitarian, [abecedarian]
egalitarianism, [abolitionism]
egg, [beg]
eggbeater, [abductor]
egghead, [abed]
eggheaded, [absentminded]
eggnog, [agog]
eggplant, [ant]
eggshell, [bagatelle]
ego, [ago]
egocentric, [aleatoric]
egomania, [abulia]
egotism, [abolitionism]
egotist, [absolutist]
egotistical, [acoustical]
egregious, [advantageous]
egress, [acquiesce]
egression, [abbreviation]
eh, [agape]
eidetic, [acoustic]
eidolon, [acetylene]
eighteen, [alexandrine]
eightfold, [ahold]
eighth, faith, interfaith, wraith
eighty, [abatis]
eisegesis, [alkalosis]
either, [altogether]
ejaculate, [ablate]
ejaculation, [abbreviation]
eject, [abject]
ejection, [abbreviation]
ejector, [abductor]

eke, [antique]
elaborate, **[adjective]**
  [accurate]
elaborate, **[verb]** [accelerate]
elan, [amazon]
elapse, [apse]
elastic, [acoustic]
elasticity, [abatis]
elate, [ablate]
elated, [abluted]
elation, [abbreviation]
elbow, [airshow]
elbowroom, [abloom]
elder, [adder]
elderly, [ably]
eldership, [airship]
eldest, [adjust]
eldritch, [backstitch]
elect, [abject]
electable, [able]
election, [abbreviation]
electioneer, [adhere]
elective, [ablative]
electoral, [admiral]
electorate, [accurate]
electric, [aleatoric]
electrical, [acoustical]
electrician, [abbreviation]
electricity, [abatis]
electrocute, [acute]
electrocution, [abbreviation]
electron, [amazon]
electronics, [administratrix]
eleemosynary, [accessory]
elegance, [abhorrence]
elegant, [abeyant]
elegiac, [amok]
elegit, [adequate]
elegy, [allergy]

element, [abandonment]
elemental, [accidental]
elementary, [accessory]
elephant, [abeyant]
elevate, [activate]
elevated, [abluted]
elevation, [abbreviation]
elevator, [abductor]
elf, [bookshelf]
elicit, [corset]
elide, [abide]
eligible, [able]
Elihu, [accrue]
eliminate, [abominate]
elimination, [abbreviation]
elision, [abscission]
elite, [accrete]
elitism, [abolitionism]
elixir, [aggressor]
elkhound, [abound]
ellipse, [apocalypse]
ellipsis, [alkalosis]
elliptical, [acoustical]
elm, helm, overwhelm, realm,
  underwhelm, whelm
elocution, [abbreviation]
elongate, [abnegate]
elongation, [abbreviation]
elope, [antelope]
eloquence, [abhorrence]
eloquent, [abeyant]
elsewhere, [anywhere]
eluant, [abeyant]
eluate, [adequate]
elucidate, [accommodate]
elucidation, [abbreviation]
elucubrate, [accelerate]
elude, [allude]
elusion, [abrasion]

elusive, [abrasive]
elute, [acute]
eluviation, [abbreviation]
e-mail, [blackmail]
emanate, [abominate]
emancipate, [anticipate]
emancipation, [abbreviation]
emarginate, [acuminate]
emasculate, [ablate]
emasculation, [abbreviation]
embalm, [balm]
embankment, [abandonment]
embarcadero, [allegro]
embargo, [ago]
embark, [aardvark]
embarrass, [actress]
embarrassment,
  [abandonment]
embassage, [acknowledge]
embassy, [absorbancy]
embattle, [accidental]
embay, [agape]
embed, [abed]
embedded, [absentminded]
embellish, [abolish]
embellishment,
  [abandonment]
ember, [amber]
embezzle, [appraisal]
embitter, [abductor]
emblaze, [ablaze]
emblazon, [anchorperson]
emblem, [addendum]
emblematic, [acoustic]
embodiment, [abandonment]
embody, [acidy]
embolden, [antiphon]
emboss, [across]
embossed, [accost]

embouchure, [abjure]
embowel, [agile]
embrace, [abase]
embracery, [accessory]
embracive, [abrasive]
embrangle, [angle]
embrasure, [admeasure]
embrittle, [accidental]
embrocation, [abbreviation]
embroider, [adder]
embroidery, [accessory]
embroil, [broil]
embryo, [airshow]
emcee, [absorbancy]
emend, [addend]
emendation, [abbreviation]
emerald, [bedraggled]
emerge, [converge]
emergence, [abhorrence]
emergency, [absorbancy]
emergent, [agent]
emerita, [aorta]
emeritus, [afflatus]
emersion, [abrasion]
emery, [accessory]
emesis, [alkalosis]
emetic, [acoustic]
emic, [academic]
emigrant, [aberrant]
emigrate, [accelerate]
emigration, [abbreviation]
émigré, [affray]
eminence, [abhorrence]
eminent, [abstinent]
emir, [adhere]
emirate, [accurate]
emissary, [accessory]
emission, [abbreviation]
emit, [acquit]

emittance, [accordance]
Emmanuel, [bagatelle]
emmer, [armor]
emollient, [abeyant]
emolument, [abandonment]
emote, [afloat]
emotion, [abbreviation]
emotional, [aboriginal]
emotionalize, [actualize]
emotionless, [acropolis]
empale, [ail]
empathetic, [acoustic]
empathic, [acidic]
empathize, [advise]
empathy, [apathy]
empennage, [arbitrage]
emperor, [adulterer]
empery, [accessory]
emphasis, [alkalosis]
emphasize, [abscise]
emphatic, [acoustic]
emphysema, [anathema]
empire, [acquire]
empiric, [aleatoric]
empirical, [acoustical]
empiricism, [abolitionism]
emplace, [abase]
emplacement, [abandonment]
employ, [ahoy]
employee, [buoy]
employment, [abandonment]
emporium, [anthurium]
empower, [airpower]
empress, [actress]
emprise, [accessorize]
emptiness, [agribusiness]
empty, [abatis]
empurple, [ample]
emulate, [ablate]

emulation, [abbreviation]
emulator, [abductor]
emulsify, [amplify]
emulsion, [abbreviation]
emulsion, [abscission]
en masse, [admass]
enable, [able]
enact, [abstract]
enamel, [abnormal]
enamor, [armor]
encaenia, [alleluia]
encage, [age]
encamp, [aid-de-camp]
encampment, [abandonment]
encapsulate, [ablate]
encapsule, [apostle]
encase, [abase]
enceinte, [ant}
enchain, [abstain]
enchant, [ant]
enchase, [abase]
enchilada, [addenda]
enchiridion, [abecedarian]
encipher, [buffer]
encircle, [acoustical]
enclasp, [clasp]
enclave, [aftershave]
enclitic, [acoustic]
enclose, [airhose]
enclosure, [admeasure]
encode, [abode]
encomiast, [aghast]
encomium, [anthurium]
encompass, [auspice]
encore, [abhor]
encounter, [abductor]
encourage, [abridge]
encouragement,
   [abandonment]

encourager, [armiger]
encroach, [abroach]
encrust, [adjust]
encrypt, [adscript]
encumbrance, [abhorrence]
encyclical, [acoustical]
encyclopedia, [abulia]
encyclopedic, [acidic]
encyst, [assist]
end zone, [alone]
end, [addend]
endanger, [armiger]
endear, [adhere]
endearment, [abandonment]
endeavor, [achiever]
endemic, [academic]
endgame, [acclaim]
endive, [alive]
endnote, [afloat]
endomorph, [corf]
endomorphic,
    [anthropomorphic]
endorse, hobbyhorse, horse,
    remorse, sawhorse,
    studhorse, warhorse,
    workhorse [see also **coarse**]
endorsement, [abandonment]
endow, [allow]
endowment, [abandonment]
endue, [accrue]
endurance, [abhorrence]
endure, [abjure]
enema, [anathema]
enemy, [academy]
energetic, [acoustic]
energize, [advise]
energy, [allergy]
enervate, [activate]
enfold, [ahold]

enforce, [coarse]
enforceable, [able]
enforcer, [aggressor]
engage, [age]
engagement, [abandonment]
engender, [adder]
engine, [allergen]
engineer, [adhere]
enginery, [accessory]
engirdle, [antipodal]
Englishman, [adman]
engraft, [abaft]
engrain, [abstain]
engrave, [aftershave]
engross, [adios]
engrossed, [aftermost]
enhance, [advance]
enhancement, [abandonment]
enhancer, [aggressor]
enigma, [anathema]
enigmatic, [acoustic]
enjambment, [abandonment]
enjoin, [adjoin]
enjoy, [ahoy]
enjoyment, [abandonment]
enkindle, [antipodal]
enlace, [abase]
enlarge, [barge]
enlargement, [abandonment]
enlighten, [anchorperson]
enlightenment,
    [abandonment]
enlist, [aerialist]
enlisted, [abluted]
enlistment, [abandonment]
enmesh, [afresh]
enmity, [abatis]
ennead, [ad]
ennoble, [able]

ennui, [colloquy]
enormity, [abatis]
enormous, [allonymous]
enough, [bluff]
enounce, [announce]
enrage, [age]
enrapture, [acupuncture]
enregister, [administer]
enrich, [backstitch]
enrichment, [abandonment]
enrobe, [bathrobe]
enroll, [areole]
enrollment, [abandonment]
ensconce, [brisance]
ensemble, [able]
enserf, [bodysurf]
ensheathe, [breathe]
enshrine, [aerodyne]
enshroud, [aloud]
ensiform, [aswarm]
ensilage, [acknowledge]
ensile, [aisle]
enslave, [aftershave]
ensnare, [affair]
ensnarl, [barrel]
ensoul, [areole]
ensue, [accrue]
ensure, [abjure]
entail, [ail]
entangle, [angle]
entanglement, [abandonment]
entasis, [abyss]
enter, [abductor]
enterprise, [accessorize]
entertain, [abstain]
entertainer, [afterburner]
entertainment, [abandonment]
enthrall, [aerosol]
enthrone, [alone]

enthuse, [amuse]
enthusiasm, [abolitionism]
enthusiast, [adjust]
enthusiast, [aghast]
enthusiastic, [acoustic]
entice, [advice]
enticed, [antichrist]
entire, [acquire]
entitle, [accidental]
entitlement, [abandonment]
entity, [abatis]
entomb, [abloom]
entourage, [arbitrage]
entrain, [abstain]
entrance, [abhorrence]
entrap, [afterclap]
entrapment, [abandonment]
entreat, [accrete]
entrechat, [aah]
entrée, [affray]
entremets, [agape]
entrench, [bench]
entrepreneur, [afterburner]
entrepreneurship, [airship]
entropy, [apocope]
entrust, [adjust]
entry, [accessory]
entryway, [airway]
entwine, [aerodyne]
enumerable, [able]
enumerate, [accelerate]
enumeration, [abbreviation]
envelop, [backup]
envelope, [antelope]
enviable, [able]
envious, [abstemious]
environment, [abandonment]
environmentalism,
  [abolitionism]

environmentalist, [adjust]
environs, sowens, summons
envisage, [acknowledge]
envision, [abrasion]
envoy, [ahoy]
envy, [anchovy]
enzyme, [airtime]
epergne, [adjourn]
epexegesis, [alkalosis]
ephemeral, [admiral]
ephod, [abroad]
epic, [acidic]
epical, [acoustical]
epicene, [alexandrine]
epicenter, [abductor]
epicontinental, [accidental]
epicure, [abjure]
epicycle, [acoustical]
epidemic, [academic]
epigone, [alone]
epigram, [aerogram]
epigraph, [allograph]
epilation, [abbreviation]
epilepsy, [absorbancy]
epileptic, [acoustic]
epilogue, [agog]
epiphany, [abalone]
episcopal, [ample]
episcopate, [adequate]
episode, [abode]
episodic, [acidic]
epistemology, [allergy]
epistle, [apostle]
epistolary, [accessory]
epitaph, [allograph]
epithet, [abet]
epitome, [academy]
epitomize, [advise]
epoch, [amok]

epochal, [acoustical]
epode, [abode]
eponym, [acronym]
eponymy, [academy]
epopee, [apocope]
epos, [across]
epoxy, [absorbancy]
epsilon, [amazon]
equal, [agile]
equality, [abatis]
equalization, [abbreviation]
equalize, [actualize]
equalizer, [adviser]
equanimity, [abatis]
equate, [accentuate]
equation, [abrasion]
equator, [abductor]
equatorial, [abaxial]
equestrian, [abecedarian]
equidistant, [abirritant]
equilateral, [admiral]
equilibrate, [accelerate]
equilibrium, [anthurium]
equinox, [bandbox]
equip, [airstrip]
equipment, [abandonment]
equipoise, [counterpoise]
equitable, [able]
equity, [abatis]
equivalence, [abhorrence]
equivalency, [absorbancy]
equivalent, [ambivalent]
equivocal, [acoustical]
equivocate, [abdicate]
era, [abracadabra]
eradicate, [abdicate]
erase, [abase]
ere, [anywhere]
erect, [abject]

erection, [abbreviation]
ergonomics, [administratrix]
eristic, [acoustic]
erode, [abode]
erogenous, [agribusiness]
eros, [across]
erosion, [abrasion]
erotic, [acoustic]
erotica, [angelica]
eroticism, [abolitionism]
err, [arbitrager]
errancy, [absorbancy]
errand, [almond]
errant, [aberrant]
errata, [aorta]
erratic, [acoustic]
erroneous, [abstemious]
error, [adulterer]
erstwhile, [anile]
eruct, [abduct]
erudite, [affright]
erudition, [abbreviation]
erupt, [abrupt]
eruption, [abbreviation]
escalade, [abrade]
escalate, [ablate]
escalator, [abductor]
escapade, [abrade]
escape, [agape]
escapee, [apocope]
escapist, [activist]
escargot, [ago]
eschatological, [acoustical]
eschatology, [allergy]
eschew, [accrue]
escort, [abort]
escrow, [allegro]
esculent, [ambivalent]
esophagus, [analogous]

esoteric, [aleatoric]
especial, [abbatial]
especially, [ably]
esperance, [abhorrence]
espionage, [arbitrage]
esplanade, [abroad]
espousal, [appraisal]
espouse, [arouse]
espresso, [also]
esprit, [accessory]
esquire, [acquire]
essay, [agape]
essayist, [activist]
essence, [accordance]
essential, [abbatial]
establish, [abolish]
establishment, [abandonment]
estate, [acetate]
esteem, [abeam]
estimate, [noun] [animate]
estimate, [verb] [acclimate]
estimation, [abbreviation]
estimator, [abductor]
estival, [adjectival]
estivate, [activate]
estoppel, [ample]
estrange, [arrange]
estrangement, [abandonment]
estrogen, [allergen]
estuary, [accessory]
etcetera, [abracadabra]
etch, [backstretch]
eternal, [abdominal]
eternity, [abatis]
ethanol, [aerosol]
ether, [altogether]
ethereal, [abaxial]
ethic, [acidic]
ethical, [acoustical]

ethicist, [assist]
ethnic, [allergenic]
ethnicity, [abatis]
ethnocentric, [aleatoric]
ethos, [across]
etiolate, [ablate]
etiology, [allergy]
etiquette, [advocate]
etymology, [allergy]
eucalyptus, [afflatus]
eugenic, [allergenic]
eugenics, [administratrix]
eulogize, [advise]
eulogy, [allergy]
eunuch, [amok]
euphemism, [abolitionism]
euphonious, [abstemious]
euphony, [abalone]
euphoria, [abulia]
euphoriant, [abeyant]
eureka, [angelica]
euthanasia, [abulia]
evacuate, [accentuate]
evacuation, [abbreviation]
evade, [abrade]
evaluate, [accentuate]
evaluation, [abbreviation]
evanesce, [acquiesce]
evanescence, [accordance]
evanescent, [adjacent]
evangel, [agile]
evangelical, [acoustical]
evangelism, [abolitionism]
evangelist, [aerialist]
evangelistic, [acoustic]
evangelization, [abbreviation]
evangelize, [actualize]
evaporate, [accelerate]
evaporation, [abbreviation]

evasion, [abrasion]
evasive, [abrasive]
eve, [achieve]
evening, [anything]
evensong, [agelong]
event, [accent]
eventful, [apocryphal]
eventide, [abide]
events, [abhorrence]
eventual, [accrual]
eventuate, [accentuate]
ever, [achiever]
everglade, [abrade]
evergreen, [alexandrine]
evermore, [abhor]
evert, [advert]
every, [accessory]
everybody, [acidy]
everyday, [agape]
everyone, [antiphon]
everything, [anything]
everywhere, [anywhere]
evict, [addict]
eviction, [abbreviation]
evidenced, [against]
evident, [abundant]
evil, [adjectival]
evince, [convince]
evitable, [able]
evoke, [artichoke]
evolution, [abbreviation]
evolutionary, [accessory]
evolutionist, [abolitionist]
evolve, [absolve]
ewe, [accrue]
ex, [annex]
exacerbate, [abate]
exact, [abstract]
exaggerate, [accelerate]

exaggeration, [abbreviation]
exalt, [asphalt]
exaltation, [abbreviation]
exam, [aerogram]
examination, [abbreviation]
examine, [abdomen]
example, [ample]
exanimate, [animate]
exasperate, [accelerate]
exasperation, [abbreviation]
excavate, [activate]
excavation, [abbreviation]
exceed, [accede]
excel, [bagatelle]
excellence, [abhorrence]
excellency, [absorbancy]
excellent, [ambivalent]
excelsior, [acupressure]
except, [accept]
exception, [abbreviation]
exceptional, [aboriginal]
excess, [access]
excessive, [abrasive]
exchange, [arrange]
exchequer, [acre]
excise tax, [anthrax]
excise, [abscise]
excision, [abrasion]
excitable, [able]
excite, [affright]
excitement, [abandonment]
exclaim, [acclaim]
exclamation, [abbreviation]
exclude, [allude]
exclusion, [abrasion]
exclusive, [abrasive]
excogitate, [acetate]
excommunicate, [abdicate]
excommunication,

[abbreviation]
excoriate, [create]
excrement, [abandonment]
excrete, [accrete]
excretion, [abbreviation]
excruciate, [create]
exculpate, [anticipate]
excursion, [abrasion]
excursive, [abrasive]
excursus, [alkalosis]
excuse, [abstruse]
excuse, [abuse]
execrate, [accelerate]
execute, [acute]
execution, [abbreviation]
executioner, [afterburner]
executive, [ablative]
executor, [abductor]
executrix, [administratrix]
exegesis, [alkalosis]
exegete, [accrete]
exegetical, [acoustical]
exemplar, [abattoir]
exemplify, [amplify]
exemplum, [addendum]
exempt, [attempt]
exemption, [abbreviation]
exenterate, [accelerate]
exercise, [abscise]
exert, [advert]
exertion, [abbreviation]
exhalant, [ambivalent]
exhale, [ail]
exhaust, [accost]
exhaustible, [able]
exhaustive, [ablative]
exhibit, [abbot]
exhibitionism, [abolitionism]
exhibitionist, [abolitionist]

exhibitor, [abductor]
exhilarate, [accelerate]
exhilaration, [abbreviation]
exhort, [abort]
exhortation, [abbreviation]
exhorter, [abductor]
exhume, [abloom]
exigent, [agent]
exile, [anile]
exist, [activist]
existence, [abhorrence]
existent, [abirritant]
existential, [abbatial]
existentialism, [abolitionism]
existentialist, [aerialist]
exit, [apposite]
exocentric, [aleatoric]
exodus, [antibias]
exonerate, [accelerate]
exorbitance, [abhorrence]
exorbitant, [abirritant]
exorcise, [abscise]
exorcism, [abolitionism]
exorcist, [assist]
exosphere, [adhere]
exotic, [acoustic]
expand, [ampersand]
expandable, [able]
expanse, [advance]
expansion, [abbreviation]
expansionism, [abolitionism]
expansionist, [abolitionist]
expansive, [abrasive]
expatiate, [create]
expatriate, [noun] [affiliate]
expatriate, [verb] [create]
expect, [abject]
expectancy, [absorbancy]
expectant, [abirritant]

expectation, [abbreviation]
expectorant, [aberrant]
expectorate, [accelerate]
expedience, [abhorrence]
expediency, [absorbancy]
expedient, [abeyant]
expedite, [affright]
expediter, [abductor]
expedition, [abbreviation]
expeditious, [adscititious]
expel, [bagatelle]
expend, [addend]
expendable, [able]
expenditure, [acupuncture]
expense, [cense]
expensive, [abrasive]
experience, [abhorrence]
experienced, [against]
experiential, [abbatial]
experiment, [abandonment]
experimental, [accidental]
experimentation,
  [abbreviation]
expert, [advert]
expertise, [antifreeze]
expertize, [absolutize]
expiate, [create]
expiation, [abbreviation]
expiration, [abbreviation]
expire, [acquire]
explain, [abstain]
explainable, [able]
explanation, [abbreviation]
explanatory, [accessory]
expletive, [ablative]
explicable, [able]
explicate, [abdicate]
explicit, [corset]
explode, [abode]

exploit, [adroit]
exploitation, [abbreviation]
exploration, [abbreviation]
exploratory, [accessory]
explore, [abhor]
explorer, [adulterer]
explosion, [abrasion]
explosive, [abrasive]
expo, [airshow]
exponent, [abstinent]
exponential, [facial]
export, [airport]
exporter, [abductor]
expose, [noun] [agape]
expose, [verb] [airhose]
exposition, [abbreviation]
expositor, [abductor]
expository, [accessory]
expostulate, [ablate]
exposure, [admeasure]
expound, [abound]
express, [acquiesce]
expression, [abbreviation]
expressionism, [abolitionism]
expressionist, [abolitionist]
expressionless, [acropolis]
expressive, [abrasive]
expresso, [also]
expressway, [airway]
expropriate, [create]
expropriation, [abbreviation]
expulsion, [abbreviation]
expunge, [challenge]
expurgate, [abnegate]
exquisite, [apposite]
exscind, [abscind]
exsiccate, [abdicate]
extant, [abirritant]

extemporaneous,
  [abstemious]
extemporize, [accessorize]
extend, [addend]
extended, [absentminded]
extension, [abbreviation]
extensive, [abrasive]
extent, [accent]
extenuate, [accentuate]
exterior, [anterior]
exterminate, [abominate]
extermination, [abbreviation]
exterminator, [abductor]
external, [abdominal]
externalize, [actualize]
extinct, [distinct]
extinction, [abbreviation]
extinguish, [abolish]
extirpate, [anticipate]
extol, [areole]
extort, [abort]
extortion, [abbreviation]
extortioner, [afterburner]
extra, [abracadabra]
extract, [abstract]
extraction, [abbreviation]
extracurricular, [angler]
extradite, [affright]
extradition, [abbreviation]
extramarital, [accidental]
extraneous, [abstemious]
extraordinary, [accessory]
extrapolate, [ablate]
extrapolation, [abbreviation]
extrasensory, [accessory]
extravagance, [abhorrence]
extravagant, [abeyant]
extravaganza, [alfalfa]
extreme, [abeam]

extremism, [abolitionism]
extremity, [abatis]
extricate, [abdicate]
extrication, [abbreviation]
extrinsic, [airsick]
extroversion, [abbreviation]
extrovert, [advert]
extrude, [allude]
exuberance, [abhorrence]
exuberant, [aberrant]
exuberate, [accelerate]
exude, [allude]
exult, [adult]
exultant, [abirritant]
exultation, [abbreviation]
exurb, [adverb]
exurbia, [abulia]
eye, [airdry]
eyeball, [aerosol]
eyebrow, [allow]
eyedrops, [chops]
eyelash, [abash]
eyelet, [aglet]
eyelid, [amid]
eyeliner, [afterburner]
eyesight, [affright]
eyestrain, [abstain]
eyewear, [affair]
eyewitness, [agribusiness]
fable, [able]
fabled, [bedraggled]
fabric, [aleatoric]
fabricate, [abdicate]
fabrication, [abbreviation]
façade, [abroad]
face, [abase]
facelift, [adrift]
face-off, [boff]
facet, [corset]

facetiae, [buoy]
facetious, [adscititious]
facial, [abbatial]
facile, [apostle]
facilitate, [acetate]
facilitator, [abductor]
facility, [abatis]
facsimile, [ably]
fact, [abstract]
faction, [abbreviation]
factious, [adscititious]
factor, [abductor]
factory, [accessory]
factual, [accrual]
faculty, [abatis]
fad, [ad]
fade, [abrade]
fadeaway, [airway]
fag, [ag]
faggot, [agate]
fagot, [agate]
fail, [ail]
fail-safe, [chafe]
failure, [ballplayer]
fain, [abstain]
faint, [acquaint]
fair, [affair]
fairground, [abound]
fairminded, [absentminded]
fairway, [airway]
fairy tale, [ail]
fairy, [accessory]
fairyland, [ampersand]
faith, [eighth]
faithful, [apocryphal]
fajita, [aorta]
fake, [awake]
faker, [acre]
falcate, [abdicate]

falcon, [awaken]
faldstool, [bascule]
fall, [aerosol]
fallacious, [adscititious]
fallacy, [absorbancy]
fallaway, [airway]
fallback, [aback]
fallibility, [abatis]
fallible, [able]
falling, [abattoir]
fallout, [about]
fallow, [afterglow]
falsehood, [adulthood]
falsetto, [aggiornamento]
falsework, [artwork]
falsie, [absorbancy]
falsify, [amplify]
falsity, [abatis]
falter, [abductor]
fame, [acclaim]
familiar, [ballplayer]
familiarity, [abatis]
familiarize, [accessorize]
family, [ably]
famine, [abdomen]
famish, [abolish]
famous, [allonymous]
fan, [adman]
fanatic, [acoustic]
fanatical, [acoustical]
fanciful, [apocryphal]
fancy, [absorbancy]
fanfare, [affair]
fanny, [abalone]
fantabulous, [acropolis]
fantail, [blackmail]
fantasize, [abscise]
fantastic, [acoustic]
fantasy, [absorbancy]

far, [abattoir]
farandole, [areole]
faraway, [airway]
farce, parse, sparse
farceur, [aggressor]
farcical, [acoustical]
fare, [affair]
farewell, [bagatelle]
farina, [alumna]
farm, [alarm]
farmer, [armor]
farmhand, [ampersand]
farmhouse, [alehouse]
farmland, [ampersand]
farmstead, [abed]
farmyard, [backyard]
farrier, [anterior]
farrow, [allegro]
farside, [abide]
farsighted, [abluted]
fart, [apart]
farther, [altogether]
farthermost, [aftermost]
farthest, [adjust]
fascia, [abulia]
fascinate, [abominate]
fascination, [abbreviation]
fascism, [abolitionism]
fascist, [assist]
fashion, [abbreviation]
fashionable, [able]
fast buck, [amok]
fast food, [allude]
fast, [aghast]
fastball, [aerosol]
fasten, [anchorperson]
fastidious, [abstemious]
fast-track, [aback]
fastuous, [ambiguous]

fat cat, [acrobat]
fat, [acrobat]
fatal, [accidental]
fatalism, [abolitionism]
fatalist, [aerialist]
fatalistic, [acoustic]
fatality, [abatis]
fate, [ate]
fateful, [apocryphal]
fathead, [abed]
father, [altogether]
fatherland, [ampersand]
fatherless, [acropolis]
fathom, [algorithm]
fathomless, [acropolis]
fatigue, [blitzkrieg]
fatso, [also]
fatten, [anchorperson]
fatty, [abatis]
fatuous, [ambiguous]
faucet, [corset]
fault, [asphalt]
faultfinder, [adder]
faultless, [acropolis]
faulty, [abatis]
fauna, [alumna]
favor, [achiever]
favorable, [able]
favorite, [accurate]
favoritism, [abolitionism]
fawn, [amazon]
fax, [anthrax]
fay, [agape]
faze, [ablaze]
fear, [adhere]
fearful, [apocryphal]
fearless, [acropolis]
fearsome, [adventuresome]
feasibility, [abatis]

feasible, [able]
feast, [beast]
feat, [accrete]
feather, [altogether]
featherbed, [abed]
featherbrain, [abstain]
featherweight, [accentuate]
feature, [acupuncture]
feces, [antifreeze]
fecund, [almond]
fecundity, [abatis]
fed, [abed]
federal, [admiral]
federalist, [aerialist]
federalize, [actualize]
federate, [adjective] [accurate]
federate, [verb] [accelerate]
federation, [abbreviation]
fedora, [abracadabra]
fee, [anastrophe]
feeble, [able]
feebleminded, [absentminded]
feed, [accede]
feedback, [aback]
feeder, [adder]
feedlot, [aeronaut]
feel, [anneal]
feeler, [angler]
feet, [accrete]
feign, [abstain]
feint, [acquaint]
feisty, [abatis]
felicitate, [acetate]
felicitous, [afflatus]
felicity, [abatis]
feline, [airline]
fell, [bagatelle]
fellate, [ablate]

fellatio, [audio]
fellow, [afterglow]
fellowship, [airship]
felon, [acetylene]
felonious, [abstemious]
felony, [abalone]
felt, [belt]
female, [blackmail]
femininity, [abatis]
feminism, [abolitionism]
fenced, [against]
fend, [addend]
fender, [adder]
fens, [cense]
fermentation, [abbreviation]
fern, [adjourn]
ferocious, [adscititious]
ferocity, [abatis]
ferret, [accurate]
ferry, [accessory]
ferryboat, [afloat]
fertile, [accidental]
fertility, [abatis]
fertilization, [abbreviation]
fertilize, [actualize]
fertilizer, [adviser]
fervent, [abeyant]
fervid, [acid]
fervor, [achiever]
fess, [acquiesce]
fester, [administer]
festival, [adjectival]
festive, [ablative]
festivity, [abatis]
fetal, [accidental]
fetch, [backstretch]
feticide, [abide]
fetid, [abluted]
fetish, [abolish]

fetishism, [abolitionism]
fetter, [abductor]
fettle, [accidental]
fettuccine, [abalone]
fetus, [afflatus]
feud, [allude]
feudal, [antipodal]
feudalism, [abolitionism]
fever, [achiever]
feverish, [abolish]
few, [accrue]
fewer, [airpower]
fey, [agape]
fiancé, [agape]
fiasco, [alfresco]
fiat, [affiliate]
fib, [bib]
fiber, [amber]
fiberboard, [aboard]
fiberglass, [admass]
fibrillate, [ablate]
fibrillation, [abbreviation]
fibroid, [adenoid]
fibrous, [actress]
fickle, [acoustical]
fiction, [abbreviation]
fictional, [aboriginal]
fictionalize, [actualize]
fictitious, [adscititious]
fiddle, [antipodal]
fiddlestick, [acoustic]
fidelity, [abatis]
fidget, [adequate]
fidgety, [abatis]
fiduciary, [accessory]
fie, [airdry]
field, [airfield]
fielder, [adder]
fieldwork, [artwork]

fiend, [archfiend]
fiendish, [abolish]
fierce, pierce
fiery, [accessory]
fiesta, [aorta]
fife, [afterlife]
fifteen, [alexandrine]
fifth, [blacksmith]
fifty, [abatis]
fig, [big]
fight, [affright]
fighter, [abductor]
figment, [abandonment]
figuration, [abbreviation]
figurative, [ablative]
figure, [ballplayer]
figurehead, [abed]
figurine, [alexandrine]
filament, [abandonment]
filar, [angler]
filbert, [advert]
filch, zilch
file, [aisle]
filial, [abaxial]
filiation, [abbreviation]
filibuster, [administer]
filigree, [accessory]
fill, [backfill]
filler, [angler]
fillet, [aglet]
fillip, [backup]
filly, [ably]
film, microfilm
filmmaker, [acre]
filmstrip, [airstrip]
filmy, [academy]
filter, [abductor]
filth, spilth
filthy, [apathy]

filtrate, [accelerate]
filtration, [abbreviation]
fin, [akin]
finagle, [angle]
final, [abdominal]
finale, [ably]
finalist, [aerialist]
finality, [abatis]
finalize, [actualize]
finance, [advance]
financial, [abbatial]
financier, [adhere]
finch, [bullfinch]
find, [affined]
finder, [adder]
fine, [aerodyne]
finery, [accessory]
finesse, [acquiesce]
finest, [adjust]
finger, [agar]
fingerboard, [aboard]
fingerhold, [ahold]
fingernail, [blackmail]
fingerprint, [blueprint]
fingertip, [airstrip]
finicky, [achy]
finis, [agribusiness]
finish, [abolish]
finite, [affright]
finitude, [altitude]
fink, [bethink]
fir, [buffer]
fire alarm, [alarm]
fire, [acquire]
firearm, [alarm]
fireball, [aerosol]
fireballer, [angler]
firebase, [abase]
fireboat, [afloat]

firebomb, [aplomb]
firebox, [bandbox]
firebrand, [ampersand]
firebreak, [awake]
firebug, [bedbug]
firecracker, [acre]
firefight, [affright]
firefighter, [abductor]
firefly, [airdry]
firehouse, [alehouse]
fireman, [abdomen]
fireplace, [abase]
fireplug, [bedbug]
firepower, [airpower]
fireproof, [aloof]
fireside, [abide]
firestorm, [aswarm]
firetrap, [afterclap]
firewater, [abductor]
firewood, [adulthood]
firework, [artwork]
firm, [affirm]
firmament, [abandonment]
first, [athirst]
firstborn, [acorn]
first-class, [admass]
firstfruit, [backup]
firstfruits, [cahoots]
firsthand, [ampersand]
fiscal, [acoustical]
fish, [abolish]
fishbowl, [areole]
fisherman, [abdomen]
fisherwoman, [abdomen]
fishery, [accessory]
fishhook, [bankbook]
fishing pole, [areole]
fishnet, [bassinet]
fishpond, [abscond]

fishtail, [blackmail]
fishy, [banshee]
fission, [anchorperson]
fissure, [acupressure]
fist, [activist]
fistfight, [affright]
fistful, [apocryphal]
fit, [acquit]
fitness, [agribusiness]
fitted, [abluted]
five, [alive]
fivefold, [ahold]
fix, [administratrix]
fixate, [ate]
fixated, [abluted]
fixation, [abbreviation]
fixative, [ablative]
fixture, [acupuncture]
fizz, frizz, his, is, quiz, showbiz, whiz
fizzle, [appraisal]
fjord, [award]
flab, [backstab]
flabbergast, [aghast]
flabby, [abbey]
flaccid, [acid]
flack, [aback]
flag, [ag]
flagellant, [ambivalent]
flagellate, **[adjective]** [aglet]
flagellate, **[verb]** [ablate]
flagellation, [abbreviation]
flagitious, [adscititious]
flagman, [abdomen]
flagpole, [areole]
flagrant, [aberrant]
flagship, [airship]
flagstaff, [allograph]
flagstick, [acoustic]

flail, [ail]
flair, [affair]
flak, [aback]
flake, [awake]
flaky, [achy]
flam, [aerogram]
flambé, [agape]
flambeau, [airshow]
flamboyance, [abhorrence]
flamboyant, [abeyant]
flame, [acclaim]
flamingo, [ago]
flammable, [able]
flan, [adman]
flank, [bank]
flanker, [acre]
flannel, [abdominal]
flap, [afterclap]
flapjack, [aback]
flappable, [able]
flapper, [barkeeper]
flappy, [apocope]
flare, [affair]
flash, [abash]
flashback, [aback]
flashbulb, [bulb]
flashcube, [boob]
flasher, [acupressure]
flashlight, [affright]
flashy, [banshee]
flask, [ask]
flat, [acrobat]
flatbed, [abed]
flatcar, [abattoir]
flatfoot, [ablaut]
flat-footed, [abluted]
flatland, [ampersand]
flat-out, [about]
flatten, [anchorperson]

flatter, [abductor]
flattery, [accessory]
flattop, [agitprop]
flatulence, [abhorrence]
flatulent, [ambivalent]
flatus, [afflatus]
flatware, [affair]
flatwise, [advise]
flaunt, [avaunt]
flavonoid, [adenoid]
flavor, [achiever]
flaw, [aah]
flawless, [acropolis]
flax, [anthrax]
flaxseed, [accede]
flay, [airplay]
flea, [ably]
fleabag, [ag]
fleabite, [affright]
fleck, [afterdeck]
fled, [abed]
fledge, [allege]
flee, [ably]
fleece, [afterpiece]
fleeced, [beast]
fleer, [adhere]
fleet, [accrete]
fleishig, [acidic]
flense, [cense]
flesh, [afresh]
fleshly, [ably]
fleshy, [banshee]
fletcher, [acupuncture]
fleury, [accessory]
flew, [accrue]
flex, [annex]
flexible, [able]
flexion, [abbreviation]
flexor, [aggressor]

flextime, [airtime]
flexuous, [ambiguous]
flexure, [acupressure]
flick, [acyclic]
flicker, [acre]
flier, [amplifier]
flight, [affright]
flighty, [abatis]
flimflam, [aerogram]
flimsy, [advisee]
flinch, [bullfinch]
fling, [anything]
flintlock, [aftershock]
flip side, [abide]
flip, [airstrip]
flippant, [abeyant]
flipper, [barkeeper]
flirt, [advert]
flirtatious, [adscititious]
flit, [acquit]
flitch, [backstitch]
flitter, [abductor]
float, [afloat]
floater, [abductor]
floc, [aftershock]
flocculate, [ablate]
flocculent, [ambivalent]
flocculus, [acropolis]
flock, [aftershock]
floe, [airshow]
flog, [agog]
flood, [acid]
floodgate, [abnegate]
floodlight, [affright]
floodplain, [abstain]
floodwater, [abductor]
floodway, [airway]
flooey, [buoy]
floor, [abhor]

floorboard, [aboard]
floozy, [advisee]
flop, [agitprop]
flophouse, [alehouse]
floppy disk, [asterisk]
floppy, [apocope]
flora, [abracadabra]
floral, [admiral]
florescence, [accordance]
floret, [accurate]
floriculture, [acupuncture]
florid, [acid]
florist, [allegorist]
floss, [across]
flossy, [absorbancy]
flotation, [abbreviation]
flotilla, [a capella]
flotsam, [adventuresome]
flounce, [announce]
flounder, [adder]
flourish, [abolish]
floury, [accessory]
flow, [airshow]
flowchart, [apart]
flower, [airpower]
flowerpot, [aeronaut]
flowery, [accessory]
flown, [alone]
flu, [accrue]
flub, [backrub]
fluctuate, [accentuate]
fluctuation, [abbreviation]
flue, [accrue]
fluency, [absorbancy]
fluent, [abeyant]
fluff, [bluff]
fluffy, [anastrophe]
flugelhorn, [acorn]
fluid, [acid]

fluidity, [abatis]
fluke, [archduke]
fluky, [achy]
flume, [abloom]
flump, [bump]
flung, [among]
flunk, [bohunk]
flunky, [achy]
fluorescence, [accordance]
fluorescent, [adjacent]
fluoridate, [accommodate]
fluoride, [abide]
fluorinate, [abominate]
fluorine, [alexandrine]
fluoroscope, [antelope]
flurry, [accessory]
flush, [airbrush]
fluster, [administer]
flute, [acute]
flutter, [abductor]
flux, [afflux]
fluxion, [abbreviation]
fly, [airdry]
flyaway, [airway]
flyboat, [afloat]
flyboy, [ahoy]
flybridge, [abridge]
flyby, [alibi]
flycatcher, [acupuncture]
flyleaf, [aperitif]
flyman, [abdomen]
flypaper, [barkeeper]
flyswatter, [abductor]
flyweight, [accentuate]
flywheel, [automobile]
foal, [areole]
foam, [astrodome]
foamy, [academy]
fob, [ab]

focal, [acoustical]
focus, [abacus]
fodder, [adder]
foe, [airshow]
fog, [agog]
fogbound, [abound]
foggy, [aggie]
foghorn, [acorn]
fogy, [aggie]
foible, [able]
foil, [broil]
foist, hoist, joist, moist, voiced
fold, [ahold]
foldaway, [airway]
foldboat, [afloat]
folder, [adder]
foldout, [about]
foliage, [acknowledge]
foliate, [affiliate]
foliated, [abluted]
foliation, [abbreviation]
folio, [audio]
folk, [artichoke]
folkish, [abolish]
folklore, [abhor]
folksinger, [arbitrager]
folksy, [absorbancy]
folktale, [blackmail]
folkway, [airway]
follicle, [acoustical]
follow, [afterglow]
follower, [airpower]
followership, [airship]
follow-up, [backup]
folly, [ably]
foment, [abandonment]
fond, [abscond]
fondant, [abundant]
fondle, [antipodal]

fondue, [accrue]
font, [avaunt]
fontina, [alumna]
food, [allude]
foodstuff, [bluff]
foofaraw, [aah]
fool, [bascule]
foolery, [accessory]
foolhardy, [acidy]
foolish, [abolish]
foolishness, [agribusiness]
foolproof, [aloof]
foot, [ablaut]
footage, [acknowledge]
football, [aerosol]
footbath, [aftermath]
footboard, [aboard]
footbridge, [abridge]
footdragger, [agar]
foothill, [backfill]
foothold, [ahold]
footle, [accidental]
footlocker, [acre]
footloose, [abstruse]
footnote, [afloat]
footpad, [ad]
footprint, [blueprint]
footrace, [abase]
footrest, [abreast]
foots, [absorbancy]
footstep, [crowstep]
footstone, [alone]
footstool, [bascule]
footwear, [affair]
footwork, [artwork]
foozle, [appraisal]
fop, [agitprop]
for, [abhor]
forage, [abridge]

forasmuch, [clutch]
foray, [affray]
forbade, [ad]
forbear, [affair]
forbearance, [abhorrence]
forbid, [amid]
forbidden, [anchorperson]
force, [coarse]
forceful, [apocryphal]
forceps, [biceps]
forcible, [able]
ford, [aboard]
Ford, [accord]
fore, [abhor]
forearm, [alarm]
forebear, [affair]
forebode, [abode]
forecast, [aghast]
forecaster, [administer]
forecheck, [afterdeck]
foreclose, [airhose]
foreclosure, [admeasure]
forecourt, [airport]
foredeck, [afterdeck]
forefather, [altogether]
forefinger, [agar]
forefront, [aberrant
forego, [ago]
foregone, [amazon]
foreground, [abound]
forehand, [ampersand]
forehead, [acid]
foreigner, [afterburner]
foreknew, [accrue]
foreknow, [albino]
foreknowledge,
   [acknowledge]
foreknown, [alone]
foreman, [abdomen]

foremost, [aftermost]
forenoon, [afternoon]
forensic, [airsick]
foreordain, [abstain]
foreordination, [abbreviation]
forepart, [apart]
forepaw, [aah]
foreplay, [airplay]
forequarter, [abductor]
forerunner, [afterburner]
foresee, [absorbancy]
foreseeable, [able]
foreseen, [alexandrine]
foreshadow, [aficionado]
foresight, [affright]
foreskin, [akin]
forest, [adjust]
forestall, [aerosol]
forestation, [abbreviation]
forester, [administer]
forestry, [accessory]
foretaste, [abased]
foretell, [bagatelle]
forethought, [aeronaut]
foretold, [ahold]
forever, [achiever]
forevermore, [abhor]
forewarn, [acorn]
forewoman, [abdomen]
foreword, [absurd]
forfeit, [adequate]
forfeiture, [abjure]
forgave, [aftershave]
forger, [armiger]
forgery, [accessory]
forget, [abet]
forgetful, [apocryphal]
forget-me-not, [aeronaut]
forgettable, [able]

forgive, give, live, olive,
    outlive, relive, sheave, sieve
    (see also **ablative**)
forgiveness, [agribusiness]
forgo, [ago]
forgot, [aeronaut]
fork, [cork]
forkball, [aerosol]
forked, [acid]
forklift, [adrift]
forlorn, [acorn]
form, [aswarm]
formal, [abnormal]
formaldehyde, [abide]
formalism, [abolitionism]
formality, [abatis]
formalize, [actualize]
format, [acrobat]
formation, [abbreviation]
formative, [ablative]
former, [armor]
formicary, [accessory]
formidable, [able]
formula, [a capella]
formulate, [ablate]
formulation, [abbreviation]
fornicate, [abdicate]
fornication, [abbreviation]
fornicator, [abductor]
forsake, [awake]
forsook, [bankbook]
forsooth, [booth]
forswear, [affair]
forsworn, [acorn]
fort, [airport]
forta, [aorta]
forte, [agape]
forth, fourth, henceforth, north
forthright, [affright]

fortification, [abbreviation]
fortified, [abide]
fortify, [amplify]
fortissimo, [airshow]
fortitude, [altitude]
fortnight, [affright]
fortress, [actress]
fortuitous, [afflatus]
fortunate, [acuminate]
forty, [abatis]
forum, [addendum]
forward, [absurd]
fossil, [apostle]
foster, [administer]
foster-child, [beguiled]
fought, [aeronaut]
foul, fowl, growl, howl, owl,
    prowl, scowl
foulmouth, [badmouth]
found, [abound]
foundation, [abbreviation]
foundational, [aboriginal]
founder, [adder]
foundry, [accessory]
fount, [account]
fountainhead, [abed]
four, [abhor]
fourfold, [ahold]
fourplex, [annex]
fourscore, [abhor]
foursome, [adventuresome]
foursquare, [affair]
fourteen, [alexandrine]
fourth, [forth]
fowl, [foul]
fox, [bandbox]
foxhole, [areole]
foxhunter, [abductor]
foxtail, [blackmail]

foxy, [absorbancy]
foyer, [ballplayer]
fracas, [abacus]
fraction, [abbreviation]
fractional, [abdominal]
fractionate, [abominate]
fracture, [acupuncture]
fragile, [agile]
fragility, [abatis]
fragment, [abandonment]
fragmentary, [accessory]
fragmentation, [abbreviation]
fragrance, [abhorrence]
fragrant, [aberrant]
frail, [ail]
frailty, [abatis]
frame, [acclaim]
framer, [armor]
framework, [artwork]
franc [bank]
France, [advance]
franchise, [advise]
franchisee, [advisee]
franchiser, [adviser]
frangible, [able]
frank, [bank]
frankfurter, [abductor]
frankincense, [cense]
frantic, [acoustic]
frap, [afterclap]
frappe, [agape]
frass, [admass]
frat, [acrobat]
fraternal, [abdominal]
fraternalism, [abolitionism]
fraternity, [abatis]
fraternization, [abbreviation]
fratricide, [abide]
fraud, [abroad]

fraudulent, [ambivalent]
fraught, [aeronaut]
fraulein, [airline]
fray, [affray]
frazzle, [appraisal]
freak, [antique]
freakish, [abolish]
freckle, [bagatelle]
free, [accessory]
freebase, [abase]
freebie, [abbey]
freeboard, [aboard]
freeborn, [acorn]
freedom, [addendum]
free-fall, [aerosol]
freehand, [ampersand]
freehearted, [abluted]
freehold, [ahold]
freelance, [advance]
freeload, [abode]
freeloader, [adder]
freestyle, [anile]
freethinker, [acre]
freeway, [airway]
freewheel, [anneal]
freewill, [backfill]
freeze, [antifreeze]
freezer, [adviser]
freight, [accelerate]
freightage, [acknowledge]
freighter, [abductor]
fremitus, [afflatus]
french, [bench]
frenetic, [acoustic]
frenzy, [advisee]
frequence, [abhorrence]
frequency, [absorbancy]
frequent, [accent]
fresco, [alfresco]

fresh, [afresh]
freshman, [abdomen]
freshwater, [abductor]
fret, [abet]
fretful, [apocryphal]
Freud, [adenoid]
friable, [able]
friar, [amplifier]
fribble, [able]
fricassee, [absorbancy]
friction, [abbreviation]
fridge, [abridge]
fried, [abide]
friends, [addend]
friendship, [airship]
frier, [amplifier]
frieze, [antifreeze]
frig, [big]
frigate, [agate]
fright, [affright]
frighten, [anchorperson]
frightful, [apocryphal]
frigid, [acid]
frigidity, [abatis]
frigorific, [anthropomorphic]
frijole, [ably]
frill, [backfill]
fringe, [binge]
frisk, [asterisk]
frisket, [advocate]
frisky, [achy]
frisson, [alone]
frittata, [aorta]
fritter, [abductor]
frivol, [adjectival]
frivolity, [abatis]
frivolous, [acropolis]
frizz, [fizz]
frizzle, [appraisal]

frizzy, [advisee]
frock, [aftershock]
frog, [agog]
frogman, [adman]
frolic, [acyclic]
from, [addendum]
front, [aberrant]
front, [aberrant]
frontage, [acknowledge]
frontal, [accidental]
frontier, [adhere]
frontiersman, [abdomen]
frontispiece, [afterpiece]
frontlet, [aglet]
frontline, [airline]
frore, [abhor]
frosh, [awash]
frost, [accost]
frostbit, [acquit]
frostbite, [affright]
frosted, [abluted]
frostwork, [artwork]
frosty, [abatis]
froth, [broadcloth]
frottage, [arbitrage]
froward, [absurd]
frown, [boomtown]
froze, [airhose]
frozen, [anchorperson]
fructify, [amplify]
fructose, [adios]
frugal, [angle]
fruit, [acute]
fruitcake, [awake]
fruitful, [apocryphal]
fruition, [abbreviation]
fruitless, [acropolis]
fruity, [abatis]
frump, [bump]

frumpy, [apocope]
frustrate, [accelerate]
frustration, [abbreviation]
fry, [airdry]
fubsy, [advisee]
fuddle, [antipodal]
fudge, [adjudge]
fuehrer, [adulterer]
fuel, [bascule]
fug, [bedbug]
fugitive, [ablative]
fulcrum, [addendum]
fulfill, [backfill]
fulfillment, [abandonment]
fulgent, [agent]
fulgurant, [aberrant]
fuliginous, [agribusiness]
full house, [alehouse]
full, [apocryphal]
fullback, [aback]
full-blown, [alone]
full-grown, [alone]
fullness, [agribusiness]
full-time, [airtime]
fully, [ably]
fulminate, [abominate]
fulsome, [adventuresome]
fulvous, [antibias]
fumble, [able]
fume, [abloom]
fumigant, [abeyant]
fumigate, [abnegate]
fumigation, [abbreviation]
fumigator, [abductor]
fun, [antiphon]
funambulism, [abolitionism]
function, [abbreviation]
functional, [aboriginal]
fund, [almond]

fundamental, [accidental]
fundamentalism, [abolitionism]
fundamentalist, [aerialist]
funeral, [admiral]
fungicide, [abide]
fungus, [analogous]
funk, [bohunk]
funky, [achy]
funnel, [abdominal]
funny bone, [alone]
funny, [abalone]
funnyman, [adman]
fur, [buffer]
furbish, [abolish]
furcation, [abbreviation]
furious, [abstemious]
furl, [aswirl]
furlong, [agelong]
furlough, [afterglow]
furnace, [agribusiness]
furnish, [abolish]
furniture, [acupuncture]
furor, [abhor]
furrier, [anterior]
furrow, [allegro]
furry, [accessory]
further, [altogether]
furtherance, [abhorrence]
furthermore, [abhor]
furthermost, [aftermost]
furthest, [adjust]
furtive, [ablative]
furuncle, [acoustical]
fury, [accessory]
fuse, [abuse]
fuselage, [arbitrage]
fusillade, [abroad]
fusion, [abrasion]

fuss, [amorphous]
fussbudget, [adequate]
fussy, [absorbancy]
fustigate, [abnegate]
futile, [accidental]
futility, [abatis]
future, [acupuncture]
futurism, [abolitionism]
futurist, [allegorist]
futuristic, [acoustic]
futurity, [abatis]
futurologist, [allergist]
fuzz, [abuzz]
fuzzy, [advisee]
gab, [backstab]
gabardine, [alexandrine]
gabble, [able]
gabby, [abbey]
gabfest, [abreast]
gable, [able]
gad, [ad]
gadabout, [about]
gadarene, [alexandrine]
gadfly, [airdry]
gadget, [adequate]
gaff, [allograph]
gaffer, [buffer]
gag, [ag]
gaga, [aah]
gage, [age]
gaggle, [angle]
gagman, [adman]
gagster, [administer]
gaiety, [abatis]
gain, [abstain]
gainsay, [agape]
gait, [abnegate]
gaiter, [abductor]
gal, [canal]

gala, [a capella]
galactic, [acoustic]
galactorrhea, [abulia]
galaxy, [absorbancy]
gale, [ail]
galilee, [ably]
gall, [aerosol]
gallant, [ant]
gallantry, [ancestry
gallbladder, [adder]]
galleria, [abulia]
gallery, [accessory]
galley, [ably]
gallivant, [ant]
gallon, [acetylene]
gallop, [backup]
gallows, [airhose]
gallstone, [alone]
Gallup, [backup]
gallus, [acropolis]
gally, [ably]
galore, [abhor]
galosh, [awash]
galumph, humph, triumph
galvanic, [allergenic]
galvanize, [agnize]
gam, [aerogram]
gambit, [abbot]
gamble, [able]
game, [acclaim]
gamecock, [aftershock]
gamekeeper, [barkeeper]
gamer, [armor]
gamesmanship, [airship]
gamester, [administer]
gammon, [abdomen]
gander, [adder]
gangbuster, [administer]
gangland, [ampersand]

gangly, [ably]
gangplank, [bank]
gangplow, [allow]
gangrene, [alexandrine]
gangster, [administer]
gangway, [airway]
gantry, [ancestry]
gap, [afterclap]
gape, [agape]
garage, [noun] [arbitrage]
garage, [noun] [dislodge]
garb, [barb]
garbage, [acknowledge]
garbageman, [abdomen]
garbanzo, [bozo]
garble, [able]
garden, [anchorperson]
gardenia, [alleluia]
garderobe, [bathrobe]
gargle, [angle]
gargoyle, [airfoil]
garibaldi, [acidy]
garish, [abolish]
garland, [almond]
garlic, [acyclic]
garment, [abandonment]
garner, [afterburner]
garnet, [acuminate]
garnish, [abolish]
garnishee, [banshee]
garnishment, [abandonment]
garniture, [acupuncture]
garret, [accurate]
garrulity, [abatis]
garrulous, [acropolis]
garter snake, [awake]
garter, [abductor]
garth, hearth
gas, [admass]

gaseous, [abstemious]
gash, [abash]
gasket, [advocate]
gaslight, [affright]
gasohol, [aerosol]
gasoline, [alexandrine]
gasp, [clasp]
gassed, [aghast]
gasser, [aggressor]
gassy, [absorbancy]
gast, [aghast]
gastric, [aleatoric]
gate, [abnegate]
gatekeeper, [barkeeper]
gatepost, [aftermost]
gateway, [airway]
gather, [altogether]
gator, [abductor]
gauche, [brioche]
gaucho, [airshow]
gaudy, [acidy]
gauge, [age]
gaunt, [avaunt]
gauntlet, [aglet]
gauze, [applause]
gavage, [arbitrage]
gave, [aftershave]
gavel, [adjectival]
gawk, [aftershock]
gay, [agape]
gaze, [ablaze]
gazebo, [airshow]
gazelle, [appraisal]
gazette, [abet]
gazpacho, [airshow]
gear, [adhere]
gearbox, [bandbox]
gearshift, [adrift]
gee, [allergy]

geek, [antique]
geese, [afterpiece]
geezer, [adviser]
geisha, [alfalfa]
gel, [bagatelle]
gelatin, [anchorperson]
gelation, [abbreviation]
gelato, [aggiornamento]
geld, handheld, held, meld,
    unparalleled, self-propelled,
    weld, withheld
gelid, [acid]
gem, [apothegm]
geminate, [adjective]
    [acuminate]
geminate, [verb] [abominate]
gemologist, [allergist]
gemology, [allergy]
gemstone, [alone]
gendarme, [alarm]
gender, [adder]
gene pool, [bascule]
gene, [alexandrine]
genealogical, [acoustical]
genealogist, [allergist]
genealogy, [allergy]
general, [admiral]
generalization, [abbreviation]
generalize, [actualize]
generally, [ably]
generate, [accelerate]
generation, [abbreviation]
generator, [abductor]
generic, [aleatoric]
generosity, [abatis]
generous, [actress]
genesis, [alkalosis]
genetic code, [abode]
genetic, [acoustic]

geneticist, [assist]
genetics, [acoustics]
genial, [abaxial]
geniculate, [aglet]
genie, [abalone]
genital, [accidental]
genitalia, [alleluia]
genitals, [annals]
genitive, [ablative]
genius, [antibias]
genocide, [abide]
genre, [abracadabra]
gent, [accent]
genteel, [anneal]
gentile, [anile]
gentility, [abatis]
gentle, [accidental]
gentleman, [abdomen]
gentler, [angler]
gentry, [ancestry]
gents, [cense]
genuflect, [abject]
genus, [agribusiness]
geocentric, [aleatoric]
geodesic, [airsick]
geographic,
 [anthropomorphic]
geographical, [acoustical]
geography, [anastrophe]
geological, [acoustical]
geology, [allergy]
geometric, [aleatoric]
geometrical, [acoustical]
geometry, [ancestry]
geophagy, [allergy]
geophysical, [acoustical]
geopolitical, [acoustical]
geopolitics, [acoustics]
geothermal, [abnormal]

geranium, [anthurium]
gerent, [aberrant]
geriatric, [aleatoric]
germ, [affirm]
germane, [abstain]
germfree, [accessory]
germicidal, [antipodal]
germicide, [abide]
germinal, [aboriginal]
germinate, [abominate]
germination, [abbreviation]
gerontology, [allergy]
gerrymander, [adder]
gerund, [almond]
gestalt, [asphalt]
gestapo, [airshow]
gestation, [abbreviation]
gesticulate, [ablate]
gesticulation, [abbreviation]
gesture, [acupuncture]
gesundheit, [affright]
get, [abet]
getaway, [airway]
getup, [backup]
geyser, [adviser]
ghastly, [ably]
ghetto, [aggiornamento]
ghost, [aftermost]
ghostwrite, [affright]
ghoul, [bascule]
giant, [abeyant]
gibber, [amber]
gibberish, [abolish]
gibbet, [abbot]
gibe, [ascribe]
giddy, [acidy]
gift, [adrift]
gifted, [abluted]
gig, [big]

gigabit, [acquit]
gigabyte, [affright]
gigahertz, hertz, megahertz
gigantic, [acoustic]
giggle, [angle]
gigolo, [afterglow]
gigot, [agate]
gild, [build]
gill, [backfill]
gimlet, [aglet]
gimme, [academy]
gimmick, [academic]
gimmickry, [accessory]
gimp, [blimp]
gin, [akin]
ginger ale, [ail]
ginger, [armiger]
gingerbread, [abed]
gingerly, [ably]
gingersnap, [afterclap]
gingham, [addendum]
gingivitis, [afflatus]
giraffe, [allograph]
girandole, [areole]
gird, [absurd]
girder, [adder]
girdle, [antipodal]
girl, [aswirl]
girlie, [ably]
girlish, [abolish]
giro, [allegro]
girt, [advert]
girth, [afterbirth]
give, [forgive]
giveaway, [airway]
giveback, [aback]
given, [antiphon]
giver, [achiever]
gizmo, [airshow]

gizzard, [absurd]
glacial, [abbatial]
glaciate, [create]
glacier, [acupressure]
glad, [ad]
glade, [abrade]
gladiator, [abductor]
gladiola, [a capella]
glair, [affair]
glamorize, [accessorize]
glamorous, [actress]
glamour,[armor]
glance, [advance]
gland, [ampersand]
glare, [affair]
glasnost, [aftermost]
glass, [admass]
glassmaker, [acre]
glassware, [affair]
glaucoma, [anathema]
glaze, [ablaze]
gleam, [abeam]
glean, [alexandrine]
glee, [ably]
glen, again]
glib, [bib]
glide, [abide]
glider, [adder]
glim, [acronym]
glimmer, [armor]
glint, [blueprint]
glisten, [anchorperson]
glitch, [backstitch]
glitter, [abductor]
glitz, [blitz]
gloat, [afloat]
glob, [ab]
global, [able]
globalism, [abolitionism]

globalist, [aerialist]
globalization, [abbreviation]
globe, [bathrobe]
glom, [aplomb]
gloom, [abloom]
gloomy, [academy]
glop, [agitprop]
glorification, [abbreviation]
glorified, [abide]
glorify, [amplify]
glorious, [abstemious]
glory, [accessory]
gloss, [across]
glossary, [accessory]
glossy, [absorbancy]
glove, [above]
glow, [afterglow]
glucose, [adios]
glue, [accrue]
glum, [addendum]
glut, [aglet]
gluten, [anchorperson]
glutton, [anchorperson]
gluttonous, [agribusiness]
gluttony, [abalone]
gnarl, [barrel]
gnarled, [bedraggled]
gnash, [abash]
gnat, [acrobat]
gnaw, [aah]
gnome, [astrodome]
gnomic, [academic]
gnosis, [alkalosis]
gnostic, [acoustic]
gnosticism, [abolitionism]
go, [ago]
goad, [abode]
goal, [areole]
goalie, [ably]

goalkeeper, [barkeeper]
goalless, [acropolis]
goalpost, [aftermost]
goaltender, [adder]
goat, [afloat]
goatee, [abatis]
gob, [ab]
gobble, [able]
go-between, [alexandrine]
goblet, [aglet]
goblin, [acetylene]
God, [abroad]
godchild, grandchild,
  stepchild, undefiled
goddess, [antibias]
godet, [abet]
godfather, [altogether]
godforsaken, [awaken]
godhead, [abed]
godhood, [adulthood]
godless, [acropolis]
godlike, [alike]
godmother, [altogether]
godparent, [aberrant]
godsend, [addend]
Godspeed, [accede]
gofer, [buffer]
goffer, [buffer]
goggle, [angle]
goiter, [abductor]
gold, [ahold]
goldbrick, [aleatoric]
goldenrod, [abroad]
goldfish, [abolish]
golf shoe, [accrue]
golf, rolf
golly, [ably]
gondola, [a capella]
gone, [amazon]

gong, [agelong]
gonorrhea, [abulia]
gonzo, [bozo]
goo, [accrue]
goober, [amber]
good, [adulthood]
goodness, [agribusiness]
goodwill, [backfill]
goody, [acidy]
gooey, [absorbancy]
gooey, [buoy]
goof, [aloof]
goofball, [aerosol]
goofy, [anastrophe]
gook, [archduke]
goon, [afternoon]
gooney, [abalone]
goop, [coop]
goose egg, [beg]
goose, [abstruse]
gopher, [buffer]
gore, [abhor]
gorgeous, [advantageous]
gorgon, [bandwagon]
gorgonize, [agnize]
gorilla, [a capella]
gormandize, [advise]
gormless, [acropolis]
gorp, [dorp]
gory, [accessory]
gosh, [awash]
gospel, [ample]
gossamer, [armor]
gossip, [backup]
gossiper, [barkeeper]
gossipy, [apocope]
got, [aeronaut]
goulash, [awash]
gourd, [aboard]

gourmand, [abscond]
gourmet, [agape]
gout, [about]
govern, [adjourn]
governess, [access]
governess, [agribusiness]
government, [abandonment]
governor, [afterburner]
gown, [boomtown]
goy, [ahoy]
grab, [backstab]
grabble, [able]
grabby, [abbey]
grace, [abase]
graceful, [apocryphal]
graceless, [acropolis]
gracious, [adscititious]
graciousness, [agribusiness]
grad, [ad]
gradation, [abbreviation]
grade, [abrade]
grader, [adder]
gradient, [abeyant]
gradual, [accrual]
gradualism, [abolitionism]
graduate, [noun and adjective] [adequate]
graduate, [verb] [accentuate]
graduation, [abbreviation]
graft, [abaft]
grail, [ail]
grain, [abstain]
grainfield, [airfield]
grainy, [abalone]
gram, [aerogram]
grammar, [armor]
grammarian, [abecedarian]
grammatical, [acoustical]
gramp, [aid-de-camp]

granary, [accessory]
grand, [ampersand]
grandbaby, [abbey]
grandchild, [brainchild]
granddad, [ad]
granddaughter, [abductor]
grandee, [acidy]
grandeur, [armiger]
grandfather, [altogether]
grandiloquence, [abhorrence]
grandiloquent, [abeyant]
grandiose, [adios]
grandioso, [also]
grandma, [aah]
grandmother, [altogether]
grandpa, [aah]
grandparent, [aberrant]
grandson, [antitoxin]
grandstand, [ampersand]
grange, [arrange]
granger, [armiger]
granita, [aorta]
granite, [acuminate]
granny, [abalone]
granola, [a capella]
grant, [ant]
grantee, [abatis]
grantor, [abductor]
granular, [angler]
granulate, [ablate]
granulation, [abbreviation]
granule, [bascule]
granulose, [adios]
grape, [agape]
grapefruit, [acute]
grapevine, [aerodyne]
graph, [allograph]
grapheme, [abeam]
graphic, [anthropomorphic]

graphical, [acoustical]
graphite, [affright]
grapple, [ample]
grasp, [clasp]
grass, [admass]
grasshopper, [barkeeper]
grassland, [ampersand]
grassroots, [cahoots]
grassy, [absorbancy]
grate, [accelerate]
grateful, [apocryphal]
gratification, [abbreviation]
gratify, [amplify]
gratin, [anchorperson]
gratis, [afflatus]
gratitude, [altitude]
gratuitous, [afflatus]
gratuity, [abatis]
gratulate, [ablate]
gravamen, [abdomen]
grave, [aftershave]
gravel, [adjectival]
gravelly, [ably]
graver, [achiever]
graveside, [abide]
gravestone, [alone]
graveyard, [backyard]
gravid, [acid]
gravida, [addenda]
gravitas, [across]
gravitate, [acetate]
gravitation, [abbreviation]
gravitational, [abdominal]
gravity, [abatis]
gravy, [anchovy]
gray, [affray]
grayish, [abolish]
graze, [ablaze]
grease, [afterpiece]

greasy, [absorbancy]
great, [accelerate]
greater, [abductor]
greathearted, [abluted]
greave, [achieve]
greed, [accede]
greedy, [acidy]
Greek, [antique]
green, [alexandrine]
greenback, [aback]
greenery, [accessory]
greenhorn, [acorn]
greenhouse, [alehouse]
greenish, [abolish]
greenmail, [ail]
greenroom, [abloom]
greenway, [airway]
greet, [accrete]
gregarious, [abstemious]
gremlin, [acetylene]
grenade, [abrade]
grenadine, [alexandrine]
grew, [accrue]
greyhound, [abound]
grid, [amid]
gridder, [adder]
griddle cake, [awake]
griddle, [antipodal]
gridiron, [adjourn]
gridlock, [aftershock]
grief, [aperitif]
grievance, [abhorrence]
grieve, [achieve]
grievous, [antibias]
grift, [adrift]
grig, [big]
grill, [backfill]
grille, [backfill]
grillwork, [artwork]

grim, [acronym]
grimace, [allonymous]
grime, [airtime]
grimy, [academy]
grin, [akin]
grinch, [bullfinch]
grind, [affined]
grinder, [adder]
grindstone, [alone]
gringo, [ago]
grip, [airstrip]
gripe, [airpipe]
grippe, [airstrip]
gripsack, [aback]
grisly, [ably]
grist, [allegorist]
gristle, [apostle]
gristmill, [backfill]
grit, [acquit]
grits, [blitz]
gritty, [abatis]
grizzle, [appraisal]
grizzly, [ably]
groan, [alone]
grocer, [aggressor]
grocery, [accessory]
groggy, [aggie]
groin, [adjoin]
groom, [abloom]
groomsman, [abdomen]
groove, [approve]
groovy, [anchovy]
grope, [antelope]
gross, [adios]
grotesque, [arabesque]
grotto, [aggiornamento]
grouch, [avouch]
grouchy, [blotchy]
ground, [abound]

groundbreaker, [acre]
groundburst, [athirst]
grounder, [adder]
groundless, [acropolis]
groundout, [about]
groundskeeper, [barkeeper]
groundswell, [bagatelle]
groundwater, [abductor]
groundwork, [artwork]
group, [coop]
groupie, [apocope]
groupthink, [bethink]
grouse, [alehouse]
grout, [about]
grove, [alcove]
grovel, [adjectival]
grow, [allegro]
growl, [foul]
grown, [alone]
grown-up, [backup]
growth, [both]
grub, [backrub]
grubby, [abbey]
grubsteak, [awake]
grudge, [adjudge]
gruel, [agile]
gruesome, [adventuresome]
gruff, [bluff]
grumble, [able]
grump, [bump]
grumpy, [apocope]
grungy, [allergy]
grunt, [aberrant]
gruntle, [accidental]
guacamole, [ably]
Guam, [aplomb]
guar, [abattoir]
guarantee, [abatis]
guarantor, [abhor]

guaranty, [abatis]
guard, [backyard]
guarded, [absentminded]
guardhouse, [alehouse]
guardian, [abecedarian]
guardianship, [airship]
guardrail, [blackmail]
guardroom, [abloom]
guardsman, [abdomen]
guava, [alfalfa]
gubernatorial, [abaxial]
guck, [amok]
guerilla, [a capella]
guernsey, [advisee]
guess, [acquiesce]
guesswork, [artwork]
guest, [abreast]
guestimate, [animate]
guff, [bluff]
guffaw, [aah]
guidance, [accordance]
guide, [abide]
guidebook, [bankbook]
guideline, [airline]
guidepost, [aftermost]
guideway, [airway]
guild, [build]
guile, [aisle]
guillotine, [alexandrine]
guilt, [atilt]
guiltless, [acropolis]
guilty, [abatis]
guinea pig, [big]
guise, [advise],
guitar, [abattoir]
guitarist, [allegorist]
gulag, [agog]
gulch, mulch
gull, [angle]

gullet, [aglet]
gullible, [able]
gully, [ably]
gulp, pulp
gum, [addendum]
gumbo, [airshow]
gumdrop, [agitprop]
gummy, [academy]
gumption, [abbreviation]
gumshoe, [accrue]
gun, [bandwagon]
gunboat, [afloat]
gunfight, [affright]
gunfighter, [abductor]
gunfire, [amplifier]
gunk, [bohunk]
gunman, [abdomen]
gunner, [afterburner]
gunnery, [accessory]
gunnysack, [aback]
gunplay, [airplay]
gunpoint, [anoint]
gunpowder, [adder]
gunrunner, [afterburner]
gunship, [airship]
gunshot, [aeronaut]
guppy, [apocope]
gurgle, [angle]
gurney, [abalone]
guru, [accrue]
gush, [airbrush]
gusher, [acupressure]
gushy, [banshee]
gust, [adjust]
gustation, [abbreviation]
gusto, [aggiornamento]
gut, [agate]
gutbucket, [advocate]
gutless, [acropolis]

gutsy, [absorbancy]
gutter, [abductor]
guttural, [admiral]
guy, [airdry]
guzzle, [appraisal]
gym suit, [backup]
gym, [acronym]
gymnasium, [anthurium]
gymnast, [adjust]
gymnastic, [acoustic]
gymnastics, [acoustics]
gynecology, [allergy]
gyp, [airstrip]
gypsum, [adventuresome]
gypsy, [absorbancy]
gyrate, [accelerate]
gyration, [abbreviation]
gyre, [amplifier]
gyro, [allegro]
gyroscope, [antelope]
haberdasher, [acupressure]
haberdashery, [accessory]
habile, [able]
habiliment, [abandonment]
habilitate, [acetate]
habit, [abbot]
habitat, [acrobat]
habitual, [accrual]
habituate, [accentuate]
habituation, [abbreviation]
habitude, [altitude]
hacienda, [addenda]
hack, [aback]
hacker, [acre]
hackle, [acoustical]
hackneyed, [accede]
hacksaw, [aah]
had, [ad]
hag, [ag]

haggard, [absurd]
haggle, [angle]
haiku, [accrue]
hail, [ail]
hailstone, [alone]
hailstorm, [aswarm]
hair, [affair]
hairbrush, [airbrush]
haircut, [advocate]
hairdo, [accrue]
hairdresser, [aggressor]
hairline, [airline]
hairlip, [airstrip]
hairpiece, [afterpiece]
hairpin, [akin]
hairsplitter, [abductor]
hairstyle, [anile]
hairstylist, [aerialist]
hairy, [accessory]
halcyon, [abecedarian]
hale, [ail]
half, [allograph]
half-and-half, [allograph]
halfback, [aback]
half-breed, [accede]
half-cocked, [blocked]
half-court, [airport]
halfhearted, [abluted]
half-mast, [aghast]
half-moon, [afternoon]
half-pint, pint
half-sole, [areole]
halftime, [airtime]
halftone, [atone]
half-truth, [booth]
halfway, [airway]
half-wit, [acquit]
halibut, [abbot]
halitosis, [alkalosis]

hall, [aerosol]
hallelujah, [alleluia]
hallmark, [aardvark]
hallow, [afterglow]
hallowed, [abode]
Halloween, [alexandrine]
hallucinate, [abominate]
hallucination, [abbreviation]
hallucinogen, [allergen]
hallucinogenic, [allergenic]
hallway, [airway]
halo, [afterglow]
halogen, [allergen]
halt, [asphalt]
halter, [abductor]
halve, [calve]
ham, [aerogram]
hamburger, [agar]
hamlet, [aglet]
hammer, [armor]
hammerlock, [aftershock]
hammock, [amok]
hamster, [administer]
hand brake, [awake]
hand, [ampersand]
handbag, [ag]
handball, [aerosol]
handbell, [bagatelle]
handbill, [backfill]
handblown, [alone]
handbook, [bankbook]
handcart, [apart]
handcuff, [bluff]
handful, [apocryphal]
handgun, [bandwagon]
handheld, [geld]
handhold, [ahold]
handicap, [afterclap]
handicapped, [adapt]

handicraft, [abaft]
handiwork, [artwork]
handkerchief, [anaglyph]
handle, [antipodal]
handlebar, [abattoir]
handler, [angler]
handmade, [abrade]
handmaiden, [anchorperson]
handout, [about]
handpick, [acidic]
handprint, [blueprint]
handrail, [blackmail]
handsaw, [aah]
handset, [abet]
handshake, [awake]
handsome, [adventuresome]
handspring, [anything]
handstand, [ampersand]
handwork, [artwork]
handy, [acidy]
handyman, [adman]
hanger, [arbitrager]
hangman, [abdomen]
hangnail, [blackmail]
hangout, [about]
hangover, [achiever]
hangup, [backup]
hanker, [acre]
hankie, [achy]
hanky, [achy]
haole, [ably]
haphazard, [absurd]
hapless, [acropolis]
happenstance, [advance]
happiness, [agribusiness]
happy, [apocope]
harass, [admass]
harassment, [abandonment]
harbinger, [armiger]

harbor, [amber]
harbormaster, [administer]
hard knocks, [bandbox]
hard up, [backup]
hard, [backyard]
hardback, [aback]
hardball, [aerosol]
hardbound, [abound]
hardcore, [abhor]
hardcover, [achiever]
harden, [anchorperson]
hardhat, [acrobat]
hardhearted, [abluted]
hardliner, [afterburner]
hardness, [agribusiness]
hard-pressed, [abreast]
hard-sell, [bagatelle]
hard-shell, [bagatelle]
hardtack, [aback]
hardtop, [agitprop]
hardware, [affair]
hardwood, [adulthood]
hardy, [acidy]
harem, [addendum]
hark, [aardvark]
harlot, [aglet]
harm, [alarm]
harmful, [apocryphal]
harmless, [acropolis]
harmonic, [allergenic]
harmonica, [angelica]
harmonious, [abstemious]
harmonize, [agnize]
harmony, [abalone]
harness, [agribusiness]
harp, [carp]
harpoon, [afternoon]
harpsichord, [award]
harrow, [allegro]

harsh, marsh
harvest, [adjust]
harvesttime, [airtime]
has, [as]
hash, [abash]
hashish, [baksheesh]
Hasidim, [acronym]
hassle, [apostle]
hassock, [amok]
haste, [abased]
hasten, [anchorperson]
hasty, [abatis]
hat, [acrobat]
hatband, [ampersand]
hatbox, [bandbox]
hatch, [armpatch]
hatchback, [aback]
hatcheck, [afterdeck]
hatchery, [accessory]
hatchet, [adequate]
hate, [ate]
hateful, [apocryphal]
hatpin, [akin]
hatred, [acid]
haughty, [abatis]
haul, [aerosol]
hauler, [angler]
haunch, carte-blanch, launch,
   ponch, prelaunch, raunch,
   stonch, staunch
haunt, [avaunt]
have, [calve]
haversack, [aback]
havoc, [amok]
hawk, [aftershock]
hawkish, [abolish]
hay, [agape]
hayloft, [aloft]
haymaker, [acre]

haymow, [allow]
hayride, [abide]
hayseed, [accede]
haystack, [aback]
haywire, [acquire]
hazard, [absurd]
hazardous, [antibias]
haze, [ablaze]
hazy, [advisee]
he, [buoy]
head, [abed]
headache, [awake]
headband, [ampersand]
headboard, [aboard]
headdress, [acquiesce]
header, [adder]
headfirst, [athirst]
headgate, [abnegate]
headgear, [adhere]
headhunter, [abductor]
headland, [almond]
headlight, [affright]
headline, [airline]
headliner, [afterburner]
headlock, [aftershock]
headlong, [agelong]
headman, [adman]
headmaster, [administer]
headmistress, [actress]
head-on, [amazon]
headphone, [alone]
headpiece, [afterpiece]
headpin, [akin]
headquarters, [bonkers]
headrest, [abreast]
headroom, [abloom]
headset, [abet]
headship, [airship]
headspace, [abase]

headstand, [ampersand]
headstone, [atone]
headstrong, [agelong]
headwaiter, [abductor]
headway, [airway]
heady, [acidy]
heal, [anneal]
healer, [angler]
health, [commonwealth]
healthy, [apathy]
heap, [asleep]
hear, [adhere]
heard, [absurd]
hearken, [awaken]
hearsay, [agape]
hearse, [adverse]
heart, [apart]
heartache, [awake]
heartbeat, [accrete]
heartbreaker, [acre]
heartburn, [adjourn]
hearten, [anchorperson]
heartfelt, [belt]
hearth, [garth]
hearthstone, [alone]
heartily, [ably]
heartland, [ampersand]
heartless, [acropolis]
heartsick, [airsick]
heartstring, [anything]
heartthrob, [ab]
heartworm, [affirm]
hearty, [abatis]
heat, [accrete]
heated, [abluted]
heater, [abductor]
heath, [beneath]
heathenism, [abolitionism]
heatstroke, [artichoke]

heave, [achieve]
heaven-ward, [absurd]
heaviness, [agribusiness]
heavy, [anchovy]
heavyhearted, [abluted]
heavyset, [abet]
heavyweight, [accentuate]
hebetate, [acetate]
hebetude, [altitude]
heck, [afterdeck]
heckle, [acoustical]
hectic, [acoustic]
heddle, [antipodal]
heder, [adder]
hedge, [allege]
hedgehog, [agog]
hedonism, [abolitionism]
hedonist, [abolitionist]
hedonistic, [acoustic]
heed, [accede]
heedless, [acropolis]
heel, [anneal]
heeler, [angler]
heelpiece, [afterpiece]
heeltap, [afterclap]
heft, [aleft]
hefty, [abatis]
hegemony, [abalone]
heifer, [buffer]
height, [affright]
heighten, [anchorperson]
heinous, [agribusiness]
heir, [affair]
heiress, [actress]
heirloom, [abloom]
heist, [antichrist]
held, [geld]
helicopter, [abductor]
helipad, [ad]

heliport, [abort]
helium, [anthurium]
helix, [administratrix]
hell bound, [abound]
hell, [bagatelle]
hellfire, [acquire]
hellhole, [areole]
hellion, [antiunion]
hellish, [abolish]
hello, [afterglow]
hell-raiser, [adviser]
helm, [elm]
helmet, [animate]
helmsman, [abdomen]
help, kelp, self-help, whelp,
    yelp
helper, [barkeeper]
helpful, [apocryphal]
helpless, [acropolis]
helpmate, [acclimate]
helpmeet, [accrete]
helve, [delve]
hem, [apothegm]
hematology, [allergy]
hematoma, [anathema]
hemisphere, [adhere]
hemistich, [acoustic]
hemline, [airline]
hemlock, [aftershock]
hemophilia, [abulia]
hemophiliac, [aback]
hemorrhage, [abridge]
hemorrhoid, [adenoid]
hemp, kemp, temp
hemstitch, [backstitch]
hen, [again]
hence, [cense]
henceforth, [forth]
henchman, [abdomen]

henotheism, [abolitionism]
henpeck, [afterdeck]
hep, [crowstep]
hepatitis, [afflatus]
heptad, [ad]
heptagonal, [aboriginal]
her, [arbitrager]
herald, [bedraggled]
herb, [adverb]
herbal, [able]
herbicide, [abide]
herd, [absurd]
herdsman, [abdomen]
here, [adhere]
hereabouts, thereabouts,
    whereabouts
hereafter, [abductor]
hereby, [alibi]
hereditary, [accessory]
heredity, [abatis]
hereinto, [accrue]
heresy, [absorbancy]
heretic, [acoustic]
heretical, [acoustical]
hereto, [accrue]
heretofore, [abhor]
heritage, [acknowledge]
hermeneutics, [acoustics]
hermit, [animate]
hernia, [abulia]
herniate, [create]
hero, [allegro]
heroic, [acidic]
heroism, [abolitionism]
herpes, [antifreeze]
herringbone, [alone]
herself, [bookshelf]
hertz, [gigahertz]
hesitance, [abhorrence]

hesitant, [abirritant]
hesitate, [acetate]
hesitation, [abbreviation]
heterodox, [bandbox]
heterogeneous, [abstemious]
heterosexual, [accrual]
heuristic, [acoustic]
hew, [accrue]
hex, [annex]
hexagon, [amazon]
hey, [agape]
heyday, [agape]
hi, [airdry]
hiatus, [afflatus]
hibachi, [blotchy]
hibernate, [abominate]
hiccup, [backup]
hick, [acidic]
hickey, [achy]
hickory, [accessory]
hid, [amid]
hidden, [anchorperson]
hide, [abide]
hide-and-seek, [antique]
hideaway, [airway]
hidebound, [abound]
hideous, [abstemious]
hideout, [about]
hiding place, [abase]
hierarch, [aardvark]
hierarchical, [acoustical]
hierarchy, [achy]
hieroglyphic,
  [anthropomorphic]
high, [airdry]
highball, [aerosol]
highbred, [abed]
highbrow, [allow]
highland, [almond]

highlight, [affright]
highness, [agribusiness]
high-strung, [among]
highway, [airway]
highwayman, [abdomen]
hijack, [aback]
hike, [alike]
hilarious, [abstemious]
hill, [backfill]
hillbilly, [ably]
hillcrest, [abreast]
hillside, [abide]
hilltop, [agitprop]
hilly, [ably]
hilt, [atilt]
him, [acronym]
himself, [bookshelf]
hind, [affined]
hinder, [adder]
hindmost, [aftermost]
hindquarter, [abductor]
hindrance, [abhorrence]
hindsight, [affright]
Hindu, [accrue]
hinge, [binge]
hint, [blueprint]
hinterland, [ampersand]
hip, [airstrip]
hipline, [airline]
hippie, [apocope]
hippopotamus, [allonymous]
hipster, [administer]
hire, [amplifier]
hired hand, [ampersand]
hirsute, [acute]
his, [fizz]
hiss, [abyss]
hissy, [absorbancy]
histamine, [alexandrine]

historic, [aleatoric]
historical, [acoustical]
history, [accessory]
histrionic, [allergenic]
histrionics, [administratrix]
hit, [acquit]
hitch, [backstitch]
hitchhike, [alike]
hither, [altogether]
hive, [alive]
hoagie, [aggie]
hoar, [abhor]
hoarse, [coarse]
hoary, [accessory]
hoax, [coax]
hob, [ab]
hobbit, [abbot]
hobble, [able]
hobby, [abbey]
hobbyhorse, [endorse]
hobnail, [ail]
hobnob, [ab]
hobo, [airshow]
hock, [aftershock]
hockey, [achy]
hod, [abroad]
hodgepodge, [dislodge]
hoe, [airshow]
hoecake, [awake]
hoedown, [boomtown]
hog, [agog]
hogan, [amazon]
hoggish, [abolish]
hogtie, [airdry]
hogwash, [awash]
hoise, [counterpoise]
hoist, [foist]
hoke, [artichoke]
hokey, [achy]

hokeypokey, [achy]
hokum, [addendum]
hold, [ahold]
holder, [adder]
holdfast, [aghast]
holdout, [about]
holdover, [achiever]
holdup, [backup]
hole, [areole]
holiday, [agape]
holiness, [agribusiness]
holistic, [acoustic]
holland, [almond]
hollandaise, [ablaze]
holler, [angler]
hollo, [afterglow]
hollow, [afterglow]
holly, [ably]
hollyhock, [aftershock]
holocaust, [accost]
hologram, [aerogram]
holograph, [allograph]
holographic,
   [anthropomorphic]
holstein, [alexandrine]
holster, [administer]
Holy Grail, [ail]
Holy Land, [ampersand]
Holy Week, [antique]
holy, [ably]
homage, [acknowledge]
hombre, [affray]
homburg, [burg]
home ec, [afterdeck]
home, [astrodome]
homebody, [acidy]
homebound, [abound]
homeboy, [ahoy]
homebrew, [accrue]

homegrown, [alone]
homeland, [ampersand]
homeless, [acropolis]
homely, [ably]
homemade, [abrade]
homemaker, [acre]
homeroom, [abloom]
homesite, [affright]
homestead, [abed]
homestretch, [backstretch]
hometown, [boomtown]
homeward, [absurd]
homework, [artwork]
homey, [academy]
homicidal, [antipodal]
homicide, [abide]
homiletic, [acoustic]
homiletics, [acoustics]
homily, [ably]
homogenize, [agnize]
homonym, [acronym]
homophobe, [bathrobe]
homophobia, [abulia]
homosexual, [accrual]
honcho, [airshow]
hone, [alone]
honest, [adjust]
honesty, [abatis]
honey, [abalone]
honeybee, [abbey]
honeycomb, [astrodome]
honeydew, [accrue]
honeymoon, [afternoon]
honeysuckle, [acoustical]
honk, [ankh]
honky, [achy]
honor, [afterburner]
honorable, [able]
honorarium, [addendum]

honorary, [accessory]
honorific, [anthropomorphic]
hooch, mooch, pooch, smooch
hood, [adulthood]
hooded, [absentminded]
hoodlum, [addendum]
hoodwink, [bethink]
hooey, [colloquy]
hoofbeat, [accrete]
hoofprint, [blueprint]
hook, [bankbook]
hooker, [acre]
hookup, [backup]
hookworm, [affirm]
hooky, [achy]
hooligan, [bandwagon]
hoop, [coop]
hoopla, [aah]
hooray, [affray]
hoosegow, [allow]
hoot, [acute]
hootenanny, [abalone]
hop, [agitprop]
hope, [antelope]
hopeful, [apocryphal]
hopeless, [acropolis]
hopper, [barkeeper]
hopsack, [aback]
hopscotch, [botch]
horde, [aboard]
horizon, [anchorperson]
horizontal, [accidental]
hormone, [alone]
horn, [acorn]
hornet, [acuminate]
horny, [abalone]
horoscope, [antelope]
horrendous, [antibias]
horrible, [able]

horrid, [acid]
horrific, [anthropomorphic]
horrify, [amplify]
horror, [adulterer]
horse race, [abase]
horse, [endorse]
horseback, [aback]
horsefeathers, [bonkers]
horsefly, [airdry]
horsehide, [abide]
horseplay, [airplay]
horsepower, [airpower]
horseradish, [abolish]
horseshoe, [accrue]
horsewhip, [airstrip]
horsy, [absorbancy]
hortative, [ablative]
hortatory, [accessory]
horticulture, [acupuncture]
hosanna, [alumna]
hose, [airhose]
hosiery, [accessory]
hospice, [auspice]
hospitable, [able]
hospital, [accidental]
hospitality, [abatis]
hospitalization, [abbreviation]
hospitalize, [actualize]
host, [aftermost]
hostage, [acknowledge]
hostel, [accidental]
hosteler, [angler]
hostess, [afflatus]
hostile, [accidental]
hostility, [abatis]
hot flash, [abash]
hot, [aeronaut]
hotblood, [acid]
hotcake, [awake]

hotdog, [agog]
hotel, [bagatelle]
hotfoot, [ablaut]
hothead, [abed]
hothouse, [alehouse]
hotshot, [aeronaut]
hound, [abound]
hour, [airpower]
hourglass, [admass]
hourly, [ably]
house, [alehouse]
houseboat, [afloat]
housebound, [abound]
housebroken, [awaken]
houseclean, [alexandrine]
housecoat, [afloat]
houseguest, [abreast]
household, [ahold]
housekeeper, [barkeeper]
housemaid, [abrade]
housemate, [acclimate]
houseparent, [aberrant]
housetop, [agitprop]
housewife, [afterlife]
housework, [artwork]
hovel, [adjectival]
hover, [achiever]
how, [allow]
howdy, [acidy]
however, [achiever]
howitzer, [aggressor]
howl, [foul]
hoy, [ahoy]
hoyden, [anchorperson]
hoyle, [broil]
hub, [backrub]
hubbub, [backrub]
hubby, [abbey]
hubcap, [afterclap]

hubris, [actress]
huckster, [administer]
huddle, [antipodal]
hue, [accrue]
hued, [allude]
huff, [bluff]
huffy, [anastrophe]
hug, [bedbug]
huge, [centrifuge]
huh, [alfalfa]
hula, [a capella]
hulk, [bulk]
hull, [agile]
hullabaloo, [accrue]
hum, [addendum]
human, [abdomen]
humane, [abstain]
humanism, [abolitionism]
humanist, [abolitionist]
humanistic, [acoustic]
humanity, [abatis]
humankind, [affined]
humble, [able]
humbug, [bedbug]
humdinger, [agar]
humdrum, [addendum]
humid, [acid]
humidifier, [amplifier]
humidify, [amplify]
humidity, [abatis]
humiliate, [create]
humiliation, [abbreviation]
humility, [abatis]
humongous, [analogous]
humor, [armor]
humorous, [actress]
hump, [bump]
humph, [galumph]
hunch, [brunch]

hundred, [acid]
hung, [among]
hunger, [agar]
hungry, [accessory]
hunk, [bohunk]
hunker, [acre]
hunt, [abeyant]
hunter, [abductor]
hup, [backup]
hurdle, [antipodal]
hurl, [aswirl]
hurly, [ably]
hurrah, [aah]
hurricane, [abstain]
hurried, [accede]
hurry, [accessory]
hurt, [advert]
hurtful, [apocryphal]
hurtle, [accidental]
husband, [almond]
husbandry, [accessory]
hush, [airbrush]
husk, [dusk]
husky, [achy]
hussy, [absorbancy]
hustle, [apostle]
hustler, [angler]
hut, [adequate]
hutch, [clutch]
hyacinth, labyrinth
hybrid, [acid]
hydrant, [aberrant]
hydrate, [accelerate]
hydraulic, [acyclic]
hydraulics, [administratrix]
hydro, [allegro]
hydroelectric, [aleatoric]
hydrogen bomb, [aplomb]
hydrogen, [allergen]

hydromancy, [absorbancy]
hydrophobia, [abulia]
hydrophobic, [acerbic]
hydroplane, [abstain]
hyena, [alumna]
hygiene, [alexandrine]
hygienic, [allergenic]
hygienist, [abolitionist]
hymen, [abdomen]
hymn, [acronym]
hymnal, [aboriginal]
hymnbook, [bankbook]
hype, [airpipe]
hyper, [barkeeper]
hyperactive, [ablative]
hyperactivity, [abatis]
hyperbola, [a capella]
hyperbole, [ably]
hyperbolic, [acyclic]
hypercritical, [acoustical]
hypertension, [abbreviation]
hyperventilate, [ablate]
hyperventilation,
  [abbreviation]
hyphenate, [abominate]
hyphenated, [abluted]
hypnosis, [alkalosis]
hypnotic, [acoustic]
hypnotism, [abolitionism]
hypnotize, [absolutize]
hypo, [airshow]
hypocenter, [abductor]
hypochondriac, [aback]
hypocrisy, [absorbancy]
hypocrite, [acquit]
hypodermic, [academic]
hypostatize, [absolutize]
hypotension, [abbreviation]
hypotenuse, [abstruse]

hypothecate, [abdicate]
hypothermia, [abulia]
hypothesis, [alkalosis]
hypothesize, [abscise]
hypothetical, [acoustical]
hyssop, [backup]
hysteria, [abulia]
hysterics, [administratrix]
ice cream, [abeam]
ice, [advice]
iceberg, [burg]
icebox, [bandbox]
icebreaker, [acre]
icehouse, [alehouse]
icicle, [acoustical]
icky, [achy]
icon, [amazon]
iconoclast, [aghast]
iconoclastic, [acoustic]
ictus, [afflatus]
icy, [absorbancy]
id, [amid]
idea, [abulia]
ideal, [anneal]
idealism, [abolitionism]
idealist, [aerialist]
idealistic, [acoustic]
idealize, [actualize
ideate, [create]
identical, [acoustical]
identifiable, [able]
identification, [abbreviation]
identify, [amplify]
identity, [abatis]]
ideologue, [agog]
ideology, [allergy]
ides, [burnsides]
idiocy, [absorbancy]
idiom, [anthurium]

idiomatic, [acoustic]
idiosyncrasy, [absorbancy]
idiot box, [bandbox]
idiot, [affiliate]
idiotic, [acoustic]
idle, [antipodal]
idol, [antipodal]
idolater, [abductor]
idolator, [abductor]
idolatrous, [actress]
idolatry, [ancestry]
idolization, [abbreviation]
idolize, [actualize]
idyllic, [acyclic]
if, [anaglyph]
iffy, [anastrophe]
igloo, [accrue]
ignite, [affright]
ignition, [abbreviation]
ignoble, [able]
ignominious, [abstemious]
ignominy, [abalone]
ignoramus, [allonymous]
ignorance, [abhorrence]
ignorant, [aberrant]
ignore, [abhor]
ilk, [bilk]
ill, [backfill]
illation, [abbreviation]
illative, [ablative]
illegal, [angle]
illegible, [able]
illegitimate, [animate]
illicit, [corset]
illiterate, [accurate]
illogical, [acoustical]
illuminate, **[adjective]**
  [acuminate]
illuminate, **[verb]** [abominate]

illuminati, [abatis]
illumination, [abbreviation]
illumine, [abdomen]
illusion, [abrasion]
illusionist, [abolitionist]
illusive, [abrasive]
illusory, [accessory]
illustrate, [accelerate]
illustration, [abbreviation]
illustrator, [abductor]
illustrious, [abstemious]
image, [acknowledge]
imagery, [accessory]
imaginable, [able]
imaginary, [accessory]
imagination, [abbreviation]
imagine, [allergen]
imago, [ago]
imam, [aplomb]
imbalance, [abhorrence]
imbecile, [apostle]
imbibe, [ascribe]
imbricate, **[adjective]**
  [advocate]
imbricate, **[verb]** [abdicate]
imbroglio, [audio]
imbue, [accrue]
imitate, [acetate]
imitation, [abbreviation]
imitator, [abductor]
immaculate, [aglet]
immanence, [abhorrence]
immanent, [abstinent]
Immanuel, [bagatelle]
immaterial, [abaxial]
immature, [abjure]
immaturity, [abatis]
immediacy, [absorbancy]
immediate, [affiliate]

immense, [cense]
immensity, [abatis]
immerge, [converge]
immerse, [adverse]
immersible, [able]
immersion, [abrasion]
immigrant, [aberrant]
immigrate, [accelerate]
immigration, [abbreviation]
imminence, [abhorrence]
imminent, [abstinent]
immobile, [able]
immobilize, [actualize]
immoderate, [accurate]
immodest, [adjust]
immolate, [ablate]
immoral, [admiral]
immorality, [abatis]
immortal, [accidental]
immortality, [abatis]
immovable, [able]
immune, [afternoon]
immunity, [abatis]
immunize, [agnize]
immutable, [able]
imp, [blimp]
impact, [abstract]
impacted, [abluted]
impair, [affair]
impale, [ail]
impalpable, [able]
impart, [apart]
impartation, [abbreviation]
impartial, [abbatial]
impasse, [admass]
impassible, [able]
impassion, [abbreviation]
impassive, [abrasive]
impatience, [abhorrence]

impatient, [abeyant]
impeach, [beach]
impeachable, [able]
impeachment, [abandonment]
impeccable, [able]
impede, [accede]
impediment, [abandonment]
impel, [bagatelle]
impend, [addend]
impendent, [abundant]
impenetrable, [able]
impenitent, [abirritant]
imperative, [ablative]
imperceptible, [able]
imperfect, [addict]
imperfection, [abbreviation]
imperial, [abaxial]
imperialism, [abolitionism]
imperil, [admiral]
imperious, [abstemious]
imperishable, [able]
impermanence, [abhorrence]
impermanent, [abstinent]
impermissible, [able]
impersonal, [aboriginal]
impersonalize, [actualize]
impersonate, [abominate]
impertinence, [abhorrence]
impertinent, [abstinent]
impervious, [abstemious]
impetigo, [ago]
impetrate, [accelerate]
impetuous, [ambiguous]
impetus, [afflatus]
impiety, [abatis]
impinge, [binge]
impish, [abolish]
implacable, [able]
implant, [ant]

implantation, [abbreviation]
implausible, [able]
implement, [abandonment]
implementation, [abbreviation]
implementer, [abductor]
implicate, [abdicate]
implication, [abbreviation]
implicit, [corset]
implode, [abode]
implore, [abhor]
implosion, [abrasion]
imply, [airdry]
impolite, [affright]
imponderable, [able]
impone, [alone]
import, [airport]
importance, [abhorrence]
important, [abirritant]
importation, [abbreviation]
importunate, [acuminate]
importune, [afternoon]
impose, [airhose]
imposition, [abbreviation]
impossibility, [abatis]
impossible, [able]
impost, [aftermost]
imposter, [administer]
imposture, [acupuncture]
impotence, [abhorrence]
impotent, [abirritant]
impound, [abound]
impoverish, [abolish]
impracticable, [able]
impractical, [acoustical]
imprecate, [abdicate]
imprecise, [advice]
imprecision, [abbreviation]
impregnate, [abominate]
impresario, [audio]

impress, [acquiesce]
impression, [abbreviation]
impressionable, [able]
impressionist, [abolitionist]
impressionistic, [acoustic]
impressive, [abrasive]
imprest, [abreast]
imprimatur, [abjure]
imprimis, [allonymous]
imprint, [blueprint]
imprison, [anchorperson]
improbable, [able]
impromptu, [accrue]
improper, [barkeeper]
impropriety, [abatis]
improve, [approve]
improvement, [abandonment]
improvisation, [abbreviation]
improvise, [advise]
imprudence, [accordance]
imprudent, [accordant]
impudence, [abhorrence]
impudent, [abundant]
impugn, [afternoon]
impulse, [convulse]
impulsion, [abbreviation]
impulsive, [abrasive]
impunity, [abatis]
impure, [abjure]
impurity, [abatis]
imputation, [abbreviation]
impute, [acute]
imputed, [abluted]
in, [akin]
inability, [abatis]
inaccessible, [able]
inaccuracy, [absorbancy]
inaccurate, [accurate]
inaction, [abbreviation]

inactive, [ablative]
inadequacy, [absorbancy]
inadequate, [adequate]
inadmissible, [able]
inadvertent, [accordant]
inadvisable, [able]
inalienable, [able]
inalterable, [able]
inane, [abstain]
inanimate, [animate]
inapplicable, [able]
inapproachable, [able]
inappropriate, [affiliate]
inaptitude, [altitude]
inarticulate, [aglet]
inasmuch, [clutch]
inattention, [abbreviation]
inattentive, [ablative]
inaudible, [able]
inaugural, [admiral]
inaugurate, [accelerate]
inauguration, [abbreviation]
inauspicious, [adscititious]
inauthentic, [acoustic]
inboard, [aboard]
inborn, [acorn]
inbound, [abound]
inbred, [abed]
inbreed, [accede]
incalculable, [able]
incandescent, [adjacent]
incant, [ant]
incantation, [abbreviation]
incapable, [able]
incapacitate, [acetate]
incapacity, [abatis]
incarcerate, [accelerate]
incarnate, **[adjective]**
  [acuminate]

incarnate, **[verb]** [abominate]
incarnation, [abbreviation]
incendiary, [accessory]
incense, [cense]
incensed, [against]
incentive, [ablative]
inception, [abbreviation]
incessant, [adjacent]
incest, [abreast]
inch, [bullfinch]
inchoate, [adequate]
inchoative, [ablative]
incidence, [abhorrence]
incident, [abundant]
incidental, [accidental]
incinerate, [accelerate]
incinerator, [abductor]
incipient, [abeyant]
incipit, [adequate]
incise, [abscise]
incision, [abrasion]
incisive, [abrasive]
incite, [affright]
inclement, [abandonment]
inclination, [abbreviation]
incline, [airline]
inclined, [affined]
include, [allude]
inclusion, [abbreviation]
inclusive, [abrasive]
incognito, [aggiornamento]
incoherence, [abhorrence]
incoherent, [aberrant]
incombustible, [able]
income tax, [anthrax]
income, [addendum]
incommunicado, [aficionado]
incomparable, [able]
incompatibility, [abatis]

275

incompatible, [able]
incompetence, [abhorrence]
incompetent, [abirritant]
incomplete, [accrete]
incomprehensible, [able]
inconceivable, [able]
inconclusive, [abrasive]
incongruous, [ambiguous]
inconsequential, [abbatial]
inconsiderate, [accurate]
inconsistency, [absorbancy]
inconsistent, [abirritant]
inconspicuous, [ambiguous]
inconstant, [abirritant]
incontinent, [abstinent]
inconvenience, [abhorrence]
inconvenient, [abeyant]
incorporate, [accelerate]
incorporated, [abluted]
incorporeal, [anneal]
incorrect, [abject]
incorrigible, [able]
incorruptible, [able]
increase, [afterpiece]
incredible, [able]
incredulous, [acropolis]
increment, [abandonment]
incriminate, [abominate]
incubate, [abate]
incubation, [abbreviation]
incubator, [abductor]
inculcate, [abdicate]
incur, [acre]
incurable, [able]
indebtedness, [agribusiness]
indecency, [absorbancy]
indecent, [adjacent]
indecision, [abrasion]
indecisive, [abrasive]

indeed, [accede]
indefatigable, [able]
indefectible, [able]
indefensible, [able]
indefinable, [able]
indefinite, [acuminate]
indelible, [able]
indelicate, [advocate]
indemnify, [amplify]
indemnity, [abatis]
indent, [accent]
indentation, [abbreviation]
indenture, [acupressure]
independence, [abhorrence]
independent, [abundant]
indescribable, [able]
indestructible, [able]
indeterminate, [acuminate]
index, [annex]
indicate, [abdicate]
indication, [abbreviation]
indicative, [ablative]
indicator, [abductor]
indices, [antifreeze]
indict, [affright]
indictment, [abandonment]
indifference, [abhorrence]
indifferent, [aberrant]
indigence, [abhorrence]
indigenous, [agribusiness]
indigent, [agent]
indigestible, [able]
indignation, [abbreviation]
indignity, [abatis]
indigo, [ago]
indirect, [abject]
indiscreet, [accrete]
indiscretion, [abbreviation]
indiscriminate, [acuminate]

indispensable, [able]
indisputable, [able]
indistinct, [distinct]
indistinguishable, [able]
indite, [affright]
individual, [accrual]
individualism, [abolitionism]
individualist, [aerialist]
individuality, [abatis]
individualize, [actualize]
indivisible, [able]
indoctrinate, [abominate]
indoctrination, [abbreviation]
indolent, [ambivalent]
indomitable, [able]
indoor, [abhor]
indubitable, [able]
induce, [abstruse]
inducement, [abandonment]
induct, [abduct]
inductee, [abatis]
induction, [abbreviation]
inductive, [ablative]
indulge, [bulge]
indulgence, [abhorrence]
indulgent, [agent]
indurate, [adjective]
   [accurate]
indurate, [verb] [accelerate]
industrial, [abaxial]
industrialist, [aerialist]
industrialization,
   [abbreviation]
industrialize, [actualize]
industrious, [abstemious]
industry, [ancestry]
indwell, [bagatelle]
inebriate, [create]
inebriated, [abluted]

inebriation, [abbreviation]
inedible, [able]
ineffable, [able]
ineffaceable, [able]
ineffective, [ablative]
ineffectual, [accrual]
inefficacious, [adscititious]
inefficiency, [absorbancy]
inefficient, [abeyant]
inelastic, [acoustic]
inelegance, [abhorrence]
inelegant, [abeyant]
ineligible, [able]
ineloquent, [abeyant]
inept, [accept]
ineptitude, [altitude]
inequality, [abatis]
inequitable, [able]
inequity, [abatis]
inerrant, [aberrant]
inert, [advert]
inertia, [noun] [abulia]
inertia, [noun] [alfalfa]
inescapable, [able]
inestimable, [able]
inevitable, [able]
inexcusable, [able]
inexhaustible, [able]
inexorable, [able]
inexpensive, [abrasive]
inexperience, [abhorrence]
inexperienced, [against]
inexplicable, [able]
inexpressible, [able]
inexpressive, [abrasive]
inextinguishable, [able]
inextricable, [able]
infallible, [able]
infamous, [allonymous]

infamy, [academy]
infancy, [absorbancy]
infant, [abeyant]
infanticide, [abide]
infantry, [ancestry]
infatuate, **[adjective]**
  [adequate]
infatuate, **[verb]** [accentuate]
infect, [abject]
infection, [abbreviation]
infectious, [adscititious]
infer, [buffer]
inference, [abhorrence]
inferential, [abbatial]
infernal, [abdominal]
inferno, [albino]
infertile, [accidental]
infertility, [abatis]
infest, [abreast]
infidel, [bagatelle]
infidelity, [abatis]
infield, [airfield]
infielder, [adder]
infiltrate, [accelerate]
infiltration, [abbreviation]
infiltrator, [abductor]
infinite, [acuminate]
infinitesimal, [abnormal]
infinitive, [ablative]
infinitude, [altitude]
infinity, [abatis]
infirm, [affirm]
infirmary, [accessory]
infirmity, [abatis]
inflame, [acclaim]
inflammable, [able]
inflammation, [abbreviation]
inflammatory, [accessory]
inflatable, [able]

inflate, [ablate]
inflated, [abluted]
Inflation, [abbreviation]
inflationary, [accessory]
inflect, [abject]
inflection, [abbreviation]
inflexible, [able]
inflict, [addict]
influence, [abhorrence]
influenced, [against]
influential, [abbatial]
influenza, [alfalfa]
influx, [afflux]
infomercial, [abbatial]
inform, [aswarm]
informal, [abnormal]
informant, [abandonment]
information, [abbreviation]
informative, [ablative]
informer, [armor]
infotainment, [abandonment]
infra, [abracadabra]
infraction, [abbreviation]
infrared, [abed]
infrastructure, [acupuncture]
infrequent, [abeyant]
infringe, [binge]
infringement, [abandonment]
infuriate, [create]
infuse, [amuse]
infusion, [abbreviation]
ingenious, [antibias]
ingenuity, [abatis]
ingenuous, [ambiguous]
ingest, [abreast]
inglorious, [abstemious]
ingot, [agate]
ingrain, [abstain]
ingrate, [accelerate]

ingratiate, [create]
ingratitude, [altitude]
ingredient, [abeyant]
ingress, [actress]
ingressive, [abrasive]
ingrown, [alone]
ingurgitate, [acetate]
inhabit, [abbot]
inhabitant, [abirritant]
inhalant, [ambivalent]
inhalation, [abbreviation]
inhale, [ail]
inhaler, [angler]
inherent, [aberrant]
inherit, [accurate]
inheritance, [abhorrence]
inhibit, [abbot]
inhibition, [abbreviation]
inhibitor, [abductor]
inhospitable, [able]
inhuman, [abdomen]
inhumane, [abstain]
inhumanity, [abatis]
inimical, [acoustical]
inimitable, [able]
iniquity, [abatis]
initial, [abbatial]
initialize, [actualize]
initiate, [create]
initiation, [abbreviation]
initiative, [ablative]
inject, [abject]
injection, [abbreviation]
injunction, [abbreviation]
injure, [armiger]
injurious, [abstemious]
injury, [accessory]
injustice, [afflatus]
ink, [bethink]

inkstand, [ampersand]
inkwell, [bagatelle]
inlaid, [abrade]
inland, [ampersand]
inlay, [airplay]
inlet, [abet]
inmate, [acclimate]
inmost, [aftermost]
inn, [akin]
innards, [billiards]
innate, [abominate]
inner, [afterburner]
innermost, [aftermost]
innersole, [areole]
innervate, [activate]
innkeeper, [barkeeper]
innocence, [abhorrence]
innocent, [acquiescent]
innocuous, [ambiguous]
innovate, [activate]
innovation, [abbreviation]
innovative, [ablative]
innovator, [abductor]
innuendo, [aficionado]
innumerable, [able]
inoculate, [ablate]
inoculation, [abbreviation]
inoffensive, [abrasive]
inoperable, [able]
inoperative, [ablative]
inopportune, [afternoon]
inordinate, [acuminate]
inorganic, [allergenic]
inpatient, [abeyant]
input, [ablaut]
inquest, [abreast]
inquietude, [altitude]
inquire, [acquire]
inquiry, [accessory]

inquisition, [abbreviation]
inquisitive, [ablative]
inroad, [abode]
insane, [abstain]
insanity, [abatis]
insatiable, [able]
inscribe, [ascribe]
inscription, [abbreviation]
inscriptive, [ablative]
inscrutable, [able]
inseam, [abeam]
insecticide, [abide]
insecure, [abjure]
insecurity, [abatis]
inseminate, [abominate]
insensible, [able]
insensitive, [ablative]
inseparable, [able]
insert, [advert]
insertion, [abbreviation]
inset, [abet]
inside, [abide]
insider, [adder]
insidious, [abstemious]
insight, [affright]
insightful, [apocryphal]
insignia, [abulia]
insignificance, [abhorrence]
insignificant, [abeyant]
insincere, [adhere]
insinuate, [accentuate]
insinuation, [abbreviation]
insipid, [acid]
insist, [assist]
insistence, [abhorrence]
insistent, [abirritant]
insofar, [abattoir]
insolation, [abbreviation]
insole, [areole]

insolence, [abhorrence]
insolent, [ambivalent]
insoluble, [able]
insolvable, [able]
insolvent, [abeyant]
insomnia, [abulia]
inspect, [abject]
inspection, [abbreviation]
inspector, [abductor]
inspiration, [abbreviation]
inspire, [acquire]
inspissate, [ate]
instability, [abatis]
install, [aerosol]
installation, [abbreviation]
installer, [angler]
installment, [abandonment]
instance, [abhorrence]
instant, [abirritant]
instantaneous, [abstemious]
instate, [acetate]
instead, [abed]
instep, [crowstep]
instigate, [abnegate]
instigation, [abbreviation]
instill, [backfill]
instillation, [abbreviation]
instinct, [distinct]
instinctive, [ablative]
institute, [acute]
institution, [abbreviation]
institutional, [aboriginal]
institutionalization,
    [abbreviation]
institutionalize, [actualize]
instruct, [abduct]
instruction, [abbreviation]
instructional, [abdominal]
instructive, [ablative]

instructor, [abductor]
instrument, [abandonment]
instrumental, [accidental]
instrumentalist, [aerialist]
insubordinate, [acuminate]
insufficiency, [absorbancy]
insufficient, [abeyant]
insulate, [ablate]
insulation, [abbreviation]
insulin, [acetylene]
insult, [adult]
insuperable, [able]
insurable, [able]
insurance, [abhorrence]
insure, [abjure]
insurgence, [abhorrence]
insurgent, [agent]
insurmountable, [able]
insurrection, [abbreviation]
insurrectionist, [abolitionist]
intact, [abstract]
intake, [awake]
intangible, [able]
integer, [armiger]
integral, [barrel]
integration, [abbreviation]
integrationist, [abolitionist]
integrity, [abatis]
intellect, [abject]
intellectual, [accrual]
intelligence, [abhorrence]
intelligent, [agent]
intelligentsia, [abulia]
intelligible, [able]
intemperance, [abhorrence]
intemperate, [accurate]
intend, [addend]
intended, [absentminded]
intense, [cense]

intensify, [amplify]
intension, [abbreviation]
intensity, [abatis]
intensive, [abrasive]
intent, [accent]
intention, [abbreviation]
intentional, [aboriginal]
inter, [abductor]
interaction, [abbreviation]
interactive, [ablative]
interbank, [bank]
interbranch, [avalanche]
intercede, [accede]
intercept, [accept]
interception, [abbreviation]
intercession, [abbreviation]
intercessor, [aggressor]
interchange, [arrange]
interchangeable, [able]
interchurch, [antichurch]
intercity, [abatis]
intercollegiate, [adequate]
intercom, [aplomb]
intercontinental, [accidental]
intercorrelation, [abbreviation]
intercourse, [coarse]
intercultural, [admiral]
interdenominational,
  [abdominal]
interdepartmental,
  [accidental]
interdependency,
  [absorbancy]
interdependent, [abundant]
interdict, [addict]
interest, [adjust]
interface, [abase]
interfaith, [eighth]
interfere, [adhere]

interim, [addendum
interior, [anterior]
interject, [abject]
interjection, [abbreviation]
interlace, [abase]
interlay, [airplay]
interlayer, [ballplayer]
interlibrary, [accessory]
interlinear, [anterior]
interlink, [bethink]
interlock, [aftershock]
interlope, [antelope]
interlude, [allude]
intermarriage, [abridge]
intermarry, [accessory]
intermediary, [accessory]
intermediate, **[adjective]**
   [affiliate]
intermediate, **[verb]** [create]
interment, [abandonment]
interminable, [able]
intermingle, [angle]
intermission, [abbreviation]
intermit, [acquit]
intermittence, [abhorrence]
intermittent, [accordant]
intermix, [administratrix]
intern, [adjourn]
internal, [abdominal]
internalize, [actualize]
international, [aboriginal]
internationalist, [aerialist]
internationalize, [actualize]
internecine, [alexandrine]
internist, [abolitionist]
internship, [airship]
interoceanic, [allergenic]
interoffice, [amorphous]
interpellate, [ablate]

interpenetrate, [accelerate]
interpersonal, [aboriginal]
interplanetary, [accessory]
interplay, [airplay]
Interpol, [areole]
interpolate, [ablate]
interpolation, [abbreviation]
interpolator, [abductor]
interpose, [airhose]
interposition, [abbreviation]
interpret, [accurate]
interpretation, [abbreviation]
interpreter, [abductor]
interracial, [abbatial]
interrelate, [ablate]
interrelated, [abluted]
interrelationship, [airship]
interreligious, [advantageous]
interrogate, [abnegate]
interrogation, [abbreviation]
interrogative, [ablative]
interrogator, [abductor]
interrupt, [abrupt]
interruption, [abbreviation]
interscholastic, [acoustic]
intersect, [abject]
intersection, [abbreviation]
intersperse, [adverse]
interstate, [acetate]
intertestamental, [accidental]
intertwine, [aerodyne]
interurban, [antiphon]
interval, [adjectival]
intervene, [alexandrine]
interview, [accrue]
interviewee, [colloquy]
interviewer, [airpower]
interweave, [achieve]
interwoven, [antiphon]

intestate, [acetate]
intestinal, [abdominal]
intimacy, [absorbancy]
intimate, **[adjective]** [animate]
intimate, **[verb]** [acclimate]
intimidate, [accommodate]
intimidator, [abductor]
into, [accrue]
intolerable, [able]
intolerance, [abhorrence]
intonate, [abominate]
intonation, [abbreviation]
intone, [atone]
intoxicant, [abeyant]
intoxicate, [abdicate]
intoxicated, [abluted]
Intoxication, [abbreviation]
intractable, [able]
intramural, [admiral]
intransigence, [abhorrence]
intransigent, [agent]
intransitive, [ablative]
intrastate, [acetate]
intravenous, [agribusiness]
intrepid, [acid]
intricate, [advocate]
intrigue, [blitzkrieg]
intrinsic, [airsick]
introduce, [abstruse]
introduction, [abbreviation]
introductory, [accessory]
introit, [adroit]
introject, [abject]
introspection, [abbreviation]
introspective, [ablative]
introversion, [abrasion]
introvert, [advert]
intrude, [allude]
intruder, [adder]

intrusion, [abbreviation]
intrusive, [abrasive]
intuit, [adequate]
intuition, [abbreviation]
intuitive, [ablative]
inundate, [accommodate]
inure, [abjure]
inurement, [abandonment]
invade, [abrade]
invalid, [acid]
invalidate, [accommodate]
invaluable, [able]
invariable, [able]
invasion, [abbreviation]
invasion, [abrasion]
invasive, [abrasive]
invective, [ablative]
invent, [accent]
invention, [abbreviation]
inventive, [ablative]
inventor, [abductor]
inventory, [accessory]
inverness, [acquiesce]
inverse, [adverse]
inversion, [abbreviation]
invert, [advert]
invertebrate, [adequate]
invest, [abreast]
investigate, [abnegate]
investigator, [abductor]
investiture, [abjure]
investment, [abandonment]
investor, [administer]
inveterate, [accurate]
inviable, [able]
invigilate, [ablate]
invigorate, [accelerate]
invincibility, [abatis]
invincible, [able]

inviolable, [able]
inviolate, [aglet]
invisible, [able]
invitation, [abbreviation]
invitational, [abdominal]
invite, [affright]
invocation, [abbreviation]
invoice, [choice]
invoke, [artichoke]
involuntary, [accessory]
involve, [absolve]
involvement, [abandonment]
invulnerability, [abatis]
inward, [absurd]
iodine, [aerodyne]
iota, [aorta]
Iran, [adman]
irascible, [able]
irate, [accelerate]
ire, [acquire]
irenic, [allergenic]
iridescence, [accordance]
iridescent, [adjacent]
iris, [actress]
irk, [artwork]
irksome, [adventuresome]
iron, [adjourn]
ironclad, [ad]
ironic, [allergenic]
ironical, [acoustical]
ironside, [abide]
irony, [abalone]
irradiance, [abhorrence]
irradiate, [create]
irrational, [aboriginal]
irreconcilable, [able]
irreducible, [able]
irrefutable, [able]
irregardless, [acropolis]

irregular, [angler]
irregularity, [abatis]
irrelevance, [abhorrence]
irrelevant, [abeyant]
irreligious, [advantageous]
irreparable, [able]
irreplaceable, [able]
irrepressible, [able]
irreproachable, [able]
irresistible, [able]
irresolute, [acute]
irresolvable, [able]
irrespective, [ablative]
irresponsibility, [abatis]
irresponsible, [able]
irreverence, [abhorrence]
irreverent, [aberrant]
irreversible, [able]
irrevocable, [able]
irrigate, [abnegate]
irrigation, [abbreviation]
irritable, [able]
irritant, [abirritant]
irritate, [acetate]
irritated, [abluted]
irritation, [abbreviation]
irrupt, [abrupt]
is, [fizz]
Islam, [balm]
island, [almond]
isle, [aisle]
isolate, [ablate]
isolation, [abbreviation]
isolationism, [abolitionism]
isolationist, [abolitionist]
issuance, [abhorrence]
issue, [accrue]
isthmus, [allonymous]
it, [acquit]

italic, [acyclic]
italicize, [abscise]
itch, [backstitch]
item, [accustom]
itemization, [abbreviation]
itemize, [advise]
iterate, [accelerate]
iterative, [ablative]
itinerant, [aberrant]
itinerary, [accessory]
itinerate, [accelerate]
itself, [bookshelf]
ivory, [accessory]
ivy, [anchovy]
jab, [backstab]
jabber, [amber]
jack, [aback]
jackal, [acoustical]
jackass, [admass]
jacket, [advocate]
jackhammer, [armor]
jackknife, [afterlife]
jackpot, [aeronaut]
jactitation, [abbreviation]
jade, [abrade]
jag, [ag]
jagged, [acid]
jaguar, [abattoir]
jail, [ail]
jailbird, [absurd]
jailbreak, [awake]
jailer, [angler]
jailhouse, [alehouse]
jalopy, [apocope]
jam, [aerogram]
jamboree, [accessory]
jangle, [angle]
janitor, [abductor]
Japanese, [antifreeze]

jape, [agape]
jar, [abattoir]
jargon, [bandwagon]
jasper, [barkeeper]
jaundice, [antibias]
jaunt, [avaunt]
java, [alfalfa]
javelin, [acetylene]
jaw, [aah]
jawbone, [alone]
jawbreaker, [acre]
jayvee, [anchovy]
jaywalk, [aftershock]
jazz, [as]
jazzy, [advisee]
jealous, [acropolis]
jealousy, [absorbancy]
jean, [alexandrine]
jeep, [asleep]
jeer, [adhere]
jeez, [antifreeze]
jell, [bagatelle]
jelly roll, [areole]
jelly, [ably]
jellybean, [alexandrine]
jellyfish, [abolish]
jeopardize, [advise]
jeopardy, [acidy]
jerk, [artwork]
jerky, [achy]
jersey, [advisee]
jest, [abreast]
jester, [administer]
Jesu, [accrue]
Jesus, [antibias]
jet lag, [ag]
jet, [abet]
jetliner, [afterburner]
jetsam, [adventuresome]

jetsetter, [abductor]
jetty, [abatis]
Jew, [accrue]
jewel, [agile]
jeweler, [angler]
jewelry, [accessory]
jibe, [ascribe]
jiffy, [anastrophe]
jig, [big]
jigger, [agar]
jiggle, [angle]
jigsaw, [aah]
jihad, [abroad]
jillion, [antiunion]
jilt, [atilt]
jimmy, [academy]
jingle, [angle]
jink, [bethink]
jinx, larynx, links, lynx,
   pharynx, sphinx
jitney, [abalone]
jitter, [abductor]
jitterbug, [bedbug]
jittery, [accessory]
jive, [alive]
job, [ab]
Job, [bathrobe]
jobber, [amber]
jobless, [acropolis]
jock, [aftershock]
jockey, [achy]
jockstrap, [afterclap]
jocular, [angler]
jocund, [almond]
joe, [airshow]
jog, [agog]
jogger, [agar]
john, [amazon]
join, [adjoin]

joinder, [adder]
joiner, [afterburner]
joint, [anoint]
joist, [foist]
joke, [artichoke]
joker, [acre]
jolly, [ably]
jolt, [bolt]
josh, [awash]
jostle, [apostle]
jot, [aeronaut]
journal, [abdominal]
journalism, [abolitionism]
journalist, [aerialist]
journalize, [actualize]
journalizer, [adviser]
journey, [abalone]
journeyman, [abdomen]
joust, oust, roust
jovial, [abaxial]
joy, [ahoy]
joyful, [apocryphal]
joyless, [acropolis]
joyous, [antibias]
joyride, [abide]
joystick, [acoustic]
jubilant, [ambivalent]
jubilate, [ablate]
jubilation, [abbreviation]
jubilee, [ably]
judge, [adjudge]
judgment seat, [accrete]
judgment hall, [aerosol]
judgment, [abandonment]
judgmental, [accidental]
judicial, [abbatial]
judiciary, [accessory]
judicious, [adscititious]
judo, [aficionado]

jug, [bedbug]
juggernaut, [aeronaut]
juggle, [angle]
juggler, [angler]
juice, [abstruse]
juicer, [aggressor]
juicy, [absorbancy]
juke, [archduke]
jukebox, [bandbox]
julienne, [again]
jumble, [able]
jumbo, [airshow]
jump, [bump]
jumper, [barkeeper]
jumpsuit, [acute]
jumpy, [apocope]
junction, [abbreviation]
juncture, [acupuncture]
jungle, [angle]
junior, [ballplayer]
juniper, [barkeeper]
junk bond, [abscond]
junk, [bohunk]
junker, [acre]
junket, [advocate]
junkie, [achy]
junkyard, [backyard]
junta, [aorta]
jurat, [acrobat]
juridical, [acoustical]
jurisdiction, [abbreviation]
jurisdictional, [aboriginal]
jurisprudence, [accordance]
jurist, [allegorist]
juror, [adulterer]
jury, [accessory]
jussive, [abrasive]
just, [adjust]
justice, [afflatus]

justifiable, [able]
justification, [abbreviation]
justified, [abide]
justify, [amplify]
jut, [adequate]
jute, [acute]
juvenile, [anile]
juxtapose, [airhose]
juxtaposition, [abbreviation]
kabob, [ab]
kale, [ail]
kaleidoscope, [antelope]
kamikaze, [advisee]
kangaroo, [accrue]
kaput, [ablaut]
karaoke, [achy]
karat, [accurate]
karate chop, [agitprop]
karate, [abatis]
karma, [anathema]
kart, [apart]
kava, [alfalfa]
kayak, [aback]
kayo, [airshow]
kazoo, [accrue]
keel, [anneal]
keen, [alexandrine]
keep, [asleep]
keeper, [barkeeper]
keepsake, [awake]
keg, [beg]
keister, [administer]
kelp, [help]
kemp, [hemp]
kennel, [abdominal]
kept, [accept]
kerchief, [aperitif]
kernel, [abdominal]
kerosene, [alexandrine]

kerygma, [anathema]
ketchup, [backup]
ketosis, [alkalosis]
kettle, [accidental]
key, [achy]
keyboard, [aboard]
keyboard, [aboard]
keyhole, [areole]
keynote, [afloat]
keynoter, [abductor]
keypad, [ad]
keypunch, [brunch]
keypuncher, [acupuncture]
khaki, [achy]
kibble [able]
kibosh, [awash]
kick, [acidic]
kickback, [aback]
kicker, [acre]
kickoff, [boff]
kickstand, [ampersand]
kid, [amid]
kidnap, [afterclap]
kidnapper, [barkeeper]
kidney bean, [alexandrine]
kidney, [abalone]
kike, [alike]
kill, [backfill]
killer, [angler]
killjoy, [ahoy]
kiln, [backfill]
kilogram, [aerogram]
kilometer, [abductor]
kilowatt, [aeronaut]
kilt, [atilt]
kilter, [abductor]
kimchi, [blotchy]
kimono, [albino]
kin, [akin]

kind, [affined]
kindergarten, [anchorperson]
kindergartner, [afterburner]
kindle, [antipodal]
kindness, [agribusiness]
kindred, [acid]
kinfolk, [artichoke]
king, [anything]
kingdom, [addendum]
kingpin, [akin]
kingship, [airship]
kinky, [achy]
kinsfolk, [artichoke]
kinship, [airship]
kinsman, [abdomen]
kiosk, [bosk]
kirtle, [accidental]
kiss, [abyss]
kit, [acquit]
kitchenette, [bassinet]
kite, [affright]
kith, [blacksmith]
kitten, [anchorperson]
kitty, [abatis]
kittykat, [acrobat]
kiwi, [colloquy]
Klan, [adman]
kleptomaniac, [aback]
klister, [administer]
kludge, [centrifuge]
klutz, [giblets]
knack, [aback]
knap, [afterclap]
knapsack, [aback]
knave, [aftershave]
knavery, [accessory]
knead, [accede]
knee, [abalone]
kneecap, [afterclap]

kneel, [anneal]
knell, [bagatelle]
knew, [accrue]
knickers, [bonkers]
knife, [afterlife]
knifepoint, [anoint]
knight, [affright]
knighthood, [adulthood]
knit, [acquit]
knitwear, [affair]
knob, [ab]
knock, [aftershock]
knockdown, [boomtown]
knocker, [acre]
knockoff, [boff]
knockout, [about]
knockwurst, [athirst]
knoll, [areole]
knot, [aeronaut]
knothole, [areole]
knotted, [abluted]
knotty, [abatis]
know, [albino]
knowledge, [acknowledge]
known, [alone]
knuckle, [acoustical]
knuckleball, [aerosol]
knuckler, [angler]
kook, [archduke]
kooky, [achy]
Koran, [adman]
kosher, [acupressure]
kowtow, [allow]
kraft, [abaft]
kremlin, [acetylene]
Ku Klux Klan, [adman]
kudo, [aficionado]
kugel, [angle]
lab, [backstab]

label, [able]
labile, [anile]
labor, [amber]
laboratory, [accessory]
laborer, [adulterer]
laborious, [abstemious]
labyrinth, [hyacinth]
lace, [abase]
lacerate, [adjective] [accurate]
lacerate, [verb] [accelerate]
laceration, [abbreviation]
lack, [aback]
lackadaisical, [acoustical]
lackey, [achy]
lackluster, [administer]
laconic, [allergenic]
lacquer, [acre]
lacrosse, [across]
lactase, [abase]
lactate, [acetate]
lactation, [abbreviation]
lactic, [acoustic]
lactose, [adios]
lad, [ad]
ladder, [adder]
laddie, [acidy]
lade, [abrade]
laden, [anchorperson]
ladies, [antifreeze]
ladle, [antipodal]
lady, [acidy]
ladybug, [bedbug]
ladyfinger, [agar]
ladylike, [alike]
ladylove, [above]
laetrile, [backfill]
lag, [ag]
lager, [agar]
laggard, [absurd]

lagoon, [afternoon]
laid, [abrade]
lain, [abstain]
laity, [abatis]
lake, [awake]
lakefront, [aberrant]
lakeshore, [abhor]
lakeside, [abide]
lam, [aerogram]
lamb, [aerogram]
lambaste, [abased]
lambent, [abeyant]
lame duck, [amok]
lame, [acclaim]
lamebrain, [abstain]
lament, [abandonment]
lamentable, [able]
lamentation, [abbreviation]
lamented, [abluted]
lamia, [abulia]
laminate, **[adjective]**
  [acuminate]
laminate, **[verb]** [abominate]
laminated, [abluted]
lamination, [abbreviation]
lamp, [aid-de-camp]
lamplighter, [abductor]
lampoon, [afternoon]
lamppost, [aftermost]
lamster, [administer]
lance, [advance]
lancer, [aggressor]
land, [ampersand]
landau, [allow]
landed, [absentminded]
landfill, [backfill]
landgrab, [backstab]
landholder, [adder]
landlady, [acidy]

landlocked, [blocked]
landlord, [award]
landlubber, [amber]
landmark, [aardvark]
landmass, [admass]
landowner, [afterburner]
landscape, [agape]
landslide, [abide]
lane, [abstain]
language, [acknowledge]
languid, [acid]
languish, [abolish]
languor, [agar]
lank, [bank]
lanky, [achy]
lanolin, [acetylene]
lantern, [adjourn]
lap, [afterclap]
lapel, [bagatelle]
lapidary, [accessory]
lapse, [apse]
laptop, [agitprop]
larceny, [abalone]
lard, [backyard]
larder, [adder]
large, [barge]
largesse, [acquiesce]
largo, [ago]
lariat, [affiliate]
lark, [aardvark]
larva, [alfalfa]
laryngitis, [afflatus]
larynx, [jinx]
lasagna, [alleluia]
lascivious, [abstemious]
lase, [ablaze]
laser, [adviser]
lash, [abash]
lass, [admass]

lassie, [absorbancy]
lassitude, [altitude]
lasso, [also]
last, [aghast]
latch, [armpatch]
latchet, [adequate]
latchkey, [achy]
late, [ablate]
latecomer, [armor]
latent, [accordant]
later, [abductor]
lateral, [admiral]
latest, [adjust]
latex, [annex]
lath, [aftermath]
lathe, [bathe]
lather, [altogether]
latinize, [agnize]
latitude, [altitude]
latrine, [alexandrine]
latter, [abductor]
lattice, [afflatus]
laud, [abroad]
laudable, [able]
laudatory, [accessory]
laugh, [allograph]
laughable, [able]
laugher, [buffer]
laughingstock, [aftershock]
laughter, [abductor]
launch, [haunch]
launcher, [acupuncture]
launchpad, [ad]
launder, [adder]
laundromat, [acrobat]
laundry, [accessory]
laureate, [affiliate]
laurel, [admiral]
lava, [alfalfa]

lavaliere, [adhere]
lavation, [abbreviation]
lavatory, [accessory]
lave, [aftershave]
lavender, [adder]
laver, [achiever]
lavish, [abolish]
law, [aah]
lawbreaker, [acre]
lawful, [apocryphal]
lawgiver, [achiever]
lawmaker, [acre]
lawman, [abdomen]
lawn, [amazon]
lawsuit, [acute]
lawyer, [ballplayer]
lax, [anthrax]
laxative, [ablative]
lay, [airplay]
layaway, [airway]
layer, [ballplayer]
layman, [abdomen]
layoff, [boff]
layout, [about]
layover, [achiever]
laypeople, [ample]
layperson, [anchorperson]
layup, [backup]
laywoman, [abdomen]
lazar, [adviser]
laze, [ablaze]
laziness, [agribusiness]
lazy, [advisee]
leach, [beach]
lead, [verb] [abed]
lead, [verb] [accede]
leaden, [anchorperson]
leader, [adder]
leadership, [airship]

leadoff, [boff]
leaf, [aperitif]
leafage, [acknowledge]
leaflet, [aglet]
leafy, [anastrophe]
league, [blitzkrieg]
leak, [antique]
leakage, [acknowledge]
leakproof, [aloofi
leaky, [achy]
lean, [alexandrine]
leap, [asleep]
leaper, [barkeeper]
leapfrog, [agog]
leapt, [accept]
learn, [adjourn]
learned, [acid]
learner, [afterburner]
lease, [afterpiece]
leaseback, [aback]
leasehold, [ahold]
leash, [baksheesh]
least, [beast]
leather, [altogether]
leatherneck, [afterdeck]
leathery, [accessory]
leave, [achieve]
lechery, [accessory]
lectern, [adjourn]
lectionary, [accessory]
lecture, [acupuncture]
led, [abed]
ledge, [allege]
ledger, [armiger]
lee, [ably]
leech, [beach]
leek, [antique]
leeward, [absurd]
leeway, [airway]

left, [aleft]
leftist, [absolutist]
leftover, [achiever]
lefty, [abatis]
leg, [beg]
legacy, [absorbancy]
legal, [angle]
legalese, [antifreeze]
legalism, [abolitionism]
legalist, [aerialist]
legalistic, [acoustic]
legality, [abatis]
legalize, [actualize]
legate, [abnegate]
legatee, [abatis]
legation, [abbreviation]
legato, [aggiornamento]
legend, [almond]
legendary, [accessory]
leggy, [aggie]
legible, [able]
legion, [allergen]
legionary, [accessory]
legionnaire, [affair]
legislate, [ablate]
legislation, [abbreviation]
legislative, [ablative]
legislator, [abhor]
legislature, [acupuncture]
legitimacy, [absorbancy]
legitimate, **[adjective]**
  [animate]
legitimate, **[verb]** [acclimate]
legitimize, [advise]
legroom, [abloom]
legume, [abloom]
legwork, [artwork]
lei, [airplay]
leisure, [admeasure]

leisurely, [ably]
lemon, [abdomen]
lemonade, [abrade]
lend, [addend]
length, strength, wavelength
lengthwise, [advise]
lengthy, [apathy]
leniency, [absorbancy]
lenient, [abeyant]
Leningrad, [ad]
lens, [cleanse]
lentil, [accidental]
leopard, [absurd]
leotard, [backyard]
leper, [barkeeper]
leprechaun, [amazon]
leprosy, [absorbancy]
leprous, [actress]
lesbian, [abecedarian]
lesbianism, [abolitionism]
lesion, [abrasion]
less, [acquiesce]
lessee, [absorbancy]
lessen, [anchorperson]
lesser, [aggressor]
lesson, [anchorperson]
lessor, [abhor]
lest, [abreast]
let, [abet]
letdown, [boomtown]
lethal, [agile]
lethargic, [acidic]
lethargy, [allergy]
letter bomb, [aplomb]
letter, [abductor]
letterhead, [abed]
letterman, [abdomen]
lettuce, [afflatus]
letup, [backup]

leukemia, [abulia]
levee, [anchovy]
level, [adjectival]
lever, [achiever]
leverage, [abridge]
levirate, [accurate]
levitate, [acetate]
levitation, [abbreviation]
Levitical, [acoustical]
levity, [abatis]
levy, [anchovy]
lewd, [allude]
lewdness, [agribusiness]
lex, [annex]
lexeme, [abeam]
lexical, [acoustical]
lexicon, [amazon]
liability, [abatis]
liable, [able]
liaison, [amazon]
liar, [amplifier]
lib, [bib]
libation, [abbreviation]
libber, [amber]
libel, [able]
libelous, [acropolis]
liberal, [admiral]
liberalism, [abolitionism]
liberality, [abatis]
liberalization, [abbreviation]
liberalize, [actualize]
liberate, [accelerate]
liberated, [abluted]
liberation, [abbreviation]
liberationist, [abolitionist]
libertine, [alexandrine]
liberty, [abatis]
libido, [aficionado]
libra, [abracadabra]

librarian, [abecedarian]
library, [accessory]
lice, [advice]
license, [accordance]
licensure, [acupressure]
licentious, [adscititious]
licit, [corset]
lick, [acyclic]
licorice, [abolish]
lid, [amid]
lido, [aficionado]
lie, [airdry]
lien, [alexandrine]
lieu, [accrue]
lieutenant, [abstinent]
life, [afterlife]
lifeblood, [acid]
lifeboat, [afloat]
lifeguard, [backyard]
lifeless, [acropolis]
lifelike, [alike]
lifeline, [airline]
lifelong, [agelong]
lifer, [buffer]
lifesaver, [achiever]
lifestyle, [aisle]
lifetime, [airtime]
lifework, [artwork]
lift, [adrift]
liftoff, [boff]
ligament, [abandonment]
ligature, [abjure]
light, [affright]
lightbulb, [bulb]
lighten, [anchorperson]
lighter, [abductor]
lightface, [abase]
lightfast, [aghast]
lighthouse, [alehouse]

lightplane, [abstain]
lightproof, [aloof]
lightweight, [accentuate]
likable, [able]
like, [alike]
likelihood, [adulthood]
likely, [ably]
liken, [awaken]
likeness, [agribusiness]
likewise, [advise]
lilac, [aftershock]
lilt, [atilt]
lily, [ably]
lima bean, [alexandrine]
limb, [acronym]
limber, [amber]
limbo, [airshow]
lime, [airtime]
limeade, [abrade]
limelight, [affright]
limerick, [aleatoric]
limestone, [atone]
limit, [animate]
limitation, [abbreviation]
limited, [abed]
limitless, [acropolis]
limo, [airshow]
limousine, [alexandrine]
limp, [blimp]
linchpin, [akin]
line, [airline]
lineage, [acknowledge]
lineage, [appanage]
lineal, [abaxial]
linear, [anterior]
linebacker, [acre]
lineman, [abdomen]
liner, [afterburner]
linesman, [abdomen]

lineup, [backup]
linger, [agar]
lingerie, [affray]
lingo, [ago]
lingua, [alfalfa]
lingual, [agile]
linguine, [abalone]
linguist, [activist]
linguistic, [acoustic]
linguistics, [acoustics]
liniment, [abandonment]
link, [bethink]
linkage, [acknowledge]
linked, [distinct]
links, [jinx]
linkup, [backup]
linoleum, [anthurium]
linseed, [accede]
lint, [blueprint]
lintel, [accidental]
lioness, [agribusiness]
lionheart, [apart]
lionize, [agnize]
lip, [airstrip]
lipid, [acid]
liposuction, [abbreviation]
lipstick, [acoustic]
liquefy, [amplify]
liqueur, [acre]
liquid, [acid]
liquidate, [accommodate]
liquidation, [abbreviation]
liquidator, [abductor]
liquidity, [abatis]
liquor, [acre]
lisp, [crisp]
list, [aerialist]
listel, [accidental]
listen, [anchorperson]

listener, [afterburner]
listless, [acropolis]
lit, [acquit]
litany, [abalone]
litchi, [blotchy]
lite, [affright]
liter, [abductor]
literacy, [absorbancy]
literal, [admiral]
literary, [accessory]
literate, [accurate]
literation, [abbreviation]
literature, [abjure]
lithe, [blithe]
lithic, [acidic]
lithify, [amplify]
lithium, [anthurium]
litho, [airshow]
lithograph, [allograph]
litigant, [abeyant]
litigate, [abnegate]
litigation, [abbreviation]
litigator, [abductor]
litigious, [advantageous]
litmus, [allonymous]
litotes, [antifreeze]
litter, [abductor]
litterbag, [ag]
litterbug, [bedbug]
little league, [blitzkrieg]
little, [accidental]
liturgical, [acoustical]
liturgy, [allergy]
livable, [able]
live, [adjective] [alive]
live, [verb] [forgive]
livelihood, [adulthood]
lively, [ably]
liver, [achiever]

liverwurst, [athirst]
livery, [accessory]
livestock, [aftershock]
livid, [acid]
lizard, [absurd]
lo, [afterglow]
load, [abode]
loaded, [absentminded]
loader, [adder]
loaf, oaf, sugarloaf
loafer, [buffer]
loan, [alone]
loaner, [afterburner]
loathe, [clothe]
loathsome, [adventuresome]
lob, [ab]
lobby, [abbey]
lobbyist, [activist]
lobe, [bathrobe]
lobster, [administer]
local, [acoustical]
locale, [canal]
locality, [abatis]
localize, [actualize]
locate, [abdicate]
location, [abbreviation]
locative, [ablative]
lock, [aftershock]
lockbox, [bandbox]
lockdown, [boomtown]
locker, [acre]
locket, [advocate]
lockjaw, [aah]
lockkeeper, [barkeeper]
locknut, [acuminate]
lockout, [about]
locksmith, [blacksmith]
lockstep, [crowstep]
lockup, [backup]

loco, [alfresco]
locomotion, [abbreviation]
locomotive, [ablative]
locus, [abacus]
locust, [adjust]
lode, [abode]
lodestar, [abattoir]
lodge, [dislodge]
loft, [aloft]
lofty, [abatis]
log, [agog]
loggerhead, [abed]
logic, [acidic]
logical, [acoustical]
logician, [abbreviation]
logistic, [acoustic]
logistics, [acoustics]
logjam, [aerogram]
logo, [ago]
loin, [adjoin]
loiter, [abductor]
loll, [aerosol]
lollipop, [agitprop]
lollygag, [ag]
lone, [alone]
loneliness, [agribusiness]
lonely, [ably]
loner, [afterburner]
lonesome, [adventuresome]
lonestar, [abattoir]
long shot, [aeronaut]
long, [agelong]
longer, [agar]
longevity, [abatis]
longhair, [affair]
longhand, [ampersand]
longhorn, [acorn]
longitude, [altitude]
longtime, [airtime]

look, [bankbook]
looker, [acre]
looking glass, [admass]
lookout, [about]
loom, [abloom]
loon, [afternoon]
loony, [abalone]
loop, [coop]
loophole, [areole]
loose, [abstruse]
loosed, [boost]
loosen, [anchorperson]
loot, [acute]
lop, [agitprop]
lope, [antelope]
loquacious, [adscititious]
lord, [award]
lordship, [airship]
lore, [abhor]
lose, [amuse]
loser, [adviser]
loss, [across]
lost, [accost]
lot, [aeronaut]
lotion, [abbreviation]
lottery, [accessory]
lotto, [aggiornamento]
loud, [aloud]
loudmouth, [badmouth]
loudness, [agribusiness]
loudspeaker, [acre]
lounge, scrounge
lousy, [advisee]
lout, [about]
loutish, [abolish]
louver, [achiever]
lovable, [able]
love child, [beguiled]
love, [above]

lovebird, [absurd]
lovebug, [bedbug]
loveliness, [agribusiness]
lovelorn, [acorn]
lovely, [ably]
lover, [achiever]
lovesick, [airsick]
low, [afterglow]
lowball, [aerosol]
lowboy, [ahoy]
lowbrow, [allow]
lowdown, [boomtown]
lower, [airpower]
lower-class, [admass]
lowlander, [adder]
lowlife, [afterlife]
lowly, [ably]
loyal, [broil]
loyalist, [aerialist]
loyalty, [abatis]
lozenge, [challenge]
lubber, [amber]
lube, [boob]
lubricant, [abeyant]
lubricate, [abdicate]
lubrication, [abbreviation]
lucent, [adjacent]
lucid, [acid]
luck, [amok]
lucky, [achy]
lucrative, [ablative]
lucre, [acre]
ludicrous, [actress]
lug, [bedbug]
luge, rouge
luggage, [acknowledge]
lukewarm, [aswarm]
lull, [agile]
lullaby, [alibi]

lulu, [accrue]
lumber, [amber]
lumberyard, [backyard]
luminaria, [abulia]
luminary, [accessory]
luminescent, [adjacent]
luminous, [agribusiness]
lump, [bump]
lumpy, [apocope]
lunacy, [absorbancy]
lunar, [afterburner]
lunatic, [acoustic]
lunch, [brunch]
luncheonette, [bassinet]
lunchroom, [abloom]
lunchtime, [airtime]
lung, [among]
lunge, [challenge]
lurch, [antichurch]
lure, [abjure]
lurid, [acid]
lurk, [artwork]
luscious, [adscititious]
lush, [airbrush]
lust, [adjust]
luster, [administer]
lustful, [apocryphal]
lustrous, [actress]
lusty, [abatis]
lute, [acute]
luxuriant, [abeyant]
luxurious, [abstemious]
luxury, [accessory]
lye, [airdry]
lynch, [bullfinch]
lynx, [jinx]
lyre, [acquire]
lyric, [aleatoric]
lyrical, [acoustical]

lyricist, [assist]
ma, [aah]
ma'am, [aerogram]
macabre, [ab]
macadam, [addendum]
macaroni, [abalone]
macaroon, [afternoon]
mace, [abase]
macerate, [accelerate]
machete, [abatis]
machinate, [abominate]
machination, [abbreviation]
machine, [alexandrine]
machinery, [accessory]
machinist, [abolitionist]
machismo, [airshow]
macho, [airshow]
mackerel, [admiral]
mackinaw, [aah]
mackintosh, [awash]
macramé, [agape]
mad, [ad]
madam, [addendum]
madame, [aerogram]
madden, [anchorperson]
made, [abrade]
mademoiselle, [bagatelle]
madhouse, [alehouse]
madman, [adman]
madness, [agribusiness]
madrigal, [angle]
maelstrom, [addendum]
maestro, [allegro]
magazine, [alexandrine]
maggot, [agate]
magi, [airdry]
magic, [acidic]
magical, [acoustical]
magician, [abbreviation]

magistrate, [accelerate]
magma, [anathema]
magnanimity, [abatis]
magnanimous, [allonymous]
magnate, [abominate]
magnesium, [anthurium]
magnet, [acuminate]
magnetic, [acoustic]
magnetism, [abolitionism]
magnetize, [absolutize]
magneto, [aggiornamento]
magnific, [anthropomorphic]
magnificat, [acrobat]
magnification, [abbreviation]
magnificence, [abhorrence]
magnificent, [acquiescent]
magnifico, [alfresco]
magnifier, [amplifier]
magnify, [amplify]
magniloquence, [abhorrence]
magniloquent, [abeyant]
magnitude, [altitude]
magnolia, [alleluia]
magus, [analogous]
maharaja, [alfalfa]
maharishi, [banshee]
mahogany, [abalone]
maid, [abrade]
maiden, [anchorperson]
maidservant, [abeyant]
mail bomb, [aplomb]
mail, [ail]
mailbag, [ag]
mailbox, [bandbox]
mailer, [angler]
mailman, [adman]
maim, [acclaim]
main, [abstain]
mainframe, [acclaim]

mainland, [ampersand]
mainline, [airline]
mainspring, [anything]
mainstay, [agape]
mainstream, [abeam]
maintain, [abstain]
maintenance, [abhorrence]
maize, [ablaze]
majestic, [acoustic]
majesty, [abatis]
major league, [blitzkrieg]
major, [armiger]
majordomo, [airshow]
majorette, [abet]
majority, [abatis]
majorly, [ably]
makable, [able]
make believe, [achieve]
make, [awake]
makeover, [achiever]
maker, [acre]
makeshift, [adrift]
makeup, [backup]
makimono, [albino]
maladapted, [abluted]
maladaption, [abbreviation]
maladaptive, [ablative]
maladjusted, [abluted]
malady, [acidy]
malaise, [ablaze]
malaria, [abulia]
malarkey, [achy]
malcontent, [accent]
male, [ail]
malediction, [abbreviation]
malefactor, [abductor]
malefic, [anthropomorphic]
maleficence, [abhorrence]
maleficent, [acquiescent]

malevolence, [abhorrence]
malevolent, [ambivalent]
malfeasance, [accordance]
malformation, [abbreviation]
malfunction, [abbreviation]
Malibu, [accrue]
malice, [acropolis]
malicious, [adscititious]
malign, [aerodyne]
malignancy, [absorbancy]
malignant, [abstinent]
malinger, [agar]
mall, [aerosol]
mallard, [absurd]
malleable, [able]
mallee, [ably]
mallet, [aglet]
malnutrition, [abbreviation]
malodor, [adder]
malodorous, [actress]
malpractice, [afflatus]
malt, [asphalt]
maltreat, [accrete]
mamma, [anathema]
mammon, [abdomen]
mammoth, [altazimuth]
mammy, [academy]
man, [adman]
mana, [alumna]
manacle, [acoustical]
manage, [appanage]
manageable, [able]
management, [abandonment]
manager, [armiger]
manana, [alumna]
manciple, [ample]
mandala, [a capella]
mandate, [accommodate]
mandatory, [accessory]

mandolin, [akin]
mandrake, [awake]
mandrel, [admiral]
mane, [abstain]
manege, [cortege]
maneuver, [achiever]
manger, [armiger]
mangle, [angle]
mango, [ago]
mangy, [allergy]
manhandle, [antipodal]
manhattan, [anchorperson]
manhole, [areole]
manhood, [adulthood]
manhunt, [abeyant]
mania, [abulia]
maniac, [aback]
maniacal, [acoustical]
manic, [allergenic]
manicotti, [abatis]
manicure, [abjure]
manicurist, [allegorist]
manifest, [abreast]
manifestation, [abbreviation]
manifesto, [aggiornamento]
manifold, [ahold]
manikin, [awaken]
manipulate, [ablate]
manipulation, [abbreviation]
manipulative, [ablative]
manipulator, [abductor]
manitou, [accrue]
mankind, [affined]
manna, [alumna]
manned, [ampersand]
mannequin, [awaken]
manner, [afterburner]
mannerism, [abolitionism]
mannerly, [ably]

mannish, [abolish]
manor, [afterburner]
manse, [advance]
mansion, [abbreviation]
mansuetude, [altitude]
manta, [aorta]
mantel, [accidental]
mantic, [acoustic]
manticore, [abhor]
mantilla, [alleluia]
mantle, [accidental]
mantra, [abracadabra]
manual, [accrual]
manufacture, [acupuncture]
manufacturer, [adulterer]
manumission, [abbreviation]
manumit, [acquit]
manure, [abjure]
manuscript, [adscript]
manyfold, [ahold]
map, [afterclap]
maple, [ample]
maquette, [abet]
marabou, [accrue]
maraschino, [albino]
marathon, [amazon]
maraud, [abroad]
marble, [able]
marbled, [bedraggled]
march, [arch]
mare, [affair]
marengo, [ago]
margarita, [aorta]
margin, [allergen]
marginal, [aboriginal]
marginalize, [actualize]
mariachi, [blotchy]
marigold, [ahold]
marijuana, [alumna]

marimba, [abracadabra]
marimbist, [activist]
marina, [alumna]
marinade, [abrade]
marinara, [abracadabra]
marinate, [abominate]
marine, [alexandrine]
mariner, [afterburner]
marionette, [bassinet]
marital, [accidental]
maritime, [airtime]
mark, [aardvark]
markdown, [boomtown]
marker, [acre]
market, [advocate]
marketable, [able]
marketeer, [adhere]
marketer, [abductor]
marketplace, [abase]
marksman, [abdomen]
marksmanship, [airship]
markup, [backup]
marlin, [acetylene]
marmalade, [abrade]
marmoreal, [abaxial]
maroon, [afternoon]
marplot, [aeronaut]
marquee, [achy]
marriage, [abridge]
marriageable, [able]
marrow, [allegro]
marry, [accessory]
marsh, [harsh]
marshal, [abbatial]
marshland, [ampersand]
marshmallow, [afterglow]
marshy, [banshee]
mart, [apart]
martial, [abbatial]

martian, [abbreviation]
martinet, [bassinet]
martingale, [ail]
martini, [abalone]
martyr, [abductor]
martyrdom, [addendum]
marvel, [adjectival]
marvelous, [acropolis]
marzipan, [amazon]
mascara, [abracadabra]
mascot, [aeronaut]
masculine, [acetylene]
mash, [abash]
mask, [ask]
masochism, [abolitionism]
masochist, [activist]
masochistic, [acoustic]
mason, [anchorperson]
masonry, [accessory]
masquerade, [abrade]
mass, [admass]
massacre, [acre]
massage, [arbitrage]
masseur, [aggressor]
masseuse, [amuse]
massive, [abrasive]
mast, [aghast]
mastectomy, [academy]
master, [administer]
masterful, [apocryphal]
masterfull, [apocryphal]
masterly, [ably]
mastermind, [affined]
masterpiece, [afterpiece]
masterstroke, [artichoke]
mastery, [accessory]
masthead, [abed]
masticate, [abdicate]
mastitis, [afflatus]

mastodon, [amazon]
masturbate, [abate]
masturbation, [abbreviation]
mat, [acrobat]
matador, [abhor]
match, [armpatch]
matchbook, [bankbook]
matchbox, [bandbox]
matchless, [acropolis]
matchlock, [aftershock]
matchmaker, [acre]
matchstick, [acoustic]
matchup, [backup]
mate, [acclimate]
material, [abaxial]
materialism, [abolitionism]
materialist, [aerialist]
materialistic, [acoustic]
materialize, [actualize]
maternal, [abdominal]
maternity, [abatis]
math, [aftermath]
mathematical, [acoustical]
mathematician, [abbreviation]
mathematics, [acoustics]
matinee, [agape]
matriarch, [aardvark]
matriarchy, [achy]
matricide, [abide]
matriculate, [ablate]
matrimonial, [abaxial]
matrimony, [abalone]
matrix, [administratrix]
matte, [acrobat]
matter, [abductor]
matter-of-fact, [abstract]
Matthew, [accrue]
mattress, [actress]
maturate, [accelerate]

maturation, [abbreviation]
mature, [abjure]
maturity, [abatis]
matzo, [alfalfa]
maudlin, [acetylene]
maul, [aerosol]
maunder, [adder]
mausoleum, [anthurium]
mauve, suave
maverick, [aleatoric]
maw, [aah]
max, [anthrax]
maxi, [absorbancy]
maxim, [adventuresome]
maximal, [abnormal]
maximin, [akin]
maximization, [abbreviation]
maximize, [advise]
maximum, [addendum]
may, [agape]
mayflower, [airpower]
mayhem, [apothegm]
mayonnaise, [ablaze]
mayoral, [admiral]
maze, [ablaze]
mazer, [adviser]
mead, [accede]
meadow, [aficionado]
meadowland, [ampersand]
meadowlark, [aardvark]
meager, [agar]
meal, [anneal]
mealtime, [airtime]
mean, [alexandrine]
meander, [adder]
meanie, [abalone]
meaningful, [apocryphal]
meaningless, [acropolis]
meantime, [airtime]

meanwhile, [anile]
measles, [annals]
measly, [ably]
measure, [admeasure]
measureless, [acropolis]
measurement, [abandonment]
meat, [accrete]
meatball, [aerosol]
meathead, [abed]
meaty, [abatis]
mecca, [angelica]
mechanic, [allergenic]
mechanical, [acoustical]
mechanics, [administratrix]
mechanism, [abolitionism]
mechanistic, [acoustic]
mechanize, [agnize]
medal, [antipodal]
medalist, [aerialist]
medallion, [antiunion]
meddle, [antipodal]
meddlesome,
  [adventuresome]
medevac, [aback]
media, [abulia]
median, [abecedarian]
mediate, [adjective] [create]
mediate, [verb] [affiliate]
mediation, [abbreviation]
mediator, [abductor]
mediatrix, [administratrix]
medic, [acidic]
medicaid, [abrade]
medical, [acoustical]
medicare, [affair]
medicate, [abdicate]
medication, [abbreviation]
medicinal, [aboriginal]
medicine man, [adman]

medieval, [adjectival]
mediocre, [acre]
mediocrity, [abatis]
meditate, [acetate]
meditation, [abbreviation]
meditative, [ablative]
medium, [addendum]
medley, [ably]
meek, [antique]
meekness, [agribusiness]
meet, [accrete]
megabuck, [amok]
megabyte, [affright]
megadose, [adios]
megahertz, [gigahertz]
megalomania, [abulia]
megalomaniac, [aback]
megaphone, [alone]
megapolis, [acropolis]
melancholic, [acyclic]
melancholy, [ably]
melanoma, [anathema]
meld, [geld]
melee, [airplay]
meliorate, [accelerate]
mellifluous, [ambiguous]
mellophone, [alone]
mellow, [afterglow]
mellowness, [agribusiness]
melodic, [acidic]
melodious, [abstemious]
melodist, [activist]
melodrama, [anathema]
melodramatic, [acoustic]
melody, [acidy]
melon, [acetylene]
melt, [belt]
meltdown, [boomtown]
member, [amber]

membership, [airship]
membrane, [abstain]
memento, [aggiornamento]
memo, [airshow]
memoir, [abattoir]
memorabilia, [abulia]
memorable, [able]
memorandum, [addendum]
memorial, [abaxial]
memorialize, [actualize]
memorization, [abbreviation]
memorize, [accessorize]
memory, [accessory]
menace, [agribusiness]
menage, [arbitrage]
menagerie, [accessory]
mend, [addend]
mendable, [able]
mendacious, [adscititious]
mendacity, [abatis]
mendicant, [abeyant]
menial, [abaxial]
meningitis, [afflatus]
menopause, [applause]
menorah, [abracadabra]
mense, [cense]
menstrual, [accrual]
menstruate, [accentuate]
menstruation, [abbreviation]
mensurable, [able]
mental, [accidental]
mentality, [abatis]
menthol, [aerosol]
mention, [abbreviation]
mentor, [abhor]
menu, [accrue]
meow, [allow]
mercantile, [automobile]
mercantilism, [abolitionism]

mercantilist, [aerialist]
mercenary, [accessory]
merchandise, [advise]
merchant, [abeyant]
merciful, [apocryphal]
merciless, [acropolis]
mercurate, [accelerate]
mercurial, [abaxial]
mercury, [accessory]
mercy, [absorbancy]
mere, [adhere]
meretricious, [adscititious]
merge, [converge]
merger, [armiger]
meridian, [abecedarian]
merino, [albino]
merit, [accurate]
meritorious, [abstemious]
mermaid, [abrade]
merriment, [abandonment]
merriness, [agribusiness]
merry-go-around, [abound]
merrymonastery, [accessory]
mesa, [alfalfa]
mesh, [afresh]
mesmerize, [accessorize]
mesne, [alexandrine]
mesquite, [accrete]
mess, [acquiesce]
message, [acknowledge]
messenger, [armiger]
messiah, [alfalfa]
messianic, [allergenic]
messiness, [agribusiness]
messy, [absorbancy]
mestiza, [alfalfa]
mestizo, [bozo]
met, [abet]
metabolic, [acyclic]

metabolism, [abolitionism]
metabolize, [actualize]
metacenter, [abductor]
metal, [accidental]
metallic, [acyclic]
metallurgy, [allergy]
metalwork, [artwork]
metamorphose, [airhose]
metamorphosis, [alkalosis]
metaphor, [abhor]
metaphorical, [acoustical]
metaphysical, [acoustical]
metaphysics, [administratrix]
metastasize, [abscise]
mete, [accrete]
meteor, [anterior]
meteoric, [aleatoric]
meteorite, [affright]
meteoroid, [adenoid]
meter, [abductor]
methadone, [alone]
methane, [abstain]
method, [acid]
methodical, [acoustical]
methodism, [abolitionism]
methodist, [activist]
methodize, [advise]
methodological, [acoustical]
methodology, [allergy]
meticulous, [acropolis]
metonymy, [academy]
metric, [aleatoric]
metrical, [acoustical]
metro, [allegro]
metronome, [astrodome]
metropolis, [acropolis]
metropolitan, [anchorperson]
mettle, [accidental]
mezzanine, [alexandrine]

miasma, [anathema]
miasmic, [academic]
mice, [advice]
microbe, [bathrobe]
microchip, [airstrip]
microcosm, [abolitionism]
microfiche, [baksheesh]
microfilm, [film]
micromanage, [appanage]
micromanagement,
  [abandonment]
micromanager, [armiger]
microorganism, [abolitionism]
microphone, [alone]
microprocessor, [aggressor]
microscope, [antelope]
microscopic, [acidic]
microwave, [aftershave]
mid, [amid]
midair, [affair]
midcourse, [coarse]
midday, [agape]
middle age, [age]
Middle East, [beast]
middle ground, [abound]
middle, [antipodal]
middle-class, [admass]
middleman, [adman]
middler, [angler]
middleweight, [accentuate]
middy, [acidy]
Mideast, [beast]
midfield, [airfield]
midget, [adequate]
midi, [acidy]
midland, [almond]
midlife, [afterlife]
midnight, [affright]
midpoint, [anoint]

midrash, [awash]
midriff, [anaglyph]
midshipman, [abdomen]
midsize, [abscise]
midsole, [areole]
midst, [amidst]
midstream, [abeam]
midsummer, [armor]
midterm, [affirm]
midtown, [boomtown]
midway, [airway]
midweek, [antique]
Midwest, [abreast]
midwife, [afterlife]
midwinter, [abductor]
midyear, [adhere]
mien, [alexandrine]
miff, [anaglyph]
miffed, [adrift]
might, [affright]
mighty, [abatis]
mignon, [alone]
migraine, [abstain]
migrant, [aberrant]
migrate, [accelerate]
migration, [abbreviation]
mikado, [aficionado]
mike, [alike]
mil, [backfill]
milady, [acidy]
mild, [beguiled]
mildew, [accrue]
mile, [aisle]
mileage, [acknowledge]
miler, [angler]
milestone, [atone]
miliaria, [abulia]
milieu, [accrue]
militant, [abirritant]

militarism, [abolitionism]
militaristic, [acoustic]
militarize, [accessorize]
military, [accessory]
militate, [acetate]
militia, [alfalfa]
militiaman, [abdomen]
milk shake, [awake]
milk, [bilk]
milkman, [abdomen]
milky, [achy]
mill, [backfill]
millage, [acknowledge]
millenarian, [abecedarian]
millennial, [abaxial]
millennialism, [abolitionism]
millennium, [anthurium]
miller, [angler]
millet, [aglet]
milligram, [aerogram]
million, [antiunion]
millionaire, [affair]
millpond, [abscond]
millrace, [abase]
millstone, [atone]
millwork, [artwork]
millwright, [affright]
mime, [airtime]
mimeograph, [allograph]
mimic, [academic]
mimicry, [accessory]
mina, [alumna]
minatory, [accessory]
mince, [convince]
mincemeat, [accrete]
mind, [affined]
minded, [absentminded]
mindful, [apocryphal]
mindless, [acropolis]

mine, [aerodyne]
minefield, [airfield]
mineral, [admiral]
minestrone, [abalone]
minesweeper, [barkeeper]
mingle, [angle]
mingy, [allergy]
miniature, [abjure]
miniaturize, [accessorize]
minibike, [alike]
minibus, [abbess]
minicamp, [aid-de-camp]
minicar, [abattoir]
minicomputer, [abductor]
minicourse, [coarse]
minimal, [abnormal]
minimax, [anthrax]
minimize, [advise]
minimum, [addendum]
minion, [antiunion]
miniseries, [antifreeze]
miniskirt, [advert]
minister, [administer]
ministerial, [abaxial]
ministration, [abbreviation]
ministry, [ancestry]
minivan, [adman]
mink, [bethink]
minnow, [albino]
minor league, [blitzkrieg]
minor, [afterburner]
minority, [abatis]
minster, [administer]
minstrel, [admiral]
mint, [blueprint]
mintage, [acknowledge]
minuend, [addend]
minuet, [abet]
minus, [agribusiness]

minuscule, [bascule]
minute, [noun] [acuminate]
minute, [verb] [acute]
minuteman, [adman]
minutia, [abulia]
minutia, [alfalfa]
minyan, [antiunion]
miracle, [acoustical]
miraculous, [acropolis]
mirage, [arbitrage]
mire, [acquire]
mirror, [adulterer]
mirth, [afterbirth]
misaddress, [actress]
misadventure, [acupuncture]
misadvise, [advise]
misaim, [acclaim]
misalign, [airline]
misallocate, [abdicate]
misallocation, [abbreviation]
misapplication, [abbreviation]
misapply, [airdry]
misapprehend, [addend]
misappropriate, [create]
misbehave, [aftershave]
misbehavior, [ballplayer]
miscalculate, [ablate]
miscalculation, [abbreviation]
miscarriage, [abridge]
miscarry, [accessory]
miscast, [aghast]
miscatalog, [agog]
miscellaneous, [abstemious]
miscellany, [abalone]
mischaracterization,
  [abbreviation]
mischaracterize, [accessorize]
mischarge, [barge]
mischievous, [antibias]

misclassification,
  [abbreviation]
misclassify, [amplify]
miscode, [abode]
miscommunication,
  [abbreviation]
miscomprehension,
  [abbreviation]
miscomputation,
  [abbreviation]
misconceive, [achieve]
misconception, [abbreviation]
misconduct, [abduct]
misconnection, [abbreviation]
misconstruction,
  [abbreviation]
misconstrue, [accrue]
miscue, [accrue]
misdeed, [accede]
misdemeanor, [afterburner]
misdial, [aisle]
misdirection, [abbreviation]
misemphasis, [alkalosis]
miser, [adviser]
miserable, [able]
misery, [accessory]
misestimate, [animate]
misevaluate, [accentuate]
misevaluation, [abbreviation]
misfile, [aisle]
misfire, [acquire]
misfit, [acquit]
misfunction, [abbreviation]
misgovern, [adjourn]
misguage, [age]
misguided, [absentminded]
mishandle, [antipodal]
mishap, [afterclap]
mishit, [acquit]

mishmash, [abash]
misidentification,
  [abbreviation]
misidentify, [amplify]
misinform, [aswarm]
misinformation, [abbreviation]
misinterpret, [accurate]
misjudge, [adjudge]
mislabel, [able]
mislay, [airplay]
mislead, [accede]
misled, [abed]
mismanage, [appanage]
mismatch, [armpatch]
misname, [acclaim]
misnomer, [armor]
miso, [also]
misogamy, [academy]
misogyny, [abalone]
misology, [allergy]
misoneism, [abolitionism]
mispackage, [acknowledge]
misperceive, [achieve]
misperception, [abbreviation]
misplace, [abase]
misplay, [airplay]
misprint, [blueprint]
mispronounce, [announce]
mispronunciation,
  [abbreviation]
misquotation, [abbreviation]
misquote, [afloat]
misread, [accede]
misrecord, [award]
misrepresent, [accent]
misroute, [about]
misrule, [bascule]
miss, [abyss]
missal, [apostle]

missend, [addend]
misshapen, [antiphon]
missile, [apostle]
missiology, [allergy]
missionary, [accessory]
missive, [abrasive]
missort, [airport]
misspeak, [antique]
misspell, [bagatelle]
misspend, [addend]
misstate, [acetate]
misstatement, [abandonment]
misstep, [crowstep]
missus, [abuzz]
missy, [absorbancy]
mist, [alchemist]
mistake, [awake]
mister, [administer]
misthrow, [allegro]
mistitle, [accidental]
mistletoe, [aggiornamento]
mistook, [bankbook]
mistranscribe, [ascribe]
mistranslate, [ablate]
mistranslation, [abbreviation]
mistreat, [accrete]
mistreatment, [abandonment]
mistress, [actress]
mistrial, [aisle]
mistrust, [adjust]
misty, [abatis]
mistype, [airpipe]
misunderstand, [ampersand]
misunderstood, [adulthood]
misusage, [acknowledge]
misuse, [abuse]
miswrite, [affright]
mite, [affright]
miter, [abductor]

mithridate, [accommodate]
miticide, [abide]
mitigate, [abnegate]
mitigation, [abbreviation]
mitt, [acquit]
mitten, [anchorperson]
mittimus, [allonymous]
mitzvah, [alfalfa]
mix, [administratrix]
mixer, [aggressor]
mixture, [acupuncture]
mnemonic, [allergenic]
mnemonics, [administratrix]
moan, [alone]
moat, [afloat]
mob, [ab]
mobile, [able]
mobilization, [abbreviation]
mobilize, [actualize]
mobster, [administer]
mocha, [angelica]
mock, [aftershock]
mocker, [acre]
mockery, [accessory]
mockingbird, [absurd]
mod, [abroad]
modal, [antipodal]
modality, [abatis]
mode, [abode]
model, [antipodal]
modem, [addendum]
moderate, [noun] [accurate]
moderate, [verb] [accelerate]
moderation, [abbreviation]
moderator, [abductor]
modern, [adjourn]
modernism, [abolitionism]
modernist, [abolitionist]
modernistic, [acoustic]

modernity, [abatis]
modernization, [abbreviation]
modernize, [agnize]
modest, [adjust]
modesty, [abatis]
modicum, [addendum]
modification, [abbreviation]
modifier, [amplifier]
modify, [amplify]
modish, [abolish]
modiste, [beast]
modular, [angler]
modulate, [ablate]
modulation, [abbreviation]
module, [bascule]
mogul, [angle]
moiety, [abatis]
moil, [broil]
moist, [foist]
moisten, [anchorperson]
moisture, [acupuncture]
moisturize, [accessorize]
mojo, [airshow]
molar, [angler]
molasses, [abuzz]
moldable, [able]
moldy, [acidy]
mole, [areole]
molecular, [angler]
molecule, [bascule]
molehill, [backfill]
molest, [abreast]
molestation, [abbreviation]
molester, [administer]
moline, [alexandrine]
moll, [aerosol]
mollycoddle, [antipodal]
molt, [bolt]
molten, [anchorperson]

molto, [aggiornamento]
mom, [aplomb]
moment, [abandonment]
momentary, [accessory]
momentous, [afflatus]
momentum, [accustom]
mommy, [academy]
monad, [ad]
monarch, [aardvark]
monarchal, [acoustical]
monarchical, [acoustical]
monarchy, [achy]
monastic, [acoustic]
monaural, [admiral]
monetarism, [abolitionism]
monetarist, [allegorist]
monetary, [accessory]
monetize, [absolutize]
money, [abalone]
monger, [agar]
mongrel, [admiral]
moniker, [acre]
monism, [abolitionism]
monist, [abolitionist]
monition, [abbreviation]
monitor, [abductor]
monitory, [accessory]
monk, [bohunk]
monkey, [achy]
monkeyshine, [aerodyne]
monochrome, [astrodome]
monocle, [acoustical]
monocular, [angler]
monocultural, [admiral]
monogamist, [alchemist]
monogamous, [allonymous]
monogamy, [academy]
monogram, [aerogram]
monograph, [allograph]

monogyny, [abalone]
monolingual, [accrual]
monolith, [blacksmith]
monolithic, [acidic]
monologue, [agog]
monomania, [abulia]
monomial, [abaxial]
mononucleosis, [alkalosis]
monophonic, [allergenic]
monoplane, [abstain]
monopolist, [aerialist]
monopolize, [actualize]
monopoly, [ably]
monorail, [blackmail]
monotheism, [abolitionism]
monotheist, [activist]
monotheistic, [acoustic]
monotone, [atone]
monotonous, [agribusiness]
monotony, [abalone]
monounsaturated, [abluted]
monseigneur, [ballplayer]
monsieur, [ballplayer]
monsingnor, [ballplayer]
monsoon, [afternoon]
monster, [administer]
monstrosity, [abatis]
monstrous, [actress]
montage, [arbitrage]
monthly, [ably]
monument, [abandonment]
monumental, [accidental]
mooch, [hooch]
mood, [allude]
moody, [acidy]
moola, [aah]
moon, [afternoon]
moonbeam, [abeam]
moonfaced, [abased]

moonlight, [affright]
moonshine, [aerodyne]
moonstruck, [amok]
moony, [abalone]
moorage, [abridge]
moose, [abstruse]
moot, [acute]
mop, [agitprop]
mope, [antelope]
moped, [abed]
mopey, [apocope]
moral, [admiral]
morale, [canal]
moralism, [abolitionism]
moralist, [aerialist]
moralistic, [acoustic]
morality, [abatis]
moralize, [actualize]
morass, [admass]
moratorium, [anthurium]
morbid, [acid]
morbidity, [abatis]
mordant, [accordant]
more, [abhor]
moreover, [achiever]
mores, [ablaze]
morganatic, [acoustic]
morgue, [cyborg]
moribund, [almond]
morn, [acorn]
morning star, [abattoir]
morocco, [alfresco]
moron, [amazon]
moronic, [allergenic]
morose, [adios]
morphine, [alexandrine]
morphologist, [allergist]
morphology, [allergy]
morrow, [allegro]

Morse code, [abode]
morsel, [apostle]
mortal sin, [akin]
mortal, [accidental]
mortality, [abatis]
mortar, [abductor]
mortarboard, [aboard]
mortgage, [acknowledge]
mortgagee, [allergy]
mortgagor, [abhor]
mortification, [abbreviation]
mortify, [amplify]
mortuary, [accessory]
mosaic, [acidic]
mosey, [advisee]
mosque, [bosk]
mosquito, [aggiornamento]
moss, [across]
mossy, [absorbancy]
most, [aftermost]
mote, [afloat]
motel, [bagatelle]
motet, [abet]
moth, [broadcloth]
mothball, [aerosol]
mother tongue, [among]
mother, [altogether]
motherboard, [aboard]
motherhood, [adulthood]
motherland, [ampersand]
motherless, [acropolis]
mothproof, [aloof]
motif, [aperitif]
motile, [accidental]
motion, [abbreviation]
motionless, [acropolis]
motivate, [activate]
motivation, [abbreviation]
motivational, [aboriginal]

motivator, [abductor]
motive, [ablative]
motley, [ably]
motor, [abductor]
motorbike, [alike]
motorboat, [afloat]
motorcade, [abrade]
motorcar, [abattoir]
motorcycle, [acoustical]
motorhome, [astrodome]
motorist, [allegorist]
motorize, [accessorize]
motormouth, [badmouth]
mottle, [accidental]
motto, [aggiornamento]
moulage, [arbitrage]
mound, [abound]
mount, [account]
mountain dew, [accrue]
mountain, [anchorperson]
mountaineer, [adhere]
mountainous, [agribusiness]
mountainside, [abide]
mountaintop, [agitprop]
mountebank, [bank]
mourn, [acorn]
mourner, [afterburner]
mournful, [apocryphal]
mouse, [alehouse]
mousetrap, [afterclap]
mousseline, [alexandrine]
mousy, [absorbancy]
mouth, [badmouth]
mouthful, [apocryphal]
mouthpiece, [afterpiece]
mouthwash, [awash]
mouthy, [apathy]
movable, [able]
move, [approve]

movement, [abandonment]
mover, [achiever]
movie, [anchovy]
moviemaker, [acre]
mow, [airshow]
mow, [allow]
mozzarella, [a capella]
much, [clutch]
muck, [amok]
muckrake, [awake]
mucky, [achy]
mucous, [abacus]
mucus, [abacus]
mud, [acid]
muddle, [antipodal]
muddy, [acidy]
mudguard, [backyard]
mudroom, [abloom]
mudslinger, [arbitrager]
muff, [bluff]
muffler, [angler]
mufti, [abatis]
mug, [bedbug]
mugger, [agar]
muggy, [aggie]
mugwump, [bump]
mulch, [gulch]
mule, [bascule]
muleteer, [adhere]
mulish, [abolish]
mull, [abnormal]
mullah, [a capella]
mulligan, [bandwagon]
multibillionaire, [affair]
multicampus, [auspice]
multichannel, [abdominal]
multicity, [abatis]
multiclient, [abeyant]
multicolor, [angler]

multicopy, [apocope]
multicultural, [admiral]
multiculturalism,
  [abolitionism]
multidimensional, [aboriginal]
multidirectional, [aboriginal]
multiethnic, [allergenic]
multifaceted, [abluted]
multifarious, [abstemious]
multifunction, [abbreviation]
multigenerational, [aboriginal]
multigrain, [abstain]
multilateral, [admiral]
multilevel, [anvil]
multileveled, [bedraggled]
multilingual, [accrual]
multimedia, [abulia]
multimillion, [antiunion]
multimillionaire, [affair]
multinational, [aboriginal]
multinomial, [abaxial]
multipartite, [affright]
multiplayer, [ballplayer]
multiple, [ample]
multiplex, [annex]
multiplicand, [ampersand]
multiplication, [abbreviation]
multiplicity, [abatis]
multiplier, [amplifier]
multiply, [airdry]
multipurpose, [auspice]
multiracial, [abbatial]
multirange, [arrange]
multirole, [areole]
multisided, [absentminded]
multiskilled, [build]
multisport, [airport]
multistate, [acetate]
multistory, [accessory]

multitalented, [abluted]
multitrack, [aback]
multitude, [altitude]
multitudinous, [agribusiness]
multiuse, [abstruse]
multivariable, [able]
multiversity, [abatis]
multivitamin, [abdomen]
multiyear, [adhere]
multure, [acupuncture]
mum, [addendum]
mumble, [able]
mummify, [amplify]
mummy, [academy]
munch, [brunch]
munchkin, [akin]
mundane, [abstain]
municipal, [ample]
municipality, [abatis]
munificent, [acquiescent]
munition, [abbreviation]
mural, [admiral]
murder, [adder]
murderer, [adulterer]
murderous, [actress]
murk, [artwork]
murky, [achy]
murmur, [armor]
muscat, [acrobat]
muscle, [apostle]
muscular, [angler]
muse, [amuse]
museum, [anthurium]
mush, [airbrush]
mushroom, [abloom]
mushy, [banshee]
music, [airsick]
musical, [acoustical]
musicale, [canal]

musicologist, [allergist]
musicology, [allergy]
musk, [dusk]
musket, [advocate]
musketeer, [adhere]
muskmelon, [acetylene]
muskrat, [acrobat]
muslin, [acetylene]
must, [adjust]
mustache, [abash]
mustachio, [audio]
mustang, [bang]
mustard, [absurd]
muster, [administer]
musty, [abatis]
mutability, [abatis]
mutable, [able]
mutate, [acetate]
mutation, [abbreviation]
mute, [acute]
mutilate, [ablate]
mutineer, [adhere]
mutinous, [agribusiness]
mutiny, [abalone]
mutt, [animate]
mutter, [abductor]
mutton, [anchorperson]
mutual, [accrual]
mutuality, [abatis]
muumuu, [accrue]
muzzle, [appraisal]
muzzy, [advisee]
my, [airdry]
myriad, [acid]
myrrh, [armor]
myself, [bookshelf]
mysterious, [abstemious]
mystery, [accessory]
mystic, [acoustic]

mysticism, [abolitionism]
mystify, [amplify]
mystique, [antique]
myth, [blacksmith]
mythical, [acoustical]
mythological, [acoustical]
mythology, [allergy]
mythos, [adios]
nab, [backstab]
nacho, [airshow]
nachos, [airhose]
nadir, [adhere]
nag, [ag]
nail, [ail]
naïve, [achieve]
naiveté, [agape]
naked, [acid]
name, [acclaim]
namebrand, [ampersand]
nameplate, [ablate]
namesake, [awake]
nance, [advance]
nanny, [abalone]
nap, [afterclap]
napalm, [aplomb]
nape, [agape]
napery, [accessory]
napkin, [awaken]
narc, [aardvark]
narcissism, [abolitionism]
narcissus, [alkalosis]
narcolepsy, [absorbancy]
narcoleptic, [acoustic]
narcosis, [alkalosis]
narcotic, [acoustic]
nard, [backyard]
narrate, [accelerate]
narration, [abbreviation]
narrative, [ablative]

narrow, [allegro]
narrowband, [ampersand]
narthex, [annex]
nasal, [appraisal]
nascent, [adjacent]
nasty, [abatis]
natal, [accidental]
natant, [accordant]
natation, [abbreviation]
natatorium, [anthurium]
nation, [abbreviation]
national, [aboriginal]
nationalism, [abolitionism]
nationalist, [aerialist]
nationalistic, [acoustic]
nationality, [abatis]
nationalization, [abbreviation]
nationalize, [actualize]
nationwide, [abide]
native, [ablative]
nativity, [abatis]
natural, [admiral]
naturalism, [abolitionism]
naturalist, [aerialist]
naturalistic, [acoustic]
naturalize, [actualize]
nature, [acupuncture]
naturopath, [aftermath]
naughty, [abatis]
nausea, [abulia]
nauseate, [create]
nauseous, [adscititious]
nautical, [acoustical]
naval, [adjectival]
nave, [aftershave]
navel, [adjectival]
navigate, [abnegate]
navigation, [abbreviation]
navigator, [abductor]

navy bean, [alexandrine]
navy, [anchovy]
nay, [agape]
naysayer, [ballplayer]
Nazarene, [alexandrine]
near, [adhere]
nearby, [alibi]
nearsighted, [abluted]
neat, [accrete]
nebbish, [abolish]
nebula, [a capella]
nebulous, [acropolis]
necessary, [accessory]
necessitate, [acetate]
necessity, [abatis]
neck, [afterdeck]
neck-and-neck, [afterdeck]
necked, [abject]
necklace, [acropolis]
necktie, [airdry]
neckwear, [affair]
necrology, [allergy]
necromancy, [absorbancy]
necropolis, [acropolis]
nectar, [abductor]
nectarine, [alexandrine]
need, [accede]
needle, [antipodal]
needlepoint, [anoint]
needless, [acropolis]
needlework, [artwork]
needy, [acidy]
nefarious, [abstemious]
negate, [abnegate]
negation, [abbreviation]
negative, [ablative]
neglect, [abject]
negligee, [agape]
negligence, [abhorrence]

negligent, [agent]
negligible, [able]
negotiable, [able]
negotiate, [create]
negotiation, [abbreviation]
neigh, [agape]
neighbor, [amber]
neighborhood, [adulthood]
neither, [altogether]
nemesis, [alkalosis]
neoliberal, [admiral]
neon, [amazon]
neonatal, [accidental]
neonate, [abominate]
neo-orthodox, [bandbox]
neoorthodoxy, [absorbancy]
neophyte, [affright]
nephew, [accrue]
nepotism, [abolitionism]
nerd, [absurd]
nerve, [conserve]
nervous, [antibias]
nervousness, [agribusiness]
nervy, [anchovy]
nescience, [abhorrence]
nescient, [abeyant]
nest, [abreast]
nester, [administer]
nestle, [apostle]
net, [bassinet]
nether, [altogether]
netherworld, [afterworld]
nettle, [accidental]
network, [artwork]
neuralgia, [alfalfa]
neuritis, [afflatus]
neurologist, [allergist]
neurology, [allergy]
neurosis, [alkalosis]

neurotic, [acoustic]
neuter, [abductor]
neutral, [admiral]
neutrality, [abatis]
neutralize, [actualize]
neutron, [amazon]
never, [achiever]
nevermore, [abhor]
new, [accrue]
newborn, [acorn]
newcomer, [armor]
newfangled, [bedraggled]
newlywed, [abed]
news, [amuse]
newsboy, [ahoy]
newsbreak, [awake]
newscast, [aghast]
newsletter, [abductor]
newsmagazine, [alexandrine]
newsman, [abdomen]
newspaper, [barkeeper]
newspeak, [antique]
newsprint, [blueprint]
newsreel, [automobile]
newsroom, [abloom]
newstand, [ampersand]
newsworthy, [noteworthy]
newsy, [advisee]
next, [context]
nexus, [alkalosis]
nib, [bib]
nibble, [able]
nibs, [dibs]
nice, [advice]
nicety, [abatis]
niche, [backstitch]
nick, [allergenic]
nickel, [acoustical]
nickelodeon, [abecedarian]

nickname, [acclaim]
nicotine, [alexandrine]
nidification, [abbreviation]
nidus, [antibias]
niece, [afterpiece]
nifty, [abatis]
niggard, [absurd]
nigger, [agar]
niggle, [angle]
nigh, [airdry]
night, [affright]
nightcap, [afterclap]
nightclub, [backrub]
nightfall, [aerosol]
nightgown, [boomtown]
nighthawk, [aftershock]
nightie, [abatis]
nightlife, [afterlife]
nightlong, [agelong]
nightmare, [affair]
nightmarish, [abolish]
nightshirt, [advert]
nightside, [abide]
nightspot, [aeronaut]
nightstand, [ampersand]
nightstick, [acoustic]
nighttime, [airtime]
nightwalker, [acre]
nihilism, [abolitionism]
nihilist, [aerialist]
nihilistic, [acoustic]
nil, [backfill]
nimble, [able]
nincompoop, [coop]
nine, [aerodyne]
ninefold, [ahold]
nineteen, [alexandrine]
ninety, [abatis]
ninja, [alfalfa]

ninny, [abalone]
nip and tuck, [amok]
nip, [airstrip]
nipple, [ample]
nippy, [apocope]
nirvana, [alumna]
nit, [acquit]
nit-pick, [acidic]
nitpicky, [achy]
nitrate, [accelerate]
nitrite, [affright]
nitrogen, [allergen]
nitwit, [acquit]
nix, [administratrix]
no, [albino]
nob, [ab]
Nobel, [bagatelle]
nobility, [abatis]
noble, [able]
nobleman, [abdomen]
nobody, [acidy]
nocturnal, [abdominal]
nocturne, [adjourn]
nocuous, [ambiguous]
nod, [abroad]
nodal, [antipodal]
noddy, [acidy]
node, [abode]
nodose, [adios]
nodule, [bascule]
noel, [bagatelle]
noetic, [acoustic]
nog, [agog]
noggin, [bandwagon]
nohow, [allow]
noise, [counterpoise]
noisemaker, [acre]
noisome, [adventuresome]
noisy, [advisee]

nomad, [ad]
nomadic, [acidic]
nomenclator, [abductor]
nomenclature, [acupuncture]
nominal, [abdominal]
nominate, [abominate]
nomination, [abbreviation]
nominative, [ablative]
nominee, [abalone]
nonabrasive, [abrasive]
nonacademic, [allergenic]
nonaccredited, [abluted]
nonachievement,
 [abandonment]
nonaction, [abbreviation]
nonactivated, [abluted]
nonaddictive, [ablative]
nonadhesive, [abrasive]
nonadjacent, [acquiescent]
nonadmission, [abbreviation]
nonaesthetic, [acoustic]
nonaffiliated, [abluted]
nonaffluent, [abeyant]
nonaggression, [abbreviation]
nonaggressive, [abrasive]
nonalcoholic, [acyclic]
nonaligned, [affined]
nonallergic, [acidic]
nonambiguous, [ambiguous]
non-answer, [aggressor]
nonantagonistic, [allergenic]
nonarbitrary, [accessory]
nonartistic, [acoustic]
nonassertive, [ablative]
nonassociated, [abluted]
nonathlete, [accrete]
nonathletic, [acoustic]
nonatomic, [academic]
nonattender, [adder]

nonauthoritarian,
 [abecedarian]
nonbeliever, [achiever]
nonbreakable, [able]
noncancerous, [actress]
noncandidate, [accommodate]
noncarcinogenic, [allergenic]
noncash, [abash]
nonchalant, [avaunt]
noncharismatic, [acoustic]
nonchristian, [antiphon]
nonchurchgoer, [airpower]
noncitizen, [artisan]
nonclinical, [acoustical]
noncombat, [acrobat]
noncombatant, [accordant]
noncombative, [ablative]
noncombustible, [able]
noncommercial, [abbatial]
noncommitment,
 [abandonment]
noncommittal, [accidental]
noncommitted, [abluted]
noncommunicative, [ablative]
noncommunist, [abolitionist]
noncompetitive, [ablative]
noncompliance, [abhorrence]
noncomplimentary,
 [accessory]
noncomprehension,
 [abbreviation]
nonconference, [abhorrence]
nonconfidence, [abhorrence]
nonconfidential, [abbatial]
nonconformist, [alchemist]
nonconformity, [abatis]
nonconfrontational,
 [abdominal]
nonconsecutive, [ablative]

nonconstructive, [ablative]
nonconsumer, [armor]
noncontagious,
  [advantageous]
noncontemporary,
  [accessory]
noncontiguous, [ambiguous]
noncontingent, [agent]
noncontractual, [accrual]
noncontradiction,
  [abbreviation]
noncontroversial, [abbatial]
nonconventional, [abdominal]
nonconvertible, [able]
noncooperation,
  [abbreviation]
noncooperative, [ablative]
noncorporate, [accurate]
noncreative, [ablative]
noncredentialed, [bedraggled]
noncritical, [acoustical]
noncumulative, [ablative]
noncustodial, [abaxial]
noncyclical, [acoustical]
nondairy, [accessory]
nondecision, [abrasion]
nondeductible, [able]
nondeductive, [ablative]
nondelinquent, [abeyant]
nondemocratic, [acoustic]
nondenominational,
  [abdominal]
nondependent, [abundant]
nondepletable, [able]
nondescript, [adscript]
nondescriptive, [ablative]
nondestructive, [ablative]
nondirective, [ablative]
nondisclosure, [admeasure]

nondiscretionary, [accessory]
nondiscrimination,
  [abbreviation]
nondiscriminatory,
  [accessory]
nondisruptive, [ablative]
nondiversified, [abide]
nondrinker, [acre]
none, [bandwagon]
noneconomic, [academic]
noneffective, [ablative]
nonelect, [abject]
nonelected, [abluted]
nonelective, [ablative]
nonemergency, [absorbancy]
nonemotional, [aboriginal]
nonentity, [abatis]
nonessential, [abbatial]
nonevent, [accent]
nonexistence, [abhorrence]
nonfactor, [abductor]
nonfamily, [ably]
nonfat, [acrobat]
nonfatal, [accidental]
nonfatty, [abatis]
nonfinancial, [abbatial]
nonflammable, [able]
nonformal, [abnormal]
nonfunctional, [abdominal]
nongay, [agape]
nonglamorous, [actress]
nongraduate, [adequate]
nongrowth, [both]
nonhandicapped, [adapt]
nonhazardous, [antibias]
nonheriditary, [accessory]
nonhomogeneous,
  [abstemious]
nonhomosexual, [accrual]

nonhostile, [accidental]
nonhuman, [abdomen]
nonincumbent, [abeyant]
noninfectious, [adscititious]
noninflammatory, [accessory]
nonintellectual, [accrual]
nonintrusive, [abrasive]
noninvolvement,
    [abandonment]
nonjudgmental, [accidental]
nonlethal, [agile]
nonliquid, [acid]
nonliterate, [accurate]
nonlogical, [acoustical]
nonmaterial, [anneal]
nonmeasurable, [able]
nonmember, [amber]
nonmilitant, [abirritant]
nonmonetary, [accessory]
nonmusician, [abbreviation]
nonnecessity, [abatis]
nonnegative, [ablative]
nonnegotiable, [able]
nonobjective, [ablative]
nonobscene, [alexandrine]
nonoperational, [abdominal]
nonoptimal, [abnormal]
non-owner, [afterburner]
nonpareil, [bagatelle]
nonparticipant, [abeyant]
nonparticipatory, [accessory]
nonpartisan, [artisan]
nonpayment, [abandonment]
nonperformance,
    [abhorrence]
nonperformer, [armor]
nonperishable, [able]
nonpermissive, [abrasive]
nonpersonal, [abdominal]

nonphilosophical, [acoustical]
nonphysical, [acoustical]
nonpoisonous, [agribusiness]
nonpolitical, [acoustical]
nonpoor, [abhor]
nonproductive, [ablative]
nonprofessional, [aboriginal]
nonprofit, [adequate]
nonprogressive, [abrasive]
nonproliferation,
    [abbreviation]
nonpurposive, [abrasive]
nonquantifiable, [able]
nonquantitative, [ablative]
nonracial, [abbatial]
nonrated, [abluted]
nonrational, [abdominal]
nonreactive, [ablative]
nonreader, [adder]
nonreciprocal, [acoustical]
nonrecurrent, [aberrant]
nonrefundable, [able]
nonregulated, [abluted]
nonrelevant, [abeyant]
nonreligious, [advantageous]
nonrenewable, [able]
nonresidency, [absorbancy]
nonresident, [abundant]
nonresidential, [abbatial]
nonresistance, [abhorrence]
nonresistant, [abirritant]
nonresponsive, [abrasive]
nonrestricted, [abluted]
nonrestrictive, [ablative]
nonreturnable, [able]
nonreusable, [able]
nonsectarian, [abecedarian]
nonsense, [abhorrence]
nonsensical, [acoustical]

nonsexist, [adjust]
nonsexual, [accrual]
non-signer, [afterburner]
nonsmoker, [acre]
nonstandard, [absurd]
nonstarter, [abductor]
nonstop, [agitprop]
nonsupport, [airport]
nontaxable, [able]
nontechnical, [acoustical]
nontheist, [activist]
nontheistic, [acoustic]
nontheological, [acoustical]
nontoxic, [airsick]
nontraditional, [abdominal]
nontransferable, [able]
nonunion, [antiunion]
nonuser, [adviser]
nonvalid, [acid]
nonverbal, [able]
nonviewer, [airpower]
nonviolence, [abhorrence]
nonviolent, [ambivalent]
nonvoter, [abductor]
nonwhite, [affright]
nonworker, [acre]
nonwriter, [abductor]
noodle, [antipodal]
nook, [bankbook]
nooky, [achy]
noon, [afternoon]
noonday, [agape]
noontide, [abide]
noontime, [airtime]
noose, [abstruse]
nope, [antelope]
nor, [abhor]
nor, [afterburner]
norm, [aswarm]

normal, [abnormal]
normalcy, [absorbancy]
normalization, [abbreviation]
normalize, [actualize]
normative, [ablative]
north star, [abattoir]
north, [forth]
northeast, [beast]
northern, [adjourn]
nose, [airhose]
nosebleed, [accede]
nosedive, [alive]
nosegay, [agape]
noseguard, [backyard]
nosepiece, [afterpiece]
nostalgia, [alfalfa]
nostalgic, [acidic]
nostril, [barrel]
nosy, [advisee]
not, [aeronaut]
notable, [able]
notarize, [accessorize]
notary, [accessory]
notation, [abbreviation]
notch, [blotch]
note, [afloat]
notebook, [bankbook]
noted, [abluted]
notepad, [ad]
notepaper, [barkeeper]
noteworthy, [newsworthy]
nothingness, [agribusiness]
notice, [afflatus]
noticeable, [able]
notification, [abbreviation]
notify, [amplify]
notion, [abbreviation]
notional, [aboriginal]
notoriety, [abatis]

notorious, [abstemious]
nougat, [agate]
nought, [aeronaut]
noumenon, [amazon]
noun, [boomtown]
nourishment, [abandonment]
nous, [abstruse]
nouveau, [airshow]
nova, [alfalfa]
novation, [abbreviation]
novel, [adjectival]
novelist, [aerialist]
novelty, [abatis]
novena, [alumna]
novice, [antibias]
now, [allow]
nowadays, [ablaze]
nowhere, [anywhere]
noxious, [adscititious]
nozzle, [appraisal]
nuance, [brisance]
nubble, [able]
nubby, [abbey]
nubile, [anile]
nuclear, [anterior]
nucleus, [abstemious]
nude, [allude]
nudge, [adjudge]
nudity, [abatis]
nugatory, [accessory]
nugget, [agate]
nuisance, [accordance]
nuke, [archduke]
null, [aboriginal]
nullify, [amplify]
nulliparous, [actress]
numb, [addendum]
number, [amber]
numen, [abdomen]

numeral, [admiral]
numerator, [abductor]
numeric, [aleatoric]
numerical, [acoustical]
numerology, [allergy]
numerous, [actress]
numismatics, [acoustics]
numskull, [acoustical]
nun, [bandwagon]
nuncio, [audio]
nuptial, [abbatial]
nurse, [adverse]
nursemaid, [abrade]
nursery, [accessory]
nurture, [acupuncture]
nut, [acuminate]
nutcase, [abase]
nutcracker, [acre]
nuthouse, [alehouse]
nutmeg, [beg]
nutpick, [acidic]
nutrient, [abeyant]
nutrition, [abbreviation]
nutritionist, [abolitionist]
nutritious, [adscititious]
nuts, [giblets]
nutshell, [bagatelle]
nutty, [abatis]
nuzzle, [appraisal]
nylon, [amazon]
oaf, [loaf]
oak, [artichoke]
oar, [abhor]
oarsman, [abdomen]
oasis, [alkalosis]
oat bran, [adman]
oat, [afloat]
oath, [both]
oatmeal, [automobile]

obbligato, [aggiornamento]
obdurate, [accurate]
obedience, [abhorrence]
obedient, [abeyant]
obeisance, [accordance]
obelisk, [asterisk]
obese, [afterpiece]
obesity, [abatis]
obey, [agape]
obfuscate, [abdicate]
obfuscation, [abbreviation]
obit, [acquit]
obituary, [accessory]
object, [addict]
objectify, [amplify]
objection, [abbreviation]
objective, [ablative]
objectivity, [abatis]
objector, [abductor]
objurgation, [abbreviation]
oblate, [ablate]
oblation, [abbreviation]
obligate, [abnegate]
obligation, [abbreviation]
obligatory, [accessory]
oblique, [antique]
obliterate, [accelerate]
obliteration, [abbreviation]
oblivion, [abecedarian]
oblivious, [abstemious]
oblong, [agelong]
obnoxious, [adscititious]
obnubilate, [ablate]
oboe, [airshow]
obscene, [alexandrine]
obscenity, [abatis]
obscurantist, [absolutist]
obscure, [abjure]
obscurity, [abatis]

obsequious, [abstemious]
observable, [able]
observance, [abhorrence]
observant, [abeyant]
observation, [abbreviation]
observatory, [accessory]
observe, [conserve]
observer, [achiever]
obsess, [abscess]
obsess, [acquiesce]
obsessed, [abreast]
obsession, [abbreviation]
obsessive, [abrasive]
obsolescence, [accordance]
obsolete, [accrete]
obstacle, [acoustical]
obstetrics, [administratrix]
obstinate, [acuminate]
obstreperous, [actress]
obstruct, [abduct]
obstruction, [abbreviation]
obstructionism, [abolitionism]
obtain, [abstain]
obtrude, [allude]
obtrusion, [abrasion]
obtrusive, [abrasive]
obtund, [almond]
obturation, [abbreviation]
obtuse, [abstruse]
obverse, [adverse]
obviate, [create]
obvious, [abstemious]
occasion, [abrasion]
occasional, [aboriginal]
occlude, [allude]
occlusion, [abrasion]
occult, [adult]
occultism, [abolitionism]
occultist, [absolutist]

occupancy, [absorbancy]
occupant, [abeyant]
occupation, [abbreviation]
occupational, [abdominal]
occupy, [airdry]
occur, [acre]
occurrence, [abhorrence]
oceanfront, [aberrant]
oceanic, [allergenic]
ochlocracy, [absorbancy]
octagon, [amazon]
octagonal, [aboriginal]
octave, [ablative]
octet, [abet]
octogenarian, [abecedarian]
octopus, [auspice]
ocular, [angler]
odd, [abroad]
oddball, [aerosol]
ode, [abode]
odeum, [anthurium]
odious, [abstemious]
odor, [adder]
odoriferous, [actress]
odorless, [acropolis]
odorous, [actress]
odyssey, [absorbancy]
of, [above]
off, [boff]
offal, [apocryphal]
offbeat, [accrete]
offend, [addend]
offender, [adder]
offense, [abhorrence]
offensive, [abrasive]
offer, [buffer]
offertory, [accessory]
offhand, [ampersand]
office, [amorphous]

officer, [aggressor]
official, [abbatial]
officiate, [create]
offscreen, [alexandrine]
offset, [abet]
offshoot, [acute]
offshore, [abhor]
offside, [abide]
offspring, [anything]
offstage, [age]
off-the-wall, [aerosol]
offtrack, [aback]
ogle, [angle]
ogre, [agar]
oh, [airshow]
ohm, [astrodome]
oil, [broil]
oilcan, [adman]
oilman, [abdomen]
oily, [ably]
oink, [bethink]
ointment, [abandonment]
okeydoke, [artichoke]
okra, [abracadabra]
old age, [age]
old, [ahold]
olden, [antiphon]
oleomargarine, [alexandrine]
olfactory, [accessory]
oligarchy, [achy]
oligopoly, [ably]
olive, [forgive]
olympiad, [ad]
ombudsman, [abdomen]
omega, [alfalfa]
omelet, [aglet]
omen, [abdomen]
omer, [armor]
ominous, [agribusiness]

omission, [abbreviation]
omit, [acquit]
omnibus, [abbess]
omnicompetent, [abirritant]
omnipotence, [abhorrence]
omnipotent, [abirritant]
omnipresence, [accordance]
omnipresent, [accordant]
omniscience, [abhorrence]
omniscient, [abeyant]
omnivorous, [actress]
omphalos, [across]
on, [amazon]
onboard, [aboard]
once, [abhorrence]
oncology, [allergy]
one, [bandwagon]
onefold, [ahold]
onerous, [actress]
oneself, [bookshelf]
onlooker, [acre]
only, [ably]
onrush, [airbrush]
onset, [abet]
onshore, [abhor]
onside, [abide]
onslaught, [aeronaut]
onstage, [age]
ontic, [acoustic]
onto, [accrue]
ontological, [acoustical]
ontology, [allergy]
onus, [agribusiness]
onward, [absurd]
onyx, [administratrix]
oodles, [annals]
ooh, [accrue]
oompah, [aah]
ooze, [amuse]

opacity, [abatis]
opalescent, [adjacent]
opaque, [awake]
opener, [afterburner]
openhearted, [abluted]
opera, [abracadabra]
operable, [able]
operand, [ampersand]
operant, [aberrant]
operate, [accelerate]
operatic, [acoustic]
operation, [abbreviation]
operative, [ablative]
operator, [abductor]
operetta, [aorta]
operose, [adios]
opiate, [affiliate]
opine, [aerodyne]
opinion, [antiunion]
opium, [anthurium]
opponent, [abstinent]
opportune, [afternoon]
opportunism, [abolitionism]
opportunist, [abolitionist]
opportunistic, [acoustic]
opportunity, [abatis]
oppose, [airhose]
opposite, [apposite]
opposition, [abbreviation]
oppress, [acquiesce]
oppression, [abbreviation]
oppressive, [abrasive]
oppressor, [aggressor]
opprobrium, [anthurium]
opt, [adopt]
optative, [ablative]
optic, [acoustic]
optical, [acoustical]
optics, [acoustics]

optimal, [abnormal]
optimism, [abolitionism]
optimist, [alchemist]
optimistic, [acoustic]
optimize, [advise]
optimum, [addendum]
option, [abbreviation]
optional, [aboriginal]
optometrist, [allegorist]
optometry, [ancestry]
opulence, [abhorrence]
opulent, [ambivalent]
opus, [auspice]
opuscule, [bascule]
opusculum, [addendum]
or, [abhor]
oracle, [acoustical]
oral, [admiral]
orange, [binge]
orangeade, [abrade]
orangish, [abolish]
orate, [accelerate]
oration, [abbreviation]
orator, [abductor]
oratorical, [acoustical]
oratorio, [audio]
oratory, [accessory]
orb, [absorb]
orbit, [abbot]
orbital, [accidental]
orbiter, [abductor]
orchard, [absurd]
orchardist, [activist]
orchestra, [abracadabra]
orchestral, [admiral]
orchestrate, [accelerate]
orchestration, [abbreviation]
orchid, [acid]
ordain, [abstain]

ordeal, [anneal]
order, [adder]
orderly, [ably]
ordinal, [aboriginal]
ordinance, [abhorrence]
ordinary, [accessory]
ordinate, [acuminate]
ordination, [abbreviation]
ordnance, [abhorrence]
ordo, [aficionado]
ordonnance, [brisance]
ordure, [armiger]
ore, [abhor]
organ, [bandwagon]
organic, [allergenic]
organism, [abolitionism]
organist, [abolitionist]
organization, [abbreviation]
organizational, [abdominal]
organize, [agnize]
organizer, [adviser]
orgasm, [abolitionism]
orgasmic, [academic]
orgiastic, [acoustic]
orgone, [alone]
orgy, [allergy]
orient, [abeyant]
oriental, [accidental]
orientate, [acetate]
orientation, [abbreviation]
oriented, [abluted]
orifice, [amorphous]
origami, [academy]
origanum, [addendum]
origin, [allergen]
original, [abdominal]
originality, [abatis]
originate, [abominate]
oriole, [areole]

ornament, [abandonment]
ornamental, [accidental]
ornate, [abominate]
ornery, [accessory]
orphanage, [appanage]
orphrey, [accessory]
ort, [abort]
orthodontics, [acoustics]
orthodox, [bandbox]
orthodoxy, [absorbancy]
orthoepy, [apocope]
orthopedic, [acidic]
orthopedics, [administratrix]
orthoscopic, [acidic]
orzo, [bozo]
oscillate, [ablate]
oscillation, [abbreviation]
osculate, [ablate]
osculation, [abbreviation]
osmosis, [alkalosis]
ossify, [amplify]
ostensible, [able]
ostensive, [abrasive]
ostentation, [abbreviation]
ostentatious, [adscititious]
ostracize, [abscise]
ostrich, [backstitch]
other, [altogether]
otherwise, [advise]
otiose, [adios]
ottava, [alfalfa]
otter, [abductor]
ouch, [avouch]
ought, [aeronaut]
ounce, [announce]
oust, [joust]
ouster, [administer]
out, [about]
outage, [acknowledge]

outbid, [amid]
outboard, [aboard]
outbound, [abound]
outbreak, [awake]
outburst, [athirst]
outcast, [aghast]
outclass, [admass]
outcoach, [abroach]
outcome, [addendum]
outcompete, [accrete]
outcrop, [agitprop]
outcry, [airdry]
outdated, [abluted]
outdid, [amid]
outdistance, [abhorrence]
outdo, [accrue]
outdone, [antiphon]
outdoor, [abhor]
outdress, [acquiesce]
outdrink, [bethink]
outdrive, [alive]
outer, [abductor]
outfield, [airfield]
outfight, [affright]
outfit, [acquit]
outflank, [bank]
outflow, [afterglow]
outgain, [abstain]
outgo, [ago]
outgrow, [allegro]
outgrowth, [both]
outguess, [acquiesce]
outgun, [bandwagon]
outhit, [acquit]
outhouse, [alehouse]
outhustle, [apostle]
outlandish, [abolish]
outlast, [aghast]
outlaw, [aah]

outlay, [airplay]
outlet, [abet]
outline, [airline]
outlive, [forgive]
outlook, [bankbook]
outman, [adman]
outmaneuver, [achiever]
outmarch, [arch]
outmuscle, [apostle]
outnumber, [amber]
outpace, [abase]
outpatient, [abeyant]
outperform, [aswarm]
outplacement, [abandonment]
outplay, [airplay]
outpoint, [anoint]
outpost, [aftermost]
outpunch, [brunch]
output, [ablaut]
outrage, [age]
outrageous, [advantageous]
outran, [adman]
outrance, [brisance]
outrank, [bank]
outreach, [beach]
outride, [abide]
outrider, [adder]
outrigger, [agar]
outright, [affright]
outrun, [pressrun]
outscore, [abhor]
outsell, [bagatelle]
outshine, [aerodyne]
outshoot, [acute]
outside, [abide]
outsider, [adder]
outskirt, [advert]
outsmart, [apart]
outspend, [addend]

outspent, [accent]
outspoken, [awaken]
outstrip, [airstrip]
outward, [absurd]
outweigh, [airway]
outwit, [acquit]
outwork, [artwork]
oval, [adjectival]
ovary, [accessory]
ovation, [abbreviation]
over, [achiever]
overabundance, [abhorrence]
overachieve, [achieve]
overachiever, [achiever]
overactive, [ablative]
overage, [age]
overall, [aerosol]
overambitious, [adscititious]
overanxious, [adscititious]
overarch, [arch]
overbill, [backfill]
overbite, [affright]
overblown, [alone]
overboard, [aboard]
overbook, [bankbook]
overbuild, [build]
overburden, [anchorperson]
overbusy, [advisee]
overcame, [acclaim]
overcast, [aghast]
overcautious, [adscititious]
overcharge, [barge]
overcoat, [afloat]
overcome, [addendum]
overcommit, [acquit]
overconfidence, [abhorrence]
overconfident, [abundant]
overcook, [bankbook]
overcool, [bascule]

overcritical, [acoustical]
overcrowd, [aloud]
overdependent, [abundant]
overdevelop, [backup]
overdo, [accrue]
overdone, [bandwagon]
overdose, [adios]
overdraft, [abaft]
overdramatize, [absolutize]
overdraw, [aah]
overdress, [acquiesce]
overdrink, [bethink]
overdrive, [alive]
overdue, [accrue]
overeager, [agar]
overearnest, [adjust]
overeat, [accrete]
overeducate, [abdicate]
overeducated, [abluted]
overemotional, [aboriginal]
overemphasis, [alkalosis]
overemphasize, [abscise]
overemphatic, [acoustic]
overenergetic, [acoustic]
overenrolled, [ahold]
overenthusiastic, [acoustic]
overestimate, [acclimate]
overexaggerate, [accelerate]
overexaggeration,
   [abbreviation]
overexcited, [abluted]
overexercise, [abscise]
overexert, [advert]
overexertion, [abbreviation]
overexpansion, [abbreviation]
overexpose, [airhose]
overextravagent, [abeyant]
overfed, [abed]
overflow, [afterglow]

overgeneralization,
   [abbreviation]
overgeneralize, [actualize]
overgenerous, [actress]
overgovern, [adjourn]
overgrown, [alone]
overhasty, [abatis]
overhaul, [aerosol]
overhead, [abed]
overheard, [absurd]
overheat, [accrete]
overindulge, [bulge]
overindulgence, [abhorrence]
overindulgent, [agent]
overinflate, [ablate]
overinflated, [abluted]
overjoyed, [adenoid]
overkill, [backfill]
overlap, [afterclap]
overlay, [airplay]
overload, [abode]
overlook, [bankbook]
overloud, [aloud]
overmanage, [appanage]
overmedicate, [abdicate]
overnight, [affright]
overopinionated, [abluted]
overoptimistic, [acoustic]
overorganize, [agnize]
overpass, [admass]
overpay, [agape]
overpayment, [abandonment]
overplay, [airplay]
overpopulate, [ablate]
overpopulation, [abbreviation]
overpower, [airpower]
overprescribe, [ascribe]
overprint, [blueprint]
overproduce, [abstruse]

overproduction, [abbreviation]
overprogram, [aerogram]
overpromote, [afloat]
overprotect, [abject]
overprotection, [abbreviation]
overprotective, [ablative]
overqualified, [abide]
overran, [adman]
overranked, [sacrosanct]
overrate, [accelerate]
overrated, [abluted]
overreach, [beach]
overreaction, [abbreviation]
overregulate, [ablate]
overregulation, [abbreviation]
override, [abide]
overripe, [airpipe]
overrule, [bascule]
overrun, [pressrun]
overseas, [antifreeze]
oversee, [absorbancy]
overseen, [alexandrine]
overseer, [anterior]
oversell, [bagatelle]
oversensitive, [ablative]
oversexed, [context]
overshadow, [aficionado]
overshoe, [accrue]
overshoot, [acute]
overshot, [aeronaut]
oversight, [affright]
oversimplify, [amplify]
oversize, [abscise]
oversleep, [asleep]
overslept, [accept]
oversold, [ahold]
overspend, [addend]
overstate, [acetate]
overstay, [agape]

overstep, [crowstep]
overstimulate, [ablate]
overstock, [aftershock]
overstride, [abide]
overstuff, [bluff]
oversubscribe, [ascribe]
oversupply, [airdry]
overt, [advert]
overtake, [awake]
overtax, [anthrax]
overthrew, [accrue]
overthrow, [allegro]
overthrown, [alone]
overtime, [airtime]
overtreat, [accrete]
overture, [abjure]
overturn, [adjourn]
overuse, [amuse]
overutilize, [actualize]
overvalue, [accrue]
overview, [accrue]
overweight, [accentuate]
overwhelm, [elm]
overwork, [artwork]
overwrite, [affright]
overzealous, [acropolis]
ovulate, [ablate]
ovulation, [abbreviation]
ow, [allow]
owe, [airshow]
owl, [foul]
own, [alone]
owner, [afterburner]
ownership, [airship]
ox, [bandbox]
oxbow, [airshow]
oxcart, [apart]
oxford, [absurd]
oxidant, [abundant]

331

oxidation, [abbreviation]
oxidize, [advise]
oxygen, [allergen]
oxygenate, [abominate]
oxymoron, [amazon]
oyster, [administer]
ozone, [alone]
pace, [abase]
pacemaker, [acre]
pacesetter, [abductor]
pachyderm, [affirm]
pacific, [anthropomorphic]
pacifism, [abolitionism]
pacifist, [activist]
pacify, [amplify]
pack, [aback]
package, [acknowledge]
packet, [advocate]
packinghouse, [alehouse]
packman, [abdomen]
pact, [abstract]
pad, [ad]
paddle, [antipodal]
paddleball, [aerosol]
paddleboard, [aboard]
paddleboat, [afloat]
padlock, [aftershock]
padre, [affray]
padrone, [abalone]
paean, [abecedarian]
pagan, [bandwagon]
paganism, [abolitionism]
page, [age]
pageant, [agent]
pager, [armiger]
paginate, [abominate]
pagination, [abbreviation]
pagoda, [addenda]
paid, [abrade]

pail, [ail]
pain, [abstain]
painful, [apocryphal]
painkiller, [angler]
painless, [acropolis]
paint, [acquaint]
paintbrush, [airbrush]
painter, [abductor]
pair, [affair]
paisley, [ably]
pajama, [anathema]
pajamas, [abuzz]
pal, [canal]
palace, [acropolis]
palaestra, [abracadabra]
palatable, [able]
palatal, [accidental]
palate, [aglet]
palatial, [abbatial]
palatine, [aerodyne]
palaver, [achiever]
pale, [ail]
paleface, [abase]
palette, [aglet]
palimony, [abalone]
palimpsest, [abreast]
palimpsest, [abreast]
palinode, [abode]
palisade, [abrade]
pall, [aerosol]
pallbearer, [adulterer]
pallet, [aglet]
palliate, [create]
pallid, [acid]
pallor, [angler]
palm, [aplomb]
palmate, [acclimate]
palmistry, [accessory]
palpable, [able]

palpate, [anticipate]
palpitate, [acetate]
palpitation, [abbreviation]
palsy, [advisee]
palter, [abductor]
paltry, [accessory]
pamper, [barkeeper]
pamphlet, [aglet]
pan, [adman]
panacea, [abulia]
panache, [abash]
panada, [addenda]
panatela, [a capella]
pancake, [awake]
pancetta, [aorta]
panchromatic, [acoustic]
pancreas, [abstemious]
panda, [addenda]
pandect, [abject]
pandemic, [academic]
pander, [adder]
pandit, [adequate]
pandora, [abracadabra]
pandowdy, [acidy]
pane, [abstain]
panel, [abdominal]
panelist, [aerialist]
panhandle, [antipodal]
panhandler, [angler]
panic, [allergenic]
panicky, [achy]
panoply, [ably]
panorama, [anathema]
panoramic, [academic]
pansexual, [accrual]
pansy, [advisee]
pant, [ant]
pantaloon, [afternoon]
pantheism, [abolitionism]

pantheist, [activist]
pantheistic, [acoustic]
pantheon, [amazon]
panther, [altogether]
pantomime, [airtime]
pantry, [accessory]
pantsuit, [acute]
pantywaist, [abased]
pap, [afterclap]
papa, [alfalfa]
papacy, [absorbancy]
papal, [ample]
paparazzi, [advisee]
papaya, [alfalfa]
paper, [barkeeper]
paperback, [aback]
paperboard, [aboard]
paperboy, [ahoy]
paperhanger, [arbitrager]
paperweight, [accentuate]
paperwork, [artwork]
papery, [accessory]
paprika, [angelica]
papyrus, [actress]
par, [abattoir]
parable, [able]
parabola, [a capella]
parabolic, [acyclic]
parabolical, [acoustical]
parachute, [acute]
parachutist, [absolutist]
paraclete, [accrete]
parade, [abrade]
paradigm, [airtime]
paradise, [advice]
paradox, [bandbox]
paradoxical, [acoustical]
paragon, [amazon]
paragraph, [allograph]

parakeet, [accrete]
paralegal, [angle]
parallel, [bagatelle]
parallelism, [abolitionism]
paralysis, [alkalosis]
paralytic, [acoustic]
paralyze, [actualize]
paramedic, [acidic]
parameter, [abductor]
paramilitary, [accessory]
paramount, [account]
paramour, [abjure]
paranoid, [adenoid]
paranormal, [abnormal]
parapet, [adequate]
paraphernalia, [alleluia]
paraphrase, [ablaze]
paraplegic, [acidic]
paraprofessional, [aboriginal]
parapsychology, [allergy]
parasite, [affright]
paratrooper, [barkeeper]
parcel, [apostle]
parch, [arch]
parchment, [abandonment]
pardon, [anchorperson]
pare, [affair]
parentage, [acknowledge]
parental, [accidental]
parenthesis, [alkalosis]
parenthetical, [acoustical]
parenthood, [adulthood]
parfait, [agape]
parietal, [accidental]
parish, [abolish]
parishioner, [afterburner]
parity, [abatis]
park, [aardvark]
parka, [angelica]

parkway, [airway]
parlance, [abhorrence]
parlando, [aficionado]
parlay, [airplay]
parley, [ably]
parliament, [abandonment]
parliamentarian,
  [abecedarian]
parliamentary, [accessory]
parlor, [angler]
parmigiana, [alumna]
parochial, [abaxial]
parody, [acidy]
parole, [areole]
paronomasia, [abulia]
paroxysm, [abolitionism]
parquet, [agape]
parricidal, [antipodal]
parricide, [abide]
parrot, [accurate]
parry, [accessory]
parse, [farce]
parser, [aggressor]
parsimonious, [abstemious]
parsimony, [abalone]
parsley, [ably]
parsnip, [airstrip]
parson, [anchorperson]
parsonage, [appanage]
part, [apart]
partake, [awake]
parted, [abluted]
partial, [abbatial]
partiality, [abatis]
partially, [ably]
participant, [abeyant]
participate, [anticipate]
participation, [abbreviation]
participative, [ablative]

participatory, [accessory]
participle, [ample]
particle, [acoustical]
particular, [angler]
partisan, [artisan]
partisanship, [airship]
partite, [affright]
partition, [abbreviation]
partner, [afterburner]
partnership, [airship]
partook, [bankbook]
partridge, [abridge]
part-time, [airtime]
parturient, [abeyant]
parturition, [abbreviation]
party, [abatis]
pass, [admass]
passable, [able]
passage, [acknowledge]
passageway, [airway]
passbook, [bankbook]
passé, [agape]
passel, [apostle]
passenger, [armiger]
passerby, [alibi]
passion fruit, [backup]
passionate, [acuminate]
passive, [abrasive]
passivism, [abolitionism]
passivist, [activist]
passivity, [abatis]
passover, [achiever]
passport, [airport]
password, [absurd]
past, [aghast]
pasta, [aorta]
paste, [abased]
pastel, [bagatelle]
Pasternak, [aback]

pasteup, [backup]
pasteurize, [accessorize]
pastor, [administer]
pastoral, [admiral]
pastorate, [accurate]
pastrami, [academy]
pastry, [accessory]
pasture, [acupuncture]
pat, [acrobat]
patch, [armpatch]
patchwork, [artwork]
patchy, [blotchy]
pate, [anticipate]
patent, [accordant]
patented, [abluted]
paternal, [abdominal]
paternalism, [abolitionism]
paternalistic, [acoustic]
paternity, [abatis]
path, [aftermath]
pathetic, [acoustic]
pathological, [acoustical]
pathologist, [allergist]
pathology, [allergy]
pathos, [across]
pathway, [airway]
patience, [abhorrence]
patient, [abeyant]
patio, [audio]
patriarch, [aardvark]
patricide, [abide]
patrimony, [abalone]
patriot, [affiliate]
patriotic, [acoustic]
patriotism, [abolitionism]
patristic, [acoustic]
patrol, [areole]
patronage, [appanage]
patsy, [absorbancy]

patter, [abductor]
pattern, [adjourn]
patty, [abatis]
paucity, [abatis]
Pauline, [alexandrine]
paunchy, [blotchy]
pauper, [barkeeper]
pause, [applause]
pave, [aftershave]
pavement, [abandonment]
pavid, [acid]
pavilion, [antiunion]
paw, [aah]
pawn, [amazon]
pawnbroker, [acre]
pawnshop, [agitprop]
pax, [anthrax]
pay, [agape]
payable, [able]
payback, [aback]
paycheck, [afterdeck]
payday, [agape]
payee, [buoy]
payload, [abode]
paymaster, [administer]
payment, [abandonment]
payoff, [boff]
payola, [a capella]
payout, [about]
payroll, [areole]
pea, [apocope]
peace, [afterpiece]
peaceable, [able]
peaceful, [apocryphal]
peacemaker, [acre]
peacenik, [allergenic]
peacetime, [airtime]
peach, [beach]
peachy, [blotchy]

peacock, [aftershock]
peak, [antique]
peal, [anneal]
peanut, [acuminate]
pear, [affair]
pearl, [aswirl]
pearly, [ably]
peasant, [accordant]
peasantry, [ancestry]
peat, [accrete]
pebble, [able]
pecan, [amazon]
peccadillo, [afterglow]
peccant, [abeyant]
pectoral, [admiral]
peculate, [ablate]
peculiar, [ballplayer]
peculiarity, [abatis]
pecuniary, [accessory]
ped, [abed]
pedagogical, [acoustical]
pedagogue, [agog]
pedagogy, [allergy]
pedal, [antipodal]
pedant, [accordant]
pedantic, [acoustic]
peddle, [antipodal]
pederast, [aghast]
pedestal, [accidental]
pedestrian, [abecedarian]
pediatrics, [administratrix]
pedicure, [abjure]
pedigree, [accessory]
pediment, [abandonment]
pedophile, [anile]
pedophilia, [abulia]
pee, [apocope]
peek, [antique]
peek-a-boo, [accrue]

peel, [anneal]
peen, [alexandrine]
peep, [asleep]
peephole, [areole]
peer, [adhere]
peeve, [achieve]
peevish, [abolish]
peewee, [colloquy]
peg, [beg]
pejorative, [ablative]
pekoe, [alfresco]
pelican, [awaken]
pellet, [aglet]
pelota, [aorta]
pelt, [belt]
pelvis, [antibias]
pen, [again]
penal, [abdominal]
penalize, [actualize]
penalty, [abatis]
penance, [abhorrence]
penchant, [abeyant]
pencil, [apostle]
pendant, [abundant]
pendulum, [addendum]
penetrable, [able]
penetrate, [accelerate]
penetration, [abbreviation]
penholder, [adder]
peninsula, [a capella]
penis, [agribusiness]
penitence, [abhorrence]
penitent, [abirritant]
penitentiary, [accessory]
penlight, [affright]
penman, [abdomen]
penmanship, [airship]
pennant, [abstinent]
penniless, [acropolis]

penny, [abalone]
penology, [allergy]
pension, [abbreviation]
pensioner, [afterburner]
pensive, [abrasive]
pent, [accent]
pentad, [ad]
pentagon, [amazon]
pentathlete, [accrete]
pentathlon, [acetylene]
Pentecost, [accost]
penthouse, [alehouse]
penult, [adult]
penultima, [anathema]
penultimate, [animate]
penury, [accessory]
people, [ample]
pep, [crowstep]
peplum, [addendum]
peppercorn, [acorn]
peppermint, [blueprint]
pepperoni, [abalone]
peppery, [accessory]
peppy, [apocope]
peptic, [acoustic]
per, [barkeeper]
peradventure, [acupuncture]
perambulate, [ablate]
percale, [ail]
perceivable, [able]
perceive, [achieve]
percent, [accent]
percentage, [acknowledge]
percentile, [anile]
percept, [accept]
perceptible, [able]
perception, [abbreviation]
perceptive, [ablative]
perceptual, [accrual]

perch, [antichurch]
perchance, [advance]
percolate, [ablate]
percolator, [abductor]
percussion, [abbreviation]
percussionist, [abolitionist]
percussive, [abrasive]
perdition, [abbreviation]
perdurable, [able]
perdure, [abjure]
peregrinate, [abominate]
peremptory, [accessory]
perennate, [abominate]
perennial, [abaxial]
perestroika, [angelica]
perfect, [addict]
perfecta, [aorta]
perfection, [abbreviation]
perfectionism, [abolitionism]
perfectionist, [abolitionist]
perfectionistic, [acoustic]
perfecto, [aggiornamento]
perfidy, [acidy]
perforate, [accelerate]
perforated, [abluted]
perforation, [abbreviation]
perform, [aswarm]
performance, [abhorrence]
performer, [armor]
perfume, [abloom]
perfunctory, [accessory]
perhaps, [apse]
pericope, [apocope]
peril, [admiral]
perilous, [acropolis]
perimeter, [abductor]
perinatal, [accidental]
period, [acid]
periodic, [acidic]

periodical, [acoustical]
peripatetic, [acoustic]
peripheral, [admiral]
periphrastic, [acoustic]
periscope, [antelope]
perish, [abolish]
perishable, [able]
perjure, [armiger]
perjury, [accessory]
perk, [artwork]
perky, [achy]
perm, [affirm]
permafrost, [accost]
permanence, [abhorrence]
permanent, [abstinent]
permeable, [able]
permeate, [create]
permissible, [able]
permission, [abbreviation]
permissive, [abrasive]
permissiveness,
    [agribusiness]
permit, [acquit]
permute, [acute]
pernicious, [adscititious]
perorate, [accelerate]
peroration, [abbreviation]
peroxide, [abide]
perpendicular, [angler]
perpetrate, [accelerate]
perpetual, [accrual]
perpetuate, [accentuate]
perpetuity, [abatis]
perphery, [accessory]
perplex, [annex]
perplexed, [context]
perplexity, [abatis]
perquisite, [apposite]
perry, [accessory]

persecute, [acute]
persecution, [abbreviation]
persecutor, [abductor]
perseverance, [abhorrence]
perseveration, [abbreviation]
persevere, [adhere]
persist, [assist]
persistence, [abhorrence]
persistent, [abirritant]
persnickety, [abatis]
person, [anchorperson]
persona, [alumna]
personable, [able]
personage, [appanage]
personal, [aboriginal]
personality, [abatis]
personalize, [actualize]
personalty, [abatis]
personate, [abominate]
personification, [abbreviation]
personify, [amplify]
personnel, [bagatelle]
perspective, [ablative]
perspicacious, [adscititious]
perspicuous, [ambiguous]
perspiration, [abbreviation]
perspire, [acquire]
persuade, [abrade]
persuader, [adder]
persuasion, [abrasion]
persuasive, [abrasive]
persuer, [airpower]
pert, [advert]
pertain, [abstain]
pertinence, [abhorrence]
pertinent, [abstinent]
perturb, [adverb]
perusal, [appraisal]
peruse, [amuse]

pervade, [abrade]
pervasive, [abrasive]
perverse, [adverse]
perversion, [abrasion]
pervert, [advert]
pervious, [abstemious]
pesky, [achy]
peso, [also]
pessimism, [abolitionism]
pessimistic, [acoustic]
pest, [abreast]
pester, [administer]
pesticide, [abide]
pestilence, [abhorrence]
pestle, [apostle]
pet, [abet]
petal, [accidental]
peter, [abductor]
petite, [accrete]
petition, [abbreviation]
petrify, [amplify]
petrol, [admiral]
petroleum, [anthurium]
petticoat, [afloat]
pettifogger, [agar]
petty, [abatis]
petulance, [abhorrence]
petulant, [ambivalent]
petunia, [alleluia]
pew, [accrue]
pewter, [abductor]
peyote, [abatis]
phalanx, thanks
phallic, [acyclic]
phallus, [acropolis]
phantasm, [abolitionism]
phantasmagoria, [abulia]
phantom, [accustom]
pharaoh, [allegro]

pharisaic, [acidic]
pharisaical, [acoustical]
pharisaism, [abolitionism]
pharisee, [absorbancy]
pharmaceutical, [acoustical]
pharmacist, [assist]
pharmacology, [allergy]
pharmacy, [absorbancy]
pharynx, [jinx]
phase, [ablaze]
phatic, [acoustic]
pheasant, [accordant]
phenom, [aplomb]
phenomena, [alumna]
phenomenal, [abdominal]
phenomenology, [allergy]
phenomenon, [amazon]
phew, [accrue]
philander, [adder]
philanderer, [adulterer]
philanthropic, [acidic]
philanthropist, [activist]
philanthropy, [apocope]
philatelic, [acyclic]
philatelist, [aerialist]
philologist, [allergist]
philology, [allergy]
philosopher, [buffer]
philosophical, [acoustical]
philosophize, [advise]
philosophy, [anastrophe]
phlegm, [apothegm]
phlegmatic, [acoustic]
phloem, [apothegm]
phobia, [abulia]
phonate, [abominate]
phone, [alone]
phonetic, [acoustic]
phonetics, [acoustics]

phonic, [allergenic]
phonics, [administratrix]
phonograph, [allograph]
phonographic,
  [anthropomorphic]
phony, [abalone]
phosphate, [ate]
photo, [aggiornamento]
photocopy, [apocope]
photogenic, [allergenic]
photograph, [allograph]
photographer, [buffer]
photographic,
  [anthropomorphic]
photojournalism,
  [abolitionism]
photojournalist, [aerialist]
photostat, [acrobat]
photosynthesis, [alkalosis]
phrase, [ablaze]
phraseology, [allergy]
phylactery, [accessory]
physical, [acoustical]
physicist, [assist]
physics, [administratrix]
physiology, [allergy]
physique, [antique]
pianist, [abolitionist]
piano, [albino]
piazza, [alfalfa]
pic, [acidic]
pica, [angelica]
picayune, [afternoon]
piccolo, [afterglow]
pick, [acidic]
picket, [advocate]
pickle, [acoustical]
pickpocket, [advocate]
pickup, [backup]

picky, [achy]
picnic, [allergenic]
pictogram, [aerogram]
pictograph, [allograph]
pictorial, [abaxial]
picture, [acupuncture]
picturesque, [arabesque]
piddle, [antipodal]
pidgin, [allergen]
pie, [airdry]
piece of cake, [awake]
piece, [afterpiece]
piecemeal, [automobile]
piecework, [artwork]
piecrust, [adjust]
pier, [adhere]
pierce, [fierce]
pietism, [abolitionism]
pietist, [absolutist]
pietistic, [acoustic]
piety, [abatis]
pig out, [about]
pig, [big]
pigeon, [allergen]
pigeonhole, [areole]
piggy, [aggie]
piggyback, [aback]
pigheaded, absentminded]
pighole, [areole]
piglet, [aglet]
pigment, [abandonment]
pigmentation, [abbreviation]
pigpen, [again]
pigskin, [akin]
pigsty, [airdry]
pigtail, [blackmail]
pike, [alike]
piker, [acre]
pilaf, [boff]

pile, [aisle]
pileup, [backup]
pilfer, [buffer]
pilgrim, [addendum]
pilgrimage, [acknowledge]
pill, [backfill]
pillage, [acknowledge]
pillar, [angler]
pillbox, [bandbox]
pillow, [afterglow]
pillowcase, [abase]
pilot, [aglet]
pimento, [aggiornamento]
pimp, [blimp]
pimple, [ample]
pin, [akin]
pinafore, [abhor]
piñata, [aorta]
pinch, [bullfinch]
pincushion, [abbreviation]
pine, [aerodyne]
pineapple, [ample]
pinecone, [alone]
ping, [anything]
pinhead, [abed]
pinhole, [areole]
pink, [bethink]
pinkie, [achy]
pinko, [alfresco]
pinnacle, [acoustical]
pinpoint, [anoint]
pinprick, [aleatoric]
pinsetter, [abductor]
pinstripe, [airpipe]
pint, [half-pint]
pinto, [aggiornamento]
pinup, [backup]
pinwheel, [automobile]
pinworm, [affirm]

pioneer, [adhere]
pious, [antibias]
pip, [airstrip]
pipe, [airpipe]
pipeline, [airline]
pipsqueak, [antique]
piquant, [abeyant]
pique, [antique]
piracy, [absorbancy]
piranha, [alumna]
pirate, [accurate]
pirouette, [abet]
piscine, [alexandrine]
pish, [abolish]
pisiform, [aswarm]
piso, [also]
piss, [abyss]
pistil, [accidental]
pistol, [accidental]
pit, [acquit]
pita, [aorta]
pitch, [backstitch]
pitcher, [acupuncture]
pitchfork, [cork]
pitchman, [abdomen]
pitchout, [about]
pitfall, [aerosol]
pith, [blacksmith]
pithy, [apathy]
pitiable, [able]
pitiful, [apocryphal]
pitiless, [acropolis]
pittance, [accordance]
pity, [abatis]
pivot, [adequate]
pivotal, [accidental]
pivotman, [adman]
pixie, [absorbancy]
pizza, [alfalfa]

pizzazz, [as]
pizzeria, [abulia]
placard, [absurd]
placate, [abdicate]
placater, [abductor]
place, [abase]
placebo, [airshow]
placed, [abased]
placekick, [acidic]
placekicker, [acre]
placement, [abandonment]
placenta, [aorta]
placid, [acid]
plagiarism, [abolitionism]
plagiarize, [accessorize]
plagiarizer, [adviser]
plague, vague
plaid, [ad]
plain, [abstain]
plaint, [acquaint]
plaintive, [ablative]
plait, [ablate]
plan, [adman]
plane, [abstain]
planeload, [abode]
planet, [acuminate]
planetarium, [anthurium]
planetary, [accessory]
plangent, [agent]
plank, [bank]
plant, [ant]
plantation, [abbreviation]
planter, [abductor]
plantigrade, [abrade]
plaque, [aback]
plasma, [anathema]
plaster, [administer]
plastic, [acoustic]
plasticize, [abscise]

plat, [acrobat]
plate, [ablate]
plateau, [aggiornamento]
platform, [aswarm]
platitude, [altitude]
platonic, [allergenic]
platoon, [afternoon]
platter, [abductor]
plaudit, [adequate]
plausible, [able]
play, [airplay]
playback, [aback]
playbook, [bankbook]
playboy, [ahoy]
player, [ballplayer]
playfield, [airfield]
playful, [apocryphal]
playgirl, [aswirl]
playground, [abound]
playhouse, [alehouse]
playmaker, [acre]
playmate, [acclimate]
playpen, [again]
playroom, [abloom]
playsuit, [acute]
plaything, [anything]
playtime, [airtime]
playwear, [affair]
playwright, [affright]
plaza, [alfalfa]
plea, [ably]
plead, [accede]
pleasant, [accordant]
pleasantry, [ancestry]
please, [antifreeze]
pleasurable, [able]
pleasure, [admeasure]
pleat, [accrete]
plebeian, [abecedarian]

plebiscite, [affright]
pled, [abed]
pledge, [allege]
plenary, [accessory]
plenitude, [altitude]
plenteous, [abstemious]
plentiful, [apocryphal]
plentifulness, [agribusiness]
plenty, [abatis]
pleonasm, [abolitionism]
plethora, [abracadabra]
pleurisy, [absorbancy]
pliability, [abatis]
pliable, [able]
pliant, [abeyant]
pliars, [bonkers]
plica, [angelica]
plicate, [abdicate]
plight, [affright]
plink, [bethink]
plod, [abroad]
plodder, [adder]
plop, [agitprop]
plot, [aeronaut]
plotline, [airline]
plotter, [abductor]
plow, [allow]
plowboy, [ahoy]
plowman, [abdomen]
plowshare, [anywhere]
ploy, [ahoy]
pluck, [amok]
plucky, [achy]
plug, [bedbug]
plum, [addendum]
plumb, [addendum]
plumber, [armor]
plume, [abloom]
plummet, [animate]

plump, [bump]
plunder, [adder]
plunge, [challenge]
plunger, [armiger]
plunk, [bohunk]
plural, [admiral]
pluralism, [abolitionism]
pluralistic, [acoustic]
plurality, [abatis]
plus, [acropolis]
plush, [airbrush]
plutocracy, [absorbancy]
plutocrat, [acrobat]
plutocratic, [acoustic]
plutonium, [anthurium]
ply, [airdry]
plywood, [adulthood]
pneuma, [anathema]
pneumatic, [acoustic]
pneumatology, [allergy]
pneumonia, [alleluia]
poach, [abroach]
poacher, [acupuncture]
pock, [aftershock]
pocketbook, [bankbook]
pocketknife, [afterlife]
pockmark, [aardvark]
pod, [abroad]
podium, [anthurium]
poem, [addendum]
poesy, [advisee]
poet, [adequate]
poetess, [afflatus]
poetic, [acoustic]
poetry, [ancestry]
pogrom, [addendum]
pogromist, [alchemist]
poi, [ahoy]
poignant, [abeyant]

poinsettia, [abulia]
point, [anoint]
pointed, [abluted]
pointer, [abductor]
poise, [counterpoise]
poison, [anchorperson]
poisonous, [agribusiness]
poke, [artichoke]
poker, [acre]
poky, [achy]
polar, [angler]
polarity, [abatis]
polarization, [abbreviation]
polarize, [accessorize]
pole, [areole]
polecat, [acrobat]
polemic, [academic]
polemical, [acoustical]
polemicist, [assist]
polemist, [alchemist]
police, [afterpiece]
policeman, [abdomen]
policy, [absorbancy]
policyholder, [adder]
polio, [audio]
polish, [abolish]
politburo, [allegro]
polite, [affright]
political, [acoustical]
politicize, [abscise]
politics, [acoustics]
polity, [abatis]
polka dot, [aeronaut]
polka, [angelica]
poll, [areole]
pollen, [acetylene]
pollinate, [abominate]
pollination, [abbreviation]
pollster, [administer]

pollutant, [accordant]
pollute, [acute]
polluter, [abductor]
pollution, [abbreviation]
polo, [afterglow]
poltergeist, [antichrist]
polyester, [administer]
polygamist, [alchemist]
polygamous, [allonymous]
polygamy, [academy]
polygenesis, [alkalosis]
polygenetic, [acoustic]
polygon, [amazon]
polygraph, [allograph]
polynomial, [abaxial]
polyp, [backup]
polyshot, [aeronaut]
polytechnic, [allergenic]
polytheism, [abolitionism]
polytheist, [activist]
polytheistic, [acoustic]
polyunsaturated, [abluted]
pomace, [allonymous]
pomegranate, [acuminate]
pommel, [abnormal]
pomp, [chomp]
pompadour, [abhor]
pompom, [aplomb]
pompous, [auspice]
ponch, [haunch]
poncho, [airshow]
pond, [abscond]
ponder, [adder]
ponderous, [actress]
Pontiac, [aback]
pontifical, [acoustical]
pontificate, [abdicate]
pontoon, [afternoon]
pony, [abalone]

ponytail, [blackmail]
pooch, [hooch]
poodle, [antipodal]
poof, [aloof]
pooh, [accrue]
pool, [bascule]
poolroom, [abloom]
poolside, [abide]
poop, [coop]
poor, [abjure]
poorhouse, [alehouse]
pop, [agitprop]
popcorn, [acorn]
pope, [antelope]
poplar, [angler]
poplin, [acetylene]
popover, [achiever]
popper, [barkeeper]
poppy, [apocope]
poppycock, [aftershock]
populace, [acropolis]
popular, [angler]
popularity, [abatis]
popularize, [accessorize]
populate, [ablate]
population, [abbreviation]
populism, [abolitionism]
populist, [aerialist]
populous, [acropolis]
porcelain, [acetylene]
porcupine, [aerodyne]
pore, [abhor]
porker, [acre]
porky, [achy]
porn, [acorn]
pornographer, [buffer]
pornographic,
   [anthropomorphic]
pornography, [anastrophe]

porosity, [abatis]
porous, [actress]
porpoise, [auspice]
porridge, [abridge]
port, [airport]
portable, [able]
portage, [acknowledge]
portal, [accidental]
portend, [addend]
portent, [accent]
portentous, [afflatus]
porter, [abductor]
porterhouse, [alehouse]
portfolio, [audio]
porthole, [areole]
portico, [alfresco]
portion, [abbreviation]
portmanteau, [aggiornamento]
portrait, [accurate]
portray, [affray]
portrayal, [ail]
posada, [addenda]
pose, [airhose]
posh, [awash]
posit, [apposite]
position, [abbreviation]
positional, [aboriginal]
positive, [ablative]
positivism, [abolitionism]
positivist, [activist]
positivistic, [acoustic]
posse, [absorbancy]
possess, [access]
possessed, [abreast]
possession, [abbreviation]
possessive, [abrasive]
possibility, [abatis]
possible, [able]
post, [aftermost]

postage, [acknowledge]
postal, [accidental]
postcard, [backyard]
postchristian, [antiphon]
postcollege, [acknowledge]
postconception,
   [abbreviation]
postdate, [accommodate]
postdepression,
   [abbreviation]
postdoctoral, [admiral]
poster, [administer]
posterior, [anterior]
posterity, [abatis]
postern, [adjourn]
postgame, [acclaim]
postgraduate, [adequate]
postgraduation, [abbreviation]
posthaste, [abased]
posthole, [areole]
posthumous, [allonymous]
postlude, [allude]
postman, [abdomen]
postmark, [aardvark]
postmaster, [administer]
postmillennial, [abaxial]
postmillennialist, [aerialist]
postmodern, [adjourn]
postmortem, [accustom]
postnatal, [accidental]
postnuptial, [abbatial]
postoperative, [ablative]
postpaid, [abrade]
postpartum, [accustom]
postpone, [alone]
postposition, [abbreviation]
postscript, [adscript]
postsecondary, [accessory]
postulant, [ambivalent]

postulate, [ablate]
postulate, [aglet]
posture, [acupuncture]
postwar, [abhor]
posy, [advisee]
pot, [aeronaut]
potable, [able]
potassium, [anthurium]
potation, [abbreviation]
potato, [aggiornamento]
potbelly, [ably]
potency, [absorbancy]
potent, [accordant]
potentate, [acetate]
potential, [abbatial]
potentiality, [abatis]
pothead, [abed]
pother, [altogether]
pothole, [areole]
potion, [abbreviation]
potlatch, [armpatch]
potluck, [amok]
potpie, [airdry]
potpourri, [accessory]
potshot, [aeronaut]
pottage, [acknowledge]
potted, [abluted]
potter, [abductor]
pottery, [accessory]
pottle, [accidental]
potty, [abatis]
pouch, [avouch]
poultice, [afflatus]
poultry, [ancestry]
pounce, [announce]
pound, [abound]
poundage, [acknowledge]
pour, [abhor]
pout, [about]

pouty, [abatis]
poverty, [abatis]
pow, [allow]
powder, [adder]
powdery, [accessory]
power, [airpower]
powerboat, [afloat]
powerful, [apocryphal]
powerhouse, [alehouse]
powerless, [acropolis]
pow-wow, [allow]
pox, [bandbox]
practicable, [able]
practical, [acoustical]
practice, [afflatus]
practicum, [addendum]
practitioner, [afterburner]
pragmatic, [acoustic]
pragmatism, [abolitionism]
pragmatist, [absolutist]
Prague, [agog]
prairie, [accessory]
praise, [ablaze]
praiseworthy, [newsworthy]
praline, [alexandrine]
prance, [advance]
prank, [bank]
prankster, [administer]
prate, [accelerate]
prattle, [accidental]
prawn, [amazon]
praxis, [alkalosis]
pray, [affray]
prayer, [affair]
prayer, [ballplayer]
prayerful, [apocryphal]
preach, [beach]
preacher, [acupuncture]
preachy, [blotchy]

preadmission, [abbreviation]
preadolescence, [accordance]
preamble, [able]
preamp, [aid-de-camp]
preapprove, [approve]
prearrange, [arrange]
preassembled, [bedraggled]
precancerous, [actress]
precarious, [abstemious]
precast, [aghast]
precatory, [accessory]
precaution, [abbreviation]
precede, [accede]
precedence, [abhorrence]
precedent, [adjective]
  [accordant]
precedent, [noun] [abundant]
precept, [accept]
precession, [abbreviation]
prechristmas, [allonymous]
precinct, [distinct]
precious, [adscititious]
precipitant, [abirritant]
precipitate, [adjective]
  [adequate]
precipitate, [verb] [acetate]
precipitation, [abbreviation]
precipitous, [afflatus]
precise, [advice]
precision, [abrasion]
preclearance, [abhorrence]
preclude, [allude]
precocious, [adscititious]
precognition, [abbreviation]
precollege, [acknowledge]
preconceive, [achieve]
preconception, [abbreviation]
precondition, [abbreviation]
precut, [advocate]

predator, [abductor]
predatory, [accessory]
predecessor, [aggressor]
predestinarian, [abecedarian]
predestinate, [abominate]
predestination, [abbreviation]
predestinator, [abductor]
predetermination,
  [abbreviation]
predetermine, [abdomen]
predicament, [abandonment]
predicate, [noun] [advocate]
predicate, [verb] [abdicate]
predication, [abbreviation]
predict, [addict]
predictable, [able]
prediction, [abbreviation]
predictive, [ablative]
predilection, [abbreviation]
predispose, [airhose]
prednisone, [alone]
predominant, [abstinent]
predominate, [adjective]
  [acuminate]
predominate, [verb]
  [abominate]
preelection, [abbreviation]
preemie, [academy]
preeminence, [abhorrence]
preeminent, [abstinent]
preempt, [attempt]
preemptive, [ablative]
preen, [alexandrine]
preexist, [activist]
preexistence, [abhorrence]
prefab, [backstab]
prefabricate, [abdicate]
preface, [amorphous]
prefer, [buffer]

preferable, [able]
preference, [circumference]
preferential, [abbatial]
prefight, [affright]
prefix, [administratrix]
preflight, [affright]
pregame, [acclaim]
pregnant, [abstinent]
preheat, [accrete]
prehistoric, [aleatoric]
prejudge, [adjudge]
prejudicial, [abbatial]
prelate, [aglet]
prelaunch, [haunch]
prelim, [acronym]
preliminary, [accessory]
prelude, [allude]
premarital, [accidental]
premature, [abjure]
premed, [abed]
premeditate, [acetate]
premeditated, [abluted]
premeditation, [abbreviation]
premier, [adhere]
premillenarian, [abecedarian]
premillennial, [abaxial]
premillennialism,
  [abolitionism]
premillennialist, [aerialist]
premise, [allonymous]
premium, [addendum]
premix, [administratrix]
premonition, [abbreviation]
prenatal, [accidental]
prenumber, [amber]
prenuptial, [abbatial]
preoccupation, [abbreviation]
preoccupied, [abide]
prep, [crowstep]

prepackage, [acknowledge]
preparation, [abbreviation]
prepare, [affair]
preplan, [adman]
preponderance, [abhorrence]
preponderate, [accelerate]
preposition, [abbreviation]
preposterous, [actress]
preppy, [apocope]
preprimary, [accessory]
prequalification,
  [abbreviation]
prerecorded, [absentminded]
preregister, [administer]
preregistration, [abbreviation]
prerequisite, [apposite]
preretirement, [abandonment]
prerogative, [ablative]
presage, [acknowledge]
presbyter, [abductor]
presbyterial, [anneal]
presbytery, [accessory]
preschool, [bascule]
preschooler, [angler]
prescience, [abhorrence]
prescient, [abeyant]
prescientific,
  [anthropomorphic]
prescribe, [ascribe]
prescription, [abbreviation]
prescriptive, [ablative]
presell, [bagatelle]
presence, [accordance]
present, [accordant]
presentable, [able]
presentation, [abbreviation]
presenter, [abductor]
preservation, [abbreviation]
preservative, [ablative]

preserve, [conserve]
preshrink, [bethink]
preside, [abide]
presidency, [absorbancy]
president, [abundant]
presidential, [abbatial]
presider, [adder]
presidio, [audio]
presidium, [anthurium]
presoak, [artichoke]
presort, [abort]
press, [acquiesce]
pressboard, [aboard]
pressman, [abdomen]
pressroom, [abloom]
pressrun, raring, run, outrun,
   overrun, siren, sovereign,
   squadron, suzerain, terrene,
   urine, veteran, warren [see
   also abdomen]
pressure, [acupressure]
pressurize, [accessorize]
prestigious, [advantageous]
presto, [aggiornamento]
presume, [abloom]
presumption, [abbreviation]
presumptuous, [ambiguous]
presuppose, [airhose]
pretax, [anthrax]
preteen, [alexandrine]
pretend, [addend]
pretender, [adder]
pretense, [cense]
pretension, [abbreviation]
pretentious, [adscititious]
pretentiousness,
   [agribusiness]
pretest, [abreast]
pretext, [context]

pretrial, [aisle]
pretty, [abatis]
pretzel, [apostle]
prevail, [ail]
prevalence, [abhorrence]
prevalent, [ambivalent]
prevaricate, [abdicate]
prevent, [accent]
preventable, [able]
preventative, [ablative]
prevention, [abbreviation]
preventive, [ablative]
preview, [accrue]
previous, [abstemious]
prevision, [abrasion]
prexy, [buoy]
prey, [affray]
priapic, [acidic]
price, [advice]
priceless, [acropolis]
pricey, [absorbancy]
prick, [aleatoric]
pricker, [acre]
pricket, [advocate]
prickle, [acoustical]
prickly, [ably]
pride, [abide]
prideful, [apocryphal]
priest, [beast]
priestess, [afflatus]
priesthood, [adulthood]
prig, [big]
prim, [acronym]
primacy, [absorbancy]
primal, [abnormal]
primarily, [ably]
primary, [accessory]
primate, [acclimate]
prime, [airtime]

primer, [armor]
primeval, [adjectival]
primipara, [abracadabra]
primitive, [ablative]
primo, [airshow]
primogenitor, [abductor]
primordial, [abaxial]
primrose, [airhose]
prince, [convince]
princely, [ably]
princess, [alkalosis]
principal, [ample]
principality, [abatis]
principalship, [airship]
principle, [ample]
principled, [bedraggled]
print, [blueprint]
printable, [able]
printer, [abductor]
printout, [about]
prior, [amplifier]
prioritize, [absolutize]
priority, [abatis]
prism, [abolitionism]
prison, [anchorperson]
prisoner, [afterburner]
prissy, [absorbancy]
pristine, [alexandrine]
privacy, [absorbancy]
private, [adequate]
privation, [abbreviation]
privative, [ablative]
privatize, [absolutize]
privilege, [acknowledge]
privity, [abatis]
privy, [anchovy]
prize, [accessorize]
prizefight, [affright]
prizewinner, [afterburner]

pro, [allegro]
pro-abortion, [abbreviation]
proabortionist, [abolitionist]
proactive, [ablative]
probability, [abatis]
probably, [able]
probate, [abate]
probation, [abbreviation]
probationary, [accessory]
probe, [bathrobe]
probity, [abatis]
problem, [addendum]
problematic, [acoustic]
problematical, [acoustical]
proboscis, [alkalosis]
procedural, [admiral]
procedure, [armiger]
proceed, [accede]
process, [alkalosis]
procession, [abbreviation]
processional, [aboriginal]
processor, [aggressor]
pro-choice, [choice]
proclaim, [acclaim]
proclamation, [abbreviation]
proclivity, [abatis]
proconsul, [apostle]
procrastinate, [abominate]
procreate, [create]
procreation, [abbreviation]
proctor, [abductor]
procurator, [abductor]
procure, [abjure]
procurement, [abandonment]
prod, [abroad]
prodigal, [angle]
prodigious, [advantageous]
prodigy, [allergy]
produce, [abstruse]

producer, [aggressor]
product, [abduct]
production, [abbreviation]
productive, [ablative]
productivity, [abatis]
proem, [apothegm]
profane, [abstain]
profanity, [abatis]
profess, [acquiesce]
professed, [abreast]
profession, [abbreviation]
professional, [aboriginal]
professionalism,
  [abolitionism]
professor, [aggressor]
proffer, [buffer]
proficiency, [absorbancy]
proficient, [abeyant]
profile, [anile]
profit, [adequate]
profitable, [able]
profiteer, [adhere]
profligacy, [absorbancy]
profligate, [agate]
profound, [abound]
profundity, [abatis]
profuse, [abstruse]
profusion, [abrasion]
progenitor, [abductor]
progeny, [abalone]
prognosis, [alkalosis]
prognosticate, [abdicate]
prognostication,
  [abbreviation]
prognosticator, [abductor]
program, [aerogram]
programmer, [armor]
progress, [noun] [access]
progress, [verb] [actress]

progression, [abbreviation]
progressive, [abrasive]
prohibit, [abbot]
prohibition, [abbreviation]
prohibitionist, [abolitionist]
prohibitive, [ablative]
project, [abject]
projectile, [accidental]
projection, [abbreviation]
projectionist, [abolitionist]
projector, [abductor]
prolapse, [apse]
prolate, [ablate]
prolegomenon, [amazon]
prolepsis, [alkalosis]
proletarian, [abecedarian]
proletariat, [affiliate]
pro-life, [afterlife]
proliferate, [accelerate]
proliferation, [abbreviation]
prolific, [anthropomorphic]
prologue, [agog]
prolong, [agelong]
prolongation, [abbreviation]
prom, [aplomb]
promenade, [abrade]
prominence, [abhorrence]
prominent, [abstinent]
promiscuity, [abatis]
promiscuous, [ambiguous]
promise, [allonymous]
promissory, [accessory]
promotable, [able]
promote, [afloat]
promoter, [abductor]
promotion, [abbreviation]
promulgate, [abnegate]
promulgation, [abbreviation]
promulgator, [abductor]

prone, [alone]
prong, [agelong]
pronoun, [boomtown]
pronounce, [announce]
pronuclear, [anterior]
pronunciation, [abbreviation]
proof, [aloof]
proofread, [accede]
proofreader, [adder]
prop, [agitprop]
propaganda, [addenda]
propagandist, [activist]
propagandize, [advise]
propagate, [abnegate]
propagation, [abbreviation]
propagator, [abductor]
propel, [bagatelle]
propellant, [ambivalent]
propeller, [angler]
propensity, [abatis]
proper, [barkeeper]
proper, [barkeeper]
property, [abatis]
prophecy, [absorbancy]
prophesy, [airdry]
prophet, [adequate]
prophetess, [afflatus]
prophetic, [acoustic]
prophetical, [acoustical]
prophylactic, [acoustic]
prophylaxis, [alkalosis]
propinquity, [abatis]
propitiation, [abbreviation]
propitiator, [abductor]
propitiatory, [accessory]
propitious, [adscititious]
propitiousness, [agribusiness]
proponent, [abstinent]
proportion, [abbreviation]

proportional, [aboriginal]
proportionate, [adjective]
  [acuminate]
proportionate, [verb]
  [abominate]
proposal, [appraisal]
propose, [airhose]
proposition, [abbreviation]
propositional, [abdominal]
propound, [abound]
proprietary, [accessory]
proprietor, [abductor]
proprietorship, [airship]
propriety, [abatis]
propulsion, [abbreviation]
prorate, [accelerate]
prosaic, [acidic]
proscribe, [ascribe]
prose, [airhose]
prosecute, [acute]
prosecution, [abbreviation]
prosecutor, [abductor]
proselyte, [affright]
proselytize, [absolutize]
proselytizer, [adviser]
prosody, [acidy]
prospect, [abject]
prospective, [ablative]
prospector, [abductor]
prospectus, [afflatus]
prosperity, [abatis]
prosperous, [actress]
prostate, [acetate]
prosthesis, [alkalosis]
prosthetic, [acoustic]
prosthetics, [acoustics]
prostitute, [acute]
prostitution, [abbreviation]
prostrate, [accelerate]

prostration, [abbreviation]
prosy, [advisee]
protagonist, [abolitionist]
protasis, [alkalosis]
protect, [abject]
protection, [abbreviation]
protectionism, [abolitionism]
protectionist, [abolitionist]
protector, [abductor]
protectorate, [accurate]
protégé, [agape]
protein, [alexandrine]
protem, [apothegm]
protest, [abreast]
protestant, [abirritant]
protestation, [abbreviation]
protocol, [aerosol]
proton, [amazon]
prototype, [airpipe]
protraction, [abbreviation]
protractor, [abductor]
protrude, [allude]
protrusion, [abrasion]
proud, [aloud]
prove, [approve]
proverb, [adverb]
proverbial, [abaxial]
provide, [abide]
providence, [abhorrence]
providential, [abbatial]
provider, [adder]
province, [abhorrence]
provincial, [abbatial]
provincialism, [abolitionism]
provision, [abrasion]
proviso, [bozo]
provisory, [accessory]
provocation, [abbreviation]
provocative, [ablative]

provoke, [artichoke]
provost, [aftermost]
prowess, [ambiguous]
prowl, [foul]
prowler, [angler]
proximate, [animate]
proximity, [abatis]
proxy, [absorbancy]
prude, [allude]
prudence, [accordance]
prudent, [accordant]
prudential, [abbatial]
prudish, [abolish]
prune, [afternoon]
prurient, [abeyant]
pry, [airdry]
psalm, [aplomb]
psalmist, [alchemist]
psalmody, [acidy]
psaltery, [ancestry]
pseud, [allude]
pseudo, [aficionado]
pseudonym, [acronym]
pshaw, [aah]
psych, [alike]
psychedelic, [acyclic]
psychiatry, [ancestry]
psychic, [acidic]
psycho, [alfresco]
psychoanalysis, [alkalosis]
psychoanalyze, [actualize]
psychobabble, [able]
psychodrama, [anathema]
psychological, [acoustical]
psychologize, [advise]
psychology, [allergy]
psychopath, [aftermath]
psychosexual, [accrual]
psychosis, [alkalosis]

psychosomatic, [acoustic]
psychotherapy, [apocope]
psychotic, [acoustic]
pub, [backrub]
puberty, [abatis]
pubescence, [accordance]
pubescent, [adjacent]
pubic, [acerbic]
public, [acyclic]
publican, [awaken]
publication, [abbreviation]
publicist, [assist]
publicity, [abatis]
publicize, [abscise]
publish, [abolish]
publishable, [able]
publisher, [acupressure]
puce, [abstruse]
puck, [amok]
pucker, [acre]
puddle, [antipodal]
pudgy, [allergy]
pueblo, [afterglow]
puerile, [admiral]
puff, [bluff]
pug, [bedbug]
pugilism, [abolitionism]
pugilist, [aerialist]
pugnacious, [adscititious]
puissance, [accordance]
puissant, [adjacent]
puke, [archduke]
pulchritude, [altitude]
pule, [bascule]
pull, [apocryphal]
pullback, [aback]
pullet, [aglet]
pulley, [ably]
pullout, [about]

pullover, [achiever]
pullulate, [ablate]
pulp, [gulp]
pulpit, [acquit]
pulpiteer, [adhere]
pulpwood, [adulthood]
pulsate, [ate]
pulsation, [abbreviation]
pulsator, [abductor]
pulse, [convulse]
pulverize, [accessorize]
pumice, [allonymous]
pummel, [abnormal]
pump, [bump]
pumpernickel, [acoustical]
pumpkin, [awaken]
pun, [bandwagon]
punch bowl, [areole]
punch, [brunch]
punchboard, [aboard]
punchy, [blotchy]
punctate, [acetate]
punctilio, [audio]
punctilious, [abstemious]
punctual, [accrual]
punctuality, [abatis]
punctuate, [accentuate]
punctuation, [abbreviation]
puncture, [acupuncture]
pundit, [adequate]
pungency, [absorbancy]
pungent, [agent]
punish, [abolish]
punishable, [able]
punishment, [abandonment]
punitive, [ablative]
punk, [bohunk]
punster, [administer]
punt, [abeyant]

punter, [abductor]
puny, [abalone]
pup, [backup]
pupil, [ample]
puppet, [adequate]
puppeteer, [adhere]
puppetry, [ancestry]
puppy, [apocope]
purchase, [antibias]
purchaser, [aggressor]
pure, [abjure]
purebred, [abed]
puree, [affray]
purgatory, [accessory]
purge, [converge]
purification, [abbreviation]
purified, [abide]
purify, [amplify]
purist, [allegorist]
puritan, [anchorperson]
puritanical, [acoustical]
puritanism, [abolitionism]
purity, [abatis]
purlieu, [accrue]
purloin, [adjoin]
purple, [ample]
purport, [airport]
purported, [abluted]
purpose, [auspice]
purposeful, [apocryphal]
purposeless, [acropolis]
purposive, [abrasive]
purr, [barkeeper]
purse, [adverse]
pursuant, [abeyant]
pursue, [accrue]
pursuit, [acute]
purtenance, [abhorrence]
purulent, [ambivalent]

purvey, [agape]
purveyance, [abhorrence]
purveyor, [ballplayer]
purview, [accrue]
pus, [auspice]
push, [ambush]
pushcart, [apart]
pusher, [acupressure]
pushover, [achiever]
pushpin, [akin]
pushy, [banshee]
pusillanimous, [allonymous]
pussy, [absorbancy]
pussycat, [acrobat]
pussyfoot, [ablaut]
put down, [boomtown]
put, [ablaut]
putative, [ablative]
putout, [about]
putrefaction, [abbreviation]
putrefy, [amplify]
putrid, [acid]
putsch, [butch]
putt, [riot]
putter, [abductor]
putty, [abatis]
puzzle, [appraisal]
puzzlement, [abandonment]
pygmy, [academy]
pyramid, [amid]
pyromania, [abulia]
pyrotechnics, [administratrix]
python, [amazon]
quack, [aback]
quackery, [accessory]
quad, [abroad]
quadrangle, [angle]
quadrant, [aberrant]
quadraphonic, [allergenic]

quadrate, [accelerate]
quadratic, [acoustic]
quadrennial, [abaxial]
quadrennium, [anthurium]
quadriceps, [biceps]
quadrilateral, [admiral]
quadriplegic, [acidic]
quadrivium, [anthurium]
quadruped, [abed]
quadruple, [ample]
quagmire, [acquire]
quail, [ail]
quaint, [acquaint]
quake, [awake]
quaker, [accrue]
qualification, [abbreviation]
qualified, [abide]
qualifier, [amplifier]
qualify, [amplify]
qualitative, [ablative]
quality, [abatis]
qualm, [aplomb]
qualmish, [abolish]
quandary, [accessory]
quantify, [amplify]
quantitative, [ablative]
quantity, [abatis]
quantum, [accustom]
quarantine, [alexandrine]
quarrel, [barrel]
quarrelsome,
    [adventuresome]
quarry, [accessory]
quart, [abort]
quarter, [abductor]
quarterback, [aback]
quarterdeck, [afterdeck]
quarterfinal, [abdominal]
quartermaster, [administer]

quartet, [abet]
quartile, [anile]
quasar, [abattoir]
quash, [awash]
quasi, [airdry]
quatrain, [abstain]
quaver, [achiever]
queasy, [advisee]
queen, [alexandrine]
queer, [adhere]
quell, [bagatelle]
quench, [bench]
query, [accessory]
quesadilla, [abulia]
quest, [abreast]
questionable, [able]
questionnaire, [affair]
queue, [accrue]
quibble, [able]
quiche, [baksheesh]
quick, [acidic]
quicken, [awaken]
quickie, [achy]
quicksand, [ampersand]
quicksilver, [achiever]
quickstep, [crowstep]
quiescent, [adjacent]
quiet, [adequate]
quietism, [abolitionism]
quietude, [altitude]
quill, [backfill]
quilt, [atilt]
quintet, [abet]
quintuple, [ample]
quintuplet, [aglet]
quip, [airstrip]
quirk, [artwork]
quit, [acquit]
quitclaim, [acclaim]

quite, [affright]
quitter, [abductor]
quiver, [achiever]
quixotic, [acoustic]
quiz, [fizz]
quizmaster, [administer]
quizzical, [acoustical]
quorum, [addendum]
quota, [aorta]
quotable, [able]
quotation, [abbreviation]
quote, [afloat]
quotient, [abeyant]
rabbi, [alibi]
rabbit, [abbot]
rabble, [able]
rabid, [acid]
rabies, [antifreeze]
raccoon, [afternoon]
race, [abase]
racecourse, [coarse]
racer, [aggressor]
racetrack, [aback]
raceway, [airway]
racial, [abbatial]
racism, [abolitionism]
racist, [assist]
rack, [aback]
racket, [advocate]
racketeer, [adhere]
raconteur, [abductor]
racquetball, [aerosol]
racy, [absorbancy]
rad, [ad]
radar, [abattoir]
radial, [abaxial]
radiance, [abhorrence]
radiant, [abeyant]
radiate, [create]

radiator, [abductor]
radical, [acoustical]
radio, [audio]
radioactive, [ablative]
radiologist, [allergist]
radiology, [allergy]
radius, [abstemious]
radix, [administratrix]
radon, [amazon]
raffle, [apocryphal]
raft, [abaft]
rafter, [abductor]
rag, [ag]
ragbag, [ag]
rage, [age]
ragged, [acid]
ragout, [accrue]
ragtag, [ag]
ragtime, [airtime]
ragweed, [accede]
rah, [aah]
raid, [abrade]
raider, [adder]
rail, [ail]
railcar, [abattoir]
railroad, [abode]
railway, [airway]
raiment, [abandonment]
rain check, [afterdeck]
rain, [abstain]
rainbow, [airshow]
raincoat, [afloat]
raindrop, [agitprop]
rainfall, [aerosol]
rainproof, [aloof]
rainspout, [about]
rainstorm, [aswarm]
rainy, [abalone]
raise, [ablaze]

raisin, [anchorperson]
rake, [awake]
rally, [ably]
ram, [aerogram]
ramble, [able]
rambler, [angler]
rambunctious, [adscititious]
ramification, [abbreviation]
ramp, [aid-de-camp]
rampage, [age]
rampant, [abeyant]
rampart, [apart]
ramrod, [abroad]
ramshackle, [acoustical]
ran, [adman]
ranch, [avalanche]
rancher, [acupuncture]
ranchero, [allegro]
rancho, [airshow]
rancid, [acid]
rancor, [acre]
rancorous, [actress]
random, [addendum]
range, [arrange]
ranger, [armiger]
rank, [bank]
ranked, [overranked]
rankle, [acoustical]
ransack, [aback]
ransom, [adventuresome]
rant, [ant]
rap, [afterclap]
rapacious, [adscititious]
rape, [agape]
rapid, [acid]
rapidity, [abatis]
rapparee, [accessory]
rappee, [agape]
rappel, [bagatelle]

rapper, [barkeeper]
rapport, [abhor]
rapt, [adapt]
rapture, [acupuncture]
rare, [affair]
rarefied, [abide]
rarefy, [amplify]
raring, [pressrun]
rarity, [abatis]
rascal, [acoustical]
rase, [ablaze]
rash, [abash]
rasp, [clasp]
raspberry, [accessory]
raspy, [apocope]
rat race, [abase]
rat, [acrobat]
ratchet, [adequate]
rate, [accelerate]
rather, [altogether]
ratify, [amplify]
ratio, [audio]
ratiocinate, [abominate]
rational, [abdominal]
rationale, [canal]
rationalism, [abolitionism]
rationalist, [aerialist]
rationality, [abatis]
rationalization, [abbreviation]
rationalize, [actualize]
rationalizer, [adviser]
rattan, [adman]
rattle, [accidental]
rattlebrain, [abstain]
rattlesnake, [awake]
rattletrap, [afterclap]
rattrap, [afterclap]
ratty, [abatis]
raucous, [abacus]

raunch, [haunch]
raunchy, [blotchy]
ravage, [acknowledge]
rave, [aftershave]
ravel, [adjectival]
ravenous, [agribusiness]
ravine, [alexandrine]
ravioli, [ably]
ravish, [abolish]
raw, [aah]
rawhide, [abide]
ray, [affray]
rayon, [amazon]
raze, [ablaze]
razor, [adviser]
razorback, [aback]
razz, [as]
reach, [beach]
reacquire, [acquire]
reacquisition, [abbreviation]
react, [abstract]
reaction, [abbreviation]
reactionary, [accessory]
reactivate, [activate]
reactivation, [abbreviation]
reactive, [ablative]
reactor, [abductor]
read, [verb] [abed]
read, [verb] [accede]
readability, [abatis]
readjust, [adjust]
readjustment, [abandonment]
readmission, [abbreviation]
readmit, [acquit]
readout, [about]
ready, [acidy]
reaffirm, [affirm]
reaffirmation, [abbreviation]
real, [anneal]

realign, [airline]
realignment, [abandonment]
realism, [abolitionism]
realist, [aerialist]
realistic, [acoustic]
reality, [abatis]
realization, [abbreviation]
realize, [actualize]
reallocate, [abdicate]
realm, [elm]
ream, [abeam]
reanalyze, [actualize]
reap, [asleep]
reaper, [barkeeper]
reappear, [adhere]
reapply, [airdry]
reappoint, [anoint]
reappointment,
    [abandonment]
reapportion, [abbreviation]
reappraisal, [appraisal]
reappraise, [ablaze]
reapprove, [approve]
rear, [adhere]
rearm, [alarm]
rearrange, [arrange]
rearrangement,
    [abandonment]
rearrest, [abreast]
reason, [anchorperson]
reasonable, [able]
reasonableness,
    [agribusiness]
reassemble, [able]
reassess, [acquiesce]
reassessment, [abandonment]
reassign, [aerodyne]
reassignment, [abandonment]
reassurance, [abhorrence]

reassure, [abjure]
reattach, [armpatch]
reauthorization, [abbreviation]
reauthorize, [accessorize]
reave, [achieve]
reawake, [awake]
reawaken, [awaken]
rebaptism, [abolitionism]
rebaptize, [absolutize]
rebate, [abate]
rebel, [able]
rebellion, [antiunion]
rebellious, [acropolis]
rebelliousness, [agribusiness]
rebid, [amid]
rebind, [affined]
reboard, [aboard]
reboot, [acute]
reborn, [acorn]
rebound, [abound]
rebounder, [adder]
rebroadcast, [aghast]
rebuff, [bluff]
rebuild, [build]
rebuilt, [atilt]
rebuke, [archduke]
rebus, [abbess]
rebut, [abbot]
rebuttal, [accidental]
recalcitrance, [abhorrence]
recalcitrant, [aberrant]
recalculate, [ablate]
recalculation, [abbreviation]
recalibrate, [accelerate]
recall, [aerosol]
recant, [ant]
recap, [afterclap]
recapitalization, [abbreviation]
recapitalize, [actualize]

recapitulate, [ablate]
recapture, [acupuncture]
recast, [aghast]
recede, [accede]
receipt, [accrete]
receivable, [able]
receive, [achieve]
receiver, [achiever]
receivership, [airship]
recension, [abbreviation]
recent, [adjacent]
receptacle, [acoustical]
reception, [abbreviation]
receptionist, [abolitionist]
receptive, [ablative]
recertify, [amplify]
recession, [abbreviation]
recessional, [aboriginal]
recessive, [abrasive]
recharge, [barge]
recheck, [afterdeck]
recidivism, [abolitionism]
recidivist, [activist]
recipe, [apocope]
recipient, [abeyant]
reciprocal, [acoustical]
reciprocate, [abdicate]
reciprocation, [abbreviation]
reciprocity, [abatis]
recirculate, [ablate]
recital, [accidental]
recitation, [abbreviation]
recitative, [ablative]
recite, [affright]
reckless, [acropolis]
reckon, [awaken]
reclaim, [acclaim]
reclamation, [abbreviation]
reclassification, [abbreviation]

reclassify, [amplify]
recline, [airline]
recliner, [afterburner]
recluse, [abstruse]
recodify, [amplify]
recognition, [abbreviation]
recognizance, [abhorrence]
recoil, [broil]
recollect, [abject]
recollection, [abbreviation]
recombinant, [abstinent]
recommend, [addend]
recommendation,
　[abbreviation]
recommission, [abbreviation]
recommit, [acquit]
recompense, [cense]
recompose, [airhose]
recomputation, [abbreviation]
recompute, [acute]
reconceptualize, [actualize]
reconcilable, [able]
reconcile, [anile]
reconciler, [angler]
reconciliation, [abbreviation]
recondite, [affright]
recondition, [abbreviation]
reconfigure, [ballplayer]
reconfirm, [affirm]
reconnaissance, [abhorrence]
reconnect, [abject]
reconnection, [abbreviation]
reconnoiter, [abductor]
reconsecrate, [accelerate]
reconsecration, [abbreviation]
reconsider, [adder]
reconstitute, [acute]
reconstruct, [abduct]
reconstruction, [abbreviation]

reconvene, [alexandrine]
reconvey, [agape]
reconvict, [addict]
reconviction, [abbreviation]
recopy, [apocope]
record, [noun] [absurd]
record, [verb] [award]
recorder, [adder]
recount, [account]
recoup, [coop]
recourse, [coarse]
recover, [achiever]
recovery, [accessory]
recreant, [abeyant]
recreate, [create]
recreation, [abbreviation]
recrimination, [abbreviation]
recrudesce, [acquiesce]
recrudescence, [accordance]
recruit, [acute]
recruiter, [abductor]
recruitment, [abandonment]
rectal, [accidental]
rectangle, [angle]
rectangular, [angler]
rectification, [abbreviation]
rectify, [amplify]
rectitude, [altitude]
rector, [abductor]
rectory, [accessory]
rectum, [accustom]
recumbent, [abeyant]
recuperate, [accelerate]
recuperation, [abbreviation]
recur, [acre]
recurrent, [aberrant]
recursion, [abrasion]
recursive, [abrasive]
recuse, [amuse]

recut, [advocate]
recycle, [acoustical]
red, [abed]
redact, [abstract]
redaction, [abbreviation]
redactor, [abductor]
redate, [accommodate]
reddish, [abolish]
redecorate, [accelerate]
redecorator, [abductor]
rededicate, [abdicate]
rededication, [abbreviation]
redeem, [abeam]
redeemer, [armor]
redefine, [aerodyne]
redeliver, [achiever]
redemption, [abbreviation]
redemptive, [ablative]
redeploy, [ahoy]
redeposit, [apposite]
redesign, [aerodyne]
redevelop, [backup]
redevelopment,
  [abandonment]
red-hot, [aeronaut]
redial, [aisle]
redirect, [abject]
redirection, [abbreviation]
rediscount, [account]
rediscover, [achiever]
rediscuss, [abacus]
redistribution, [abbreviation]
redistrict, [addict]
redline, [airline]
redneck, [afterdeck]
redness, [agribusiness]
redo, [accrue]
redolence, [abhorrence]
redolent, [ambivalent]

redouble, [able]
redound, [abound]
redraft, [abaft]
redraw, [aah]
redress, [acquiesce]
redshirt, [advert]
redskin, [akin]
reduce, [abstruse]
reduction, [abbreviation]
reductionism, [abolitionism]
reductionist, [abolitionist]
redundancy, [absorbancy]
redundant, [abundant]
reduplicate, [noun] [advocate]
reduplicate, [verb] [abdicate]
reduplication, [abbreviation]
redwood, [adulthood]
reecho, [alfresco]
reed, [accede]
reeducate, [abdicate]
reeducation, [abbreviation]
reef, [aperitif]
reefer, [buffer]
reek, [antique]
reel, [anneal]
reelect, [abject]
reelection, [abbreviation]
reemphasize, [abscise]
re-enact, [abstract]
reenactment, [abandonment]
reenergize, [advise]
reenforce, [coarse]
reenlist, [aerialist]
reenroll, [areole]
reenter, [abductor]
reentry, [ancestry]
reestablish, [abolish]
reevaluate, [accentuate]
reevaluation, [abbreviation]

reexamination, [abbreviation]
reexamine, [abdomen]
refashion, [abbreviation]
refection, [abbreviation]
refer, [buffer]
referable, [able]
referee, [accessory]
reference, [circumference]
referendum, [addendum]
referent, [aberrant]
referral, [admiral]
refigure, [ballplayer]
refile, [anile]
refill, [backfill]
refillable, [able]
refinance, [advance]
refind, [affined]
refine, [aerodyne]
refinement, [abandonment]
refinery, [ancestry]
refinish, [abolish]
refinisher, [acupressure]
refit, [acquit]
reflect, [abject]
reflection, [abbreviation]
reflective, [ablative]
reflector, [abductor]
reflex, [annex]
reflexive, [abrasive]
reflux, [afflux]
refocus, [abacus]
refold, [ahold]
reforestation, [abbreviation]
reform, [aswarm]
reformable, [able]
reformat, [acrobat]
reformation, [abbreviation]
reformatory, [accessory]
reformer, [armor]

reformulate, [ablate]
refortify, [amplify]
refract, [abstract]
refraction, [abbreviation]
refractor, [abductor]
refractory, [accessory]
refrain, [abstain]
refresh, [afresh]
refresher, [acupressure]
refreshment, [abandonment]
refried, [abide]
refrigerant, [aberrant]
refrigerate, [accelerate]
refrigeration, [abbreviation]
refrigerator, [abductor]
refuel, [bascule]
refuge, [centrifuge]
refugee, [allergy]
refulgence, [abhorrence]
refulgent, [agent]
refund, [almond]
refurbish, [abolish]
refusal, [appraisal]
refuse, [amuse]
refusenik, [allergenic]
refutable, [able]
refutation, [abbreviation]
refute, [acute]
regain, [abstain]
regal, [angle]
regale, [ail]
regalia, [alleluia]
regard, [backyard]
regardless, [acropolis]
regatta, [aorta]
regency, [absorbancy]
regenerate, [adjective]
    [accurate]
regenerate, [verb] [ablate]

regeneration, [abbreviation]
regenerator, [abductor]
regent, [agent]
regime, [abeam]
regimen, [abdomen]
regiment, [abandonment]
regimental, [accidental]
regimentation, [abbreviation]
region, [allergen]
regional, [aboriginal]
regionalism, [abolitionism]
regionalize, [actualize]
register, [administer]
registered, [absurd]
registrant, [aberrant]
registrar, [abattoir]
registration, [abbreviation]
registry, [ancestry]
regnal, [abdominal]
regnant, [abstinent]
regress, [acquiesce]
regression, [abbreviation]
regressive, [abrasive]
regret, [abet]
regretful, [apocryphal]
regroup, [coop]
regular, [angler]
regularity, [abatis]
regulate, [ablate]
regulation, [abbreviation]
regulator, [abductor]
regulatory, [accessory]
regurgitate, [acetate]
regurgitation, [abbreviation]
rehab, [backstab]
rehabilitate, [acetate]
rehabilitation, [abbreviation]
rehash, [abash]
rehearsal, [apostle]

rehearse, [adverse]
reheat, [accrete]
rehire, [acquire]
rehydrate, [accelerate]
reify, [amplify]
reign, [abstain]
reignite, [affright]
reimburse, [adverse]
reimbursement,
  [abandonment]
rein, [abstain]
reincarnate, [abominate]
reincarnation, [abbreviation]
reindeer, [adhere]
reinflate, [ablate]
reinforce, [coarse]
reinforcement, [abandonment]
reinjure, [armiger]
reinspect, [abject]
reinstall, [aerosol]
reinstate, [acetate]
reinstatement, [abandonment]
reinsurance, [abhorrence]
reinsure, [abjure]
reinsurer, [adulterer]
reintegrate, [accelerate]
reinterpret, [accurate]
reinterpretation, [abbreviation]
reinvasion, [abrasion]
reinvent, [accent]
reinvention, [abbreviation]
reinvest, [abreast]
reinvestigate, [abnegate]
reinvestigation, [abbreviation]
reinvestment, [abandonment]
reissue, [accrue]
reiterate, [accelerate]
reject, [abject]
rejection, [abbreviation]

rejoice, [choice]
rejoin, [adjoin]
rejoinder, [adder]
rejuvenate, [abominate]
rejuvenation, [abbreviation]
rekey, [achy]
rekindle, [antipodal]
relabel, [able]
relapse, [apse]
relate, [ablate]
relation, [abbreviation]
relational, [aboriginal]
relationship, [airship]
relative, [ablative]
relativism, [abolitionism]
relativist, [activist]
relativistic, [acoustic]
relativity, [abatis]
relativize, [advise]
relax, [anthrax]
relaxant, [acquiescent]
relaxation, [abbreviation]
relay, [airplay]
relearn, [adjourn]
release, [afterpiece]
relegate, [abnegate]
relegation, [abbreviation]
relent, [accent]
relentless, [acropolis]
relevance, [abhorrence]
relevancy, [absorbancy]
relevant, [abeyant]
reliability, [abatis]
reliable, [able]
reliance, [abhorrence]
reliant, [abeyant]
relic, [acyclic]
relict, [addict]
relief, [aperitif]

relieve, [achieve]
reliever, [achiever]
religion, [allergen]
religionist, [abolitionist]
religious, [advantageous]
relinquish, [abolish]
relish, [abolish]
relive, [forgive]
reload, [abode]
relocate, [abdicate]
relocation, [abbreviation]
relucent, [adjacent]
reluctance, [abhorrence]
reluctant, [abirritant]
reluctate, [acetate]
rely, [airdry]
remain, [abstain]
remainder, [adder]
remake, [awake]
remand, [ampersand]
remanufacture, [acupuncture]
remark, [aardvark]
remarkable, [able]
remarriage, [abridge]
remarry, [accessory]
rematch, [armpatch]
remedial, [abaxial]
remedy, [acidy]
remember, [amber]
remembrance, [abhorrence]
remind, [affined]
reminisce, [abyss]
reminiscence, [accordance]
reminiscent, [adjacent]
remint, [blueprint]
remise, [advise]
remiss, [abyss]
remissible, [able]
remission, [abbreviation]

remit, [acquit]
remittal, [accidental]
remittance, [accordance]
remittent, [accordant]
remobilize, [actualize]
remodel, [antipodal]
remonstrate, [accelerate]
remonstration, [abbreviation]
remorse, [endorse]
remorseful, [apocryphal]
remote control, [areole]
remote, [afloat]
remount, [account]
removable, [able]
removal, [adjectival]
remove, [approve]
remunerate, [accelerate]
remuneration, [abbreviation]
renaissance, [brisance]
rename, [acclaim]
renascent, [adjacent]
rend, [addend]
render, [adder]
rendezvous, [accrue]
rendition, [abbreviation]
renegade, [abrade]
renege, [big]
renegotiable, [able]
renegotiate, [create]
renegotiation, [abbreviation]
renew, [accrue]
renewable, [able]
renewal, [agile]
renitency, [absorbancy]
renitent, [abirritant]
renominate, [abominate]
renounce, [announce]
renovate, [activate]
renovation, [abbreviation]

renovator, [abductor]
renown, [boomtown]
renowned, [abound]
rent, [accent]
rental, [accidental]
renter, [abductor]
renumber, [amber]
renunciation, [abbreviation]
reoccupy, [airdry]
reoccur, [acre]
reoperate, [accelerate]
reorchestrate, [accelerate]
reorder, [adder]
reorganization, [abbreviation]
reorient, [accent]
rep, [crowstep]
repackage, [acknowledge]
repaint, [acquaint]
repair, [affair]
repairable, [able]
repairman, [adman]
reparable, [able]
reparation, [abbreviation]
repartee, [abatis]
repartition, [abbreviation]
repast, [aghast]
repatriate, [create]
repay, [agape]
repayment, [abandonment]
repeal, [anneal]
repeat, [accrete]
repeatable, [able]
repeated, [abluted]
repel, [bagatelle]
repellent, [accent]
repent, [accent]
repentant, [accordant]
repercussion, [abbreviation]
repertoire, [abattoir]

repertory, [accessory]
repetend, [addend]
repetition, [abbreviation]
repetitious, [adscititious]
repetitive, [ablative]
rephrase, [ablaze]
repine, [aerodyne]
replace, [abase]
replacement, [abandonment]
replant, [ant]
replantation, [abbreviation]
replay, [airplay]
replenish, [abolish]
replenishment,
  [abandonment]
replete, [accrete]
repletion, [abbreviation]
replica, [angelica]
replicate, **[adjective or noun]**
  [advocate]
replicate, **[verb]** [abdicate]
replication, [abbreviation]
reply, [airdry]
repo, [airshow]
repopulate, [ablate]
report, [airport]
reporter, [abductor]
repose, [airhose]
reposit, [apposite]
reposition, [abbreviation]
repository, [accessory]
repossess, [acquiesce]
repossession, [abbreviation]
re-possessor, [aggressor]
repower, [airpower]
reprehend, [addend]
reprehensible, [able]
represent, [accent]
representation, [abbreviation]

representative, [ablative]
repress, [acquiesce]
repressed, [abreast]
repression, [abbreviation]
repressive, [abrasive]
reprieve, [achieve]
reprimand, [ampersand]
reprint, **[blueprint]**
reprisal, [appraisal]
reprise, **[noun]** [antifreeze]
reprise, **[verb]** [accessorize]
repristinate, [abominate]
repro, [allegro]
reproach, [abroach]
reprobate, [abate]
reprobation, [abbreviation]
reprocess, [acquiesce]
reproduce, [abstruse]
reproducible, [able]
reproduction, [abbreviation]
reproductive, [ablative]
reprogram, [aerogram]
reprogrammable, [able]
reproof, [aloof]
reprove, [approve]
reprover, [achiever]
reptile, [anile]
republican, [awaken]
republication, [abbreviation]
republish, [abolish]
repudiate, [create]
repudiation, [abbreviation]
repugn, [afternoon]
repugnance, [abhorrence]
repugnant, [abstinent]
repulse, [convulse]
repulsion, [abbreviation]
repulsive, [abrasive]
repurchase, [antibias]

reputable, [able]
reputation, [abbreviation]
repute, [acute]
request, [abreast]
requiem, [anthurium]
require, [acquire]
requirement, [abandonment]
requisite, [apposite]
requisition, [abbreviation]
requital, [accidental]
requite, [affright]
reread, [accede]
reroof, [aloof]
reroute, [about]
resale, [blackmail]
rescale, [ail]
reschedule, [bascule]
rescind, [abscind]
rescission, [abrasion]
rescript, [adscript]
rescue, [accrue]
reseal, [automobile]
research, [antichurch]
resect, [abject]
resection, [abbreviation]
reseed, [accede]
resell, [bagatelle]
reseller, [angler]
resemblance, [abhorrence]
resemble, [able]
resend, [addend]
resent, [accent]
resentful, [apocryphal]
resentment, [abandonment]
reservation, [abbreviation]
reserve, [conserve]
reservist, [activist]
reservoir, [abattoir]
reset, [abet]

reshape, [agape]
reshuffle, [apocryphal]
reside, [abide]
residence, [abhorrence]
residency, [absorbancy]
resident, [abundant]
residential, [abbatial]
residual, [accrual]
residue, [accrue]
resign, [aerodyne]
resignation, [abbreviation]
resile, [aisle]
resilience, [abhorrence]
resilient, [abeyant]
resin, [anchorperson]
resist, [assist]
resistance, [abhorrence]
resistant, [abirritant]
resistor, [administer]
resolute, [acute]
resolution, [abbreviation]
resolvable, [able]
resolve, [absolve]
resonance, [abhorrence]
resonant, [abstinent]
resonate, [abominate]
resort, [abort]
resound, [abound]
resource, [coarse]
resourceful, [apocryphal]
respect, [abject]
respectable, [able]
respectful, [apocryphal]
respective, [ablative]
respiration, [abbreviation]
respirator, [abductor]
respire, [acquire]
respite, [adequate]
resplendence, [abhorrence]

resplendent, [abundant]
respond, [abscond]
respondent, [abundant]
response, [brisance]
responsibility, [abatis]
responsible, [able]
responsive, [abrasive]
rest stop, [agitprop]
rest, [abreast]
restart, [apart]
restate, [acetate]
restaurant, [aberrant]
restful, [apocryphal]
restitution, [abbreviation]
restive, [ablative]
restless, [acropolis]
restock, [aftershock]
restoration, [abbreviation]
restore, [abhor]
restrain, [abstain]
restrainable, [able]
restrainer, [afterburner]
restraint, [acquaint]
restrict, [addict]
restricted, [abluted]
restriction, [abbreviation]
restrictive, [ablative]
restructure, [acupuncture]
resubmit, [acquit]
result, [adult]
resultant, [accordant]
resume, [verb] [abloom]
resume', [noun] [agape]
resumption, [abbreviation]
resurface, [amorphous]
resurge, [converge]
resurgence, [abhorrence]
resurgent, [agent]
resurrect, [abject]

resurrection, [abbreviation]
resuscitate, [acetate]
resuscitation, [abbreviation]
resuscitator, [abductor]
retail, [blackmail]
retain, [abstain]
retainer, [afterburner]
retake, [awake]
retaliate, [create]
retaliation, [abbreviation]
retard, [backyard]
retardant, [accordant]
retardation, [abbreviation]
retarded, [absentminded]
retch, [backstretch]
retention, [abbreviation]
retest, [abreast]
rethink, [bethink]
reticence, [abhorrence]
reticent, [acquiescent]
retile, [anile]
retina, [alumna]
retinal, [aboriginal]
retire, [acquire]
retiree, [accessory]
retirement, [abandonment]
retold, [ahold]
retool, [bascule]
retort, [abort]
retouch, [clutch]
retrace, [abase]
retract, [abstract]
retractable, [able]
retraction, [abbreviation]
retrain, [abstain]
retranslate, [ablate]
retranslation, [abbreviation]
retread, [abed]
retreat, [accrete]

retrench, [bench]
retrial, [aisle]
retribution, [abbreviation]
retributive, [ablative]
retrievable, [able]
retrieval, [adjectival]
retrieve, [achieve]
retriever, [achiever]
retroactive, [ablative]
retrofire, [acquire]
retrofit, [acquit]
retrograde, [abrade]
retrogression, [abbreviation]
retrospect, [abject]
retrospective, [ablative]
return, [adjourn]
returnable, [able]
retype, [airpipe]
reunification, [abbreviation]
reunion, [antiunion]
reunite, [affright]
reusable, [able]
revalue, [accrue]
revamp, [aid-de-camp]
reveal, [anneal]
revealer, [angler]
reveille, [ably]
revel, [adjectival]
revelation, [abbreviation]
revelator, [abductor]
revelry, [accessory]
revenge, [avenge]
revengeful, [apocryphal]
revenue, [accrue]
reverberate, [accelerate]
reverberation, [abbreviation]
revere, [adhere]
reverence, [abhorrence]
reverenced, [against]

reverend, [almond]
reverent, [aberrant]
reverential, [abbatial]
reverie, [accessory]
reversal, [apostle]
reverse, [adverse]
reversible, [able]
reversion, [abrasion]
revert, [advert]
review, [accrue]
reviewer, [airpower]
revile, [aisle]
revise, [advise]
revision, [abrasion]
revisionist, [abolitionist]
revisit, [apposite]
revitalization, [abbreviation]
revitalize, [actualize]
revival, [adjectival]
revivalism, [abolitionism]
revivalist, [aerialist]
revive, [alive]
revivify, [amplify]
revocable, [able]
revocation, [abbreviation]
revoke, [artichoke]
revolt, [bolt]
revolution, [abbreviation]
revolutionary, [accessory]
revolutionist, [abolitionist]
revolve, [absolve]
revolver, [achiever]
revote, [afloat]
revue, [accrue]
revulsion, [abbreviation]
reward, [award]
rewash, [awash]
rewind, [affined]
reword, [absurd]

rework, [artwork]
rewrap, [afterclap]
rewrite, [affright]
rezone, [alone]
rhapsody, [acidy]
rheostat, [acrobat]
rhetoric, [aleatoric]
rhetorical, [acoustical]
rheumatism, [abolitionism]
rhinoceros, [actress]
rhubarb, [barb]
rhyme, [airtime]
rhythm, [algorithm]
rhythmic, [academic]
rialto, [aggiornamento]
rib, [bib]
ribald, [bedraggled]
rice, [advice]
rich, [backstitch]
riches, [abuzz]
rickety, [abatis]
rickshaw, [aah]
ricotta, [aorta]
rid, [amid]
riddance, [abhorrence]
ridden, [anchorperson]
riddle, [antipodal]
ride, [abide]
rider, [adder]
ridge, [abridge]
ridicule, [bascule]
ridiculous, [acropolis]
rife, [afterlife]
riff, [anaglyph]
riffle, [apocryphal]
rifle, [apocryphal]
riflemen, [abdomen]
rift, [adrift]
rig, [big]

rigger, [agar]
right, [affright]
righteous, [antibias]
rightful, [apocryphal]
right-to-life, [afterlife]
rigid, [acid]
rigidity, [abatis]
rigmarole, [areole]
rigor, [agar]
rigorous, [actress]
rim, [acronym]
rind, [affined]
ring, [anything]
ringer, [arbitrager]
ringleader, [adder]
ringlet, [aglet]
ringmaster, [administer]
ringside, [abide]
ringworm, [affirm]
rink, [bethink]
rinse, [convince]
Rio Grande, [ampersand]
riot, [adequate]
riotous, [afflatus]
rip, [airstrip]
ripe, [airpipe]
ripen, [antiphon]
rip-off, [boff]
ripple effect, [abject]
ripple, [ample]
ripsaw, [aah]
ripsnorter, [abductor]
riptide, [abide]
rise, [accessorize]
risen, [anchorperson]
riser, [adviser]
risk, [asterisk]
risky, [achy]
risqué, [agape]

rite, [affright]
ritual, [accrual]
ritualism, [abolitionism]
ritualist, [aerialist]
ritualistic, [acoustic]
ritzy, [absorbancy]
rival, [adjectival]
rivalry, [accessory]
rive, [alive]
river, [achiever]
riverbank, [bank]
riverbed, [abed]
riverboat, [afloat]
riverfront, [aberrant]
riverside, [abide]
rivet, [adequate]
roach, [abroach]
road, [abode]
roadblock, [aftershock]
roadkill, [backfill]
roadside, [abide]
roadster, [administer]
roadway, [airway]
roadwork, [artwork]
roadworthy, [newsworthy]
roam, [astrodome]
roar, [abhor]
roast, [aftermost]
roaster, [administer]
rob, [ab]
robber, [amber]
robbery, [accessory]
robe, [bathrobe]
robot, [aeronaut]
robotic, [acoustic]
robotics, [acoustics]
robust, [adjust]
rock and roll, [areole]
rock, [aftershock]

rocker, [acre]
rocket, [advocate]
rocketry, [ancestry]
rockhound, [abound]
rocky, [achy]
rod, [abroad]
rode, [abode]
rodent, [accordant]
rodeo, [audio]
roe, [allegro]
roebuck, [amok]
rogue, [brogue]
roguish, [abolish]
roil, [broil]
role, [areole]
roll, [areole]
rollback, [aback]
roller, [angler]
rollick, [acyclic]
rollout, [about]
romaine, [abstain]
romance, [advance]
romantic, [acoustic]
romanticist, [assist]
romanticize, [abscise]
romp, [chomp]
romper, [barkeeper]
roof, [aloof]
roofline, [airline]
rooftop, [agitprop]
rook, [bankbook]
rookie, [achy]
room, [abloom]
roommate, [acclimate]
roomy, [academy]
roost, [boost]
rooster, [administer]
root, [acute]
rope, [antelope]

rosary, [accessory]
rose, [airhose]
roseate, [adequate]
rosebud, [acid]
rosebush, [ambush]
rosemary, [accessory]
roster, [administer]
rostrum, [addendum]
rosy, [advisee]
rot, [aeronaut]
rotary, [accessory]
rotatable, [able]
rotate, [acetate]
rotation, [abbreviation]
rote, [afloat]
rotisserie, [accessory]
rotor, [abductor]
rototill, [backfill]
rototiller, [angler]
rotten, [anchorperson]
rotund, [almond]
rotunda, [addenda]
roturier, [agape]
roué, [agape]
rouge, [luge]
rough, [bluff]
roughage, [acknowledge]
roughen, [antiphon]
roughneck, [afterdeck]
roughness, [agribusiness]
roughrider, [adder]
roughshod, [abroad]
roulette, [abet]
round, [abound]
roundabout, [about]
rounded, [absentminded]
roundup, [backup]
rouse, [arouse]
roust, [joust]

rout, [about]
route, [about]
route, [acute]
router, [abductor]
routine, [alexandrine]
rove, [alcove]
rover, [achiever]
row, [allegro]
rowboat, [afloat]
rowdy, [acidy]
royal, [broil]
royalist, [aerialist]
royalty, [abatis]
rub, [backrub]
rubber check, [afterdeck]
rubber, [amber]
rubberneck, [afterdeck]
rubbery, [accessory]
rubbish, [abolish]
rubble, [able]
rubdown, [boomtown]
ruble, [able]
rubric, [aleatoric]
ruby, [abbey]
ruckus, [abacus]
rudder, [adder]
rudderless, [acropolis]
ruddy, [acidy]
rude, [allude]
rudiment, [abandonment]
rue, [accrue]
rueful, [apocryphal]
ruff, [bluff]
ruffian, [abecedarian]
ruffle, [apocryphal]
rug, [bedbug]
rugby, [abbey]
rugged, [acid]
ruination, [abbreviation]

ruinous, [agribusiness]
rule, [bascule]
ruler, [angler]
ruly, [ably]
rum, [addendum]
rumba, [alfalfa]
rumble, [able]
ruminate, [abominate]
rummage, [acknowledge]
rummy, [academy]
rumor, [armor]
rump, [bump]
rumple, [ample]
rumpus, [auspice]
run, [pressrun]
runabout, [about]
runagate, [abnegate]
runaround, [abound]
runaway, [airway]
runback, [aback]
rundle, [antipodal]
rung, [among]
runner, [afterburner]
runoff, [boff]
runt, [aberrant]
runway, [airway]
rupee, [apocope]
rupture, [acupressure]
rural, [admiral]
ruse, [noun] [abstruse]
ruse, [noun] [amuse]
rush, [airbrush]
russet, [corset]
rust, [adjust]
rustic, [acoustic]
rustle, [apostle]
rusty, [abatis]
rut, [accurate]
rutabaga, [alfalfa]

ruth, [booth]
ruthless, [acropolis]
rye, [airdry]
sabbath, [altazimuth]
sabbatical, [acoustical]
saber, [amber]
sable, [able]
sabotage, [arbitrage]
saboteur, [abductor]
sac, [aback]
saccate, [abdicate]
sacerdotal, [accidental]
sacerdotalism, [abolitionism]
sack, [aback]
sackcloth, [broadcloth]
sacker, [acre]
sackful, [apocryphal]
sacral, [admiral]
sacrament, [abandonment]
sacramental, [accidental]
sacramentalism, [abolitionism]
sacramentalist, [aerialist]
sacred, [acid
sacrifice, [advice]
sacrificial, [abbatial]
sacrilege, [acknowledge]
sacrilegious, [advantageous]
sacroiliac, [aback]
sacrosanct, [overranked]
sad, [ad]
saddle, [antipodal]
saddlebag, [ag]
sadism, [abolitionism]
sadist, [activist]
sadistic, [acoustic]
sadomasochism,
    [abolitionism]
sadomasochist, [activist]
sadomasochistic, [acoustic]

safari, [accessory]
safe house, [alehouse]
safe, [chafe]
safeguard, [backyard]
safety, [abatis]
sag, [ag]
saga, [alfalfa]
sagacious, [adscititious]
sagacity, [abatis]
sage, [age]
sahib, [bib]
said, [abed]
sail, [ail]
sailboard, [aboard]
sailboat, [afloat]
sailer, [angler]
sailor, [angler]
saimin, [akin]
saint, [acquaint]
sainted, [abluted]
sainthood, [adulthood]
sake, [awake]
saks, [anthrax]
salacious, [adscititious]
salad, [acid]
salamander, [adder]
salami, [academy]
salary, [accessory]
sale, [ail]
sales tax, [anthrax]
salesclerk, [artwork]
salesgirl, [aswirl]
salesman, [abdomen]
salesmanship, [airship]
salespeople, [ample]
salesperson, [anchorperson]
salesroom, [abloom]
salient, [abeyant]
saline, [alexandrine]

saliva, [alfalfa]
salivate, [activate]
sally, [ably]
salmon, [abdomen]
salmonella, [a capella]
salon, [amazon]
saloon, [afternoon]
salsa, [alfalfa]
salt, [asphalt]
saltcellar, [angler]
saltine, [alexandrine]
saltpeter, [abductor]
saltshaker, [acre]
saltwater, [abductor]
salty, [abatis]
salutary, [accessory]
salutation, [abbreviation]
salutatorian, [abecedarian]
salute, [acute]
salvage, [acknowledge]
salvation, [abbreviation]
salve, [calve]
salvific, [anthropomorphic]
salvo, [airshow]
same, [acclaim]
samp, [aid-de-camp]
sample, [ample]
sampler, [angler]
sanctification, [abbreviation]
sanctifier, [amplifier]
sanctify, [amplify]
sanctimonious, [abstemious]
sanction, [abbreviation]
sanctity, [abatis]
sanctuary, [accessory]
sanctum, [accustom]
sand, [ampersand]
sandal, [antipodal]
sandbag, [ag]

sandbar, [abattoir]
sandblast, [aghast]
sandbox, [bandbox]
sander, [adder]
sandlot, [aeronaut]
sandman, [adman]
sandpaper, [barkeeper]
sandpile, [anile]
sandpiper, [barkeeper]
sandstone, [alone]
sandstorm, [aswarm]
sandwich, [backstitch]
sandy, [acidy]
sane, [abstain]
sang, [bang]
sanitarium, [anthurium]
sanitary, [accessory]
sanitation, [abbreviation]
sanitize, [absolutize]
sanitorium, [anthurium]
sanity, [abatis]
sank, [bank]
sap, [afterclap]
sapid, [acid]
sapience, [abhorrence]
sapient, [abeyant]
sapphire, [acquire]
sarcasm, [abolitionism]
sarcastic, [acoustic]
sarcoma, [anathema]
sardine, [alexandrine]
sardonic, [allergenic]
sash, [abash]
sashimi, [academy]
sass, [admass]
sassafras, [admass]
sassy, [absorbancy]
sat, [acrobat]
satanic, [allergenic]

satanism, [abolitionism]
satchel, [agile]
satellite, [affright]
satiable, [able]
satiety, [abitis]
satin, [anchorperson]
satire, [acquire]
satirical, [acoustical]
satirist, [allegorist]
satirize, [accessorize]
satisfaction, [abbreviation]
satisfactory, [ancestry]
satisfy, [amplify]
satrap, [afterclap]
saturate, [accelerate]
saturated, [abluted]
saturation, [abbreviation]
sauce, [across]
sauceman, [adman]
saucer, [aggressor]
saucy, [absorbancy]
sauerkraut, [about]
sauna, [alumna]
saunter, [abductor]
sausage, [acknowledge]
sauté, [agape]
savage, [acknowledge]
savagery, [accessory]
savant, [avaunt]
savate, [aeronaut]
save, [aftershave]
saver, [achiever]
savings, [bank]
savior, [ballplayer]
savory, [accessory]
savvy, [anchovy]
saw, [aah]
sawdust, [adjust]
sawhorse, [endorse]

sawmill, [backfill]
sawtooth, [booth]
saxophone, [alone]
say, [agape]
scab, [backstab]
scad, [ad]
scaffold, [bedraggled]
scalar, [angler]
scald, [bald]
scale, [ail]
scall, [aerosol]
scallion, [antiunion]
scallop, [backup]
scalp, [alp]
scalpel, [ample]
scaly, [ably]
scam, [aerogram]
scamp, [aid-de-camp]
scamper, [barkeeper]
scampi, [apocope]
scan, [adman]
scandal, [antipodal]
scandalize, [actualize]
scandalous, [acropolis]
scanner, [afterburner]
scansion, [abbreviation]
scant, [ant]
scanty, [abatis]
scape, [agape]
scapegoat, [afloat]
scar, [abattoir]
scarcity, [abatis]
scare, [anywhere]
scarecrow, [allegro]
scarf, [barf]
scarify, [amplify]
scarlet, [aglet]
scarp, [carp]
scary, [accessory]

scat, [acrobat]
scatback, [aback]
scathe, [bathe]
scatter, [abductor]
scatterbrain, [abstain]
scavenge, [avenge]
scavenger, [armiger]
scenario, [audio]
scene, [alexandrine]
scenery, [accessory]
scenic, [allergenic]
scent, [accent]
scented, [abluted]
scepter, [abductor]
schadenfreude, [addenda]
schedule, [bascule]
schema, [anathema]
schematic, [acoustic]
scheme, [abeam]
schemer, [armor]
scherzando, [aficionado]
scherzo, [also]
schiller, [angler]
schism, [abolitionism]
schismatic, [acoustic]
schizoid, [adenoid]
schizophrenia, [abulia]
schizophrenic, [allergenic]
schlepp, [crowstep]
schlock, [aftershock]
schmooze, [amuse]
schnitzel, [apostle]
scholar, [angler]
scholarly, [ably]
scholarship, [airship]
scholastic, [acoustic]
school, [bascule]
schoolhouse, [alehouse]
schoolmarm, [alarm]

schoolmate, [acclimate]
schoolroom, [abloom]
schoolwork, [artwork]
schooner, [afterburner]
schottische, [abolish]
science, [abhorrence]
scientific, [anthropomorphic]
scientist, [absolutist]
scintilla, [a capella]
scintillate, [ablate]
scintillation, [abbreviation]
sciolism, [abolitionism]
scission, [abrasion]
scissor, [adviser]
scissors, [bonkers]
sclaff, [allograph]
sclerosis, [alkalosis]
scoff, [boff]
scoffer, [buffer]
scold, [ahold]
scoliosis, [alkalosis]
sconce, [brisance]
scone, [alone]
scoop, [coop]
scooper, [barkeeper]
scoot, [acute]
scooter, [abductor]
scope, [antelope]
scorch, [blowtorch]
scorcher, [acupuncture]
score, [abhor]
scoreboard, [aboard]
scorecard, [backyard]
scorekeeper, [barkeeper]
scoreless, [acropolis]
scorer, [adulterer]
scorn, [acorn]
scornful, [apocryphal]
scorpion, [abecedarian]

scotch, [blotch]
scoundrel, [admiral]
scour, [airpower]
scourge, [converge]
scout, [about]
scoutmaster, [administer]
scow, [allow]
scowl, [foul]
scrabble, [able]
scraggly, [ably]
scraggy, [aggie]
scram, [aerogram]
scramble, [able]
scrap, [afterclap]
scrapbook, [bankbook]
scrapper, [barkeeper]
scrappy, [apocope]
scratch, [armpatch]
scratchy, [blotchy]
scrawl, [aerosol]
scrawny, [abalone]
scream, [abeam]
screamer, [armor]
screech, [beach]
screed, [accede]
screen, [alexandrine]
screenplay, [airplay]
screw, [accrue]
screwball, [aerosol]
screwdriver, [achiever]
screwup, [backup]
screwy, [colloquy]
scribble, [able]
scribe, [ascribe]
scrimmage, [acknowledge]
scrip, [airstrip]
script, [adscript]
scriptural, [admiral]
scripture, [acupressure]

scriptwriter, [abductor]
scroll, [areole]
scrotum, [accustom]
scrouge, [centrifuge]
scrounge, [lounge]
scroungy, [allergy]
scrub, [backrub]
scrubby, [abbey]
scruff, [bluff]
scruffy, [anastrophe]
scrum, [addendum]
scrumptious, [adscititious]
scrunch, [brunch]
scruple, [ample]
scrupulous, [acropolis]
scrutable, [able]
scrutiny, [abalone]
scuba, [alfalfa]
scud, [acid]
scuff, [bluff]
scuffle, [apocryphal]
scullery, [accessory]
scullion, [antiunion]
sculptor, [abductor]
sculpture, [acupuncture]
scum, [addendum]
scumbag, [ag]
scumble, [able]
scupper, [barkeeper]
scurrilous, [acropolis]
scurry, [accessory]
scurvy, [anchovy]
scut, [adequate]
scuttle, [accidental]
scuttlebutt, [abbot]
scuzzy, [advisee]
scythe, [blithe]
sea, [absorbancy]
seacoast, [aftermost]

seafood, [allude]
seal, [anneal]
sealant, [ambivalent]
sealer, [angler]
sealing wax, [anthrax]
seam, [abeam]
seaman, [abdomen]
seamless, [acropolis]
seamster, [administer]
seamstress, [actress]
séance, [brisance]
seaplane, [abstain]
seaport, [airport]
sear, [adhere]
search, [antichurch]
searchable, [able]
searchlight, [affright]
seascape, [agape]
seashell, [bagatelle]
seashore, [abhor]
seasick, [airsick]
seaside, [abide]
season, [anchorperson]
seasonable, [able]
seasonal, [aboriginal]
seat, [accrete]
seatrain, [abstain]
seaward, [absurd]
seawater, [abductor]
seaweed, [accede]
seaworthy, [newsworthy]
sebaceous, [adscititious]
secede, [accede]
secession, [abbreviation]
secessionist, [abolitionist]
seclude, [allude]
secluded, [absentminded]
seclusion, [abrasion]
second, [almond]

secondary, [accessory]
second-class, [admass]
secondhand, [ampersand]
secrecy, [absorbancy]
secret, [accurate]
secretariat, [affiliate]
secretary, [accessory]
secrete, [accrete]
secretion, [abbreviation]
sect, [abject]
sectarian, [abecedarian]
section, [abbreviation]
sectional, [abdominal]
sector, [abductor]
secular, [angler]
secularism, [abolitionism]
secularist, [allegorist]
secularize, [accessorize]
secund, [almond]
secure, [arbitrager]
security, [abatis]
sedan, [adman]
sedate, [accommodate]
sedation, [abbreviation]
sedative, [ablative]
sedentary, [accessory]
seder, [adder]
sediment, [abandonment]
sedition, [abbreviation]
seditious, [antibias]
seduce, [abstruse]
seduction, [abbreviation]
see, [absorbancy]
seed, [accede]
seeder, [adder]
seedy, [acidy]
seek, [antique]
seeker, [acre]
seem, [abeam]

seen, [alexandrine]
seep, [asleep]
seepage, [acknowledge]
seer, [adhere]
seersucker, [acre]
seesaw, [aah]
seethe, [breathe]
segmentation, [abbreviation]
segregate, [abnegate]
segregated, [abluted]
segregation, [abbreviation]
segregationist, [abolitionist]
segue, [airway]
seidel, [antipodal]
seigneur, [ballplayer]
seine, [abstain]
seismic, [academic]
seismograph, [allograph]
seismographer, [buffer]
seismologist, [allergist]
seismology, [allergy]
seize, [antifreeze]
seizure, [admeasure]
selah, [a capella]
seldom, [addendum]
select, [abject]
selected, [abluted]
selection, [abbreviation]
selective, [ablative]
self, [bookshelf]
self-abasement,
  [abandonment]
self-absorption, [abbreviation]
self-actualization,
  [abbreviation]
self-addressed, [abreast]
self-advancement,
  [abandonment]
self-aggrandizement,

[abandonment]
self-analysis, [alkalosis]
self-appointed, [abluted]
self-assessment,
[abandonment]
self-betterment,
[abandonment]
self-condemnation,
[abbreviation]
self-confidence, [abhorrence]
self-confident, [abundant]
self-conscious, [adscititious]
self-contempt, [attempt]
self-contradiction,
[abbreviation]
self-control, [areole]
self-controlled, [ahold]
self-critical, [acoustical]
self-criticism, [abolitionism]
self-deceive, [achieve]
self-deception, [abbreviation]
self-deluded, [absentminded]
self-delusion, [abrasion]
self-denial, [aisle]
self-destruct, [abduct]
self-determination,
[abbreviation]
self-development,
[abandonment]
self-directed, [abluted]
self-discipline, [acetylene]
self-doubt, [about]
self-employed, [adenoid]
self-employment,
[abandonment]
self-esteem, [abeam]
self-evaluation, [abbreviation]
self-evident, [abundant]
self-examination,

[abbreviation]
self-existence, [abhorrence]
self-existent, [abirritant]
self-feed, [accede]
self-fulfillment,
[abandonment]
self-glorification,
[abbreviation]
self-glory, [accessory]
self-government,
[abandonment]
self-gratification,
[abbreviation]
self-hate, [ate]
self-hatred, [acid]
self-help, [help]
self-hypnosis, [alkalosis]
self-identity, [abatis]
self-image, [acknowledge]
self-improvement,
[abandonment]
self-incrimination,
[abbreviation]
self-indulgence, [abhorrence]
self-indulgent, [agent]
self-inflicted, [abluted]
self-insurance, [abhorrence]
self-insure, [abjure]
self-interest, [adjust]
selfish, [abolish]
selfishness, [agribusiness]
self-justification,
[abbreviation]
selfless, [acropolis]
self-love, [above]
self-made, [abrade]
self-management,
[abandonment]
self-mastery, [accessory]

self-motivated, [abluted]
self-oriented, [abluted]
self-portrait, [accurate]
self-preservation,
    [abbreviation]
self-promotion, [abbreviation]
self-propelled, [geld]
self-protection, [abbreviation]
self-protective, [ablative]
self-realization, [abbreviation]
self-regulation, [abbreviation]
self-reliant, [abeyant]
self-renewal, [accrual]
self-respect, [abject]
self-restraint, [acquaint]
self-revelation, [abbreviation]
self-righteous, [antibias]
self-rule, [bascule]
self-sacrifice, [advice]
self-satisfaction,
    [abbreviation]
self-satisfied, [abide]
self-serve, [conserve]
self-starter, [abductor]
self-study, [acidy]
self-styled, [beguiled]
self-sufficiency, [absorbancy]
self-sufficient, [abeyant]
self-surrender, [adder]
self-taught, [aeronaut]
self-will, [backfill]
self-willed, [build]
self-worth, [afterbirth]
sell, [bagatelle]
sellout, [about]
seltzer, [aggressor]
semantic, [acoustic]
semantics, [acoustics]
semblance, [abhorrence]

semen, [abdomen]
semester, [administer]
semiannual, [accrual]
semiarid, [acid]
semiautomatic, [acoustic]
semi-calm, [balm]
semicircle, [acoustical]
semicolon, [acetylene]
semiconductor, [abductor]
semiconscious, [adscititious]
semifinal, [abdominal]
semiformal, [abnormal]
semigloss, [across]
semiliterate, [accurate]
semimonthly, [ably]
seminal, [abdominal]
seminar, [abattoir]
seminarian, [abecedarian]
seminary, [accessory]
semiprivate, [adequate]
semipro, [allegro]
semiprofessional, [aboriginal]
semiretirement,
    [abandonment]
sempre, [affray]
senate, [acuminate]
senator, [abductor]
senatorial, [anneal]
send, [addend]
send-off, [boff]
senile, [anile]
senility, [abatis]
senior, [ballplayer]
seniority, [abatis]
sennit, [acuminate]
senora, [abracadabra]
senorita, [aorta]
sensate, [ate]
sensation, [abbreviation]

sensational, [abdominal]
sensationalism, [abolitionism]
sensationalist, [aerialist]
sensationalize, [actualize]
sense, [cense]
sensed, [against]
senseless, [acropolis]
sensibility, [abatis]
sensible, [able]
sensitive, [ablative]
sensitivity, [abatis]
sensitize, [absolutize]
sensor, [abhor]
sensory, [accessory]
sensual, [accrual]
sensualism, [abolitionism]
sensuality, [abatis]
sensualize, [actualize]
sensuous, [ambiguous]
sent, [accent]
sententia, [abulia]
sententious, [adscititious]
sentience, [abhorrence]
sentient, [abeyant]
sentiment, [abandonment]
sentimental, [accidental]
sentimentalism, [abolitionism]
sentimentality, [abatis]
sentinel, [aboriginal]
sentry, [ancestry]
separate, [adjective]
  [accurate]
separate, [verb] [accelerate]
separation, [abbreviation]
separationist, [abolitionist]
separatism, [abolitionism]
separatist, [absolutist]
separatistic, [acoustic]
septet, [abet]

septic, [acoustic]
sepulchre, [acre]
sequel, [agile]
sequence, [abhorrence]
sequential, [abbatial]
sequester, [administer]
sequitur, [abductor]
serac, [aback]
serape, [agape]
seraphim, [acronym]
serenade, [abrade]
serendipity, [abatis]
serene, [alexandrine]
serenity, [abatis]
serf, [bodysurf]
serfdom, [addendum]
sergeant, [agent]
serial, [abaxial]
serialize, [actualize]
seriate, [create]
series, [antifreeze]
serigraph, [allograph]
serious, [abstemious]
seriousness, [agribusiness]
sermon, [abdomen]
sermonette, [bassinet]
serpent, [abeyant]
serpentine, [alexandrine]
serpiginous, [agribusiness]
serrate, [accelerate]
serration, [abbreviation]
serry, [accessory]
serum, [addendum]
servant, [abeyant]
servanthood, [adulthood]
serve, [conserve]
server, [achiever]
service, [antibias]
serviceman, [adman]

servitude, [altitude]
sesame, [academy]
session, [abbreviation]
set, [abet]
setback, [aback]
setoff, [boff]
setout, [about]
settee, [abatis]
setter, [abductor]
settle,]accidental]
settlement, [abandonment]
setup, [backup]
sevenfold, [ahold]
seventeen, [alexandrine]
seventy, [abatis]
sever, [achiever]
several, [admiral]
severance, [abhorrence]
severe, [adhere]
severity, [abatis]
sew, [also]
sewage, [acknowledge]
sewer, [airpower]
sewing, [alexandrine]
sewn, [alone]
sex, [annex]
sexagenarian, [abecedarian]
sexed, [context]
sexism, [abolitionism]
sexist, [activist]
sexploitation, [abbreviation]
sexpot, [aeronaut]
sextant, [abirritant]
sextet, [abet]
sextuple, [ample]
sextuplet, [aglet]
sexual, [accrual]
sexuality, [abatis]
sexy, [absorbancy]

shabby, [abbey]
shack, [aback]
shackle, [acoustical]
shade, [abrade]
shadow, [aficionado]
shady, [acidy]
shaft, [abaft]
shag, [ag]
shaggy, [aggie]
shake, [awake]
shakedown, [boomtown]
shakeout, [about]
shaker, [acre]
shaky, [achy]
shale, [ail]
shallow, [afterglow]
shalom, [astrodome]
sham, [aerogram]
shaman, [abdomen]
shamanism, [abolitionism]
shamanist, [abolitionist]
shamble, [able]
shambles, [annals]
shame, [acclaim]
shamefaced, [abased]
shameful, [apocryphal]
shameless, [acropolis]
shammy, [academy]
shampoo, [accrue]
shamrock, [aftershock]
shanghai, [airdry]
shank, [bank]
shanty town, [boomtown]
shanty, [abatis]
shape, [agape]
shapely, [ably]
shard, [backyard]
share, [affair]
sharecrop, [agitprop]

shareholder, [adder]
shark, [aardvark]
sharp, [carp]
shatter, [abductor]
shave, [aftershave]
shaver, [achiever]
shaw, [aah]
shawl, [aerosol]
she, [banshee]
sheaf, [aperitif]
shear, [adhere]
sheath, [beneath]
sheathe, [breathe]
sheave, [noun] [forgive]
sheave, [verb] [achieve]
shed, [abed]
sheen, [alexandrine]
sheep, [asleep]
sheepfold, [ahold]
sheepherder, [adder]
sheepish, [abolish]
sheepskin, [akin]
sheer, [adhere]
sheet, [accrete]
shekel, [acoustical]
shelf, [bookshelf]
shell, [bagatelle]
shellac, [aback]
shelter, [abductor]
shelve, [delve]
Sheol, [areole]
shepherd, [absurd]
sherbet, [abbot]
sherlock, [aftershock]
sherry, [accessory]
shibboleth, [altazimuth]
shift, [adrift]
shiftless, [acropolis]
shifty, [abatis]

shikari, [accessory]
shill, [backfill]
shimmer, [armor]
shimmy, [academy]
shin, [akin]
shindig, [big]
shine, [aerodyne]
shiner, [afterburner]
shingle, [angle]
shingles, [annals]
shininess, [agribusiness]
shinny, [abalone]
shinsplints, [convince]
shiny, [abalone]
shipbuilder, [adder]
shiplap, [afterclap]
shipman, [abdomen]
shipmate, [acclimate]
shipment, [abandonment]
shipshape, [agape]
shipwreck, [afterdeck]
shipyard, [backyard]
shirk, [artwork]
shirt, [advert]
shirtsleeve, [achieve]
shirttail, [blackmail]
shit, [acquit]
shiva, [alfalfa]
shivaree, [accessory]
shiver, [achiever]
shoal, [areole]
shock, [aftershock]
shocker, [acre]
shockproof, [aloof]
shod, [abroad]
shoddy, [acidy]
shoe, [accrue]
shoehorn, [acorn]
shoelace, [abase]

shofar, [abattoir]
shone, [alone]
shoofly, [airdry]
shook, [bankbook]
shoot, [acute]
shooter, [abductor]
shooting star, [abattoir]
shop, [agitprop]
shopkeeper, [barkeeper]
shoplift, [adrift]
shoplifter, [abductor]
shopper, [barkeeper]
shopping cart, [apart]
shoptalk, [backtalk]
shopworn, [acorn]
shore, [abhor]
shorefront, [aberrant]
shoreline, [airline]
shorn, [acorn]
short, [abort]
shortage, [acknowledge]
shortbread, [abed]
shortcake, [awake]
shortchange, [arrange]
shortcut, [advocate]
shorten, [anchorperson]
shortfall, [aerosol]
shorthand, [ampersand]
shorthanded, [absentminded]
shortlist, [aerialist]
shortrange, [arrange]
shortsighted, [abluted]
shortstop, [agitprop]
short-wave, [aftershave]
shot, [aeronaut]
shotgun, [bandwagon]
should, [adulthood]
shoulder, [adder]
shout, [about]

shove, [above]
shovel, [adjectival]
shovelful, [apocryphal]
show, [airshow]
showbiz, [fizz]
showboat, [afloat]
showbread, [abed]
showcase, [abase]
showdown, [boomtown]
shower, [airpower]
showgirl, [aswirl]
showman, [abdomen]
shown, [alone]
showpiece, [afterpiece]
showplace, [abase]
showroom, [abloom]
showstopper, [barkeeper]
showy, [colloquy]
shrank, [bank]
shrapnel, [abdominal]
shred, [abed]
shrew, [accrue]
shrewd, [allude]
shriek, [antique]
shrill, [backfill]
shrimp, [blimp]
shrine, [aerodyne]
shrink, [bethink]
shrinkage, [acknowledge]
shrivel, [adjectival]
shroud, [aloud]
shrub, [backrub]
shrubbery, [accessory]
shrug, [bedbug]
shrunk, [bohunk]
shtick, [acoustic]
shuck, [amok]
shucks, [afflux]
shudder, [adder]

shuffle, [apocryphal]
shuffleboard, [aboard]
shul, [apocryphal]
shun, [abbreviation]
shunned, [almond]
shunpike, [alike]
shunt, [abeyant]
shush, [airbrush]
shut, [adequate]
shutdown, [boomtown]
shutoff, [boff]
shutout, [about]
shutter, [abductor]
shuttle, [accidental]
shy, [airdry]
shyness, [agribusiness]
shyster, [administer]
sib, [bib]
sic, [airsick]
sick, [airsick]
sicken, [awaken]
sickish, [abolish]
sickle, [acoustical]
sickly, [ably]
sickness, [agribusiness]
sickroom, [abloom]
side, [abide]
sidearm, [alarm]
sidebar, [abattoir]
sidecar, [abattoir]
sidekick, [acidic]
sidelight, [affright]
sideline, [airline]
sidereal, [abaxial]
sidesaddle, [antipodal]
sideshow, [airshow]
sidestep, [crowstep]
sidestroke, [artichoke]
sideswipe, [airpipe]

sidetrack, [aback]
sidewalk, [aftershock]
sidewall, [aerosol]
sideway, [airway]
sideways, [ablaze]
sidle, [antipodal]
siege, [besiege]
sierra, [abracadabra]
sieve, [forgive]
sift, [adrift]
sigh, [airdry]
sight, [affright]
sightly, [ably]
sightsee, [absorbancy]
sigil, [backfill]
sigma, [anathema]
sign, [aerodyne]
signage, [appanage]
signal, [abdominal]
signalman, [abdomen]
signature, [abjure]
signet, [acuminate]
significance, [abhorrence]
significant, [abeyant]
signified, [abide]
signify, [amplify]
sign-off, [boff]
signor, [abhor]
signora, [abracadabra]
signpost, [aftermost]
silage, [acknowledge]
silence, [abhorrence]
silencer, [aggressor]
silent, [ambivalent]
silhouette, [abet]
silicone, [alone]
silk, [bilk]
silken, [awaken]
silkworm, [affirm]

silky, [achy]
sill, [backfill]
silly, [ably]
silo, [afterglow]
silt, [atilt]
silver, [achiever]
silversmith, [blacksmith]
silverware, [affair]
similar, [angler]
similarity, [abatis]
simile, [ably]
similitude, [altitude]
simmer, [armor]
simony, [abalone]
simper, [barkeeper]
simple, [ample]
simpleminded,
   [absentminded]
simplex, [annex]
simplicity, [abatis]
simplification, [abbreviation]
simplify, [amplify]
simplistic, [acoustic]
simply, [ably]
simulate, [ablate]
simulated, [abluted]
simulation, [abbreviation]
simulator, [abductor]
simulcast, [aghast]
simultaneous, [abstemious]
sin, [akin]
since, [convince]
sincere, [adhere]
sincerity, [abatis]
sine, [aerodyne]
sinew, [accrue]
sinewy, [colloquy]
sinfonia, [abulia]
sinful, [apocryphal]

sing, [anything]
singe, [binge]
single, [angle]
single-handed,
   [absentminded]
single-minded,
   [absentminded]
singsong, [agelong]
singular, [angler]
singularity, [abatis]
sinister, [administer]
sink, [bethink]
sinkage, [acknowledge]
sinker, [acre]
sinkhole, [areole]
sinless, [acropolis]
sinner, [afterburner]
sinter, [abductor]
sinus, [agribusiness]
sip, [airstrip]
sir, [aggressor]
sire, [acquire]
siren, [pressrun]
sirloin, [adjoin]
sis, [abyss]
sissy, [absorbancy]
sister, [administer]
sisterly, [ably]
sit, [acquit]
sitcom, [aplomb]
site, [affright]
sitter, [abductor]
situate, [accentuate]
situation, [abbreviation]
situational, [abdominal]
situs, [afflatus]
sitzmark, [aardvark]
six, [administratrix]
sixfold, [ahold]

sixpence, [abhorrence]
sixpenny, [abalone]
sixteen, [alexandrine]
sixty, [abatis]
sizable, [able]
size, [abscise]
sizzle, [appraisal]
sizzler, [angler]
skat, [aeronaut]
skate, [abdicate]
skateboard, [aboard]
skater, [abductor]
skedaddle, [antipodal]
skeet, [accrete]
skeeter, [abductor]
skeleton, [anchorperson]
skelter, [abductor]
skeptic, [acoustic]
skeptical, [acoustical]
skepticism, [abolitionism]
sketch, [backstretch]
sketchy, [blotchy]
skew, [accrue]
skewer, [airpower]
skibob, [ab]
skid, [amid]
skill, [backfill]
skilled, [build]
skillet, [aglet]
skillful, [apocryphal]
skim, [acronym]
skimmer, [armor]
skimp, [blimp]
skimpy, [apocope]
skin, [akin]
skinflint, [blueprint]
skinhead, [abed]
skinned, [abscind]
skinny, [abalone]

skintight, [affright]
skip, [airstrip]
skipjack, [aback]
skipper, [barkeeper]
skirmish, [abolish]
skirt, [advert]
skirted, [abluted]
skit, [acquit]
skitter, [abductor]
skittish, [abolish]
skive, [alive]
skivvy, [anchovy]
skoal, [areole]
skulk, [bulk]
skull, [acoustical]
skullcap, [afterclap]
skullduggery, [accessory]
skunk, [bohunk]
sky, [airdry]
skybox, [bandbox]
skycap, [afterclap]
skyhook, [bankbook]
skylight, [affright]
skyline, [airline]
skyrocket, [advocate]
skyscraper, [barkeeper]
skywalk, [aftershock]
skyward, [absurd]
skyway, [airway]
skywrite, [affright]
slab, [backstab]
slack, [aback]
slacken, [awaken]
slacker, [acre]
slain, [abstain]
slake, [awake]
slalom, [addendum]
slam, [aerogram]
slammer, [armor]

slander, [adder]
slanderous, [actress]
slanguage, [acknowledge]
slant, [ant]
slap, [afterclap]
slapjack, [aback]
slapshot, [aeronaut]
slapstick, [acoustic]
slash, [abash]
slasher, [acupressure]
slat, [acrobat]
slate, [ablate]
slather, [altogether]
slattern, [adjourn]
slaughter, [abductor]
slaughterhouse, [alehouse]
slaughterous, [actress]
slave, [aftershave]
slaveholder, [adder]
slavery, [accessory]
slavish, [abolish]
slaw, [aah]
slay, [airplay]
sleave, [achieve]
sleaze, [antifreeze]
sleazebag, [ag]
sleazeball, [aerosol]
sleazy, [advisee]
sled, [abed]
sledge, [allege]
sledgehammer, [armor]
sleek, [antique]
sleep, [asleep]
sleeper, [barkeeper]
sleepless, [acropolis]
sleepwalker, [acre]
sleepwear, [affair]
sleepy, [apocope]
sleet, [accrete]

sleeve, [achieve]
sleeveless, [acropolis]
sleevelet, [aglet]
sleigh, [airplay]
sleight, [affright]
slender, [adder]
slept, [accept]
sleuth, [booth]
slew, [accrue]
slice, [advice]
slick, [acyclic]
slicker, [acre]
slid, [amid]
slide, [abide]
slider, [adder]
sliding scale, [ail]
slight, [affright]
slim, [acronym]
slime, [airtime]
slimeball, [aerosol]
slimnastics, [acoustics]
slimy, [academy]
sling, [anything]
slingshot, [aeronaut]
slink, [bethink]
slinky, [achy]
slip, [airstrip]
slipcase, [abase]
slipcover, [achiever]
slipknot, [aeronaut]
slippage, [acknowledge]
slipper, [barkeeper]
slippery, [accessory]
slipshod, [abroad]
slipsole, [areole]
slipup, [backup]
slipware, [affair]
slit, [acquit]
slither, [altogether]

sliver, [achiever]
slob, [ab]
slobber, [amber]
slobbish, [abolish]
slog, [agog]
slogan, [bandwagon]
sloop, [coop]
slop, [agitprop]
slope, [antelope]
sloppiness, [agribusiness]
sloppy, [apocope]
slopwork, [artwork]
slosh, [awash]
slot, [aeronaut]
slotback, [aback]
sloth, [broadcloth]
slothful, [apocryphal]
slouch, [avouch]
slouchy, [blotchy]
slough, [accrue]
slovenly, [ably]
slow, [afterglow]
slowdown, [boomtown]
slowpoke, [artichoke]
sludge, [adjudge]
slug, [bedbug]
slugfest, [abreast]
sluggard, [absurd]
sluggardly, [ably]
slugger, [agar]
sluggish, [abolish]
sluice, [abstruse]
slum, [addendum]
slumber, [amber]
slumberous, [actress]
slumlord, [award]
slump, [bump]
slumpflation, [abbreviation]
slung, [among]

slunk, [bohunk]
slur, [angler]
slurp, [burp]
slush, [airbrush]
slushy, [banshee]
slut, [aglet]
sly, [airdry]
smack, [aback]
smacker, [acre]
small, [aerosol]
smallpox, [bandbox]
smarmy, [academy]
smart, [apart]
smarten, [anchorperson]
smash, [abash]
smashup, [backup]
smatter, [abductor]
smear, [adhere]
smell, [bagatelle]
smelly, [ably]
smelt, [belt]
smelter, [abductor]
smidgen, [allergen]
smile, [aisle]
smirch, [antichurch]
smirk, [artwork]
smite, [affright]
smith, [blacksmith]
smithereens, teens
smock, [aftershock]
smog, [agog]
smoggy, [aggie]
smoke bomb, [aplomb]
smoke, [artichoke]
smokehouse, [alehouse]
smokejack, [aback]
smokestack, [aback]
smoky, [achy]
smolder, [adder]

smooch, [hooch]
smooth, soothe, ultrasmooth
smorgasbord, [aboard]
smote, [afloat]
smother, [altogether]
smudge, [adjudge]
smug, [bedbug]
smuggle, [angle]
smuggler, [angler]
smut, [animate]
smutty, [abatis]
snack, [aback]
snaffle, [apocryphal]
snafu, [accrue]
snag, [ag]
snail, [ail]
snake, [awake]
snakebite, [affright]
snap, [afterclap]
snappy, [apocope]
snapshot, [aeronaut]
snare, [affair]
snarl, [barrel]
snatch, [armpatch]
snazzy, [advisee]
sneak, [antique]
sneaker, [acre]
sneaky, [achy]
sneer, [adhere]
sneeze, [antifreeze]
snicker, [acre]
snide, [abide]
sniff, [anaglyph]
sniffle, [apocryphal]
sniffler, [angler]
snifter, [abductor]
snip, [airstrip]
snipe, [airpipe]
snippet, [adequate]

snippy, [apocope]
snips, [apocalypse]
snitch, [backstitch]
snivel, [adjectival]
snob, [ab]
snobbery, [accessory]
snobbish, [abolish]
snooker, [acre]
snoop, [coop]
snoopy, [apocope]
snoot, [acute]
snooty, [abatis]
snooze, [amuse]
snore, [abhor]
snorkel, [acoustical]
snort, [abort]
snot, [aeronaut]
snotty, [abatis]
snout, [about]
snow, [albino]
snowball, [aerosol]
snowbank, [bank]
snowbird, [absurd]
snowblower, [airpower]
snowboard, [aboard]
snowbound, [abound]
snowcap, [afterclap]
snowcapped, [adapt]
snowdrift, [adrift]
snowflake, [awake]
snowman, [adman]
snowmelt, [belt]
snowmobile, [automobile]
snowpack, [aback]
snowplow, [allow]
snowscape, [agape]
snowshoe, [accrue]
snowstorm, [aswarm]
snowsuit, [acute]

snowy, [colloquy]
snub, [backrub]
snuff, [bluff]
snuffer, [buffer]
snuffy, [anastrophe]
snug, [bedbug]
snuggle, [angle]
so, [also]
soak, [artichoke]
soap, [antelope]
soapbox, [bandbox]
soapy, [apocope]
soar, [abhor]
sob, [ab]
sober, [amber]
sobriety, [abatis]
so-called, [appalled]
soccer, [acre]
sociability, [abatis]
sociable, [able]
social, [abbatial]
socialism, [abolitionism]
socialist, [aerialist]
socialistic, [acoustic]
socialite, [affright]
socialize, [actualize]
societal, [accidental]
society, [abatis]
sociological, [acoustical]
sociologist, [allergist]
sociology, [allergy]
sociopath, [aftermath]
sociopathic, [acidic]
sociopolitical, [acoustical]
sock, [aftershock]
socket, [advocate]
sod, [abroad]
soda pop, [agitprop]
soda, [addenda]

sodality, [abatis]
sodbuster, [administer]
sodden, [anchorperson]
sodium, [anthurium]
sodomize, [advise]
sodomy, [academy]
soffit, [adequate]
soft, [aloft]
softball, [aerosol]
softboiled, [bedraggled]
softcore, [abhor]
softhearted, [abluted]
softpedal, [antipodal]
softsell, [bagatelle]
softshoe, [accrue]
softspoken, [awaken]
software, [affair]
softy, [abatis]
soggy, [aggie]
soil, [broil]
soiree, [agape]
sojourn, [adjourn]
sojourner, [afterburner]
solace, [acropolis]
solar, [angler]
solarium, [anthurium]
solatium, [anthurium]
sold, [ahold]
solder, [adder]
soldier, [armiger]
sole, [areole]
solecism, [abolitionism]
solemn, [addendum]
solemnify, [amplify]
solemnity, [abatis]
solemnize, [agnize]
solicit, [corset]
solicitation, [abbreviation]
solicitor, [abductor]

solicitous, [afflatus]
solicitude, [altitude]
solid, [acid]
solidarity, [abatis]
solidify, [amplify]
solidity, [abatis]
solipsism, [abolitionism]
solipsist, [assist]
solitaire, [affair]
solitary, [accessory]
solitude, [altitude]
solo, [afterglow]
soloist, [activist]
solon, [acetylene]
solstice, [afflatus]
soluble, [able]
solution, [abbreviation]
solvable, [able]
solve, [absolve]
solvent, [abeyant]
soma, [anathema]
somatic, [acoustic]
somber, [amber]
sombrero, [allegro]
some, [adventuresome]
somebody, [acidy]
somehow, [allow]
someone, [antiphon]
someplace, [abase]
somersault, [asphalt]
sometime, [airtime]
sometimes, [times]
someway, [airway]
somewhat, [adequate]
somewhere, [anywhere]
somnambulate, [ablate]
somnambulism, [abolitionism]
somnifacient, [abeyant]
somnolent, [ambivalent]

son, [antitoxin]
sonar, [abattoir]
sonata, [aorta]
song, [agelong]
songbook, [bankbook]
songfest, [abreast]
songster, [administer]
songwriter, [abductor]
sonic, [allergenic]
sonnet, [acuminate]
sonny, [abalone]
sonogram, [aerogram]
sonorous, [actress]
sonship, [airship]
soon, [afternoon]
sooner, [afterburner]
soot, [ablaut]
soothe, [smooth]
soothsayer, [ballplayer]
sop, [agitprop]
sophism, [abolitionism]
sophist, [activist]
sophisticate, [abdicate]
sophisticate, [advocate]
sophisticated, [abluted]
sophistication, [abbreviation]
sophistry, [ancestry]
sophomore, [abhor]
sophomoric, [aleatoric]
soporific, [anthropomorphic]
soppy, [apocope]
soprano, [albino]
sorbet, [agape]
sorcerer, [adulterer]
sorceress, [actress]
sorcery, [accessory]
sordid, [absentminded]
sore throat, [afloat]
sore, [abhor]

395

sorehead, [abed]
soreness, [agribusiness]
sorority, [abatis]
sorrow, [allegro]
sorrowful, [apocryphal]
sorry, [accessory]
sort, [abort]
sorter, [abductor]
sortie, [abatis]
sortilege, [acknowledge]
sortition, [abbreviation]
soteriology, [allergy]
sottish, [abolish]
soubise, [antifreeze]
soubrette, [abet]
soufflé, [airplay]
sough, [allow]
sought, [aeronaut]
souk, [archduke]
soul, [areole]
soulless, [acropolis]
sound, [abound]
soundboard, [aboard]
soundman, [adman]
soundstage, [age]
soup, [coop]
soupy, [apocope]
sour, [airpower]
source, [coarse]
sourcebook, [bankbook]
sourdough, [aficionado]
sous, [accrue]
souse, [alehouse]
south, [badmouth]
southbound, [abound]
southeast, [beast]
southern, [adjourn]
southland, [ampersand]
southpaw, [aah]

southward, [absurd]
southwest, [abreast]
souvenir, [adhere]
souvlakia, [abulia]
sovereign, [pressrun]
sovereignty, [abatis]
soviet, [abet]
sow, [allow]
sowbelly, [ably]
sowens, [environs]
soy, [ahoy]
soybean, [alexandrine]
sozzled, [bedraggled]
spa, [aah]
space suit, [backup]
space walk, [artichoke]
space, [abase]
spacecraft, [abaft]
spaceflight, [affright]
spaceman, [adman]
spaceship, [airship]
spacious, [adscititious]
spaciousness, [agribusiness]
spackle, [acoustical]
spade, [abrade]
spadille, [backfill]
spaetzle, [a capella]
spaghetti, [abatis]
spaghettini, [abalone]
spall, [aerosol]
spallation, [abbreviation]
span, [adman]
spandex, [annex]
spangle, [angle]
spaniel, [agile]
spank, [bank]
spanker, [acre]
spanner, [afterburner]
spar, [abattoir]

spare, [affair]
spareribs, [dibs]
sparge, [barge]
spark, [aardvark]
sparkle, [acoustical]
sparkler, [angler]
sparky, [achy]
sparrow, [allegro]
sparse, [farce]
sparsity, [abatis]
spasm, [abolitionism]
spasmodic, [acidic]
spastic, [acoustic]
spat, [acrobat]
spate, [anticipate]
spatial, [abbatial]
spatter, [abductor]
spatula, [a capella]
spawn, [amazon]
spayed, [abrade]
spaz, [as]
speak, [antique]
speakeasy, [advisee]
speaker, [acre]
speakerphone, [alone]
spear, [adhere]
speargun, [bandwagon]
spearhead, [abed]
spearman, [abdomen]
spearmint, [blueprint]
spec, [afterdeck]
special, [abbatial]
specialist, [aerialist]
specialization, [abbreviation]
specialize, [actualize]
specialty, [abatis]
specie, [banshee]
species, [antifreeze]
specific, [anthropomorphic]

specification, [abbreviation]
specificity, [abatis]
specify, [amplify]
specimen, [abdomen]
specious, [adscititious]
speck, [afterdeck]
speckle, [acoustical]
specs, [annex]
spectacle, [acoustical]
spectacular, [angler]
spectator, [abductor]
specter, [abductor]
spectrum, [addendum]
speculate, [ablate]
speculation, [abbreviation]
speculative, [ablative]
speculator, [abductor]
sped, [abed]
speech, [beach]
speechwriter, [abductor]
speed, [accede]
speedball, [aerosol]
speedboat, [afloat]
speedometer, [abductor]
speedster, [administer]
speedup, [backup]
speedway, [airway]
speedy, [acidy]
speleology, [allergy]
spell, [bagatelle]
spellbind, [affined]
spellbinder, [adder]
spellbound, [abound]
spelunker, [acre]
spencer, [aggressor]
spend, [addend]
spender, [adder]
spendthrift, [adrift]
spent, [accent]

sperm, [affirm]
spermicide, [abide]
spew, [accrue]
sphere, [adhere]
spherical, [acoustical]
sphinx, [jinx]
spiccato, [aggiornamento]
spice, [advice]
spicy, [absorbancy]
spider, [adder]
spiderweb, [bleb]
spiel, [anneal]
spiff, [anaglyph]
spiffy, [anastrophe]
spigot, [agate]
spike, [alike]
spikenard, [backyard]
spill, [backfill]
spillage, [acknowledge]
spillover, [achiever]
spillway, [airway]
spilt, [atilt]
spilth, [filth]
spin, [akin]
spinach, [backstitch]
spinal, [abdominal]
spindle, [antipodal]
spindly, [ably]
spindrift, [adrift]
spine, [aerodyne]
spineless, [acropolis]
spinet, [acuminate]
spinner, [afterburner]
spinster, [administer]
spinto, [aggiornamento]
spiracle, [acoustical]
spiral, [admiral]
spirant, [aberrant]
spire, [acquire]

spirit, [accurate]
spirited, [abluted]
spiritism, [abolitionism]
spiritist, [absolutist]
spiritistic, [acoustic]
spiritless, [acropolis]
spiritual, [accrual]
spiritualism, [abolitionism]
spiritualist, [aerialist]
spiritualistic, [acoustic]
spirituality, [abatis]
spiritualization, [abbreviation]
spiritualize, [actualize]
spit, [acquit]
spitball, [aerosol]
spite, [affright]
spiteful, [apocryphal]
spitfire, [acquire]
spittle, [accidental]
spittoon, [afternoon]
splash, [abash]
splashboard, [aboard]
splashdown, [boomtown]
splashy, [banshee]
splat, [acrobat]
splatter, [abductor]
splay, [airplay]
spleen, [alexandrine]
splendent, [abundant]
splendid, [absentminded]
splendidness, [agribusiness]
splendiferous, [actress]
splendor, [adder]
splice, [advice]
splint, [blueprint]
splinter, [abductor]
split screen, [alexandrine]
split, [acquit]
splitter, [abductor]

splotch, [blotch]
splurge, [converge]
splutter, [abductor]
spoil, [broil]
spoilage, [acknowledge]
spoiler, [angler]
spoilsport, [airport]
spoke, [artichoke]
spoken, [awaken]
spokesman, [abdomen]
spokesperson,
  [anchorperson]
spokeswoman, [abdomen]
spoliate, [create]
spoliation, [abbreviation]
spondee, [acidy]
sponge, [challenge]
spongy, [allergy]
sponson, [antitoxin]
sponsor, [aggressor]
sponsorship, [airship]
spontaneity, [abatis]
spontaneous, [abstemious]
spoof, [aloof]
spook, [archduke]
spooky, [achy]
spool, [bascule]
spoon, [afternoon]
spoonful, [apocryphal]
spoony, [abalone]
spoor, [abjure]
sporadic, [acidic]
spore, [abhor]
sport, [airport]
sportive, [ablative]
sportscast, [aghast]
sportscaster, [administer]
sportsman, [abdomen]
sportsmanship, [airship]

sportswear, [affair]
sportswoman, [abdomen]
sportswriter, [abductor]
sporty, [abatis]
spot, [aeronaut]
spotless, [acropolis]
spotlight, [affright]
spotter, [abductor]
spotty, [abatis]
spousal, [appraisal]
spouse, [alehouse]
spout, [about]
spraddle, [antipodal]
sprag, [ag]
sprain, [abstain]
sprat, [acrobat]
sprawl, [aerosol]
spray, [affray]
spread, [abed]
spreadable, [able]
spreader, [adder]
spreadsheet, [accrete]
spree, [accessory]
sprig, [big]
sprightly, [ably]
spring, [anything]
springald, [bedraggled]
springboard, [aboard]
springe, [binge]
springtime, [airtime]
springwater, [abductor]
springy, [aggie]
sprinkle, [acoustical]
sprinkler, [angler]
sprint, [blueprint]
sprinter, [abductor]
sprite, [affright]
spritz, [blitz]
spritzer, [aggressor]

sprocket, [advocate]
sprout, [about]
spruce, [abstruse]
sprung, [among]
spry, [airdry]
spud, [acid]
spume, [abloom]
spumoni, [abalone]
spun, [bandwagon]
spunk, [bohunk]
spunkiness, [agribusiness]
spunky, [achy]
spur, [barkeeper]
spurious, [abstemious]
spurn, [adjourn]
spurt, [advert]
sputnik, [allergenic]
sputter, [abductor]
sputum, [accustom]
spy, [airdry]
spyglass, [admass]
spymaster, [administer]
squab, [ab]
squabble, [able]
squad, [abroad]
squadron, [pressrun]
squalid, [acid]
squall, [aerosol]
squaller, [angler]
squalor, [angler]
squander, [adder]
squanderer, [adulterer]
square root, [backup]
square, [affair]
squash, [awash]
squat, [aeronaut]
squatty, [abatis]
squaw, [aah]
squawk, [aftershock]

squeak, [antique]
squeaker, [acre]
squeaky, [achy]
squeal, [anneal]
squealer, [angler]
squeamish, [abolish]
squeegee, [allergy]
squeeze, [antifreeze]
squelch, [belch]
squib, [bib]
squid, [amid]
squiggle, [angle]
squinch, [bullfinch]
squint, [blueprint]
squire, [acquire]
squirm, [affirm]
squirmy, [academy]
squirrel, [aswirl]
squirt, [advert]
squish, [abolish]
squishy, [banshee]
stab, [backstab]
stabile, [anile]
stability, [abatis]
stabilization, [abbreviation]
stabilize, [actualize]
stabilizer, [adviser]
stable, [able]
staccato, [aggiornamento]
stack, [aback]
stacker, [acre]
stadia, [abulia]
stadium, [anthurium]
staff, [allograph]
staffer, [buffer]
stag, [ag]
stage, [age]
stagecoach, [abroach]
stagecraft, [abaft]

stagehand, [ampersand]
stage-struck, [amok]
stagflation, [abbreviation]
stagger, [agar]
stagnant, [abstinent]
stagnate, [abominate]
stagy, [allergy]
staid, [abrade]
stain, [abstain]
stainless, [acropolis]
stair, [affair]
staircase, [abase]
stairway, [airway]
stairwell, [bagatelle]
stake, [awake]
stakeholder, [adder]
stakeout, [about]
stalactite, [affright]
stalag, [agog]
stalagmite, [affright]
stale, [ail]
stalemate, [acclimate]
stalk, [aftershock]
stalked, [blocked]
stall, [aerosol]
stallion, [antiunion]
stalwart, [advert]
stamen, [abdomen]
stamina, [alumna]
stammer, [armor]
stamp, [aid-de-camp]
stampede, [accede]
stance, [advance]
stand, [ampersand]
standard, [absurd]
standardization, [abbreviation]
standardize, [advise]
standby, [alibi]
standish, [abolish]

standoff, [boff]
standoffish, [abolish]
standout, [about]
standpat, [acrobat]
standpipe, [airpipe]
standpoint, [anoint]
standstill, [backfill]
stank, [bank]
stanza, [alfalfa]
staple, [ample]
stapler, [angler]
star, [abattoir]
starboard, [absurd]
starch, [arch]
stardom, [addendum]
stardust, [adjust]
stare, [affair]
stargaze, [ablaze]
stargazer, [adviser]
stark, [aardvark]
starless, [acropolis]
starlet, [aglet]
starlets, [giblets]
starlight, [affright]
starry, [accessory]
starship, [airship]
starstruck, [amok]
start, [apart]
starter, [abductor]
startle, [accidental]
starvation, [abbreviation]
starve, [carve]
stash, [abash]
stasis, [alkalosis]
stat, [acrobat]
statant, [accordant]
state, [acetate]
statehood, [adulthood]
statehouse, [alehouse]

stateliness, [agribusiness]
stately, [ably]
statement, [abandonment]
state-of-the-art, [apart]
stateside, [abide]
statesman, [abdomen]
statesmanship, [airship]
statewide, [abide]
static, [acoustic]
staticky, [achy]
station, [abbreviation]
stationary, [accessory]
stationery, [accessory]
stationmaster, [administer]
statism, [abolitionism]
statistic, [acoustic]
statistical, [acoustical]
statistician, [abbreviation]
statistics, [acoustics]
stative, [ablative]
statuary, [accessory]
statue, [accrue]
statuesque, [arabesque]
statuette, [abet]
stature, [acupuncture]
status, [afflatus]
statute, [acute]
statutory, [accessory]
staunch, [haunch]
stave, [aftershave]
stay, [agape]
stead, [abed]
steadfast, [aghast]
steadfastness, [agribusiness]
steadiness, [agribusiness]
steady, [acidy]
steak, [awake]
steal, [anneal]
stealth, [commonwealth]

steam, [abeam]
steamboat, [afloat]
steamer, [armor]
steamfitter, [abductor]
steamroller, [angler]
steamship, [airship]
steamy, [academy]
steed, [accede]
steel, [anneal]
steeliness, [agribusiness]
steely, [ably]
steep, [asleep]
steeple, [ample]
steeplechase, [abase]
steeplejack, [aback]
steer, [adhere]
stein, [aerodyne]
stellar, [angler]
stem, [apothegm]
stemware, [affair]
stench, [bench]
stenographer, [buffer]
stenographic,
    [anthropomorphic]
stenography, [anastrophe]
stenotype, [airpipe]
step, [crowstep]
stepbrother, [altogether]
stepchild, [brainchild]
stepdaughter, [abductor]
stepfamily, [ably]
stepfather, [altogether]
stepladder, [adder]
stepmother, [altogether]
stepparent, [aberrant]
stepsister, [administer]
stepson, [antitoxin]
stepwise, [advise]
stereo, [audio]

stereophonic, [allergenic]
stereotype, [airpipe]
stereotypical, [acoustical]
sterile, [admiral]
sterility, [abatis]
sterilization, [abbreviation]
sterilize, [actualize]
stern, [adjourn]
sternness, [agribusiness]
sternum, [addendum]
sternway, [airway]
steroid, [adenoid]
stethoscope, [antelope]
stevedore, [abhor]
stew, [accrue]
steward, [absurd]
stewardess, [antibias]
stewardship, [airship]
stick, [acoustic]
stickball, [aerosol]
sticker, [acre]
stickiness, [agribusiness]
stickle, [acoustical]
stickman, [abdomen]
stickpin, [akin]
stickum, [addendum]
stickup, [backup]
stickwork, [artwork]
sticky, [achy]
stiff, [anaglyph]
stiffness, [agribusiness]
stifle, [apocryphal]
stigma, [anathema]
stigmatic, [acoustic]
stigmatize, [absolutize]
stile, [aisle]
stiletto, [aggiornamento]
still, [backfill]
stillbirth, [afterbirth]

stillborn, [acorn]
stillman, [abdomen]
stillness, [agribusiness]
stillroom, [abloom]
stilly, [ably]
stilt, [atilt]
stilted, [abluted]
stimulant, [ambivalent]
stimulate, [ablate]
stimulation, [abbreviation]
stimulus, [acropolis]
sting, [anything]
stinger, [arbitrager]
stingray, [affray]
stingy, [allergy]
stink, [bethink]
stinker, [acre]
stinkpot, [aeronaut]
stinky, [achy]
stint, [blueprint]
stipend, [addend]
stipple, [ample]
stipulate, [ablate]
stipulation, [abbreviation]
stir, [administer]
stirp, [burp]
stirrup, [backup]
stitch, [backstitch]
stiver, [achiever]
stock, [aftershock]
stockade, [abrade]
stockbreeder, [adder]
stockbroker, [acre]
stockholder, [adder]
stock-keeper, [barkeeper]
stockman, [abdomen]
stockpile, [anile]
stockpot, [aeronaut]
stockroom, [abloom]

stocky, [achy]
stockyard, [backyard]
stodge, [dislodge]
stodginess, [agribusiness]
stodgy, [allergy]
stoic, [acidic]
stoicism, [abolitionism]
stoke, [artichoke]
stoker, [acre]
stole, [areole]
stolen, [acetylene]
stolid, [acid]
stoma, [anathema]
stomach, [amok]
stomachache, [awake]
stonch, [haunch]
stone, [atone]
stonecutter, [abductor]
stonemason, [anchorperson]
stonewall, [aerosol]
stoneware, [affair]
stonework, [artwork]
stony, [abalone]
stood, [adulthood]
stooge, [centrifuge]
stool, [bascule]
stoop, [coop]
stop, [agitprop]
stopgap, [afterclap]
stop-keeper, [barkeeper]
stoplight, [affright]
stopover, [achiever]
stoppage, [acknowledge]
stopper, [barkeeper]
stopwatch, [blotch]
storage, [abridge]
store, [abhor]
storefront, [aberrant]
storehouse, [alehouse]

storeroom, [abloom]
storewide, [abide]
stork, [cork]
storm, [aswarm]
stormy, [academy]
story, [accessory]
storyboard, [aboard]
storybook, [bankbook]
storyteller, [angler]
stoup, [coop]
stout, [about]
stouthearted, [abluted]
stove, [alcove]
stover, [achiever]
stow, [aggiornamento]
stowage, [acknowledge]
stowaway, [airway]
straddle, [antipodal]
strafe, [chafe]
straggle, [angle]
straggler, [angler]
straggly, [ably]
straight, [accelerate]
straightedge, [allege]
straighten, [anchorperson]
straightforward, [absurd]
straightjacket, [advocate]
straightway, [airway]
strain, [abstain]
strainer, [afterburner]
strait, [accelerate]
straitlaced, [abased]
strake, [awake]
strand, [ampersand]
stranded, [absentminded]
strange, [arrange]
stranger, [armiger]
strangle, [angle]
stranglehold, [ahold]

strangulate, [ablate]
strangulation, [abbreviation]
strap, [afterclap]
straphanger, [arbitrager]
strapless, [acropolis]
strappado, [aficionado]
strapper, [barkeeper]
stratagem, [addendum]
strategic, [acidic]
strategist, [allergist]
strategize, [advise]
strategy, [allergy]
strath, [aftermath]
stratification, [abbreviation]
stratify, [amplify]
stratosphere, [adhere]
stratum, [accustom]
stratus, [afflatus]
straw, [aah]
strawberry, [accessory]
strawhat, [acrobat]
stray, [affray]
streak, [antique]
streaker, [acre]
streaky, [achy]
stream, [abeam]
streamer, [armor]
streamline, [airline]
streamlined, [affined]
streamliner, [afterburner]
street, [accrete]
streetcar, [abattoir]
streetlight, [affright]
streetscape, [agape]
streetwalker, [acre]
streetwise, [advise]
strength, [length]
strenuous, [ambiguous]
strenuousness, [agribusiness]

strep, [crowstep]
stress, [acquiesce]
stressful, [apocryphal]
stressor, [aggressor]
stretch, [backstretch]
stretcher, [acupuncture]
stretto, [aggiornamento]
strew, [accrue]
strewn, [afternoon]
stria, [abulia]
striation, [abbreviation]
stricken, [awaken]
strict, [addict]
stricture, [acupuncture]
stride, [abide]
strident, [accordant]
strider, [adder]
stridulate, [ablate]
stridulous, [acropolis]
strife, [afterlife]
strike, [alike]
strikebreaker, [acre]
strikeout, [about]
strikeover, [achiever]
striker, [acre]
stringent, [agent]
stringer, [arbitrager]
stringy, [aggie]
strip, [airstrip]
stripe, [airpipe]
stripper, [barkeeper]
striptease, [antifreeze]
stripteaser, [adviser]
strive, [alive]
strobe, [bathrobe]
strode, [abode]
stroke, [artichoke]
stroll, [areole]
stroller, [angler]

strong, [agelong]
strongbox, [bandbox]
stronghold, [ahold]
strongman, [adman]
strop, [agitprop]
strophe, [anastrophe]
strophic, [anthropomorphic]
stroud, [aloud]
strove, [alcove]
struck, [amok]
structural, [admiral]
structure, [acupuncture]
structured, [absurd]
strudel, [antipodal]
struggle, [angle]
strum, [addendum]
strumpet, [adequate]
strung, [among]
strut, [accurate]
strychnine, [aerodyne]
stub, [backrub]
stubble, [able]
stubborn, [adjourn]
stubbornness, [agribusiness]
stubby, [abbey]
stucco, [alfresco]
stuck, [amok]
stud, [abluted]
student, [accordant]
studhorse, [endorse]
studio, [audio]
studious, [abstemious]
study, [acidy]
stuff, [bluff]
stuffer, [buffer]
stuffy, [anastrophe]
stultify, [amplify]
stumble, [able]
stumblebum, [addendum]

stumblingblock, [aftershock]
stump, [bump]
stumpage, [acknowledge]
stumpy, [apocope]
stun, [bandwagon]
stung, [among]
stunk, [bohunk]
stunned, [almond]
stunt, [abirritant]
stuntman, [abdomen]
stuntwoman, [abdomen]
stupe, [coop]
stupefy, [amplify]
stupendous, [antibias]
stupid, [acid]
stupidity, [abatis]
stupor, [barkeeper]
sturdy, [acidy]
sturgeon, [allergen]
stutter, [abductor]
sty, [airdry]
style, [aisle]
stylet, [abet]
stylish, [abolish]
stylist, [aerialist]
stylistic, [acoustic]
stylite, [affright]
stylize, [actualize]
stylus, [acropolis]
stymie, [academy]
styptic, [acoustic]
suasion, [abrasion]
suave, [mauve]
sub, [backrub]
subatomic, [academic]
subcategory, [accessory]
subchapter, [abductor]
subclass, [admass]
subconscious, [adscititious]

subcontractor, [abductor]
subculture, [acupuncture]
subdistrict, [addict]
subdivide, [abide]
subdivision, [abrasion]
subdue, [accrue]
subfile, [anile]
subfloor, [abhor]
subgrade, [abrade]
subgroup, [coop]
subhead, [abed]
subhuman, [abdomen]
subject, [noun] [addict]
subject, [verb] [abject]
subjective, [ablative]
subjectivism, [abolitionism]
subjectivity, [abatis]
subjectivize, [advise]
subjugate, [abnegate]
subjugation, [abbreviation]
subjunctive, [ablative]
sublease, [afterpiece]
sublet, [abet]
sublevel, [adjectival]
sublimate, [acclimate]
sublimation, [abbreviation]
sublime, [airtime]
subliminal, [abdominal]
submarine, [alexandrine]
submerge, [converge]
submerse, [adverse]
submersible, [able]
submersion, [abrasion]
submission, [abbreviation]
submissive, [abrasive]
submit, [acquit]
subnormal, [abnormal]
suboptimal, [abnormal]
suboptimum, [addendum]

subordinate, [noun]
  [acuminate]
subordinate, [verb]
  [abominate]
subordination, [abbreviation]
subpanel, [aboriginal]
subpar, [abattoir]
subparagraph, [allograph]
subplot, [aeronaut]
subpoena, [alumna]
subreption, [abbreviation]
subreptitious, [antibias]
subrogate, [abnegate]
subrogation, [abbreviation]
subroutine, [alexandrine]
subscale, [blackmail]
subscribe, [ascribe]
subscriber, [amber]
subscript, [adscript]
subscription, [abbreviation]
subsection, [abbreviation]
subsector, [abductor]
subsequent, [abeyant]
subservient, [abeyant]
subset, [abet]
subside, [abide]
subsidiary, [accessory]
subsidize, [advise]
subsidy, [acidy]
subsist, [assist]
subsistence, [abhorrence]
subsoil, [airfoil]
subspecialty, [abatis]
substance, [abhorrence]
substandard, [absurd]
substantial, [abbatial]
substantiate, [create]
substantiation, [abbreviation]
substantive, [ablative]

substate, [acetate]
substation, [abbreviation]
substitute, [acute]
substitution, [abbreviation]
substitutionary, [accessory]
substratum, [accustom]
substructure, [acupuncture]
subsume, [abloom]
subteen, [alexandrine]
subtend, [addend]
subterfuge, [centrifuge]
subterranean, [abecedarian]
subtext, [context]
subtheme, [abeam]
subtitle, [accidental]
subtle, [accidental]
subtlety, [abatis]
subtotal, [accidental]
subtract, [abstract]
subtrahend, [addend]
suburb, [adverb]
suburban, [antiphon]
suburbanize, [agnize]
suburbia, [abulia]
subversion, [abrasion]
subvert, [advert]
subway, [airway]
succeed, [accede]
success, [acquiesce]
successful, [apocryphal]
succession, [abbreviation]
successive, [abrasive]
successor, [aggressor]
succinct, [distinct]
succor, [acre]
succubus, [abbess]
succulent, [ambivalent]
succumb, [addendum]
such, [clutch]

suck, [amok]
sucker, [acre]
suckle, [acoustical]
sucrose, [adios]
suction, [abbreviation]
sudatorium, [anthurium]
sudden, [anchorperson]
suddenness, [agribusiness]
sudoriferous, [actress]
sudorific, [anthropomorphic]
sue, [accrue]
suede, [abrade]
suet, [adequate]
suffer, [buffer]
suffice, [advice]
sufficiency, [absorbancy]
sufficient, [abeyant]
suffix, [administratrix]
suffocate, [abdicate]
suffocation, [abbreviation]
suffrage, [abridge]
suffragette, [abet]
suffuse, [amuse]
sugar, [agar]
sugarcane, [abstain]
sugarcoat, [afloat]
sugarloaf, [loaf]
sugarplum, [addendum]
sugary, [accessory]
suggest, [abreast]
suggestion, [abbreviation]
suggestive, [ablative]
suicidal, [antipodal]
suicide, [abide]
suit, [acute]
suitability, [abatis]
suitable, [able]
suitcase, [abase]
suite, [accrete]

suiter, [abductor]
suitor, [abductor]
sukiyaki, [achy]
sulcate, [abdicate]
sulfur, [buffer]
sulk, [bulk]
sulky, [achy]
sullage, [acknowledge]
sullen, [acetylene]
sully, [ably]
sultan, [anchorperson]
sultriness, [agribusiness]
sultry, [ancestry]
sum, [adventuresome]
summa, [anathema]
summand, [ampersand]
summarize, [accessorize]
summary, [accessory]
summation, [abbreviation]
summer, [armor]
summertime, [airtime]
summit, [animate]
summon, [abdomen]
summons, [environs]
sump, [bump]
sumptuous, [ambiguous]
sun, [antitoxin]
sunbath, [aftermath]
sunbathe, [bathe]
sunblock, [aftershock]
sunbonnet, [acuminate]
sunbow, [airshow]
sunburn, [adjourn]
sunburst, [athirst]
sundae, [acidy]
sundeck, [afterdeck]
sunder, [adder]
sundial, [aisle]
sundown, [boomtown]

sundress, [acquiesce]
sundries, [antifreeze]
sundry, [accessory]
sunflower, [airpower]
sung, [among]
sunglass, [admass]
sunk, [bohunk]
sunken, [awaken]
sunlamp, [aid-de-camp]
sunlight, [affright]
sunny, [abalone]
sunrise, [accessorize]
sunroof, [aloof]
sunroom, [abloom]
sunscreen, [alexandrine]
sunseeker, [acre]
sunset, [abet]
sunshade, [abrade]
sunshine, [aerodyne]
sunspot, [aeronaut]
sunstroke, [artichoke]
sunsuit, [acute]
suntan, [adman]
sup, [backup]
Super Bowl, [areole]
super, [barkeeper]
superabundance,
  [abhorrence]
superabundant, [abundant]
superb, [adverb]
supercede, [accede]
supercharge, [barge]
supercharger, [armiger]
supercomputer, [abductor]
superconfident, [abundant]
supercool, [bascule]
supercritical, [acoustical]
Superdome, [astrodome]
superefficient, [abeyant]

superego, [ago]
superfast, [aghast]
superficial, [abbatial]
superfluity, [abatis]
superfluous, [antibias]
superglue, [accrue]
superheavyweight,
 [accentuate]
superhero, [allegro]
superhighway, [airway]
superhuman, [abdomen]
superimpose, [airhose]
superintelligent, [agent]
superintend, [addend]
superintendent, [accent]
superior, [anterior]
superiority, [abatis]
superlative, [ablative]
superman, [adman]
supermarket, [advocate]
supermodel, [antipodal]
supermom, [aplomb]
supernal, [abdominal]
supernatural, [admiral]
superperson, [anchorperson]
superpower, [airpower]
supersensitive, [ablative]
supersmart, [apart]
supersonic, [allergenic]
supersophisticated, [abluted]
superspy, [airdry]
superstar, [abattoir]
superstition, [abbreviation]
superstitious, [adscititious]
superstore, [abhor]
superstructure, [acupuncture]
supertanker, [acre]
superthin, [akin]
supertight, [affright]

supervise, [advise]
supervision, [abrasion]
supervisor, [adviser]
supine, [aerodyne]
supper, [barkeeper]
suppertime, [airtime]
supplant, [ant]
supplanter, [abductor]
supple, [ample]
supplement, [abandonment]
supplemental, [accidental]
supplementary, [accessory]
supplicant, [abeyant]
supplicate, [abdicate]
supply, [airdry]
support, [airport]
supporter, [abductor]
supportive, [ablative]
suppose, [airhose]
supposition, [abbreviation]
suppository, [accessory]
suppress, [acquiesce]
suppressant, [adjacent]
suppression, [abbreviation]
supremacist, [assist]
supremacy, [absorbancy]
supreme, [abeam]
surcharge, [barge]
surd, [absurd]
sure, [abjure]
surefire, [acquire]
surely, [ably]
surety, [abatis]
surf, [bodysurf]
surface, [amorphous]
surfboard, [aboard]
surfboarder, [adder]
surfeit, [adequate]
surfer, [buffer]

surge, [converge]
surgeon, [allergen]
surgery, [accessory]
surgical, [acoustical]
surmise, [advise]
surmount, [account]
surname, [acclaim]
surpass, [admass]
surplus, [acropolis]
surprise, [accessorize]
surreal, [anneal]
surrealism, [abolitionism]
surrealist, [aerialist]
surrealistic, [acoustic]
surrender, [adder]
surreptitious, [adscititious]
surrey, [accessory]
surrogate, [abnegate]
surrogate, [agate]
surround, [abound]
surtax, [anthrax]
surtout, [accrue]
surveil, [ail]
surveillance, [abhorrence]
survey, [agape]
surveyor, [ballplayer]
survival, [adjectival]
survive, [alive]
survivorship, [airship]
susceptibility, [abatis]
susceptible, [able]
susceptive, [ablative]
sushi, [banshee]
suspect, [abject]
suspend, [addend]
suspender, [adder]
suspense, [cense]
suspenseful, [apocryphal]
suspension, [abbreviation]

suspicion, [abbreviation]
suspicious, [adscititious]
suspire, [acquire]
suss, [alkalosis]
sustain, [abstain]
sustainable, [able]
sustainer, [afterburner]
sustenance, [abhorrence]
suture, [acupuncture]
suzerain, [pressrun]
svelte, [belt]
swab, [ab]
swaddle, [antipodal]
swag, [ag]
swagger, [agar]
swain, [abstain]
swale, [ail]
swallow, [afterglow]
swam, [aerogram]
swami, [academy]
swamp, [chomp]
swan, [amazon]
swank, [bank]
swap, [agitprop]
swarm, [aswarm]
swart, [abort]
swash, [awash]
swashbuckle, [acoustical]
swastika, [angelica]
swat, [aeronaut]
swatch, [blotch]
swath, [broadcloth]
swear, [affair]
sweat suit, [backup]
sweat, [abet]
sweatband, [ampersand]
sweatbox, [bandbox]
sweater, [abductor]
sweatpants, [advance]

sweatshirt, [advert]
sweatshop, [agitprop]
sweaty, [abatis]
swede, [accede]
sweep, [asleep]
sweeper, [barkeeper]
sweepstake, [awake]
sweet, [accrete]
sweetbread, [abed]
sweeten, [anchorperson]
sweetener, [afterburner]
sweetheart, [apart]
sweetness, [agribusiness]
swell, [bagatelle]
swellhead, [abed]
swelter, [abductor]
swept, [accept]
swerve, [conserve]
swift, [adrift]
swig, [big]
swill, [backfill]
swim, [acronym]
swimsuit, [acute]
swimwear, [affair]
swindle, [antipodal]
swine, [aerodyne]
swing, [anything]
swinger, [arbitrager]
swingman, [adman]
swipe, [airpipe]
swirl, [aswirl]
swish, [abolish]
switch, [backstitch]
switchblade, [abrade]
switchboard, [aboard]
switchman, [abdomen]
swith, [blacksmith]
swither, [altogether]
swivel, [adjectival]

swizzle, [appraisal]
swollen, [acetylene]
swoon, [afternoon]
swoop, [coop]
swoosh, [cartouche]
sword, [aboard]
swordsman, [abdomen]
swordsmanship, [airship]
swore, [abhor]
sworn, [acorn]
swum, [addendum]
swung, [among]
sycamore, [abhor]
sycophant, [abeyant]
syllabic, [acerbic]
syllable, [able]
syllabus, [abbess]
syllogism, [abolitionism]
syllogist, [allergist]
syllogize, [advise]
symbiosis, [alkalosis]
symbiotic, [acoustic]
symbol, [able]
symbolic, [acyclic]
symbolical, [acoustical]
symbolism, [abolitionism]
symmetric, [aleatoric]
symmetrical, [acoustical]
symmetry, [ancestry]
sympathetic, [acoustic]
sympathize, [advise]
sympathizer, [adviser]
sympathy, [apathy]
symphonic, [allergenic]
symphony, [abalone]
symposium, [anthurium]
symptom, [accustom]
symptomatic, [acoustic]
synagogue, [agog]

synapse, [apse]
synchromesh, [afresh]
synchronize, [agnize]
syncopate, [anticipate]
syncopated, [abluted]
syncopation, [abbreviation]
syncope, [apocope]
syncretic, [acoustic]
syncretism, [abolitionism]
syncretize, [absolutize]
syndicalism, [abolitionism]
syndicate, [noun] [advocate]
syndicate, [verb] [abdicate]
syndication, [abbreviation]
syndrome, [astrodome]
synecdoche, [achy]
synergism, [abolitionism]
synergistic, [acoustic]
synergy, [allergy]
synod, [acid]
synonym, [acronym]
synonymous, [allonymous]
synopsis, [alkalosis]
synoptic, [acoustic]
syntax, [anthrax]
synthesis, [alkalosis]
synthesize, [abscise]
synthesizer, [adviser]
synthetic, [acoustic]
syphilis, [acropolis]
syringe, [binge]
system, [accustom]
systematic, [acoustic]
systematize, [absolutize]
systemic, [academic]
tab, [backstab]
tabard, [absurd]
tabby, [abbey]
tabernacle, [acoustical]

table, [able]
tableau, [afterglow]
tablecloth, [broadcloth]
tablespoonful, [apocryphal]
tabletop, [agitprop]
tableware, [affair]
tabloid, [adenoid]
taboo, [accrue]
tabor, [amber]
taboret, [abet]
tabular, [angler]
tabulate, [ablate]
tacet, [abet]
tach, [aback]
tacit, [corset]
taciturn, [adjourn]
tack, [aback]
tackboard, [aboard]
tackle, [acoustical]
tacky, [achy]
taco, [alfresco]
tacometer, [abductor]
tact, [abstract]
tactful, [apocryphal]
tactfulness, [agribusiness]
tactic, [acoustic]
tactical, [acoustical]
tactician, [abbreviation]
tactics, [acoustics]
tactile, [accidental]
tactless, [acropolis]
tad, [ad]
tadpole, [areole]
taffeta, [aorta]
taffy, [anastrophe]
tag, [ag]
tagalong, [agelong]
tagboard, [aboard]
tail, [ail]

tailback, [aback]
tailbone, [alone]
tailcoat, [afloat]
tailgate, [abnegate]
taillight, [affright]
tailor, [angler]
tailpiece, [afterpiece]
tailpipe, [airpipe]
tailspin, [akin]
tailwind, [abscind]
taint, [acquaint]
take, [awake]
takedown, [boomtown]
takeoff, [boff]
takeout, [about]
takeover, [achiever]
tale, [ail]
talebearer, [adulterer]
talent, [ambivalent]
talented, [abluted]
talesman, [abdomen]
talisman, [abdomen]
talk, [aftershock]
talkathon, [amazon]
talkative, [ablative]
talky, [achy]
tall, [aerosol]
talleyho, [airshow]
tallow, [afterglow]
tally, [ably]
tallyman, [abdomen]
talon, [acetylene]
tamale, [ably]
tamarisk, [asterisk]
tambourine, [alexandrine]
tame, [acclaim]
tamp, [aid-de-camp]
tamper, [barkeeper]
tamperproof, [aloof]

tampon, [amazon]
tan, [adman]
tandem, [addendum]
tangent, [agent]
tangential, [abbatial]
tangerine, [alexandrine]
tangible, [able]
tangle, [angle]
tangled, [bedraggled]
tango, [ago]
tank, [bank]
tanker, [acre]
tanner, [afterburner]
tannery, [accessory]
tantalize, [actualize]
tantamount, [account]
tap, [afterclap]
tape, [agape]
taper, [barkeeper]
tapestry, [ancestry]
tapeworm, [affirm]
tapioca, [angelica]
taproot, [acute]
taps, [apse]
tar, [abattoir]
tarantula, [a capella]
tardo, [aficionado]
tardy, [acidy]
tare, [affair]
target, [agate]
tarlatan, [anchorperson]
tarmacadam, [addendum]
tarn, [barn]
tarnation, [abbreviation]
tarnish, [abolish]
tarok, [aftershock]
tarot, [allegro]
tarp, [carp]
tarpaulin, [acetylene]

tarrier, [anterior]
tarry, [accessory]
tart, [apart]
tartan, [anchorperson]
tartar, [abductor]
task, [ask]
taskmaster, [administer]
tassel, [apostle]
taste, [abased]
tasteful, [apocryphal]
tasteless, [acropolis]
taster, [administer]
tasty, [abatis]
tat, [acrobat]
tatter, [abductor]
tattle, [accidental]
tattler, [angler]
tattletale, [blackmail]
tattoo, [accrue]
tatty, [abatis]
taunt, [avaunt]
taupe, [antelope]
taut, [aeronaut]
tautological, [acoustical]
tautology, [allergy]
tavern, [adjourn]
tawny, [abalone]
tax, [anthrax]
taxable, [able]
taxation, [abbreviation]
taxeme, [abeam]
tax-exempt, [attempt]
taxi, [absorbancy]
taxicab, [backstab]
taxidermist, [alchemist]
taxidermy, [academy]
taxiway, [airway]
taxonomy, [academy]
taxpayer, [ballplayer]

tea, [abatis]
teach, [beach]
teachable, [able]
teacher, [acupuncture]
teacup, [backup]
teahouse, [alehouse]
teakettle, [accidental]
teal, [anneal]
team, [abeam]
teammate, [acclimate]
teamster, [administer]
teamwork, [artwork]
teapot, [aeronaut]
tear, [adhere]
tearaway, [airway]
teardown, [boomtown]
teardrop, [agitprop]
tearful, [apocryphal]
teargas, [admass]
tearjerker, [acre]
tearoom, [abloom]
tearstain, [abstain]
teary, [accessory]
tease, [antifreeze]
teaser, [adviser]
teaspoon, [afternoon]
teaspoonful, [apocryphal]
tech, [afterdeck]
technical, [acoustical]
technicality, [abatis]
technician, [abbreviation]
technique, [antique]
technocrat, [acrobat]
technological, [acoustical]
technology, [allergy]
technophobia, [abulia]
tedious, [abstemious]
tediousness, [agribusiness]
tedium, [anthurium]

tee, [abatis]
teem, [abeam]
teen, [alexandrine]
teenage, [age]
teens, [smithereens]
teeny, [abalone]
teenybop, [agitprop]
teenybopper, [barkeeper]
teepee, [apocope]
teeter, [abductor]
teethe, [breathe]
teetotal, [accidental]
teetotaler, [angler]
tefillin, [acetylene]
telecast, [aghast]
telecaster, [administer]
telecommunication,
  [abbreviation]
telecommute, [acute]
teleconference, [abhorrence]
telecourse, [coarse]
telefacsimile, [ably]
telegenic, [allergenic]
telegram, [aerogram]
telegraph, [allograph]
telegraphic, [anthropomorphic]
telegraphy, [anastrophe]
telekinesis, [alkalosis]
telemarketer, [abductor]
telemetry, [ancestry]
teleological, [acoustical]
teleology, [allergy]
telepathy, [apathy]
telephone pole, [areole]
telephone, [alone]
telephonic, [allergenic]
telephony, [abalone]
telephoto, [aggiornamento]
teleplay, [airplay]

teleportation, [abbreviation]
teleprinter, [abductor]
telescope, [antelope]
telescopic, [acidic]
telesis, [alkalosis]
teletext, [context]
telethon, [amazon]
teletype, [airpipe]
teletypewriter, [abductor]
televangelism, [abolitionism]
televangelist, [aerialist]
teleview, [accrue]
televise, [advise]
television, [abrasion]
televisual, [accrual]
telex, [annex]
telic, [acyclic]
tell, [bagatelle]
teller, [angler]
telltale, [blackmail]
telos, [across]
temerity, [abatis]
temp, [hemp]
temper, [barkeeper]
temperament, [abandonment]
temperamental, [accidental]
temperance, [abhorrence]
temperate, [accurate]
temperature, [abjure]
tempest, [adjust]
tempestuous, [ambiguous]
template, [aglet]
temple, [ample]
tempo, [airshow]
temporal, [admiral]
temporality, [abatis]
temporarily, [ably]
temporary, [accessory]
temporize, [accessorize]

tempt, [attempt]
temptation, [abbreviation]
tempter, [abductor]
temptress, [actress]
tempura, [abracadabra]
ten, [again]
tenable, [able]
tenace, [abase]
tenacious, [adscititious]
tenacity, [abatis]
tenant, [abstinent]
tend, [addend]
tendency, [absorbancy]
tendentious, [adscititious]
tender, [adder]
tenderfoot, [ablaut]
tenderhearted, [abluted]
tenderize, [accessorize]
tenderloin, [adjoin]
tenderness, [agribusiness]
tendonitis, [afflatus]
tenebrific, [anthropomorphic]
tenebrous, [actress]
tenement, [abandonment]
tenet, [acuminate]
tennies, [antifreeze]
tennis, [agribusiness]
tenor, [afterburner]
tenpin, [akin]
tense, [cense]
tensile, [apostle]
tension, [abbreviation]
tensity, [abatis]
tent, [accent]
tentacle, [acoustical]
tentative, [ablative]
tenuity, [abatis]
tenuous, [ambiguous]
tenuousness, [agribusiness]

tenure, [ballplayer]
tenuto, [aggiornamento]
tepid, [acid]
tequila, [a capella]
teraph, [bluff]
teraphim, [acronym]
teriyaki, [achy]
term, [affirm]
terminal, [aboriginal]
terminate, [abominate]
termination, [abbreviation]
terminator, [abductor]
terminology, [allergy]
terminus, [agribusiness]
termite, [affright]
ternary, [accessory]
terra, [abracadabra]
terrace, [actress]
terrain, [abstain]
terrene, [pressrun]
terrestrial, [abaxial]
terrible, [able]
terribleness, [agribusiness]
terrific, [anthropomorphic]
terrify, [amplify]
territorial, [abaxial]
territorialize, [actualize]
territory, [accessory]
terror, [adulterer]
terrorism, [abolitionism]
terrorist, [allegorist]
terrorize, [accessorize]
terse, [adverse]
terseness, [agribusiness]
tertiary, [accessory]
tessellate, [ablate]
tessellation, [abbreviation]
test case, [abase]
test, [abreast]

testable, [able]
testament, [abandonment]
testate, [acetate]
testator, [abductor]
tested, [abluted]
testicle, [acoustical]
testify, [amplify]
testimonial, [abaxial]
testimony, [abalone]
testosterone, [alone]
testy, [abatis]
tetanus, [agribusiness]
tetchy, [blotchy]
tether, [altogether]
tetherball, [aerosol]
tetrarch, [aardvark]
tetrarchy, [achy]
tetrazzini, [abalone]
text, [context]
textbook, [bankbook]
textual, [accrual]
texture, [acupuncture]
than, [adman]
thanatologist, [allergist]
thanatology, [allergy]
thank, [bank]
thankful, [apocryphal]
thankfulness, [agribusiness]
thanklessness, [agribusiness]
thanks, [phalanx]
that, [acrobat]
thataway, [airway]
thatch, [armpatch]
thatcher, [acupuncture]
thaumaturgist, [allergist]
thaumaturgy, [allergy]
thaw, [aah]
the, [alfalfa]
theater, [abductor]

theatrical, [acoustical]
theatrics, [administratrix]
thee, [buoy]
theft, [aleft]
theirs, [bonkers]
theism, [abolitionism]
theist, [activist]
theistic, [acoustic]
them, [algorithm]
thematic, [acoustic]
theme, [abeam]
then, [again]
thence, [cense]
theocentric, [aleatoric]
theocracy, [absorbancy]
theocrat, [acrobat]
theocratic, [acoustic]
theodicy, [absorbancy]
theogony, [abalone]
theologian, [allergen]
theological, [acoustical]
theologize, [advise]
theologue, [agog]
theology, [allergy]
theonomy, [academy]
theophany, [abalone]
theorem, [addendum]
theoretical, [acoustical]
theorist, [allegorist])
theorize, [accessorize]
theory, [accessory]
theosophical, [acoustical]
theosophy, [anastrophe]
therapeutic, [acoustic]
therapy, [apocope]
there, [affair]
thereabout, [about]
thereabouts, [hereabouts]
thereby, [alibi]

therefore, [abhor]
therefrom, [addendum]
therein, [akin]
thereof, [above]
thereon, [amazon]
thereto, [accrue]
theretofore, [abhor]
thereunder, [adder]
thereupon, [amazon]
therm, [affirm]
thermal, [abnormal]
thermometer, [abductor]
thermonuclear, [anterior]
thermos, [allonymous]
thermostat, [acrobat]
thesaurus, [actress]
thesis, [alkalosis]
thespian, [abecedarian]
theurgy, [allergy]
thew, [accrue]
they, [agape]
thick, [acidic]
thicken, [awaken]
thicket, [advocate]
thickhead, [abed]
thickheaded, [absentminded]
thickness, [agribusiness]
thief, [aperitif]
thievery, [accessory]
thigh, [airdry]
thimble, [able]
thimblerig, [big]
thin, [akin]
thine, [aerodyne]
thing, [anything]
thingamajig, [big]
think, [bethink]
thinner, [afterburner]
thinnest, [adjust]

third, [absurd]
thirdhand, [ampersand]
thirst, [athirst]
thirsty, [abatis]
thirteen, [alexandrine]
thirty, [abatis]
this, [abyss]
thistle, [apostle]
thither, [altogether]
thole, [areole]
thong, [agelong]
thorax, [anthrax]
thorn, [acorn]
thornless, [acropolis]
thorny, [abalone]
thorough, [allegro]
thoroughbred, [abed]
thoroughfare, [affair]
thoroughness, [agribusiness]
those, [airhose]
thou, [allow]
though, [airshow]
thought, [aeronaut]
thoughtful, [apocryphal]
thoughtless, [acropolis]
thoughtway, [airway]
thousand, [almond]
thrall, [aerosol]
thrash, [abash]
thrasher, [acupressure]
thread, [abed]
threadbare, [affair]
threat, [abet]
threaten, [anchorperson]
three, [accessory]
threefold, [ahold]
threescore, [abhor]
threesome, [adventuresome]
thresh, [afresh]

threshhold, [ahold]
threw, [accrue]
thrice, [advice]
thrift, [adrift]
thriftiness, [agribusiness]
thrifty, [abatis]
thrill, [backfill]
thriller, [angler]
thrive, [alive]
throat, [afloat]
throaty, abatis]
throb, [ab]
thrombosis, [alkalosis]
throne, [alone]
throng, [agelong]
throttle, [accidental]
through, [accrue]
throughout, [about]
throughput, [ablaut]
throw, [allegro]
throwaway, [airway]
throwback, [aback]
thrown, [alone]
thrust, [adjust]
thruster, [administer]
thud, [acid]
thug, [bedbug]
thumb, [addendum]
thumbnail, [blackmail]
thumbprint, [blueprint]
thumbscrew, [accrue]
thumbtack, [aback]
thump, [bump]
thunder, [adder]
thunderbolt, [bolt]
thunderclap, [afterclap]
thundercloud, [aloud]
thunderhead, [abed]
thunderous, [actress]

thundershower, [airpower]
thunderstorm, [aswarm]
thunderstrike, [alike]
thunderstroke, [artichoke]
thunderstruck, [amok]
thunk, [bohunk]
thurifer, [buffer]
thus, [antibias]
thwack, [aback]
thwart, [abort]
thy, [airdry]
thyme, [airtime]
thyroid, [adenoid]
tic, [acoustic]
tick, [acoustic]
ticked, [addict]
ticker, [acre]
ticket, [advocate]
tickle, [acoustical]
tickler, [angler]
ticklish, [abolish]
ticktock, [aftershock]
tidal wave, [aftershave]
tidal, [antipodal]
tidbit, [acquit]
tide, [aide]
tidewater, [abductor]
tidy, [acidy]
tie, [airdry]
tieback, [aback]
tiebreaker, [acre]
tier, [adhere]
tiff, [anaglyph]
tiffany, [abalone]
tiger, [agar]
tight, [affright]
tighten, [anchorperson]
tightfisted, [abluted]
tightness, [agribusiness]

tightrope, [antelope]
tightwad, [abroad]
tiki, [achy]
tile, [aisle]
till, [backfill]
tillable, [able]
tillage, [acknowledge]
tiller, [angler]
tilt, [atilt]
timber, [amber]
timberland, [ampersand]
timberline, [airline]
timbre, [amber]
timbrel, [admiral]
time, [airtime]
timekeeper, [barkeeper]
timeless, [acropolis]
timeliness, [agribusiness]
timely, [ably]
timepiece, [afterpiece]
timer, [armor]
times, [sometimes]
timesaver, [achiever]
timeshare, [anywhere]
timetable, [able]
timework, [artwork]
timeworn, [acorn]
timid, [acid]
timidity, [abatis]
timorous, [actress]
timpani, [abalone]
tin, [akin]
tincture, [acupuncture]
tinder, [adder]
tinderbox, [bandbox]
tinfoil, [airfoil]
ting, [anything]
tinge, [binge]
tingle, [angle]

tingly, [ably]
tinhorn, [acorn]
tinker, [acre]
tinkle, [acoustical]
tinnitus, [afflatus]
tinny, [abalone]
tinsel, [apostle]
tint, [blueprint]
tinware, [affair]
tinwork, [artwork]
tiny, [abalone]
tip, [airstrip]
tipper, [barkeeper]
tipsy, [absorbancy]
tiptoe, [aggiornamento]
tiptop, [agitprop]
tirade, [abrade]
tire, [acquire]
tireless, [acropolis]
tirelessness, [agribusiness]
tiresome, [adventuresome]
tissue, [accrue]
tit, [acquit]
titan, [anchorperson]
titanic, [allergenic]
tithe, [blithe]
tither, [altogether]
titillate, [ablate]
titillation, [abbreviation]
title, [accidental]
titleholder, [adder]
titter, [abductor]
tittle, [accidental]
titular, [angler]
tizzy, [advisee]
to, [accrue]
to, [aorta]
toad, [abode]
toadstool, [bascule]

toast, [aftermost]
toaster, [administer]
toastmaster, [administer]
toasty, [abatis]
tobacco, [alfresco]
toboggan, [bandwagon]
toccata, [aorta]
tocsin, [antitoxin]
today, [agape]
toddle, [antipodal]
toddler, [angler]
toe, [aggiornamento]
toehold, [ahold]
toepiece, [afterpiece]
toeplate, [ablate]
toffee, [anastrophe]
tofu, [accrue]
tog, [agog]
toga, [alfalfa]
together, [altogether]
togetherness, [agribusiness]
toggle, [angle]
toil, [broil]
toilet, [aglet]
toiletry, [ancestry]
toilette, [abet]
toilsome, [adventuresome]
token, [awaken]
tokenism, [abolitionism]
told, [ahold]
tolerable, [able]
tolerance, [abhorrence]
tolerant, [aberrant]
tolerate, [accelerate]
toleration, [abbreviation]
toll, [areole]
tollbooth, [booth]
tollgate, [abnegate]
tollhouse, [alehouse]

tollway, [airway]
tomahawk, [aftershock]
tomato, [aggiornamento]
tomb, [abloom]
tomboy, [ahoy]
tombstone, [alone]
tomcat, [acrobat]
tome, [astrodome]
tomentose, [adios]
tomentum, [accustom]
tomfool, [bascule]
tomfoolery, [accessory]
tommyrot, [aeronaut]
tomorrow, [allegro]
ton, [bandwagon]
tonal, [abdominal]
tone, [atone]
toneless, [acropolis]
toner, [afterburner]
tonetic, [acoustic]
tongue, [among]
tonic, [allergenic]
tonight, [affright]
tonnage, [appanage]
tonsil, [apostle]
tonsillectomy, [academy]
tonsillitis, [afflatus]
tonsorial, [abaxial]
tontine, [alexandrine]
tony, [abalone]
too, [accrue]
took, [bankbook]
tool, [bascule]
toolbox, [bandbox]
toolholder, [adder]
toolmaker, [acre]
toolroom, [abloom]
toolshed, [abed]
toot, [acute]

tooth, [booth]
toothache, [awake]
toothbrush, [airbrush]
toothpaste, [abased]
toothpick, [acidic]
toothsome, [adventuresome]
toothy, [apathy]
tootsie, [absorbancy]
top hat, [acrobat]
top, [agitprop]
topaz, [as]
topcoat, [afloat]
tope, [antelope]
topflight, [affright]
topiary, [accessory]
topic, [acidic]
topical, [acoustical]
topknot, [aeronaut]
topless, [acropolis]
topographer, [buffer]
topography, [anastrophe]
topological, [acoustical]
topology, [allergy]
topos, [across]
topper, [barkeeper]
topple, [ample]
tops, [chops]
topside, [abide]
topsoil, [airfoil]
topspin, [akin]
toque, [artichoke]
torch, [blowtorch]
torchbearer, [adulterer]
torchlight, [affright]
tore, [abhor]
tormentor, [abductor]
torn, [acorn]
tornado, [aficionado]
torpedo, [aficionado]

torpid, [acid]
torpor, [barkeeper]
torque, [cork]
torrent, [aberrant]
torrential, [abbatial]
torrid, [acid]
torsion, [abbreviation]
torso, [also]
tort, [abort]
tortellini, [abalone]
tortilla, [alleluia]
tortoise, [afflatus]
tortuous, [ambiguous]
torture, [acupuncture]
torturous, [actress]
toss, [across]
toss-up, [backup]
tostada, [addenda]
tot, [aeronaut]
total, [accidental]
totalitarian, [abecedarian]
totalitarianism, [abolitionism]
totality, [abatis]
tote, [afloat]
totem, [accustom]
totter, [abductor]
tottle, [accidental]
touch, [clutch]
touchable, [able]
touchback, [aback]
touchdown, [boomtown]
touché, [agape]
touchiness, [agribusiness]
touchline, [airline]
touchstone, [atone]
touch-tone, [atone]
touchy, [blotchy]
tough, [bluff]
toughen, [antiphon]

toughie, [anastrophe]
toupee, [agape]
tour, [abjure]
tourism, [abolitionism]
tourist, [allegorist]
touristy, [abatis]
tournament, [abandonment]
tournedos, [aficionado]
tourney, [abalone]
tourniquet, [advocate]
tousle, [appraisal]
tout, [about]
tow bar, [abattoir]
tow, [aggiornamento]
toward, [absurd]
towboat, [afloat]
towel, [agile]
towelette, [abet]
tower, [airpower]
towhead, [abed]
town, [boomtown]
township, [airship]
townspeople, [ample]
towrope, [antelope]
toxemia, [abulia]
toxic, [airsick]
toxicology, [allergy]
toxin, [antitoxin]
toxophilite, [affright]
toy, [ahoy]
trace, [abase]
traceable, [able]
tracer, [aggressor]
trachea, [abulia]
track, [aback]
trackball, [aerosol]
trackless, [acropolis]
tract, [abstract]
tractable, [able]

tractate, [acetate]
traction, [abbreviation]
tractor, [abductor]
trade, [abrade]
trademark, [aardvark]
trader, [adder]
tradition, [abbreviation]
traditional, [aboriginal]
traditionalism, [abolitionism]
traditionalist, [aerialist]
traduce, [abstruse]
traffic stop, [agitprop]
traffic, [anthropomorphic]
tragedy, [acidy]
tragic, [acidic]
trail, [ail]
trailblazer, [adviser]
trailer, [angler]
trailhead, [abed]
train, [abstain]
trainee, [abalone]
trainload, [abode]
trait, [accelerate]
traitor, [abductor]
trajectory, [accessory]
tram, [aerogram]
trammel, [abnormal]
tramp, [aid-de-camp]
trample, [ample]
trampoline, [alexandrine]
tramway, [airway]
trance, [advance]
tranquil, [agile]
tranquility, [abatis]
tranquilize, [actualize]
tranquilizer, [adviser]
transact, [abstract]
transaction, [abbreviation]
transcend, [addend]

transcendence, [abhorrence]
transcendent, [abundant]
transcendental, [accidental]
transcontinental, [accidental]
transcribe, [ascribe]
transcriber, [amber]
transcript, [adscript]
transcription, [abbreviation]
transcultural, [admiral]
transduce, [abstruse]
transducer, [aggressor]
transfer, [buffer]
transferee, [accessory]
transference, [abhorrence]
transferor, [abhor]
transfiguration, [abbreviation]
transfigure, [ballplayer]
transfix, [administratrix]
transform, [aswarm]
transformation, [abbreviation]
transformational, [abdominal]
transformer, [armor]
transfusion, [abrasion]
transgress, [acquiesce]
transgression, [abbreviation]
transgressor, [aggressor]
transient, [abeyant]
transistor, [administer]
transit, [corset]
transition, [abbreviation]
transitional, [aboriginal]
transitive, [ablative]
transitory, [accessory]
translate, [ablate]
translation, [abbreviation]
translator, [abductor]
transliterate, [accelerate]
translucent, [adjacent]
transmigrate, [accelerate]

transmission, [abbreviation]
transmit, [acquit]
transmitter, [abductor]
transmutation, [abbreviation]
transmute, [acute]
transnational, [aboriginal]
transparency, [absorbancy]
transparent, [aberrant]
transpire, [acquire]
transplant, [ant]
transponder, [adder]
transport, [airport]
transportation, [abbreviation]
transpose, [airhose]
transposition, [abbreviation]
transsexual, [accrual]
transubstantiation,
  [abbreviation]
transvestite, [affright]
trap, [afterclap]
trapshooter, [abductor]
trash, [abash]
trashman, [abdomen]
trashy, [banshee]
trauma, [anathema]
traumatic, [acoustic]
traumatize, [absolutize]
travail, [ail]
travel, [adjectival]
traveler, [angler]
travelogue, [agog]
traverse, [adverse]
travesty, [abatis]
trawler, [angler]
tray, [affray]
treacherous, [actress]
treachery, [accessory]
tread, [abed]
treadmill, [backfill]

treason, [anchorperson]
treasonable, [able]
treasure, [admeasure]
treasurer, [adulterer]
treasury, [accessory]
treat, [accrete]
treatable, [able]
treatise, [afflatus]
treatment, [abandonment]
treaty, [abatis]
treble, [able]
tree, [ancestry]
treetop, [agitprop]
trek, [afterdeck]
trellis, [acropolis]
tremble, [able]
tremendous, [antibias]
tremor, [armor]
tremulous, [acropolis]
trench, [bench]
trenchant, [abeyant]
trencher, [acupuncture]
trend, [addend]
trendsetter, [abductor]
trendy, [acidy]
trepan, [adman]
trepid, [acid]
trepidation, [abbreviation]
trespass, [admass]
trespass, [auspice]
trespasser, [aggressor]
tress, [acquiesce]
trestle, [apostle]
trey, [affray]
triad, [ad]
triage, [arbitrage]
trial, [aisle]
triangle, [angle]
triangular, [angler]

triangulate, [ablate]
triarchy, [achy]
triathlete, [accrete]
triathlon, [acetylene]
triaxial, [abaxial]
tribal, [able]
tribalism, [abolitionism]
tribe, [ascribe]
tribulation, [abbreviation]
tribunal, [abdominal]
tribune, [afternoon]
tributary, [accessory]
tribute, [acute]
triceps, [biceps]
trichotomy, [academy]
trick, [aleatoric]
trickery, [accessory]
trickle, [acoustical]
trickster, [administer]
tricky, [achy]
tricycle, [acoustical]
tried, [abide]
trifle, [apocryphal]
trigger, [agar]
trigonometry, [ancestry]
trilateral, [admiral]
trill, [backfill]
trim, [acronym]
trimmer, [armor]
Trinidad, [ad]
trinitarian, [abecedarian]
trinket, [advocate]
trinomial, [anneal]
trio, [audio]
trip, [airstrip]
tripartite, [affright]
tripe, [airpipe]
triple, [ample]
triplet, [aglet]

triplex, [annex]
triplicate, [abdicate]
triplicate, [advocate]
tripod, [abroad]
tripper, [barkeeper]
tristate, [acetate]
trite, [affright]
tritheism, [abolitionism]
tritheist, [activist]
tritheistic, [acoustic]
triturate, [accelerate]
trituration, [abbreviation]
triumph, [galumph]
triumphal, [apocryphal]
triumphant, [abeyant]
triumvir, [achiever]
triumvirate, [accurate]
triune, [afternoon]
trivet, [adequate]
trivia, [abulia]
trivial, [abaxial]
trivialize, [actualize]
trod, [abroad]
trodden, [anchorperson]
troika, [angelica]
troll, [areole]
trolley car, [abattoir]
trolley, [ably]
trolleybus, [abbess]
trombone, [alone]
tromp, [chomp]
troop, [coop]
trooper, [barkeeper]
trope, [antelope]
trophy, [anastrophe]
tropical, [acoustical]
trot, [aeronaut]
troth, [broadcloth]
trotter, [abductor]

troubadour, [abhor]
troubadour, [adore]
trouble, [able]
troubled, [bedraggled]
troublemaker, [acre]
troubleshoot, [acute]
troubleshooter, [abductor]
troublesome,
    [adventuresome]
trough, [boff]
trounce, [announce]
troupe, [coop]
trouper, [barkeeper]
trouser, [adviser]
trout, [about]
trove, [alcove]
trover, [achiever]
trowel, [agile]
truancy, [absorbancy]
truant, [abeyant]
truce, [abstruse]
truck, [amok]
trucker, [acre]
truckle, [acoustical]
truckline, [airline]
truckload, [abode]
truculence, [abhorrence]
truculent, [ambivalent]
trudge, [adjudge]
true, [accrue]
truebred, [abed]
truehearted, [abluted]
truffle, [apocryphal]
truism, [abolitionism]
trull, [admiral]
truly, [ably]
trump, [bump]
trumpet call, [aerosol]
trumpet, [adequate]

trumpeter, [abductor]
truncate, [abdicate]
trundle, [antipodal]
trunk, [bohunk]
truss, [actress]
trust, [adjust]
trustable, [able]
trustee, [abatis]
trusteeship, [airship]
trustful, [apocryphal]
trustfulness, [agribusiness]
trustworthy, [newsworthy]
trusty, [abatis]
truth, [booth]
truthful, [apocryphal]
try, [airdry]
tryout, [about]
tryst, [allegorist]
tsar, [abattoir]
tsunami, [academy]
tub, [backrub]
tuba, [alfalfa]
tubby, [abbey]
tube, [boob]
tuberculosis, [alkalosis]
tuck, [amok]
tucker, [acre]
tug, [bedbug]
tugboat, [afloat]
tuition, [abbreviation]
tulip, [backup]
tumble, [able]
tumbler, [angler]
tumbleweed, [accede]
tumid, [acid]
tummy, [academy]
tumor, [armor]
tump, [bump]
tumult, [adult]

tumultuous, [ambiguous]
tumurous, [actress]
tun, [antiphon]
tuna, [alumna]
tundra, [abracadabra]
tune, [afternoon]
tuner, [afterburner]
tunic, [allergenic]
tunnel, [abdominal]
turbid, [acid]
turbo, [airshow]
turbojet, [abet]
turboprop, [agitprop]
turbot, [abbot]
turbulence, [abhorrence]
turbulent, [ambivalent]
turd, [absurd]
tureen, [alexandrine]
turf, [bodysurf]
turgid, [acid]
turgidity, [abatis]
turgidness, [agribusiness]
turkey, [achy]
turmoil, [airfoil]
turn, [adjourn]
turnabout, [about]
turnaround, [abound]
turncoat, [afloat]
turndown, [boomtown]
turnip, [backup]
turnkey, [achy]
turnoff, [boff]
turnout, [about]
turnover, [achiever]
turnpike, [alike]
turnspit, [acquit]
turnstile, [anile]
turntable, [able]
turpentine, [aerodyne]

turpitude, [altitude]
turquoise, [counterpoise]
turret, [accurate]
turtle, [accidental]
turtledove, [above]
turtleneck, [afterdeck]
tush, [ambush]
tusk, [dusk]
tussle, [apostle]
tutelage, [acknowledge]
tutor, [abductor]
tutorial, [abaxial]
tutti, [abatis]
tutu, [accrue]
tuxedo, [aficionado]
twaddle, [antipodal]
twain, [abstain]
tweak, [antique]
tweed, [accede]
tweet, [accrete]
tweeter, [abductor]
tweezer, [adviser]
tweezers, [bonkers]
twelve, [delve]
twenty, [abatis]
twerp, [burp]
twice, [advice]
twiddle, [antipodal]
twig, [big]
twilight, [affright]
twill, [backfill]
twin, [akin]
twine, [aerodyne]
twinge, [binge]
twinkle, [acoustical]
twirl, [aswirl]
twist, [activist]
twisted, [abluted]
twister, [administer]

twit, [acquit]
twitch, [backstitch]
twitchy, [blotchy]
twitter, [abductor]
twittery, [accessory]
two, [accrue]
twofold, [ahold]
twosome, [adventuresome]
two-two, [atone]
tycoon, [afternoon]
type, [airpipe]
typecast, [aghast]
typeface, [abase]
typeset, [abet]
typesetter, [abductor]
typewriter, [abductor]
typhoid, [adenoid]
typhoon, [afternoon]
typical, [acoustical]
typify, [amplify]
typist, [activist]
typo, [airshow]
typographer, [buffer]
typographical, [acoustical]
typography, [anastrophe]
typological, [acoustical]
typology, [allergy]
tyrannical, [acoustical]
tyrannize, [agnize]
tyranny, [abalone]
tyrant, [aberrant]
ubiquitous, [afflatus]
ubiquity, [abatis]
udder, [adder]
ugh, [bedbug]
ugly, [ably]
ukulele, [ably]
ulcer, [aggressor]
ulcerate, [accelerate]

ulceration, [abbreviation]
ullage, [acknowledge]
ulterior, [anterior]
ultimacy, [absorbancy]
ultimate, [animate]
ultimatum, [accustom]
ultra, [abracadabra]
ultracareful, [apocryphal]
ultracasual, [accrual]
ultra-cautious, [adscititious]
ultraclean, [alexandrine]
ultraconservative, [ablative]
ultracool, [bascule]
ultracritical, [acoustical]
ultradistant, [abirritant]
ultradry, [airdry]
ultraefficient, [abeyant]
ultraexclusive, [abrasive]
ultrafast, [aghast]
ultraglamorous, [actress]
ultraheavy, [anchovy]
ultrahitch, [backstitch]
ultrahuman, [abdomen]
ultraleftist, [absolutist]
ultraliberal, [admiral]
ultramilitant, [abirritant]
ultramodern, [adjourn]
ultranationalism,
   [abolitionism]
ultranationalistic, [acoustic]
ultraorthodox, [bandbox]
ultrapatriotic, [acoustic]
ultrapowerful, [apocryphal]
ultraprecise, [advice]
ultraprofessional, [aboriginal]
ultraradical, [acoustical]
ultrarefined, [affined]
ultrarevolutionary,
   [accessory]

ultraright, [affright]
ultrarightist, [absolutist]
ultrasegregationist,
   [abolitionist]
ultrasmart, [apart]
ultrasmooth, [smooth]
ultrasound, [abound]
ultraviolent, [ambivalent]
ultraviolet, [aglet]
ultrawide, [abide]
ululate, [ablate]
umbilical, [acoustical]
umbra, [abracadabra]
umbrage, [abridge]
umbrella, [a capella]
umlaut, [about]
ump, [bump]
umpire, [acquire]
umpteen, [alexandrine]
unabated, [abluted]
unable, [able]
unacceptable, [able]
unaccepted, [abluted]
unaccountable, [able]
unadulterated, [abluted]
unaffected, [abluted]
unaffiliated, [abluted]
unafraid, [abrade]
unaided, [absentminded]
unallocated, [abluted]
unalterable, [able]
unambiguous, [ambiguous]
unambitious, [adscititious]
unanimity, [abatis]
unanimous, [allonymous]
unanswerable, [able]
unanticipated, [abluted]
unapologetic, [acoustic]
unappreciated, [abluted]

unapproachable, [able]
unappropriated, [abluted]
unassailable, [able]
unassembled, [bedraggled]
unassisted, [abluted]
unassociated, [abluted]
unattainable, [able]
unattractive, [ablative]
unaudited, [abluted]
unavailable, [able]
unavoidable, [able]
unaware, [affair]
unbearable, [able]
unbeatable, [able]
unbeaten, [anchorperson]
unbelief, [aperitif]
unbelievable, [able]
unbeliever, [achiever]
unbendable, [able]
unbiased, [adjust]
unbiblical, [acoustical]
unborn, [acorn]
unbound, [abound]
unbounded, [absentminded]
unbowed, [aloud]
unbreakable, [able]
unbroken, [awaken]
unbudgeted, [abluted]
unburden, [anchorperson]
unbusinesslike, [alike]
uncalculated, [abluted]
uncanny, [abalone]
uncarpeted, [abluted]
uncertain, [anchorperson]
uncertainty, [abatis]
uncertified, [abide]
unchangeable, [able]
uncharacteristic, [acoustic]
uncharted, [abluted]

unchaste, [abased]
unchristian, [antiphon]
uncial, [abbatial]
uncirculated, [abluted]
uncivil, [adjectival]
unclad, [ad]
unclarified, [abide]
uncle, [acoustical]
unclean, [alexandrine]
uncoil, [uncoil]
uncomfortable, [able]
uncommercial, [abbatial]
uncommitted, [abluted]
uncommon, [abdomen]
uncommunicative, [ablative]
uncompetitive, [ablative]
uncompleted, [abluted]
uncomplicated, [abluted]
uncomplimentary, [accessory]
unconditional, [aboriginal]
unconfessed, [abreast]
unconscionable, [able]
unconscious, [adscititious]
unconsecrated, [abluted]
unconstitutional, [aboriginal]
uncontested, [abluted]
uncontrollable, [able]
uncontrolled, [ahold]
unconventional, [aboriginal]
unconverted, [abluted]
uncool, [bascule]
uncooperative, [ablative]
uncoordinated, [abluted]
uncork, [cork]
uncorrected, [abluted]
uncorroborated, [abluted]
uncouple, [ample]
uncouth, [booth]
uncover, [achiever]

uncreative, [ablative]
uncredentialed, [bedraggled]
uncritical, [acoustical]
unction, [abbreviation]
uncut, [advocate]
undated, [abluted]
undaunted, [abluted]
undebatable, [able]
undecided, [absentminded]
undecorated, [abluted]
undedicated, [abluted]
undefeated, [abluted]
undefended, [absentminded]
undefiled, [brainchild]
undefined, [affined]
undelegated, [abluted]
undeliverable, [able]
undemocratic, [acoustic]
undemonstrative, [ablative]
undeniable, [able]
undependable, [able]
under, [adder]
underachiever, [achiever]
underactive, [ablative]
underage, [age]
underappreciated, [abluted]
underarm, [alarm]
underbid, [amid]
underbody, [acidy]
underbrush, [airbrush]
underbudgeted, [abluted]
undercard, [backyard]
undercarriage, [abridge]
undercharge, [barge]
underclass, [admass]
underclassman, [abdomen]
undercoat, [afloat]
undercool, [bascule]
undercover, [achiever]

undercurrent, [aberrant]
undercut, [advocate]
underdog, [agog]
undereducated, [abluted]
underemphasis, [alkalosis]
underemphasize, [abscise]
underemployed, [adenoid]
underemployment,
  [abandonment]
underestimate, [acclimate]
underexpose, [airhose]
underfinance, [advance]
underfoot, [ablaut]
underfund, [almond]
undergarment, [abandonment]
undergo, [ago]
undergraduate, [adequate]
underground, [abound]
underhanded, [absentminded]
underhandy, [acidy]
underinflated, [abluted]
underlay, [airplay]
underline, [airline]
underling, [anything]
undermanned, [ampersand]
undermine, [aerodyne]
undermined, [affined]
undermost, [aftermost]
underneath, [beneath]
underpants, [advance]
underpass, [admass]
underpay, [agape]
underpin, [akin]
underplay, [airplay]
underpopulated, [abluted]
underranked, [overranked]
underrate, [accelerate]
underrepresented, [abluted]
underscore, [abhor]

undersea, [absorbancy]
undersecretary, [accessory]
undersell, [bagatelle]
undershirt, [advert]
undersigned, [affined]
underskirt, [advert]
understaffed, [abaft]
understand, [ampersand]
understate, [acetate]
understated, [abluted]
understood, [adulthood]
understudy, [acidy]
undertake, [awake]
undertaker, [acre]
undertone, [alone]
undertow, [aggiornamento]
undervalue, [accrue]
underwater, [abductor]
underway, [airway]
underwear, [affair]
underweight, [accentuate]
underwhelm, [elm]
underworld, [afterworld]
underwrite, [affright]
underwriter, [abductor]
undesignated, [abluted]
undesirability, [abatis]
undeveloped, [abrupt]
undigestible, [able]
undignified, [abide]
undiplomatic, [acoustic]
undirected, [abluted]
undisciplined, [abscind]
undisputed, [abluted]
undivided, [absentminded]
undo, [accrue]
undocumented, [abluted]
undone, [antiphon]
undoubted, [abluted]

undress, [acquiesce]
undressed, [abreast]
undrinkable, [able]
undulate, [adjective] [aglet]
undulate, [verb] [ablate]
undulation, [abbreviation]
unearth, [afterbirth]
unedited, [abluted]
uneducable, [able]
uneducated, [abluted]
unelectable, [able]
unemotional, [aboriginal]
unemploy, [ahoy]
unemployable, [able]
unemployed, [adenoid]
unemployment,
    [abandonment]
unenforceable, [able]
unenthusiastic, [acoustic]
unequal, [accrual]
unequivocal, [acoustical]
unessential, [abbatial]
unethical, [acoustical]
uneven, [antiphon]
uneventful, [apocryphal]
unexamined, [abscind]
unexpected, [abluted]
unexplainable, [able]
unexploited, [abluted]
unexplored, [aboard]
unexpressed, [abreast]
unexpressive, [abrasive]
unfair, [affair]
unfaithful, [apocryphal]
unfamiliar, [ballplayer]
unfashionable, [able]
unfasten, [anchorperson]
unfathomable, [able]
unfavorable, [able]

unfit, [acquit]
unfold, [ahold]
unforeseen, [alexandrine]
unforgettable, [able]
unforgivable, [able]
unformulated, [abluted]
unfortunate, [acuminate]
unfounded, [absentminded]
unfriendly, [ably]
unfrozen, [anchorperson]
unfruitful, [apocryphal]
unfulfilled, [build]
unfunded, [absentminded]
unfurl, [aswirl]
unglue, [accrue]
unglued, [allude]
ungodliness, [agribusiness]
ungodly, [ably]
ungraceful, [apocryphal]
ungracious, [adscititious]
ungrad, [ad]
ungrateful, [apocryphal]
unguard, [backyard]
unguarded, [absentminded]
unhappily, [ably]
unhappy, [apocope]
unhealthful, [apocryphal]
unhealthy, [apathy]
unhelpful, [apocryphal]
unheralded, [absentminded]
unhitch, [backstitch]
unholy, [ably]
unhook, [bankbook]
unhurt, [advert]
unicameral, [admiral]
unicorn, [acorn]
unicycle, [acoustical]
unidentified, [abide]
unidimensional, [aboriginal]

unidirectional, [aboriginal]
unification, [abbreviation]
uniform, [aswarm]
uniformity, [abatis]
unify, [amplify]
unilateral, [admiral]
unimportant, [accordant]
unimpressed, [abreast]
unincorporated, [abluted]
unindicted, [abluted]
uninfected, [abluted]
uninhabited, [abluted]
uninhibited, [abluted]
uninspected, [abluted]
uninstructed, [abluted]
uninsulated, [abluted]
uninsurable, [able]
unintelligent, [agent]
unintelligible, [able]
unintended, [absentminded]
unintentional, [abdominal]
uninterested, [abluted]
uninterrupted, [abluted]
unintimidated, [abluted]
uninvited, [abluted]
Union Jack, [aback]
union, [antiunion]
unionization, [abbreviation]
unionize, [agnize]
unique, [antique]
unirrigated, [abluted]
unisex, [annex]
unison, [antitoxin]
unissued, [allude]
unit, [acuminate]
unitarian, [abecedarian]
unitary, [accessory]
unite, [affright]
united, [abluted]

unitrust, [adjust]
unity, [abatis]
universal, [apostle]
universalism, [abolitionism]
universalize, [actualize]
universe, [adverse]
university, [abatis]
unjust, [adjust]
unjustifiable, [able]
unjustified, [abide]
unkempt, [attempt]
unkind, [affined]
unknowable, [able]
unknown, [alone]
unlabeled, [bedraggled]
unlawful, [apocryphal]
unleaded, [absentminded]
unlearn, [adjourn]
unlearned, [acid]
unleash, [baksheesh]
unless, [acquiesce]
unliberated, [abluted]
unlike, [alike]
unlikely, [ably]
unlimited, [abluted]
unlinked, [distinct]
unlisted, [abluted]
unload, [abode]
unlock, [aftershock]
unloose, [abstruse]
unloosen, [anchorperson]
unlovable, [able]
unlovely, [ably]
unlucky, [achy]
unmanageable, [able]
unmanly, [ably]
unmanned, [ampersand]
unmannerly, [ably]
unmasculine, [acetylene]

unmask, [ask]
unmedicated, [abluted]
unmentionable, [able]
unmerciful, [apocryphal]
unmerited, [abluted]
unmitigated, [abluted]
unmodified, [abide]
unmotivated, [abluted]
unnatural, [admiral]
unnecessary, [accessory]
unnerve, [conserve]
unobstructed, [abluted]
unobtainable, [able]
unobtrusive, [abrasive]
unoccupied, [abide]
unofficial, [abbatial]
unorthodox, [bandbox]
unpack, [aback]
unpaid, [abrade]
unpalatable, [able]
unparalleled, [geld]
unpardonable, [able]
unpatriotic, [acoustic]
unpave, [aftershave]
unperfect, [addict]
unpersuasive, [abrasive]
unpile, [aisle]
unpin, [akin]
unplaced, [abased]
unplanned, [ampersand]
unpleasant, [accordant]
unpolitical, [acoustical]
unpopular, [angler]
unprecedented, [abluted]
unpredictable, [able]
unpretentious, [adscititious]
unprincipled, [bedraggled]
unprintable, [able]
unprocessed, [abreast]

unproductive, [ablative]
unprofessional, [abdominal]
unprofitable, [able]
unprotected, [abluted]
unpublishable, [able]
unqualified, [abide]
unquenchable, [able]
unquestionable, [able]
unranked, [overranked]
unrated, [abluted]
unravel, [adjectival]
unread, [abed]
unreal, [anneal]
unrealistic, [acoustic]
unreality, [abatis]
unreasonable, [able]
unreceptive, [ablative]
unrecognizable, [able]
unreconcilable, [able]
unrecorded, [absentminded]
unredeemable, [able]
unrefined, [affined]
unregenerate, [accurate]
unreliable, [able]
unremarkable, [able]
unrepentant, [accordant]
unreported, [abluted]
unrepresented, [abluted]
unrequited, [abluted]
unreserve, [conserve]
unresolvable, [able]
unresponsive, [abrasive]
unrest, [abreast]
unrestraint, [acquaint]
unrewarded, [absentminded]
unripe, [airpipe]
unrivaled, [bedraggled]
unromantic, [acoustic]
unruffled, [bedraggled]

unruly, [ably]
unsaddle, [antipodal]
unsafe, [chafe]
unsaid, [abed]
unsalable, [able]
unsalvageable, [able]
unsanitary, [accessory]
unsatisfactory, [accessory]
unsatisfied, [abide]
unsaturated, [abluted]
unsavory, [accessory]
unscented, [abluted]
unscholarly, [ably]
unscramble, [able]
unscrew, [accrue]
unscripted, [abluted]
unscriptural, [admiral]
unscrupulous, [acropolis]
unsearchable, [able]
unseasonable, [able]
unseat, [accrete]
unseeded, [absentminded]
unseemly, [ably]
unseen, [alexandrine]
unsegregated, [abluted]
unselfish, [abolish]
unsellable, [able]
unsettle, [accidental]
unshackle, [acoustical]
unshakable, [able]
unshaken, [awaken]
unshaven, [antiphon]
unsightly, [ably]
unsigned, [affined]
unsinkable, [able]
unskilled, [build]
unskillful, [apocryphal]
unsnap, [afterclap]
unsociable, [able]

unsocial, [abbatial]
unsold, [ahold]
unsolicited, [abluted]
unsophisticated, [abluted]
unsound, [abound]
unspeakable, [able]
unspecified, [abide]
unspectacular, [angler]
unspiritual, [accrual]
unspoken, [awaken]
unsportsmanlike, [alike]
unspotted, [abluted]
unstable, [able]
unstated, [abluted]
unsteady, [acidy]
unstick, [acoustic]
unstoppable, [able]
unstrap, [afterclap]
unstuck, [amok]
unsubstantiated, [abluted]
unsuccessful, [apocryphal]
unsuitable, [able]
unsung, [among]
unsupportable, [able]
unsure, [acupressure]
unsurpassable, [able]
unsurpassed, [aghast]
unsustainable, [able]
unsympathetic, [acoustic]
unsystematic, [acoustic]
untainted, [abluted]
untalented, [abluted]
untamable, [able]
untangle, [angle]
untapped, [adapt]
untaught, [aeronaut]
unteachable, [able]
untenable, [able]
untended, [absentminded]

unthinkable, [able]
untie, [airdry]
until, [backfill]
untimely, [ably]
unto, [accrue]
untold, [ahold]
untouchable, [able]
untraditional, [abdominal]
untranslated, [abluted]
untreated, [abluted]
untried, [abide]
untroubled, [bedraggled]
untrue, [accrue]
untrustworthy, [newsworthy]
untruthful, [apocryphal]
untypical, [acoustical]
unusual, [accrual]
unutterable, [able]
unveil, [ail]
unverifiable, [able]
unvisited, [abluted]
unwanted, [abluted]
unwarranted, [abluted]
unwary, [accessory]
unwearable, [able]
unwed, [abed]
unwelcome, [addendum]
unwholesome,
    [adventuresome]
unwieldy, [acidy]
unwind, [affined]
unwinnable, [able]
unwise, [advise]
unworkable, [able]
unworldly, [ably]
unworthy, [newsworthy]
unwrap, [afterclap]
unwritten, [anchorperson]
unzip, [airstrip]

up, [backup]
upbeat, [accrete]
update, [accommodate]
upheaval, [anvil]
uphill, [backfill]
uphold, [ahold]
upholster, [administer]
upholstery, [accessory]
uplift, [adrift]
uplink, [bethink]
upload, [abode]
upon, [amazon]
upper, [barkeeper]
upper-class, [admass]
uppercut, [advocate]
uppermost, [aftermost]
uppity, [abatis]
upraise, [ablaze]
upright, [affright]
uprightness, [agribusiness]
uproar, [abhor]
uproot, [acute]
upscale, [ail]
upset, [abet]
upshot, [aeronaut]
upstage, [age]
upstairs, [backstairs]
upstart, [apart]
upstate, [acetate]
upstream, [abeam]
upstroke, [artichoke]
upsurge, [converge]
uptake, [awake]
uptick, [acoustic]
uptight, [affright]
uptime, [airtime]
uptown, [boomtown]
uptrend, [addend]
upturn, [adjourn]

upward, [absurd]
uranium, [anthurium]
urban sprawl, [aerosol]
urbane, [abstain]
urbanization, [abbreviation]
urbanize, [agnize]
urge, [converge]
urgency, [absorbancy]
urgent, [agent]
urinal, [abdominal]
urinary, [accessory]
urinate, [abominate]
urination, [abbreviation]
urine, [pressrun]
urn, [adjourn]
us, [antibias]
usage, [acknowledge]
use, [noun] [abstruse]
use, [verb] [abuse]
useful, [apocryphal]
usefulness, [agribusiness]
useless, [acropolis]
usher, [acupressure]
usherette, [abet]
usual, [accrual]
usufruct, [abduct]
usurer, [adulterer]
usurp, [burp]
usurpation, [abbreviation]
usury, [accessory]
utensil, [apostle]
uterus, [actress]
utilitarian, [abecedarian]
utilitarianism, [abolitionism]
utility, [abatis]
utilization, [abbreviation]
utilize, [actualize]
utmost, [aftermost]
utopia, [abulia]

utopianism, [abolitionism]
utter, [abductor]
utterance, [abhorrence]
uttermost, [aftermost]
vacancy, [absorbancy]
vacant, [abeyant]
vacate, [abdicate]
vacation, [abbreviation]
vacationland, [ampersand]
vaccinate, [abominate]
vaccination, [abbreviation]
vaccine, [alexandrine]
vacillate, [ablate]
vacillation, [abbreviation]
vacuity, [abatis]
vacuous, [ambiguous]
vacuum, [abloom]
vagabond, [abscond]
vagarious, [abstemious]
vagary, [accessory]
vagile, [agile]
vagina, [alumna]
vaginal, [abdominal]
vagrancy, [absorbancy]
vagrant, [aberrant]
vague, [plague]
vail, [ail]
vain, [abstain]
vainglorious, [abstemious]
vainglory, [accessory]
valance, [abhorrence]
vale, [ail]
valedictorian, [abecedarian]
valedictory, [accessory]
valence, [abhorrence]
valentine, [aerodyne]
valet, [airplay]
valetudinarian, [abecedarian]
valiant, [abeyant]

valid, [acid]
validate, [accommodate]
validation, [abbreviation]
validity, [abatis]
vallate, [ablate]
valley, [ably]
valor, [angler]
valuable, [able]
valuate, [accentuate]
valuation, [abbreviation]
valuator, [abductor]
value, [accrue]
valueless, [acropolis]
valvula, [a capella]
vamoose, [abstruse]
vamp, [aid-de-camp]
vampire, [acquire]
van, [adman]
vandal, [antipodal]
vandalism, [abolitionism]
vandalize, [actualize]
vane, [abstain]
vanguard, [backyard]
vanilla, [a capella]
vanish, [abolish]
vanity, [abatis]
vantage, [acknowledge]
vapid, [acid]
vapidity, [abatis]
vapor, [barkeeper]
vaporize, [accessorize]
vaporizer, [adviser]
vaporous, [actress]
variability, [abatis]
variable, [able]
variableness, [agribusiness]
variance, [abhorrence]
variant, [abeyant]
variate, [create]

variation, [abbreviation]
varicose, [adios]
variegate, [abnegate]
variegated, [abluted]
variegation, [abbreviation]
variety, [abatis]
variorum, [addendum]
various, [abstemious]
varlet, [aglet]
varmint, [abandonment]
varnish, [abolish]
varsity, [abatis]
vary, [accessory]
vas, [admass]
vascular, [angler]
vase, [abase]
vasectomy, [academy]
vassal, [apostle]
vast, [aghast]
vastitude, [altitude]
vat, [acrobat]
vatic, [acoustic]
vaticinal, [aboriginal]
vaticinate, [abominate]
vaticination, [abbreviation]
vaudeville, [adjectival]
vault, [asphalt]
vaulted, [abluted]
vaulter, [abductor]
vaunt, [avaunt]
vaunted, [abluted]
veal, [anneal]
vector, [abductor]
vedette, [abet]
veep, [asleep]
veer, [adhere]
vegetable, [able]
vegetarian, [abecedarian]
vegetation, [abbreviation]

vegetative, [ablative]
veggie, [allergy]
vehement, [abandonment]
vehicle, [acoustical]
vehicular, [angler]
veil, [ail]
veiled, [bedraggled]
vein, [abstain]
velleity, [abatis]
vellum, [addendum]
velocity, [abatis]
velodrome, [astrodome]
velour, [abjure]
velure, [abjure]
velvet, [adequate]
velveteen, [alexandrine]
velvety, [abatis]
venal, [abdominal]
vend, [addend]
vendee, [acidy]
vendetta, [aorta]
vendor, [adder]
vendue, [accrue]
veneer, [adhere]
venerate, [accelerate]
veneration, [abbreviation]
venereal, [abaxial]
venery, [accessory]
vengeance, [abhorrence]
vengeful, [apocryphal]
venial, [abaxial]
venire, [accessory]
venison, [antitoxin]
venom, [addendum]
venomous, [allonymous]
vent, [accent]
ventilate, [ablate]
ventilation, [abbreviation]
ventilator, [abductor]

ventriloquism, [abolitionism]
ventriloquist, [activist]
venture, [acupressure]
venturesome,
   [adventuresome]
venturous, [actress]
venue, [accrue]
veracious, [adscititious]
veracity, [abatis]
veranda, [addenda]
verb, [adverb]
verbal, [able]
verbalization, [abbreviation]
verbalize, [actualize]
verbatim, [accustom]
verbiage, [acknowledge]
verbicide, [abide]
verbigeration, [abbreviation]
verbose, [adios]
verboten, [anchorperson]
verdant, [accordant]
verdict, [addict]
verdure, [armiger]
verge, [converge]
veridical, [acoustical]
verifiable, [able]
verification, [abbreviation]
verify, [amplify]
verily, [ably]
veritable, [able]
verity, [abatis]
verjuice, [abstruse]
vermicelli, [ably]
vermin, [abdomen]
verminous, [agribusiness]
vermouth, [booth]
vernacular, [angler]
vernal, [abdominal]
versatile, [accidental]

versatility, [abatis]
verse, [adverse]
versickle, [acoustical]
versification, [abbreviation]
version, [abrasion]
versus, [alkalosis]
vertebra, [abracadabra]
vertebrate, [accelerate]
vertebrate, [accurate]
vertex, [annex]
vertical, [acoustical]
vertigo, [ago]
verve, [conserve]
very, [accessory]
vesper, [barkeeper]
vespers, [bonkers]
vessel, [apostle]
vest, [abreast]
vestiary, [accessory]
vestibule, [bascule]
vestige, [acknowledge]
vestment, [abandonment]
vestry, [ancestry]
vesture, [acupuncture]
vet, [abet]
veteran, [pressrun]
veterinarian, [abecedarian]
veto, [aggiornamento]
vex, [annex]
vexation, [abbreviation]
vexed, [context]
via, [alfalfa]
viability, [abatis]
viable, [able]
viaduct, [abduct]
vial, [aisle]
vibe, [ascribe]
vibraharp, [carp]
vibraharpist, [activist]

vibrancy, [absorbancy]
vibrant, [aberrant]
vibrate, [accelerate]
vibration, [abbreviation]
vibrato, [aggiornamento]
vibrator, [abductor]
vicar, [acre]
vicarious, [abstemious]
vice, [advice]
viceroy, [ahoy]
vicinage, [appanage]
vicinity, [abatis]
vicious, [adscititious]
vicissitude, [altitude]
victim, [accustom]
victimize, [advise]
victor, [abductor]
victorious, [abstemious]
victory, [accessory]
victual, [accidental]
video game, [acclaim]
video, [audio]
videocassette, [abet]
videocast, [aghast]
videodisk, [asterisk]
videotape, [agape]
videotext, [context]
vie, [airdry]
Viet Nam, [aerogram]
view, [accrue]
viewer, [airpower]
viewfinder, [adder]
viewpoint, [anoint]
vigil, [agile]
vigilance, [abhorrence]
vigilant, [ambivalent]
vigilante, [abatis]
vignette, [abet]
vigor, [agar]

vigoroso, [also]
vigorous, [actress]
vile, [aisle]
vilification, [abbreviation]
vilify, [amplify]
vilipend, [almond]
villa, [a capella]
village, [acknowledge]
villager, [armiger]
villain, [acetylene]
villainous, [agribusiness]
vim, [acronym]
vinaigrette, [accurate]
vincible, [able]
vindicate, [abdicate]
vindication, [abbreviation]
vindictive, [ablative]
vindictiveness, [agribusiness]
vine, [aerodyne]
vinedresser, [aggressor]
vinegar, [agar]
vineyard, [absurd]
vinification, [abbreviation]
vinify, [amplify]
vino, [albino]
vinosity, [abatis]
vinous, [agribusiness]
vintage, [acknowledge]
vintner, [afterburner]
vinyl, [abdominal]
viol, [aisle]
viola, [a capella]
violate, [ablate]
violation, [abbreviation]
violence, [abhorrence]
violent, [ambivalent]
violet, [aglet]
violin, [akin]
violoncello, [afterglow]

viper, [barkeeper]
viperish, [abolish]
viperous, [actress]
virago, [ago]
viral, [admiral]
virgin, [allergen]
virginal, [abdominal]
virginity, [abatis]
virile, [admiral]
virility, [abatis]
virtual, [accrual]
virtually, [ably]
virtue, [accrue]
virtueless, [acropolis]
virtuosity, [abatis]
virtuoso, [also]
virtuous, [ambiguous]
virulence, [abhorrence]
virulent, [ambivalent]
virus, [actress]
visa, [alfalfa]
visage, [acknowledge]
visceral, [admiral]
viscosity, [abatis]
viscount, [account]
vise, [advice]
visibility, [abatis]
visible, [able]
vision, [abrasion]
visionary, [accessory]
visit, [apposite]
visitation, [abbreviation]
visitor, [abductor]
visor, [adviser]
vista, [aorta]
visual, [accrual]
visualization, [abbreviation]
visualize, [actualize]
vita, [aorta]

vital, [accidental]
vitalist, [aerialist]
vitality, [abatis]
vitalize, [actualize]
vitamin, [abdomen]
vitiate, [create]
viticulture, [acupuncture]
vitrify, [amplify]
vitriolic, [acyclic]
vituperate, [accelerate]
vituperation, [abbreviation]
vituperative, [ablative]
vivache, [agape]
vivacious, [adscititious]
vivid, [acid]
vividness, [agribusiness]
vivify, [amplify]
viviparous, [actress]
vivisect, [abject]
vivisection, [abbreviation]
vixen, [antitoxin]
vizard, [absurd]
vocable, [able]
vocabular, [angler]
vocabulary, [accessory]
vocal, [acoustical]
vocalist, [aerialist]
vocalize, [actualize]
vocation, [abbreviation]
vocational, [abdominal]
vocative, [ablative]
vociferate, [accelerate]
vociferous, [actress]
vodka, [angelica]
vogue, [brogue]
voguish, [abolish]
voice, [choice]
voiced, [foist]
voiceprint, [blueprint]

void, [adenoid]
voidable, [able]
volant, [ambivalent]
volante, [agape]
volar, [angler]
volatile, [accidental]
volatility, [abatis]
volcanic, [allergenic]
volcano, [albino]
volition, [abbreviation]
volitional, [aboriginal]
volitive, [ablative]
volleyball, [aerosol]
volplane, [abstain]
volt, [bolt]
voltage, [acknowledge]
voltmeter, [abductor]
voluble, [able]
volume, [addendum]
volumeter, [abductor]
voluminous, [agribusiness]
voluntary, [accessory]
volunteer, [adhere]
volunteerism, [abolitionism]
voluptuary, [accessory]
voluptuous, [ambiguous]
vomit, [animate]
voodoo, [accrue]
voodooism, [abolitionism]
voracious, [adscititious]
voracity, [abatis]
vortex, [annex]
vortical, [acoustical]
votary, [accessory]
vote, [afloat]
voter, [abductor]
votive, [ablative]
vouch, [avouch]
voucher, [acupuncture]

vouchsafe, [chafe]
vow, [allow]
vowel, [agile]
voyage, [acknowledge]
voyeur, [ballplayer]
vulgar, [agar]
vulgarity, [abatis]
vulgarize, [accessorize]
vulgate, [abnegate]
vulnerable, [able]
vulture, [acupuncture]
vulva, [alfalfa]
wacko, [alfresco]
wacky, [achy]
wad, [abroad]
waddle, [antipodal]
waddy, [acidy]
wade, [abrade]
wader, [adder]
wadi, [acidy]
wafer, [buffer]
waffle, [apocryphal]
wag, [ag]
wage, [age]
wager, [armiger]
waggery, [accessory]
waggish, [abolish]
waggle, [angle]
wagon, [bandwagon]
wagoner, [afterburner]
wahine, [abalone]
wahoo, [accrue]
waif, [chafe]
wail, [ail]
wainscot, [afloat]
wain-wright, [affright]
waist, [abased]
waistband, [ampersand]
waistline, [airline]

wait, [accentuate]
waiter, [abductor]
waitress, [actress]
waive, [aftershave]
waiver, [achiever]
wake, [awake]
wakeful, [apocryphal]
wale, [ail]
walk, [aftershock]
walkathon, [amazon]
walkaway, [airway]
walker, [acre]
walk-on, [amazon]
walkout, [about]
walkway, [airway]
wall, [aerosol]
wallaby, [abbey]
wallah, [a capella]
wallboard, [aboard]
wallet, [aglet]
walleye, [airdry]
wallflower, [airpower]
wallop, [backup]
wallow, [afterglow]
wallpaper, [barkeeper]
wally, [ably]
walnut, [acuminate]
walrus, [actress]
wamble, [able]
wampum, [addendum]
wan, [amazon]
wand, [abscond]
wander, [adder]
wanderer, [adulterer]
wanderlust, [adjust]
wane, [abstain]
wangle, [angle]
wanigan, [bandwagon]
want, [avaunt]

wanton, [anchorperson]
wapiti, [abatis]
war game, [acclaim]
war, [abhor]
warble, [able]
ward, [award]
warden, [anchorperson]
wardrobe, [bathrobe]
wardroom, [abloom]
ware, [affair]
warehouse, [alehouse]
wareroom, [abloom]
warf, [corf]
warfare, [affair]
warhead, [abed]
warhorse, [endorse]
warlike, [alike]
warlock, [aftershock]
warlord, [award]
warm, [aswarm]
warmer, [armor]
warmhearted, [abluted]
warmonger, [agar]
warm-up, [backup]
warn, [acorn]
warp, [dorp]
warpath, [aftermath]
warplane, [abstain]
warrant, [aberrant]
warrantee, [abatis]
warranty, [abatis]
warren, [pressrun]
warrior, [anterior]
warship, [airship]
wart, [abort]
wartime, [airtime]
wary, [accessory]
was, [abuzz]
wash, [awash]

washable, [able]
washbasin, [anchorperson]
washboard, [aboard]
washbowl, [areole]
washcloth, [broadcloth]
washout, [about]
washrag, [ag]
washroom, [abloom]
washtub, [backrub]
wassail, [apostle]
wassailer, [angler]
waste, [abased]
wasteband, [ampersand]
wastebasket, [advocate]
wasted, [abluted]
wasteful, [apocryphal]
wasteland, [ampersand]
wastepaper, [barkeeper]
wastewater, [abductor]
watch, [blotch]
watchband, [ampersand]
watchdog, [agog]
watcher, [acupuncture]
watchful, [apocryphal]
watchmaker, [acre]
watchman, [abdomen]
watchword, [absurd]
water break, [awake]
water, [abductor]
watercolor, [angler]
watercooler, [angler]
watercourse, [coarse]
watercraft, [abaft]
watercress, [acquiesce]
waterfall, [aerosol]
waterfront, [aberrant]
waterline, [airline]
waterlog, [agog]
waterloo, [accrue]

waterman, [abdomen]
watermark, [aardvark]
watermelon, [acetylene]
waterpower, [airpower]
waterproof, [aloof]
waterscape, [agape]
watershed, [abed]
waterspout, [about]
watertight, [affright]
waterway, [airway]
waterwheel, [automobile]
watery, [accessory]
watt, [aeronaut]
wattage, [acknowledge]
wattle, [accidental]
wave, [aftershave]
wavelength, [length]
waver, [achiever]
wavy, [anchovy]
wax, [anthrax]
way, [airway]
waybill, [backfill]
wayfarer, [adulterer]
waylay, [airplay]
wayside, [abide]
wayward, [absurd]
we, [colloquy]
weak, [antique]
weaken, [again]
weakness, [agribusiness]
weakside, [abide]
weal, [anneal]
wealth, [commonwealth]
wealthy, [apathy]
wean, [alexandrine]
wear, [affair]
wearable, [able]
wearisome, [adventuresome]
weary, [accessory]

weasel, [appraisal]
weather, [altogether]
weathercast, [aghast]
weathercaster, [administer]
weathercock, [aftershock]
weatherize, [accessorize]
weatherman, [adman]
weatherperson,
  [anchorperson]
weatherproof, [aloof]
weatherworn, [acorn]
weave, [achieve]
web, [bleb]
webfoot, [ablaut]
wed, [abed]
wedding cake, [awake]
wedding, [anything]
wedge, [allege]
wedgie, [allergy]
wedgy, [allergy]
wedlock, [aftershock]
wee, [colloquy]
weed, [accede]
weeder, [adder]
weedy, [acidy]
week, [antique]
weekday, [agape]
weekdays, [ablaze]
weekend, [addend]
weeklong, [agelong]
weeknight, [affright]
weenie, [abalone]
weep, [asleep]
weevil, [adjectival]
weigh, [airway]
weight, [accentuate]
weighted, [abluted]
weightless, [acropolis]
weighty, [abatis]

weirdo, [aficionado]
welcome, [addendum]
weld, [geld]
welder, [adder]
welfarism, [abolitionism]
well, [bagatelle]
well-adjusted, [abluted]
well-bred, [abed]
well-defined, [affined]
well-founded, [absentminded]
well-grounded,
  [absentminded]
wellness, [agribusiness]
well-off, [boff]
well-read, [abed]
well-rounded, [absentminded]
well-spoken, [awaken]
well-to-do, [accrue]
well-wisher, [acupressure]
welt, [belt]
weltanschauung, [among]
welter, [abductor]
welterweight, [accentuate]
wench, [bench]
wept, [accept]
were, [airpower]
west, [abreast]
westbound, [abound]
westernization, [abbreviation]
westernize, [agnize]
westward, [absurd]
wet suit, [backup]
wet, [abet]
wetback, [aback]
whack, [aback]
whacko, [alfresco]
whacky, [achy]
whale, [ail]
whaler, [angler]

wham, [aerogram]
whammy, [academy]
wharf, [corf]
what, [adequate]
whatever, [achiever]
whatnot, [aeronaut]
whatsit, [corset]
whatsoever, [achiever]
wheat, [accrete]
whee, [colloquy]
wheedle, [antipodal]
wheel, [anneal]
wheelbarrow, [allegro]
wheelbase, [abase]
wheelchair, [anywhere]
wheezy, [advisee]
whelm, [elm]
whelp, [help]
when, [again]
whence, [cense]
whenever, [achiever]
where, [anywhere]
whereabout, [about]
whereabouts, [hereabouts]
whereas, [as]
whereby, [alibi]
wherefore, [abhor]
wherein, [akin]
whereof, [above]
wherever, [achiever]
wherewithal, [aerosol]
whet, [abet]
whether, [altogether]
whetstone, [alone]
whew, [accrue]
whey, [airway]
which, [backstitch]
whichever, [achiever]
whicker, [acre]

whiff, [anaglyph]
whiffet, [adequate]
whiffle, [apocryphal]
while, [aisle]
whim, [acronym]
whimper, [barkeeper]
whimsical, [acoustical]
whimsy, [advisee]
whine, [aerodyne]
whip, [airstrip]
whipcord, [award]
whiplash, [abash]
whippersnapper, [barkeeper]
whippy, [apocope]
whipsaw, [aah]
whirl, [aswirl]
whirligig, [big]
whirlpool, [bascule]
whirlwind, [abscind]
whirly, [ably]
whish, [abolish]
whisk, [asterisk]
whisker, [acre]
whiskey, [achy]
whisper, [barkeeper]
whistle, [apostle]
whistler, [angler]
whit, [acquit]
White House, [alehouse]
white, [affright]
whitecap, [afterclap]
whitehead, [abed]
white-hot, [aeronaut]
whitener, [afterburner]
whiteness, [agribusiness]
whiteout, [about]
whitesmith, [blacksmith]
whitetail, [blackmail]
whitewall, [aerosol]

whitewash, [awash]
whither, [altogether]
whittle, [accidental]
whiz, [fizz]
who, [accrue]
whoa, [airshow]
whodunit, [acuminate]
whole, [areole]
wholehearted, [abluted]
wholesale, [blackmail]
wholesaler, [angler]
wholesome, [adventuresome]
wholestick, [acoustic]
whom, [abloom]
whomp, [chomp]
whoop, [coop]
whoopee, [apocope]
whoopla, [aah]
whoosh, [cartouche]
whop, [agitprop]
whopper, [barkeeper]
whore, [abhor]
whorehouse, [alehouse]
whose, [amuse]
whump, [bump]
why, [airdry]
wick, [acidic]
wicked, [acid]
wickedness, [agribusiness]
wicker, [acre]
wicket [advocate]
wide, [abide]
wide-awake, [awake]
widen, [anchorperson]
wider, [adder]
widespread, [abed]
widget, [adequate]
widow, [aficionado]
widower, [airpower]

widowerhood, [adulthood]
widowhood, [adulthood]
width, [bandwidth]
wieldy, [acidy]
wiener, [afterburner]
wienerwurst, [athirst]
wienie, [abalone]
wife, [afterlife]
wig, [big]
wiggle, [angle]
wiggly, [ably]
wiglet, [aglet]
wigwam, [aplomb]
wild, [beguiled]
wildcat, [acrobat]
wildcatter, [abductor]
wilderness, [agribusiness]
wildfire, [acquire]
wildflower, [airpower]
wildlife, [afterlife]
wile, [aisle]
will, [backfill]
willed, [build]
willful, [apocryphal]
willow, [afterglow]
willowy, [colloquy]
wilt, [atilt]
wily, [ably]
wimp, [blimp]
win, [akin]
wince, [convince]
winch, [bullfinch]
wind, [abscind]
wind, [affined]
windblown, [alone]
windbreak, [awake]
windbreaker, [acre]
windburn, [adjourn]
windchill, [backfill]

windfall, [aerosol]
windjammer, [armor]
windmill, [backfill]
window, [aficionado]
windowpane, [abstain]
windowsill, [backfill]
windpipe, [airpipe]
windproof, [aloof]
windscreen, [alexandrine]
windshield, [airfield]
windstorm, [aswarm]
windsurf, [bodysurf]
windswept, [accept]
windup, [backup]
windward, [absurd]
windy, [acidy]
wine, [aerodyne]
wineglass, [admass]
winepress, [acquiesce]
winery, [accessory]
wineshop, [agitprop]
wineskin, [akin]
wing, [anything]
wingback, [aback]
wingman, [abdomen]
wingspan, [adman]
wink, [bethink]
winless, [acropolis]
winner, [afterburner]
winnow, [albino]
wino, [albino]
winsome, [adventuresome]
winter, [abductor]
wintergreen, [alexandrine]
wintertime, [airtime]
wipe, [airpipe]
wipeout, [about]
wire, [acquire]
wireless, [acropolis]

wirephoto, [aggiornamento]
wiretap, [afterclap]
wiretapper, [barkeeper]
wiry, [accessory]
wisdom, [addendum]
wise, [advise]
wiseacre, [acre]
wiseass, [admass]
wisecrack, [aback]
wish, [abolish]
wishbone, [alone]
wishful, [apocryphal]
wisp, [crisp]
wispy, [apocope]
wistful, [apocryphal]
wit, [acquit]
witch, [backstitch]
witchcraft, [abaft]
withal, [aerosol]
withdraw, [aah]
withdrawal, [agile]
withdrawn, [amazon]
withdrew, [accrue]
wither, [altogether]
withheld, [geld]
withhold, [ahold]
within, [akin]
without, [about]
withstand, [ampersand]
withstood, [adulthood]
witless, [acropolis]
witness, [agribusiness]
witticism, [abolitionism]
witty, [abatis]
wizard, [absurd]
wizardry, [accessory]
wobble, [able]
woe, [airshow]
woebegone, [amazon]

woeful, [apocryphal]
woke, [artichoke]
wolverine, [alexandrine]
woman, [abdomen]
womanhood, [adulthood]
womanize, [agnize]
womanizer, [adviser]
womankind, [affined]
womanly, [ably]
womb, [abloom]
womenfolk, [artichoke]
won, [bandwagon]
wonder, [adder]
wonderful, [apocryphal]
wonderland, [ampersand]
wonderment, [abandonment]
wonderwork, [artwork]
wondrous, [actress]
wonk, [ankh]
woo, [accrue]
wood, [adulthood]
woodchopper, [barkeeper]
woodchuck, [amok]
woodcraft, [abaft]
woodcutter, [abductor]
wooded, [absentminded]
woodenhead, [abed]
woodland, [almond]
woodlot, [aeronaut]
woodman, [abdomen]
woodpecker, [acre]
woodpile, [anile]
woodshed, [abed]
woodwind, [abscind]
woodwork, [artwork]
woodworker, [acre]
woody, [acidy]
woofer, [buffer]
wool, [abaxial]

word, [absurd]
wordless, [acropolis]
wordplay, [airplay]
wordsmith, [blacksmith]
wordy, [acidy]
work, [artwork]
workable, [able]
workaday, [agape]
workaholic, [acyclic]
workbench, [bench]
workbook, [bankbook]
workday, [agape]
worker, [acre]
workfare, [affair]
workforce, [coarse]
workhorse, [endorse]
working-class, [admass]
workingman, [abdomen]
workload, [abode]
workmanlike, [alike]
workmanship, [airship]
workout, [about]
workpiece, [afterpiece]
workplace, [abase]
workroom, [abloom]
workstation, [abbreviation]
worktable, [able]
workweek, [antique]
world, [afterworld]
worldliness, [agribusiness]
worldly, [ably]
worldview, [accrue]
worldwide, [abide]
worm, [affirm]
wormwood, [adulthood]
wormy, [academy]
worrisome, [adventuresome]
worry, [accessory]
worrywart, [abort]

worse, [adverse]
worsen, [anchorperson]
worship, [backup]
worshipful, [apocryphal]
worst, [athirst]
worsted, [abluted]
wort, [advert]
worth, [afterbirth]
worthiness, [agribusiness]
worthless, [acropolis]
worthwhile, [aisle]
worthy, [newsworthy]
would, [adulthood]
wound, [no other words with this ending]
wounded, [absentminded]
wove, [alcove]
wow, [allow]
wrack, [aback]
wraith, [faith]
wrangle, [angle]
wrangler, [angler]
wrap, [afterclap]
wraparound, [abound]
wrapper, [barkeeper]
wrath, [aftermath]
wrathful, [apocryphal]
wreak, [antique]
wreath, [beneath]
wreathe, [breathe]
wreck, [afterdeck]
wreckage, [acknowledge]
wrecker, [acre]
wren, [again]
wrench, [bench]
wrest, [abreast]
wrestle, [apostle]
wrestler, [angler]
wretch, [backstretch]

wretched, [acid]
wriggle, [angle]
wriggler, [angler]
wring, [anything]
wringer, [arbitrager]
wrinkle, [acoustical]
wrist, [allegorist]
wristband, [ampersand]
wristlet, [aglet]
wristlock, [aftershock]
wristwatch, [blotch]
writ, [acquit]
write, [affright]
writer, [abductor]
writhe, [blithe]
wrong, [agelong]
wrongdoer, [airpower]
wrongful, [apocryphal]
wrongheaded, [absentminded]
wrote, [afloat]
wroth, [broadcloth]
wrought, [aeronaut]
wrung, [among]
wry, [airdry]
wunderkind, [blueprint]
xenophile, [anile]
xenophobe, [bathrobe]
xenophobia, [abulia]
xerography, [anastrophe]
xerox, [bandbox]
xylography, [anastrophe]
xylophone, [alone]
yacht, [aeronaut]
yahoo, [accrue]
yakitori, [accessory]
yam, [aerogram]
yammer, [armor]
yank, [bank]
yap, [afterclap]

yard, [backyard]
yardage, [acknowledge]
yardman, [abdomen]
yardmaster, [administer]
yardstick, [acoustic]
yarmulke, [angelica]
yarn, [barn]
yashmak, [aback]
yawn, [amazon]
ye, [buoy]
year, [adhere]
yearbook, [bankbook]
yearly, [ably]
yearn, [adjourn]
yeast, [beast]
yeh, [agape]
yellow, [afterglow]
yelp, [help]
yelper, [barkeeper]
yen, [again]
yenta, [aorta]
yeoman, [abdomen]
yep, [crowstep]
yes, [acquiesce]
yeshiva, [alfalfa]
yesterday, [agape]
yesteryear, [adhere]
yet, [abet]
yip, [airstrip]
yippee, [apocope]
yodel, [antipodal]
yoga, [alfalfa]
yogi, [aggie]
yogurt, [advert]
yoke, [artichoke]
yolk, [artichoke]
yon, [amazon]
yonder, [adder]
yore, [abhor]

you, [accrue]
young, [among]
younger, [agar]
youngest, [adjust]
youngster, [administer]
younker, [acre]
your, [ballplayer]
yourself, [bookshelf]
youth quake, [awake]
youth, [booth]
youthful, [apocryphal]
yuck, [amok]
yucky, [achy]
yuk, [amok]
Yule, [bascule]
yuletide, [abide]
yummy, [academy]
yuppie, [apocope]
zag, [ag]
zany, [abalone]
zap, [after clap]
zapper, [barkeeper]
zeal, [anneal]
zealot, [aglet]
zealous, [acropolis]
zebra, [abracadabra]
zeitgeist, [antichrist]
zenith, [altazimuth]
zeppelin, [acetylene]
zero, [allegro]
zest, [abreast]
zestful, [apocryphal]
zesty, [abatis]
zig, [big]
ziggurat, [acrobat]
zigzag, [ag]
zilch, [filch]
zinc, [bethink]
zinger, [arbitrager]

zip, [airstrip]
zipper, [barkeeper]
zippy, [apocope]
zirconia, [abulia]
zit, [acquit]
zither, [altogether]
zodiac, [aback]
zombie, [abbey]
zone, [alone]
zonk, [ankh]
zoo, [accrue]
zookeeper, [barkeeper]
zoological, [acoustical]
zoology, [allergy]
zoom, [abloom]
zucchini, [abalone]
zwieback, [aback]
zygote, [afloat]